Frommer's

Alaska

by Charles P. Wohlforth

with Melissa Rivers on Cruises
and Peter Oliver on Wilderness Adventures

Macmillan • USA

ABOUT THE AUTHORS

Charles P. Wohlforth is a life-long Alaskan who has been a writer and journalist since 1986. He lives in Anchorage, where he is active in civic affairs.

Her mother didn't want **Melissa Rivers** to grow up thinking of Texas (her birthplace) as the center of the Universe, so the precocious teen was packed off to the Orient to do a stint as an exchange student. Melissa has been thoroughly addicted to travel ever since, and over the past decade has co-authored and edited dozens of travel guidebooks and penned magazine and newspaper articles too numerous to count. She spends each summer completing research in Alaska, fall in British Columbia, winter island hopping in the Caribbean, and a few precious months each spring at home in Oregon.

Peter Oliver writes about sports and the outdoors for a number of publications, including *Backpacker,* the *New York Times, Skiing, Summit,* and *USA Today.* He was awarded the 1995 Lowell Thomas Award for ski journalism. His most recent book is *Bicycling: Touring and Mountain Biking Basics* (W. W. Norton). He lives in Warren, Vermont.

MACMILLAN TRAVEL

A Simon & Schuster Macmillan Company
1633 Broadway
New York, NY 10019

Find us online at **http://www.mgr.com/travel** or
on America Online at **Keyword: Frommer's.**

ISBN 0-02-860897-6
ISSN 1042-8283

Editor: Ian Wilker
Production Editor: Amy DeAngelis
Design by Michele Laseau
Digital Cartography by Ortelius Design

SPECIAL SALES

Bulk purchases (10+ copies) of Frommer's Travel Guides are available to corporations at special discounts. The Special Sales Department can produce custom editions to be used as premiums and/or for sales promotion to suit individual needs. Existing editions can be produced with custom cover imprints such as corporate logos. For more information write to Special Sales, Simon & Schuster, 1230 Avenue of the Americas, New York, NY 10020.

Manufactured in the United States of America

Contents

List of Maps

ACKNOWLEDGMENTS

Many people all over Alaska helped in my travels and writing—hospitable, friendly people, helping out the way Alaskans traditionally do. But a few people in particular made this book possible. My wife, Barbara, was almost a coauthor, visiting sights and hotels and keeping our family in order and happy as we traveled together. She made dozens of follow-up phone calls, had valuable insights, and was endlessly patient over months of deadline work. My young son, Robin, and even younger daughter, Julia, provided lots of unique perspectives for "our travel book," and made the discoveries of travel a joy, as only children can. I had several assistants in my research whose work also was invaluable, and is found all over this book, including Kathryn Gerlek, Laura Mathews, Eric Troyer, Dean Mitchell, Mark Handley, and Catherine Reardon. Many other friends checked my work and offered advice and travel tips on their favorite places, and I'm grateful and indebted to all of them.

—*Charles P. Wohlforth*

AN INVITATION TO THE READER

In researching this book, we discovered many wonderful places—hotels, restaurants, shops, and more. We're sure you'll find others. Please tell us about them, so we can share the information with your fellow travelers in upcoming editions. If you were disappointed with a recommendation, we'd love to know that, too. Please write to:

Charles P. Wohlforth
Frommer's Alaska, 4th Edition
Macmillan Travel
1633 Broadway
New York, NY 100019

AN ADDITIONAL NOTE

Please be advised that travel information is subject to change at any time—and this is especially true of prices. We therefore suggest that you write or call ahead for confirmation when making your travel plans. The authors, editors, and publisher cannot be held responsible for the experiences of readers while traveling. Your safety is important to us, however, so we encourage you to stay alert and be aware of your surroundings. Keep a close eye on cameras, purses, and wallets, all favorite targets of thieves and pickpockets.

WHAT THE SYMBOLS MEAN

✪ Frommer's Favorites

Hotels, restaurants, attractions, and entertainment you should not miss.

Ⓢ Super-Special Values

Hotels and restaurants that offer great value for your money.

The following abbreviations are used for credit cards:

AE	American Express	EURO	Eurocard
CB	Carte Blanche	JCB	Japan Credit Bank
DC	Diners Club	MC	MasterCard
DISC	Discover	V	Visa
ER	enRoute		

The Best of Alaska

As a child, when my family would travel outside Alaska for vacations, I often met other children who would ask, "Wow, you live in Alaska? What's it like?" I never did well with that question. To me, the place I was visiting was far simpler and easier to describe than the one I was from. The Lower 48 seemed a fairly homogenous land of freeways and fast food, a well-mapped network of established places. Alaska, on the other hand, wasn't—and isn't—even completely explored. Natural forces of vast scale and subtlety still were shaping the land in their own way, inscribing a different story on each of an infinite number of unexpected places. Each region, whether populated or not, was unique far beyond my ability to explain. Unlike the built environment where human endeavor held sway, Alaska was so large and new, unconquered and exquisitely real, as to defy description.

Now, as an adult, I'm faced with the same question again. It's my job, in some sense, to help capture Alaska between the covers of this book. I'm not the first writer to run into an adjective crisis when trying to describe the state—words like spectacular, majestic, vast, or magnificent all are quickly exhausted from the excessive workout they get. But I have comforted myself with the thought that all I really need to write is an introduction. The rest of the answer to the question—what Alaska really is like—is up to you, the reader, to find on your own journey of discovery. This volume only aims to help show the way.

The book's goal is to give you an idea of the best places to look, and to help take care of the details on the way, as you make your own discoveries. When you get home, if your trip has been especially successful, you may find that you, also, are at a loss for words about what you've seen and experienced.

The structure of the book is intended to make it a useful tool in your exploration. This first chapter just gives broad-brush ideas about some of the best Alaska has to offer (the entries aren't in any particular order). Chapter 2 provides an overview of the people, history, and natural history of the state. Chapters 3 and 4 have practical information for planning a trip. Chapter 5, by Melissa Rivers, is a self-contained guide to voyaging to Alaska on a cruise. Chapter 6, by Peter Oliver, serves the same function for joining outdoors adventures. The following chapters, 7 through 11, cover each of the state's regions in detail, broken into subregions or towns.

Good luck, and may your Alaskan trip be indescribable.

1 The Best Views

You can find your own best views almost anywhere in Alaska. But here are some of the sorts of visions you may have in Alaska:

- **From the Chugach Mountains over Anchorage, at sunset:** The city sparkles below, on the edge of an orange-reflecting Cook Inlet, far below the mountainside where you stand. Beyond the pink and purple silhouettes of mountains on the other side of the Inlet, the sun is spraying warm, dying light into puffs of clouds. It's midnight. (Chapter 8)
- **Northern Brooks Range, looking out over the North Slope:** The Brooks Range is a cracked gray rampart of unnamed peaks standing between the broad Interior of Alaska and the wet plain of the Arctic tundra. Looking north from the north side, gray gives way to green, smudging in the vast distance, and a thin line of the blue Arctic Ocean on the far horizon, more than 100 miles away. (Chapter 11)
- **Polychrome Pass, Denali National Park:** Riding in a bus rising up the narrow park road on a cliff face, you're too nervous to notice the horizon. And then, there it is—a great valley of green tundra, mountain peaks receding in every direction, and, on either side of the valley, mountains of colored rock standing like gates. (Chapter 9)
- **Punchbowl Cove, Misty Fjords National Monument:** A sheer granite cliff rises smooth and implacable 3,150 feet straight up from the water. A pair of bald eagles wheels and soars across its face, providing the only sense of scale. They look the size of gnats. Stand on the deck of your boat all day and gaze and you still won't get used to anything being quite that big. (Chapter 7)
- **The Northern Lights, Alaska's Interior or Southcentral region:** Blue, purple, green, and red lines spin from the center of the sky, draping long tendrils of slow-moving light. Flashing, bright, sky-covering waves wash across the dome of stars like ripples driven by a gust of wind on a pond. Looking around, your companions' faces are rosy in a silver, snowy night, all gazing straight up with their mouths open. (Chapter 10)
- **A Breaching Humpback Whale, Glacier Bay National Park:** Everyone is holding his or her breath on deck, scanning the wavy green water, waiting for the whale to surface again where someone said he saw it. Then it suddenly appears, and before people have time to gasp, its entire huge body is hanging in the air over the water and crashes down with a huge splash. (Chapter 7)
- **A First Sight of Alaska:** Flying north from Seattle, you're in clouds, so you concentrate on a book. When you look up, the light from the window has changed. Down below, the clouds are gone, and under the wing, where you're used to seeing roads, cities, and farms on most flights, instead you see only high, snowy mountain peaks, without the slightest mark of human presence, stretching as far as the horizon. Welcome to Alaska.

2 The Best of Cruising Alaska

by Melissa Rivers

Alaska is one of the world's top cruise destinations, well served by a variety of cruise lines running many different kinds of ships through the scenic Inside Passage, Prince William Sound, and the coast of the Kenai Peninsula. Which line, ship, and itinerary is best for you will depend on what you most want from your cruise experience.

Here are some of the highlights of cruising Alaska. For details on all these ships and places, see Chapter 5.

- **The Best Ships:** I get this question all the time and it's a hard one to answer because I have so many favorites, each for a different reason. The *Crystal Symphony* and sister ship *Crystal Harmony* are my favorite luxury liners. The gourmet cuisine is incredible, as are the cabins, the casino, the entertainment, the ship facilities, and the level of service. The twin *Crown Princess* and *Regal Princess* are favorites because of their outstanding onboard entertainment and the array of shore excursions available. The enormous *Legend of the Seas* has the most onboard facilities of the ships in Alaska, including the very best spa and fitness facilities afloat. Holland America leads the pack when it comes to onboard activities, and my favorites among their many ships are the twins *Statendam* and *Ryndam.* My top choice for families with kids or active travelers who appreciate plenty of sports amenities would be Norwegian Cruise Line's *Windward.* The best in the small-ship category would be the *Spirit of '98,* for its period decor, added amenities (cozy lounges, in-room TVs and VCRs, etc.), and limited onboard entertainment.
- **The Best Cruising Itinerary:** There's no contest. The best Alaskan itinerary is the 14-day trip aboard World Explorer Cruises' *Universe.* The ship itself isn't much, but the itinerary includes seven ports of call (Ketchikan, Wrangell, Sitka, Juneau, Skagway, Valdez, and Seward) plus days cruising Yakutat Bay / Hubbard Glacier, Glacier Bay, the Gulf of Alaska, and the Inside Passage—all for about the same cost as the standard week-long itinerary on other lines.
- **The Best Port of Call:** For years, my favorite Alaskan cruising port was Ketchikan, but lately it has become as commercialized as some ports in the Caribbean, with many of the same duty-free shops encroaching to push out the old mom-and-pop places. **Skagway,** which is admittedly very commercial-minded (but for the most part one of the cheapest shopping ports in Alaska), is now my favorite port of call, in part because of the enthusiastic characters who live and work there and in part because of the array of great entertainment and outdoor options readily available.
- **The Best Natural Sights from On Board:** When it comes to glaciers, my favorite area is Prince William Sound's **College Fjord:** The number and variety of glaciers there far outrank Glacier Bay. On the other hand, when it comes to the sheer scenic beauty of Alaska, the thickly forested peaks, mist-shrouded crags, tremendously quiet inlets, lichen-encrusted cliffs, and shimmering waterfalls of **Misty Fjords National Monument** are hard to beat (even though you won't find a glacier there).

3 The Best Glaciers

More than 100 times more of Alaska is covered by glacier ice than is settled by human beings. There are plenty of glaciers, and after a couple weeks, you may be a glacier connoisseur. Here are some favorites.

- **Childs Glacier, Cordova:** Out the Copper River Highway from Cordova, this is a participatory glacier-viewing experience. The glacier is cut by the Copper River, a quarter mile broad; standing on the opposite shore, unless you're up in the viewing tower, you have to be ready to run like hell when the creaking, popping ice gives way and a huge berg falls into the river. Waves created by the falling ice have thrown boulders and people around the picnic area and left salmon high up in the tree branches. (Chapter 8)

- **Exit Glacier, Seward:** This is a family glacier—not so large, not so dramatic, but you can drive near it and walk the rest of the way on a gravel path. Then it towers above like a huge blue sculpture, the spires of broken ice close enough to breath a freezer-door chill down on watchers. (Chapter 8)
- **Grand Pacific Glacier, Glacier Bay National Park:** Two vast glaciers of deep blue meet at the top of an utterly barren fjord—they rubbed and creased the gray rock for thousands of years before just recently releasing it to the air again. Boats that pull close to the glaciers seem surrounded by the intimidating walls of ice on three sides. (Chapter 7)
- **College Fjords, Prince William Sound:** In this area of western Prince William Sound you can see a couple of dozen glaciers in a day. Some of these are the amazing tidewater glaciers that dump huge, office-building–sized spires of ice into the ocean, each setting off a terrific splash and outward radiating sea wave. (Chapter 8)

4 The Most Beautiful Drives & Train Rides

There aren't many highways in Alaska, and all are worth exploring. You'll find a description of each in Chapter 10. Here are some highlights:

- **Richardson Highway, Thompson Pass:** Just out of Valdez heading north, the Richardson Highway rises quickly from sea level to more than 2,600 feet, switching back and forth on the side of a mountain. With each turn, the drop down the impassable slope becomes more amazing. It's too steep to see anything over the edge in places—it's as if the road is hanging up in the sky. At the top, the highway levels in a high alpine valley, well above tree line, where tundra gives way to towers of rock and a glacier hanging down on one side. (Chapter 8)
- **Richardson Highway, Alaska Range:** North of Glennallen, the highway rises again, through a low boreal forest of black spruce, past small lakes and roaring rivers, and suddenly bursts through the tree line between a series of mountains. Then for miles it traces the edge of huge, alpine lakes, broad and slate gray in reflection of the sky and the barren rock all around. On the opposite side it begins to descend, parallel with the silver skein of the Alaska Pipeline and a river now running in the opposite direction from those on the other side of the range. (Chapter 10)
- **Seward Highway, Turnagain Arm:** Just south of Anchorage, the highway has been chipped into the side of the Chugach Mountains over the surging gray water of Turnagain Arm. Above, Dall sheep pick their way along the cliffs, within easy sight. Below, white beluga whales chase salmon through the turbid water. (Chapter 8)
- **Alaska Railroad, Anchorage to Seward:** The line follows the same stretch of Turnagain Arm as the Seward Highway, then splits off as it rises into the mountains of the Kenai Peninsula, rumbling close along the face of a glacier and clinging to the edge of a vertically walled gorge with a roaring river at bottom. When it descends, the line follows a series of sparkling alpine lakes into a spruce forest and finally emerges at tidewater in Seward. (Chapter 8)
- **The Roads Around Nome:** You can't drive to Nome, but 250 miles of gravel roads radiate from the Arctic community into tundra populated only by musk oxen, bears, reindeer, birds, and other wildlife. There isn't anywhere much to drive to except an abandoned steam railroad train and a remote, undeveloped hot spring. (Chapter 11)
- **Top of the World Highway:** Leading over the top of rounded, tundra-clothed mountains from Dawson City, Yukon Territory, to the intersection with the

Taylor Highway, near Chicken, the gravel Top of the World seems to float on a waving sea of terrain, with mountains receding to the infinite horizon in every direction. (Chapter 10)

- **Yukon and White Pass Route Railway, Skagway to Summit:** A steam engine pulls historic cars up the narrow-gauge tracks for a few miles, then a diesel takes over for the haul up a steep grade chiseled into the granite mountains. The train is a sort of mechanical mountain goat, balancing on trestles and steep rock walls far above deep gorges below. (Chapter 7)

5 The Best Salmon & Halibut Fishing

- **Copper River Valley, Cordova:** The Copper itself is silty with glacial run-off, but feeder streams and rivers are rich with trout, Dolly Varden, and salmon. (Chapters 6 and 8)
- **Gustavus:** Charter boats from Gustavus get big halibut without long trips in the area of Icy Strait, and also see humpback whales feeding virtually without fail on the same trip, off Point Adolphus. (Chapter 7)
- **Homer:** The halibut aren't the easiest to find or the very largest, but they're easy and large enough, and Homer has one of the state's largest charter fishing fleets, accessible on the road network. (Chapter 8)
- **Kodiak Island:** Why do you think the bears are so big? It's because they live on an island that's crammed with spawning salmon in the summer. Kodiak has the best roadside salmon fishing in Alaska, and the remote fishing, at lodges or fly-in stream banks, is so hot that anglers complain their arms get too tired from fighting a big salmon on every cast. Kodiak is a good port for halibut fishing, too. (Chapter 11)
- **Prince of Wales Island:** Fly-in trips to the nation's third-largest island and stays at its luxurious fishing lodges yield some of the most prolific salmon fishing anywhere. (Chapter 7)
- **Sheenjek River, Arctic National Wildlife Refuge:** The grayling aren't big—they never are—but they're abundant. (Chapter 6)
- **The Kenai River:** The biggest king salmon—up to 98 pounds—come from the swift Kenai River. Big fish are so common in the second run of kings that there's a special, higher standard for what makes a trophy from this river. Silvers and reds add to a mad, summer-long fishing frenzy on the river and from its banks. (Chapter 8)
- **Unalaska/Dutch Harbor:** For lots of really enormous fish, nowhere else compares to Unalaska, in the Aleutian Archipelago. Halibut approaching 400 pounds are hauled in, right close to shore, and some fishermen throw back 70- and 100-pound fish to wait for a bigger one. (Chapter 11)
- **Wood-Tikchik State Park, Southwestern Alaska:** Hard to get to, relatively unknown, the park reportedly has some of the best lake fishing for trout and Dolly Varden in the state.

6 The Best Tips for Cooking Salmon

Now that you've caught a Pacific salmon, you need to know how to cook it—or order it in a restaurant—to avoid spoiling the sublime flavor.

- **Freeze as little as possible:** It's a sad fact that salmon loses some of its richness and gets more "fishy" as soon as it's frozen. It's still wonderful, but eat as much as you can fresh, because it'll never be better.

- **Choose the best fish:** The finest restaurants advertise where their salmon come from on the menu—in early summer, Copper River reds and kings are the richest in flavor; later in the summer, Yukon River salmon are best. King, red, and silver are the only salmon you should find in a restaurant. The oil in the salmon gives it the rich, meaty flavor; the fish from the Copper and Yukon are high in oil.
- **Keep it simple:** When ordering salmon or halibut in a restaurant, avoid anything with cheese, heavy sauces, or brown sugar. When salmon is fresh, it's best with just a little lemon, dill weed, and pepper and salt—or without anything on it, grilled over alder or mesquite coals.
- **Don't overcook it:** Salmon should be cooked just until the moment the meat changes color through to the bone. A few minutes more and the texture and flavor are lost. That's why those huge, barbecue salmon bakes often are not as good as they should be—it's too hard to cook hundreds of pieces of fish just right and serve them all hot.
- **Filets, not steaks:** Salmon is cut two ways in Alaska—length-wise filets or crosswise steaks. The filet is cut with the grain of the flesh, keeping the oil and moisture in the fish.

7 The Best Guided Wilderness Adventures

by Peter Oliver

Here are a few of the guided wilderness trips available. More choices, and details on these, are in chapter 6.

- **Chitistone Canyon Backpacking, Wrangell–St. Elias National Park:** This is a rigorous, rewarding backpack of 7 to 12 days, through deep canyons and heavily glaciated country. (St. Elias Alpine Guides, ☎ and fax 907/277-6867)
- **Prince William Sound Sea Kayaking, Southcentral Alaska:** The Sound is recovering from the notorious 1989 oil spill. Its islands and coves still offer some of the best kayaking in Alaska. (Alaska Wilderness Sailing Safaris, ☎ 907/835-5175, fax 907/835-5679)
- **Sheenjek River Rafting, Arctic National Wildlife Refuge:** One of the wildest of 26 wild and scenic rivers in Alaska, the Sheenjek cuts a wide path through the Brooks Range. (Alaska Discovery, ☎ 800/586-1911; or Alaska Wilderness Journeys, ☎ 800/349-0064)
- **Tatshenshini River Rafting, Southeastern Alaska and the Yukon Territory:** This is one of the most renowned white-water-rafting trips in the world, through the heavily glaciated mountains of Southeast Alaska. (Mountain Travel • Sobek, ☎ 800/227-2384; or Chilkat Guides Ltd., ☎ 907/766-2491)
- **Wild River Valley Dog Mushing, the Brooks Range:** For anyone interested in experiencing the Alaskan wilderness to its fullest, dog mushing in the Brooks Range is about as full as it gets. (Sourdough Outfitters, ☎ 907/692-5252)

8 The Best Sea Kayaking

Sea kayaking, which is like backpacking on the sea, is hugely popular. Here are some areas for trips you'll find more fully described in Chapter 6, and in the individual regional chapters:

- **Glacier Bay National Park:** Cruise ships frequent the main bay, but to escape the crowds, explore the smaller inlets—Muir Inlet, Johns Hopkins Inlet, and Tarr Inlet—a kayak is the way to go.

- **Kodiak Island:** The coast is pocked with coves and inlets and is abundant with bird life. Fly south to the bays of Kodiak National Wildlife Refuge, famous for excellent fishing and bears.
- **Misty Fjords National Monument:** Coves, inlets, and canals framed by high granite walls are the principal features of Misty Fjords. There's also lots of rain, but you can stay relatively dry by reserving public-use cabins for overnight stays.
- **Prince William Sound:** Probably the best place to start for exploring the fjords and glaciers that feed the Sound is Whittier.
- **Shuyak Island, Kodiak Archipelago:** Whether exploring the protected bays or rugged coastline of this island north of Kodiak, Shuyak kayakers are assured of seeing plenty of bird and sea life.

9 The Best Bear Viewing

There are lots of places to see bears in Alaska. But if your goal is to make sure that you see a bear, and potentially, lots of bears, these are the best places:

- **Anan Bear Observatory:** Accessed from Wrangell or Petersburg by float plane, Anan offers a relatively undiscovered chance to see bears feeding in a salmon stream from close at hand. There's even a Forest Service cabin to spend the night. In 1995 the Forest Service was considering a lottery system, but Anan will still be less visited than the other places on this list. (Chapter 7)
- **Denali National Park:** Although you won't see bears from as close as at one of the coastal salmon creeks, most every bus that drives the park road as far as the Eielson Visitor Center sees at least some grizzlies. Sometimes you're lucky enough to see bears feeding, hunting, or interacting. (Chapter 9)
- **Katmai National Park:** The Brooks Camp Lodge is the one place I'm aware of where you can put your feet up and sip a cold drink while watching bears wander by, within a few yards. As is the case at other bear observatories, the bears are drawn to the area during salmon spawning by a natural barrier for the fish that makes for an easy meal for the bears—in this case, a waterfall on the Brooks River. Wooden platforms allow visitors to watch in safety, and no permit is needed, although rooms at the lodge or sites in the campground aren't easy to get. Or fly in to remote locations, most notably the McKenzie River, and you're certain to see large grizzlies working salmon-choked streams. (Chapters 6 and 11)
- **Kodiak Archipelago:** At least two air-taxi operators guarantee you'll see the huge Kodiak brown bear or you get your money back. It's a safe bet for them. The float planes fly till they find a bear, then land on floats and watch from perfect safety, often at close range. (Chapter 11)
- **McNeil River State Game Sanctuary:** On the west side of Cook Inlet, accessed from Homer, McNeil is an opportunity to watch dozens of bears feeding in a waterfall of leaping salmon, and behaving naturally, while standing closer than you could in any zoo, without any protection between you and the bear. Over years of careful management, the bears have learned to ignore the few humans lucky enough to win a permit from a special lottery for the opportunity to see them. (Chapter 7)
- **Pack Creek, Admiralty Island:** The bears of the island, the most thickly populated with bears of any land in the world, have learned to ignore the daily visitors who stand on the platforms at Pack Creek. People can watch from close by as the mothers and cubs catch salmon from the creek. You have to win a permit in a lottery or buy a slot from a guide service or air-taxi that owns them. Access is from Juneau. (Chapter 7)

10 The Best Marine Mammal Viewing

You've got a good chance of seeing marine mammals almost anywhere you go boating in Alaska, but in some places it's almost guaranteed.

- **Frederick Sound, Petersburg:** A humpback gave Steve Berry's whale-watching trips the ultimate recommendation in 1995—when it jumped right into his boat. Berry and other charter operators see whales whenever they look for them out of Petersburg, and he has hydrophones for listening to their songs. They also see otters and baby seals sitting on icebergs floating in front of LeConte Glacier. (Chapter 7)

- **Kenai Fjords National Park, Seward:** You don't have to go all the way into the park—you're pretty well assured of sea otters and sea lions in Resurrection Bay, near Seward. But the best chance for humpbacks comes with longer trips, among the towering fjords and glaciers of the park. (Chapter 8)

- **Point Adolphus, Gustavus:** Humpback whales show up on schedule off the point in Icy Strait, just a few miles from little Gustavus, a town of luxurious country inns. You also have a good chance of seeing whales and sea lions in Glacier Bay National Park, which is on the other side of Gustavus, but there you have to watch from a greater distance. (Chapter 7)

- **Prince William Sound:** Otters, seals, and sea lions are easy—you'll see them on most trips out of Valdez, Whittier, or Cordova—but you also have a better chance of seeing both humpback and killer whales In the Sound than in most other parts of the state. There aren't fail-safe humpback spots, as there are in Southeast Alaska, but when one of the orca pods is handy, the local skippers know where to find it. (Chapter 8)

- **Sitka Sound:** Occasional whales and lots and lots of otters show up on the wildlife cruises in the island-dotted waters around Sitka. In the late fall the migrating whales are so common, I'm told, you can easily watch them from shore. (Chapter 7)

11 The Best Encounters with Native Culture

Alaska's Native people live all over the state, and you can learn about their cultures just by meeting them. Here are some of the best, organized ways to encounter Native culture:

- **Chilkat Dancers, Haines:** The Tlingit dancers of Haines started a Native cultural heritage renaissance in Southeast Alaska in the 1950s. Their dance performances are authentically loose—children learn their new parts by being thrown into the dance and picking it up, just as their grandparents would have done. The troupe's totem-carving studio is wonderfully casual, standing open for visitors to wander in and meet Tlingit artists. (Chapter 7)

- **Dig Afognak, Kodiak Archipelago:** The Koniag people's attempt to reclaim their culture from more than 200 years of suppression has turned to the work of archeology, which visitors are invited to join in. The digs on Afognak Island, north of Kodiak, are serious scientific work, but helpers who pay their own way are needed. Here you can live in the same remote wilderness where the ancient Koniag made their home while you help unearth clues to their way of life for their present-day descendants, who live on the land today. (Chapter 11)

- **NANA Museum of the Arctic, Kotzebue:** Eskimos of this still-traditional city/village proudly show off their Inupiat way of life with a combination of high-tech and age-old entertainment, part of a tour that includes a ride around Kotzebue and a demonstration of crafts and survival techniques. It's the best place for a formal presentation of Eskimo culture. (Chapter 11)

- **Saxman Totem Park:** Just south of Ketchikan, a Tlingit Native corporation owns a major totem pole collection and clan house, and provides tours and cultural demonstrations for visitors. Another totem park, north of town, is more picturesque, but Saxman is special for its living culture. The informal part of the experience is the best part, for in the workshop you can meet carver Nathan Jackson, recognized in 1995 as a National Cultural Heritage Fellow by first lady Hillary Clinton, as he works on new masterpieces of Tlingit culture. (Chapter 7)

12 The Best Museums & Historic Sites

- **Anchorage Museum of History and Art:** Alaska's largest museum doesn't have anything close to its richest collection, but it has the room and expertise to tell the story of Native and white history in Alaska, and to showcase the history of contemporary Alaskan art and culture. The best temporary shows come here too, and there are Native dance demonstrations in the lovely atrium in the summer. (Chapter 8)

- **Pratt Museum, Homer:** This independent museum would have no chance to be so good in any other small town of Homer's size, but the Pratt benefits from being situated in Alaska's leading community of visual artists, which also has an active intellectual life in natural history—not to mention an obsession with anything to do with the sea. Consequently, the Pratt explains the life of the ocean in an articulate way you'll find nowhere else in Alaska. (Chapter 8)

- **Sitka National Historic Park:** There are several fascinating historic sites and a rich museum in Sitka, and you should see all of them, but the site of the 1804 battle between the Tlingits and Russians, in a totem pole park and seaside stand of old-growth forest, has an especially deep impact. You can really appreciate what the Native people were fighting for when they resisted assimilation in this beautiful land. Inside the visitor center, Native craftspeople carry on their traditional work, as if to demonstrate who were the final victors in that struggle. (Chapter 7)

- **The State Museum, Juneau:** The museum is far too small for its purpose of representing the natural history of Alaska and the culture and history of each of its peoples, yet it succeeds in a way that startles, with discoveries all through the galleries. Here a rich collection on Alaska is boiled down to essences and displayed in a thoughtful and creative way that teaches the meaning of the place far more deeply than a book can. It's an indispensable stop to make sure you understand what you see while in Alaska. (Chapter 7)

- **University of Alaska Museum, Fairbanks:** The wealth of the university's study of Alaska, in all its forms, is put on display in a somewhat cluttered gallery with significant objects and serious explanations of what you're looking at. As the museum reminds you, here you see something real—from the equipment that makes UAF the world's leading center of study on the aurora borealis to the petrified bison that stands above everything. (Chapter 10)

13 The Best Places to Have Fun with Kids

- **Alaskaland, Fairbanks:** Younger children will be in heaven riding the little train, playing in the huge playground, playing miniature golf, riding on the merry-go-round, watching water swoosh through the gold-mining display, seeing the historic dioramas in the riverboat, and looking at the airplanes in the aviation museum. Adults will learn and have a good time, too. Older children and teens will think it's dumb and hokey—but they hate everything. (Chapter 10)

- **Chief Shakes Island, Wrangell:** The little island in the Wrangell small-boat harbor is a significant cultural resource for adults, too. But there's something about crossing a long, wooden foot bridge over a sea otter playground to a grassy little island with totem poles that's especially memorable for children. Totems are a form of art children can really appreciate, and the lawn behind the clan house is a casual setting for a picnic or play. My son still talked about our visit months afterward. (Chapter 7)
- **El Dorado Gold Mine, Fairbanks:** There are as many places to go gold panning in Alaska as there are entrepreneurs with a gold claim near a road, but none is more educational or fun than the El Dorado mine, north of Fairbanks, where visitors ride a train through a permafrost tunnel to see how commercial mining worked historically and still does today. It's fun for adults too, and you find plenty of gold. (Chapter 10)
- **The Alaska Botanical Garden, Anchorage:** In my experience, children don't enjoy only activities that are noisy and fun; like adults, they also need peace and respite. The new botanical garden in Anchorage is integrated into a forest, with lots of trails and quiet, hidden spots to explore. (Chapter 8)
- **The Alaska ferry system:** Riding the ferries is fun and unforgettable for children. Over the long hours steaming up the Inside Passage, children can explore freely over the decks and corridors of the ships. Some boats have playrooms. The children on a voyage always find each other and make new friends, roving around the vessels while their parents read a book or look out the window. All members of our family, from our three-year-old up, have made lasting friendships on the ferry. (Chapter 7)
- **The Alaska Zoo, Anchorage:** The animals' enclosures are along gravel paths through the woods—a child can easily imagine she is exploring the forest, finding the bears, musk ox, tigers, and elephants. A charmingly ramshackle boardwalk leads right through the waterfowl area, where the swans and geese are liable to demand a toll. This is the best place for kids to actually see Alaska wildlife in close-up. (Chapter 8)
- **The Imaginarium, Anchorage:** Half indoor playground, half science museum, the Imaginarium sneaks up on kids with lessons about how the world works. For that rare experience that kids would choose all on their own, but that's also good for them, this is the place to go. (Chapter 8)

14 The Best Places for the Gold Rush Centennial

- **Dawson City, Yukon Territory:** A group of prospectors made the Klondike gold strike in 1896, returned to tell of it in 1897, and tens of thousands of greedy gold seekers arrived after their arduous stampede in 1898. Gold is still coming out of the Yukon Territory around Dawson City, but the town is mostly dedicated to preserving and sharing the history of the gold-rush phenomenon. Celebrations and commemorations of the centennial are planned till the turn of the century. (Chapter 10)
- **Skagway:** The little town at the top of Lynn Canal was where most of the gold-rush stampeders got off the boat to head over the mountains to the Klondike. Spared of fire, flood, or even of much significant economic development other than tourism, Skagway contains a large collection of gold rush–era buildings protected

by the National Park Service. The whole town is one big museum and gift shop. (Chapter 7)

- **Nome:** The great Nome gold rush came next after the Klondike, in turn-of-the-century years when stampeders sloshed back and forth across the unsettled territory in search of riches. Gold came from the hills and from the very beach sand in front of the town. Although few buildings remain from the gold-rush period, the spirit and industry of that time remain authentically alive in Nome, unlike the other gold-rush towns in Alaska. (Chapter 11)

- **Fairbanks:** The gold rush in Fairbanks, just after the turn of the century, was one of the last major stampedes of the era. It's not entirely done yet—there was another rush to stake claims north of town recently. The town is large enough to provide lots of interesting and fun activities exploiting gold-rush history. (Chapter 10)

15 The Best Winter Destinations

- **Alyeska Resort, Girdwood:** Alaska's premier downhill skiing area has lots of snow over a long season, fantastic views, new lifts, and a luxurious new hotel (see "The Best Hotels," below). Sled-dog and snowmobile rides, cross-country skiing, and other activities are available, too. (Chapter 8)

- **Anchorage:** The Fur Rendezvous and Iditarod sled-dog races keep a winter-carnival atmosphere going through much of February and March. But those who enjoy winter sports will enjoy Anchorage most, with some of the best Nordic skiing anywhere, close access to the Alyeska Resort and two other downhill skiing areas, NCAA Division I hockey, and other activities and events. Culturally, much more happens in winter than summer. You'll also find Alaska's best hotel accommodations at bargain prices. (Chapter 8)

- **Chena Hot Springs Resort:** A 90-minute ride from Fairbanks and you're out in the country, where the northern lights are clear on a starry winter afternoon and night. The resort has lots of activities to get out into the snowy countryside, or you can just relax in the hot mineral springs. (Chapter 10)

- **Fairbanks:** The Interior's hub doesn't worry about extreme cold—it makes the most of winter, with sled-dog races, an extraordinary ice-carving festival, and outdoor activities. (Chapter 10)

- **Sitka:** Much of what makes Sitka attractive is just as good in winter, but with fewer crowds and lower prices. The historic sites are open year round, and in the late fall and early winter the humpback whale watching is exceptional, as the whales stop off on their migration. (Chapter 7)

16 The Best Unspoiled Small Towns

- **Cordova:** This fishing town off the beaten track is a forgotten treasure, caught at some mythical point in the past when Norman Rockwell's paintings were relevant. That atmosphere combines with the best birdwatching, fishing, scenic grandeur, and other outdoor activities to make Cordova one of Alaska's most charming and attractive destinations. (Chapter 8)

- **Gustavus:** It's a lovely little town near Glacier Bay National Park, except it isn't really a town. There's no local government or town center, just a collection of luxurious country inns and lodges in a setting of great scenic beauty, close to some of the best fishing, whale watching, and sea kayaking in Alaska. (Chapter 7)

- **Homer/Halibut Cove/Seldovia:** Homer is overrun by tourists, but somehow that's just part of the mix that contributes to, instead of taking away from, an energetic and creative community. Nearby Seldovia and Halibut Cove provide the other side of the coin, with perfectly preserved, quiet maritime lifestyles with the engines set on dead slow. (Chapter 8)
- **Kodiak:** This hub for an area with the biggest bears, most plentiful salmon, richest wilderness sea kayaking waters, and much other natural beauty is virtually untouched by visitors. Commercial fishing runs Kodiak, not tourism. The narrow, winding streets, Russian and Native historic sites, and wonderfully hospitable people are there waiting for those willing to go off the beaten track. (Chapter 11)
- **Petersburg:** The town is so easy to get to, right on the Inside Passage ferry route, it's incredible it has kept its quaint, small-town identity as perfectly as it has. Part of the formula is a conspicuous lack of catering to tourists. But it's got a wonderfully diverse choice of outdoor activities. (Chapter 7)

17 The Most Bizarre Community Events

- **Bering Sea Ice Golf Classic, Nome:** The greens are Astroturf, as the sea ice won't support a decent lawn in mid-March. Hook a drive and you could end up spending hours wandering among the pressure ridges, but you must play the ball as it lies. (Chapter 11)
- **Cordova Ice Worm Festival:** The truth is, ice worms do exist. Really. This winter carnival celebrates them in February. The highlight is the traditional annual march of the ice worm down the main street, a costume with dozens of feet sticking out. (Chapter 8)
- **Midnight Sun Baseball Game, Fairbanks:** The semi-pro baseball game, without lights, doesn't begin until 10:30pm on June 21, the longest day of the year. (Chapter 10)
- **Nome Polar Bear Swim/Bathtub Race:** Nome has so *many* strange community events. Memorial Day is marked by the polar bear swim, sea ice permitting. Labor Day is celebrated by a bathtub race down Front Street, with water in the tubs. (Chapter 11)
- **Pillar Mountain Golf Classic, Kodiak:** The course is one hole, par is 70, elevation gain is 1,400 feet. Having a spotter in the deep snow of late March is helpful, but use of two-way radios and dogs is prohibited. Also, no cutting down power poles, and cursing tournament officials carries a $25 fine. (Chapter 11)
- **World Extreme Skiing Championships, Valdez:** As far as I can tell, extreme skiing is the act of hurling yourself off the side of a vertical mountain with skis on, and landing upright. They make a competition of the daredevil plunge each March. (Chapter 8)

18 The Best Hotels

- **Alyeska Prince Hotel, Girdwood:** The first sight of this new ski resort hotel (☎ 800/880-3880)—designed in a château style and standing in an undeveloped mountain valley—is enough to make you catch your breath. Wait till you get inside and see the starscape and polar bear diorama in the lobby atrium, or the large swimming pool, with its high-beamed ceiling and wall of windows looking out on the mountain. The cozy rooms are full of cherry wood. A tram carries skiers and diners to the top of the mountain. (Chapter 8)

- **The Grand Aleutian Hotel, Unalaska/Dutch Harbor:** Not long ago it wasn't much of a distinction to be the best hotel in the Alaska Bush. Then the UniSea fish company built this large, lodge-style, luxury hotel (☎ 800/891-1194), which is competitive with the best in the state. Offering this level of service in this remote Aleutian archipelago setting is quite an accomplishment, and creates a unique opportunity for those who want to stay in a fine hotel and see the Bush, with the best unexploited fishing, wildlife watching, and rare-bird watching. (Chapter 11)
- **Hotel Captain Cook, Anchorage:** This is the grand old hotel of downtown Anchorage (☎ 907/276-6000), with a heavy nautical theme and teak paneling and furniture that carries through to the smallest detail in the rooms. It also remains the state's standard of service and luxury. Every facility is available, every detail considered. The rooms and restaurants have stunning views from three high-rise towers located in the best part of Anchorage's downtown area. (Chapter 8)
- **Kenai Princess Lodge, Cooper Landing:** The Princess Cruise Line has built three good hotels in Alaska, but this one (☎ 907/595-1425) is like no other. Perched on a mountainside above the Kenai River, each room has the feel of a wilderness cabin, with a wood stove stocked with firewood, a balcony overlooking the valley, and a pervasive forest scent emanating from the cedar walls. There are lots of perfect little details. But, of course, it's not a wilderness cabin—it has all the comforts of a top hotel. A wonderfully romantic retreat. (Chapter 8)
- **Land's End, Homer:** The hotel itself (☎ 907/235-2500) has some nice touches, but it wouldn't be in a class with the others on this list if not for the location. The low, wood buildings lie like a string of driftwood beached on the tip of Homer Spit, out in the middle of Kachemak Bay. Nothing stands between the rooms or restaurant and the ocean, across the beach. Sometimes whales and otters swim along the shore, just outside the windows. (Chapter 8)
- **Westmark Cape Fox Lodge, Ketchikan:** Standing in its own little forest atop a rocky promontory that dominates downtown Ketchikan, this cleanly luxurious hotel (☎ 907/225-8001) has the feel of a mountain lodge or resort. A funicular tram carries visitors to the Creek Street boardwalks, or you can take the wooded, cliffside path. Exceptional views of the city and Tongass Narrows through the trees are offered from rooms and common areas accented with rich red cedar and masterpieces of Tlingit art, mostly by National Heritage Fellow Nathan Jackson. For its setting and perfect execution of an understated theme, this hotel is the most attractive in Alaska. (Chapter 7)

19 The Best Moderately Priced Lodgings

- **All Seasons Bed and Breakfast, Fairbanks:** This is a small country inn (☎ 907/451-6649) on a quiet street a couple of blocks from the downtown center. It was recently completely remodeled for its function, and great details like a screened-in porch were added. The rooms are comfortable and simply elegant. (Chapter 10)
- **Harborview Bed and Breakfast/Seaview Apartments, Seward:** When the friendly hosts (☎ 907/224-3217) showed me their large, very clean, bright, attractively decorated rooms, and the beachfront apartments they rent for an incredible bargain price, I kept waiting for the other shoe to drop. It never did—they simply take pride in offering much better for much less than others. (Chapter 8)
- **Log Cabin Bed and Breakfast, Kenai:** This lodge (☎ 907/283-3653), with huge picture windows overlooking a beaver pond, was built specifically for its function as the family business. The rooms have character and the whole experience is more like a top-priced wilderness lodge, except that it's quite inexpensive. (Chapter 8)

- **Motel Nord Haven, Healy (near Denali Park):** It's in an area dominated by hotels with so-so rooms renting for sky-high rates, but you'd count this attractive new hotel (☎ 907/683-4500) as having very good rooms for reasonable rates if you came across it almost anywhere. (Chapter 9)
- **The New York Hotel, Ketchikan:** An old building right on the water (☎ 907/225-0246) has been lovingly restored into just a few charming rooms, decorated with antiques and with views out on the town's most attractive, historic district. (Chapter 7)
- **The Northern Lights Inn, Cordova:** Located in a historic hillside house with just a few rooms, the inn (☎ 907/424-5356) is operated by an old Cordova family with lots of hospitality and energy. The upstairs rooms have every amenity and are furnished with antiques, but rent for very low rates. (Chapter 8)
- **Snowshoe Inn, Anchorage:** This small, converted apartment building (☎ 907/258-SNOW) has just what's called for: bright, immaculate rooms, a hospitable and meticulous couple as owner-operators, a central location on a quiet downtown side street, and low prices. (Chapter 8)
- **Snowshoe Motel & Fine Arts and Gifts, Tok:** This is just a roadside motel (☎ 907/883-4511) behind a gift shop on the Alaska Highway. But for the price, and the area, the suitelike rooms are an exceptional value. (Chapter 10)

20 The Best Bed-and-Breakfasts

- **Alaska Ocean View Bed and Breakfast, Sitka:** Here a family has set out to turn their home (☎ 907/747-8310) into perfect accommodations. Among other details, the elaborate feminine decor in each room matches a unique packet of souvenir wildflower seeds given to each guest. (Chapter 7)
- **Aurora Winds B&B Resort, Anchorage:** An enormous house on the hillside above Anchorage (☎ 907/346-2533) has rooms so completely and theatrically decorated you'll feel as if you're sleeping in a movie set. Details like a fully equipped computer room behind a secret door in one room make this the most excessively luxurious B&B in Alaska. (Chapter 8)
- **Captain's Quarters Bed & Breakfast, Ketchikan:** On a hill where some of the streets are staircases, the ocean-facing rooms (☎ 907/225-4912) have unbelievable views of Tongass Narrows. The decor matches—a nautical theme, all in oak, lovingly crafted by the hands of the meticulous proprietor. (Chapter 7)
- **Cliff House Bed and Breakfast, Valdez:** With a spectacular location atop a wooded rock outcropping right on the ocean, but with downtown right at hand beyond the thick screen of trees, the house (☎ 907/835-5244) is an architectural masterpiece for the way it fits its surroundings. The rooms are luxurious. (Chapter 8)
- **Forget-Me-Not Lodge and the Aurora Express Bed and Breakfast, Fairbanks:** This family bought an old-fashioned railroad train, hauled it up the side of a mountain above Fairbanks, and remodeled the cars in luxurious, theme decor as a bed-and-breakfast (☎ 907/474-0949). The story of why they did it is as improbable as Hollywood's worst scripts, but the sight of the rail cars in this incongruous location and their extraordinary interiors will enable you to believe anything. (Chapter 10)
- **Pearson's Pond Bed and Breakfast, Juneau:** Diane Pearson (☎ 907/789-3772) takes the prize for the most obsessive attention to detail at any bed-and-breakfast in Alaska. Not only are the bathrooms stocked with condoms, but the private pond, with a fountain spraying, is stocked with fish. (Chapter 7)

- **Skagway Inn:** Each Victorian room is named for a woman documented by police records to have worked in the building when it was a gold-rush brothel. Yet today the place (☎ 907/983-2289) has the genteel feeling of an English country inn, and the area's best restaurant serves meals in the evening in the breakfast room. (Chapter 7)

21 The Best Wilderness Lodges

- **Camp Denali, Kantishna, Denali National Park:** This lodge (☎ 907/ 683-2290), on private land at the end of the national park road, is more than a place to relax and get into the wilderness—it also has a highly regarded program of natural-history education. The difference from other lodges is like that between listening to a symphony as a naive music lover or understanding it as a trained musician. (Chapter 9)
- **Gustavus Inn at Glacier Bay:** Gustavus has several exceptional country inns, all similar to wilderness lodges, and this (☎ 907/697-2254) is the best of that superb collection. The rooms are charming, the grounds lovely, the meals incomparable, and the hospitality warm and welcoming. The natural surroundings in the area offer extraordinary outdoor opportunities for fishing, whale watching, sea kayaking, hiking, and biking. (Chapter 7)
- **Kachemak Bay Wilderness Lodge, near Homer:** This is the state's original ecotourism lodge (☎ 907/235-8910), and still one of the best. The lodgings are completely comfortable while also fitting in with their rich maritime wilderness surroundings. The food is famous. But the hosts, Mike and Diane McBride, with their deep knowledge of the area and its natural history, make the experience one of the best to be had of any kind in Alaska. (Chapter 8)
- **Riversong Lodge, northwest of Anchorage:** Fishing and wilderness treks to Lake Clark National Park are the outdoor attractions of this lodge (☎ 907/274-2710), but the food is what makes it famous. Kirsten Dixon is hailed as one of the best chefs in Alaska, drawing people out to the wilderness just for the meals. (Chapter 6)
- **Ultima Thule Lodge, Wrangell–St. Elias National Park:** The rugged surroundings in the park and the enthusiasm of the proprietors provide a seemingly limitless range of outdoor activities on mountains, glaciers, rivers, ocean, horseback—you get the idea. Once back in the lodge (☎ 907/258-0636), your stay is in comfort, with a skylight over your bed to watch the midnight sun or, in winter, the northern lights. (Chapter 6)

2 Alaska: Experiment in Magnificence

An old photo album opens, breathing a scent of dust and dried glue. Inside, pale images speak wanly of shrunken mountains and glaciers, a huge blue sky, water and trees, a moose standing way off in the background. No family photographer can resist the drive to capture Alaska's vastness in the little box of a camera, and none, it seems, has ever managed it. Then, turning the page, there it is—not in another picture of the landscape, but reflected in a small face at the bottom of the frame. My own face, as a child. For anyone who hasn't experienced that moment, the expression is merely enigmatic—slightly dazed, happy but abstracted, as if hearing a far-off tone. But if you've been to Alaska, that photograph captures something familiar: It's an image of discovery, revelation, even conversion. I've seen it on the fresh, pale faces in photographs stamped with the dates of my family's first explorations of Alaska more than 30 years ago. And then, researching this book, I got to see it once again, on my own young son's face. And I knew that, like me, he had discovered something about himself in Alaska.

So what am I talking about? If I could tell you, you wouldn't need to come here. There are some things you can't learn until they reach inside and rearrange you—and this is one of them.

Tour guides try to get it across with statistics. Not much hope of that, although some of the numbers do give you a general idea of scale. Once you've driven across the continental United States, and know how big that is, seeing a map of Alaska placed on top of the area you crossed, just about spanning it, provides some notion of size. Alaskans always like to threaten that we'll split in half and make Texas the third-largest state. Alaska has about 600,000 residents. If you placed each of them an equal distance apart, no one would be within a mile of anyone else. Of course, that couldn't happen. No one has ever been to some parts of Alaska.

But none of that expresses what really matters. It's not just a matter of how big Alaska is, or how few people it contains. It's not an intellectual conception at all. None of that crosses your mind when you see a chunk of ice the size of an office building fall from a glacier and send up a huge splash and wave surging outward. There's no point thinking about comparisons or abstract concepts of scale when you hike for a couple of days to stand on top of a mountain, and from there see more mountaintops, layered off as far as the horizon, in unnamed, seemingly infinite multiplicity. Intellect disappears altogether when you're walking in the woods and meet a bear—an animal large enough to eat you, fast enough to outrun the fastest man on earth, nimble enough to outclimb you, and tough enough to withstand a slug from all but the heaviest guns. Instead, the hair on your neck stands on end and you freeze, and until the bear decides what to do with you, you're nothing more than potential prey, like our long-forgotten ancestors from before civilization.

A realization of what Alaska means doesn't have to be anything so dramatic or pronounced. It can come at the end of a long day driving an Interior Alaska highway, as your car climbs into yet another mountain range, the sun still hanging high in what should be night, storm systems arranged before you across the landscape, when you realize that you haven't seen another car in an hour. Or standing on an Arctic Ocean beach, it could happen when you look around at the sea of empty tundra behind you, the sea of green water before you, and your own place on an endless line of gravel at what seems to be the edge of the world. Or you might simply be sitting on the sun-warmed rocks of a beach in Southeast or Southcentral Alaska when you discover that you're occupying only one of many worlds—a world of intermediate size, lying in magnitude between the tiny tide-pool universes of life all around you and the larger world seen by an eagle gliding through the air high above, in which you occupy only one of many little beaches encompassed by pockets of rock and forest.

What's the soul alchemy of such a moment? I suppose it's different for each person, but for me it has something to do with realizing my actual size in the world, how I fit in, what it means to be just another medium-sized mammal, unable to sustain the illusions supplied by civilization. On returning to the city from the wilderness, there's a reentry process, like walking from a vivid movie to the mundane, gray street outside—it's the movie that seems more real. For a while it's hard to take human institutions seriously after you've been deep into Alaska.

Some people never do step back across that boundary. They live their lives out in the wilderness away from people. Others compromise, living in Alaskan cities and walking out into the mountains when they can, the rest of the time just maintaining a prickly notion of their own independence. But anyone can make the same discovery, if he or she has the courage to come to Alaska and the time to let the place sink in. You don't have to be an outdoors enthusiast or a young person. You only have to be open to wonder, and able to slow down long enough to see it. Then, in a quiet moment when you least expect it, things may suddenly seem very clear, and all that you left behind oddly irrelevant.

How you find your way back to where you started is your affair.

1 The Regions in Brief

SOUTHEAST ALASKA   The Southeast Panhandle is the relatively narrow strip of mountains and islands that lies between Canada and the Gulf of Alaska. To Alaskans, it's the Southeast, but to the rest of the country it's more like the northernmost extension of the lush Pacific Northwest. It's a land of huge rain-forest trees, glacier-garbed mountains, and countless islands ranging in size from the nation's third largest to tiny, one-tree islets strewn like confetti along the channels and fjords. The water is the highway of Southeast Alaska, as the land is generally too steep and rugged to build roads, but there are lots of towns and villages reachable by the ferry system or cruise ships. Southeast contains Juneau, Alaska's capital and third-largest city, and Ketchikan, next in size to Juneau. Southeast's towns are as quaint and historic as any in Alaska, especially Sitka, which preserves the story of Russian America and its conflict with the indigenous Native people. Nowhere in Alaska is Native

Alaska

MILEAGE CHART Approximate driving distances in miles between cities.	Anchorage	Circle	Eagle	Fairbanks	Haines	Homer	Prudhoe Bay	Seward	Skagway	Tok	Valdez
Anchorage		520	501	358	775	226	847	126	832	328	304
Circle	520		541	162	815	746	1972	646	872	368	526
Eagle	501	541		379	620	727	868	627	579	173	427
Fairbanks	358	162	379		653	584	489	484	710	206	364
Haines	775	815	620	653		1001	1142	901	359	447	701
Homer	226	746	727	584	1001		1073	173	1058	554	530
Prudhoe Bay	847	1972	868	489	1142	1073		973	1199	695	853
Seward	126	646	627	484	901	173	973		958	454	430
Skagway	832	872	579	710	359	1058	1199	958		504	758
Tok	328	368	173	206	447	554	695	454	504		254
Valdez	304	526	427	364	701	530	853	430	758	254	

Chukchi Sea

RUSSIA

Little Diomede Island

Nome

Norton Sound

St. Lawrence Island

Yukon Delta National Wildlife Refuge

St. Matthew Island

Bering Sea

Nunivak Island

Bethel

Yukon Delta National Wildlife Refuge

Attu Island

Pribilof Islands

Bristol Bay

Cape St. Stephen

Rat Islands

Alaska Peninsula

Unimak Island

Cold Bay

Adak

Atka Island
Atka

Dutch Harbor

Fort Glen

Unalaska

Unimak

Adak Island

Aleutian Islands

PACIFIC

2170

culture—here, Tlingit and Haida—richer or closer to hand. Nor is any region much richer in opportunities for boating or seeing marine wildlife. The weather is wet and temperate.

SOUTHCENTRAL ALASKA   As a region, Southcentral is something of a catch-all, weaker in identity than other parts of the state. The area is roughly defined by the arc of the Gulf of Alaska from the straight portion of the Canadian border, on the east, to Cook Inlet and the end of the road network, to the west. It's a micro-cosm of the state, containing Prince William Sound, which is similar to the wooded island habitat of Southeast; the Kenai Peninsula, a roaded fishing, boating, and out-doors mecca; Anchorage, the state's modern, major city; the Matanuska and Susitna valleys, an agricultural and suburban region of broad flatlands between steep moun-tains; and the Copper River country, a rugged and sparsely populated region along the border with Canada with much in common with the Interior. Southcentral dominates the state, with most of its population and a more highly developed transportation system, including a network of highways and the Alaska Railroad. Southcentral's weather is influenced by the ocean, keeping it from being very hot or very cold. The coastal areas are wet, while farther inland is drier.

THE INTERIOR   The vast central part of the state is crossed by highways and riv-ers that act as highways. There are huge, generally flat areas lying between the Alaska Range, which contains Mount McKinley, North America's tallest peak, and the Brooks Range, a continental divide between the Interior's great rivers and the Arc-tic. The region's dominant city is Fairbanks, Alaska's second largest, which lies on the Chena River in the middle of the state. The natural environment is drier and less abundant than Southeast or Southcentral. Consequently, the Athabascans, the Interior's first people, are less numerous and traditionally lacked the rich natural endowments of Southeast's Native peoples. Summers can be hot and winters very cold in the Interior, because of the distance from the ocean.

THE BUSH   Bush Alaska is linked by lifestyle rather than by geography. One good definition would be that the Bush is that part of the state that's closer to the wilder-ness than to civilization. It's also the only part of the state where Native people outnumber whites and other relative newcomers. In many Bush villages, reachable only by small plane, people still live according to age-old subsistence hunting-and-gathering traditions. "Rural Alaska" is a synonym for the Bush. The Bush region includes the majority of Alaska outside the road network, ranging from the north end of the Canadian border all the way around the coast, out the Aleutians, and the Alaska Peninsula and Kodiak Island, at the border of the Southcentral region. But some towns in each of the other regions also could be called "Bush villages." The Bush con-tains many regions, including the Arctic, Northwest, and Southwest Alaska.

2 Natural History: Rough Drafts & Erasures

In 1986, Hubbard Glacier, north of Yakutat, suddenly decided to surge forward, cutting off Russell Fjord from the rest of the Pacific Ocean. A group of warm-hearted but ill-advised wildlife lovers set out to save the marine mammals that had been trapped behind the glacier. Catching a dolphin from an inflatable boat isn't that easy—they didn't accomplish much, but they provided a lot of entertainment for everyone watching. Then the water burst through the dam of ice and the lake became a fjord again, releasing the animals anyway.

Currently, the Bering Glacier is galloping into a wetland, destroying a migratory bird stopover. Meares Glacier is plowing through old-growth forest. On the other side of the ledger, Malaspina Glacier is retreating. It has so much dirt on it that trees and brush have grown to maturity, only to topple as the ice melts underneath the dirt. And on a larger scale, all the land of Glacier Bay—mountains, forests, sea floor—is rising $1^1/_2$ inches a year as it rebounds from the weight of melted glaciers that 100 years ago were a mile thick and 65 miles longer.

Yet these new and erased lands are just small corrections around the margins compared to what the earth has done before in setting down, wiping out, and rewriting the natural history of Alaska. In the last Ice Age, 15,000 years ago, much of what is Alaska today was one huge glacier. At the tops of granite mountains in Southeast Alaska, especially in the northern Lynn Canal, it's possible to see a sort of high-water mark—the highest point the glaciers came in the Ice Age. Even looking from the deck of a boat, thousands of feet below, you can see where mountain shoulders, rounded by the passage of ice, are much smoother than the sharp, craggy peaks just above, which stuck above that incredible sheet of ice.

Some children worry about the bogeyman or being caught in a house fire at age seven. When I was that age, living with my family in Juneau—and I learned how Gastineau Channel was formed, and we went to see Mendenhall Glacier, and I was told how it was really a river of ice, advancing and retreating—I developed a deeper fear: ice. I was afraid that while I slept, another Ice Age would come and grind away the city of Juneau.

It's possible that a glacier *could* get Juneau—the city fronts on the huge Juneau Ice Field—but there would be at least a few centuries' warning before it hit. Glaciers are essentially just snow that doesn't get a chance to melt. It accumulates at higher altitudes until it gets deep enough to compress into ice and starts oozing down the side of the mountain. When the ice reaches the ocean, or before, the melt and calving of icebergs at the leading edge reaches a point of equilibrium with the snow that's still being added at the top. The glacier stops advancing, becoming a true river of ice, moving a snow flake from the top of the mountain to the bottom in a few hundred years. When conditions change—more snow or colder long-term weather, for example—the glacier gets bigger. That's called advancing, and the opposite is retreating. Sometimes, something strange will happen under the glacier—in the case of Bering Glacier, it started to float on a cushion of water—and it will surge forward, several feet or even dozens of feet a day in extreme cases. But most of the time the advance or retreat is measured in inches or feet a year. Today Alaska's 100,000 glaciers cover about 5% of its land mass.

Despite my early glacier phobia, I never had a similar fear of earthquakes. Living in Anchorage, I'd been through enough of them that, as early as I can remember, I generally didn't bother to get out of bed when they hit.

It's all part of living in a place that isn't quite done yet. Any part of Alaska could have an earthquake, but the Pacific Rim from Southcentral Alaska to the Aleutians is the shakiest. That's because this is where Alaska is still under construction. The very rocks that make up the state are something of an ad hoc conglomeration, still in the process of being assembled. They've been gathered from all over the Pacific and slammed together to make a single land mass—a thrift-store grab bag of land from tropical waters and beyond carried north by a terrestrial conveyor belt called the Pacific tectonic plate.

Here's how it works. The center of the Pacific plate is expanding, with underwater volcanoes and cracks that constantly ooze new rock. That forces the existing sea floor to spread, at perhaps an inch a year. At the other side of the Pacific plate, there's not enough room for the sea floor that's being created, and the crust bends and cracks as it's forced downward into the planet's great, molten recycling mill of magma. Land masses that are along for the ride smash into the continent that's already there. When one hits—the so-called Yakutat block is still in the process of docking—a mountain range gets shoved up. Earthquakes and volcanoes are a byproduct.

Living in such an unsettled land is a matter of more than abstract interest. The Mount Spurr volcano, which erupted most recently in 1992, turned day to night in Anchorage, dropping a blanket of ash all over the region, choking lungs and machines. A Boeing 747 full of passengers flew into the plume and lost power in all its engines, falling in darkness for several minutes before pilots were able to restart the clogged jets. After that incident, the airport was closed until aviation authorities could find a way to keep volcanic plumes and planes apart. More than 80 volcanoes have been active in Alaska in the last 200 years. Earthquakes over 7 on the Richter scale—larger than the 1994 Los Angeles quake—have occurred every 15 months, on average, over the last century.

The worst of the quakes, on March, 27, 1964, was the strongest ever to hit North America. It ranked 9.2 on the Richter scale, lowering an entire region of the state some 10 feet and moving it even farther laterally. No other earthquake has ever moved so much land.

There are lots of tales about what people did when the quake hit—it lasted a good 10 minutes, long enough for a lot to happen. My wife, Barbara, a one-year-old at the time, is said to have found it hilariously funny while everyone else ran around in panic. A family friend rushed out into the street from bathing, stark naked; a neighbor who had been doing laundry when the earth started shaking met him there and handed him a pair of socks she had happened to carry with her.

The earthquake destroyed much of Anchorage and several smaller towns and killed more than 130 people, mostly in sea waves created by underwater landslides. In Valdez, the waterfront was swept clean of people. In the Prince William Sound village of Chenega, built on a hill along the water, people started running for higher ground when the wave came. About half made it. Families were divided by just yards between those who ran fast enough and those who were caught by the water and disappeared. But the earthquake could have been much worse—it occurred in the early evening, on Good Friday, when most public buildings were empty. An elementary school in Anchorage that broke in half and fell into a hole didn't have anyone inside at the time.

The Interior and Arctic parts of the state are less susceptible to earthquakes and, since they receive little precipitation, they don't have glaciers either. But there's still a sense of living on a land that's not quite sure of itself, as most of northern Alaska is solid only by virtue of being frozen. When it thaws, it turns to mush. The phenomenon is caused by permafrost, a layer of earth a little below the surface that never thaws—or at least, you'd better hope it doesn't. Buildings erected on permafrost without some mechanism for dispersing their own heat—pilings, or even refrigerator coils—thaw the ground below and sink into a self-made quicksand. You occasionally run across such structures. There's one in Dawson City, Yukon Territory, still left from the gold rush, that leans at an alarming angle with thresholds and lower tiers of siding disappearing into the ground.

Building sewer and water systems in such conditions is a challenge still unmet in much of Alaska's Bush, where village toilets are often "honey buckets" and the septic systems are sewage lagoons on the edge of town where the buckets are dumped. Disease caused by the unsanitary conditions sweeps the villages as if rural Alaska were a Third World country, but the government has been slow to provide the funds required to solve the problem.

The Arctic, and much of the Interior, are a sort of swampy desert. Most of the time the tundra is frozen in white; snow blows around, but not much falls. That water melts in the summer and stands on the surface, on top of the permafrost, creating ponds—Alaska is a land of 10 million lakes, with 3 million larger than 20 acres. Migratory birds arrive to feed and paddle around those shallow circles of enigmatic deep green and sky blue. Flying over the Arctic in a small plane is disorienting, for no pattern maintains in the flat green tundra and irregularly shaped patches of water stretching as far as the eye can see. Pilots find their way by following landmarks like tractor tracks etched into the tundra. Although few and far between, the tracks remain clearly delineated for decades after they're made, appearing as a pair of narrow, parallel ponds reaching from one horizon to the other.

The permafrost also preserves much older things. The meat of prehistoric mastodons, still intact, has been unearthed from the frozen ground. On the Arctic Coast, the sea eroded ground near Barrow that contained ancient ancestors of the Eskimos who still inhabit the same neighborhood. In 1982 they found a family that apparently was crushed by sea ice up to 500 years ago. Two of the bodies were well preserved, sitting in the home they had occupied and wearing the clothes they had worn the day of the disaster, perhaps around the same time as Columbus was sailing to America.

Sea ice is the frozen ocean that extends from northern Alaska to the other side of the world. At the very top of the world it never thaws, but the water opens for a few months of summer along the shore. Then, in September, when the ocean water falls below 29°, ice forms along the beach and expands from the North Pole's permanent ice pack until the two sides meet. The clash of huge ice floes creates towering pressure ridges, small mountains of steep ice that are difficult to cross. The Eskimo blanket toss—the game of placing a person in the center of a walrus-skin blanket and bouncing him or her high in the air—traditionally got hunters high enough to see over the pressure ridges so they could spot game. At its extreme, in March, the ice extends solidly all the way to the Pribilof Islands, and it's possible to drive a dog team across the Bering Sea to Siberia. The National Weather Service keeps track of the ice pack and issues predictions, as crabbing boats like to tempt its south-moving edge in the fall. Ice even interferes with shipping in Cook Inlet, around Anchorage, although the floes never form a solid pack. Walking on the downtown coastal trail at night, you can hear their eerie crunch and squeal as they tumble together in the fast tidal currents.

The Arctic and Interior are relatively barren biologically compared to the southern coastal areas of the state. Polar bears wander the Arctic ice pack, but they, like the Eskimos, feed more on marine mammals than on anything found on the shore. A 1,200-pound adult polar bear can make a meal of a walrus, and even eat a whale that happens to wash up, although they mostly feed on seals. In the summer huge herds of caribou come north to their eastern Arctic calving grounds, but they migrate south when the cold, dark winter falls unremittingly on the region. In Barrow, the sun doesn't rise for more than 80 days in the winter; in February, the average daily high temperature is −12° Fahrenheit, and the average low is −24°.

By comparison, southern coastal Alaska is warm and biologically rich. Temperate rain forest ranges up the coast from Southeast Alaska into Prince William Sound. Bears, deer, moose, wolves, and even big cats live among the massive western hemlock, Sitka spruce, and cedar. This old-growth forest, too wet to burn in forest fires, is the last vestige of the virgin, primeval woods that seemed so limitless to the first white settlers who arrived on the continent in the 17th century. The trees grow on and on, sometimes rising more than 200 feet high and a dozen feet in diameter, and falling only after hundreds of years. The trunks rot on the damp moss of the forest floor and return to soil to feed more trees.

Standing among these giants one feels dwarfed by their age and size, living things of so much greater life span and magnitude than any person. Part of the mystery and grandeur also comes from the knowledge that, here at least, Alaska *does* seem permanent. That sense helps explain why cutting the rain forest is so controversial. Just one of these trees contains thousands of dollars worth of wood, a prize that drives logging as voraciously as the federal government, which owns most of the coastal forest, may choose to allow.

The rivers of the great coastal forests bring home runs of big salmon, clogging in spawning season like a busy sidewalk at rush hour. The fish spawn only once, returning by a precisely tuned sense of smell to the streams where they were hatched as many as seven years before. When the fertilized eggs have been left in the stream gravel, the fish often conveniently die on the beach, making themselves a smörgåsbord for bears. The huge Kodiak brown bear, topping 1,000 pounds, owes everything to the millions of salmon that return to the island each summer. By comparison, the brown bears of the Interior—living on berries or an occasional ground squirrel— are mere midgets, their weight counted in the hundreds of pounds. Forest-dwelling black bears instead grow to only a few hundred pounds.

But rain forest covers only a small fraction of Alaska. In fact, only a third of Alaska is forested at all, and most of this is the boreal forest that covers the central part of the state, behind the rain shadow of coastal mountains that intercept moist clouds off the oceans. Ranging from the Kenai Peninsula, south of Anchorage, to the Brooks Range, where the Arctic begins, this is a taiga of smaller, slower-growing, hardier trees. In well-drained areas, on hillsides and southern land less susceptible to permafrost, the boreal forest is a lovely, broadly spaced combination of straight, proud white spruce and pale, spectral paper birch. Along the rivers, poplar and cottonwood grow, with deep-grained bark and branches that spread in an oaklike matrix—if they could speak, it would be as wise old men. Where it's wet and swampy—over more and more land as you go north—all that will grow is the glum black spruce, which struggles to become a gnarled stick a mere three inches thick in 100 years, if it doesn't burn first. As the elevation grows, the spruce shrink, turning into weirdly bent, ancient shrubs just before the tree line and the open alpine tundra.

Forest fires tear through as much as several million acres of Alaska's boreal forest each summer. In most cases, forest managers do no more than note the occurrence on a map. Unlike the rain forest, there's little commercially valuable timber in these thin stands, and, anyway, it isn't possible to halt the process of nature's self-immolation over the broad expanse of Alaska. The boreal forest regenerates through fire—it was made to burn. The wildlife that lives in and eats it needs new growth from the burns as well as the shelter of older trees. When the forest is healthiest and most productive the dark green of the spruce is broken by streaks and patches of light-green brush in an ever-changing succession.

This is the land of the moose. They're as big as a large horse, with a long, bulbous nose and big eyes that seem to know, somehow, just how ugly they are. Their flanks look like a worn-out shag carpet draped over a saw horse. But moose are survivors. They thrive in land that no one else wants. In the summer they wade out into the swampy tundra ponds to eat green muck. In the winter they like nothing better than an old burn, where summer lightning has peeled back the forest and allowed a tangle of willows to grow—a moose's all-time favorite food. Eaten by wolves, hunted and run over by man, stranded in the snows of a hard winter, the moose always come back, as if just to show that same self-pitying expression on their faces.

Or so you can imagine, until you get up close. Then you can smell the beast's foul scent and see, if the moose is under stress, the ears turn back and the whites of the eyes showing, and you know that this huge animal is no teddy bear—it could easily kill you. During a hard winter, moose starve in the deep snow, show up dead in people's driveways, even, in one case I know, die on their feet and rot that way, propped up on all fours. When they wander into the city in search of food and the easy walking on roads and railroad tracks, they're under stress and dangerous. In Anchorage's snowy winter of 1994–95, a man who tried to walk around a starving moose on a public sidewalk was knocked down and trampled to death.

Anthropomorphizing wild animals—thinking of them in human terms—is a way of making nature seem more predictable and friendly. Whether you're afraid of bears, moose, earthquakes, or even glaciers, the evolving natural history of Alaska can make for an unsettling home. Thinking of wild animals as furry people is a useful, if dangerous crutch—dangerous because the best protection from wild animals is to take them seriously and keep your distance.

It's not that nature is malicious, it's just brutally indifferent. In a land where environmental forces seem as willing to erase as to create, any animal, human beings included, is far from indelible. Our species has only begun to scratch the edges of Alaska—we're still barely guests. Only 160,000 acres of Alaska today shows any sign of human habitation. More than 100 times that much land is covered by glacier ice. Who knows, in another 15,000 years, the whole thing may be erased by another Ice Age—rain forests, salmon streams, mountains, cities—ground to oblivion under a mile-thick sheet of ice, as it was 15,000 years ago.

3 Politics & History: Living a Frontier Myth

The occupations of prospector, trapper, and homesteader—rugged individualists relying only on themselves in a limitless land—would dominate Alaska's economy if the state's image of itself were accurate. Alaskans talk a lot about the Alaskan spirit of independence, yearn for freedom from government, and declare that they just don't understand us Outside when they insist on locking up Alaska's lands in parks and wilderness status. The bumper sticker says, simply, WE DON'T GIVE A DAMN HOW THEY DO IT OUTSIDE. A state full of self-reliant frontiersmen can't be tied down and deterred from their manifest destiny by a bunch of Washington bureaucrats. At the extreme, there has even been a movement to declare independence as a separate nation so Alaskans could extend the frontier, extracting its natural resources unfettered by bunny-hugging easterners.

But just because you wear a cowboy hat doesn't mean you know how to ride a horse. In Las Vegas you find a lot more hats than horsemen, and Alaska is full of self-reliant frontier pioneers who spend rush hour in traffic jams and worry more about urban drug dealing and air pollution than where to catch their next meal or dig the mother lode. As for self-reliance and independence from

Alaska Timeline

- **Perhaps up to 30,000 years ago** First human explorers arrive in Alaska from Asia.
- **1741** Vitus Bering, on a mission originally chartered by Peter the Great, finds Alaska; ship's surgeon and naturalist Georg Steller goes ashore for a few hours, the first white to set foot in Alaska.
- **1743** Enslaving the Aleuts, Russian fur traders enter the Aleutian Islands; Aleuts are massacred when they try to revolt—their cultural traditions are eliminated and they are relocated as far south as California for their hunting skills.
- **1772** Unalaska, in the Aleutian Islands, becomes a permanent Russian settlement.

continues

■ **1776–79** British Capt. James Cook makes voyages of exploration to Alaska, seeking the Northwest Passage from the Pacific to the Atlantic, and draws charts of the coast.

■ **1784** Russians build settlement at Kodiak.

■ **1799** Russians establish settlement at present-day Sitka, which later becomes their capital; Tlingits attack fort and destroy it, but are later driven off in a counterattack; the Russian-America Company receives a 20-year exclusive franchise to govern and exploit Alaska.

■ **1821** Russian naval officers are placed in control of Russian-America Company, which begins to decline in profitability.

■ **1824** Boundaries roughly matching Alaska's current borders are set by treaty between Russia, Britain, and the United States.

■ **1839** The British Hudson's Bay Company, surpassing Russia in trade, begins leasing parts of Southeast Alaska, and subsequently extends trading outposts into the Interior.

■ **1843** First overtures are made by American officials interested in buying Alaska from the Russians—so U.S. instead of British power could expand there.

■ **1867** In need of money and fearful Russia couldn't hold onto Alaska anyway, Tsar Alexander II sells Alaska to the U.S.; Secretary of State William Seward negotiates the deal, for a price of $7.2 million, roughly 2¢ an acre; the American flag is raised in Sitka and the U.S. miltary assumes government of Alaska.

■ **1870** The Alaska Commercial Company receives a

continues

government—Alaska has the highest per capita state spending of any state in the nation, with no state income or sales taxes and an annual payment of almost $1,000 a year to every man, woman, and child just for living here. The state government provides such socialistic benefits as retirement homes and automatic income for the aged; it owns various businesses, ranging from a dairy to a subsidized mortgage lender; it has built schools in the smallest communities, operates a state ferry system and a radio and television network, and owns nearly a third of the land mass of Alaska. And although the state government has run huge deficits in recent years, digging deeply into savings to maintain its lavish style, the independent, self-reliant citizens have successfully resisted any taxes or significant cuts in services.

That conflict between perception and reality grows out of the story of a century of development of Alaska. The state is a great storehouse of minerals, oil, timber, and fish. A lot of wealth has been extracted and many people have gotten rich. But it has always been because the federal government let them do it. Every acre of Alaska belonged to the U.S. government from the day Secretary of State William Seward bought Alaska from Russia in 1867. Since then the frontier has never been broader than Uncle Sam made it.

But today, amid deep conflicts about whether areas should remain natural or be exploited for natural resources, federal control stands out far more clearly than it did 100 years ago, when the gold rush was on and the government offered the land and its wealth to anyone with strength enough to take it. Alaskans who want to keep receiving the good things that government brings today equate the frontier spirit of the past with their own financial well-being, whether that means working at a mining claim or at a desk in a glass office tower. But other Americans feel they own Alaska too, and they don't necessarily believe in giving it away anymore. They may want the frontier to stay alive in another sense— unconquered and still wild.

White colonization of the territory came in boom and bust waves of migrants arriving with the goal of making a quick buck and then clearing out— without worrying about the people who already lived there. Although the gold-rush pioneers are celebrated today, the Klondike rush of 1898 that opened up and populated the territory was motivated entirely by greed and was a mass importer of crime, inhumanity, and, for the Native people, massive epidemics of new diseases that killed off whole villages. Like the Russians 150 years before, who had made slaves of the Natives, the new white population considered the indigenous people less than human. Segregation was overcome only after World War II. Native land was taken and their culture suppressed by missionaries who forbade telling the old stories or even speaking in their own languages. Meanwhile, the salmon that fed the people of the territory were overfished by a powerful, Outside-owned canning industry with friends in Washington and Juneau.

It was only with World War II, and the Japanese invasion of the Aleutian Islands, that Alaska developed an industry not based on exploitation of natural resources—military spending. It was another boom. To this day the federal government remains a key industry, which, if removed, would send the economy into a tailspin.

The fight for Alaska statehood also came after the war. Alaskans argued that they needed local, independent control of natural resources, pointing to the example of overfishing in the federally managed salmon industry. Opponents said that Alaska would never be able to support itself, always requiring large subsidies from the federal government, and therefore should not be a state. The discovery of oil on the Swanson River, on the Kenai Peninsula, in 1957, helped tip the balance, and in 1959 Alaska finally joined the union as the 49th state. To aid the new state in becoming self-sufficient, Alaska was given a right to select 104 million acres of land for state ownership from the total 365 million acres of land mass, virtually all of which still remained in federal hands. But to this day the federal government still spends a lot more in Alaska than it receives from the state in taxes.

From the beginning the new state government relied on oil revenues to support itself and to start extending services to the vast, undeveloped expanse of Alaska. Anchorage boomed in the 1960s in a period of buoyant optimism. Leaders believed that the age-old problems of the wide-open frontier—poverty, lack of basic services, impenetrable remoteness—would succumb to the new government and new money, while the land still remained wide-open. Then the pace of change redoubled, with the discovery of the largest oil field in North America at Prudhoe Bay in 1968—that land had been a wise state selection in the federal land-grant entitlement.

monopoly on harvesting seals in the Pribilof Islands and soon expands across the territory (the company remains a presence in the Alaska Bush today).

- **1879** Naturalist and writer John Muir explores Southeast Alaska by canoe, discovering Glacier Bay with Native guides.
- **1880** Joe Juneau and Richard Harris, guided by local Natives, find gold on Gastineau Channel, founding city of Juneau; gold strikes begin to come every few years across the state.
- **1884** Military rule ends in Alaska, but residents still have no right to elect a legislature, governor, or congressional representative, or make laws.
- **1885** Christian missionaries meet to divide up the territory, parceling out each region to a different religion; they begin to fan out across Alaska to convert Native peoples, largely suppressing their traditional ways.
- **1897** After prospectors arrive in Seattle with a ton of gold, the Klondike gold rush begins; gold rushes in Nome and Fairbanks follow within a few years; Americans begin to populate Alaska.
- **1906** Alaska's first, nonvoting, delegate in Congress takes office; the capital moves from Sitka to Juneau.
- **1910** The Iditarod Trail, a sled-dog mail route, is blazed from Knik, on Cook Inlet, to Nome.
- **1913** The first territorial legislature convenes, although it has few powers; the first automobile drives route of Richardson Highway, from Valdez to Fairbanks.

continues

- 1914 Federal construction of the Alaska Railroad begins; the first tents go up in the river bottom that will be Anchorage, along the rail line.
- 1917 Mount McKinley National Park established.
- 1920 The first flights connect Alaska to the rest of the U.S. by air; aviation quickly becomes the most important means of transportation in the territory.
- 1923 President Warren Harding drives final spike on the Alaskan Railroad at Nenana, then dies on the way home, purportedly from eating bad Alaskan seafood.
- 1925 Leonhard Seppala and other dog mushers relay diphtheria serum on the Iditarod Trail to fight an epidemic in Nome; Seppala and his lead dog, Balto, become national heroes.
- 1934 Federal policy of forced assimilation of Native cultures is officially discarded, and New Deal efforts to preserve Native cultures begin.
- 1935 New Deal "colonists," broke farmers from all over the U.S., settle in the Matanuska Valley north of Anchorage.
- 1940 A military build-up begins in Alaska; bases built in Anchorage accelerate city's growth into major population center.
- 1942 Japanese invade Aleutians, taking Attu and Kiska islands and bombing Unalaska/Dutch Harbor (a U.S. counterattack the next year drives out the Japanese); Alaska Highway links Alaska to the rest of the country overland for the first time, but is open to civilians only after the war.

continues

The state government received as much money in a single payment from the oil companies bidding on leases on the North Slope as it had spent in total for the previous six years. This was going to be the boom of all booms.

The oil bonanza on the North Slope would change Alaska more than any other event in its history—change that came in many unexpected ways. Once, opening the frontier had only meant letting a few prospectors scratch the dirt in search of a poke of gold—nothing to make a federal case over. But getting the oil to market, from one of the most remote spots on the globe, would require allowing the world's largest companies to build across Alaska a pipeline that, when completed, could credibly claim to be the largest privately financed construction project in world history. With the stakes suddenly so much higher, it came time to figure out exactly who owned which parts of Alaska. That wouldn't be easy—much of the state had never even been mapped, much less surveyed, and there were some outstanding claims that had to be settled.

Alaska Natives, who had lost land, culture, and health in two centuries of white invasion, finally saw their luck start to turn. It wouldn't be possible to resolve the land issues surrounding the pipeline until their claims to land and compensation were answered. Native leaders cannily used that leverage to assure that they got what they wanted. In the early 1970s America had a new awareness of the way its first people had been treated in the settlement of the West. When white frontiers expanded, Native traditional homelands were stolen. In Alaska, with the powerful lure of all that oil providing the impetus, Native people were able to insist on a fairer resolution. In 1971, with the support of white Alaskans, Congress passed the Alaska Native Claims Settlement Act, called ANCSA, which transferred 44 million acres of land and $962.5 million to corporations whose shareholders were all the Native peoples of Alaska. Those corporations would be able to exploit their own land for their shareholders' profit. Some Natives complained that they'd received only an eighth of the land they had owned before white contact, but it was still the richest settlement any of the world's indigenous people had received.

It was a political deal on a grand scale. It's unlikely Natives would have gotten their land at all but for the desire of whites to get at the oil, and their need of Native support. Nor could the pipeline have overcome environmental challenges without the Natives' dropping their objections. Even with Native support in place, legislation authorizing the pipeline passed the U.S. Senate by only one vote, cast by Vice President Spiro Agnew.

But there were other side effects of the deal that white Alaskans didn't like so well. After the Native settlement passed, the state—which still hadn't received much of its land entitlement—and the Native corporations both had a right to select the land they wanted. But that didn't mean the issue was resolved. There still remained the question of who would get what—and of the wild lands that Congress, influenced by a strong, new environmental movement, wanted to maintain as national parks and wilderness and not give away. That issue wasn't settled until 1980, when the Alaska National Interest Lands Conservation Act passed, setting aside an additional 106 million acres—nearly a third of the state—for conservation. Alaska's frontier-minded population screamed bloody murder over the "lock-up of Alaska," but the act was only the last, tangible step in a process started by the coming of big oil and the need its arrival created to draw lines on the map, tying up the frontier.

When construction of the $8 billion pipeline finally got underway in 1974, a huge influx of new people chasing the high-paying jobs put any previous gold rush to shame. The newcomers were from a different part of the country than previously, too. Alaska had been a predominately Democratic state, but oil workers from Texas, Oklahoma, and other Bible-belt states helped shift the balance of Alaska's politics, and now it's solidly Republican. In its frontier days, Alaska had a strong, Libertarian streak—on both the liberal and the conservative side—but now it became more influenced by fundamentalist conservatism. A hippie-infested legislature of the early 1970s legalized marijuana for home use. Conservatives at the time, who thought the government shouldn't butt into its citizens' private lives, went along with them. After the pipeline, times changed and Alaska developed tough anti-drug laws. As the election of 1996 approached, even Alaska's senior U.S. senator, Republican Ted Stevens, who since 1968 had guided the state through its most tumultuous years in Congress, was considered too liberal by the Christian right group that had taken over his own state party apparatus.

- 1957 Oil is found on Kenai Peninsula's Swanson River.
- 1959 Alaska becomes a state.
- 1964 The largest earthquake ever to strike North America shakes South-central Alaska, killing 131 people, primarily in tsunami waves.
- 1968 Oil is found at Prudhoe Bay, on Alaska's North Slope.
- 1970 Environmental lawsuits tie up work to build the Alaska pipeline, which is needed to link the North Slope oil field to markets.
- 1971 Congress acknowledges and pays the federal government's debt to Alaska's indigenous people with the Alaska Native Claims Settlement Act, which transfers 44 million acres of land and almost $1 billion to new Native-owned corporations.
- 1973 The first Iditarod Trail Sled Dog Race runs more than 1,000 miles from Anchorage to Nome.
- 1974 Congress clears away legal barriers to construction of the trans-Alaska pipeline; Vice President Spiro Agnew casts the deciding vote in the U.S. Senate.
- 1977 The trans-Alaska pipeline is completed and begins providing up to 25% of the U.S. domestic supply of oil.
- 1980 Congress sets aside almost a third of Alaska in new parks and other land-conservation units; awash in new oil wealth, the state legislature abolishes all taxes paid by individuals to state government.
- 1982 Alaskans receive their first Alaska Permanent Fund dividends, interest paid on an oil-wealth savings account.

continues

■ **1985** Declining oil prices send the Alaska economy into tailspin; tens of thousands leave the state and most of the banks collapse.

■ **1989** The tanker *Exxon Valdez* hits Bligh Reef in Prince William Sound, spilling 11 million gallons of North Slope crude in the worst oil spill ever in North America.

■ **1994** A federal jury in Anchorage awards $5 billion to 10,000 fishermen, Natives, and others hurt by the Exxon oil spill; Exxon appeals.

Growth also brought urban problems, just as it has anywhere else. As the pipeline construction boom waned with completion in 1977, a boom-town atmosphere of gambling and street prostitution went with it, but other big-city problems remained. No longer could residents of Anchorage and Fairbanks go to bed without locking their doors. Both cities were declared "nonattainment" areas by the Environmental Protection Agency because of air pollution near the ground in cold winter weather, when people leave their cars running during the day to keep them from freezing. We got live television, but also serial murderers.

But the pipeline seemed to provide limitless wealth to solve the problems. For fear that too much money would be wasted, the voters altered the state constitution to bank a large portion of the new riches; the politicians in Juneau could spend only half the Permanent Fund's earnings, after paying out half the annual income as dividends to every citizen of the state. The fund now contains over $15 billion in savings and has become one of the largest sectors of the economy simply by virtue of paying out more than half a billion a year in dividends to everyone who lives at least a year in the state. All major state taxes—except those on the oil industry—were canceled, and people got used to receiving everything free from government.

Then, in 1985, oil prices dropped, deflating the overextended economy like a pin in a balloon. Housing prices crashed and thousands of people simply walked away from their mortgages. All but a few of the banks in the state went broke. Condominiums that had sold for $100,000 sold for $20,000 or less a year later. It was the bust that always goes with the boom, but even after so many previous examples, it still came as a surprise to many. The spending associated with the *Exxon Valdez* oil spill in 1989 restarted the economy, and it generally has been on an even keel ever since, but the wealth of the earlier oil years never returned.

Meanwhile, the oil from Prudhoe Bay started running out. Oil revenues, an irreplaceable 85% of the state budget, started an irrevocably downward trend in the early 1990s. The oil companies downsized. An economic precipice appeared in the distance, drawing ever closer.

That's where Alaska finds itself today—its citizens, spoiled by past wealth, are looking at a future far beyond their control. Culture moves slower than politics or events, and Alaskans still see themselves as those gold-rush prospectors or wildcat oil drillers, adventuring in an open land and striking it rich by their own devices. But today the state's future is as little in its own hands as it has ever been. There may be more oil in protected wilderness areas on the North Slope, and there certainly is plenty of natural gas that could be exploited. But whether those projects occur will be decided in corporate board rooms around the world and in Congress, not in Alaska. Ultimately, an economy based on exploiting natural resources is anything but independent.

Haggling over one plot of land or another will always continue, but the basic lines have been drawn on the map. The frontier has been carved up and regulated—today it's mostly just a state of mind. Or a myth we like to believe about ourselves.

4 The People: Three Ways to Win an Argument in Alaska

#1: WAIT FOR SPRING

A small town in Alaska in March. Each time it snows, you have to throw shovels of it farther over your head to dig out. The air in the house is stale and out the window all you see is black, white, and gray. Everyone's ready to go nuts with winter. It's time for a good political ruckus. No one can predict exactly what will set it off— it could just be an ill-considered letter to the editor in the local newspaper, or it could be something juicier, like a controversial development proposal. At some point, when the cabin fever gets bad enough, it almost doesn't matter what sparks the inferno. Alaskans can generate outrage about almost anything, with a ritual of charges and countercharges, conspiracy theories and impassioned public testimony.

It's particularly amusing when some outsider is involved, thinking he's at the town council meeting in a normal political process to get some project approved, only to wind up on the receiving end of a public hearing from hell. I'll never forget a sorry businessman who was trying to lease some land from the town of Homer. He endured hours of angry public testimony one night. He was sweating, the only person in the packed city hall meeting room wearing a tie, surrounded by flannel shirts, blue jeans, and angry faces. Finally, he stood up at his chair and, in a plaintive tone of frustration near tears, declared, "You're not very professional as a community!" For once, no one could disagree.

He gave up. He didn't know that if he had only waited a couple of months, the opposition would dry up as soon as the salmon started running. Then most of the city council meetings would be canceled and those that weren't would be brief and sparsely attended. If anything really important came up, the council would be smart enough to postpone it till fall. In the summer Alaskans have more important things to attend to than government.

The sun shines deep into the night so you can catch fish and tourists, not sit inside. It's the season when the money is made. The streets are full of new people, like a bird rookery refreshed by migrants. Everyone stays awake late pounding nails, playing softball, and fly casting for reds. Office workers in Anchorage depart straight from work for a three-hour drive down to the Kenai Peninsula, fish through the night, catch a quick nap in the car in the wee hours, and make it to work on time the next morning, with fish stories to share at the coffee machine. Sleep is expendable—you don't seem to need it that much when the sky is light at night.

In the Native villages of the Bush, everyone has gone to fish camp. Families load everything in an aluminum river boat and leave town, headed upriver and back to a time of purer cultural traditions. On the banks and beaches they set up wall tents and spruce-log fish-drying racks, maybe a basketball hoop and campfire, too. The huge extended families work as a unit. Men gather in the salmon and the women gut them with a few lightning strokes of a knife and hang them to dry on the racks. Children run around in a countryside paradise, watched by whatever adults are handiest.

Suddenly, August comes. For the first time in months you can see the stars. It comes as a shock the first time you have to use your car headlights. The mood gets even more frantic. There's never enough time in the summer to do everything that needs to get done. Construction crews can count the days now till snow and cold will shut them down. Anything that's not done now won't be done until next May. Labor Day approaches as fast as 5pm on a busy business day.

As September turns to October, everything had better be done. The last tourists are gone and T-shirt shops are closed for the season. The commercial fishing boats are tied up back in the harbor and the fishermen preparing for vacation. Deckhands and cannery workers are already back at college. For the first time in months, people can slow down long enough to look at each other and remember where they left off in the spring. It's time to catch up on sleep, think longer thoughts, make big decisions. The hills of birch turn bright yellow, the tundra becomes brick red, and the sky turns gray—there's the smell of wood smoke in the air—and one day it starts to snow.

It's not the velvet darkness of midwinter that gets you. December is bearable, even if the sun rises after the kids get to school, barely cruises along the horizon, and sinks before they start for home. Nowhere is Christmas more real than Alaska, singing carols with cheeks tingling from the cold. January isn't so hard. You're still excited about the skiing. The phone rings in the middle of the night—it's a friend telling you to put on your boots and go outside to see the northern lights. February is a bit harder to take, but most towns have a winter carnival to divert your attention from the cold.

March is when bizarre things start to happen. People are just holding on for the end of winter and you never know what will set them off. That's when you'd better hunker down and lay low, watch what you say, bite your tongue when your spouse lets hang a comment you'd like to jump on like a pike hitting fresh bait. Hold on—just until the icicles start to melt, the mud shows around the snowbanks, and the cycle starts fresh.

#2: BE HERE FIRST

There's a simple and effective way to win an argument in Alaska—state how long you've lived here. If it's longer than your adversary, he'll find it difficult to put up a fight. This is why, when speaking in public, people will often begin their remarks by stating how many years they've been in Alaska. It's a badge of authenticity and status in a place with a young, transient population that's grown fast. No one cares where you came from, or who you were back there, and there's no such thing as class in Alaska—anyone who tries to act superior will quickly find that no one else notices. But if you haven't made it through a few winters, you probably don't know what you're talking about.

It's also traditional—although, sadly, a fading tradition—to treat strangers as friends until they prove otherwise. The smaller the town you visit, the more strongly you'll find that hospitality still alive. Visitors can find it pleasantly disorienting to arrive in a small town and have everyone in the street greet them with a smile. These traditions of hospitality and respect for experience run deepest in Alaska's Native people. (Alaskans use the word "Native" to mean all the indigenous peoples of Alaska.) But instead of beginning a conversation by stating how long they've lived here, Natives—who've always been here—try to find a relation with a new person by talking about where their families are from.

The first people to come to the Americas arrived in the area between Nome and Kotzebue, probably first crossing a land bridge from Asia through the dry Bering Sea, 20,000 to 30,000 years ago, in pursuit of migrating game. Several waves of immigrants came, the last of which probably arrived about 6,000 years ago. Those who kept going south from Alaska were the ancestors of the Incas in South America, the Cherokee in North America, and all the other indigenous people of the hemisphere. Those who stayed in Alaska became the Eskimos—the Inupiat of the Arctic, the Yup'ik of the west, the Aleuts of the Aleutian Islands, and the Chugach, Koniag, and Eyak of Southcentral. They also became the Athabascans of the Interior, and the Tlingit, Haida, and Tsimshian of Southeast Alaska, who are known as Indians rather than Eskimos.

The Native groups of Alaska have a lot in common culturally, but before the white invasion they had well-defined boundaries and didn't mix much. They didn't farm and the only animal they domesticated was the dog—dog teams and boats were the primary means of transportation and commerce. But they generally were not nomadic, and no one lived in igloos. Where there was no wood, houses were built of sod. Typically, a family-connected tribal group would have a winter village and a summer fish camp for gathering and laying up food. Elders guided the community in important decisions. A gifted shaman led the people in religious matters, relating to the spirits of animals, trees, and even the ice that populated their world. Stories passed on through generations explained the world.

Those oral traditions kept Native cultures alive. Twenty distinct Native languages were spoken—some elders still speak only their Native language yet today. The languages break into three major groups: The Eskimo-Aleut language group, spoken by coastal people from the Arctic Ocean to the Gulf of Alaska, includes Inupiaq, in the Arctic; Yup'ik, in southwest, the Yukon–Kuskokwim Delta area; Aleut, in the Aleutian Islands; and Sugpiaq, in Southcentral Alaska. There are 12 Athabascan and Eyak languages in the central part of the state. In Southeast Alaska, Tlingit was spoken across most of the Panhandle. Haida was spoken on southern Prince of Wales Island and southward into what's now British Columbia.

The first arrival of whites was often violent and destructive, spanning a 100-year period that started in the 1740s with the coming of the Russian fur traders, who enslaved and massacred the Aleuts, to the 1840s when whalers and other mariners met the Inupiat of the Arctic. There were many battles, but nonviolent destruction of oral traditions was more influential. Christian missionaries, with the support of government assimilation policy, drove the old stories and even Native languages underground. Lela Kiana Oman, who has published traditional Inupiat stories to preserve them, told me of her memories of her father secretly telling the ancient tales at night to his children. She was forbidden to speak Inupiaq in school, and did not see her first traditional Native dance until age 18.

Oman's work is part of today's Native cultural renaissance. It's not a moment too soon. In some villages, children know more about the geography of Beverly Hills they see on television than about their own culture. Some don't share a language with their own grandparents. But schools in many areas have begun requiring Native language classes. For the Aleut, whose cultural traditions were almost completely wiped out, the process of renewal involves a certain amount of invention. On the other hand, some villages remain, especially deep in the country of the Yukon–Kuskokwim Delta, where Yup'ik is still the dominant language and most of the food comes from traditional subsistence hunting and gathering, altered only by the use of modern materials and guns.

Alaska Natives also are fighting destruction fueled by alcohol and other substance-abuse problems, which have created an epidemic of suicide, accidents, and domestic violence in the Bush. Statistically, virtually every Alaska Native in prison is there because of alcohol. A sobriety movement is attacking the problem one person at a time. One of its goals is to use traditional Native culture to fill a void of rural despair where alcohol now flows in. Politically, a "local option" law provides individual communities the choice of partial or total alcohol prohibition; it has been used in many villages and towns, but remains a divisive battle in others, where Native residents tend to support going dry but whites more often vote against.

An Alaska Glossary

If Alaska feels like a different country from the rest of the United States, one reason may be the odd local usage that makes English slightly different here—different enough, in fact, that the Associated Press publishes a separate style-book dictionary just for Alaska. Here are some Alaskan words you may run into:

break up   When God set up the seasons in Alaska, He forgot one—spring. While the rest of the United States enjoys new flowers and baseball, Alaskans are looking at melting snowbanks and mud. Then, in May, summer miraculously arrives. Break up officially occurs when the ice goes out in the Interior's rivers, but it stands for the time period of winter's demise and summer's initiation.

bunny boots   If you see people wearing huge, bulbous white rubber boots in Alaska's winter, it's not necessarily because they have enormous feet. Those are bunny boots, super-insulated footwear originally designed for Arctic air force operations—they're the warmest thing in the world.

cheechacko   A newcomer or greenhorn. Not used much anymore, because almost everyone is one.

dry or damp   Many towns and villages have invoked a state law that allows them to outlaw alcohol completely—to go dry—or to outlaw sale but not possession—to go damp.

Lower 48   The rest of the United States. Why don't we include Hawaii and say "Lower 49?" They're newcomers to the Union—it didn't become a state until 1960. (Alaska made it in 1959.)

Native   When capitalized, the word refers to Alaska's indigenous people. "American Indian" isn't used much in Alaska, "Alaska Native" being the preferred term.

Native corporation   In 1971 Congress settled land claims from Alaska's Natives by turning over land and money; corporations were set up, with Natives as shareholders, to receive the property. Most of the corporations still thrive.

There are social and political tensions between Natives and whites on many levels and over many issues. Some urban, white hunters and sport fishermen, for example, feel they should have the same rights to fish and game as the Natives. Rural Natives, who have so far won the day, maintain that subsistence hunting and fishing are an integral part of their cultural heritage, far more important than sport, and should take priority. Darker conflicts exist too, and it's impossible to discount the charges of racism that Native Alaskans raise.

Alaska Natives have become a minority in their own land. In 1880 Alaska contained 33,000 Natives and 430 whites. By 1900, with the gold rush, the numbers were roughly equal. Since then, whites have generally outnumbered Natives in ever-greater numbers. Today there are about 94,000 Alaska Natives—22,000 of whom live in the cities of Anchorage and Fairbanks—out of a total state population of about 600,000 people of all races. Consequently, Alaska Natives learn to walk in two worlds. The North Slope's Inupiat, who hunt the bowhead whale from open boats as their forefathers did, must also know how to negotiate for their take in international diplomatic meetings. And they have to use the levers of government to protect the whale's environment from potential damage by the oil industry. The 1971 Alaska Native Claims Settlement Act, which ceded 44 million acres of land and

oosik   The huge penile bone of a walrus. Knowing this word could save you from being the butt of any of a number of practical jokes people like to play on cheechakos.

Outside   Anywhere that isn't Alaska. This is a widely used term in print, and is capitalized, like any other proper noun.

PFD   No, not personal floatation device, Permanent Fund Dividend. When Alaska's oil riches started flowing in the late 1970s, the voters set up a savings account called the Permanent Fund; half the annual interest is paid annually to every man, woman, and child in the state. With more than $15 billion in investments, the fund now yields nearly $1,000 in dividends to each Alaskan annually—and as a consequence the fund has never been raided by the politicians.

pioneer   A white settler of Alaska who has been here longer than most other people can remember—25 or 30 years usually does it.

salmon   There are five species of Pacific salmon, each with two names. The king or Chinook is the largest, growing up to 90 pounds in some areas; the silver or coho is next in size, a feisty sport fish; the red or sockeye has rich red flesh; the pink or humpy and the chum or dog are smallish and not as tasty, mostly ending up in cans and dog lots.

Southeast   Most people don't bother to say "Southeast Alaska." The region may be to the northwest of everyone else in the country, but it's southeast of most Alaskans, and that's all we care about.

tsunami   Earthquake-caused sea waves are often called tidal waves, but it's a bit of a misnomer. The most destructive waves of the 1964 Alaska earthquake were tsunami waves caused by underwater upheavals like landslides.

village   A small, Alaska Native settlement in the Bush, usually tightly bound by family and cultural tradition.

almost $1 billion to Alaska Natives, created a new class, the corporate Native, responsible for representing rural needs but also obliged to function as an executive for large, far-reaching business concerns. Outnumbered by white voters, Bush politicians in the legislature must be especially skilled, sticking together, crossing political boundaries and forming coalitions to protect their constituencies.

Non-Natives traveling to the Bush also walk in two worlds, but they may not even know it. In a Native village, a newly met friend will ask you in for a cup of coffee; it can be rude not to accept. Looking a person in the eye in conversation also can be rude—that's how Native elders look at younger people who owe them respect. If a Native person looks down, speaks slowly, and seems to mumble, that's not disrespect, but the reverse. Fast-talking non-Natives have to make a conscious effort to slow down and leave pauses in conversation, because Natives usually don't jump in or interrupt—they listen, consider, and then respond. Of course, most Native people won't take offense at your bad manners—they're used to spanning cultures, and they know whites, or gussocks, may not know how to act in a village.

But urban visitors who miss cultural nuances rarely overlook the apparent poverty of many villages. Out on a remote landscape of wind-swept tundra, swampy in summer and frozen in winter, they may secretly wonder why Natives stay there, enduring the hardships of rural Alaskan life when even the most remote villager can see on cable television how easy it is in southern California. Save your pity. As Yup'ik leader Harold Napoleon has said, "We're poor, all right, but we've got more than most people. Our most important asset is our land and our culture, and we want to protect it come hell or high water."

Alaska's Natives may be outnumbered, but they've been here a lot longer than anyone else. My money is on them.

#3: BE A REAL ALASKAN

Alaska's history books are full of the stories of economic booms, the people who came, what kind of wealth they were after, and how they populated and developed the land. In a largely empty place you can make it into history just by showing up. But every wave is followed by a trough—the bust that comes after the boom—when those who came just for the money go back where they came from. Those are the times when the real Alaskans—those who live here for the love of the place, not only the money— are divided from the rest. The real Alaskans stay; the others leave. It's the perfect way to settle an argument.

Other people have other definitions of what it takes to be a real Alaskan. One definition, which I once read on a place mat in a diner in Soldotna, holds that to be a real Alaskan you have know how to fix a tractor. Similar definitions require various feats in the outdoors, hunting, fishing, or shooting, and even acts in the bar room or the bedroom. They all assume that a real Alaskan is a big, tough, white, male bulldozer-driving type of guy. But those can be the first to leave when the economy goes down the tubes.

The first group to leave were the Russians sent by the tsar and the Russian-America Company. On October 18, 1867, their flag came down over Castle Hill in Sitka in a solemn ceremony, got stuck, and had to be untangled by a soldier sent up the pole. The territory was virtually empty of Russians before the check was even signed, as Congress didn't much like the idea of the purchase and took a while to pay. The gold-rush Stampeders were the next to leave. The population of Nome went from 12,500 to 852 after the Stampede was over. The oil years have seen the same phenomenon, as people who can't find work in the bust years pack up and leave.

But each time the boom has gone bust since the gold rush, enough have stayed so that Alaska ended up with more people than it had before the boom began. Over the long term the population has kept growing dramatically. It doubled from 1890 to 1900—the gold rush; doubled again by 1950 because of World War II and the Cold War; doubled again by 1964, with statehood and the early oil years; and doubled again by 1983, because of the trans-Alaska pipeline and the arrival of big oil. Since then, it has grown another 20%.

Each set of migrants has been similar—young, coming mostly from the West, but from other parts of the United States, too. Most people who have come to Alaska have been white—minority populations are smaller than in the country as a whole— but there are strong minority communities in Anchorage. Little pockets of immigration have grown around the state—in Kodiak, the canneries are run by a tight Filipino community started by just a few pioneer immigrants. Today the population of Alaska as a whole is young and relatively well paid and educated. Six times as many babies are born as people die.

Historically, old people often moved somewhere warmer when they retired. Some migrate annually, spending only the summer in Alaska—they are called snowbirds. Over the years the state government set out to keep more old people in the state, to help build the continuity and memory a community needs. Special retirement homes were built, local property-tax breaks were granted to the elderly, and the legislature created a "Longevity Bonus" entitlement whereby elders who'd been in the state at least 25 years were automatically paid $250 a month for life. When a court ruled that the state couldn't impose a residency requirement of more than one year for the program, Alaska began to import thousands of new elderly people who were coming north to take advantage of the hand-outs. Now the bonus is being phased out.

It wasn't the first time Alaska has tried to reward real Alaskans just for staying. When the Permanent Fund Dividend program started in the 1970s, to distribute some of the state's new oil riches to the citizens, it was designed to provide more money for each year of residency. A 1-year greenhorn would get $50 and a 20-year pioneer $1,000. The Supreme Court threw out the plan—apparently being a "real Alaskan" isn't a special category of citizen in the U.S. Constitution.

Alaskans have always been well paid. Until recently, the popular explanation always held that prices are higher because of shipping costs, so salaries needed to match. That's still true in rural Alaska, and for some purchases in the large cities. But generally, fierce competition in the retail trade has driven prices down. Large national chains moved in all at once in 1994. Today the cost of living in Anchorage, Fairbanks, and Juneau compares favorably to most parts of the country. Wages have gone down a little, largely because all those new retail jobs lowered average pay, but the federal government still pays a premium to its Alaskan employees, and oil workers, fishermen, and other skilled workers make a very good living.

Prices for hotel rooms and restaurant meals also remain quite high. The best explanation is the seasonal nature of the economy—tourism operators need to make their full income in the high summer season. The other explanation is that they'll charge what the market can bear, and empty hotel rooms are in high demand in the summer.

The non-Native part of Alaska, 100 years old with the anniversary of the gold rush, hasn't had time to develop a culture of its own, much less an Alaskan accent. It's a melting pot of the melting pot, with a population made up of odds and ends from all over the United States. People tend to judge each other on the basis of their actions, not on who they are or where they came from. New arrivals to Alaska have been able to reinvent themselves since the days when Soapy Smith, a small-time con man, took over Skagway with a criminal gang and had the territorial governor offer to make him the town marshall—all in the period of a year. Everyone arrives with a clean slate and a chance to prove himself or herself, but on occasion, that ability to start from scratch has created some embarrassing discoveries, when the past does become relevant. There have been a series of political scandals uncovered by reporters who checked the résumés of well-known politicians, only to find out they had concocted their previous lives out of thin air. One leading legislative candidate's husband found out about her real background from such a news story.

If an Alaskan culture hasn't had time to develop, Alaska does have traditions, or at least accepted ways of thinking—among them tolerance and equality, hospitality, independence, and a propensity for violence. Several years ago, in Homer, there was a gunfight over a horse that left a man lying dead on a dirt road. In the newspaper the next week the editorial called for people not to settle their differences with guns. A couple of letters to the editor shot back, on the theme, "Don't you tell *us* how to settle our differences." Guns are necessary tools in Alaska. They're also a religion. I have friends who exchanged handguns instead of rings when they got married.

The tradition of tolerance of newcomers has made Alaska a destination for oddballs, religious cults, hippies, and people who just can't make it in the mainstream. Perhaps the most interesting of the religious groups that formed its own community is the Old Believers, who in recent decades built villages of brightly painted, gingerbreadlike houses around Kachemak Bay, near Homer. Their resistance to convention dates back to Peter the Great's reforms to Russian Orthodoxy in the 18th century, which they reject. After centuries of persecution, in Alaska have they found a place where they can live without interference—in fact, they've thrived as fishermen and boat builders. You see them around town, in their 18th-century Russian peasant dress. Even the girls' high school basketball team wears long dresses, with their numbers stitched to the bodice.

Nikolaevsk was the first of the Russian Old Believer villages. In the public school there, they don't teach about dinosaurs or men landing on the moon—that's considered heresy. Yet other Old Believers rebelled, convinced that Nikolaevsk was making too many compromises and was bound to lose the next generation to decadent American ways. They broke off and formed another village, farther up the bay, unreachable except by all-terrain vehicle, and adhered to stricter rules. They, in turn, suffered another schism and another village was formed, farther up the bay, virtually inaccessible and with even-stricter rules. The process continues. The fight against assimilation may inevitably be hopeless, as children will ultimately do as they please, but it's the Old Believers' own struggle. No one in Homer pushes them to change. No one pays any attention at all, except to buy their fish and their top-quality boats.

After several decades, it looks as if the Old Believers are here to stay. Whether they speak English or not, I'd say they're real Alaskans.

5 Recommended Books

Coming into the Country, by John McPhee (Bantam, 1976), is the classic portrait of Alaska, telling the stories of the trappers and prospectors of the upper Yukon region, around Eagle. Covering much of the same territory, *Tisha,* by Richard Specht (Bantam, 1976), is probably the most popular novel of Alaska. Based closely on a true story, it's the tale of a young white schoolteacher in Chicken in the 1920s and 1930s who courageously insisted on treating the Natives as equals. Of course, no one has surpassed Jack London's 1904 *Call of the Wild* and his short stories as classic adventure yarns; he based his work on a winter prospecting on the Klondike. *Road Song,* by Natalie Kusz (Farrar Straus and Giroux, 1990), is her harrowing memoir of her family's attempt to settle in rural Alaska in 1968.

The best firsthand accounts of early Alaska are still fresh. John Muir chronicled his voyage of discovery in Southeast in *Travels in Alaska.* Libby Bearman's journals and letters about living on the Pribilof Islands in 1879 and 1880, recently reprinted by Oak Council Books, are strongly authentic and reveal a powerful personality.

For deeper insight into Native culture, *Fifty Years below Zero,* a memoir by Charles Brower (University of Alaska Press reprint, 1994), is a vivid standard. Brower came to the Arctic as a whaler in 1884 and stayed 60 years, beginning as a lone student of the Inupiat and becoming a North Slope leader. *The Wake of the Unseen Object,* by Tom Kizzia (Henry Holt, 1991), is a more recent journey into the Bush, eloquently describing the lives of Alaska's Natives as they are today.

Several writers have recorded Native stories and legends in their own words. *Two Old Women,* by Velma Wallis (Harper Perennial, 1994), is one of the most popular; it's based on Athabascan legend, telling a suspenseful story of survival and renewal. *The Epic of Qayaq; The Longest Story Ever Told by My People,* by Lela Kiana Oman (Carlton University Press, 1995), is an Inupiat story originally told over many nights, like Homer's *Odyssey.*

Planning a Trip to Alaska 3

Planning a trip to Alaska can be a bit more complicated than traveling in the rest of the United States. Besides the vast distances and range of climatic conditions, Alaska travel in the high summer season usually requires long advance preparations and reservations. This chapter provides the general information you'll need to get started.

1 Visitor Information & Money

VISITOR INFORMATION

The **Alaska Division of Tourism,** Dept. 801 (P.O. Box 110801), Juneau, AK 99811-0801 (☎ **907/465-2010**), provides a free *Official State Guide and Vacation Planner* with information on traveling to all parts of Alaska, including advertising from many tourism-related businesses. Other sources of state-wide information are the **Alaska Tourism Marketing Council** (☎ **907/563-2289**) and the **Alaska Visitors Association** (☎ **907/561-5733**).

The Alaska Department of Transportation provides an updated recording with **weather and road information** for various regions of the state (☎ **800/478-7675**).

For outdoors information, the **Alaska Public Lands Information Centers** are centralized sources on all government-owned lands—which takes in more than 85% of the state. The centers are operated cooperatively by seven land agencies. The Anchorage center is at 605 W. Fourth Ave., Ste. 105, Anchorage, AK 99501 (☎ **907/ 271-2737;** fax 907/271-2744). See the Fairbanks and Tok listings in Chapter 10 for the centers there. Information on a center in Ketchikan is in Chapter 7.

ON THE NET   As this is being written, Alaska information on the Internet is expanding exponentially, with new towns and businesses publishing e-mail addresses and World Wide Web sites daily. Here are some of the more established starting points on the Web.

The **Alaska Information Cache,** http://www.neptune.com. alaska/alaska.html, e-mail akcache@alaska.neptune.com, is an award-winning travel information service. The **Governor's Office** has a Web site at http://www.state.ak.us, and will respond to questions by e-mail at Tony_Knowles%gov@state.ak.us. The **Anchorage Convention and Visitors Bureau** has a Web page at http:// www.alaska.net/~acvb, and receives e-mail at acvb@alaska.net.

The **Alaska Railroad** Web page is http://alaska.net/~akrr, e-mail at akrr@alaska.net. The **Alaska Marine Highway** ferry system is at http://www.dot.state.ak.us/external/amhs/home.html. For fishing and wildlife information, try the **Alaska Department of Fish & Game** at http://ccl.alaska.edu/local/adfg/gallery/galhome.html. The **University of Alaska System** is at http://www.alaska.edu/. The **University of Alaska Anchorage** is http://orion.alaska.edu/www/cwis.html and **University of Alaska Fairbanks** is http://zorba.uafadm.alaska.edu/.

MONEY

HOW MUCH MONEY YOU'LL NEED   Alaska is an expensive place to get to, get around, and stay in. A good, standard motel room is rarely available for less than $90 to $100. Airfare from Seattle to Anchorage fluctuates wildly with competition among the airlines, but a $400 round-trip is a fair deal. You can easily pay that again to get to an Alaska Bush community. Even the train is expensive, with a one-way fare from Anchorage to Fairbanks, a 350-mile trip, at $135 on the least luxurious of three choices of cars. A couple ordering a good salmon dinner, appetizers, and wine would be lucky to get out of a fine restaurant for less than $90 to $100, including tip. One reason cruise ships have become so popular is that, for this quality level, they're comparable in price on a daily basis to independent travel; see Chapter 5 for details on cruising.

To travel at a standard American comfort level, a couple should allow $100 per person, per day, for room and board. The cost of an activity such as flightseeing, wild-life cruises, or guided fishing typically is $75 to $150 per person. Also add ground transportation—you may need to rent a car, the best way to see much of the state, for around $55 a day (weekly rentals are less, and check for sales). You also will likely need train and ferry tickets. Two weeks for a couple, then, will cost in the neighborhood of $4,500, including airfare to Alaska, two $100-per-person activities, and $500 for ground transportation, but without going to the Bush. For high luxury, you can spend much more—as much, in fact, as you might be willing to spend.

Of course, you also can trim down your costs by cutting your demands. You'll learn more about the real Alaska staying in bed-and-breakfast accommodations than in a standard hotel room, and expect to pay $65 to $85 for a decent room with a shared bath. The breakfast cuts your food costs. And there are plenty of family restaurants where you can eat a modest dinner for two for $25, with a tip and a glass of beer. Traveling in that style will bring the cost of room and board down to about $60 per person, per day, for a couple. Leaving the rest of the costs the same, with airfare, ground transportation, and activities, that couple would spend about $3,300 for two weeks.

Another way to save money is to travel in the shoulder season, before and after the peak summer season. Hotel and guided activity prices drop significantly, typically 25% or more. May and September are solidly in the shoulder season, and sometimes you get bargains as late as June 15 or as early as August 15. Traveling in the winter is a whole different experience, but certainly saves a lot of money—where hotels are open, rates are typically half of peak rates, or less. For other considerations on off-season and shoulder-season travel, see "When to Go," later in this chapter.

You can save the most money by giving up a private room every night and cooking some of your own meals. Camping is a fun way to really see Alaska, and costs only $8 a night in state and Forest Service campgrounds. Hostels are available in most towns, typically around $12 a night. Thousands of young people come to Alaska each summer and spend almost nothing, replenishing their funds when necessary with stints working at a fish cannery or restaurant—low-wage, long-hour jobs are usually available in the summer (see "Tips for Students" under "Tips for Special Travelers," later in this chapter). Retired recreational vehicle owners travel for a cost little greater than staying at home, except for the fuel to navigate the beast down the road. A family can have the experience of a lifetime by driving the Alaska Highway or taking the family car up the Inside Passage on a state ferry, and camping at night. Unfortunately, most people don't have the time for these options. It adds a week to each end of your trip to drive to Alaska, and puts thousands of miles and heavy wear and tear on your vehicle. Depending on where you start from, I wouldn't attempt it with less than five to seven weeks for the trip.

HOW TO CARRY YOUR MONEY   There are few special warnings to be given about money in Alaska other than the caution you'd use in any other part of the United States. Don't carry enough cash to tempt a criminal, or to ruin your trip if it's lost, but make sure you have enough before going to very small towns, villages, or on rural highways. A few towns still lack automatic-teller machines (ATMs) and have businesses that don't take credit or charge cards. The "Fast Facts" section for each town in this book will tell you if there's an ATM and where to find it; most towns that are too small to be in this volume also are too small to have an ATM. Alaska ATMs generally are all on the Cirrus and Plus networks and other major ATM networks. In larger towns, you'll find that every business you'd expect to take credit or charge cards at home will accept them here. Bed-and-breakfasts often don't take credit or charge cards, however, and few businesses of any kind will take an out-of-state personal check. Traveler's checks are good just about anywhere.

When I travel around Alaska, I carry at least $100 in cash, plus a couple of different kinds of credit/charge cards and an ATM card. I use a credit or charge card (preferably earning frequent-flier miles) whenever I can, and stop at an ATM machine whenever my emergency cash falls under $100. If I'm going to a really small town for a while, I load up on cash first. I've rarely run into a problem with this system, and it saves the cost and inconvenience of using traveler's checks.

2 When to Go

CLIMATE & SEASONS

Nothing makes a bigger difference in the success of your vacation than the weather, and the weather in Alaska is extreme and unpredictable. We're the first to get whatever Arctic Siberia or the void of the North Pacific have to throw at North America. The extremes of recorded temperatures are a high of 100°F and low of –80°F. A single spring day in the Southcentral or Southeast region can include snow flurries, sun, rain, and a combination of all three at once. Statistics give means and averages of the climate, but that doesn't mean your vacation couldn't be made perfect by weeks of unbroken sunny weather or ruined by weeks of unbroken rain. All you can do is play the averages and hope for the best.

JUNE, JULY & AUGUST   Summer in Alaska is a miraculous time when the sun refuses to set and people are energized with limitless energy. The sun dips below the horizon in Anchorage for only about four hours on June 21, the longest day of the year, and the sky is light all night. The state fills with people coming to visit and to work in the seasonal fishing, timber, and construction industries. Weather gets warmer, although how warm depends on where you go (see the chart below). June is the driest of the three summer months, July the warmest, and August generally the rainiest month of the brief summer, but warmer than June. In most respects June is the best summer month to make a visit, but it does have some drawbacks to consider: Vestiges of winter linger in some areas until mid-month; in the Arctic, snow doesn't all melt till mid-June; in Southcentral Alaska, trails at high elevation or in the shade may be too muddy or snowy; and not all activities or facilities at Denali National Park open until late June. It's also the worst time for mosquitoes. The salmon-fishing season depends on where you are. July is generally its height, followed by August and September, but there are salmon, somewhere, all summer.

Summer also is the season of crowds and high prices. Most operators in the visitor industry have only these 90 days to make their year's income, and they charge whatever the market will bear. July is the absolute peak of the tourist season, when everything is booked solidly and crowds are most prevalent; you must book well ahead to travel in Alaska in July. Before June 15 and after August 15 the season begins to decline, providing occasional bargains and more elbow room. But the length and intensity of the visitor season varies widely in different areas, and in some places it stays very busy from Memorial Day to Labor Day.

MAY & SEPTEMBER   More and more visitors are coming to Alaska during these shoulder months to take advantage of the lower prices, absence of crowds, and special beauty.

May is the drier of the two months, and can be as warm as summer, if you're lucky, but as you go farther north and earlier in the month, your chances increase of finding cold, mud, and even snow. In Alaska we don't have spring—the melt of snow and resultant seas of mud are called *break up*. Many outdoor activities aren't possible during break up, which can extend well into May. Before May 15, most tourist-oriented activities and facilities are still closed, and a few don't open until Memorial Day or June 1. Where visitor facilities are open, they often have significantly lower prices. Also, the first visitors of the year always receive an especially warm welcome. The very earliest salmon runs start in May, but the bulk of the fishing season is later.

Sometime from late August to mid-September, weather patterns change, bringing clouds, frequent rainstorms, and cooling weather, and signaling the trees and tundra to turn bright, vivid colors. For a week the bright-yellow birches of the boreal forest make September the most lovely time of year. But the rain and the nip in the air, similar to late October or November in New England, mean you'll likely have to bundle up, and September is generally the wettest month of the year. Most tourist-oriented businesses stay open, with lower prices, till September 15, except in the Arctic. After September 15, it's pot luck; some areas close up tight, but the silver salmon fishing hits prime time on the Kenai Peninsula and the season stays active till the end of the month. A lucky visitor can come in September and hit a month of crisp, sunny, perfect weather, and have the state relatively to him- or herself. Or it can be cold and rain all month.

WINTER   One of the most spectacular trips I ever took was a train ride from Fairbanks to Anchorage in January. Outside the windows, Mount McKinley stood clear and so vivid that I felt as if I could reach out and touch it in a vast, smooth landscape of pale blue and rich orange. A young woman from South Africa was on the train. When I asked her why she came to Alaska in January, she only had to point out the window. She said, "Alaska is all about snow and ice."

She was right, but visitors and the people who serve them generally haven't figured that out yet. Some towns—such as Skagway and Dawson City—close down completely. In others—most places on the ocean, for example—most activities and attractions are closed for the season, but some services remain open. Where facilities are open, hotel prices are often less than half of what you'd pay in the high season. Quite luxurious rooms sometimes go for the cost of a budget motel. Visitors who seek out places of interest can have an exceptional and memorable time, enjoying some of the best alpine, Nordic, and backcountry skiing, dog mushing, and aurora and wildlife watching available anywhere, at any time. Some of the best spots to go: Chena Hot Springs Resort, outside Fairbanks; Alyeska Resort, south of Anchorage; and in the late fall and early winter, Sitka, where humpback whales congregate.

ALASKA'S CLIMATE, BY MONTHS & REGIONS

	Jan.	Feb.	March	April	May	June	July	Aug.	Sept.	Oct.	Nov.	Dec.

Anchorage: Southcentral Alaska

	Jan.	Feb.	March	April	May	June	July	Aug.	Sept.	Oct.	Nov.	Dec.
Average high/low	21/8	26/12	33/18	43/29	54/39	62/47	65/52	63/50	55/42	41/29	27/15	23/10
Hours of light*	6:30	9:15	12	15:30	17:45	19:30	18:15	15:30	12	9:30	7	5:30
Sunny days†	12	10	13	12	11	10	9	9	9	10	10	10
Rainy or snowy days	8	8	8	6	7	8	11	13	14	12	10	11
Precipitation‡	0.8	0.8	0.7	0.7	0.7	1.1	1.7	2.4	2.7	2	1.1	1.1

Barrow: Arctic Alaska

	Jan.	Feb.	March	April	May	June	July	Aug.	Sept.	Oct.	Nov.	Dec.
Average high/low	-7/-19	-12/-24	-9/-21	5/-9	24/14	38/30	45/34	42/33	34/27	18/9	3/-7	-5/-17
Hours of light*	0:00	6:00	12:00	20:00	24:00	24:00	24:00	20:00	13:00	7:30	0:00	0:00
Sunny days†	7	18	21	18	8	9	11	5	4	6	8	4
Rainy or snowy days	4	4	4	4	4	5	9	11	11	11	6	5
Precipitation‡	0.2	0.2	0.2	0.2	0.2	0.3	1	1	0.6	0.5	0.3	0.2

Cold Bay: Aleutian Archipelago

	Jan.	Feb.	March	April	May	June	July	Aug.	Sept.	Oct.	Nov.	Dec.
Average high/low	33/24	32/23	35/25	38/29	44/35	50/41	55/46	56/47	52/43	44/35	39/30	35/27
Hours of light*	8:00	10:00	12:00	14:30	16:30	17:30	16:30	14:00	12:30	9:00	8:00	7:00
Sunny days†	8	6	8	4	3	3	3	2	4	6	6	7
Rainy or snowy days	19	17	18	16	17	16	17	20	21	23	22	21
Precipitation‡	2.8	2.3	2.2	2	2.3	2.1	2.5	3.2	4.4	4.3	4.2	3.7

Fairbanks: Interior Alaska

	Jan.	Feb.	March	April	May	June	July	Aug.	Sept.	Oct.	Nov.	Dec.
Average high/low	-2/-18	7/-14	24/-2	41/20	59/38	70/50	72/53	66/47	55/36	32/18	11/-6	2/-15
Hours of light*	6:45	9:00	11:00	15:30	19:00	21:00	19:00	16:00	13:45	9:00	6:00	4:00
Sunny days†	15	14	17	14	16	13	12	10	10	9	12	12
Rainy or snowy days	8	7	6	5	7	11	12	12	10	11	11	9
Precipitation‡	0.5	0.4	0.4	0.3	0.6	1.4	1.9	2	0.9	0.9	0.8	0.8

Juneau: Southeast Alaska

	Jan.	Feb.	March	April	May	June	July	Aug.	Sept.	Oct.	Nov.	Dec.
Average high/low	29/19	34/23	39/27	47/32	55/39	61/45	64/48	63/47	56/43	47/37	37/27	32/23
Hours of light*	7:30	9:30	12:00	14:30	17:00	18:15	17:30	15:30	12:30	10:00	7:30	6:30
Sunny days†	8	7	7	8	8	8	8	9	6	4	6	5
Rainy or snowy days	18	17	18	17	17	15	17	17	20	24	20	21
Precipitation‡	4.5	3.7	3.3	2.8	3.4	3.1	4.2	5.3	6.7	7.8	4.9	4.4

Valdez: Prince William Sound

	Jan.	Feb.	March	April	May	June	July	Aug.	Sept.	Oct.	Nov.	Dec.
Average high/low	26/15	30/18	36/22	44/30	52/38	59/44	62/48	61/46	54/40	43/33	32/22	28/18
Hours of light*	6:30	9:15	12:00	15:15	17:45	19:30	18:00	15:15	12:30	9:45	7:00	5:45
Sunny days†	9	9	11	11	9	8	8	10	8	8	10	7
Rainy or snowy days	17	14	16	14	17	15	17	17	20	20	16	18
Precipitation‡	5.6	5.1	4.7	3.2	3.8	3.1	3.8	6	8.4	8	5.5	6.8

*Hours of light is an approximation of the possible daylight on the 20th day of each month.
†Sunny days includes the average observed clear and partly cloudy days per month.
‡Precipitation is the average water equivalent of rain or snow.

WHAT TO WEAR

SUMMER You're not going to the North Pole, and you don't need a down parka or winter boots weighing down your luggage. But you do need to be ready for a variety of weather, from sunny, 80° days to windy, rainy 50° outings on the water. The way Alaskans prepare for such a range is with layers.

WINTER Normal alpine and Nordic skiing garb are adequate for skiing in Southcentral Alaska. Cross-country skiing in the Interior may require you to dress more warmly than you're accustomed to. Snowmobiling or dog mushing in winter requires the warmest possible clothing; you'll need the stoutest Sorel or air force bunny boots, insulated snow pants, thermal underwear, a heavy down parka with a hood, thick mittens (not gloves), and a wool hat or face-covering mask. Expect to spend at least $500 on a full winter outfit adequate for backcountry winter travel. You can buy what you need in Anchorage or Fairbanks when you arrive. If you're not planning anything so rugged, you can get by in a city with a normal great coat, gloves, and wool socks; if you're like most Alaskans, you'll just make a quick dash from car to heated building when really cold weather hits.

ALASKA CALENDAR OF EVENTS

Here are some of the biggest community events of the year in Alaska's cities and towns. You'll also find fishing derbies going on all summer almost anywhere you go in Alaska. The dates, in many cases, are predictions: Don't plan a vacation around them. Instead, call the organizers or visitor information centers listed in each of the towns for late details.

January
- **Russian Orthodox Christmas,** Kodiak and Sitka. Celebrated with solemn ceremonies and the starring ceremony, in which a star is carried through the streets from house to house. January 7.

February
- **The Cordova Iceworm Festival,** a winter carnival in Cordova on Prince William Sound; the big iceworm or, to be precise, ice centipede, marches in a parade. First full weekend in the month.
- **The Yukon Quest International Sled Dog Race** starts or finishes in Fairbanks. (Fairbanks has the start in even-numbered years; Whitehorse, Yukon Territory, in odd years.) The challenge of the 1,000-mile race is equal to the Iditarod. Mid-month.
- ✪ **The Anchorage Fur Rendezvous,** a huge, city-wide winter carnival, over 10 days. The main event is the **World Champion Sled Dog Race,** a three-day sprint event of about 25 miles per heat. Second and third weekends of the month.
- **The Nenana Ice Classic** starts with a weekend celebration; the classic is a sweepstakes on who can guess closest to the exact date and time ice will go out on the Tanana River. You can buy tickets all over Alaska. Last weekend in the month.

March
- ✪ **The Iditarod Trail Sled Dog Race.** The famous race starts with much fanfare from **Anchorage,** then the teams are loaded in trucks a few miles out of town; the **Iditarod Re-start,** in **Wasilla,** is the real beginning of the race. Here the dogs are unloaded from trucks for the continuous 1,000-mile run to Nome. The event enlivens Wasilla at the end of a long winter, and the area makes the most of it. First

Saturday in March. The finish in Nome is the biggest event of the year in the Arctic, drawing world media attention and turning Nome into a huge party for a few days.

- **The Bering Sea Ice Golf Classic** showcases Nome's well-developed sense of humor—six holes are set up on the sea ice. Various similar silly events take place all year—you can get a list from the visitors center. Mid-month.
- **The North American Sled Dog Championships,** in Fairbanks, a sprint with two 20-mile heats and one 30-mile heat, begins and ends downtown. Mid-month.
- ✪ **The Ice Art Competition,** also in Fairbanks, brings carvers from all over the world to create spectacular sculptures out of immense chunks cut from Fairbanks lakes. Toward the end of the month.
- **The World Extreme Skiing Championships,** Valdez. Held on the vertical faces of mountains north of Valdez; it's a daredevil competition, and someone seems to get killed or seriously injured every year. March 30–April 1.

April

- **King of the Hill Snowboard Competition,** Valdez. This high-risk event takes place after the extreme skiing races; it's the same kind of thing, on snowboards. April 9–13, 1996.
- **The Alaska Folk Festival,** Juneau. A community-wide celebration drawing musicians, whether on the bill or not, from all over the state. April 8–14, 1996.

May

- **The Copper River Delta Shorebird Festival** revolves around the coming of dizzying swarms of shorebirds that use the delta, and the beaches near the town, as a migratory stop-over; it's an opportunity to see immense waves of birds. The whole community gets involved to host bird watchers and put on a full schedule of educational and outdoor activities. May 1–5, 1996.
- **Kachemak Bay Shorebird Festival,** Homer. Includes guided bird watching, art activities, and other events. May 10–12, 1996.
- **Little Norway Festival,** Petersburg, celebrating the May 17, 1814, declaration of independence of Norway from Sweden. The town goes wild and lots of community events are planned. May 16–18, 1996.
- ✪ **The Crab Festival,** Kodiak. Includes a carnival, fleet parade, and various competitions, as well as a solemn service for lost fishermen, which occurs at the fishermen's memorial by the boat harbor. May 23–Memorial Day weekend.
- **The Polar Bear Swim,** Nome. Occurs in the Bering Sea on Memorial Day, ice permitting.

June

- **Kenai River Festival,** Kenai. Food, music, crafts, and games. Early in the month.
- **Celebration,** Juneau. Modestly titled gathering of some 1,000 Native dancers at the Juneau Centennial Hall. June 6–8, 1996.
- ✪ **The Sitka Summer Music Festival,** a chamber music series that began in 1972, is one of Alaska's most important cultural events, drawing musicians from all over the world. June 7–28, 1996.
- **Midnight Sun Baseball Game,** Fairbanks. A summer-solstice event—the local semi-pro baseball team, the **Fairbanks Goldpanners,** plays a game under the midnight sun, beginning at 10:30pm. June 21.
- **Solstice Gathering,** Eagle Summit. On the Steese Highway, 107 miles out of Fairbanks, an informal gathering occurs to celebrate the solstice at the 3,624-foot Eagle Summit highway pass. June 21.

- **Midnight Sun Festival,** Nome. Celebrates the summer solstice, when Nome gets more than 22 hours of direct sunlight, with a parade, beauty pageant, and similar events. June 21.

July

- **The Yukon Gold Panning Championships and Canada Day Celebrations,** Dawson City. July 1.
- ✪ **Independence Day.** Most of the small towns in Alaska make a big deal of the 4th of July. Nowhere is there a bigger celebration than in Seward. The whole town explodes with visitors, primarily from Anchorage. Besides the parade and many small town festivities, the main attraction is the **Mount Marathon Race.** Run every year since it started as a bar bet in 1915, the racers go from the middle of town straight up rocky Mount Marathon to its 3,022-foot peak, then tumble down again. **Seldovia, Kenai, Ketchikan, Skagway,** and **Juneau** also have exceptional 4th of July events.
- **The Fairbanks Summer Arts Festival.** Besides offerings for the public in music, dance, theater, opera, ice skating, and the visual arts, there are opportunities for instruction for all levels, without the requirement for audition tapes. July 26 August 6, 1996.

August

- ✪ **Southeast Alaska State Fair** and **Bald Eagle Music Festival,** Haines. The area's biggest summer event, it's a regional small-town get-together, with livestock, cooking, a logging show, parade, music, and other entertainments. August 7–11, 1996.
- **Concert on the Lawn,** Homer. Put on by KBBI radio, this is a day-long, outdoor music festival that brings together the whole town. August 10 or 11, 1996.
- **Prince William Sound Community College Theater Conference,** Valdez. Brings famous playwrights and directors to the community for seminars and events. August 16–19, 1996.
- **Blueberry Arts Festival,** Ketchikan. Has booths, music, and food, and is put on by the Ketchikan Area Arts and Humanities Council. August 10, 1996.
- ✪ **Alaska State Fair,** Palmer. The biggest event of the year for the Matanuska Valley, and one of the biggest for Anchorage. It's a typical mid-sized fair, except for the huge vegetables. The good soil and long days in the Valley grow cabbages the size of a bean-bag chair. A mere beach-ball-sized cabbage wouldn't even make it into competition. August 23–September 2, 1996.

October

- **Alaska Day Festival,** Sitka. Alaska Day, commemorating the Alaska purchase, on October 18, 1867, is a big deal in this former Russian and U.S. territorial capital city. October 14–18, 1996.

November

- **Athabascan Fiddling Festival,** Fairbanks. Draws together musicians and dancers from the Interior region for performances and workshops. November 8–11, 1996.
- **Great Alaska Shootout Men's Basketball Tournament,** Anchorage. The University of Alaska Seawolves host a roster of the nation's top-ranked NCAA Division I teams at the Sullivan Arena. November 27–30, 1996.
- **Christmas Tree Lighting,** Anchorage. Takes place in town square, with Santa arriving behind a team of real reindeer. It's usually followed by a performance of *The Nutcracker* in the Alaska Center for the Performing Arts. The Saturday after Thanksgiving, November 30, 1996.
- **Winter Arts Faire,** Ketchikan. First Saturday after Thanksgiving.

December

- **Christmas,** Anchorage. A full schedule of community Christmas festivities, including crafts fairs and performances, takes place all month. Similar events take place all over the state.

3 Health, Safety & Traveler's Insurance

HEALTH

You'll find modern, full-service hospitals in each of Alaska's larger cities, and even in some small towns that act as regional centers. There's some kind of clinic even in tiny villages. Travelers who don't plan to spend time in the outdoors need take no health precautions beyond what they'd do when traveling anywhere else. If you'll be doing any hiking, boating, camping, or other outdoor activities, the tips below may be more relevant.

HYPOTHERMIA   Sometimes known as exposure, hypothermia is a potentially fatal lowering of core body temperature. It can sneak up on you, and it's most dangerous when you don't realize how cold you are, on a damp mountain hike or wet boating trip. It doesn't have to be very cold if you're wet and not adequately dressed in wool. Among the symptoms are cold extremities, shivering, being uncommunicative, poor judgment or coordination, and sleepiness. The cure is to warm the victim up—getting indoors, forcing him to drink hot liquids, and, if shelter is unavailable, applying body heat from another person, skin on skin, in a sleeping bag, if possible.

INSECT BITES   The good news is that Alaska has no poisonous snakes or spiders. The bad news is the mosquitoes and other biting insects. They're not dangerous, but they *can* ruin a trip. Insect repellent is a necessity, as is having a place where you can get away from them. Hikers in the Interior, where mosquitoes are worst, use head nets. Mosquitoes can go through light fabric, which is why people in the Bush wear heavy Carharts even on the hottest days. Wasps, hornets, and other stinging insects are common in Alaska. If you're allergic, be ready with your serum.

PLANTS   Two shrubs common in Alaska can cause a rash. Pushki, also called cow parsnip, is a large-leafed plant growing primarily in open areas, up to shoulder height by late summer, with white flowers. The celerylike stalks break easily and the sap has the quality of intensifying the burning power of the sun on skin. Wash it off quickly. Devil's Club, a more obviously dangerous plant, grows on steep slopes and has ferocious spines that can pierce through clothing.

SHELLFISH   Don't eat mussels or clams you pick or dig from the seashore unless the local office of the **Alaska Department of Fish and Game** (☎ **907/465-6085**) indicates that the area is safe. Most of Alaska's remote beaches are not tested, and so are not safe. The risk is paralytic shellfish poisoning, a fatal malady caused by a naturally occurring toxin. It causes paralysis of breathing. A victim can be kept alive with artificial respiration—the kiss of life—until medical help is obtained. People have even been saved that way for days, until the toxin works its way out of the body.

SWIMMING   Ask about lake water before swimming in it. In recent years some lakes have been infested with a bug that causes an itchy rash.

WATER   Authorities advise against drinking unpurified river or lake water.

SAFETY

I've listed a few important safety tips for traveling in Alaska, but the most important safety advice is to be cautious and use common sense. People who are hurt while visiting Alaska often are doing stupid things that they wouldn't think of doing at home—like the otherwise intelligent woman from Australia a few years ago who climbed into the polar bear cage at the Alaska Zoo to get a better picture.

BEARS Being eaten by a bear is probably the least likely way for your vacation to end. Deaths from dog bites are much more common, for example. But bears are one of those deep-seated fears, and if you're spending any time in the outdoors, you should be prepared. Use common sense—if you see a bear from a car, don't get out, and if you're near the car, get in. The first rule of defense is equally simple—don't attract bears. All food must be kept in airtight containers when you're camping, and be careful when you're cooking and cleaning up not to spread food odors. Never keep food in your tent. When walking through brush or thick trees, make lots of noise to avoid surprising a bear or moose—singing, loud conversation, and bells all work. Never intentionally approach a bear. At all costs, avoid coming between a bear and cubs or a bear and food. If you see a bear, stop, wave your arms, make noise, and group together so you look larger to the bear. Stand your ground to avoid enticing the bear to chase; depart only by slowly backing away, at an angle. If the bear follows, stop. Almost every time, if you stand still, the bear will turn and walk off. Once in a great while the bear may bluff a charge; even less often it may attack. Fall and play dead, rolling into a ball face down with your hands behind your neck. The bear should lose interest, but you have to stay still till it's gone. In very rare instances the bear may not lose interest, especially in the case of a black bear, because it's planning to make a meal of you—then fight back for all you're worth. Most Alaskans carry a gun for protection in bear country; some carry pepper spray that's available in sporting-goods stores. In either case, you have to hold back the weapon as a last resort, when the bear is quite close and in the process of an attack. If you take a gun, it had better be a big one. Even a .45-caliber handgun won't stop a bear in time if you don't get off a precise shot. A .300-Magnum rifle or 12-gauge shotgun loaded with rifled slugs is the weapon of choice.

BOATING Going out on the water is more hazardous in Alaska than in most other places, and you should only go with an experienced, licensed operator unless you really know what you're doing. The weather can be severe and unpredictable, and there's no margin for error if you fall into the water or capsize—you have only minutes to get out and get warm before hypothermia and death. A life jacket will keep you afloat, but it won't keep you alive in 40°F water.

CRIME Sadly, crime rates are not low in Alaska's major cities, although muggings are rare. Take the normal precautions you'd take at home. You're safe in daylight hours anywhere tourists commonly go, less so late at night leaving a rough bar. Women need to be especially careful on their own, as Alaska has a disproportionately high rate of rape. Most women I know avoid walking by themselves at night in Alaskan towns and cities, especially in wooded or out-of-the-way areas. The late-night sunlight can be deceiving—just because it's light doesn't mean it's safe. Assaults occur in big towns and small. Women should never hitchhike alone.

SUMMER DRIVING Keep your headlights on for safety. Make sure you've got a good spare and jack, especially if driving a gravel highway. For remote driving, take a first-aid kit, emergency food, a tow rope, and jumper cables. Drivers are required to pull over at the next pull-out whenever five or more cars are trailing on a two-lane highway, regardless of how fast they're going. This saves the lives of people who otherwise will try to pass. When passing a truck going the other way on a gravel highway, slow down or stop and pull as far as possible to the opposite side of the road to avoid losing your windshield to a flying rock. Always think about the path of rocks you're kicking up toward others' vehicles.

WINTER DRIVING   Drivers on Alaska's highways in winter should be prepared for cold-weather emergencies far from help. Take all the items listed for rural summer driving, plus a flashlight, matches and materials to light a fire, chains, a shovel, and an ice scraper. A camp stove to make hot beverages is also a good idea. If you're driving a highway between November and April, take along gear adequate to keep you safe from the cold even if you have to wait 24 hours with a dead car at –40°F—parkas, boots, hats, mittens, blankets, and sleeping bags. Other vehicles come by rarely. All Alaska roads are icy all winter. Studded tires are a necessity—nonstudded snowtires or so-called all-weather tires aren't adequate. Also, never leave your car without starting it for more than four hours in extreme cold. Alaskans generally have electrical head-bolt heaters installed to keep the engine warm overnight; you'll find outlets everywhere on rural highways.

TRAVELER'S INSURANCE

Travel insurance falls into three categories: (1) health and accident, (2) trip cancellation, and (3) lost luggage.

First, review your present policies—you may already have adequate coverage between them and what's offered by credit/charge-card companies. Many card companies insure their users in case of a travel accident, providing the transit ticket was purchased with their card. Sometimes fraternal organizations have policies protecting members in case of sickness or accidents abroad.

Many homeowner's insurance policies cover theft of luggage during travel and loss of documents—your passport or airline ticket, for instance. Coverage is usually limited to about $500. To submit a claim on your insurance, remember that you'll need police reports or a statement from a medical authority that you did suffer the loss or experience the illness for which you're seeking compensation.

Some policies (and this is the type you should have) provide advances in cash or transfers of funds so you won't have to dip into your precious travel funds to settle medical bills.

If you've booked a charter flight, you'll probably have to pay a cancellation fee if you cancel a trip suddenly, even if caused by an unforeseen crisis. It's possible to get insurance against such a possibility. Some travel agencies provide this coverage, and often flight insurance against a canceled trip is written into tickets paid for by credit or charge cards from such companies as Visa and American Express. Many tour operators or insurance agents provide this type of insurance.

The following companies offer such policies:

Access America, 6600 W. Broad St., Richmond, VA 23230 (☎ **804/285-3300,** or 800/284-8300), offers a comprehensive travel insurance/assistance package, including medical and on-the-spot hospital payments, medical transportation, baggage insurance, trip cancellation/interruption insurance, and collision-damage insurance for a car rental. Their 24-hour hotline connects you to multilingual coordinators who can offer advice on medical, legal, and travel problems. Packages begin at $27.

Wallach & Co., 107 W. Federal St. (P.O. Box 480), Middleburg, VA 22117-0480 (☎ **703/687-3166,** or 800/237-6615), offers a policy called Healthcare Abroad (MEDEX). It covers 10 to 90 days at $3 per day; the policy includes accident and sickness coverage to the tune of $100,000. Medical evacuation is also included, along with $25,000 dismemberment and/or death compensation. Provisions for trip cancellation and lost or stolen luggage can also be written into the policy at a nominal cost.

Travel Guard International, 1145 Clark St., Stevens Point, WI 54481 (☎ **800/ 826-1300**), offers a comprehensive seven-day policy that covers basically everything for $52: emergency assistance, accidental death, trip cancellation/interruption, medical coverage abroad, and lost luggage. However, there are restrictions you should understand before accepting the coverage.

4　Tips for Special Travelers

FOR TRAVELERS WITH DISABILITIES　The Americans with Disabilities Act, along with economic competition, have sped the process of retrofitting hotels and even bed-and-breakfasts to be accessible for people with disabilities. They're often the best rooms in the house. Hotels without such facilities now are the exception; however, check when making reservations.

There are several Alaska agencies for people with disabilities. **Challenge Alaska,** 720 W. 58th Ave., Anchorage, AK 99518 (☎ **907/563-2658**), is a nonprofit organization dedicated to providing accessible outdoors activities. They have a skiing center on Mount Alyeska (☎ **907/783-2925**), in Girdwood, and also offer summer camping, sea kayaking, fishing, and other trips. **Access Alaska,** 3710 Woodland Dr., Suite 900, Anchorage, AK 99517 (☎ **907/248-4777,** or 800/770-4488 in Alaska; TTY/TDD 907/248-8799), advocates for people with disabilities, and offers referrals and tour information packets. **Alaska Welcomes You! Inc.,** P.O. Box 91333, Anchorage, AK 99509-1333 (☎ **907/349-6301** or 800/349-6301), offers three- and eight-day packages for people with disabilities and reasonably priced, accessible tours in Southcentral Alaska from 90 minutes to all day. Trips include rafting, boating, flightseeing, and fishing.

FOR SENIORS　People over age 65 get reduced admission prices to most Alaska attractions, and many accommodations have special senior rates. National parks offer special rates for people over 62 with a Golden Age Passport, which you can obtain at any of the parks. Most towns have a senior citizens center where you'll find activities and help with any special needs. The **Anchorage Seniors Center** (☎ **907/258-7823**) offers guidance for visitors, as well as free RV parking and use of the restaurant, showers, gift shop, and fitness room; a big band plays Friday nights for dancing. **Elderhostel,** 75 Federal St., Boston, MA 02110-1941 (☎ **617/ 426-8056**), operates learning vacations for groups of senior citizens.

FOR GAY & LESBIAN TRAVELERS　Anchorage and Juneau have active gay and lesbian communities. In Anchorage, **Identity Inc.** (☎ **907/258-4777**) offers referrals, publishes a newsletter, and sponsors pot-luck dinners. The **S.E. Alaska Gay/ Lesbian Alliance** (☎ **907/586-4297**) is a similar organization in Juneau. **Apollo Travel Agency,** 1207 W. 47th Ave., Anchorage, AK 99503 (☎ **907/561-0661**), is a member of the International Gay Travel Agencies Association, and can guide you to businesses, such as bed-and-breakfast accommodations and tours, that cater specifically to gays and lesbians. **Equinox Wilderness Expediters,** 618 W. 14th Ave., Anchorage, AK 99501 (☎ **907/274-9087**), offers wilderness trips ranging from three days to three weeks by canoe, kayak, rafting, or hiking; male- or female-only trips are available. The *Gayellow Pages National Edition* (☎ **212/674-0120**) has a couple of pages of listings in Alaska.

FOR STUDENTS   Most museums offer free or greatly reduced admission for students and anyone under 18, although sometimes you have to ask. Make sure to bring a student identification card. There are hostels in most major towns in Alaska, mostly open in the summer only. You'll find them listed in the text for each town. Ten hostels in Alaska are affiliated with **Hostelling International–American Youth Hostels,** 733 15th St. NW, Suite 840, Washington, DC 20005 (☎ **202/783-6161**). Membership costs $25 for adults, $10 for youths 17 and under; or you can buy their directory of hostels in North America for $5.95.

Many students travel to Alaska for summer work. It's usually possible to get a job in a fish cannery in most coastal towns. Work on the slime line is hard and unpleasant and the pay is low, but if the season is good you can work long hours and earn considerably more than at a normal summer job. If you camp and keep your expenses low, you can take home decent money for your summer's work. Stay on shore unless you're really desperate for money—offshore fish-processing ships are a truly miserable and dangerous place to work, and if the ship doesn't get any fish you don't make any money. Don't come north expecting to make fabulous wages. The stories of college students making huge crew shares on fishing boats are legends—there are lots of experienced fishermen to take those jobs before boats hire raw hands they have to train. Jobs are often available in the tourism industry, too. Before heading north in search of summer work, contact the **Alaska Department of Labor Job Service,** P.O. Box 107024, Anchorage, AK 99510 (☎ **907/269-4800**), to check on the current job market and to find out if there are likely to be openings when you arrive, and where.

FOR FAMILIES   I researched most of this book while traveling with my wife, Barbara, three-year-old boy, Robin, and eight-month-old girl, Julia. They made many of the best discoveries, and I've tried to include my advice for families throughout the text. I've left out places that were hostile to kids.

Alaska is a great place to take a family. The magnificent scenery is something even young children can understand and internalize. Also, an Alaska vacation is largely spent outdoors, which is where kids like to be. Robin hadn't had enough ferry riding after we'd been doing it for weeks, and both children enjoyed camping immensely. When Julia realized everyone was going to sleep in the tent with her, on her level, her face lit up. The hillside towns of Southeast Alaska, overhung with mountains and huge trees, are magical places for kids. I was amazed at how the children could teach adults to slow down and find joy in new discoveries.

There are drawbacks to Alaska as a family destination, too. The primary one is the expense. Airlines offer insignificant discounts for children these days. Activities like flightseeing and tour-boat cruises, which also tend to have less-than-generous children's discounts, will cost too much for most families. Many bed-and-breakfasts simply are not practical for a family because the rooms tend to be too small. Hotel rooms are expensive in Alaska, especially those with enough space and a kitchenette. Restaurants that aren't too fancy to take the kids often are too smoky. A car camping trip solves many of those problems, with stops in a hotel every few days to get everyone cleaned up. But the highways in Alaska are long, and children will require a gradual approach to covering ground. The worst day we endured was when we had to get back to Anchorage from Fairbanks and Julia just couldn't stand to be in her car seat another minute—and we had five hours left.

You must be careful in choosing your itinerary and activities with children. There are the obvious things, like allowing time to play, explore, and rest, but also remember that children often don't enjoy activities like wildlife watching. It takes a long time to find the animals, and when you do they're usually off in the distance—kids often don't have the visual skills to pick out the animals from the landscape. Be careful never to overtax children with walks and hiking trips; it'll just make everyone miserable. Short sea-kayaking excursions, on the other hand, are great for children who are old enough, riding in the front of a double-seat boat with a parent in back.

If you're flawed mortals like us, after the end of a few weeks on the road you'll be getting on each other's nerves. We found success in leaving time for low-key kid activities, like beachcombing and playing in the park, while one grownup could split off and do something else. One of us would watch the children while the other visited the museum or went on a special, more expensive activity. Of course, if you want to save your marriage, you'll have to be scrupulously fair about who gets to go flightseeing and who has to stay behind, changing diapers, as you won't have my all-purpose excuse—research.

5 Package Tour or Do-It-Yourself?

Hundreds of thousands of visitors come to Alaska each year on package tours, leaving virtually all their travel arrangements in the hands of a single company that takes complete responsibility for ushering them through the state for a single, lump-sum fee. But more and more visitors are cutting the apron strings and exploring Alaska on their own, and finding a more relaxed, spontaneous experience. There are advantages and disadvantages to each approach, and which way you choose to visit depends on how you value those pros and cons. Unfortunately, some people make the choice based on expectations that aren't valid, so it's important to know what you're getting into either way.

A package provides security. You'll know in advance how much everything will cost, you don't have to worry about making hotel and ground transportation reservations, you're guaranteed to see the most popular highlights of each town you visit, and you'll have someone telling you what you're looking at. If there are weather delays or other travel problems, it's the tour company's problem, not yours. Everything happens on schedule, and you never have to touch your baggage other than to unpack when it magically shows up in your room. If you sometimes feel like you're a member of a herd on a package tour, you may also feel more secure, knowing there is safety in numbers. And there will be others on the way—predominantly older people—to make new friends with.

If you're short on time, packages make the most of it—most travel at an exhausting pace, getting passengers up early, covering a lot of ground, and scheduling sights and activities solidly through the day with only the minimum time allocated to each, just enough to get a taste of what it's about. Of course, that's also a disadvantage. On a package you'll meet few if any Alaska residents, since most of the tour companies hire college students from Outside to fill summer jobs, and you won't have time to dig in and learn about a place you're especially interested in, because it's always time to get back on the bus for the next stop. For visiting wilderness, such as Denali National Park, the quick and superficial approach can, in my opinion, spoil the whole point of going to a destination that's about an experience, not just seeing a particular object or place.

Studies by Alaska tourism experts have found that many people choose packages to avoid risks that don't really exist. Alaska still has the reputation of being an untamed frontier land—and in some sense it is—but that doesn't mean it's a dangerous or uncomfortable place to travel. Visitors who sign up for a tour to avoid having to spend the night in an igloo or deal with the wild-eyed proprietor of a frontier roadhouse without indoor plumbing may wish they'd been a bit more adventurous when they arrive and find that Alaska has the same facilities as are found in any other state. Except for tiny Bush villages that you won't be visiting anyway, you can find the standard American hotel room anywhere you go. And there are enough other travelers that the tourism infrastructure is well developed even in small towns—you're never far from help unless you want to be.

It's also possible for an independent traveler to obtain some of the predictability a package tour provides. You can reserve accommodations and activities and control your expenses by using a good travel agent experienced in Alaska travel. Several based in Alaska, which I've listed below and in the regional chapters, are experienced in booking trips for independent travelers who want to know where they're going to be, what they're going to be doing, and how much it will cost in detail before they leave home. Using this book to get a good outline of what you want to do first is a good idea before you consult a travel agent. But independent travelers never have the complete security of those on package tours. Once you're on the road, weather delays and other cancellations will confound the best-laid plans, and you'll be on your own to adjust your arrangements. If you can't relax and enjoy a trip knowing that could happen—and plenty of people feel that way—then a package tour is the way to go.

LARGE TOUR COMPANIES

Three major tour companies dominate the Alaska package-tour market with "vertically integrated" operations that allow them to take care of everything you do while in Alaska with tight quality control. Each also offers tours as short as a couple of hours to independent travelers who want to combine their own exploring with a more structured experience. All can be booked through any travel agent. All three companies also have storefront offices in Anchorage on Fourth Avenue between E and F streets, as well as other local offices and tour desks around the state.

Holland America Westours / Gray Line of Alaska. 300 Elliot Ave., Seattle, WA 98119. ☎ **800/628-2449.**

The Holland America cruise line became the giant of Alaska tourism by buying local companies. It acquired the Gray Line and Westours tour companies to carry visitors in buses, trains, and boats, and the Westmark hotel chain to put them up for the night. Gray Line is primarily the face the company puts to the public. Chances are, any major tour you sign up for other than Princess or Alaska Sightseeing (see below) will put you on a Gray Line coach and in exclusively Westmark hotels. Descriptions of Westmark hotels are in each of the towns where they're found. The quality is not consistent—the Westmark Cape Fox in Ketchikan is among the best in the state while the hotel in Skagway is below usually accepted standards. Most are adequate properties with standard American rooms. On a package, you don't spend much time in the room, as schedules generally are tightly planned and daily departures early. You'll find a description of the company's rail cars on the Anchorage–Denali–Fairbanks run in Chapter 9. Gray Line coaches are first rate, especially several super-luxurious, extra-long vehicles that bend in the middle. The company can take you virtually anywhere you want to go in Alaska, and some of its boat excursions—from Juneau to Skagway and on the Yukon River from Dawson City, for example—are unparalleled.

✪ **Princess Cruises and Tours.** 2815 Second Ave., Suite 400, Seattle, WA 98121-1299. ☎ **800/835-8907.**

The Princess cruise line has built its land-tour operation from the ground up instead of buying it, as Holland America did, and the result is a smaller but consistently top-quality collection of properties. The Princess hotels in Fairbanks, Denali National Park, and Cooper Landing, on the Kenai Peninsula, are all exceptionally good. Princess operates its own coaches and has the best rail cars on the Alaska Railroad route to Denali. Descriptions of each hostelry can be found in the appropriate chapter. The company's network of tours is less extensive than Holland America's, but covers much of the state.

Alaska Sightseeing/Cruise West. Fourth and Battery Bldg., Suite 700, Seattle, WA 98121. ☎ **800/666-7375.**

This relatively small company, started by Alaska-based tourism pioneers, offers a more intimate experience compared to the Princess and Holland America giants. The land tours are marketed primarily as add-ons to small-vessel cruises, but are available separately. The buses are less luxurious than the major competition. The company doesn't own its own hotels, and uses the Alaska Railroad's cars on the train ride to Denali National Park. Tours cover only the state's hot spots—Anchorage, Southeast, Fairbanks and Denali, Prince William Sound, and the Kenai Peninsula.

SMALL & SPECIALTY TOURS

There are a seemingly infinite number of small tour operators in Alaska. Contact the tourism marketing council, listed above, or a travel agent, for more ideas.

FOR BIRDWATCHERS   A trip to Alaska is an unsurpassed opportunity for birders. Those interested in adding exceptional birds to a life list will want to travel to Nome, Gambell Island, or the Aleutian Archipelago, the only places in North America, and in some cases the only places anywhere, to see some species. Here are two operators which may be leading birdwatching tours: **Questers Worldwide Nature Tours,** 257 Park Ave. S., New York, NY 10010 (☎ **212/673-3120**); or **Victor Emanual Nature Tours,** P.O. Box 33008, Austin, TX 78764 (☎ **512/328-5221**).

FOR CAMPERS   Traveling in a van with only 12 adults and camping at night, **Camp Alaska Tours,** P.O. Box 872247, Wasilla, AK 99687 (☎ **907/376-9438,** or 800/376-9438), offers trips lasting 6 to 22 days, with hiking, rafting, kayaking, and an opportunity to see the outdoors with a new group of outdoors-oriented friends.

FOR CYCLISTS   Tours of Alaska and the Yukon Territory, with train and boat trips included, and Canondale bikes, are offered by Anchorage-based **Alaska Bicycle Adventures,** 2734 Iliamna Ave., Anchorage, AK 99517-1216 (☎ **907/243-2329,** or 800/770-7242).

FOR PHOTOGRAPHERS   In Talkeetna, **Alaska Photo Tours,** P.O. Box 141, Talkeetna, AK 99676-0141 (☎ **907/733-3051,** or 800/799-3051), offers guided trips for small groups of photographers with everything arranged to capture wildlife and scenery on film.

FOR RV OWNERS   Several companies offer caravans to Alaska each summer, with activities planned along the way. One long-time operator is **Point South RV Tours,** 11313 Edmonson Ave., Moreno Valley, CA 92555 (☎ **800/421-1394**).

FOR SLOWER-PACED TRAVEL   A company with a mini-coach accessible for people with disabilities, **Alaska Snail Trails,** P.O. Box 210894, Anchorage, AK 99501-2211 (☎ **907/337-7517,** or 800/348-4543), specializes in tours that slow down and allow a more leisurely chance to look at Alaska.

FOR WOMEN   A small Anchorage company, **Sourdough Sidekicks,** HC 83, Box 2444, Eagle River, AK 99577 (☎ **907/694-9694**), offers week-long van tours for up to eight women, designed around the interests of the participants.

CUSTOM TOURS & ALASKAN TRAVEL AGENCIES

Any travel agency can book a trip to Alaska. Here are some good Alaska-based firms that specialize in setting up trips around the state for independent travelers and groups and creating special packages.

- **Alaska Rainforest Tours,** 369 S. Franklin St., Suite 200, Juneau, AK 99801 (☎ **907/463-3466**).
- **All Ways Travel,** 302 G St., Anchorage, AK 99501 (☎ **907/276-3644**).
- **Eagle Custom Tours of Alaska,** 329 F St., Suite 206, Anchorage, AK 99501 (☎ **907/277-6228**).
- **World Express Tours,** 200 W. 34th Ave., Suite 412, Anchorage, AK 99503-3969 (☎ **800/544-2235**).

6 Planning Your Own Itinerary

Many visitors to Alaska feel compelled to cover the whole state, traveling to each region, and plan everything around seeing certain famous wilderness parks. By doing so, they spend a lot more time and money covering ground than necessary. Each of Alaska's regions, by itself, has most of what you're coming to Alaska for—wildlife, mountains, glaciers, historic sites, cute little towns—and you can have a better trip touring one or two regions than spending precious time going from region to region. The glaciers of Southcentral Alaska are just as impressive as those of Southeast, and you can see bears in the Interior, Southcentral, or Southeast. There's no law that says you have to go to Denali or Glacier Bay national parks. I met a couple who were afraid of flying, desperately trying to find a way to Glacier Bay National Park by boat—not a simple proposition. When I asked why they didn't just take the boat from Juneau to see the glacier in Tracy Fjord instead, they didn't have much of an answer. It wasn't that there was anything in Glacier Bay they were particularly anxious to see—in fact, they weren't sure what was there—but they knew that that was where they were supposed to go.

I think half the joy of traveling independently is discovering places off the beaten track where most tourists don't go. If you follow a set itinerary of places you're "supposed" to go see, you don't get that pleasure. I offer suggested itineraries here and at the beginning of each regional chapter only to spark ideas. You'll find lots of ideas within these pages, and I hope you can find Alaska on your own.

In the interest of showing as much as I can about how to link the towns, these itineraries are fast-paced. I recommend reducing stops and lengthening the visit to each town that especially interests you rather than trying to do any more.

If You Have 1 Week

If you have only a week, you need to chose an Alaska region to explore. If you try to cover the whole state, you'll just be moving around without doing anything.

In **Southeast Alaska,** try flying to Sitka, spending a day looking at the historic sights and a day on the water, meeting the sea otters; then catch the ferry on the third day for Juneau, perhaps taking the "local" that stops off at all the little villages on the way. In Juneau, take a look at the sights in town and Mendenhall Glacier, or take a hike, for one day. The next day, fly to Gustavus, spending the night at one of the charming inns there, and the following day take in Glacier Bay National Park on a boat tour, or go whale watching or sea kayaking off Point Adolphus. Another night in Gustavus, and it's time to fly home.

In **Southcentral and Interior Alaska,** you can fly to Anchorage and spend a day taking in the city, with a visit to the museum or zoo or a bike ride on the coastal trail. Next day, take the train to Seward and take a boat ride into Kenai Fjords National Park. Spend the night in Seward and enjoy the town and Exit Glacier the next day, perhaps taking a hike or a sea-kayak paddle, returning to Anchorage on the train that evening. Next morning, fly to Fairbanks and rent a car, spending the first day exploring the city and the next driving out into the country to soak at Chena Hot Springs Resort. The next day, go horseback riding, hiking, or rafting at the resort. The next day, it's time to drive back to Fairbanks and catch a plane home.

If You Have 2 Weeks

Starting in **Southeast Alaska,** take the ferry from Bellingham or Prince Rupert or fly to Ketchikan, spend at least a full day exploring there, and another day to get out on the water, fishing or visiting Misty Fjords National Monument. Go north on the ferry to Sitka, taking two full days to see the historic sights and really explore the town, perhaps taking a hike or getting out on the water. Catch another ferry north, to Haines, spending at least one full day there to see the eagles and the quaint town, and take a flightseeing trip to Glacier Bay National Park. Then, the next day, rent a car and drive 450 miles, over one of the most beautiful parts of the Alaska Highway, to Tok, where you can stay in a motel, rising as early as possible the next day for the 187-mile drive over the Taylor and Top of the World highways to Dawson City. The next day, finish explorations of Dawson City. The following day, drive 435 miles to Skagway. You have a full day to enjoy Skagway the next day, perhaps riding the Yukon and White Pass Route railway. Then take the car on the ferry to Haines, return it there, fly to Juneau, and catch a flight home from Juneau.

Starting in **Southcentral Alaska,** fly to Anchorage, spend two days exploring the city, perhaps taking a hike in the Chugach Mountains or a flightseeing trip to Denali National Park on a classic DC-3. Then rent a car and drive down the Kenai Peninsula, stopping in Cooper Landing or Soldatina for king salmon fishing for a day, or continuing all the way to Homer, a 235-mile drive from Anchorage. In Homer, spend the next day visiting galleries and then take the boat to the waterside community of Halibut Cove to have dinner and spend the night. The next day, go sea kayaking or wildlife watching on the water, or take a hike in Kachemak Bay State Park. The following day, return to Homer and spend another day there, going for a halibut-fishing trip, or drive back up the highway and stop in Girdwood for the night. The next morning, drive to Portage, take the train through the mountains to Whittier, and take a tour-boat cruise to see the glaciers of Prince William Sound, returning that evening to Anchorage and turning in the car. A day of rest or activities in Anchorage is in order. The next day, take the train to Denali National Park, spending the afternoon with a rafting excursion or other activities at the park entrance. Next day, get up early for a bus trip into the park, to see wildlife and go for a walk on the tundra. The next day, catch the train to Fairbanks and spend the following day sightseeing. Then fly back to Anchorage and fly home.

If You Have 3 Weeks

Use the two-week itinerary for **Southeast Alaska,** but add two days in Petersburg, two days in Juneau, and three days in Glacier Bay National Park and Gustavus.

Use the two-week itinerary for **Southcentral Alaska,** but instead of taking the train to Denali, keep the rental car and drive to Denali; then spend an additional two days exploring the Interior Highways around Fairbanks or relaxing at Chena Hot Springs Resort. Then drive the Richardson Highway to Valdez, spend the night there, and take the ferry to Cordova. Spend the next day there, visiting the Copper River Delta and Childs Glacier. The next day, fly back to Valdez and drive to Anchorage, catching the flight home the next day. Or add the one-week Southeast itinerary to the Southcentral itinerary.

Or, in either case, you can add a two- or three-day excursion to the Bush, flying to Kotzebue, taking the Native culture tour there, then flying to Nome and exploring the tundra roads and gold-rush historic sights, and returning to Anchorage on the third or fourth day.

Alaska by the Numbers

This chart shows some comparative indicators for 17 of Alaska's most popular destinations. The first column is the name of the destination, next is population. The third column "TI," stands for my own "Touristy Index." It shows how many visitors come to the destination for each year-round resident—it's just to give you an idea of your chances of meeting local residents as opposed to other tourists. The "Transportation" column shows ways of getting to each destination. The fifth column is average annual precipitation, in water equivalent (in inches), and the final column is average annual snowfall (in inches).

Place	Population	TI*	Transportation	Precip.	Snow
Anchorage	240,258	2.3	Road, air, rail	15.4	69
Barrow	3,986	0.9	Air	4.7	28
Denali National Park	35	8,605.7	Road, rail	15.0	54.8
Fairbanks	33,281	7.7	Road, air, rail	10.4	68
Glacier Bay National Park	258	993.8	Air	53.9	70.2
Homer	4,349	30.9	Road, air, ferry	24.9	58
Juneau	29,078	14.1	Air, ferry	52.9	100
Kenai	6,535	24.5	Road, air	18.9	59.3
Ketchikan	8,478	45.6	Air, ferry	155.2	37
Kodiak	7,229	1.5	Air, ferry	74.3	80
Kotzebue	3,004	6.3	Air	9.0	47.6
Nome	4,184	5.6	Air	15.6	56
Petersburg	3,419	11.1	Air, ferry	105.8	102
Seward	2,732	90.8	Road, rail, ferry, air	67.7	79.9
Sitka	9,052	25.9	Air, ferry	86.8	40.7
Skagway	751	424.6	Road, ferry, air	23.0	35.7
Valdez	4,713	26.4	Road, air, ferry	61.5	320

*"TI" stands for Touristy Index, which is the ratio of summer visitors to year-round residents—for example, for each year-round resident of Anchorage there are 2.3 tourist visits each summer.

If You Have 6 Weeks

You have time to drive to Alaska, or to ride up on the ferry, exploring each little Southeast Alaska town, then seeing each of the other regions in depth.

An Alaska Native Culture Tour

A roughly two-week itinerary concentrating only on Alaska's Native culture could start in Ketchikan, with a visit to the Tlingit totem pole collections, clan houses, and carving studio. Then fly or take the ferry to Sitka and see the national historic site where the Tlingits fought off the Russians, and the Sheldon Jackson Museum. Proceed to Haines, for the Chilkat Dancers and the Sheldon Museum. Backtrack to Juneau, make a stop at the state museum, and fly to Anchorage. There, visit the Anchorage Museum of History and Art, the Native art co-ops and workshop downtown, and the Eklutna spirit houses. Fly to Kotzebue for the Tour Arctic culture tour, and take a scheduled Bush plane to Kiana or one of the other outlying Inupiat villages to see Native culture in the flesh. Return to Anchorage and go to Fairbanks for the University of Alaska Museum and the Riverboat Discovery Athabascan village demonstration.

Whales, Otters, Sea Birds & Bears

A 10-day **Southeast Alaska** itinerary to concentrate only on seeing wildlife could start in Petersburg, with whale watching and seals, or Gustavus and Glacier Bay, the other sure-fish whale-watching area, also good for other marine mammals and birdwatching. If you're traveling in the fall, don't miss the eagles in Haines. Then, in midsummer, travel to Juneau and make a trip to the Pack Creek bear observatory on Admiralty Island. Then travel to Sitka for sea otters, sea birds, and possibly more whales.

In **Southcentral Alaska,** for a 10-day trip concentrating only on wildlife, start in Anchorage, then go to Kenai Fjords National Park, out of Seward, for whales, otters, sea lions, and sea birds. Then travel to Homer and fly out to the McNeil River bear sanctuary, or, if you haven't been able to obtain a permit for McNeil River, to Katmai National Park for bear viewing, in mid- to late summer. Return to Anchorage. Those interested in seeing more mammals can then go to Denali National Park. Birdwatchers will enjoy a side trip to Unalaska, in the Aleutians, or Nome, where they can add to a life list birds they're unlikely to see anywhere else.

A Winter Itinerary

Arrive in Anchorage in February, during the Fur Rendezvous sled-dog races, or in March, to see the start of the Iditarod. If you're a Nordic skier, go to Kincaid Park and, after checking with the Alaska Public Lands Information Center for avalanche conditions, rent a car and make a day trip into Chugach State Park or to Turnagain Pass, south of Anchorage, or ski into one of many public cabins in Chugach National Forest. Alpine or Nordic skiers will want to spend at least a few days in Girdwood at the Alyeska Resort. Besides exceptional skiing, this is a good place for a sled-dog ride, and there are others at each stop on the itinerary. After Girdwood, catch the train from Anchorage to Fairbanks, spending the night in Fairbanks and catching the sled-dog races or ice-carving festivals in February or March. The following day, take the van out to the Chena Hot Springs Resort, for outdoors explorations, swimming, and aurora watching, returning and flying out of Fairbanks when your trip is over.

7 Getting There & Getting Around

BY PLANE   Anchorage is the main entry hub for Alaska. It's served by several major carriers to the rest of the United States, primarily through Seattle, including **United Airlines** (☎800/241-6522), **Delta Air Lines** (☎ 800/221-1212), and **Alaska Airlines** (☎ 800/426-0333; TDD 800/682-2221). There usually is a charter or seat wholesaler in operation with below-market deals on economy seats—in the middle of the night and with few amenities. Use a travel agent to get the best price, as the route is highly competitive and prices are volatile. Some airlines also continue to Fairbanks.

Alaska Airlines is the primary carrier to Southeast Alaska, and has the most jet flights to most Alaska small towns and to Magadan, Khabarovsk, and Vladivostok, in the Russian Far East. Fanning out from Alaska's network, **Era Aviation,** which can be booked at the same number, flies to communities with commuter service. There are a number of other regional commuter carriers, which you can book through a travel agency.

To fly to the smallest villages, or to fly between some small towns without returning to a hub, you take a **Bush plane.** The legendary Alaska Bush pilot is alive and well, connecting Alaska's villages by small plane and flying air-taxi routes to fishing sites, lodges, remote cabins, or just about anywhere else you might want to go. An authentic Alaskan adventure is to be had from many small towns by taking a **Bush mail plane** round-trip to a village and back. The ticket price is generally a fraction of the cost of a flightseeing trip, and you'll have at least a brief chance to look around a Native village. Cordova, Kodiak, Nome, Barrow, and even Fairbanks and Anchorage are places from which you can do this.

BY SHIP   The most popular way to get to Alaska is on a **cruise ship.** Chapter 5, "Cruising Alaska's Coast," provides an in-depth look at coming to the state that way.

The **Alaska Marine Highway System** (☎ 800/642-0066; TDD 800/764-3779) is the lowest-cost way to get to Alaska. The big blue, white, and gold ferries ply the Inside Passage from Bellingham, Wash., and Prince Rupert, B.C., to the towns of Southeast Alaska, with road links to the rest of the state at Haines and Skagway. For a complete discussion of using the ferries, see Chapter 7, "Southeast Alaska." Smaller ferries also connect towns of Prince William Sound and the Kenai Peninsula, in Southcentral Alaska, to Kodiak Island and the Aleutian Archipelago—a long haul in open ocean, but a unique adventure few people will share.

BY RAIL   You can't get to Alaska by train, but you can get close. **Amtrak** (☎ 800/872-7245) connects Seattle and Vancouver, B.C., to Bellingham, Wash., where you can catch the Alaska ferry north at a dock a short walk from the depot. Or you can get to the ferry dock in Prince Rupert, B.C., with connections on **Via Rail Canada** (☎ 800/561-3949) and **B.C. Rail** (☎ 800/663-8238). Within Alaska, you can travel the **Alaska Railroad** (☎ 800/544-0552) from Seward, on Resurrection Bay in Southcentral Alaska, north to Anchorage, in summer only; and from Anchorage north to Denali National Park and Fairbanks year round. For a full description of the service available, see Chapter 9, "Denali National Park," and the section on Seward in Chapter 8, "Southcentral Alaska."

BY CAR   Driving to Alaska is a great adventure, but it requires thousands of miles on the road and you have to be ready to spend plenty of time. Anchorage is almost

2,500 miles from Seattle by car, 3,700 miles from Los Angeles, and 4,650 miles from New York City. Some of the drive is frankly dull, but there are spectacular sections of the 1,400-mile **Alaska Highway** too, and few experiences give you a better feel for the size and personality of Alaska. Putting your car on the ferry cuts the length of the trip considerably, but raises the cost. Details on the Alaska section of the Alaska Highway, and other highways, are contained in Chapter 10, "The Alaskan Interior." *The Milepost,* published by Vernon Publications, contains mile-by-mile logs of all Alaska highways and approaches, but its commercial listings are sold as advertisements and thus are not objective. Inexpensive road maps also are widely available; there are few roads, so the map found in the back of this volume will be perfectly adequate.

Renting a car in Alaska is the easiest way to see the Interior and Southcentral part of the state. All major car-rental companies are represented in Anchorage, and individual town listings provide details on which firms are in each. Base rates for major rental companies are in the range of $55 a day. You can save money by using a travel agent, reserving far in advance, renting by the week, or using a down-market franchise or independent rental company that rents older cars. One-way rentals between Alaska towns are attractive, but you generally pay steep drop-off charges, so a more popular plan is to fly into and out of Anchorage and use it as a base to pick up and return the car.

FAST FACTS: Alaska

American Express   There are four American Express offices in Alaska: at 5011 Jewel Lake Rd., Suite 102, Anchorage, AK 99502 (☎ 907/266-6600); 202 Center St., Suite 103, Kodiak, AK 99615 (☎ 907/486-6084); 8745 Glacier Ave., Suite 328, Juneau, AK 99801 (☎ 907/789-0999); and at Front Street and Federal Way (P.O. Box 1786), Nome, AK 99762 (☎ 907/443-2211).

Area Code   All of Alaska is in area code **907.** In the Yukon Territory, the area code is 403. When placing a toll call within the state, you must dial 1, the area code, and the number. See "Telephone," below, for important tips.

Banks & ATM Networks   Bank of America, Key Bank, and First Interstate all have branches in Alaska. There are Alaska-based banks in most towns, as noted in the listings for each. Automatic-teller machines are widely available, except in tiny towns. They generally are connected to the Plus and Cirrus networks, as well as other networks.

Business Hours   In the larger cities, major grocery stores are open 24 hours a day, with wide-ranging product lines in addition to food. At a minimum, **stores** are open Monday through Friday from 10am to 6pm, on Saturday afternoon, and often are closed on Sunday, but many are open much longer hours, especially in summer. **Banks** may close an hour earlier and may not be open on Saturday. Under state law, **bars** don't have to close until 5am, but many communities have an earlier closing, generally around 2am.

Emergencies   Generally, you can call **911** for medical, police, or fire emergencies. On remote highways there sometimes are gaps in 911 coverage. A widely available brochure called **"Help Along the Way"** provides emergency phone numbers on all stretches of rural highways and the location of emergency phone boxes. You can write for a free copy from the state Office of Emergency Medical Services, P.O. Box H-06C, Juneau, AK 99811. Dialing 0 will generally get an operator, who can connect you to emergency services. In addition, CB Channels 9 and 11 are monitored for emergencies on most highways, and Channels 14 and 19 in some areas.

Liquor Laws   The minimum drinking age in Alaska is 21. Some rural communities have laws prohibiting the importation and possession of alcohol, or only the sale (but not possession) of alcohol. Generally, these are the smaller Bush villages. Check the listings for the towns you'll visit for details.

Maps   For driving maps, see "Getting There and Getting Around," earlier in this chapter, or just use the map in the back of this book. The Alaska Public Lands Information Centers have free maps with outdoors information; for campers, their map showing all the public campgrounds in the state is invaluable. For outdoors trips, get topographic maps from the U.S. Geological Survey, at the public lands centers or directly from 4230 University Dr., Anchorage, AK 99508 (☎ 907/786-7011). *The Alaska Atlas and Gazetteer,* published by DeLorme Mapping, P.O. Box 298, Freeport, ME 04032 (☎ 207/865-4171), contains topographical maps of the entire state, most at 1:300,000 scale, marked with trails, public cabins and other features, and much other useful information. It's widely available in Alaska.

Newspapers & Magazines   The state's dominant newspaper is the *Anchorage Daily News;* it's available everywhere, but not easy to find in Southeast Alaska. Seattle newspapers and *USA Today* are often available, and in Anchorage you can get virtually any newspaper. *Alaska* magazine is the largest monthly; it's a general-interest popular magazine with features on the state and the outdoors. For subscriptions, write P.O. Box 37027, Boone, Iowa, 50037-2027.

Pets   Bringing a pet to Alaska will make life much more difficult. Most hotels don't allow pets, and in the wilderness it isn't safe to let dogs run loose, as they may create dangerous conflicts with moose and bears. All but the smallest towns have veterinarians.

Taxes   There is no state sales tax, but most local governments have a sales tax and bed tax on accommodations. The tax rates are listed in each town section.

Telephone   Making toll calls can be a headache for visitors. Before you leave for Alaska, contact your long-distance company for instructions on how to use your phone card and charges. Your MCI, Sprint, or AT&T phone cards may not work. The easiest and cheapest solution is to bring one of the privately issued, by-the-minute cards. Target carries one that operates at 25¢ per minute, a good deal since the Smile-and-Dial cards sold in Alaska charge at least 29¢ per minute for calls to the Lower 48.

Time Zone   Although the state naturally spans five time zones, in the 1980s Alaska's central time zone was stretched so the entire state would lie all in one zone, known as Alaska time. It's one hour earlier than the U.S. West Coast's Pacific time. Daylight saving time follows the national pattern.

4 For Foreign Visitors

This chapter will provide some specifics about getting to the United States as economically and effortlessly as possible, plus some helpful information about how things are done in Alaska—from receiving mail to making a local or long-distance telephone call.

1 Preparing for Your Trip

ENTRY REQUIREMENTS

DOCUMENT REGULATIONS Canadian citizens may enter the United States without visas; they need only proof of residence.

British subjects and citizens of New Zealand, Japan, and most Western European countries traveling on valid passports may not need a visa for less than 90 days of holiday or business travel to the United States, providing that they hold a round-trip or return ticket and enter the country on an airline or cruise line participating in the visa-waiver program. (Citizens of these visa-exempt countries who first enter the United States may then visit Mexico, Canada, Bermuda, and/or the Caribbean islands and then reenter the United States, by any mode of transportation, without needing a visa. Further information is available from any U.S. embassy or consulate.)

Citizens of countries other than those stipulated above, including citizens of Australia, must have two documents: (1) a valid passport with an expiration date at least six months later than the scheduled end of their visit to the United States; and (2) a tourist visa, available without charge from the nearest U.S. consulate.

To obtain a visa, the traveler must submit a completed application form (either in person or by mail) with a $1^1/_2$-inch-square photo and demonstrate binding ties to a residence abroad. Usually you can obtain a visa at once or within 24 hours, but it may take longer during the summer rush from June to August. If you cannot go in person, contact the nearest U.S. embassy or consulate for directions on applying by mail. Your travel agent or airline office may also be able to provide you with visa applications and instructions. The U.S. consulate or embassy that issues your visa will determine whether you will be issued a multiple- or single-entry visa and any restrictions regarding the length of your stay.

MEDICAL REQUIREMENTS No inoculations are needed to enter the United States unless you're coming from, or have stopped over in, areas known to be suffering from epidemics, especially of cholera or yellow fever.

If you have a disease requiring treatment with medications containing narcotics or drugs requiring a syringe, carry a valid signed prescription from your physician to allay any suspicions that you're smuggling drugs.

CUSTOMS REQUIREMENTS Every adult visitor may bring in free of duty: 1 liter of wine or hard liquor; 200 cigarettes *or* 100 cigars (but no cigars from Cuba) *or* 3 pounds of tobacco; and $100 worth of gifts. These exemptions are offered to travelers who spend at least 72 hours in the United States and who have not claimed them within the preceding six months. It's altogether forbidden to bring into the country foodstuffs (particularly cheese, fruit, cooked meats, and canned goods) and plants (vegetables, seeds, tropical plants, and so on). Foreign tourists may bring in or take out up to $10,000 in U.S. or foreign currency with no formalities; larger sums must be declared to Customs on entering or leaving.

INSURANCE

There is no national health-care system in the United States. Because the cost of medical care is extremely high, I strongly advise every traveler to secure health insurance coverage before setting out. You may want to take out a comprehensive travel policy that covers (for a relatively low premium) sickness or injury costs (medical, surgical, and hospital); loss or theft of your baggage; trip-cancellation costs; guarantee of bail in case you are arrested; and costs associated with accidents, repatriation, or death. Such packages (for example, "Europe Assistance" in Europe) are sold by automobile clubs at attractive rates, as well as by insurance companies and travel agencies.

MONEY

CURRENCY & EXCHANGE The U.S. monetary system has a decimal base: one American **dollar** ($1) = 100 **cents** (100¢).

Dollar bills commonly come in $1 ("a buck"), $5, $10, $20, $50, and $100 denominations (the last two are not welcome when paying for small purchases and are not accepted in taxis). There are also $2 bills (seldom encountered).

There are six denominations of coins: 1¢ (one cent, or a "penny"), 5¢ (five cents, or a "nickel"), 10¢ (ten cents, or a "dime"), 25¢ (twenty-five cents, or a "quarter"), 50¢ (fifty cents, or a "half dollar"), and the rare $1 piece.

Note: The "foreign-exchange bureaus" so common in Europe are rare even at airports in the United States, and nonexistent outside major cities. Try to avoid having to change foreign money, or traveler's checks not denominated in U.S. dollars, at a small-town bank, or even a branch bank in a big city. In fact, leave any currency other than U.S. dollars at home—it may prove more nuisance to you than it's worth.

TRAVELER'S CHECKS Traveler's checks denominated in U.S. dollars are readily accepted at most hotels, motels, restaurants, and large stores, but the best place to change traveler's checks is at a bank. Do not bring traveler's checks denominated in other currencies.

CREDIT CARDS The method of payment most widely used is credit cards: Visa (BarclayCard in Britain), MasterCard (EuroCard in Europe, Access in Britain, Chargex in Canada), American Express, Diners Club, Discover, and Carte Blanche. You can save yourself trouble by using "plastic money" rather than cash or traveler's checks in most hotels, motels, restaurants, and retail stores (a growing number of food and liquor stores now accept credit cards). You must have a credit card to rent a car.

It can also be used as proof of identity (it often carries more weight than a passport), or as a "cash card," enabling you to draw money from banks and automatic-teller machines (ATMs) that accept it.

SAFETY

GENERAL   While tourist areas are generally safe, crime is on the increase everywhere, and U.S. urban areas tend to be less safe than those in Europe or Japan. Visitors should always stay alert. This is particularly true in large U.S. cities. It is wise to ask the city's or area's tourist office if you're in doubt about which neighborhoods are safe.

Remember that hotels are open to the public, and in a large hotel, security may not be able to screen everyone entering. Always lock your room door—don't assume that once inside your hotel you are automatically safe and no longer need be aware of your surroundings.

In Alaska, you still must be careful. Advice is provided in the section on safety in Chapter 3. As a rule, the smaller the town you are in, the safer you are.

DRIVING   Safety from crime while driving is particularly important on U.S. highways before you reach Alaska. Question your rental agency about personal safety, or ask for a brochure of traveler safety tips when you pick up your car. Obtain from the agency written directions, or a map with the route marked in red, to show you how to get to your destination. If possible, arrive and depart during daylight hours.

Alaska, thankfully, lags behind the rest of the States in highway crime, and such incidents as carjackings are still rare enough in the state to make front-page news. On rural two-lane roads without many cars, there are unlikely to be many predators on the prowl for tourists to rob. Even if you have that fear, you will need help from another driver in case of a major breakdown, as the distances between settlements can be large. On the other hand, sexual assault is more prevalent in Alaska than in other parts of the country, and women traveling alone must use extra caution.

2 Getting To & Around the U.S.

Travelers from overseas can take advantage of the **APEX (advance-purchase excursion) fares** offered by the major U.S. and European carriers.

Some large airlines (for example, American Airlines, Delta, Northwest, TWA, and United) offer travelers on their transatlantic and transpacific flights special discount tickets under the name **Visit USA,** allowing travel between any U.S. destinations at minimum rates. They are not on sale in the United States—they must be purchased before you leave your foreign point of departure. This system is the best, easiest, and fastest way to see the United States at low cost. You should obtain information well in advance from your travel agent or the office of the airline concerned, since the conditions attached to these discount tickets can be changed without advance notice.

The visitor arriving by air, no matter what the port of entry, should cultivate patience and resignation before setting foot on U.S. soil. Getting through Immigration control may take as long as two hours on some days, especially summer weekends. Add the time it takes to clear Customs and you'll see that you should make very generous allowance for delay in planning connections between international and domestic flights—an average of two to three hours at least.

In contrast, travelers arriving by car or by rail from Canada will find border-crossing formalities streamlined to the vanishing point. And air travelers from Canada,

Bermuda, and some places in the Caribbean can sometimes go through Customs and Immigration at the point of departure, which is much quicker and less painful.

The United States is a nation of cars and the most cost-effective, convenient, and comfortable way to travel through the country is by driving. The Interstate highway system connects cities and towns all over the country, and in addition to these high-speed, limited-access roadways, there's an extensive network of federal, state, and local highways and roads. Another convenience of traveling by car is the easy access to inexpensive motels at Interstate-highway off-ramps. Such motels are almost always less expensive than hotels and motels in downtown areas.

For further information about travel to and around Alaska, see "Getting There" and "Getting Around" in Chapter 3.

FAST FACTS: For the Foreign Traveler

Accommodations   It's always a good idea to make hotel reservations as soon as you know your trip dates. Reservations usually require a deposit of one night's payment. In the Lower 48, major downtown hotels, which cater primarily to business travelers, commonly offer weekend discounts of as much as 50% to entice vacationers to fill up the empty hotel rooms. However, resorts and hotels near tourist attractions tend to have higher rates on weekends.

Throughout Alaska, hotels are particularly busy during the summer months and book up in advance, especially on holiday weekends. If you don't have a reservation, it's best to look for a room in midafternoon. If you wait until later in the evening, you run the risk that hotels will already be filled.

Automobile Organizations   Auto clubs will supply maps, suggested routes, guidebooks, accident and bail-bond insurance, and emergency road service. The major auto club in the United States, with 955 offices nationwide, is the **American Automobile Association (AAA).** Members of some foreign auto clubs have reciprocal arrangements with the AAA and enjoy its services at no charge. If you belong to an auto club in your home country, inquire about AAA reciprocity before you leave. The AAA can provide you with an **International Driving Permit** validating your foreign license. You may be able to join the AAA even if you aren't a member of a reciprocal club. To inquire, call 800/AAA-HELP. In addition, some automobile-rental agencies now provide these services, so you should inquire about their availability when you rent your car.

Automobile Rentals   To rent a car you need a major credit card and a valid driver's license. Sometimes a passport or an international driver's license is also required if your driver's license is in a language other than English. You usually need to be at least 25, although some companies do rent to younger people but may add a daily surcharge. Be sure to return your car with the same amount of gasoline you started out with, as rental companies charge excessive prices for gas. Keep in mind that a separate motorcycle driver's license is required in most states.

Business Hours   See "Fast Facts: Alaska" in Chapter 3.

Electricity   The United States uses 110–120 volts, 60 cycles, compared to 220–240 volts, 50 cycles, as in most of Europe. In addition to a 110-volt transformer, small appliances of non-American manufacture, such as hairdryers or shavers, will require a plug adapter with two flat, parallel pins.

Emergencies   Call **911** to report a fire, call the police, or get an ambulance. This is a toll-free call (no coins are required at a public telephone).

Check the local directory to find an office of the **Traveler's Aid Society,** a nationwide nonprofit social-service organization geared to helping travelers in difficult straits. Their services might include reuniting families separated while traveling, providing food and/or shelter to people stranded without cash, or even emotional counseling. If you're in trouble, seek them out.

Mail   If you want to receive mail on your vacation and you aren't sure of your address, your mail can be sent to you, in your name, **c/o General Delivery** (Poste Restante) at the main post office of the city or region where you expect to be. The addressee must pick it up in person and produce proof of identity (driver's license, credit card, passport, etc.).

Domestic **postage rates** are 23¢ for a postcard and 32¢ for a letter. Check with any local post office for current international postage rates to your home country.

Generally found at intersections, **mailboxes** are blue with a red-and-white stripe and carry the inscription U.S. MAIL. If your mail is addressed to a U.S. destination, don't forget to add the five-figure **postal code,** or ZIP (Zone Improvement Plan) code, after the two-letter abbreviation of the state to which the mail is addressed (AK for Alaska, CA for California, and so on).

Taxes   In the United States there is no VAT (value-added tax) or other indirect tax at the national level. Every state, and each city in it, is allowed to levy its own local tax on all purchases (including hotel and restaurant checks and airline tickets) and services. Taxes are already included in the price of certain services, such as public transportation, cab fares, telephone calls, and gasoline.

There is no state sales tax in Alaska, but many communities have imposed their own sales and bed taxes.

Telephone, Telegraph, and Fax   The telephone system in the United States is run by private corporations, so rates, especially for long-distance service and operator-assisted calls, can vary widely—even on calls made from public telephones. Local calls usually cost 25¢.

Generally, hotel surcharges on long-distance and local calls are astronomical. You're usually better off using a **public pay telephone.** Outside metropolitan areas, public telephones are more difficult to find. Stores and gas stations are your best bet.

Most **long-distance and international calls** can be dialed directly from any phone. For calls to Canada and other parts of the United States, dial 1 followed by the area code and the seven-digit number. For international calls, dial 011 followed by the country code (Australia, 61; Republic of Ireland, 353; New Zealand, 64; United Kingdom, 44), city code, and the telephone number of the person you wish to call.

Note that all calls to area code 800 are toll free. However, calls to numbers in area codes 700 and 900 (chat lines, bulletin boards, "dating" services, etc.) can be very expensive—usually a charge of 95¢ to $3 or more per minute, and they sometimes have minimum charges that can run as high as $15 or more.

For **reversed-charge (collect) calls,** and for **person-to-person calls,** dial 0 (zero, *not* the letter "O") followed by the area code and number you want; an operator will then come on the line and you should specify what you want. If your operator-assisted call is international, ask for the overseas operator.

For **local directory assistance** ("information"), dial 411; for **long-distance information,** dial 1, then the appropriate area code and 555-1212.

Like the telephone system, **telegraph** services are provided by private corporations like ITT, MCI, and above all, Western Union. You can bring your telegram in to the nearest Western Union office (there are hundreds across the country), or dictate it over the phone (☎ 800/325-6000). You can also telegraph money, or have it telegraphed to you, very quickly over the Western Union system. (Note, however, that this service can be very expensive—the service charge can run as high as 15% to 25% of the amount sent.)

If you need to send a **fax,** almost all shops that make photocopies offer fax service as well.

Time   The United States is divided into six time zones. From east to west these are eastern standard time (EST), central standard time (CST), mountain standard time (MST), Pacific standard time (PST), **Alaska standard time (AST),** and Hawaii standard time (HST). Always keep changing time zones in your mind if you are traveling (or even telephoning) long distances in the U.S. For example, noon in Anchorage (AST) is 1pm in Seattle (PST), 2pm in Phoenix (MST), 3pm in Chicago (CST), 4pm in New York City (EST), and 11am in Honolulu (HST). **Daylight saving time** is in effect from 1am on the first Sunday in April until 2am on the last Sunday in October except in Arizona, Hawaii, part of Indiana, and Puerto Rico.

Tipping   This is part of the American way of life, on the principle that you must expect to pay for any service you get (many service personnel receive little direct salary and must depend on tips for their income). Here are some rules of thumb:

In **hotels,** tip bellhops $1 per piece and tip the chamber staff $1 per day. Tip the doorman or concierge only if he or she has provided you with some specific service (for example, calling a cab for you or obtaining difficult-to-get theater tickets).

In **restaurants, bars, and nightclubs,** tip the service staff 15% of the check, tip bartenders 10% to 15%, tip checkroom attendants $1 per garment, and tip valet-parking attendants $1 per vehicle. Tip the doorman only if he has provided you with some specific service (such as calling a cab for you). Tipping is not expected in cafeterias and fast-food restaurants.

Tip **cab drivers** 15% of the fare.

As for **other service personnel,** tip redcaps at airports or railroad stations $1 per piece and tip hairdressers and barbers 15% to 20%.

Tipping ushers in cinemas, movies, and theaters and gas-station attendants is not expected.

Toilets   Foreign visitors often complain that public toilets (or "restrooms") are hard to find in most U.S. cities. True, there are none on the streets, but the visitor can usually find one in a bar, restaurant, hotel, museum, department store, or service station—and it will probably be clean (although service-station restrooms sometimes leave much to be desired). Note, however, that a growing number of restaurants and bars display a notice like RESTROOMS ARE FOR THE USE OF PATRONS ONLY. You can ignore this sign or, better yet, avoid arguments by paying for a cup of coffee or a soft drink, which will qualify you as a patron. The cleanliness and safety of toilets at public transportation depots is open to question. Some public places are equipped with pay toilets, which require you to insert one or more coins into a slot on the door before it will open. In restrooms with attendants, leaving at least a 25¢ tip is customary.

5 Cruising Alaska's Coast

by Melissa Rivers

Alaska is now the top cruise destination in North America, and the third-ranked cruise destination in the world. In 1994 nearly 400,000 people visited the 49th state by ship (one-third of the total arrivals); by 1996 this number is expected to jump to half a million as more lines join the ranks of those sailing Alaska's coast, increasing capacity dramatically.

The reason for this popularity is fairly simple—Alaska, one of the nation's last great frontiers, retains much of its natural scenic beauty. Wildlife and wilderness abound along the state's breathtaking coastline and are readily witnessed from the relative comfort of a deck chair or observation lounge. Snowcapped peaks; islands dotting the waterway cloaked in an emerald rain forest of hemlock, spruce, and cedar; glacially carved fjords and calm coves where brown and black bears, bald eagles, and Sitka black-tailed deer feed at the waterline; milky-green waters peppered with icebergs fallen from immense tidewater glaciers; gray and orca whales spouting in the distance—these are among the awe-inspiring sights the state holds in store.

1 Selecting the Right Cruise

With all the diversification and growth in the cruise industry today, there is literally a cruise out there to suit every taste. The trick comes in tracking down the one best suited to you.

Cruising experiences vary widely depending on the type of ship selected. There are casual and elegant cruises; learning cruises where you attend lectures to learn about the art, culture, and wildlife of the region; adventure-oriented cruises that incorporate time spent ashore in remote areas, hiking, birding, or exploring tide pools; and luxury cruises where gourmet dining, gambling, and other entertainment compete with the setting for attention.

When it comes time to choose a particular cruise, you can defer to the judgment of a trusted travel agent who knows your preferences inside and out—if you're lucky enough to know such a person. Otherwise, start by asking yourself and the cruise lines a few pertinent questions to help you narrow the field. Once you've made your choice, book the cruise through a travel agency for the very best price available (many discounts are available only through travel agents—and cruise operators won't take direct bookings). Check the *Yellow Pages,* the World Wide Web, or the travel section in a big-city newspaper for agencies that specialize in cruises.

How large is the ship?   The size of the vessel dictates whether it will be a luxury cruise in a scenic setting or a casual cruise with a concentrated focus *on* the setting. It also dictates what the ship has to offer in the way of amenities, activities, and dining, as well as the number of other passengers and crew it can carry.

If your primary goal is to see Alaska's wilderness and wildlife up-close, then smaller, shallow-draft ships will suit you. These vessels offer an experience that focuses on the scenic beauty and abundant wildlife of the state; they are often accompanied by one or more naturalists and offer few, if any, diversions to pull you away from deckside observations. Bow thrusters and their smaller size allow these ships to navigate narrow passages, nosing up to sheer cliff faces, bird rookeries, cascading waterfalls, and bobbing icebergs. Wildlife are not as intimidated by these ships, and tend to stay put, continuing their activity rather than making a beeline away from the ship—you can watch porpoises playing in the bow wake or, if you're lucky, humpbacks feeding scant yards away. The deck is also closer to the waterline, giving passengers a more intimate view of whales, dolphins, otters, seals, sea lions, and shorebirds.

The small-ship cruise is generally a more casual experience; the 75 to 100 passengers on board seldom dress up for dinner, and the close quarters tends to encourage quick camaraderie. In some cases, the cost of the cruise includes shore excursions, often utilizing Zodiacs (motorized inflatable boats) to tender to shore for hikes.

If you're looking for the traditional cruise experience—to be entertained, stuffed with gourmet cuisine, and pampered in a nice setting—opt for one of the megaliners. The larger cruise ships, some over a dozen stories high, are floating resorts that afford an array of entertainment options and a much higher level of comfort and personalized attention. The primary drawback of large ships is that the size tends to keep Alaska's wilderness and wildlife at a distance. Marine creatures veer away from the louder engines, and even those that do range close must be viewed from decks several stories above the water. However, the more powerful engines are faster, making it easier to squeeze in more ports along the way. Less maneuverability means that the big ships must stay farther away from intriguing glaciers and shorelines, and their deeper drafts and broader beams keep them out of many pristine fjords, inlets, and narrows. They also carry between 1,000 and 2,000 passengers, so disembarkation in the various ports of call can be a lengthy process, and once you've descended on that small Alaskan town with the rest of the horde, you might feel uncomfortably like a salmon trying to return upstream. While they tend to be more stable in rough water, the larger ships' itineraries frequently take them into open ocean, passing, say, from Sitka across the Gulf to Seward, where the rock and roll of the water is noticeable.

What is the itinerary and how much time is spent in the various ports?   Most ships sail from Vancouver, British Columbia, on 7-day trips that are either round-trip with stops in Ketchikan, Sitka, and Juneau, or north- or southbound between Vancouver and Seward (near Anchorage) with additional stops in smaller ports such as Haines, Skagway, or Valdez. More and more vessels are sailing to Alaska from San Francisco and Seattle, offering itineraries of 7 to 12 days.

Land tours are frequently sold in conjunction with the cruise, allowing inland visits to stunning destinations such as Denali National Park, Fairbanks, and Nome, making it easy to stretch the holiday out and see the Interior of the state as well. (If a cruise line doesn't offer land tours, contact the tour operators listed in Chapter 3, "Planning a Trip to Alaska.") It's better to schedule land trips at the beginning of your vacation—they're fast-paced and can be extremely tiring. The cruise will give you a chance to catch your breath and relax. This makes southbound trips from Seward a good choice. However, on northbound trips, the beauty of the scenery grows exponentially the farther north you travel, so northbound itineraries are a favorite.

Be aware that not all Alaskan cruises visit Glacier Bay, or the historic gold-rush town of Skagway, or head as far north as Seward. Ask to be certain which ports of call to expect, and how much time the ship stays in port—port calls range from a few hours to a full day. If you're pretty sure the Native and Russian cultures and historic interest of Sitka will thrill you, be sure you'll be in port long enough to satisfy your curiosity. If you'll get bored looking at glaciers for hours on end, don't select an itinerary that spends a full day in Glacier Bay.

How much time is spent on open waters?   Most of your time in Alaska will be spent cruising the calm, protected waterways of the Inside Passage. However, if the itinerary starts or ends in San Francisco or Seward (i.e., Anchorage), the ship will be traveling a larger portion of the time on the open ocean, which tends to be rougher water and creates noticeable rolling even on the largest, most stable vessels. If you or someone you're planning to travel with is susceptible to motion sickness, choose an Inside Passage itinerary, which spends most of the time in calm, protected waterways. If the thrill of the open ocean appeals to you, select one of the north- or southbound itineraries (most often referred to as the "Glacial Route").

How much does it cost and what's not included?   In figuring your vacation budget, this becomes an important factor because of the number of expenses not covered in the typical cruise package. Airfare to and from your port of embarkation and disembarkation is often extra, as is any necessary lodging before or after the cruise and all gratuities and port taxes. Other extras are of a personal nature and might include money set aside for laundry, alcoholic beverages and soft drinks, gambling, duty-free shopping, and shore excursions. Shore excursions in Alaska are pricey and can easily become as costly as the cruise itself.

What facilities does the ship feature?   Would the lack of a hot tub, fitness center, spa, sports courts, casino, or shopping arcade leave you feeling deprived? If so, pick one of the larger ships that offer these and many other facilities. If a good book to read, an informative lecture on the sights, and a pair of binoculars and an unobstructed view from a deck chair is enough, you'll be happy on one of the small ships.

What activities and entertainment does the ship offer?   Activities on smaller ships are usually limited by the available public space but often include recent-release videos, group-oriented games (Bingo, poker, etc.), and perhaps an evening dance or social hour. They typically offer a lecture series during the trip, usually conducted by a trained naturalist who concentrates on the natural history of Alaska. Lectures on the flora, fauna, and geography of Alaska are also becoming more popular on the larger ships, and lines are hiring naturalists or Alaskan lecturers on a seasonal basis to teach passengers about the region.

Larger ships are able to offer a broader selection of activities to entertain their passengers. There may be shipboard classes—self-enrichment, personal finance, photography, and art are popular topics, often taught by well-known specialists. Fitness instruction, be it aerobics, sit-and-be-fit, or weight-training classes, are also part of the package. Planned activities run the gamut, from craft classes to golf putting or ping-pong tournaments, to singles or newlywed gatherings; there may also be recent-release movies, glitzy floor shows, and the like.

What are the meals like?   Meals are a big part of the cruise experience. The larger the ship, the more choice you'll find in the foods served aboard. Ask about the selection of restaurants and snack bars and the types of cuisine that will be available,

Glaciers 101

Glaciers are constantly on the move, sculpting the landscape below, grinding the shale and other rock forms and pushing rubble and silt ahead and to the sides. This sediment is known as morain. *Terminal* morain is the accumulation of rubble at the front of a glacier. *Lateral* morain lines the sides of glaciers; a dark area in a glacier's center—seen when two glaciers flow together, pushing their ice and crushed rubble together—is *median* morain. When seen from above, glaciers that have run together (known as "piedmont" glaciers) resemble a highway interchange, edged by road slush, with the median morain looking like dividing lines between lanes. Hanging glaciers are just that—hanging high above on rounded hillsides. Tidewater glaciers are the kind most often gracing the postcards; they hang at the water's edge, like Margerie in Glacier Bay. There are also alpine, *cirque* (or bowl), glaciers high in the mountains, and valley glaciers that don't reach the sea at any point.

"Galloping" glaciers may sometimes surge either forward or backward as much as 10 to 150 feet a day. Some are receding or retreating glaciers, like the Mendenhall Glacier in Juneau, which is backing away (literally melting away) at the rate of about 30 feet a year. Hubbard Glacier became a galloping glacier for a brief time in 1986, moving forward rapidly to block in Yakutat Bay for a few months.

When large chunks break off the face of a tidewater glacier and splash into the water below, the phenomenon is known as *calving*. Icebergs of different sizes have different names: Very large chunks are icebergs, pieces of moderate size are known as "growlers," and tiny pieces are known as "bergie bits."

---

how many meals are served each day, and whether or not you must dine at set times or can take meals at your leisure. If you have any special dietary requirements, be sure that the line is informed well in advance; almost every ship can easily meet your needs. When booking your cruise on a larger vessel, you'll be asked ahead of time to schedule your preferred dinner hour since most feature two seatings each evening.

What are the cabins like?   Cabins (also known as staterooms) come in all sizes and configurations. Some come with minibars, broad view windows, verandas, bathtubs in roomy bathrooms, TVs and VCRs, sitting areas, and big beds. Others offer just the basics—narrow upper and/or lower bunks, postage-stamp bathrooms, a porthole, and limited storage space. Consider carefully what would make you comfortable during your time at sea, how much time you might actually spend in your cabin, and what amenities you require or might easily do without.

Is the cruise formal or casual?   If you don't care to get dressed up, select a less formal cruise typical of small ships. If, on the other hand, the chance to put on your finery seems an integral part of the cruise experience, select one of the larger, more elegant ships.

How many passengers and crew does the ship carry?   A large number of passengers provides the chance to meet lots of different people and ensures a certain amount of anonymity, but keep in mind that you'll be disembarking with all those other passengers in the same small ports that may be visited by other megaliners on the same day, leading to massive crowding. Smaller passenger lists tend to lead to a congenial group atmosphere, engendering fast and firm friendships. However, smaller ships necessarily carry smaller crews, which means less personalized attention and pampering.

What are the other passengers usually like? Each cruise attracts a fairly specific audience, and you'll be more comfortable if you find out ahead of time. Most of your fellow passengers will be American retirees, though more and more ships are attracting a younger crowd. On small ships you'll find a more physically active bunch highly interested in nature. You'll find few families or single travelers though. Larger ships cater to a more diverse group; singles, newlyweds, families, and couples over 55. The more expensive the trip, the more seasoned the travelers will be. The less expensive the cruise, the more likely you are to find passengers complaining rigorously because the budget cruise isn't just like the "Loveboat" they saw on television for years. Certain lines, such as Crystal and Cunard, have a strong following among European and Asians, so you'll find a broader international mix on their cruises.

Does the ship have a children's program? More parents are taking their kids along on cruises to Alaska, and more lines are adding youth counselors to keep the kids entertained while their parents relax. Some ships even provide a supervised nursery or guaranteed babysitting. Ask whether the program is dependent on the number of children booked on any given cruise, and if it is, whether or not it will be available for your children on the dates of your cruise.

Is shipboard life heavily scheduled? If you're aboard to relax and catch up on reading and sleep, you may be annoyed at having to wake up early to eat breakfast at a set time. The larger the vessel, the less likely you'll have to stick to someone else's schedule.

How far in advance do I need to book? Many itineraries sell out six or more months in advance. Once you've selected the cruise that's right for you, inquire to be sure there will be space available when you're ready to purchase your cruise package. The addition of new ships' and new lines' joining the ranks in Alaska in 1996 brings more variety, but don't count on the additional space remaining available up to the last minute; plan to book your cabin of choice well in advance, or be prepared to accept whatever cabin category remains available.

As cruising here continues to grow in popularity, sailings frequently sell out, so plan to book in advance; you'll also find early-booking discounts of 10% to 25% if you book at least 120 days prior to sailing.

2 Cruise Practicalities

WHEN TO GO   The Alaska cruise season stretches from mid-May through mid-September, with the driest days falling in May and June, the warmest and longest days falling in July and August (considered peak season, so these are the most expensive months to cruise). The least expensive cruises are typically the first and last runs of the season.

TIPS ON PACKING   See Chapter 3, "Planning a Trip to Alaska," for general advice on packing for Alaska's variable weather. A swimsuit is a must for cruising on a ship equipped with a heated pool or hot tubs. You'll also need to bring along enough dressy clothing for the number of formal evenings (usually two per 7-day itinerary and three on 7- to 10-day trips); dress suits or tuxedos are fine for men, cocktail dresses or evening gowns for women. Sports jackets and, on some lines, ties for men and dresses or pant suits for women are suitable for less formal evenings. Anything but swimsuits, shorts, and in some cases jeans, is suitable for casual evenings. You may even want to pack something special if your itinerary includes a theme night— maybe a 1950s night, or country-and-western, pirate, or masquerade night. Check ahead to see what sort of costume will be appropriate for the cruise you select.

Don't leave home without a pair of binoculars (though some smaller vessels provide enough to loan to passengers), a camera and plenty of film, sunglasses, and sunblock.

Travel documents, medications, passports, traveler's checks, jewelry, and other valuables or personal items you might need within easy reach should be packed in a carry-on bag since your luggage will be inaccessible during embarkation and disembarkation. This carry-on can also serve as an overnight bag for short land excursions to Denali as well.

CUSTOMS & IDENTIFICATION DOCUMENTS   When transiting through Vancouver, British Columbia, you'll have to clear Immigration and Customs. See Chapter 3, "Planning a Trip to Alaska," for details.

TIPPING   Gratuities are entirely discretionary, but these days most cruise lines will provide tipping guidelines and envelopes at the close of the cruise. It's customary to tip approximately $10 per passenger per day on cruises, and on the last full day of the cruise these tips are usually given directly to the people who provided the service. A general breakdown is $3 to $5 per day each for the cabin and dining attendants, $1.50 to $2 per day for the busboy (also called the assistant waiter), and $5 to $10 per week to the maître d' and wine steward (assuming you ordered wine). Those lines that pool tips will inform you of the proper procedure for tipping. Gratuities to other ship personnel for good service are entirely up to you; bar tabs include an automatic gratuity of 15%, but tips for room service are not included. Tips for shore personnel (local tour guides or bus drivers) are at your discretion as well, but most people tip $1 for two to four hours of sightseeing, $2 for longer day trips or highway tours. Longshoremen and skycaps are usually tipped $1 per bag when assisting with luggage, though there are posted signs at Vancouver's piers stating that tipping is not necessary.

3 Cruise Lines & Ships

The departure dates and cruise prices included in all of the ship reviews below are for *1996*. At press time dates and prices for 1997 were simply unavailable; however, there's remarkable consistency from one year to the next. If you're planning a cruise for the summer of 1997, the figures in this chapter may be off by a few days or dollars, but should nonetheless give you a good basis for comparison.

SMALL SHIPS

These are the casual, shallow-draft vessels that can get in and out of tight areas. They're usually under 200 feet in length and carry 100 or so passengers. In addition to the lines reviewed below, **Clipper Cruises** (☎ 800/325-0100) and **Glacier Bay Tours and Cruises** (☎ 800/451-5952) operate small-ship cruises in Alaska. (Glacier Bay's ships are briefly described in the Glacier Bay National Park section of Chapter 7.)

Alaska Sightseeing / Cruise West. 4th and Battery Building, Suite 700, Seattle, WA 98121. ☎ **206/441-8687**, or 800/426-7702. Fax 206/441-4757.

Established in 1973, Alaska Sightseeing / Cruise West now operates the largest fleet of small ships cruising the Pacific Northwest and Alaska, including the 101-passenger *Spirit of '98*, the 84-passenger *Spirit of Discovery*, the 82-passenger *Spirit of Alaska*, and an array of smaller overnight and day-cruise yachts. American owned and operated, the line's young crews are energetic and infectiously enthusiastic. A cruise coordinator, trained to lecture on the flora, fauna, geology, and history of the region, accompanies each trip, giving passengers the opportunity to learn about Alaska

in depth. Local fishermen and Native Alaskans come aboard in some ports to entertain and teach about the culture and industry of the state as well. ASCW also operates a variety of reasonably priced land tours so that you can see more of the state than
its scenic coastline.

ASCW ships' best point is their small size and ability to navigate tight areas such
as Desolation Sound in British Columbia and visit tiny ports such as Petersburg,
places the larger ships simply dare not venture. Open bow areas on each vessel,
accessed through the lounge, are the best observation points. Guests tend to congregate there and on the more sheltered sundeck aft to watch for wildlife, the star of
the show on small-ship cruises. During the day, wildlife sightings are announced over
the shipwide intercom system. You can even sign up for a crew member to wake
you during the night if you don't want to miss the northern lights or any wildlife
sightings.

While at sea, days are filled watching wildlife (there are binoculars aboard for your
use during the cruise) or reading a book from the small Alaska reference library in
the lounge. Onboard activities, while limited (perhaps lectures, videos, Bingo, or a
mini-casino night), include more than most ships of this size. There's nothing
special for the kids to do, so ASCW cruises are not really suitable for families with
children unless the kids are really enthralled by nature.

Breakfast, lunch, and dinner are served at set times at one unassigned seating, so
you're free to mingle with the other passengers. If you feel like sleeping in, you'll miss
breakfast—no room service is available. The fare is primarily home-style American,
utilizing fresh products purchased in ports along the way. Presentation is basic, but
the cuisine is tasty and varied, a surprising achievement considering the tiny galley
and limited crew. Following the evening meal, the chef will describe the two entrees
available for dinner the next evening, and guests make their selection before retiring
to their compact cabin for the night.

✪ **Spirit of '98.** Passenger capacity: 101. Crew compliment: 23. 49 cabins, all outside. Ship
facilities: dining room, open-access bow area, sundeck, lounge (with full bar, small library, and
audiovisual equipment), video library, exercise bike, gift shop. Activities: lectures and videos on
Alaska, board games, Bingo, horse racing, casino, and other theme nights. Itineraries: Week-long
cruises between Seattle and Juneau visit Desolation Sound, Misty Fjords National Monument,
Tracy Arm, and the Inside Passage, and stop in Ketchikan, Sitka, Skagway, and Haines. Northbound departures: 5/11, 5/25, 6/8, 6/22, 7/6, 7/20, 8/3, 8/17, 8/31, 9/14. Southbound
departures: 5/4, 5/18, 6/1, 6/15, 6/29, 7/13, 7/27, 8/10, 8/24, 9/7. Cruise only, $2,249–$5,229
per person, double occupancy. Single and triple prices available on request.

The *Spirit of '98*, flagship of the Alaska Sightseeing / Cruise West line, was built in
1984 and refurbished stem to stern in 1995, but its decor is strictly period, with a
strong Victorian flavor inside and a riverboat design outside. Pressed-tin ceilings,
paisley carpeting, balloon-back chairs, and plenty of polished woodwork are in
keeping with the '98's turn-of-the-century theme in the public areas. The tight cabins
were greatly improved as well, and now have coordinated burgundy or navy-blue
comforters and carpeting, swag curtains around large windows, platform beds with
wooden headboards, sconce lighting, framed naturalist prints, and light-oak desk and
cabinets trimmed in cherry-stained walnut. Televisions with built-in VCRs were
added, and a video library is available for your entertainment. If you prefer not to
use the air conditioning in the cabin, simply open the window to allow in fresh
breezes. Bathrooms are tight, but have full showers. Several cabins have queen-size
beds, two are outfitted as triples, and two have bunks. I prefer the pie-shaped rooms
both fore and aft.

The Bottom Line: The *Spirit of '98* has slightly more public space to enjoy than does the *Spirit of Discovery*. A favorite area is Soapy's Parlour, an intimate lounge tucked behind the dining room where you'll usually find freshly baked cookies and tea in the afternoon. The full bar in the main lounge is also more comfortable since it's equipped with bar stools (guests stand at the bar on the *Discovery*). Darker colors used in the period decor, while charming, somehow make the ship feel smaller overall than it actually is, and additional lighting doesn't quite manage to compensate.

Spirit of Discovery. Passenger capacity: 84. Crew compliment: 21. 43 cabins, all outside. Ship facilities: dining room, open-access bow area, sundeck, lounge (with full bar, small library, and audiovisual equipment), video library, exercise bike, gift shop. Activities: lectures and videos on Alaska, board games, Bingo, horse racing, casino, and other theme nights. Itinerary: Week-long cruises run between Seattle and Juneau, with cruising days in Desolation Sound, LeConte and Misty fjords, Glacier Bay, and the Inside Passage, and port days in Sitka, Petersburg, and Ketchikan. Northbound departures: 5/4, 5/18, 6/1, 6/15, 6/29, 7/13, 7/27, 8/10, 8/24, 9/7. Southbound departures: 5/11, 5/25, 6/8, 6/22, 7/6, 7/20, 8/3, 8/17, 8/31, 9/14. Cruise only, $2,125–$3,699 per person, double occupancy. Two single cabins are available (otherwise solo passengers pay 175% of the twin rate).

Decor lends the *Spirit of Discovery*, launched in 1976 and extensively refurbished in 1992, a more streamlined, modern appearance. Lighter colors used in carpets, wood veneer, and wall coverings and plenty of light flooding through big picture windows reflecting off shiny brass and mirrored surfaces give the lounge and dining room a more spacious, airy feel. Cabins are very snug (slightly smaller than those on the '98), but comfortable, and feature cheery pastel color schemes, picture windows that open to ocean breezes in all categories, a radio/public address system, individual heating and cooling, tight head with shower and toilet (the sink is in the main room), and lower twin or double platform beds (though deluxe cabins have queen-size beds and Cabins 101 and 102, situated forward on the main deck, have bunks). Storage space is ample.

The Bottom Line: The young American captain and crew of the *Discovery* are particularly enthusiastic, always upbeat and fun to be around. It's nice that the vessel is equipped with a couple of single cabins, but single passengers may feel like third wheels since most passengers come paired up. Engine noise reverberates in the dining room, making normal conversation difficult during meals.

SPECIAL EXPEDITIONS

720 Fifth Ave., New York, NY 10019. ☎ **212/765-7740** or 800/762-0003. Fax 212/265-3770.

Sven-Olof Lindblad, son of adventure-travel pioneer Lars-Eric Lindblad, followed in his father's footsteps with the formation of Special Expeditions in 1984. His company specializes in environmentally sensitive, soft-adventure vacations to remote places in the world, including Alaska. The trips are explorative and informal in nature, designed to appeal to the intellectually curious traveler seeking a vacation that's educational as well as relaxing. Expeditions aboard Lindblad's ships are led by four to five top naturalists, botanists, anthropologists, biologists, and geologists who lecture on all aspects of the area visited and guide forays into the natural world for a closer look. Educational films and slide presentations shown aboard the ship precede nature hikes and quick jaunts aboard Zodiacs (motorized inflatable rafts) for firsthand inspection. An afternoon hike through a mushroom- and fern-laden forest to a natural hot spring might be followed by floating peacefully just yards away from a raft of dozing sea otters.

Trips aboard the *Sea Lion* and *Sea Bird* in Alaska are anything but the traditional cruise experience; you'll find no casino, no disco, no dance lounges, no massage or fitness rooms, no telephones or TVs, no room service or laundry room, no recent-release movies, and no late-night buffet here. Instead, your days aboard are spent learning about and observing the world around you (bring your own binoculars), either from the ship or on shore excursions (included in the cruise package). On-board presentations and meals (featuring hearty but basic American fare at single open sittings) fall at set times, which are posted in a daily program and announced over the shipwide intercom system. Other than that, the schedule remains loose enough to diverge a bit to search out whales or stop for a cookout in a quiet cove just because it's a gorgeous day. Passengers tend to be younger and more physically active, but even so, the ships become very quiet not long after dinner; everyone crashes early to store up energy for the next day's adventures. It's a casual experience suited for an easygoing crowd bent on learning about Alaska.

MV *Sea Bird* and MV *Sea Lion*. Passenger capacity: 70. Crew compliment: 22. 37 cabins, all outside. Ship facilities: dining room, bar and library in observation lounge, open bow area, sundeck, gift shop. Activities: lectures, educational videos; wheelhouse open for tours; books, cards, and board games on loan from library. Itinerary: Week-long "Coastal Wilderness" cruises run from Sitka to Ketchikan, with visits to Haines, Glacier Bay, Bartlett Cove, Tracy Arm, Petersburg, Misty Fjords, and numerous off-the-beaten-path coves, inlets, and islands. Departures: 6/1, 6/8, 6/15, 6/16, 6/22, 6/30, 7/6, 7/7, 7/13, 7/14, 7/20, 7/21, 7/27, 7/28, 8/3, 8/4, 8/10, 8/17, 8/18, 8/24, 8/25. Cruise/air package, $2,990–$4,190 per person, double occupancy. Also, a 12-day Alaska/D.C. combination round-trip cruise departing 8/31 from Seattle, Wash., with visits to Sitka, Point Adolphus (for whale watching) in Glacier Bay, Tracy Arm, Kupreanof Island, Ketchikan, Alert Bay and Johnstone Straight (B.C.), and the San Juan Islands, Wash.; cost, $3,590–$5,080 per person, double occupancy. Solo passengers pay 150% of the per-person double-occupancy rate in the smallest cabins only. No cabins are set up for third or fourth passengers.

These are very intimate, shallow-draft ships (smaller than most of their competition), more like cruising yachts than ocean-going vessels, and as such are able to visit pristine off-the-beaten-path areas larger ships can't reach. The *Sea Lion* and *Sea Bird* are identical twins down to their decor schemes and furniture. Public and private areas are very compact and informal. Public space is limited to open sundeck and bow areas, the dining room, and an observation lounge that serves as the nerve center for activities. The lounge is where you'll find the bar, a library of atlases and books on Alaska's culture, geology, history, plants, and wildlife, a gift shop tucked into a closet, and audiovisual aids for the many naturalists' presentations.

Postage-stamp cabins are tight and functional rather than fancy; they feature twin or double beds, a closet (there are also drawers under the bed for extra storage), a speaker for shipwide announcements, and a sink and mirror in the main room, and, behind a folding door, a Lilliputian head with a toilet opposite the shower nozzle. All cabins are located outside and have picture windows that open to fresh breezes. Rather than embue a sense of claustrophobia, the compactness of these tiny vessels seems to engender quick camaraderie among guests and crew.

The Bottom Line: Large passengers will find it very difficult to negotiate showers in the closet-size bathrooms. There are no facilities for children and no cabins large enough to accommodate more than two, so these ships are not really suitable for families. However, the curious, adventuresome traveler looking for an up-close, in-depth look at Alaska will find that these ships fit the bill perfectly. The caliber of expedition leaders is outstanding. Best of all, a choice of soft-adventure shore excursions is included in the cost of the cruise.

CLASSIC LINERS

With gracefully curved bow and stern, enclosed promenades, and the genteel decor of an earlier era, these older vessels built decades ago for transatlantic cruising are still going strong. They usually carry under 1,000 passengers. On a classic liner you'll feel you're really on a ship, rather than a huge floating resort.

HOLLAND AMERICA LINE/WESTOURS

300 Elliott Ave. W., Seattle, WA 98119. ☎ **206/281-3535** or 800/426-0327. Fax 800/628-4855.

Founded in 1873, Holland America Line now operates one of the largest cruise fleets in the world, and continues to grow, with several new ships now under construction and due to be launched in the next couple of years. Expansion of its fleet allows it to offer an unprecedented number of Alaska departures (117 in 1996). This summer Holland America will operate the *Rotterdam, Noordam, Nieuw Amsterdam, Statendam, Ryndam* (all reviewed below), and *Westerdam* (to be reviewed in a future edition) in Alaska. One of the pioneers in cruising Alaska, Holland America has also developed the most extensive land-tour operation (Westours, Inc.) in Alaska, so you'll have plenty of choices of shore excursions and land-tour extensions.

Holland America stands out from the crowd in many ways. Its ships offer more activities than any other line—so many, in fact, that the selection can prove to be overwhelming and frustrating at times because you'll invariably find yourself wanting to take part in two or more activities scheduled at the same time. Naturalists accompany every cruise in Alaska, lecturing on the flora and fauna to enhance your trip through the region. In addition to Bingo, fashion and talent shows, horse racing, board and card games, dance or cooking classes, tours of the bridge, and art auctions, there are a variety of enrichment lectures to choose from, covering everything from photography to finance to nutrition. An extensive fitness program—Passport to Fitness—has the added bonus of awards for participation.

The carefully trained Indonesian and Filipino crews are incredibly cheerful, friendly, and solicitous, so service consistently receives outstanding ratings from passengers. Holland America's ships are always immaculately clean. The mixed international cuisine served aboard the vessels is well prepared, attractively presented, and extensive in selection. Room service is available at all hours, and you can get anything from the daily menu delivered to your cabin during lunch and dinner hours (as far as I'm aware, this is the only line to do this as standard practice). Holland America also garnered rave reviews in the past for its entertainment, but I've overheard a number of loyal passengers grumbling about a downward slide in the quality of entertainment recently.

Holland America features some of the lowest cruise fares in Alaska, especially with its early-booking discount of 25% and discounts for third and forth passengers per cabin. The *Rotterdam* offers single cabins; on other ships, solo passengers pay 150% to 190% the per-person double-occupancy rate for a standard double cabin.

⑤ SS *Rotterdam*. Passenger capacity: 1,100. Crew compliment: 628. 307 outside cabins and 268 inside cabins. Ship facilities: two dining rooms, café with an ice-cream bar, five bars, bilevel show theater, two entertainment lounges, casino, disco, video room, spa and salon, indoor and outdoor pools, whirlpools, men's and women's saunas, library, children's video arcade, shops, photo service, shore-excursions desk, coin laundries, medical facility. Activities: extensive onboard activities (up to 250 per seven-day cruise), deck sports (shuffleboard, ping-pong, volleyball, tennis). Itinerary: Seven-day Glacier Discovery Cruises between Vancouver (B.C.) and Seward, with visits to Ketchikan, Juneau, Sitka, Yakutat Bay and Hubbard Glacier, Valdez, and College and

Harriman fjords. Northbound departures: 5/19, 6/2, 6/16, 6/30, 7/14, 7/28, 8/11, 8/25, 9/8. Southbound departures: 5/26, 6/9, 6/23, 7/7, 7/21, 8/4, 8/18, 9/1, 9/15. Cruise only, $1,025–$3,900 per person, double occupancy. Also, a week-long Glacier Bay Inside Passage round-trip cruise departing 9/22 from Vancouver, B.C., with visits to Ketchikan, Juneau, Glacier Bay, Sitka, and the Inside Passage; cruise only, $975–$3,350 per person, double occupancy. Single cabins, early-booking discounts of 25%, and discounts for third and fourth passengers are available.

The SS *Rotterdam*, flagship of Holland America's rapidly expanding line, is a classic *grande dame* in every sense of the term, from the elegant, old-world decor (trimmed out in polished wood and brass you don't find on newer vessels) to the graceful curves of bow and stern. The ship, commissioned in 1958 and last refurbished in 1995, simply exudes the gentility and grace of an earlier era. The partially enclosed promenade, a sweeping central staircase, a smoking room, raised door seals, spacious rooms decked out in rich wood trim, and other hints attest to the ship's days as a transoceanic vessel.

Of the many public areas, the Ritz Carlton lounge is the most stunning—a curved staircase takes you to the balcony area for the best view of an elaborate wall-to-wall mural of the Aegean Sea and a look at the gold-leaf dance floor below. The entertainment lounge at the opposite end of the ship is tiered and has a balcony, so everyone in the house has a view of the shows.

As with most classic liners, cabins are nicely proportioned on the large size; all are equipped with well-lit dressing tables, ample storage space, full bathrooms with shower (some have deep baths), a small sitting area, telephone, and television (movies, news, shore talks, and simulcasts of the evening show are featured). The bathrooms show the age of the ship fairly clearly in the marble sink shelf, tilework, and steampipe towel racks (used to heat the bath towels in earlier days), and other period fittings. Cabins 1 to 25, on the highest deck, have partially obstructed views; Cabins 31 to 34, located one deck down, offer the most expansive view through windows overlooking the bow of the ship (book one of these only if you have cruise experience and know that your stomach can handle the extra motion felt in this part of the ship). Several inside and outside single cabins are available.

The Bottom Line: Among Holland America's well-heeled repeat passengers (and there are many), the *Rotterdam* is the ship of choice, which probably explains why it's assigned the round-the-world voyages. Rumor has it that 1996 will be the ship's final season cruising in Alaska because it will be decommissioned or sold by 1997, so book early for this last chance. The dining rooms, situated low in the ship, are very stable and quiet, but it's a shame there are no windows to look out on the sea. There's a children's activity room and an organized activity program for the kids, but the *Rotterdam* would not be my choice for families with younger children.

ROYAL CRUISE LINE

One Maritime Plaza, Suite 1400, San Francisco, CA 94111. ☎ **415/956-7200** or 800/227-5628. Fax 415/956-1656.

Established in 1971, Royal Cruise Line found its niche by developing worldwide air/sea packages utilizing refurbished classic ships and gearing its cruises to an older, more affluent audience. The line does a fine job of catering to mature cruisers, providing a high percentage of single cabins, numerous hosts to entertain the single females aboard (they originated the host program at sea), healthy low-fat meals developed in conjunction with the American Heart Association (RCL was also the first to introduce such a program), one sitting for dinner, and an enrichment series and entertainment geared toward more mature tastes.

Sadly, Royal Cruise Line (under parent company Kloster Cruises) appears to be experiencing financial difficulties, and it's reflected in the cruise experience. The line generated both headlines and headaches in the spring of 1995 when the crew of the

Royal Odyssey went on strike, shutting services down entirely. They did go back to work, but the problem has yet to be fully resolved, and the tension aboard remains thick, even uncomfortable. It's also fairly obvious that the line is cutting costs where it can, noticeable in a lack of fresh flower arrangements throughout public areas (easy enough to live with), and more important, in the overall quality of the food (not as easy to live with). At press time, the line was up for sale, and things may improve if new owners step in with a needed monetary infusion.

MS *Royal Odyssey.* Passenger capacity: 750. Crew compliment: 410. 333 outside cabins (9 with a veranda) and 81 inside cabins. Ship facilities: dining room, café, two snack bars, ice-cream bar, four bars, two entertainment lounges, tiny casino, disco, spa and salon, pool, three heated whirl-pools, basketball/paddle-tennis court, enclosed golf-driving net, saunas and steam rooms, library, card room, movie theater, duty-free and photo shops, shore-excursion desk (note that choices in shore excursions are very limited), onboard cruise consultant, medical facility. Activities: limited lecture series, language classes, demonstrations, dance and fitness classes; organized shuffleboard, ping-pong, and board games. Itineraries: Seven-day cruises between Vancouver (B.C.) and Anchorage, with visits to Ketchikan, Juneau, Skagway, Hubbard Glacier, Columbia Glacier, and College Fjord. Northbound departures: 7/17, 7/31, 8/14. Southbound departures: 7/24, 8/7, 8/21. Cruise only, $1,798–$7,498 per person, double occupancy. Also, 10-day positioning cruises between San Francisco and Vancouver (B.C.), with visits to Glacier Bay, Skagway, Juneau, Sitka, and Ketchikan. Northbound departure: 5/26 only. Southbound departure: 8/28 only (this one includes a stop in Victoria). Cruise only, $2,598–$8,778 per person, double occupancy. Also, a 12-day round-trip cruise from San Francisco, departing 5/14 only, stops in Victoria, Ketchikan, Juneau, Skagway, Sitka, and Vancouver, and includes a day in Glacier Bay; cruise only, $2,928–$10,168 per person, double occupancy. Early-booking discounts of 15%–30%, single cabins, and third-passenger berths are available.

Formerly known as the *Royal Viking Sea* and built in 1973 for world cruising, the 750-passenger MS *Royal Odyssey* is a mid-sized classic liner with spacious cabins and public areas, a broad promenade and plenty of deck space, a dining room large enough to seat all passengers at one dinner sitting (a big convenience), and several lounges and a disco with view windows perched high in the ship. The ship was cosmetically refurbished in early 1995, adding 15 new cabins (7024A and 7025A were favorites), a salon, aerobics room, massage rooms, saunas, and steam rooms, and complimentary laundry rooms. The interior decor was also spiffed up with polished marble floors in the foyers and lighter colors throughout to brighten and modernize the overall look. However, the ship still has the original pipes that pump out rusty water occasionally and other mechanical (namely engine) problems that should have been attended to as part of the refurbishment.

New inside cabins added in the recent refurbishment are a bit claustrophobic, but the older ones are extremely generous in space and layout. Huge deluxe cabins on Deck 7 feature broad view windows, extensive storage space, minirefrigerators, and bathrooms with full bathtubs and built-in hairdryers. Penthouse suites on Deck 9 have balconies, minibars, larger bathrooms, and VCRs. All cabins are equipped with twin or queen-size beds (pullman berths are available in some cabins as well), a sitting area, desk with lockable drawers for valuables, color TV, three-channel music and TV systems, telephone, and individual climate control. Twenty-four-hour room service and valet laundry service are a phone call away; there are also complimentary laundry facilities aboard.

Enrichment lectures are a plus—health and well-being, photography, jazz, country-and-western music, and the natural history of Alaska are topics of the 1996 series. Its diminutive size—28,000 tons and 676 feet—gives this older ship an intimate appeal, but does mean that it creaks and rocks noticeably on rough open seas (and there are at least four days in open water on the 12-day Alaska itinerary from San Francisco). The ship's best asset, though, is its primarily Greek crew, who are genuinely charming and very eager to please; they've garnered awards for top service in the industry for years.

Service remains high because of the passenger-to-crew ratio (averaging less than two passengers for each crew member), but the food is disappointing. By consensus, my dinner partners and I found the pastas, seafood, and Greek dishes to be the most reliable selections; salads and vegetables were usually a letdown. The morning cinnamon buns, however, were too tasty to resist and quickly became a highlight of the cruise.

The Bottom Line: The charming, attentive crew and the feel of family they engender is the best thing going for Royal Cruise Lines. Another big plus is the convenience and relaxed pace of single-seating dining in the extended dining room. Food quality, on the other hand, was lacking at the time I cruised, but may improve under new ownership. The boxy entertainment lounge is cramped, and floor space limits the productions showcased there (don't miss the Greek show put on by the crew). There are very few shore excursions to choose from, perhaps because the older passengers prefer to stay on the ship rather than get off and explore all the ports of call. With more single cabins than most cruise liners and gentlemen hosts to dance and dine with single female passengers, an Alaskan cruise on the *Royal Odyssey* would be a top choice for conservative, mature single passengers who appreciate slightly longer itineraries incorporating more time at sea to simply relax.

WORLD EXPLORER CRUISES

555 Montgomery St., San Francisco, CA 94111-2544. ☎ 415/393-1145 or 800/854-3835. Fax 415/391-1145.

If immersion in Alaska is what you're after, World Explorer Cruises is your answer. This line has created its own niche by focusing on educational and cultural cruises of greater length that visit more ports than any other line cruising in the state. It was the originator of the "eco-cruise" in Alaska, and now almost every line has followed its example by adding naturalists or Alaskan lectures to the staff roster. World Explorer continues to stand apart from the crowd by hiring top educators from institutions all over the United States to lead seminars and provide entertaining and informative lectures on the culture, history, geology, glaciers, flora, and fauna of Southeast and Southcentral Alaska. It also hires talented performers from around the globe to provide classical and folk entertainment; a Chinese pianist or American violin virtuoso might be followed the next night by a Russian balalaika player, flamenco guitarist, or a Native Alaskan drummer. Even the 40-plus shore excursions are soft-adventure oriented and educational in nature.

During the summer in Alaska, World Explorer operates the SS *Universe,* which, during the academic year, serves the Institute for Shipboard Education (affiliated now with the University of Pittsburgh) on two around-the-world Semester-at-Sea voyages full of eager college students. Those students are rather rough on the ship (and it shows), but World Explorer scrubs and polishes before moving the *Universe* to Alaska for passenger cruises. The cruise experience it strives to provide is informal, educational, and entertaining rather than luxurious, and this intimate, age-worn vessel suits that purpose well.

As we went to press, World Explorer announced they had leased a larger, faster ship than the old SS *Universe.* I can't offer a full ship review this edition, but if your goal is to learn about this beautiful frontier, this is the cruise for you. The cultural entertainment, educational activities, and caliber of World Explorer's lectures are outstanding.

MODERN CRUISE SHIPS

This generation saw the beginning of many changes in shipbuilding; cabins got a bit smaller to make room for expanded public facilities. Sports courts, more elaborate spas, pools and whirlpools, open atriums, glass walls, forward observation lounges, and cabin balconies for better sea views are among the additions. Modern cruise ships are larger (20,000 to 60,000 gross tons) and outfitted to handle more passengers (anywhere from 750 to 1,300). **Celebrity Cruises'** *Horizon* (☎ **800/445-0063**) will be joining the ranks in Alaska in 1996. **Carnival's** *Tropical* (☎**800/438-6744**) will also be running in Alaska in 1996.

CUNARD LINE

555 Fifth Ave., New York, New York 10017-2453. ☎ **718/361-4000** or 800/5-CUNARD. Fax 718/786-0038.

Cunard got its start in Britain in 1840 carrying mail, special cargo, and diplomats for the Crown. Hallmarks in Cunard's long history include being the first line to operate ships with radios (Marconi actually ran his first ship-to-shore experiments on a Cunard vessel), the first with truly fast steam engines used on transatlantic crossings, and among the pioneers of vacation cruising, offering sailings in the Mediterranean as early as 1928. Cunard was also among the first to scout out Alaska as a cruise destination, and has been cruising here since 1976. If the intimate *Crown Dynasty* (reviewed below) is fully booked, check to see if a cabin aboard Cunard's more luxurious—and more expensive—*Sagafjord* or *Sea Goddess II* (to be reviewed in a future edition) is available.

MS *Crown Dynasty*. Passenger capacity: 850. Crew compliment: 340. 268 outside cabins and 124 inside cabins. Ship facilities: dining room, café, five bars, two entertainment lounges, casino, disco, spa and salon, pool, three whirlpools, men's and women's saunas and steam rooms, library, children's activity room, duty-free and gift shops, medical facility. Activities: limited lecture series and onboard activities; craft and dance classes, shuffleboard, ping-pong, Bingo, passenger talent competition, board games. Itinerary: Seven-day cruises between Vancouver (B.C.) and Seward visit Ketchikan, the Brothers Islands for whale watching, North and South Sawyer glaciers in Tracy Arm Fjord, Juneau, Sitka, and Hubbard Glacier northbound; and Hubbard Glacier, Juneau, Skagway, Wrangell, Ketchikan, and Misty Fjords southbound. Northbound departures: 5/20, 6/3, 6/17, 7/1, 7/15, 7/29, 8/12, 8/26, 9/9. Southbound departures: 5/27, 6/10, 6/24, 7/8, 7/22, 8/5, 8/19, 9/2, 9/16. Air/sea packages $1,495–$4,415 per person, double occupancy. Solo passengers pay 150%–200% of the per-person double-occupancy rate. A 20% early-booking discount is available.

The MS *Crown Dynasty*, launched in 1993, feels as if it had been constructed specifically for viewing wildlife in Alaska—broad decks, an open bow (on other vessels of this size the bow is a working area accessible to crew only, and on this one you can peer over the side to watch porpoises playing in the wake), and deck chairs set behind protective glass windscreens makes viewing the passing scenery much more comfortable. The lack of an enclosed forward observation lounge is hardly noticeable. It's a quietly elegant ship, outfitted with lots of nicely laid out facilities, from the tiered dining room offering a view from every table to the well-stocked fitness center at the top and front of the ship offering gorgeous views to take your mind off the workout. If you'd rather relax, there's a whirlpool tub beneath a skylight in the gym, and two more out on the sundeck next to the pool. There's a play center for children on the sundeck, but no supervised program of activities unless there are several families with younger children aboard.

Inside it seems like a small luxury hotel. A five-story glass-walled atrium, winding brass-railed staircases, soaring windows, and skylights brighten pastel oil and

Alaskan Cruises at a Glance

Legend:
★ outstanding/excellent
● good
◐ fair
○ could stand improvement/not available/mediocre

	food	entertainment	ship amenities	cabin amenities	onboard activities	shore excursions	passenger to crew ratio	family/youth program	Alaskan Ports of Call — Ketchikan
Crystal Harmony/Symphony	★	★	★	★	●	◐	1.76	●	✓
LUXURY LINERS									
Legend of the Seas	★	★	★	★	●	◐	2.50	★	✓
Star Princess	●	★	★	★	★	★	2.48	★	✓
Crown/Regal Princess	●	★	★	★	★	★	2.28	●	✓
MEGALINERS (1400-2200)									
Windward	★	★	★	●	●	★	2.5	★	✓
Statendam/Ryndam	★	●	★	●	★	★	2.22	●	✓
Nieuw Amsterdam/Noordam	★	◐	★	●	★	★	2.36	●	✓
Crown Dynasty	◐	◐	★	●	○	●	2.5	◐	✓
MODERN LINER (750-1300)									
Universe	○	★	○	○	★	●	2.42	◐	✓
Royal Odyssey	○	○	◐	●	◐	○	1.83	○	✓
Rotterdam	★	◐	●	●	★	★	1.75	◐	✓
CLASSIC LINER (200-1200)									
Sea Lion & Sea Bird	◐	◐	○	○	◐	★	3.18	○	✓
Spirit of Discovery	◐	○	○	○	◐	●	4.0	○	✓
Spirit of 98	◐	○	◐	○	◐	●	4.39	○	✓
SMALL SHIPS (cap. <200)									

THE SHIP — food · entertainment · ship amenities · cabin amenities · onboard activities · shore excursions · passenger to crew ratio · family/youth program

THE ITINERARY — Alaskan Ports of Call — Ketchikan

Petersburg																
Wrangell	✓	✓														
Sitka	✓	✓	✓		✓			✓				✓	✓			✓
Juneau	✓	✓		✓	✓	✓	✓	✓	✓			✓	✓	✓		✓
Haines	✓		✓	✓		✓	✓									✓
Skagway	✓				✓	✓		✓				✓	✓	✓		✓
Valdez				✓	✓	✓		✓	✓							✓
Seward				✓	✓	✓	✓	✓	✓	✓		✓	✓			✓
Natural Sights																
Desolation Sound	✓															
Misty Fjords	✓	✓	✓		✓		✓			✓				✓		✓
Tracy Arm/Endicott Arm	✓	✓	✓		✓	✓	✓									✓
Glacier Bay	✓	✓	✓		✓	✓		✓	✓	✓		✓	✓			✓
Yakutat Bay/Hubbard Glacier					✓	✓	✓	✓	✓					✓		✓
College Fjord					✓	✓		✓	✓			✓	✓			✓
THE COST	$2,249–$4,149	$2,125–$3,799	$2,990–$5,080	$975–$3,900	$1,349–$8,135	$995–$3,395	$1,495–$4,415	$1,280–$4,050	$1,530–$7,574	$1,499–$2,959		$1,549–$4,549	$1,449–$4,449	$1,599–$5,749		$1,999–$14,306
Number of Days	7	7	7-12	7	7-12	7-14	7-10	7-12	7-12	7		7	7	7		7-13

watercolor paintings and murals that echo the cool, muted tones of the interior decor. Judicious use of mirrors, glass, marble, and gleaming brass bring lots of light to the interior, creating a more open feel without seeming tinny and echoing as do some of the other new ships.

Its middling size has advantages; the ship feels cozy and is easy to learn your way around in within a matter of hours. It's rare when passengers don't see whales, but there are no guarantees; to make it that much easier, though, whale sightings are usually announced by the officer on duty over the public address system. An Alaskan lecturer uses the same shipwide system to talk about the ecology, flora, and fauna of the region and relate history and current statistics on the ports of call, but you can only hear what's being said in public areas and on outside decks (no in-cabin broadcasts). The ship's size, however, does limit the amount of planned activities on board.

The cuisine (which at the time I cruised was good, but not outstanding as I'd come to expect from Cunard) is European-influenced, featuring fish, fowl, beef, and vegetarian selections. Breakfast and lunch are served in the dining room and the indoor/outdoor café, dinner only in the dining room at two assigned seatings (6 and 8:30pm). Go to the dining room for better-quality food, but expect the attentive service to be excruciatingly slow at times. A limited room service menu is available around the clock on all but the final day of the cruise.

Most staterooms have broad-view windows (though some views are obstructed by lifeboats on Decks 6 and 7). None of the staterooms has a bathtub, and only a select few have a veranda. However, all, even in the least expensive category, are very attractive and are outfitted with twin beds (most can be pushed together to form a double bed), a TV, sitting area, desk, in-room safe, and ample closet space (though drawer space is somewhat limited). For the best view, select one of the seven cabins at the front of the ship looking out over the bow, but be aware that you'll experience a good bit more motion here than midship. A few inside cabins equipped with bunks are suitable for families. Cabins on Deck 2 have small porthole windows and tend to be noisier when on rough seas because they're located so close to the waterline.

The Bottom Line: The *Crown Dynasty* is a prime choice for those interested in seeing Alaska's wildlife while cruising in style; whale watching is built into the itinerary. With over 30 nationalities among the crew and staff compliment, language difficulties are rare for the largely international passenger list. The ship is family friendly, and the kids will find plenty to do (however, children under 18 aren't permitted in the gym). There are no hosts aboard to dance with single female passengers.

HOLLAND AMERICA LINE/WESTOURS

300 Elliott Ave. W., Seattle, WA 98119. ☎ **206/281-3535** or 800/426-0327. Fax 800/628-4855.

See my review of this line and the company history under "Classic Liners," above.

MS *Nieuw Amsterdam* and MS *Noordam*. Passenger capacity: 1,250. Crew compliment: 530. 411 outside cabins and 194 inside cabins. Ship facilities: dining room, café with an ice-cream bar, five bars, entertainment lounge, casino, disco, spa and salon, exercise room, two pools, whirlpool, men's and women's saunas, library, card room, children's activity room with video arcade, deck sports (shuffleboard, ping-pong, volleyball, tennis), shops, coin laundries, medical facility. Activities: extensive onboard activities (up to 250 per seven-day cruise). Itineraries: Seven-day Glacier Bay Inside Passage cruises from Vancouver (B.C.), with stops in Ketchikan, Juneau, Sitka, and Glacier Bay. *Nieuw Amsterdam* departures: 5/16 (5/13 from Los Angeles for a 10-day cruise), 5/23, 5/30, 6/6, 6/13, 6/20, 6/27, 7/4, 7/11, 7/18, 7/25, 8/1, 8/8, 8/15, 8/22, 8/29, 9/5, 9/12, 9/19; cruise only, $1,280–$4,000 (10-day cruise from Los Angeles, $1,579–$3,949). *Noordam* departures: 9/17, 9/24; cruise only, $1,280–$3,500. Seven-day Glacier Discovery cruises between Vancouver (B.C.) and Seward, with visits to College and

Harriman fjords, and stops in Ketchikan, Juneau, Sitka, Hubbard Glacier, and Valdez. *Noordam* northbound departures: 5/14, 5/28, 6/11, 6/25, 7/9, 7/23, 8/6, 8/20, 9/3. *Noordam* southbound departures: 5/21, 6/4, 6/18, 7/2, 7/16, 7/30, 8/13, 8/27, 9/10. Cruise only, $1,330–$4,050 per person, double occupancy. Early-booking discounts of 25% and discounts for third and fourth passengers are available. Solo passengers pay 150%–190% of the per-person double-occupancy rate.

Launched in 1983 and 1984 respectively, the *Nieuw Amsterdam* and the *Noordam* are identical other than their collection of decorative art and antiques, their differing names, and the color schemes of their public rooms. The *Nieuw Amsterdam* follows a Dutch seafaring theme while the *Noordam* features an antique Oriental theme. Equipped with more spacious public areas and bigger gyms than the *Rotterdam* (though overall these ships are smaller in tonnage), window-encased dining rooms located on higher decks designed for sea views, forward view lounges on the top floor, and expanded cafés with double buffet lines, these twins fall mid-range in the Holland America line in terms of price and style (they're not quite as fancy as the newer vessels reviewed below). Seating configurations in their bilevel entertainment lounges could be better for viewing the fine productions staged there, but shows and lectures are also broadcast on stateroom TVs, eliminating the need to show up early for the best seat in the house. Photo displays set up at the entrance of the Lido café on the *Nieuw Amsterdam* and *Noordam* tend to clog traffic at mealtimes.

Both ships were refurbished in stages during 1994 and 1995, updating colors of carpets and upholstery to soothing jewel tones. Inside cabins, which are about average in size and storage space, tend toward cool teal color schemes while outside cabins feature terra-cottas or deep blues. Cabins on the upper four decks feature rectangular view windows (though many on the Navigation Deck have obstructed views) and twin beds that can be pushed together to form one bed. Those on lower decks have portholes and twin beds in a fixed L configuration; you may also notice engine vibrations more on these lower decks. My favorite cabins (100 to 103) are actually the four handicapped-accessible rooms overlooking the bow of the ship; they're very spacious, have picture windows framing the broadest views, and are available to anyone when not booked by handicapped passengers. All cabins are well laid out and provide ample storage area, multichannel music, TVs, telephones, individual climate control, lockable drawers, and tiled bathrooms with deep tubs (showers only in the lower price categories).

The Bottom Line: Both these ships are very comfortable, and while they're more modern and feature larger public areas and newer facilities, they also cater to 100 or so more people than does the *Rotterdam*. The crowd is younger overall, so either the *Nieuw Amsterdam* or the *Noordam* would be a fine choice for families with children. Neither is as glamorous as the newer ships reviewed below, though.

✪ MS *Ryndam* and MS *Statendam*. Passenger capacity: 1,300. Crew compliment: 586. 485 outside cabins (129 with a veranda) and 148 inside cabins. Ship facilities: dining room, café with an ice-cream bar, six bars, entertainment lounge, casino, disco, spa and salon, aerobics room, gym, two pools (one with retractable roof), two whirlpools, men's and women's saunas and steam rooms, library, card room, children's activity center with video arcade, deck sports (shuffleboard, ping-pong, tennis courts), shore-excursion desk, duty-free shops, photo service, coin laundries, medical facility. Activities: extensive onboard activities. Itineraries: *Statendam,* seven-day Glacier Bay Inside Passage cruises from Vancouver (B.C.), with stops in Ketchikan, Juneau, Sitka, and Glacier Bay. Departures: 5/13 (5/8 or 5/10 for a 10- or 12-day cruise beginning in San Diego or San Francisco), 5/20, 5/27, 6/3, 6/10, 6/17, 6/24, 7/1, 7/8, 7/15, 7/22, 7/29, 8/5, 8/12, 8/19, 8/26, 9/2, 9/9, 9/16, 9/23 (continuing from Vancouver to San Francisco or San Diego). Cruise only, $1,530–$6,950 (from $1,859 from/to San Francisco and from $2,079 from/to San Diego) per person, double occupancy. *Ryndam,* seven-day Glacier Discovery cruises between Vancouver (B.C.) and Seward, with visits to College and Harriman fjords, and stops at Ketchikan, Juneau, Sitka, Hubbard Glacier, and Valdez. Northbound departures: 5/12, 5/26, 6/9, 6/23, 7/7, 7/21, 8/4, 8/18, 9/1, 9/15. Southbound departures: 5/19, 6/2, 6/16, 6/30, 7/14, 7/28, 8/11, 8/25, 9/8, 9/22. Cruise only, $1,580–$7,000 per person, double occupancy. Early booking discounts of 25% and discounts for third and fourth passengers are available. Solo passengers pay 150%–190% of the per-person double-occupancy rate.

Two of a set of quadruplets, the *Statendam* and the *Ryndam*, introduced in 1993 and 1994 respectively, are glitzier than their older sibling ships, especially in their soaring grand atriums and their view lounges-cum-discos. Copious use of glass, high ceilings, shining metal trim, and lighter colors brighten them and make them feel more open and modern than the *Noordam* and *Nieuw Amsterdam* (but then, at almost twice the tonnage, their public areas are bound to feel much larger). They also feature bigger, better designs in their show lounges, more elegant two-story dining rooms with walls of glass, and better traffic flow through in their Lido buffets. The ships vary only slightly in their decor, sports facilities, and collection of antiques showcased; the *Statendam* feels a bit more formal and has a cushioned running track in place of sports courts, while the *Ryndam* feels slightly homier and has practice tennis courts.

These lovely vessels also feature large penthouses and a number of plush suites and deluxe staterooms with verandas not found on Holland America's older vessels. Extras like minibars, refrigerators, VCRs, whirlpool baths and showers, sitting areas, and floor-to-ceiling windows are available in these upper-level categories. Standard cabins are comparable in design and amenities to those on the *Nieuw Amsterdam* and the *Noordam*, but every room has the added convenience of configurations that allow the twin beds to be pushed together to form one double bed (even in the smallest inside cabins, which manage not to feel too confining). Another plus is that every outside cabin is equipped with a bathtub (shower only, in the inside cabins).

The Bottom Line: Of Holland America's numerous ships sailing in Alaska, these are the most inviting and technologically advanced. Prior to the introduction of the *Veendam* in late 1995 (which won't sail in Alaska in 1996), these, along with sibling ship *Maasdam* (also sailing elsewhere in the world) were Holland America's most glamorous offerings. The addition of escalators, a coffee bar, a juice bar in the gym, and a retractable dome over one of the pools are improvements in design.

NORWEGIAN CRUISE LINE

95 Merrick Way, Coral Gables, FL 33134. ☎ **305/447-9660** or 800/327-9020. Fax 305/448-7936.

Founded in 1968 as Norwegian Caribbean Line, NCL is now a division of Kloster Cruises Ltd., parent company of Royal Cruise Line (reviewed above). However, the sibling lines couldn't be more different than night and day. While RCL caters to the more mature, and often single, passenger, NCL concentrates on appealing to families and younger, more active passengers. This line is an innovator in many areas. It's the first I've run across that offers designated no-smoking rooms (fully half of all cabins aboard). It's also the first to introduce full-scale Broadway productions (such as *George M.!*, *Dreamgirls*, and *The Pirates of Penzance*) as part of its entertainment roster. Another point that sets NCL apart is its intriguing selection of soft-adventure shore excursions (including hiking, biking, kayaking, scuba diving for certified divers, and wet-suit snorkeling) in addition to all the popular standards. At press time, NCL was operating only one ship, the *Windward*, in Alaska.

✪ **MS Windward.** Passenger capacity: 1,300. Crew compliment: 520. 529 outside cabins (48 with a veranda) and 92 inside cabins. Ship facilities: three main dining rooms, specialty bistro, sports bar with a snack counter, casino, six bars/lounges, show lounge, observation lounge/disco, fitness center with aerobics room, small gym, men's and women's saunas and steam rooms, two heated pools, two whirlpools, terraced sundeck, basketball/volleyball court, shuffleboard, ping-pong room, golf driving cage, jogging track, library/card room, shore-excursion desk, duty-free and photo shops, tuxedo rentals, onboard cruise consultant, medical facility. Activities: Alaskan lecturer, wine tastings, art auctions, trap shooting, cooking demonstrations, craft and dance classes, incentive fitness program, daily quizzes, board games, lotto, and Bingo among other activities. Itineraries: Seven-day Glacier Bay cruises (focusing on—what else—Glacier Bay) and Misty Fjord cruises (visiting Sawyer Glacier and Misty Fjord) from Vancouver, with stops at Skagway, Haines, Juneau, and Ketchikan. Glacier Bay departures: 5/6, 5/13, 5/20, 5/27, 6/3, 6/24, 7/1, 7/15, 7/22, 8/12, 8/26, 9/2, 9/9. Misty Fjords departures: 6/10, 6/17, 7/8, 7/29, 8/5, 8/19. Cruise only, $1,499–$2,959 per person, double occupancy. Early-booking discounts of 15%, and third- and fourth-person discounts are available. Solo passengers pay 150%–200% of the per-person double-occupancy rate.

Making its maiden voyage in June 1993, the shiny new *Windward* is unique in many ways. It's a very family-friendly vessel: There's at least one full-time youth-activity coordinator, a kid's activity room, a television lounge with video games, the all-important ice-cream bar, and guaranteed babysitting aboard (note, however, that kids under 16 aren't allowed in the fitness center, nor those under 18 in the casino or disco). It's also well equipped for the sports-minded and active vacationer—in addition to a small aerobics room and a gym packed with weights and other fitness equipment, there are two heated pools, an unobtructed rubberized jogging/walking track, a sports bar with walls of TV screens showing ESPN, and a good selection of sports facilities (listed above). Miles of glass bring the outside in on this ship, and there are plenty of view lounges for relaxation. Windscreens wrap around the sports deck, protecting it and the terraced pool deck, so these areas remain warm even when you're cruising next to glaciers.

Dining is a treat on the *Windward;* instead of one or two mega dining rooms there are three more intimate dining rooms and a romantic specialty bistro when you're ready for a change of pace. Request a table in The Terraces or Sun Terrace for panoramic sea views. Dinners follow a theme (Viking, Northern Lights, Klondike, International, etc.) as do the extravagant late-night buffets (don't miss the unique "Galley Raid" for a chance to meet the chefs and watch ice carving and cooking demonstrations as you pass through the galley piling your plate high).

Cabins, done in cheery peaches and teals, are fairly standard in size (averaging 160 square feet) and vary little other than in the style of window in the different categories. About 85% of the cabins are outside, and most have picture windows. Suites have floor-to-ceiling windows, and a number of them have private balconies. All are equipped with multichannel TVs, telephones, small dressing tables, soundproofed doors, individual climate control, and sitting areas that are actually big enough to stretch out in to watch TV or enjoy a meal (room service is available around the clock, from a menu of soups, salads, sandwiches, and sweets). Closet and drawer space is quite limited, so pack light. There's no guest laundry aboard, but valet laundry service is available. There's no need to pack a hairdryer because you'll find one built-in on the wall of the tight bathroom (a nice touch, but it fails to make up for the total lack of cabinets and shelf space for toiletries).

The Bottom Line: Entertainment and dining are fun on this ship, and receive rave reviews consistently. The ratio of crew to passengers is not quite as strong as on a few other lines (around 2^1/$_2$ to 1), but service is still good and the international crew and Norwegian officers are geniunely friendly. Shipwide announcements are fairly frequent—noisesome to some, helpful to others. A youth-activities program is available at all times regardless of the number of children aboard, so it's a great line for families. While other lines have dropped trap shooting for environmental concerns (anything that ends up in the ocean is a pollutant), the *Windward* still offers this classic cruise activity.

MEGASHIPS

More like floating cities than ships, these vessels are enormous, weighing in at 60,000 or more gross tons and housing 1,400 to 2,200 passengers. They are also outfitted with loads of fun facilities and lots of extras smaller ships just don't have room for.

PRINCESS CRUISES

10100 Santa Monica Blvd., Los Angeles, CA 90067-4189. ☎ **310/553-1770** or 800/421-0522. Fax 310/284-2857.

What started as a one-ship company cruising Alaska and the Mexican Riviera in 1965 has steadily grown to be ranked among the largest cruise lines in the world. The selection of two Princess ships for "The Love Boat" television series in 1975 not only popularized cruising as a romantic, all-inclusive vacation option, but catapulted this company to the forefront, and it continues to build and upgrade its fleet to keep up with growing demand. A billion-dollar expansion will see the introduction of the 77,000-ton super-ship *Sun Princess* making its inaugural cruise in December 1995; it promises to be the largest and most innovative cruise ship afloat for a time. The *Sun* will be joining the *Crown, Golden, Regal, Sky,* and *Star Princesses* in 1996 on Alaskan itineraries ranging from 7 to 12 days. The *Crown Princess, Regal Princess,* and *Star Princess* are reviewed below; other ships will be reviewed in coming editions.

Princess works hard to maintain its "Love Boat" reputation through all this growth, responding well to passenger suggestions by banning smoking in the main dining and show areas, adding children's activities and youth counselors, putting terry-cloth robes and fruit baskets in every cabin, and even a heart-shaped chocolate placed on the pillow at night. These are highly popular, fun cruises on a mass-market level, which means that the line can afford to present elaborate Broadway-style shows (one of its strongest points), hire top entertainers, showcase bountiful buffets, adorn its ships with loads of interesting art and fresh flower arrangements, and provide quality Italian-influenced cuisine.

As one of the pioneers in Alaska, it has also built the largest land-tour operation and offers an array of shore excursions and land-cruise tours rivaled only by Holland America / Westours, so your choices with this line are extensive. These outstanding excursions are really the only way you'll see much Alaskan wildlife since the focus on board is on the cruise experience; a naturalist does lecture on whales and such during the cruise, but the ships don't typically go in search of wildlife (unless it's of personal interest to the captain), so you'll be on your own to spot things from the high decks.

MV *Crown Princess* and MV *Regal Princess*. Passenger capacity: 1,590. Crew compliment: 696. 618 outside cabins (184 with a balconette) and 177 inside cabins. Ship facilities: Enormous bilevel dining room, café, pizzeria, pâtisserie, wine and caviar bar, disco, casino/observation lounge, six bars/lounges, tiered show theater with balcony, movie theater, aerobics room, gym, salon with men's and women's saunas and steam rooms, two pools (one heated), four whirlpools, basketball/volleyball court, shuffleboard, ping-pong, jogging track, library, card room, shore-excursion desk, duty-free and photo shops, coin laundries, medical facility. Activities: life-enhancement and naturalist lectures, language lessons, cooking demonstrations, galley and bridge tours, craft and dance classes, incentive fitness program, passenger talent show, daily quizzes, board games, Bingo, and horse racing, among other activities. Itineraries: Seven-day cruises between Seward and Vancouver (B.C.), with cruising days in College Fjord, Glacier Bay, and the Inside Passage, and stops in Skagway, Juneau, and Ketchikan. Departures (northbound *and* southbound—the two ships depart the same day headed in opposite directions): 5/11, 5/18, 5/25, 6/1, 6/8, 6/15, 6/22, 6/29, 7/6, 7/13, 7/20, 7/27, 8/3, 8/10, 8/17, 8/24, 8/31, 9/7, 9/14. Cruise only, $1,549–$4,549 per person, double occupancy. Early-booking discounts can bring fares down by $550–$750 per person, and third- and fourth-passenger discounts are 50%. Solo passengers pay 160%–200% of the per-person double-occupancy rate.

The *Crown Princess* and the *Regal Princess,* designed by an Italian architect and introduced in 1991 and 1992 respectively, are dramatic in appearance because of their aqualinear, almost dolphinlike appearance of sweeping exterior lines and graceful curves. They are essentially identical in personality and in their sleek, modern decor, though the *Crown* tends to feel somewhat more formal than the *Regal* because of its interior color schemes and art collection. Catering to the whims of up to 1,600 passengers a week, these are super-ships (among the largest afloat in Alaska) equipped with virtually every facility you can imagine. One of their best features is the large number of dining and entertainment areas to choose from, ensuring something to please virtually anyone's taste in cuisine and music. Their massive size does mean miles of corridors and 14 decks, all of which take time to explore; expect to get turned around the first few days. A good portion of the space on these ships is alloted to expansive public areas and more facilities than you can sample thoroughly in one week.

Cabins, which are 190 to 210 square feet in the standard category (spacious as cabins on megaliners go), are well laid out, and attractively decorated in light colors and cherry-stained furniture; many feature glass doors that open onto narrow balconettes (a Princess trademark), and those that don't are outfitted with picture windows. All have multichannel color TVs, telephones, safes, minirefrigerators, and twin beds that convert to a double bed. A walk-in closet/dressing area in the hallway leading to the tight bathroom features floor-to-ceiling drawers, but there's no door on the hanging section (I got very tired of looking at my wardrobe). Four of the ships' 10 handicapped-accessible cabins (nos. 101, 102, 104, and 106) are situated near the disco, but triple doors in the hallway suffice to block the night noise.

The Bottom Line: The charming Italian officers and hardworking international crew are pros at providing individualized attention, an amazing feat considering the number of passengers they deal with week in and week out. And the mass-produced meals are pretty good, also amazing since the chefs and galley crew turn out around 9,600 meals each day (this doesn't include the daily meals they prepare for the large crew). These twins lack a formal children's area found on other Princess vessels, but a full activities program is available when there are at least 15 youngsters onboard. *A warning:* The water temperature fluctuates dramatically, so set the shower a little cooler than normal, and prepare yourself for the shock of marine toilets that sound like rockets blasting.

✪ **MV** *Star Princess.* Passenger capacity: 1,490. Crew compliment: 600. 510 outside cabins (50 with a balconette) and 165 inside cabin. Ship facilities: bilevel dining room, café, pizzeria, pâtisserie, wine and caviar bar, disco/observation lounge, six bars/lounges, tiered show theater with balcony, aerobics room, gym, salon with men's and women's saunas and steam rooms, two pools (one heated), four whirlpools, large children and teen activity centers, children's pool, basketball/volleyball court, shuffleboard, ping-pong, jogging track, library, card room, movie theater, shore-excursion desk, duty-free and photo shops, coin laundries, medical facility. Activities: extensive—life-enhancement and naturalist lectures, cooking demonstrations, galley and bridge tours, craft and dance classes, incentive fitness program, passenger talent show, daily quizzes, board games, Bingo, and horse racing, among other activities. Itineraries: Seven-day cruises between Seward and Vancouver (B.C.), with cruising days in College Fjord, Glacier Bay, and the Inside Passage, and stops in Skagway, Juneau, and Ketchikan. Northbound departures: 5/13, 5/27, 6/10, 6/24, 7/8, 7/22, 8/5, 8/19, 9/2. Southbound departures: 5/20, 6/3, 6/17, 7/1, 7/15, 7/29, 8/12, 8/26, 9/9. Cruise only, $1,449–$4,449 per person, double occupancy. Early-booking discounts are available, as well as 50% discounts for third and fourth passengers. Solo passengers pay 160%–200% of the per-person double-occupancy rate.

At 63,500 gross tons, the *Star Princess,* christened by actress Audrey Hepburn in March 1989, is slightly smaller than the *Crown* and the *Regal* (each weighing in at a whopping 70,000 tons) and carries just 100 fewer passengers. It's similar to its younger siblings in many respects—a million-dollar collection of contemporary art adorning public areas, a three-story central atrium surrounded by boutiques and specialty bars, a huge bilevel theater showcasing Princess's outstanding shows, the same fun pizzeria and specialty bar on an upper deck where you'll also find the whirlpools, heated swimming pools, and a swim-up bar—but there are a few minor differences. I found the *Star*'s forward observation lounge/disco, aptly named "Windows on the World" because of the panoramic view found there, more inviting than the cavernous casino/observation/dancing lounge on the *Crown* and the *Regal.* The atrium, however, seemed darker, almost foreboding, unlike the brightly lit bilevel fitness center which appears larger than its counterparts on the *Crown* and the *Regal.*

While a good percentage of cabins on the *Crown* and *Regal* have little balconies, only a few in the suite category do aboard the *Star.* Otherwise, standard cabins are almost exactly the same in generous size, overall layout, and in-room amenities as on the bigger twins (see the review above for details). Tubs are found in suite categories only; all other cabins feature showers. Lower twin beds can be put together to make one bed in all but a few cabins; some also have upper berths to accommodate third and fourth passengers. My favorites were Cabins 103 to 105 on Baja Deck because of their foreward location and view. However, I'd recommend booking a cabin near the middle of the ship to avoid walking extra miles of corridor.

The Bottom Line: When it comes down to it, the primary reason to pick the *Star* over the *Crown* or *Regal* (or vice versa, for that matter) would be that its departure dates better fit your schedule. The *Star* is equally luxurious and comfortable, and the differences between the ships so minor as not to matter much. The bonus of extensive youth facilities and a staffed nursery does make the *Star* a better option for families, though.

ROYAL CARIBBEAN CRUISES LTD.

1050 Caribbean Way, Miami, FL 33132. ☎ **305/379-4731** or 800/327-6700.

A pioneer in modern cruise vacationing since its inception in 1969, Royal Caribbean Cruises has grown to become one of the largest cruise lines in the world, operating nine ships on 60 itineraries calling at more than 150 ports on five continents. The line has set many standards for the industry as a whole; it was the first to build a ship designed specifically for warm-water cruising in the Caribbean, first to introduce air/sea inclusive packages, first to introduce view lounges perched on the highest deck, first to add an incentive-based fitness program to its roster of activities, and first to build a "megaship" (as the massive *Sovereign of the Seas* was dubbed by journalists when it was introduced in 1988). It continues to set trends in cruising, both in design innovation and introduction of improved passenger services and itineraries.

The *Legend of the Seas* is the first of six megaships to be launched in the next few years, increasing overall capacity for RCCL to almost 25,000 berths by 1998. Even through this tremendous growth spurt, the line deftly maintains its well-deserved reputation for excellence in service, entertainment, cuisine, and family fun throughout the fleet. If the *Legend* (reviewed below) is fully booked, consider passage on RCCL's *Song of Norway,* cruising in Alaska in 1996 on 10- and 12-day itineraries.

✪ **MS *Legend of the Seas*.** Passenger capacity: 1,804. Crew compliment: 720. 575 outside cabins (231 with a balcony) and 327 inside cabins. Ship facilities: dining room, café, snack bar, espresso bar, six bars/lounges, champagne and caviar bar, entertainment theater, disco, casino, conference center, extensive spa and salon, aerobics room, weight room, two pools (one inside with a retractable roof), four whirlpools, men's and women's saunas and steam rooms, observatory, cushioned jogging track, putting course, shuffleboard, ping-pong, library, card room, children's activitiy room, video-games room, teen center/disco, duty-free shops, photo services, tuxedo rental, medical facility. Activities: Incentive-fueled fitness program; dance and gaming classes; health, beauty, and cooking demonstrations; lecture series; art auctions; and organized games and sports; among other activities. Itineraries: Seven-day round-trip voyages from Vancouver (B.C.) cruise Yakutat Bay/Hubbard Glacier and Misty Fjord, and stop in Skagway, Haines, Juneau, and Ketchikan. Departures: every Sunday 5/12 to 9/8. Cruise only, $1,599–$5,749 per person, double occupancy. Early-booking discounts of up to 30%, and third- and fourth-passenger discounts, are available. Solo passengers pay 150% of the per-person double-occupancy rate.

The sparkling new *Legend of the Seas*, launched in early 1995 at a cost of approximately $360 million, is elegant down to the last well-planned detail, from the $4-million art collection decorating the interior to the wide array of onboard facilities. Plenty of nice touches—a sumptuous spa with lots of health and beauty treatments; loads of fine shopping, dining, and entertainment options; luxurious appointments such as triple sheeting on every bed (all of which convert to a double-bed configuration in every cabin)—give the *Legend* the feel of a top-flight shore-based resort.

This megaship soars 10 stories above the waterline and features a 7-story glass-walled atrium at its heart with glass elevators and winding brass-trimmed staircases providing access to the various levels. At the peak is the Viking Crown, RCCL's signature lounge and the highest bar afloat, affording a 360° view of the passing scenery. You'll also appreciate the view through the glass walls of the bilevel dining room. Actually, other than in the windowless casino and show lounge, there are great views to be found virtually everywhere on this ship.

Glass windbreaks shelter an observatory (complete with stargazing equipment), cushioned jogging and walking tracks, a fancy 18-hole miniature putting course (the only course at sea to date; a minimal fee is charged), and a pool bar, whirlpools, and outdoor swimming pool. A crystal-roofed solarium, decked out as a luxurious Roman bath, features statues and fountains around the heated pool and whirlpools and an extensive fitness center, salon, and spa (a broad assortment of body therapies is available). A teen disco, a playroom, and a video arcade provide plenty to keep the kids happily occupied while you relax, gamble, attend one of the many activities (there are around 200 to select from each week, including informative nature lectures), or dance the night away in one of numerous lounges and bars. The ship employs four youth counselors to organize children's activities for 5- to 17-year-olds—so many activities, in fact, that the kids get their own daily program delivered to their cabin.

Five executive chefs and a galley crew of 75 work around the clock, turning out up to nine meals a day, so it's a safe bet you'll never get hungry or fail to find something that appeals to those taste buds. The cuisine is primarily continental with a strong Italian influence (plenty of pastas and tangy herb sauces); fresh Alaskan products are a highlight, and the dinner menu always presents a vegetarian selection and a detailed breakdown of fat and calorie content on lowfat recommendations. Meals are served in several dining areas, so there's loads of freedom as to when you dine and choice as to what you'll eat. Lighter fare is served at breakfast, lunch, teatime, and dinner in the solarium (an unusual and convenient bonus—on most ships you must either go to the dining room or order room service for dinner). Room service is, of course, available at any hour and the menu is fairly extensive.

Cabins are well proportioned and extremely quiet (other than a few located forward on Deck 6 above an entertainment lounge). They have ample storage space, well-lit bathrooms of moderate size, TVs with plenty of movie, news, and information channels (several of the shows, and excursion and disembarkation talks, are rebroadcast in-room just in case you missed something). All outside cabins on Decks 7 and 8 (and a few aft on Deck 6) have balconies and can sleep up to four quite comfortably. Of those, the best are located across the back of the ship; these are considered deluxe because they're larger, feature balconies broad enough for sunbathing, and have upgraded amenities (bathrobes, better toiletries, bigger TVs, and a minirefrigerator).

The Bottom Line: The *Legend* is an enormous vessel that, surprisingly, manages not to feel overwhelmingly crowded. Entertainment productions featured in the exceedingly comfortable show lounge are lavish and very well done. Hands down, this ship hosts the best spa afloat in Alaskan waters. The quality of the youth programs and kids-only facilities and the fact that there seem to be many more children on this than on other ships sailing in Alaska makes the *Legend* my top choice for families. However, high passenger capacity means that embarkation/disembarkation procedures and booking shore excursions are tedious at best. There are no gentlemen hosts aboard, but gallant officers are sometimes on hand in the disco after hours to dance or chat with single female passengers.

LUXURY SHIPS

High-dollar cruising is still in style, and there are several lines meeting the demands of discerning travelers in this field. These are floating five-star resorts, equipped with every shoreside amenity you could want for the complete luxury vacation and a large enough crew to ensure personalized service and attention. **Seabourn Cruise Line** (☎ 415/391-7444) will be joining the ranks cruising Alaska in 1996; their Seabourn *Pride* definitely falls within the luxury category.

CRYSTAL CRUISES

2121 Ave. of the Stars, Suite 200, Los Angeles, CA 90067. ☎ **310/785-9300.** Fax 310/785-0011.

Established in 1988, Los Angeles–based Crystal Cruises may be the new kid on the block when it comes to cruising, but the company is already setting new standards in the industry. Its goal was to redefine luxury cruising, and it has accomplished this with flying colors. The deep pockets of Japanese parent company NYK Line (the largest shipping line in the world) allowed American-managed Crystal Cruises to build two incredible vessels, the $200-million *Crystal Harmony* and the $250-million *Crystal Symphony,* with exacting attention to detail, furnishing the ships with the finest of everything to provide first-class service to a discerning clientele.

In addition to being among the most technologically advanced ships afloat, Crystal's vessels feature the highest ratio of staterooms and penthouses with verandas, two specialty restaurants for alternative dining, the largest (and only) Caesars Palace at Sea casinos, true concierge service available to all passengers, a business center (for vacationers who can't let go of the outside world), and a library (stocked with an extensive collection of books, audio tapes, and videos).

This line spares no expense, from sumptuous flower arrangements to the very best in linens, crystal, china, and silver service. Guests sleep on down pillows under soft European duvets, step off the bed onto linen mats, nap wrapped in mohair blankets, and wander about in thick terry robes. A cadre of European chefs produce incredible gourmet fare, always fresh, utilizing the best ingredients, and as pleasing to the eye as to the palate. You'll find no rotating menus here, and with around 25,000 bottles in the cellar, there's sure to be a wine to complement every meal.

Even Crystal's onboard activities are tonier, with current hit movies, golf and bridge clinics, art auctions, wine tastings, and classes in needlepoint, calligraphy, aerobics, and ballroom dance. The enrichment lecture series is also a cut above, featuring such notables as Wolfgang Puck, Jacques Pepin, Pierre Salinger, Judith Krantz, and Caspar Weinberger in addition to local lecturers (from teachers and librarians to historians and anthropologists) aboard to broaden your knowledge of Alaska. Crystal sees to it that gentlemen hosts are available to entertain single female passengers, and they provide a cruise consultant on every sailing to help guests select future Crystal itineraries (which are deeply discounted when booked aboard the ship).

✪ *Crystal Harmony* **and** *Crystal Symphony*. Passenger capacity: 960. Crew compliment: 545. *Crystal Harmony:* 480 outside cabins (260 with a veranda) and 19 inside cabins. *Crystal Symphony:* 480 cabins, all outside (342 with a veranda). Ship facilities: dining room, café, two specialty restaurants, pâtisserie, snack bar, ice-cream bar, four bars, two entertainment lounges, casino, disco, spa and salon, two pools (one with a retractable cover), two whirlpools, basketball/paddle-tennis court, enclosed golf driving net, men's and women's saunas and steam rooms, library, card room, movie theater, shore-excursion desk, duty-free and photo shops, complimentary laundry facilities, medical facility. Activities: enrichment lecture series, craft and dance classes, demonstrations, shuffleboard, ping-pong, and board games, among other activities. Itineraries: Seven-day round-trip cruises from Vancouver (B.C.), stopping at Juneau, Skagway, Haines, Glacier Bay, Ketchikan, and Misty Fjords. Departures: 5/12 (5/6 for a 13-day cruise beginning in Los Angeles), 5/19. Cruise only, $1,999–$8,199 per person, double occupancy ($3,499–$14,306 for the 13-day cruise from Los Angeles). Later in the season, 10- and 11-day cruises between Vancouver (B.C.) and Anchorage, cruising in Tracy Arm, College Fjord, and Yakutat Bay, and stopping at Juneau, Skagway, Haines, Glacier Bay, Ketchikan, Misty Fjords, Sitka, Wrangell, Valdez, Homer, and Seward. Northbound departures (11 days): 5/26, 6/16, 7/7, 7/28, 8/18; cruise only, $3,199–$13,609 per person, double occupancy. Southbound departures (10 days): 6/6, 6/27, 7/18, 8/8; cruise only, $2,899–$12,407 per person, double occupancy. Some single cabins are available, and standard cabins are offered to solo passengers at 115% of the per-person double-occupancy rate. Early-booking discounts of 10%–17^1/$_2$% are available.

While they were constructed a few years apart (the *Harmony* made its debut in 1990, the *Symphony* in 1995), these vessels are virtual twins, with only minor differences in the size of public areas (the *Harmony* has slightly more interior public space; the *Symphony* has more exterior deck space) and placement of lounges and dining areas. Each features two specialty restaurants—Japanese and Italian on the *Harmony* and Chinese and Italian on the *Symphony*—in addition to an elegant tiered dining room, a café, a pâtisserie, a snack bar, and an ice-cream bar.

These vessels were built to pamper affluent travelers with demanding tastes. The plush staterooms were obviously well thought-out and are equipped with safes, minirefrigerators, telephones with voice mail, well-lit dressing tables, hydraulically lifted coffee/dining tables, plenty of drawer space, closet with automatic lighting, and remote-control multichannel TVs with videocassette players. And every piece of furniture is rounded, so there are no sharp corners to bump if the ship rocks. Bathrooms are long and narrow, but extremely functional, outfitted with double sinks, a deep oval tub with an adjustable shower head, a built-in hairdryer, a makeup mirror, and a telephone (on the *Harmony,* in penthouse suites only).

The few inside cabins available on the *Harmony* are only slightly smaller than the outside cabins, which average at least 200 square feet in size, and most have a veranda; those that don't have large picture windows. Penthouses on both ships are enormous (measuring between 360 and 982 square feet), pricey, and immensely popular (they always sell out first), perhaps because they're equipped with Jacuzzi bathtubs, bidets, and lots of other extras, perhaps because each is attended by a white-gloved butler who sees to every detail. This is not to say that the rest of the European hotel and dining staff are not as attentive, for they are, and somehow every passenger walks away feeling he or she received VIP treatment during the cruise.

The Bottom Line: This high-ticket line shines in many ways. For the price, passengers are treated to the ultimate in pampering service, luxurious accommodations, outstanding gourmet cuisine, the best casino afloat (the drinks are free for gamblers, as they are in any land-based Caesars establishment), and top-quality entertainment (from classical recitals to Broadway-worthy musical reviews). These ships are fast, so transit between ports is quick, allowing for more time in the ports of call. The kids' activity room is rather small on the *Harmony* (though spacious on the *Symphony*), and there's no supervised program unless there are enough children aboard to warrant it; however, both ships are family friendly (though children that misbehave among the typically well-to-do international passengers will stand out like a sore thumb). Shipwide announcements are kept to a minimum for the comfort of guests.

4 The Seafarer's Alaska

Below is a primer on the sights and places you'll encounter on your Alaskan voyage, presented as you'd find them along a south-to-north cruise itinerary beginning in British Columbia (as the majority of cruises do), and ending in Seward, in Southcentral Alaska (the primary northernmost terminus). Included are the major sights of natural and historical interest along the way and the ports of call, both large and small, visited by ships cruising in Alaska.

No one cruise hits every port, and not all travel south to north; skip around as needed. In each port-of-call section, I've listed a few of the top shore excursions available as well as what little advice on seeing the port on your own that space allows; the "On Your Own" sections highlight what's really important to cruise passengers on a short visit, but independent types should consult Chapter 7, "Southeast Alaska," for more information.

SHORE EXCURSIONS   Excursions, while expensive, are an essential part of the Alaska cruise experience. Try to budget for at least one flightseeing tour, an excursion that focuses on the wildlife of the area, and perhaps a fishing charter. These are essential for a well-rounded introduction to what Alaska has to offer.

City tours give an overview of the history, culture, and sights of interest and are a good way to get your feet wet before setting out on your own to explore and shop. Land-based tours in the major ports of call usually include a quick introduction to the town and some free time for shopping, in addition to whatever special focus the tour takes.

Alaskan port cities are small and easily explored on foot (other than a few outlying sights of interest), but if you skip the organized tours and strike forth on your own you'll miss the narrative on the area's history, much of which is flamboyantly colorful. If you can do without historical background, head for the visitor information center and pick up a walking tour map before heading out to explore the museums, galleries, and souvenir shops on your own.

Prices listed are an approximate range, and vary by ship (same tour, different charge, depending on the ship making your arrangements) for 1995 shore excursions; they may be up to 5% more expensive in 1996. The same tours are generally cheaper (up to 25% less) when made independently ashore, but the cruise-tour offices will tell you that they don't know the operators and cannot guarantee your satisfaction with these tours, nor can they guarantee that you'll be delivered back to the ship prior to departure time. Weather should also be a consideration; if flightseeing or boat tours are canceled because of inclement conditions, you'll receive a refund on those tours booked aboard ship, but you may not on tours booked independently, making the gamble yours to bear. Another consideration is that tours with limited capacity frequently sell out well before you reach port. You'll find operators on every pier selling a range of independent tours.

PORTS OF CALL & SIGHTS ALONG THE WAY
PORT OF CALL—VICTORIA

Cruises that start in Los Angeles, San Francisco, and Seattle typically stop first in Victoria on Vancouver Island on the way up to Alaska. High tea, flowering gardens, and Victorian architecture set the prim and proper tone for this, the capital of British Columbia. Most cruisers leave wishing they'd had a few days to explore.

Culture & History Tours

CITY TOUR WITH HIGH TEA OR CASTLE VISIT (2^1/$_2$–3 hours; $20–$30)   This guided excursion aboard a double-decker bus takes you by the major sights of the Inner Harbour, downtown, and residential areas; the variation comes in with either a stop at Craigdarroch Castle or for afternoon high tea.

CITY TOUR & BUTCHART GARDENS (3^1/$_2$–4 hours; $30–$40)   After an abbreviated tour of the sights in Victoria, the bus makes the 13-mile trip out the Saanich Peninsula to world-renowned Butchart Gardens in Brentwood Bay, where you'll have two hours or so to explore the 130-acre grounds.

Victoria on Your Own

Take the shuttle to the Inner Harbor, located about a mile from the pier. From the drop point next to the Empress, you'll find more than enough things to see and do, all within walking distance, to fill your day in Victoria.

Flower baskets, milling crowds, and street performers liven the scene at the **Inner Harbour** under the watchful eye of the grand ✪ **Empress Hotel** (famed setting for English-style high tea; call 604/384-8111 ahead of time for reservations and ask about the dress code) and the lovely **Parliament Buildings** (call 604/387-3046 for information on free tours). You can pick up a map of the city at the **Visitors Information Center,** on the waterfront at 812 Wharf St. (☎ 604/953-2033).

There are plenty of kitschy attractions on the harbor as well, but skip them in favor of the ✪ **Royal British Columbia Museum,** 675 Belleville St. (☎ 604/ 387-3014), one of this museum-lover's top picks in North America. Behind the museum is **Thunderbird Park** with Native totem poles and a ceremonial house. **Helmcken House,** 10 Elliot St. (☎ 604/361-0021), next to the park, is one of the oldest houses in British Columbia; it was the home of a pioneer doctor, and there are lots of torturous-looking medical tools to marvel over.

You'll have to take a cab to see **Craigdarroch Castle,** 1050 Joan Crescent (☎ 604/592-5323), the elaborate home of a millionaire coal-mining magnate. A cab ride and several free hours will be required for a visit to world-famous ✪ **Butchart Gardens,** 800 Benvenuto Ave. in Brentwood Bay (☎ 604/652-5256), 13 miles north of downtown Victoria, a 130-acre estate featuring English, Italian, Japanese, water, and rose gardens.

Government Street running north from the Inner Harbour holds sway with shoppers; it's lined with boutiques, curio shops, galleries, coffeehouses, and restaurants. Among the multitudes, my recommendations are **Beautiful B.C.,** 910 Government St. (☎ 604/384-7773), for art and souvenirs; **Hill's Indian Crafts,** 1008 Government St. (☎ 604/385-3911), for Native art; the **Irish Linen Store,** 1090 Government St. (☎ 604/383-6812), for fine linens and china; **Murchie's,** 1110 Government St. (☎ 604/383-3112), for packaged teas; and **Roger's Chocolates,** 913 Government St. (☎ 604/384-7021), for sweets.

PORT OF CALL—VANCOUVER

The majority of Alaska cruises are either week-long round-trips out of Vancouver, B.C., or seven-day one-way runs between Vancouver and Seward, Alaska. In either case, Vancouver is generally a transit point, and unless you're booked on a pre- or postcruise extension, you won't have much time for sightseeing. There are two piers used by the cruise ships in Vancouver: **Canada Place,** in the heart of downtown, within walking distance of several sights of interest, and **Ballantyne Pier,** set in an industrial section over a mile east of downtown.

Vancouver is electrifying, a city where you can find any type of cuisine, hear almost every language, and purchase goods shipped in from around the globe. There are literally hundreds of attractions here, but time is a factor, so I'll list only the top choices to hit (see "Vancouver on Your Own," below).

Culture & History Tours

CITY TOUR   (3 hours, $20–$30)   Very few lines offer a tour in Vancouver, but those that do use a motorcoach to drive you around pointing out the major sights, including Gastown (where Vancouver got its start), Chinatown (the second largest in North America), Stanley Park (1,000 verdant acres in the heart of the city), high-end residential areas, and Queen Elizabeth Park, where you'll stop to tour the Bloedell Conservatory. This tour generally ends at the Vancouver International Airport.

Vancouver on Your Own

With flights in or out on the day of embarkation/disembarkation, there's not really enough time to do a full-blown walking tour of Vancouver; sights tend to be a bit spread out anyway. However, here are the best areas to pick and choose from as your time allows. Expect to spend anywhere from one to three hours in each area, and keep transit time in mind when mapping out your plans in this port.

The cobblestone streets and historic buildings of ✪ **Gastown** are just blocks east of the pier at Canada Place, and if you only have a few hours, this is the area I recommend visiting. Gastown is the birthplace of Vancouver, established by "Gassy" Jack Deighton, who built a saloon here in 1867 to serve the loggers and trappers living in the area. His statue stands in Maple Tree Square at the intersection of Water, Alexander, and Carrall streets. A steam-powered clock is another draw here; you'll find it near the corner of Water and Cambie streets. There are also loads of boutiques, galleries, and bistros to explore in Gastown.

Vancouver has the second-largest **Chinatown** in North America; it stretches between Carrall, East Hastings, East Pender, and Gore streets. In addition to photogenic Chinese gates, bright-red buildings, and open-air markets, you'll find the amazing 6-foot-wide **Sam Kee Building,** at 8 W. Pender St., and the lovely ✪ **Dr. Sun Yat-sen Garden,** at 578 Carrall St. (☎ 604/689-7133), worth a look.

Within the confines of **Stanley Park,** 1,000 acres nestled in the heart of downtown Vancouver, are rose gardens, totem poles, a yacht club, a kids' water park, miles of wooded hiking trails, great vantage points for views of Lions Gate Bridge, and the outstanding ✪ **Vancouver Aquarium** (☎ 604/682-1118).

Nirvana for shopping fanatics, Vancouver features **Granville Island,** 15 minutes from downtown Vancouver across False Creek (☎ 604/666-5784), with its vibrant daily market and streets lined with fine-art studios; and **Robson Street,** chock-a-block with boutiques, souvenir shops, coffeehouses, and eateries, and miles of shops to suit every need in **Pacific Centre Mall** (it fills the city blocks between Robson, Dunsmuir, Howe, and Granville streets).

ALONG THE WAY: ALASKA-BOUND ON THE INSIDE PASSAGE

As the ship pulls out of Vancouver and rounds the bend headed north, so begins your voyage up the **Inside Passage,** the scenic, island-dotted waterway that stretches along the coastline of British Columbia and Southeast Alaska's panhandle. In all but a few areas the sailing is extremely smooth here because the waterway is protected from the pounding of the open ocean. The first section encountered after departing Vancouver is the **Strait of Georgia,** named by intrepid explorer Capt. George Vancouver in honor of George III. On the left is **Vancouver Island** (at 285 miles long and 80 miles wide, the largest island on the west coast), and on the right is British Columbia's **"Sunshine Coast,"** a string of tiny resort communities. Just past the mainland pulp-mill city of Powell River is **Desolation Sound,** a pristine wilderness area of islands and fjords accessible only by boat; a few of the smaller cruise vessels venture in.

You may notice the ship slowing at **Discovery Passage,** a narrow channel between Campbell River (world-famous for fishing tournaments) and Cape Mudge. **Seymour Narrows** is the tightest portion of the passage, with fierce tides that must be transited when slack for navigational safety, so all types of boats and ships creep along here waiting for slack tide, then zip across the narrows as quickly as traffic allows. The next area of great interest is ✪ **Johnstone Strait;** orcas (killer whales) abound here, so this is the very best location to go on deck and watch for their tall black dorsal fins and distinctive white saddle patches—an awesome sight beheld virtually every time I've been through.

Next, it's time to transit **Queen Charlotte Sound,** which, because there are no islands blocking it from the ocean, can at times be a rough crossing (take a pill well before reaching this point if you're susceptible to seasickness). The waterway narrows again at **Fitz Hugh Sound,** and it's along this passage that you'll pass **Bella Bella,** named for the Native Kwakiutl tribe that dwells there. This is one of the largest Indian villages on the west coast. **Prince Rupert** will be the final city you'll pass in British Columbia before crossing the international border near the Triple Islands (where the Alaskan pilot zips out to board the ship as it passes) and into the **Alexander Archipelago.** Welcome to Alaska!

On your right is the southern tip of ✪ **Misty Fjords National Monument Wilderness,** a 2.3-million-acre wilderness reserve and the southernmost point of Alaska. Named for the thick mists and fogs that shroud the place, giving it an air of mystery and intrigue, the area has a largely untouched coast frosted with evergreen forests that drop to meet glacialy carved bays, inlets, and coves. The area is home to bald eagles, pigeon guillemots, glaucous gulls, brown and black bears, wolves, mountain goats, beavers, river otters, and Sitka black-tailed deer, so wildlife spottings are frequent. No roads lead in, so the area remains largely pristine. Smaller ships like those run by Alaska Sightseeing / Cruise West enter and travel to the head of Rudyerd Bay, skimming past a glaucous gull rookery in Punchbowl Cove; several of the larger ships don't venture in here yet, though more are adding Misty Fjords to their itineraries every year.

Misty Fjords is just one small portion of the **Tongass National Forest,** 17 million acres that stretch from Yakutat to Ketchikan (encompassing most of the Alexander Archipelago). Tongass is the largest national forest in the United States, and like other national forests, is set aside for multiple use, meaning that tourism and recreation must coexist with mining and logging here. (See "The Tongass Battleground" in Chapter 7 for more information.) Mining isn't really evident at the shoreline, but the effects of logging are clearly visible as you cruise past large stands of old-growth timber next to clear-cut swathes, pulp mills that fuel a healthy chunk of Alaska's economy, and barges pulling broad rafts of felled logs. The clear-cut scars just above the shoreline are painful to look at, but for the most part the preserve continues to be a lush, inviting area to cruise through.

Those ships not visiting Misty Fjords usually cruise north up Nicholas Passage, with **Prince of Wales Island** on the port (left) side, before reaching **Revillagigedo Island** to stop in the port at Ketchikan; ships that do cruise Misty Fjords use the Revillagigedo Passage to reach the port city. (For more on Prince of Wales Island, see "A Side Trip to Prince of Wales Island," in the Ketchikan section of Chapter 7.)

PORT OF CALL—KETCHIKAN

Known as "Alaska's First City"—it's the first one encountered on the marine route north—Ketchikan is also called the "Salmon Capital of the World" because of the number of canneries based here. The largest totem pole collection in the world and a historic red-light district once provided the distinctive flavor for the city, but that flavor is quickly being overshadowed by commercialization—specifically, an influx of major duty-free chain stores such as Little Switzerland and Columbian Emeralds catering to cruise passengers (fishermen, backpackers, and other land-bound visitors don't normally visit these shops). Ketchikan is also the rain capital of Southeast Alaska (rainfall averages 156 inches per year), so carry an umbrella just in case.

Culture & History Tours

TOTEM BIGHT STATE HISTORICAL PARK TOUR (2¹/₂ hours; $25–$37) This tour takes you by bus through the Tongass National Forest to see the historic Native campsite where a ceremonial clan house and totem poles are set amid the rain forest. There's a fair amount of walking involved, making the tour a poor choice for anyone with mobility problems.

SAXMAN NATIVE VILLAGE TOUR (2¹/₂ hours; $40–$50) This modern-day Native village situated 3 miles outside Ketchikan is home to hundreds of Tlingit, Tsimshian, and Haida, and is a center for the revival of Native arts and culture. The tour includes either a Native legend or a performance by the Cape Fox dancers in the park theater and a guided walk through the grounds to see the totem poles and learn to read their stories. Craftsmen are sometimes on hand in the working sheds to demonstrate totem-pole carving.

The Alaskan Outdoors

MISTY FJORDS FLIGHTSEEING (1¹/₂–2 hours, $125–$180) Everyone gets a window seat aboard the Bush float planes that run these quick flightseeing jaunts over Misty Fjords National Monument to see the sparkling fjords, cascading waterfalls, thick forests, and rugged mountains dotted with wildlife before landing on a serene wilderness lake. This is one of the cheaper flightseeing tours in Alaska, but doesn't take in the tremendous icefields and glaciers of the state.

✪ **SPORT FISHING** (4–6 hours, $140–$160) If catching one of Alaska's famed salmon is your goal, Ketchikan is the most likely spot to do it on an Inside Passage itinerary. Chartered fishing boats come with tackle, bait, fishing gear, and crew to help you strike king and coho around the end of June or pink, chum, and silver from July through mid-September. Fishing licenses are an additional $10 and are sold on the boat; you may also need to purchase a king salmon tag at $10.

Ketchikan on Your Own

Most of the top sights in Ketchikan can be covered on foot, but you'll need to take a taxi to a few. For detailed descriptions, see "Exploring Ketchikan" in the Ketchikan section of Chapter 7.

Your first stop should be the **Ketchikan Visitor Information Center,** on the pier, to pick up a walking-tour map. Then continue heading south down the pier to the new green-roofed ✪ **Southeast Alaska Visitors Center,** at 50 Main St. (☎ **907/ 228-6220**), to see the interesting interpretive displays and watch the short film; it's a great introduction to the region.

Next, head up Mill Street to the triangular **Whale Park** for a look at the totem poles. There are more totem poles on Stedman Street at the rear of the park. Native heritage and local history are showcased in the **Tongass Historical Museum,** 629 Dock St. (☎ **907/225-5600**), which shares space with the library up the hill on the left.

On your left as you exit the museum is **Creek Street,** the former red-light district, built on pilings over the creek. Now the wood frames are filled with souvenir shops, cafés, and galleries. **Dolly's House Museum,** at 24 Creek St. (☎ **907/247-2452**), preserves the bawdier nature of the district.

To continue the walking tour, backtrack to the **Westmark Tramway.** For $1, this funicular whisks you from Creek Street up to the Cape Fox Westmark Inn, a great view spot overlooking Ketchikan. Pass through the lobby to see the fascinating group of totem poles at the hotel's entrance, then take the stairway leading down the steep hillside on your left to continue on. At the foot of the staircase is Venetia Avenue, which intersects with Park Avenue at the bottom of the hill. Turn right on Park Avenue and follow it through the quiet residential section until you cross the bridge over Ketchikan Creek. A sharp right immediately past the bridge will lead you to the **Deer Mountain Salmon Hatchery** in **City Park.** This hatchery currently releases hundreds of thousands of smolts (hatchling salmon) into local waters every year.

On the right past the hatchery is yet another bridge. This one leads to the door-way of the **Totem Heritage Center,** 601 Deermount St. (☎ **907/225-5900**), where aging Tlingit and Haida totem poles that would otherwise have been abandoned to the elements are preserved and displayed. Ask attendants to show you the two educational videos for a better understanding of this ancient art form. When you finish up here, either call for a cab back to the pier or walk down Deermont Street to the intersection at Stedman Street, turn right, and follow Stedman as it winds back to the waterfront (it's a 15- to 20-minute walk).

Ketchikan is brimming with galleries, souvenir outlets, and duty-free shops. **The Trading Post,** 201 Main St. (☎ **907/225-2349**), has a good selection of souvenir items and a better selection of Native crafts. Another option for Native carvings, prints, and basketry is **Hide-A-Way Gifts,** 18 Creek St. (☎ **907/225-8626**); you might even see a weaver or carver at work here. The better galleries in town are **Scanlon Gallery,** 318 Mission St. (☎ **907/247-4730**), for fine arts, and the **Soho Coho,** 5 Creek St. (☎ **907/225-5954**), for eclectic pieces. **Little Switzerland,** 328 Mission St. (☎ **907/225-5911**), is the leader of the duty-free pack; crystal, china, fragrances, leather goods, crafts, and jewelry are beautifully displayed here.

ALONG THE WAY: A FORK IN THE MARINE HIGHWAY

Clarence Strait is the route farther north. At the convergence with Sumner Strait, larger vessels typically head back out toward sea to wind past **Cape Decision** (the point where Capt. George Vancouver made the decision to turn back in 1793, leaving off his quest for the Inland Passage) and continue the voyage north up Chatham Sound bound for Sitka. A few of the smaller vessels, though, frequently turn inland here to visit the small fishing seaports of Wrangell and Petersburg for a taste of Alaskan towns that remain as yet largely untainted by mass tourism.

PORT OF CALL—WRANGELL

Wrangell began as a fortified Russian fur-trading post and was a jump-off point during the Klondike gold rush, but it's the area's strong Native history, seen in the ceremonial house surrounded by totem poles on Chief Shakes Island and the 8,000-year-old petrolyphs strewn on the beach, that stands out most clearly for visitors today. Much less visited than other ports of call, this town retains a relaxed, intimate atmosphere. Nobody ever seems to be in a hurry here—there's time to stop and give directions or chat about life in a small Alaskan town over a beer in the local saloon.

Culture & History Tours

WRANGELL CITY TOUR   (1½ hours, $20)   This quick tour is a fine introduction to this small island community. The tour guide will stop the bus at Petroglyph Beach to see the ancient rock carvings and on Chief Shakes Island to explore the tribal house and look at the totem poles before making a pass through downtown to drop you off at the museum or back at the ship.

The Alaskan Outdoors

STIKINE RIVER JETBOAT   (3–3½ hours, $130–$145)   Following the route of fur traders and prospectors of long ago, participants traverse open water, back sloughs, and clear tributaries to reach Shakes Lake where the maneuverable jet boat navigates amid icebergs that have fallen from Shakes Glacier at the head of the lake. Colorful alpine meadows, lichen-coated cliffs, and cascading waterfalls cry out to be photographed on this wilderness tour.

STIKINE RIVER / LECONTE GLACIER FLIGHTSEEING   (1¼ hours, $120) After transfering to Wrangell Airport and boarding a small land-based airplane, you'll be treated to a 45-minute flight up the Stikine River to the Alaska-Canada border before veering west to the Stikine Icefield to see LeConte Glacier, the southernmost glacier on the continent. Weather permitting, the pilot will descend toward the glacier face for a closer view of the iridescent blue crevasses before returning over Frederick Sound to the airport.

Wrangell on Your Own

At the end of the dock, take a sharp right and cut through the warehouse parking area, a short-cut to Outer Drive. First stop will be the **Information Center** in the A-frame next to the totem pole at the corner of Outer Drive and Lynch Street. Pick up a map there and continue on around Outer Drive to the intersection of Front Street. Hang a right again and follow the street across the footbridge to tiny ✪ **Chief Shakes Island** to see the many Tlingit totem poles surrounding a re-created clan house (which should be open for a guided tour since your ship is in town).

Backtrack on Front Street to Episcopal Avenue and turn right again to see another collection of totem poles at **Kiksadi Totem Park.** After a brief respite in the park, continue on up Episcopal Avenue to the intersection of Case Avenue, where you'll turn left this time. This avenue quickly becomes Church Street, where, at no. 318, you'll find the temporary quarters of the **Wrangell Museum** (☎ 907/874-3770). It's a typical small-town collection portraying the history and industry of Wrangell.

At this point, continue on down Church Street, which eventually becomes Second Street and finally winds around as McCormack Street before intersecting Evergreen Avenue at the ferry terminal. Turn right on Evergreen, and after a quarter mile or so you'll find **Our Collections Museum,** Evergreen Avenue (☎ 907/874-3646), on the left. Run by grandmotherly Elva Bigelow, this private museum showcases 60 years of family and town memorabilia, from old dolls, clothes, and kitchen gadgets to a model of the townsite as it appeared in the 1960s. Donations are welcomed.

After finishing up your chat with Mrs. Bigelow (and she does love to chat), continue north on Evergreen and watch for the path on the left leading down to **Petroglyph Beach,** named for the scattered rocks carved with ancient geometric and animal designs. For years visitors used to take rubbings of the rocks, but the practice is now discouraged since it wears away the images.

It's about a mile south down Evergreen Avenue to the dock. Now it's time to make your way back into town to return to the ship or browse the curio shops along Front Street (though I found none to really recommend, nor are there any particularly worthwhile restaurants).

PORT OF CALL—PETERSBURG

Across the channel on Mitkof Island is Petersburg, a hardworking community made up primarily of proud descendants of the town's Norwegian founders. The first image here is of its canneries perched on pilings and ringed on the water side by fishing vessels and private boats in a small harbor. Above the harbor, boardwalks and wooden bridges lead to the main street in town, and houses on pilings hang over a slough. There's no mistaking this for anything but a true Alaskan fishing seaport.

Culture & History Tours

LITTLE NORWAY (2 hours, $25)   The Norwegian heritage of Petersburg is the focus of this excursion, which takes in a performance by the Leikarring Dancers at the Sons of Norway Hall and a bus tour through the port area, downtown, the residential section, and the muskeg at the back of the village.

WATERFRONT WALK (1½ hours, $10)   A guide strolls you through Hammer Slough, Singh Lee Alley, the bustling port area (with a stop to see the workings of a seafood-processing plant), and downtown before ending the tour at Eagle's Roost Park to watch the eagles feeding and soaring over Frederick Sound.

The Alaskan Outdoors

LECONTE GLACIER FLIGHTSEEING (45 minutes, $105)   This quick trip by floatplane takes in the Stikine Icefield, the Coastal Mountains, and the ice-filled bay below the towering face of LeConte Glacier.

✪ **COMMERCIAL TRAWLING** (3 hours, $100)   This adventure aboard a gillnetter owned and operated by Syd and Vara Wright is a rare up-close view of what commercial fishing in Alaska is all about. Syd directs you on methods of trawling for shrimp, crab, and sole; then Vara takes over, preparing the catch for an all-you-can-eat feast aboard the boat. There are few better storytellers than Syd, and he won't take much coaxing. This is an absolute favorite, not-to-be-missed excursion.

Petersburg on Your Own

If you arrive in the late morning or early afternoon, you'll be fascinated by the sight of all manner of fishing vessels pulling into the harbors of Petersburg. Take a few minutes to watch the folks unloading salmon, halibut, shrimp, and an array of fishing gear for a glimpse of what life here revolves around.

Since **Hammer Slough,** to the south of the pier area, will likely be the first area to draw your attention ashore, we'll start there. Turn right at the end of the dock parking lot to walk along the boardwalk streets and see the old wood-frame houses that hang out over the slough. When you've snapped enough photos, backtrack from this point to the dock and keep heading straight past it on the boardwalk. You'll pass the **Sons of Norway Hall** (stop to notice the rose malling on the exterior, and check the performance schedule if you're interested in cutural dancing) and a working model of a Viking ship on your right as you make your way into town via **Singh Lee Alley,** which intersects Main Street (also known as Nordic Drive) downtown.

Turn left on Main Street and make your way past the seafood-processing plants along the waterfront. After a few blocks, turn right on Fram Street and stop in at the **visitor information center,** on the corner of Fram and First streets (☎ 907/ 772-3646), to pick up a map (though you probably won't need it to get your bearings in this tiny village). One more block up the hill is the **Clausen Memorial Museum,** at the corner of Fram and Second streets (☎ 907/772-3598), a small-town museum focusing on the Norwegian heritage and strong fishing tradition of this community.

Bop back down the hill to Main and turn left to continue on past canneries to ✪ **Eagle's Roost Park,** where you'll find both young and mature bald eagles perched in the trees or swooping down to scoop fish out of Wrangell Narrows. There's a grassy area and a few benches near the street, but the better spot to watch is down the winding wooden staircase on the rocky beach.

If you're ready to shop for Scandinavian mementos, head back down Main Street to **Diamante,** Main Street at Fram Street (☎ 907/772-4858), or the **Trading Union,** Main Street at Dolphin (☎ 907/772-3881), or stop by **Husfliden,** located in the loft of the Sons of Norway Hall, on the way back to the ship.

PORT OF CALL—SITKA

If your ship heads out to Chatham Strait instead of inland, it is bound for Sitka on Baranof Island. Once the capital of tsarist Russia in the New World, Sitka retains much of the influence of its original settlers (both Tlingit Natives and the Russians they battled against to retain control of this verdant island). The town is bounded by the Alaska Marine Highway and by towering mountain peaks. There's no pier facility here for large ships, so passengers on all but the smallest vessels must tender into the small-boat harbor in the heart of town.

Culture & History Tours

SITKA HISTORICAL & RAPTOR REHABILITATION CENTER TOUR

(3 hours, $40)   This bus excursion hits all the historic sights of this former "Russian capital," including St. Michael's Cathedral, the Russian Cemetery, Castle Hill, and Sitka's National Historic Park, before visiting the Raptor Rehabilitation Center where volunteers work to heal injured bald eagles and other raptors before returning them to the wild. The tour concludes with a performance of traditional Russian dances by the New Archangel Dancers at Centennial Hall downtown.

The Alaskan Outdoors

✪ **SEA OTTER & WILDLIFE QUEST**   (3 hours, $85–$95)   Board a comfortable excur;ion jet boat built specifically for wildlife viewing to make the 50-mile round-trip journey to Salisbury Sound. A naturalist accompanies you to point out the various animals you'll encounter—sea lions, harbor seals, porpoises, brown bears, Sitka black-tailed deer, eagles, puffins, sea otters, humpbacks, or orcas—and to explain the delicate balance of the marine ecosystem of the region. They're so sure you'll see a whale, bear, or otter that they offer a partial cash refund if you don't. This is another favorite of mine.

Sitka on Your Own

Since you'll probably arrive by tender at the visitor's dock in Crescent Harbor, our tour begins there. The building to the left of the dock is the **Centennial Building,** and it's there you'll find the **Sitka Convention and Visitor Bureau** and can pick up a map. The **Isabel Miller Museum** (☎ 907/747-6455), chronicling life in Sitka, is also housed in this building.

Head left down Harbor Drive in front of the Centenial Building. At the first intersection look to your right and you'll see **St. Michael's Cathedral,** a Russian Orthodox church, at 224 Lincoln St. Lincoln Street is lined with boutiques and galleries, but hold off until you've seen the sights so you won't be stuck carrying bags around all day. Continue west down Lincoln and you'll find the pathway to **Castle Hill** (where the famous transfer of Alaska from Russian to American hands took place) on the left; watch for the signs. **Totem Square,** with its Russian double-headed eagle-crested totem, sits across Katlian Avenue in front of the Pioneers Home.

Retrace your steps on Lincoln to Barracks Street and turn left to reach the old **Russian blockhouse** (it'll be on your left after you cross Seward Street) and the **Russian cemetery** (which will be on your right). When you've finished looking around there, turn left on Seward Street and follow it as it winds east to intersect Lake Street. Make a right here, then a left on Lincoln Street to reach the **Russian Bishop's House** (☎ 907/747-6281), one of the last vestiges of Russian occupation of the area.

Continue on east on Lincoln Street and you'll come to Sheldon Jackson College (James Michener stayed here when he wrote *Alaska*) and the intriguing **Sheldon Jackson Museum** (☎ 907/747-8981). Housed within the octagonal structure is a priceless collection of Native artifacts—other than the Smithsonian's, no other collection can match this one.

A few more blocks down Lincoln Street and you'll reach the ✪ **Sitka National Historical Park** (☎ 907/747-6281), where the Tlingit and Russian residents battled for control of the island; there are hiking trails lined with 15 incredible totem poles (some ancient, others replicas) and a fine interpretive center featuring displays of Native artifacts, films on the history of Sitka, and workshops where you can see demonstrations of Native weaving, carving, and silver etching.

Last stop in Sitka (whew!) is the ✪ **Raptor Rehabilitation Center,** Sawmill Creek Boulevard (☎ 907/747-8662), where bald eagles, owls, and other raptors are brought to be treated and recuperate after injuries before being released again into the wild. Just outside the park visitor center at the side of the upper parking lot is a footpath that leads over a bridge at Indian River and on to Saw Creek Road. Turn left at the road and follow the paved sidewalk to the unpaved driveway on the right which leads to the Raptor Center. I'm usually pooped at this point and call for a cab back to the dock, but it's possible to walk back; at the drive, turn right on Saw Creek, follow it to the junction of Lake Street where you'll turn left and continue on until it twists into Harbor Drive, and you've made it back to the dock.

You don't have to be on a tour to see fine dance performances at Centennial Hall. Whenever ships are in, traditional Russian dances are performed by the **New Archangel Dancers** several times a day. Two Native dance troupes, the **Gajaa Heen Dancers** and the **Noow Tlein Dancers,** also perform Native Tlingit dances and songs on a regular basis. A schedule of performances is posted in the Centennial Building; tickets are $6 for the Russian performance, $5 for the Native performance.

The **Bayview Trading Company,** 407 Lincoln St. (☎ 907/747-6228), has it all under one roof; the **Russian American Company** offers an array of arts and handcrafts from Russia, **MacDonald's Wharf** sells a selection of smoked salmon, and the **Goldsmith Gallery** features carved Native jewelry, Arctic opals, and natural gold nuggets in a variety of settings. The better galleries in Sitka are the **Artist Cove Gallery,** 241 Lincoln St. (☎ 907/747-6990), and **Impressions Gallery,** 239 Lincoln St. (☎ 907/747-5502); both showcase the works of Alaskan artists, both Native and non.

ALONG THE WAY: BEARS & GLACIERS

Frederick Sound at the foot of **Admiralty Island** (home of the Kootznoowoo Wilderness, an important brown bear refuge) is another marine-highway fork. Some ships cruise up Chatham Strait along the western shore of Admiralty Island on their way to Sitka. Many more, though, head up Stephens Passage on the eastern side of the island so that they can cruise into the **Tracy Arm–Fords Terror Wilderness.** Notice the geological changes as you proceed into the fjord, the lush vegetation dropping away to smooth rock as you near the twin North and South Sawyer glaciers at the head of Tracy Arm. Endicott Arm, another glacially carved fjord in this wilderness area, is frequently visited as an alternative if weather conditions or iceberg-choked waters necessitate a change. Both are spectacular, with waterfalls dancing down sheer rock palisades and fields of springtime wildflowers lying below snowcapped peaks. Watch for eagles, goats, bears, porpoises, and seals.

PORT OF CALL—JUNEAU

There is no road or railway leading into bustling Juneau (it's only accessible by plane or boat), still the little town functions as the capital of Alaska. Juneau is literally hemmed in by the Gastineau Channel and a ring of tall mountain peaks; a concentration of glaciers and the massive Juneau Icefield are within scant miles of the city proper.

Culture & History Tours

CITY & GLACIER TOUR   (2¹⁄₂–3 hours, $28–$30)   This narrated motorcoach excursion passes the capitol building, the governor's mansion, and other sights of interest in downtown before heading out to Mendenhall Glacier, the highlight of the trip, to see the glacier, walk the nature trails, and take in the glaciology exhibits at the visitor center. A stop at the Gastineau Salmon Hatchery is usually included.

GOLD HISTORY TOUR   (1¹⁄₂ hours, $32–$35)   Juneau's gold-rush history comes to life as you pan for gold near the ruins of a mine. A costumed prospector-guide recounts colorful tales of the discovery of gold here.

The Alaskan Outdoors

✪ **WILDERNESS LODGE ADVENTURE**   (3 hours, $165)   This favorite trip combines flightseeing over glaciers and an icefield with a stop at the Taku Glacier Lodge for a traditional all-you-can-eat salmon bake. After a hearty lunch, you can hike the nature trails around the wilderness lodge before reboarding the floatplane for the flight back to Juneau. Keep an eye out for the resident black bears, Scarface and cub, who show up from time to time to see what's left for them on the grill.

HELICOPTER GLACIER FLIGHT   (2 hours, $145–$155)   This is one of the most popular excursions in Alaska because it involves a helicopter flight and a chance to walk on the face of a glacier. After transferring to the airport by bus, guests are outfitted with ice boots and board helicopters bound for Mendenhall Glacier. After about 20 minutes on the glacier, you'll soar over the jagged peaks carved by the massive Juneau Icefield before turning back for the airport and town. If touching a glacier appeals to you, here's the chance.

Juneau on Your Own

Whether you dock at the pier or tender in from the harbor, you'll end up on the wharf downtown. If you look up at the mountain and to the right from the far end of the pier (near the small fish-processing plant), you'll see the ruins of the **Alaska-Juneau Stamp Mill** on the side of Mount Roberts. About midway down the wharf is a blue building housing a **visitor information center;** stop in to pick up a map of Juneau before striking out to see the sights. There's also a visitor information center housed in the **log cabin** at Third and Seward streets, downtown; here you can see an informative video orientation on the city and pick up a copy of "55 Free Things to See and Do in Juneau," and a walking-tour map.

The full walking tour takes several hours to complete but hits the **State Office Building** (referred to by locals not employed by the government as the S.O.B., **St. Nicholas Church** (a picturesque octagonal Russian Orthodox church built in 1894), the **House of Wickersham** (built in 1898 and open for historical tours), the **Juneau-Douglas City Museum** (it houses a collection of mining memorabilia), the turn-of-the-century **governor's mansion,** the **Evergreen Cemetery** (where Juneau's founders are buried), the **Federal Building** (the post office is inside) and **Founder's Monument,** the fascinating **Alaska State Museum,** and the **Centennial Building,** before winding back along the waterfront.

If your time is limited, follow South Franklin Street toward downtown, branch left at the Y intersection at Admiralty (which becomes Marine Way and Egan Drive), and pass through the Centennial Building to reach the ✪ **Alaska State Museum.** It's small, but one of the finest museums you'll find in the state. The walk there takes about 15 minutes, and you'll need at least an hour to see the well-rounded exhibits.

Locals claim that **Mendenhall Glacier,** 12 miles wide and 1¹/₂ miles high, is the most visited glacier in the world (you'd hear the same thing about Portage Glacier outside Anchorage, too). No matter; it's the most popular sight in Juneau. The glacier is 13 miles from downtown, so you'll need transportation to get there. Cabs are readily available, but cost about the same as narrated tours. A city bus from the lot in front of the information center at the wharf will cost only $1.25 and will drop you off at a spot about a 25-minute walk from the glacier viewing center; however, timing is everything in making the connection back to town, so pay close attention to the schedule.

If time allows, there are some good performances to check out in Juneau. **Karagod,** a true Russian dance company, performs in Centennial Hall, at 101 Eagan Dr. (☎ **907/586-5283**), about a seven-minute walk from the pier, daily at 11am and 3:30pm; the cost is $10 for adults and $4 for children. Another performance of great interest takes place at the **Naa Kahidi Theater,** in Sealaska Cultural Art Park in front of the main dock area; Natives in traditional costume sing songs, tell stories, and dance for guests at 2 and 8pm Tuesday through Saturday (the cost is $15 for adults and $9 for children). On the lighter side, and of much greater interest to children (though it's too loud for younger ones), is the **Lady Lou Review** (☎ 907/586-3686), a campy musical revue about life in Alaska during the Klondike gold rush. It's presented in the Voices Theater in Merchant Wharf next to Marine Park. Show times vary with ship schedules, so call for specifics; tickets are $16 for adults, half that for kids.

The works of top Alaskan artists Rie Muñoz, Byron Birdsall, and others are featured at the **Decker Gallery,** 233 S. Franklin St. (☎ 907/463-5536). Another favorite is the **Rainsong Gallery,** 291 S. Franklin St. (☎ 907/463-3337), which showcases traditional and contemporary Alaskan art. **Taku Smokeries,** 230 S. Franklin St. (☎ 907/463-FISH), ships smoked or flash-frozen salmon and halibut filets anywhere in the United States. Items of fur, from slippers and parkas to Eskimo dolls, are available at **Alaska International Fur and Memeluck Doll Company,** 126 Seward St. (☎ 907/463-2627). There are also tons of souvenir shops to browsethrough lining South Franklin Street, all within about five minutes of the wharf.

PORT OF CALL—HAINES

Surrounded by towering snowcapped peaks reminiscent of the Swiss Alps, Haines is an idyllic, happy-go-lucky town, as close to humorist Tom Bodett's "End of the Road" as you'll get—this side of Homer, anyway. (See the Kenai Penninsula section in Chapter 8.) Local watering holes really are the place to catch up on who's doing what. Everyone knows everyone, and while you'll instantly be recognized as an outsider, you'll be welcomed with genuine hospitality. They love having guests, and so few still visit that the locals haven't become jaded or hardened by tourism (and it's my fervent hope things stay this way).

Culture & History Tours

HAINES CITY & CULTURAL TOUR   (3 hours, $32)   This narrated drive introduces you to Fort Seward, Alaska's first U.S. military installation, the Alaska Indian Art Center where Tlingit culture and arts thrive, and the fine artifact collection at the Sheldon Museum and Cultural Center. The tour varies from cruise line to cruise line, but may also include a dog-sled demonstration or stop at the American Bald Eagle Interpretive Center.

✪ **CHILKAT DANCERS & SALMON BAKE**   (3½ hours, $50)   Enter a replica of a Chilkat Native tribal house on the parade grounds of Fort Seward to be regaled with Native legends and dances performed by the renowned Tlingit Indian Dancers. Following the performance, you'll feast on alderwood-smoked salmon filets, barbecued ribs, and salad buffet before returning to the ship. Most ports feature salmon bakes, but this is the one to plan for.

The Alaskan Outdoors

GLACIER FLIGHTSEEING   (1½ hours, $115)   Here's yet another chance to fly over the Juneau Icefield and Glacier Bay, and if the weather is clear, see majestic Mount Fairweather. This one is a bit less expensive, too.

CHILKAT NATURE HIKE   (4 hours, $41)   The narrative on Alaskan old-growth rain forests and spotting scopes provided to view bald eagles set this nature hike apart. The 4.8-mile round-trip hike is moderate in difficulty.

FORT SEWARD / CHILKAT RIVER BIKE RIDE   (2 hours, $42)   This moderate 6-mile guided ride takes in the sights and history of Fort Seward before pedaling along the Chilkat River estuary to see wildflowers, eagles, and other wildlife. There are some small hills to deal with, but this is the easiest bike trip in town.

Haines on Your Own

From Port Chilkoot dock, walk across the road and up the hill to the parade grounds of **Fort William Seward.** The log cabin and Native tribal house on the parade grounds are worth a picture or two, as are the surrounding whitewashed period homes that once housed the officers stationed here at Alaska's first military post. The cultural rebirth of the Tlingit Native tribe began here; you may find carvers, weavers, and other Native craftsmen at work southeast of the parade grounds in the **Alaska Indian Arts Center** (☎ 907/766-2160), just behind the **Chilkat Center for the Arts,** the setting for performances of the famed Chilkat Indian Dancers (they sometimes perform in the tribal house as well).

Backtrack to the dock to catch the shuttle into town to pick up a map at the **Haines Visitor Center,** Second Avenue (☎ 907/766-2234, or 800/458-3579). From here you've a choice to make between museums. You can head north down Second Avenue and turn right at Main Street to see the exhibits on local history and Native culture at the ✪ **Sheldon Museum and Cultural Center,** 11 Main St. (☎ 907/766-2368). You can also head south on Second Avenue to Haines Highway; at the junction is the new **American Bald Eagle Foundation Natural History Museum** (☎ 907/776-3094), a natural-history museum full of stuffed bald eagles and other creatures set in a woodland scene.

Haines has some fine galleries worth perusal. Delicate wooden bowls, silver jewelry, watercolors, and Native carvings are showcased at **Chilkat Valley Arts,** 307 Willard St. (☎ 907/766-2990). Artist Tresham Gregg demonstrates Native carving techniques at his studio in the **Sea Wolf Gallery,** on the parade grounds of Fort Seward; his work is also displayed at the **Whale Rider Gallery,** on Portage Street near Port Chilkoot (☎ 907/766-2540).

PORT OF CALL—SKAGWAY

Skagway, a gold-rush boomtown with false-fronted shops, saloons, and a brothel, has been restored to look much as it did when high-hoped prospectors passed through this staging ground on their way up the Chilkoot or White Pass trails in search of gold in the Yukon. The tiny town retains its days-of-yore flavor with the help of enthusiastic locals more than willing to share tales of the town's rough-and-tumble beginnings. With all the wonderful things to see and do here, I never get enough of Skagway—it's my favorite port in Alaska.

Culture & History Tours

✪ **SKAGWAY BY STREETCAR** (1½–2 hours, $35)   This is as much performance art as it is a historical tour of Skagway. Guides in period costume relate spellbinding tales and an insider's view of this boomtown as you tour the sights aboard vintage motor touring cars. In addition to seeing the Historic District, the Lookout, and the Goldrush Cemetery, guests watch a fascinating multimedia presentation on Skagway's history and become honorary members of the Arctic Brotherhood. Hands down, this is the best city tour offered in Alaska.

WHITE PASS & YUKON ROUTE (3 hours, $78)   Ride the narrow-gauge railway aboard vintage parlor cars from the dock past waterfalls and parts of the famous "Trail of '98" to White Pass Summit, the international boundary between Canada and the United States.

The Alaskan Outdoors

✪ **TRAIN RIDE / TRAIL HIKE TO A GLACIER** (8 hours, $200)   One of Skagway's larger-than-life characters is Buckwheat, leader of Packer Expeditions offering hiking tours through the Tongass National Forest to the foot of Denver or

Laughton Glacier. Following an hour-long ride on the White Pass and Yukon nar-row-gauge railroad, participants strap on fanny packs full of water and snacks for a 5-mile round-trip hike over uneven, sometimes difficult, but stunningly beautiful terrain. Gung-ho Buckwheat and his guides point out flora and fauna, encouraging the group to forage for edible berries and watch for bear and moose tracks along the way. Following a Bush lunch (crackers, cheese, smoked salmon, and luncheon meats), the group crosses the border into Canada before the return trip to Skagway via van. This is one of my top choices in Alaskan shore excursions.

✪ **CHILKAT BALD EAGLE PRESERVE FLIGHTSEEING & FLOAT TRIP**
(5¹/₂ hours, $205)   This excursion combines two of my favorite activities—flightseeing over the icefields of Glacier Bay and wildlife watching on a gentle float trip through the Chilkat Bald Eagle Preserve. After the 45-minute flightseeing trip from Skagway to Haines, vans carry participants to a pull-out point up the Chilkat Valley for a picnic on the pebbly beach before embarking in 18-foot inflatable rafts for the smooth float (no white water) through the preserve. Carry a camera and binoculars to capture the eagles, wolves, moose, and bears you might see.

Skagway on Your Own

One of the first stops to make in Skagway is the **National Park Service Visitor Center,** at Second Avenue and Broadway Street (☎ **907/983-2921**), to visit with rangers, look at town maps, and see the 30 minute film on Skagway's gold-mining history (shown daily at 11am and 3pm). The **White Pass and Yukon Railway Depot, Soapy's Parlor,** and the **Mascot Saloon** are visited on free guided walking tours of the town that depart from the visitor center at least four times each day (at 9:30 and 11am, and 2 and 4pm; the number of tours will probably increase in 1996). The park rangers are wonderful at relating the colorful tales of the town.

Housed at City Hall for years, the **Trail of '98 Skagway Historical Museum and Archives** (☎ **907/983-2420**) moved into the driftwood-faced ✪ **Arctic Brotherhood Hall** on Broadway Street during the winter of 1995–96. This is probably the most photographed building in Alaska. Gold-mining tools and gambling paraphernalia are among the artifacts displayed. Up in the air at press time was where the displaced **Skagway Convention and Visitors Bureau Information Center** (☎ **907/ 983-2854**), once housed in the Arctic Brotherhood Hall, was to be located; call for its new location. Wherever it moves, you'll want to stop by to pick up a historical **walking-tour map** that describes the quaint gold rush–era homes and false-fronted buildings that dot this little town.

Skagway excels in entertainment as well. In addition to the Red Onion jazz sessions extemporaneously put on by band members from the various ships in town, there are a couple of performances you might want to fit into your busy schedule. The *Days of '98 Show* featured at Eagle Hall, Sixth Avenue and Broadway Street (☎ **907/983-2545**), is a rowdy musical comedy about the life of con man Soapy Smith and his reign over Skagway during the Klondike gold rush. Morning and matinee shows usually work best with cruise schedules. Even better is the 24-minute multimedia presentation *The Skagway Story,* at the Skagway Mercantile building, 270 Second Ave. (☎ **907/983-2908**), an introduction to the town's colorful history narrated by storyteller extraordinaire Steve Hites.

There are two fine galleries in Skagway: the **David Present Gallery** (☎ **907/ 983-2873**), for incredible carvings by Present himself and a selection of other fine crafts produced primarily by Alaskans; and **Inside Passage Arts** (☎ **907/983-2585**), which showcase Native arts of Southeast Alaska. Both are located on the west side of Broadway. Also on Broadway (at Fifth Avenue) is **Corrington's Museum of Alaska History,** located in Corrington's gift shop (☎ 907/983-2580), a free museum of Alaska artifacts (many for sale) and a good collection of ivory, soapstone, and jade pieces. For general souvenirs and shirts, you'll find the best prices and a huge selection at the new **Skagway Outlet Store,** at the corner of Broadway and Seventh (☎ 907/983-3331).

ALONG THE WAY: GLACIERS, GLACIERS EVERYWHERE

After backtracking down the Lynn Canal, it's time to cruise west along Icy Strait to the entrance of **Glacier Bay National Park and Preserve.** This famous park contains 3.3 million acres of Alaska's southeastern panhandle and is accessible only by air or by water; cruise-ship passengers are by far the largest percentage of visitors. Sixteen tidewater glaciers run down from the Fairweather Range to meet the sea here; the masses who have flocked here by ship since the 1880s and returned home with tales of beautiful glaciers have spread word of this natural spectacle far and wide. Many glaciers, including Johns Hopkins, Margerie, and Grand Pacific, are fairly active, retreating steadily up the mountain ranges, providing ample entertainment as they calve off large portions, which drop into the icy waters below with a tremendous boom and a gratifying splash.

This microcosm of Alaskan climatic zones and ecosystems is a prime wildlife-viewing area: seals and sea lions bask in the sun atop icebergs; gargantuan whales feed on microscopic krill, brown bears and bald eagles feed on fish at the shoreline, mountain goats and western red cedar cling precariously to the sheer, glacier-carved walls of the narrow fjord inlets. Otters, porpoises, sea lions, orcas and minke whales, and an array of shorebirds (including the adulated puffin) are often glimpsed here as well. Even the endangered peregrine falcon shows up from time to time, but it's the humpback that thrills visitors most. ✪ **Point Adolphus,** near the entrance to the bay, is considered the best spot for humpback viewing, and it's there that I most often witness them feeding in the Glacier Bay area.

Glacier Bay is the farthest northern point visited by most seven-day round-trip cruises out of Vancouver, B.C. Other cruises continue, following the curve of Alaska's coastline northwest. Those that continue on usually make a stop in **Yakutat Bay** to view Hubbard Glacier. On the way into Yakutat Bay, you'll pass the northernmost reaches of the Tongass National Forest on your right and, on your left, **Malaspina Glacier,** which, at 3,937 square miles (larger than Switzerland), is the largest glacier in Alaska and one of the largest glaciers on the planet. On a clear day, it's an incredible sight.

At 92 miles long and 6 miles wide, **Hubbard Glacier** is far bigger than its more famous relations in Glacier Bay. It begins in the icefields of Canada, beyond the rugged range of the **St. Elias Mountains** that serve as the borderline between Canada and the United States. This tidewater glacier once filled Yakutat Bay, but has receded 34 nautical miles from the mouth of the bay over the last 100 years. In 1986, Hubbard made headlines because it began surging forward at the rate of 120 feet a day, temporarily blocking off a fjord. The red dusting on the glacier is volcanic ash from the 1992 eruption of Mount Spurr, some 80 miles away. Today the glacier is fairly active, dropping icebergs that form large sheets of ice occupied by seals and kittiwakes. An impressive sight, it's more often than not viewed from a distance because the waters leading up to its face are frequently choked with ice and are treacherous to navigate.

The **Chugach National Forest** is a bit west along the arched coastline, and at the heart of this forest is **Prince William Sound.** Badly damaged by the horrendous

Where the Whales Are

Humpbacks, orcas, belugas, and minkes—just some of Alaska's cetacean residents—can seem to be both everywhere and nowhere all within one day spent cruising off Alaska's coast. They'll pop up when you least expect them and prove maddeningly elusive when you're looking the hardest. When they're encountered somewhere along the route, the captain or officer on watch on most cruise ships will make a shipwide announcement to let passengers know where to look, but the ship probably won't stop to let you watch for a while. On a few cruise lines, though, whales are a primary focus of the trip, so their ships will visit areas favored by whales and spend time waiting there for an encounter, or will monitor marine-traffic radio broadcasts and deviate from course to go where whale sightings have been reported.

The top spot to see **orca** (the distinctive black-and-white whales with upright dorsal fins) is Robson Bight, an area in **Johnstone Strait** (between Vancouver Island and mainland British Columbia) where these "killer whales" tend to cruise slowly near the shoreline, rubbing their bellies on the rounded stones of the sloping beach. Some ships pass through at night, but most will time their transit, when possible, to match the best viewing hours in the day. **Beluga** (the small white or milky-gray whales with rounded beaks) frequently follow salmon to feed in **Turnagain Arm** near Anchorage; if your cruise starts or ends in Seward, you'll most likely take a bus transfer between Anchorage and Seward, driving along this arm a good portion of the way. **Humpback** whales (those singing gentle giants with long flippers and enormous tail fins) tend to congregate to feed on the rich supply of krill off Point Adolphus and other spots in and near **Glacier Bay.** The waters around the **Brothers Islands** are another good area for frequent humpback encounters.

Most lines (Princess, Holland America, Norwegian, and Royal Caribbean among them) don't generally focus on whale watching, but do offer onboard lectures about whales and announce sightings made along the course. Others (including Alaska Sightseeing, Crystal, Cunard, and Special Expeditions) intentionally build time into their cruise itineraries to spend in these areas watching for whales. There are also numerous whale-and-wildlife-watching day trips in the various ports of call—some even offer guarantees, so of you really want to see whales, you can in Alaska.

Exxon Valdez oil spill in 1989, the area and its abundant wildlife are once again beautiful to behold. Within the confines of the sound is ✪ **College Fjord.** This is my absolute favorite area for viewing glaciers, both for the sheer concentration of glaciers and the clear demonstration of different stages of change they bring to the landscape. The scenic 16-mile fjord is dotted by glaciers named for top institutions—Harvard, Yale, Crescent, Amherst, Wellesley, Smith, and Vassar—that joined forces to research the area. Some glaciers have retreated more recently than others, leaving carved cliffs and hillsides just now coming alive with pioneering vegetation, including alder. Other areas are thick with spruce and cedar and a carpet of undergrowth.

After cruising back into the main body of the Sound, some ships head for the port of Valdez. The steep vertical face of the **Columbia Glacier,** which flows out of the Chugach Mountains, will be on your left as you sail into Valdez Arm. Ice in this 4-mile-long glacier is estimated to be up to 10,000 years old.

PORT OF CALL—VALDEZ

In the tiny community of Valdez, the southern terminus of the Alaska pipeline, you'll find your attention drawn to the surrounding 5,000-foot peaks of the Chugach Mountains. If not for the crude storage tanks on the opposite shore, this northernmost year-round ice-free port could almost appear to be a Swiss alpine village on the shore of Lake Geneva.

Culture & History

PIPELINE TOUR   (2–2¹/₂ hours, $25)   If the pipeline project and Alaska's "black gold" are of interest, sign up for the tour of Alyeska Pipeline Service Company's terminal. You may observe giant tankers taking on their crude-oil cargo as you tour this stainless-steel facility.

THOMPSON PASS / WORTHINGTON GLACIER   (2¹/₂–3 hours, $35)   This tour by bus takes you past the old townsite (destroyed in the earthquake of 1964), through narrow Keystone Canyon, and up to Thompson Pass to get a look at where the Trans-Alaska Pipeline is buried before reaching Worthington Glacier. The bus then drops you at the ship or in town for shopping.

The Alaskan Outdoors

✪ **CANYON RAFTING**   (2¹/₄ hours, $65–$70)   You can't beat the rafting in Keystone Canyon, so Valdez would be my choice above other ports of call to experience a rafting trip. There are a few "hickups" along the way, but it's a mild run for the most part and the sheer canyon walls and waterfalls pounding into the Lowe River are stunning. Knowledgeable guides and all equipment are provided.

HELICOPTER SAFARI   (1¹/₂ hours, $160–$170)   This quick chopper adventure zips you over the Trans-Alaska Pipeline, over the crevasses of the Columbia Glacier, and over Prince William Sound for a broader view, but the highlight for most is landing on the face of Shoup Glacier to walk about for 15 minutes.

Valdez on Your Own

Valdez is tiny and there's really not much to see while you're in town. A shuttle bus carries passengers from the pier to the **Tourist Information Center** in town and back. Other than a few overpriced souvenir outlets, the **Valdez Museum,** 217 Egan Ave. (☎ **907/835-2764**), with very good displays on local history, is pretty much the only sight of interest. For shopping, check out the temporary kiosks set up on the pier.

PORT OF CALL—SEWARD

Following Valdez, the final stop is generally Seward, a quiet seaport village and popu-lar summer destination for boaters and fishermen attracted by its small-boat harbor and the number of fishing derbies. Outdoors enthusiasts are drawn by its proximity to Kenai Fjords National Park and other public wilderness lands. Seward is a major port for coal destined for the Pacific Rim and a major cargo-transfer point— the Alaska Railroad's southern terminus is here—so the pier area has a distinctly industrial look.

Because sailing around the Kenai Peninsula and up Cook Inlet into Anchorage adds another full day to itineraries (not to mention higher mooring fees in Anchor-age), Seward has become the northern terminus of choice for cruise lines. Cruises that include Anchorage either start or end in Seward. A three-hour bus ride along Turnagain Arm and through the Chugach National Forest is the favored connection between Seward and Anchorage. It's a pretty ride, but does cut the time you'll have to sightsee in either city unless you book a pre- or post-cruise extension (available predominantly for Anchorage only).

Culture & History

Sorry, there are no culture and history shore excursions to speak of in Seward. Most folks interested in such fill their time with a trip to the big city instead.

ANCHORAGE CITY TOUR   (3¹/₂–9 hours, $30–$70)   At least a portion of the trip is spent aboard a restroom-equipped motorcoach for the three-hour drive through the Chugach National Forest and along Turnagain Arm between Seward and Anchorage. Once you hit Anchorage, the bus makes a circuit through the downtown area pointing out sights of interest, better shops, and popular restaurants. You'll then be free for a few hours to shop, eat, or visit the fascinating Museum of History and Art. The tour is either an all-day round-trip affair from Seward or a half-day trip that ends in Anchorage (either downtown at Egan Center or at the Anchorage Airport).

The Alaskan Outdoors

EXIT GLACIER   (3 hours, $35)   This excursion does include a quick orientation trip through town before heading out the Resurrection River Valley to Exit Glacier. After a short hike along nature trails, you'll come to the face of this land-based glacier. (*Note:* Chunks fall off the glacier regularly, making it far too dangerous to get close enough to touch, and park rangers are on hand to see that you don't try it.)

PORTAGE GLACIER   (2–8 hours, $30–$70)   If you haven't had your fill of glaciers, here's another chance. This tour is typically done en route to Anchorage via motorcoach, but is also available as a day-long round-trip excursion from Seward. A stop is made in the Kenai Mountains to board the MV *Ptarmigan,* an enclosed cruiser, for an hour-long sojourn to Portage Glacier. This little vessel comes within 300 yards or so of the face, providing a great chance for up-close pictures of the spires, morain, and deep-blue crevasses of the glacier.

RESURRECTION BAY WILDLIFE CRUISE   (4 hours, $65)   Board a 90-foot touring vessel for a 50-mile narrated tour into Resurrection Bay and the Kenai Fjords area. The highlight of this one is wildlife watching; the region is teeming with birds and sea mammals, so chances are good that you'll see eagles, puffins, kittiwakes, cormorants, harbor seals, otters, sea lions, porpoises, and maybe even humpbacks.

MOUNT MCKINLEY FLIGHTSEEING   (3 hours, $290)   If the tour hasn't been canceled because of weather conditions (as it frequently is), you'll board a private airplane at the Seward Airport and swoop over the dramatic valleys of the Kenai Peninsula to watch for wildlife before heading over Anchorage and up the Susitna Valley and Kahiltna River to towering Mount McKinley, the highest peak in North America. On the return flight you'll pass over Prince William Sound for a different perspective.

Seward on Your Own

As with most Alaskan towns, Seward is small enough to negotiate on foot. Your first stop should be the **visitor information booth** on the pier to pick up a map. From there it's about a half-mile walk into town, or you can hop a shuttle on the pier for a quick orientation trip through town before striking out on your own. The **small-boat harbor,** on the other side of the industrial tracks, is the first picturesque area of Seward you'll encounter. Boutiques and little eateries line the waterfront street across from the harbor. The **Kenai Fjords National Park Headquarters,** on Fourth Avenue (☎ 907/224-3175), is also located here; stop in to see the informative films on the wildlife and geography of the park and the major earthquake that changed the face of Seward in 1964.

All other sights of interest are located downtown within blocks of each other. Displays of historical interest are found at the **Resurrection Bay Historical Society Museum,** at Third Avenue and Jefferson Street (☎ **907/224-3902**), and at the **Seward Community Library,** at Fifth Avenue at Adams Street (☎ **907/224-3646**). Ongoing oceanographic and aquaculture studies are the subjects of interest at the University of Alaska's **Institute of Marine Science,** at Third and Railway avenues (☎ **907/224-5261**). While the famous race doesn't actually run here, you'll find the **Iditarod Trailhead** in the small park nearby on Railroad Avenue.

As long as you're downtown, you can pick up souvenirs at the **Alaska Shop,** Fourth Avenue at Washington Street (☎ **907/224-5420**). Also worth a peek in the area is the **Bardarson Studio,** at the Smallboat Harbor (☎ **907/224-8068**), for its selection of Alaskan art.

6

Outside in Alaska

by Peter Oliver

You hear stories, plenty of them. People get hold of pictures or maps of Alaska's boundless wildlands and they become, as the British say, a bit touched. They get ideas. Then they go out and do things to make more domesticated humans shake their heads incredulously. That's the way the stories—some true, some imaginatively reinvented—are born.

There is the story, for example, of a robust California woman determined to travel the entire length (roughly 2,300 miles) of the Yukon River on cross-country skis. Two-thirds of the way through her journey, the spring break-up of the river ice began prematurely. Undeterred, she laid over in a Native community and enlisted the help of village elders in building a canoe by hand. When the ice break-up was complete a month or so later, she boarded her newly handcrafted canoe and finished the trip.

Less admirable but no less astonishing is the story of a fellow, reportedly pumped full of amphetamines, who tried to paraglide over the unclimbable, 3,000-foot icefall above the Root Glacier in Wrangell–St. Elias National Park. Competing in a multiday race through the roadless, virtually trail-less wilderness from Nabesna to McCarthy, he decided he could win by taking a shortcut. Instead, he crash-landed among the treacherous seracs of the icefall before eventually straggling into McCarthy. Upon arrival, he was immediately disqualified.

Fortunately, a person needn't go to such extremes to experience the Alaskan wilderness—unless, of course, for the sake of a good story. But it's instructive to know the possibilities. The limits of what you can do in the vast Alaskan backcountry are defined not strictly by the land itself but by time, imagination, hardiness, and, to some degree, sanity.

The wilderness stats are dizzying. Alaska is the land of North America's biggest mountain (20,320-foot Mount McKinley), its biggest glacier (the 2,250-square-mile Bering Glacier), its biggest national park (13,188,000-acre Wrangell–St. Elias), and its biggest *state* park (Wood-Tikchik, at 1.6 million acres). National wildlife refuges cover 76 million acres, roughly equal to the geographic area of New Mexico. There are more than 3,000 rivers in Alaska, 26 of which are officially protected as Wild and Scenic Rivers, adding up to a total water mileage many times greater than the state's meager highway mileage of about 5,000. Think of it this way: If you really want to go places in Alaska, you're better off in a canoe than in a car. Or better still, in a sea kayak, given a tidal shoreline estimated at over 47,000 miles. Talk about an abundance of wilderness opportunity!

It's an abundance that can be as intimidating and downright scary as it is inspiring. Yet it's also surprisingly accessible and, under proper guidance, surprisingly manageable. Accessibility comes about thanks to the hundreds of Bush planes that flock the Alaskan skies more regularly than eagles or migratory waterfowl. Manageability is the mandate of wilderness outfitters and lodge operators, many of whom can deliver a remarkably high level of luxury in the heart of a land that remains decidedly precivilized.

How far you choose to push the envelope of possibility is entirely your call. Wilderness lodges are the way to go for anyone insistent upon such creature comforts as meals with fresh ingredients, a warm bed at night, and a roof to keep out the rain. Yet, inevitably, lodges, to a greater or lesser degree, impinge in subtle ways upon the intimacy between adventurer and wilderness.

Extended trips, involving camping in various forms, intensify the wilderness experience. Not incidental in that process is a unique bonding that develops among participants. Shut off for days from the whir and dither of the civilized world, groups in the wilderness have a way of forming cohesive social units, from which lasting friendships often evolve. However, the physical demands, the ubiquitous grime, and wilderness inconveniences (not least of which is the awkwardness of going to the bathroom *al fresco*) limit the appeal of camping trips for many people.

Anyone intent on setting off into the Alaskan wilds must start with the daunting enterprise of choosing an activity. Fishing, hiking, and water sports—canoeing, kayaking, and rafting—draw the most comers, but there are plenty of other ways to go, some obvious, others improbable. Surely it goes without saying that mountaineering attracts many enthusiasts to a state with more 14,000-foot peaks than any other in the United States. But there are less likely ways to spend time in the Alaskan outdoors—scuba diving, for one. A growing number of Anchorage-area coldbloods these days are not only probing undersea Alaska but—hard to imagine—prefer to do so in *winter,* when the sea water (so they claim) is not much colder but considerably clearer than in summer.

Don't forget that it is wilderness that spends most of its time under the shroud of winter, which is not necessarily a bad thing. Ironically, winter makes the Alaskan wilderness even more accessible than in summer. Impassible bogs and thickets, wind-whipped lakes, and fast-running rivers become solidified and smoothed over by snow and ice in winter. Dog mushing, snowmobiling, snowshoeing, and skiing, both downhill and cross-country—all draw their share of winter outdoor activists to Alaska. Sure it's cold, and –50°F is not uncommon. But it isn't always cold everywhere; average February temperatures in Southeast, for example, are well above freezing. And it need not be a debilitating cold if you dress for it and if you don't do some oddball thing like go scuba diving in the frigid winter sea. What you get in return is a white-cloaked (and bug-free!) Alaska of raw, fearsome beauty and the northern lights at full intensity.

Settling on an activity gets you only halfway there; you must also choose a place. That's no easy matter either, given that abundance and variety of wild country. Still, it's imperative to wrench yourself from the notion that all of Alaska's wilderness can be experienced in one mad-dash, see-Alaska rush. A vulgar comparison would be going to a multiplex cinema and watching a few minutes of 12 different movies. That's no way to treat Alaska.

Be willing to commit yourself to a specific region. Choose the arid wilds of the Brooks Range or the North Slope; the mountains of the Interior; the fjords and inlets of that unfathomably long coastline; the glaciers of Southeast. Full immersion in one region, for several days or more, is the fast track to a deeper, more fulfilling understanding of what wild Alaska is all about. It makes economic sense, too. Roaming around the Alaskan outback does not come cheaply.

At one time, wild Alaska was pretty much the exclusive province of leather-tough wilderness jocks. That isn't so any more. You don't necessarily need to be young, fit, and athletic. You don't need he-man skills or backcountry know-how. A willingness to give the great Alaskan outdoors a go is the only real prerequisite. Ordinary people of all ages are capable of amazing stuff once they give themselves a chance. Snow-cat skiing guide Chris Nettles tells the story of a four-year-old boy, skis locked in a snow-plow, who skied the pants off the adults in his group, racking up 20,000 vertical feet in a day. Mountain-bike guide Robert Kozler, a robust, athletic 30-year-old, recalls approaching near-total exhaustion trying to keep pace with a rider in his 70s.

There are, certainly, activities inappropriate for older people or children. In some cases, a lack of certain skills and/or a lack of physical fitness, regardless of your age, may get you into serious trouble or at least a state of inconsolable discomfort. Alaska can be a punishing, uncompromising beast toward those who embark on adventures that are surely out of their league. But with so much to choose from, heading off on an adventure for which you're ill-suited is inexcusable. Select a trip that you know you can handle—or which a guide or outfitter is confident you can handle—and the Alaskan wilderness can be remarkably obliging.

Not every story that comes from the Alaskan outback is peopled with expeditionary adventurers engaged in Odyssean feats. More common is the story of two self-described "unfit inhabitants of a New York apartment" who wrote in thanks to dog musher Ruth Hirsiger. Expressing initial trepidation about taking on the Alaskan winter and driving their own dog teams, the New Yorkers completed a four-day trip saying they "wished to turn around and do it all over again." More common than any heady rush of "man vs. the wilderness" accomplishment is the resonant, lasting sentiment expressed by outdoor writer John Barsness, after a fishing trip to Kodiak. Wrote Barsness in an article in *Alaska* magazine: "Not all of me leaves Alaska; some part is always getting there. Some particle, perhaps a piece of my heart, floats through the sky, over glacial mountains and silver rivers. Another, the part that is cousin of fish, always swims upstream, past the bears and gravel bars, into an Alaska that never ends." In other words, any story about the Alaskan wilds is not so much a story about doing anything—about catching a fish, or climbing a mountain, or running a river. It's about being there.

1 Preparing for the Alaskan Wilderness

Most of the information agencies you'll want to turn to when planning a wilderness adventure are listed under "Visitor Information" in Chapter 3 or under the "Outside in . . . " sections near the beginning of each regional chapter.

Depending on where you're going, specific public lands agencies may be of help. These include **Alaska State Parks,** P.O. Box 107001, Anchorage, AK 99510 (☎ 907/762-2617); the federal **Bureau of Land Management (BLM),** 701 C St. (P.O. Box 13), Anchorage, AK 99513 (☎ 907/271-5076); **Chugach National Forest,** 201 E. Ninth Ave., Suite 206, Anchorage, AK 99501 (☎ 907/271-2599); **Tongass National Forest,** USDA Public Affairs Office, P.O. Box 21628, Juneau, AK 99802 (☎ 907/586-8806); and the **U.S. Fish and Wildlife Service,**

1101 E. Tudor Rd., Anchorage, AK 99503 (☎ **907/786-3486**), which manages national wildlife refuges.

The **U.S. Geological Survey,** 4230 University Dr., Anchorage, AK 99508 (☎ **907/786-7011**), is the primary source for topographical maps. You can also find USGS maps at the public lands information centers. Another source is the *Alaska Atlas & Gazetteer,* available in many bookstores and shops in Alaska or by calling 800/225-5669; it includes excellent, large-scale topographical maps of the entire state.

Choosing the best time to travel in the Alaskan wilderness depends on several variables, among them: temperature, bugs, daylight, and the principal activity you plan to engage in during your trip. Most outfitters operate June through August and begin closing up shop (or severely curtailing activities) after Labor Day. By September the hunting season (primarily for moose or Dall sheep) occupies the attention of many pilots, outfitters, and lodges that stay in business. See the "When to Go" section in Chapter 3 for details.

For river-based activities, early summer, when waters are swollen by snowmelt and rivers run faster, may be preferable. However, glacially fed rivers may actually surge later, as warming temperatures melt glacial ice. For land-based activities—like backpacking or mountain biking—later in the summer, when the bugs diminish, fall colors begin to emerge, and trails are relatively dry, may be the best time. In most parts of Alaska, however, precipitation—possibly in the form of snow—tends to increase later in the summer.

Regardless of when you go, be sure to allow extra time in your schedule, especially toward the end of your travels. The Alaskan wilderness doesn't run on a fixed schedule. Most adventures require some kind of small-plane shuttling to and/or from remote locations. Small planes require relatively good weather to fly; if the weather socks in, you may well find your group waiting an extra day for a pickup. Reliable outfitters prepare for this possibility with extra food, and you, in building extra time into your schedule, should prepare for it, too.

WHERE TO GO

Picking the perfect trip from among so many choices might seem hopeless, but you can narrow things down relatively quickly by assessing four variables: the type of activity you're interested in, the geography, the climate, and how much you want to rough it.

In a state interlaced with thousands of rivers and streams, you can go almost anywhere for canoeing, kayaking, and rafting. However, rivers in the north, particularly in the Brooks Range and the Alaska National Wildlife Refuge, typically feature the longest stretches of unspoiled wilderness. Popular northern rivers, including the Alatna, the John, the Kobuk, the Noatak, and the Sheenjek, are for the most part relatively gentle and are suitable for canoeing. White-water–hungry rafters and kayakers generally stick to rivers farther south—among them the Alsek and the Tatshenshini (which begin in Yukon), the Copper, the Nenana, and the Talkeetna.

Hiking and backpacking opportunities are plentiful throughout the state, but they may not involve the sort of clearly marked trails hikers elsewhere in the United States are accustomed to. In the late 19th century one traveler over the Chilkoot Pass in Southeast Alaska wrote the following: "A trail in Alaska should not be confused with the ordinary highway of settled states. When a trail is spoken of as existing between two points in Alaska it has no further meaning than that a man . . . may travel that way over the natural surface of the ground." In 100 years things haven't changed much.

The most developed trail systems are in Chugach State Park and Tongass National Forest, and on the Kenai Peninsula. There are virtually no trails in the Far North, but the springy tundra of the foothills and mountains mean that you can go more or less where you want to go without a trail to follow. (The swampy ground and slippery tussocks of the low Arctic tundra north of the Brooks Range, on the other hand, can be a nightmare to hike in in the summer; it's actually easier to traverse in the winter when it's frozen solid—but then, of course, you've got –40°F cold and blasting wind to contend with.) Stream crossings probably present the biggest challenge and hazard to safe travel. Snow-fed streams tend to be highest in spring and early summer, but some glacially fed streams may rise later in the summer, when warm temperatures melt glacial ice.

With the highest concentration of roads and trails radiating north and south from Anchorage, cyclists—mountain bikers and road riders—will want to concentrate their attention in that area. Sea kayakers can obviously go wherever there is sea, but the fjords of Southeast, Prince William Sound, the Katmai coast, and the Kodiak Archipelago rank at the top of the list.

Wherever you go in Alaska, the landscape has a way of astonishing you in one way or another. The mountain ranges of the north tend to be stark, arid, and more treeless the farther north you go, while glaciers and deep forests are more prevalent in the south. In large part this reflects a difference in climate. If you have a deep aversion to rain, head north, where summer days are usually dry and often surprisingly mild. Rain is a given the farther south you go; if you're planning any outdoor activities in Southeast, industrial-strength rain gear is a must.

The difference in climate between north and south may go far in determining how you'll spend your nights in the outdoors. Cabins and fixed, floored tents are common accommodations offered by outfitters who operate in southern Alaska, where good dry tent sites can be hard to find. Not so in the north, where tenting is the norm, as it must be; cabins and lodges are few and far, far between. The most comfortable way to go, of course, is to base yourself in a wilderness lodge, most of which are concentrated in the Southwest (tons of fishing lodges), the Interior (usually not far from Denali National Park), in the Southeast, and in Southcentral.

It's fairly safe to say that no matter where you go in Alaska, you'll encounter wildlife. Moose, Dall sheep, bears, caribou, eagles, and waterfowl are the most likely sightings. If you're interested in large caribou herds, you must head north, while the biggest bears (though by no means the only bears) are in Southeast, the Kodiak Archipelago, and elsewhere where fish and berries, staples of the ursine diet, are more plentiful.

The really legendary fishing is nearest to the coastlines, but it's fairly safe to say that you'll find good fishing almost anywhere you go, save for rivers and lakes milky with glacial silt. Good fishing in Alaska is less a matter of location than it is a matter of the time of year. Salmon runs change with the season: King salmon, which get the prize for size, can run in June but the real monsters in the Kenai River, for example, run in July; sockeyes (reds) can run as early as May, the smaller species— cohos and the unloved chums—run later. Grayling are usually abundant near where feeder streams meet larger rivers, while rainbow trout are most common in lakes and streams of the Interior and the Kenai Peninsula. There's no shortage of guides or charter-boat operators who can take you to some fish-rich hot spot. For a list of fishing guides in a given area, see the regional chapters later in this book.

WHAT TO BRING

Obviously, your packing list will be determined by the activity and time of the year you choose. If you're signing on with an outfitter, the outfitter should supply a detailed list of the gear you'll need. Stick religiously to the list; forgetting something so simple as extra socks can bring on great misery should you accidentally step into an ice-cold river. It needs to be emphasized that this is no place to try to develop skill in planning and executing a wilderness trip—if you're going out without the help of professional outfitters and guides, you need to know exactly what to bring and exactly how to deal with the curves wilderness can deal you. Some of these, like hordes of mosquitoes, can be unpleasant; others, like bears, stream crossings, injuries, and sudden extreme cold, can easily be life-threatening.

Proper clothing, enabling you to adapt to the changing moods of Alaskan weather, should be your primary concern. Essential clothing items include: heavy-duty rain gear, warm outer coat, wool cap, at least one pair of gloves, wool sweater or fleece pullover, one or more sets of long underwear, several pairs of wool socks and synthetic liners, sun hat, shorts, sturdy hiking boots, and more comfortable footwear—sturdy nylon-and-rubber waterproof sandals are great—for lounging around camp.

Other than clothing, items you'll want to have along include: sunglasses, insect repellent, sunscreen, a small knife, binoculars, a camera, and pepper spray or a gun if you're venturing into bear country (and most of Alaska is bear country). Depending on the trip you choose, it may be necessary to bring a sleeping bag and pad, tent, rubber boots (for river trips), and fishing gear. Fishing and/or camping equipment may be available for rent from outfitters or Alaska sporting-goods stores (see "Planning an Independent Wilderness Adventure," later in this chapter).

ALASKA'S WILDERNESS TRAVEL OUTFITTERS

Ralph Waldo Emerson, after venturing deep into the Adirondack woods of New York, praised the men who had guided him as "doctors of the wilderness." You'll find many reliable wilderness doctors in Alaska, too—people who know the Alaskan backcountry and can safely lead you through it. But there are many fly-by-nighters as well. It doesn't take much to print a color brochure, sign up for an 800 number, advertise in magazines, and call yourself a wilderness outfitter. Proceed with caution.

What should you look for in an outfitter? The top outfitters put together well-organized, air-tight trips, never leaving you wondering, for example, how to get from the airport to some rendezvous point. Experienced guides, reliable equipment (no leaky rafts, for example), and responsiveness to your needs (such as unusual diets) are other strong points. The best guides have not only backcountry skills but "people" skills as well—when in remote environments, perhaps waiting out a storm, a cheerful, helpful attitude can make a difference. An area of weakness for many outfitters, even the good ones, is naturalist training. A good boatman may get you down the river smoothly and a good fishing guide may know all the hot spots. But when you have questions about a particularly intriguing flower, or animal, or geological curiosity, it's a decided bonus when a correct and satisfying answer is forthcoming.

QUESTIONS TO ASK A PROSPECTIVE TRIP ORGANIZER

What level of fitness and experience is required? For extended wilderness trips, the top outfitters are likely to beat you to the punch, over the phone or through questionnaires: How fit are you and how much experience do you have in the activity you're interested in? For many trips, you hardly have to be a hard-bodied outdoorsperson in order to participate. However, misjudging your fitness and ability can not only be a hazard to you but to your fellow participants as well. Be sensible and don't get your heart set on a specific trip. Discuss options—Alaska offers plenty—with prospective outfitters, trying to settle on a trip that's right for you. If you don't have outdoors experience, start with a trip no more than a few days long—you might not like it, and you could save yourself a lot of money and misery if you ease yourself into this kind of travel. This is a less critical issue if you're planning a lodge- or inn-based trip; however, the rigorousness of activities can vary substantially from one lodge to the next.

What are the outfitter's credentials?   When embarking on a wilderness trip, the quality of the outfitter means everything. No one wants lousy food, musty tents, or surly attitudes, but those concerns are merely asides to the main concern, which is safety. At least one guide on any trip should have CPR, emergency-medical, and wilderness-response training. Generally speaking, the longer an outfitter has been in operation, the better, although that's not certainly so. Make sure the outfitter has the permits and licenses required by the state, and ask about accreditation by professional organizations (for example, for mountaineers, the American Mountain Guides Association).

Can the outfitter provide a list of references?   This is a crucial one, especially since I only have space here to list a few of the many Alaska-based outfitters who have superb reputations. Any reputable outfitter can provide references of previous clients who've taken the trip you're considering—call them up and ask how things went.

What meals and accommodations are involved?   The range here is enormous, and terms can be misleading. One man's "luxurious" cabin is another man's hovel; "gourmet" is strictly a matter of interpretation. The most comfortable accommodations and the freshest food tend to be found at wilderness lodges, but don't count on it. Food for raft trips can be of a surprisingly high caliber; support rafts are capable of carrying large coolers with fresh meats, vegetables, and even beer and wine. Backpacking meals, by contrast, are usually pretty bare-bones, and don't expect any backpacking guide to haul around an ice chest or a chilled case of beer for your enjoyment over the evening campfire. Tents, incidentally, are not always tents in the strictest sense of the word. Many outfitters make use of large wood- or metal-framed tents that may include wood floors, full beds, heat, and even electricity.

What is included in the price?   Typically, package prices include almost everything except airfare to and from Alaska. "Almost" is the key word. Usually not included are tips, alcoholic beverages, gear rental (such as packs, tents, boots, rain gear), fishing licenses, and expenses (such as lodging, meals, and car rentals) you might incur before or after the period covered by your package. For example, the cost of a layover night in Anchorage between the arrival of your flight and the beginning of your wilderness trip would probably not be included. Traveling à la carte in Alaska in summer can be expensive, so be sure you know exactly what you're getting when you book.

What about children?   Because of the physical demands of wilderness travel and often because backcountry partners (such as canoe partners) must be matched by size, strength, and ability, some trip organizers set age limits. On multiday camping trips, each participant is usually expected to pull his or her own weight—in some cases, literally. Teenagers may be physically up to that responsibility, but children under 10, on any extended camping trip, probably aren't. If you really want to bring young children along, ask the outfitter about trip options.

How far must I book in advance? Some popular trips may be fully booked as much as a year in advance. Tourism statistics show that Alaska travelers tend to plan and book their vacations several months in advance. This does not mean that you're out of luck if you start planning late in the game. However, the later you plan, the more flexible you'll have to be if the trip or lodge of first choice is full. Keep a couple of factors in mind. First, some operators offer discounts for early bookings. Second, smaller groups make for better wilderness experiences, but there are also fewer openings for last-minute planners. Requirements for deposits and prepayments vary widely from one company to the next; deposits are usually partially or completely refundable if you cancel well in advance—say, 60 days or so.

RECOMMENDED OUTFITTERS

The following are among the most reliable companies leading trips into the Alaskan wilderness:

Alaska Discovery. 5449 Shaune Dr., Suite 4, Juneau, AK 99801. ☎ **907/780-6226** or 800/586-1911. Fax 907/780-4220.

Based in Southeast Alaska, this company offers primarily Southeast trips involving water activities—canoeing, kayaking, and rafting. Trips tend to be of moderate difficulty.

Alaska Wilderness Journeys. P.O. Box 220204, Anchorage, AK 99522. ☎ **907/349-2964** or 800/349-0064. Fax 907/349-2964.

Originally a river-oriented outfitter, this company has broadened its scope to include backpacking and mountain biking as well as river trips.

Alaska Wildland Adventures. P.O. Box 389, Girdwood, AK 99587. ☎ **907/783-2928** or 800/334-8730. Fax 907/783-2130.

With lodges on the Kenai Peninsula and in the Denali area, Alaska Wildland gears its program toward the softer side of adventure travel, including "safaris" specifically for seniors.

American Wilderness Experience. P.O. Box 1486, Boulder, CO 80306. ☎ **303/444-2622** or 800/444-0099. Fax 303/333-3999.

A.W.E. is an adventure-travel clearinghouse, and its catalog features selected trips from numerous outfitters.

Mountain Travel • Sobek. 620 Fairmount Ave., El Cerrito, CA 94530. ☎ **510/527-8100** or 800/227-2384. Fax 510/525-7710.

This is perhaps the granddaddy of adventure-travel companies. The company guides its own trips and also acts as an agent for other outfitters. River-running is a strong suit.

Sierra Club Outings. 730 Polk St., San Francisco, CA 94109. ☎ **415/923-5630.** Fax 415/923-0636.

In addition to its activities as an environmentalist organization, the Sierra Club oversees a large international outings program. Trips tend to be on the more strenuous side, with emphasis on wildlife viewing and naturalist activities.

Sourdough Outfitters. P.O. Box 90, Bettles, AK 99726. ☎ **907/692-5252.** Fax 907/692-5612.

Sourdough features an extensive program of moderate to strenuous trips in the Brooks Range, summer and winter. The company also provides support service for self-guided trips.

WILDERNESS HAZARDS

The wilderness is not so much a dangerous place as an unfamiliar place for most people. That said, lack of familiarity can lead to bad wilderness behavior and that, in turn, *can* be dangerous. Common sense is often a reliable guide—if you're cold, for example, put on more clothing—but it can lead you astray, too. The best guideline for getting along in the wilderness, then, is to heed the advice and instructions of those in the know (like the guides on a guided trip) and use common sense when you've got nothing else to go by. Once again, you shouldn't be out on your own in Alaskan wilderness unless you have extensive outdoors experience and survival skills. You have to be ready, able, and willing to deal with the worst—and if you are, this is one of the very few places left on the planet where you can experience the exhilaration of having to deal with a land on its terms, not yours.

There are half a dozen principal hazards to be most concerned about in the Alaskan wilds: bears, bugs, hypothermia, stream crossings, and *giardia lamblia*, known colloquially in Alaska as beaver fever. The first three are ably addressed in the "Health" and "Safety" sections of Chapter 3; I'll say a little more about the last two.

GIARDIA Generally blamed on parasites carried by dog feces, giardia is a prevalent problem in streams throughout Alaska as well as the Lower 48. The symptoms are nausea, cramps, headaches, and diarrhea—and you don't want anything to do with them. The larger the river and the nearer you are to civilization, the more apt the water is to be contaminated. Conversely, small feeder streams in remote environments may be perfectly safe to drink from. If you're on a guided trip, follow the guide's advice regarding the purity of a particular stream. But to be safe, I strongly recommend making a policy of purifying all water you plan to drink from streams; you can use iodine tablets or, better yet, a filtering system. Both are available from sporting-goods stores, and you can get reusable, simple-to-use filters today that don't cost an arm and a leg.

CROSSING STREAMS & RIVERS This can be a lot more daunting in Alaska than you'd think on the face of it. This is cold, really *cold,* water; furthermore, the silt in glacially fed streams makes the water opaque and it can be difficult to gauge depth. And if you're hiking over tundra, a hard rain can change the character of a stream quickly—the permafrost won't absorb water, and thus a gentle creek can become a roaring river in a matter of hours. You'll want to be careful with your trip routing, picking a path that will lead you to the easiest places to cross rivers and streams. If you go out with a professional outfitter they'll take care of this for you, but even if you're going out on your own, it's a good idea to enlist the services of an outfitter in picking your itinerary—see "Planning an Independent Wilderness Adventure," later in this chapter.

If you can't find a place to rock-hop across a stream, scout along the banks for a wide place in the stream. If you can find one, a long stick will be useful in checking depth as you wade across. I like to pack a sure-footed pair of Tevas or some such waterproof sandal—they serve double duty as camp shoe and river footwear. Tie your boots and socks up in your pack and wade across; putting on your dry socks and boots afterward will be a near-religious experience.

REMINDER Finally, remember that the wilderness is wild—no phones, no hospital around the corner, no 911 number to call. In an emergency, help may be days away. Be prepared with extra prescription medications, extra eyeglasses, and basic first-aid equipment.

2 Traveling in the Alaskan Wilderness

What follows are recommended vacation possibilities in the Alaskan wilderness, culled from literally hundreds of trips and lodges you might want to consider. The prevailing variable to keep in mind is that almost anything can change—the dates, prices, activities included, and so on. If you don't like what's being offered, ask about options; many outfitters are very flexible. Customization and adaptation are norms rather than exceptions, often though not always contingent on how much you're willing to spend.

The difficulty ratings listed here are, as suggested, relative within this listing. They may not jibe with rating systems used by individual trip organizers. As a rough guideline, "easy" means pretty much anybody can do it, "moderate" means some degree of physical fitness is required, and "strenuous" means that you ought to be in good shape and should probably have at least some backcountry experience, or you're going to have a lousy time.

Traveling around in the wilderness is not cheap. If you're looking for bargain-basement deals in adventure travel, you've probably come to the wrong place in coming to Alaska. Small-plane flying to and from remote locations adds considerably to the bottom-line cost of many trips. In addition, the shortness of the Alaskan summer means that outfitters have perhaps a three-month window of opportunity within which to ply their trade. Finally, the cost of living in general in Alaska is high. But if prices might seem high, be comforted by the fact that few wilderness outfitters are getting rich in Alaska. They aren't in it for the money. Most do what they do because they love to do it.

SOUTHEAST

Chitistone Canyon Backpacking. St. Elias Alpine Guides, P.O. Box 111241, Anchorage, AK 99511. ☎ and fax **907/277-6867.** Approximate cost: $1,873. Dates: July–Aug. Trip length: 11 days. Group size: 2–6. Begins and ends in: Anchorage. Relative difficulty: Strenuous.

Upon being met by Bob Jacobs in McCarthy, the tiny former mining town at the confluence of the Root and Kennicott glaciers in Wrangell–St. Elias National Park, you might have good reason to be skeptical. The first impression is not impressive. Bob, head of St. Elias Alpine guides, drives an ancient tin can of a truck nicknamed Moondog, with not all of its body parts firmly attached, and Bob himself can come across as something of an eccentric. But he happens to be a sober-minded, preeminent alpinist who knows this neck of the Alaskan woods better than any other living being.

You'd have a hard time getting Bob to single out a favorite backpacking trip in the Wrangell–St. Elias region, given his abiding affection for just about every square inch of this exquisite wilderness. Yet stoke him with a beer or two and he might let slip that the hike through Chitistone Canyon into the high country around Skolai Pass is about as good as backpacking gets.

This is a classic, all-in-everything trip. It begins in a canyon framed by sheer, 4,000-foot cliffs and passes by sweeping, deep-valley glaciers and waterfalls hundreds of feet high. It rises to high, tundra meadows—the grazing lands of Dall sheep—and traverses Skolai Pass before reaching the broad basin of Skolai Creek. Severe rock walls, hanging glaciers, distant peaks reaching to over 16,000 feet—all are part of the backdrop.

It's a breathtaking trek and not at all easy. This is backpacking recommended for experienced, well-conditioned backpackers. Much of the trail—if it can be called a trail—links animal tracks, making surefootedness essential. This is true, alpine wilderness, where the weather can change faster than the time it takes to draw a deep breath and where self-sufficiency instincts are the key not just to comfort but to survival. You'll have to get by on backpacker food—nutritionally adequate, culinarily forgettable—and you may find yourself quarantined in a wet tent for two days waiting for a storm to pass. Total misery is not out of the question. So why bother? The rewards—the scenery, the wildlife, the challenge, the sense of accomplishment—exceed the limits of the imagination. It's as good as backpacking gets.

Muir Inlet Sea Kayaking. Alaska Discovery, 5449 Shaune Dr., Suite 4, Juneau, AK 99801. ☎ **907/780-6226** or 800/586-1911. Fax 907/780-4220. Approximate cost: $1,500. Dates: Mid-June to mid-Aug. Trip length: 5 days. Group size: Up to 10. Begins and ends in: Gustavus. Relative difficulty: Moderate.

Consider this syllogism: Kayaks are an essential part of Alaskan history, and Glacier Bay is one of the world's quintessential sea-kayaking regions; ergo, Glacier Bay sea kayaking has a long history. Not so—200 years ago, Glacier Bay was a mass of impassible glacial ice. It wasn't until glaciation in the area went into full retreat through the 1800s, at the astonishingly rapid rate of about half a mile a year, that the bay exposed itself as a navigable inland passage.

Glacier Bay has since become a frenzy of natural activity. Glaciers are literally coming and going, huge blocks of ice exploding into the water in a calving process Tlingit natives called "white thunder." Where glaciers have receded, wildlife has flourished; as John Muir, the naturalist for whom Muir Inlet is named, said himself: "Out of all the cold darkness and glacial crushing and grinding comes this warm, abounding beauty and life." Whales, sea lions, bears, wolves, mountain goats, moose, eagles—it is abounding life indeed. This convolution of nature draws a sizable human audience, their access enabled by deep channels in the bay allowing cruise ships to venture far inland. Muir Inlet, however—with its strong tides and narrow entry—does not present cruise ships with easy passage. As a result, sea kayakers can have this northeastern finger of the bay pretty much to themselves.

Glacier Bay is wet country. In 1982 naturalist Harry Fielding Reid grumbled about the certainty of rain in Glacier Bay: "If the sun shines, if the stars appear, if there are clouds, or if there are none; these are all sure indications [of rain]. If the barometer falls, it will rain; if the barometer rises, it will rain; if the barometer remains steady, it will continue to rain." Don't regard this as a deterrent but simply as likelihood to prepare for. You bring the rain gear, Alaska Discovery provides a solidly waterproof tent, and you're in business. And you never know—it might not rain. Reid might just have been having a bad day.

A relaxed kayaking itinerary, involving at most 40 miles in $3\frac{1}{2}$ days, leaves ample opportunity for beachcombing and hiking. If you're a total newcomer to paddling, you should take a guided or solo day trip before you embark on a multiday trip like this one—you won't have the option of dropping out if you don't like it. But very likely you'll love it: The skill to propel a stable, two-person kayak can be learned within minutes, and there's no tricky water on this trip to give novices hesitation. All you'll need is an eagerness to experience the natural frenzy of Glacier Bay away from the cruise-ship crowds.

Tatshenshini River Rafting. Mountain Travel • Sobek, 6420 Fairmount Ave., El Cerrito, CA 94530. ☎ **510/527-8100** or 800/227-2384. Fax 510/525-7710. Approximate cost: $1,875. Dates: July–Aug. Group size: Up to 12. Begins and ends in: Haines. Relative difficulty: Moderate.

Edward Abbey, the late, great gonzo environmentalist, once described a break from rafting on the Tatshenshini thusly: "We lie in the sunshine, on the warm grass, and stare at the mountains, range after range, standing beyond the dark forest. Now and then, so remote as to be barely audible, comes the rumble of readjustments, the clash and crash of falling ice. Flowers and ice, sunlight and snow . . . "

Whitewater and icebergs, too. The river begins in southwestern Yukon Territory as a fast stream with Class IV rapids. From there it flows for more than 100 miles through glacier-draped mountains, broadening to 2 miles wide before emptying into Alsek Bay, filled with icebergs freshly calved from tidewater glaciers. It's rich country and, as such, a rich haven of wildlife, most prominently such fish-hunting raptors as eagles and ospreys.

Sobek, a modern pioneer of guided rafting trips, was the first company to take paying guests down the "Tat"—a trip that has since come to be considered a river-running classic. So classic, in fact, that increased popularity has forced the National Park Service to institute a permit system for the section of the river that runs through Glacier Bay National Park. But it has hardly become a water-borne traffic jam; the permitting assures at the very least that you won't have to share evening campsites with other river runners. Your sense of privacy should remain undefiled. Your sense of wonder should become elevated, too, on a trip that ends, in Abbey's words, where "the river blends with the bay and the bay with the sea, and the sea melts, without dividing line, into a golden sky."

ANCHORAGE & SOUTHCENTRAL ALASKA

Anchorage Area Mountain Biking. Birch Bark Mountain Biking Adventures, P.O. Box 111591, Anchorage, AK 99511. ☎ **907/345-9055.** Fax 907/345-9723. Dates: June–Sept. Trip length: 3 days or more. Group size: Up to 8. Begins and ends in: Anchorage. Relative difficulty: Easy to moderate.

Maybe it's the lack of roads and trails. Maybe it's the many other Alaskan activities that vie for the attention of sporting people. For whatever reason, mountain biking has yet to catch on big in Alaska. There is, to be sure, a solid corps of local wild-and-crazies with scars and broken body parts to show for their adventurous efforts. But mountain-bike mania, on a California or Colorado scale, hasn't yet swept north to Alaska.

Alaska is hardly a mountain-biking wasteland, however, and some of the best riding can be found right in the Anchorage area. Don't be fooled into thinking that because the Chugach Mountains are close to the city they are somehow less rugged or more citified than other mountains in Alaska. Glaciers, rocky escarpments, fast-running mountain streams, waterfalls, bears, moose—all are within minutes of the metropolitan area. The one concession to civilization is a well-defined—and on weekends, well-used—trail system, a bonus for mountain bikers.

This trip has no fixed program, no weekly schedule or set daily itinerary. Go over daily options each morning with Peter Krabacher, proprietor of Birch Bark Mountain Biking Adventures, who will then gear you up with bikes, helmets, lunches, and a guide. You can ride for a day or a week, returning each evening to Anchorage after daily outings. A good strategy for a three-day program is to start easy, increasing the challenge of each daily ride. The trail along Eklutna Lake is wide and relatively flat, a good 24-mile warm-up ride. More challenging is the shorter but steeper climb right out of Anchorage to the summit of Flattop Mountain, with views on a clear day of Mount McKinley to the north and Cook Inlet to the south. After that, you may want to venture farther afield, to the 24-mile Johnson Pass Trail or the longer Resurrection Pass Trail (see below) on the Kenai Peninsula.

You can stay anywhere you want in Anchorage, but Krabacher's comfortable, well-appointed bed-and-breakfast is a good choice. Well removed from the heart of downtown, it isn't ideal for anyone keen on evenings spent dining or shopping in

Anchorage. On the other hand, you can pop out the door and be on your way up Flattop within minutes. That's not a bad back yard.

Hatcher Pass Snowcat Skiing, Glacier Snow Cat Skiing & Tours, P.O. Box 874234, Wasilla, AK 99687. ☎ and fax **907/373-3118.** Approximate cost: $1,200. Dates: Jan–Apr. Trip length: 5 days. Group size: 12. Begins and ends in: Anchorage. Relative difficulty: Moderate to strenuous.

The shortage of ski areas in a state as mountainous and snowy as Alaska is something of a mystery. This shortage has fueled a healthy renegade attitude among Alaskan skiing enthusiasts who feel liberated to go wherever they feel like going—not necessarily where there are lifts—and whose tracks can often be spotted in outlandishly hard-to-ski places. At Thompson Pass, north of Valdez and home of the annual World Extreme Skiing Championship, self-guided heli-skiing is the current rage. Gather together your best skiing buddies, scrape up the bucks (about $25 a head) for a helicopter ride to some remote mountaintop, and bon voyage! Great stuff, but for anyone unfamiliar with the terrain and not well schooled in dealing with the deadly hazards (avalanches, crevasses) of big-mountain skiing, to go about this unguided is risk-taking on a grand scale.

Fortunately, there are safer ways to go backcountry skiing in Alaska, with guided snowcat skiing at Hatcher Pass ranking at the top of that list. Hatcher Pass is less than a two-hour drive north of Anchorage, but it's far enough into the Interior to be only minimally affected by the moderating (that is, dampening) influences of Alaska's coastal climate. That can mean cold weather, but it can also mean wonderfully light, dry snow—nearly 500 inches' worth in an average winter. That snow covers roughly 1,500 acres and 2,000 vertical feet of skiable terrain—not eye-popping numbers, but plenty of skiing when you only have to share it with 11 other skiers in the snowcat. It's ideal for strong intermediates eager to improve their powder-skiing skills.

Don't fret too much about the cold; the snowcat is heated, and there's a warming hut where you can hole up between runs if you want to. You can also keep warm by logging 20,000 vertical feet or more in a day. The Motherlode, originally built in the 1930s when mining was active at Hatcher Pass, provides daily meals and nightly accommodations. You could spend a few dollars more to stay in fancier digs in nearby Wasilla, but the Motherlode (renovated since the mining days) has a comfortable, funky feel and a knock-out view from the dining room. After five days of Hatcher Pass skiing, maybe then you'll be ready to take on the steeps and deep snow of Thompson Pass. Maybe.

Kenai Peninsula Rafting and Wilderness, Alaska Wildland Adventures, P.O. Box 389, Girdwood, AK 99587. ☎ **907/783-2928** or 800/334-8730. Fax 907/783-2130. Approximate cost: $1,195 (for cabins), $995 (for tents). Dates: June to mid-Sept. Trip length: 4 days. Group size: 4–10. Begins and ends in: Anchorage. Relative difficulty: Easy.

On a weekend day when the salmon are running, the Kenai River can turn into a combat-fishing zone. Fisticuffs are not out of the question as fishermen standing shoulder to shoulder attempt to assert their perceived right to occupy particular patches of fish-infested waters.

Fortunately, there are kinder, gentler ways to experience the Kenai. Start from Cooper Landing on a relaxed float by raft along the upper stretches of the Kenai River. Expect to see plenty of birds, the occasional moose, and perhaps a couple of fishermen, toe to toe, whaling at one another. From there the river picks up steam, gaining Class III force through a lower canyon before spilling into glacier-fed Skilak Lake, where the color of the water changes from aquamarine to turquoise, depending on the wind and the light of day.

Cross the lake to a small backcountry lodge, in the heart of the two-million acre Kenai Wildlife Refuge, and the sense of removal from civilization becomes quickly and dramatically complete. One Alaska Wildland Adventures employee recalls arriving one time at the unoccupied lodge to see on the front window the unmistakable imprint of two giant and muddy bear paws.

This may be considered rustic living, in that the absence of running water makes an outhouse imperative. But accommodations in outlying log cabins or wood-framed "cabin" tents are remarkably comfortable and the food borders on gourmet. From the lodge, kayaking on the lake or hiking to tundral ridges, for exceptional views of the Kenai Peninsula backcountry, are the main activities for the next couple of days. Or you can simply while away your time reading or card-playing in the main lodge, waiting for that bear to come banging at the window.

Resurrection Pass Backpacking. Chugach Hiking Tours. ☎ **907/278-4553.** Approximate cost: $500. Dates: June–Aug. Trip length: 6 days. Group size: 4–8. Begins and ends in: Anchorage. Relative difficulty: Moderate.

The trail over Resurrection Pass is quite probably Alaska's most popular backpacking trip. The Chilkoot Trail in Southeast Alaska is the only real contender, and since more than half of it is actually in Yukon Territory, its true-Alaskan credentials are suspect. Both trails share a common history, having been cut in the late 1800s by prospectors sniffing around for rich gold deposits. The gold is gone and so are the prospectors, but the land remains relatively unscathed—clear lakes with good fishing and stark mountains that appear much more substantial than topological maps indicate. A 5,000-foot peak sounds modest until you come upon its tundra-covered flanks and sharp crags sequestering patches of summer-resistant snow.

The trek southward from Hope to Cooper Landing on the Kenai River covers 40 miles, and you're assured of seeing other backcountry travelers along the way. The trail is well formed and gradual enough to have become popular among local mountain bikers, some of whom roar over the full length of the trail in one day. There are several public-use cabins along the way to indulge those with an aversion to tent camping, further broadening the appeal of hiking the trail. Nevertheless, this is hardly a teeming thoroughfare of recreational activity, and particularly on weekdays early in the summer the sense of wilderness isolation can be complete. You're more apt to encounter mountain bikers and horseback riders later in the summer, when trails are fully clear of snow.

This is a trip geared to people with little or no backpacking experience. "This is," says Cable Starling, proprietor of Chugach Hiking Tours, "about learning how to backpack and learning about Alaska." That's a learning process that begins with proper gearing and packing, includes the selection of appropriate food for the trip, and continues onto the trail, with the business of maintaining camp and preparing meals. It is learning in which, as Starling says, "everybody is an equal participant." If all of that sounds like some laborious wilderness clinic, forget about it. The hiking is fairly easy, at least by rigorous Alaskan backpacking standards. The beauty of the landscape is nonstop entertainment, and Starling himself makes for engaging backcountry company. It may be learning, but it's quite the classroom. And if you want to learn more, keep on going. A good trail, with fewer people but more bears, continues on for 30 miles from Cooper Landing, the southern terminus of the Resurrection Pass Trail, to Seward.

Prince William Sound Sailing and Sea Kayaking. Alaska Wilderness Sailing Safaris, P.O. Box 1313, Valdez, AK 99686. ☎ **907/835-5175.** Fax 907/835-5679. Approximate cost: $1,200. Dates: June–Aug. Trip length: 7 days. Begins and ends in: Anchorage. Relative difficulty: Moderate.

Prince William Sound is a name that will forever live in ecological infamy. The 1989 *Exxon Valdez* spill imprinted images on the national consciousness of oil-smothered bird carcasses, blackened beaches, and courtrooms filled with finger-pointing trial combatants. Despite the comedy of errors that the spill and subsequent cleanup efforts proved to be (see "The *Exxon Valdez:* What Wasn't Learned," in Chapter 8, on the spill), Prince William Sound is well on its way to regaining its dignity as one of Alaska's great natural preserves.

You can make of this trip what you want. A base camp on tiny Growler Island, in the heart of the Sound, is the beginning and end of each day's activities. It's your choice each day as to whether to go sailing or kayaking (experience in either is not necessary as lessons are offered), and it's your call as to how devotedly you want to pursue either. Sailing trips, aboard a 40-foot sloop, can cover more territory, to permit viewing of, among other natural phenomena, the Columbia Glacier insistently pushing into the sea or (depending on the season) pods of migrating whales, sea otters, and eagles. On the other hand, kayaks—primarily stable, idiot-proof two-person inflatables—are better for exploring shorelines, pocked with hidden coves and sea caves. Sedentary boat time can be relieved by short hikes through moss-floored rain forests or along alpine ridges.

The logistics of getting to and from the Growler Island camp call for a close encounter with mainstream Alaskan tourism: a tour-bus, train, and tour-boat combo (see Valdez section under "The Kenai Peninsula," in Chapter 8, for information on Stan Stephens Cruises). That means two full days devoted to coming and going. It's scenic, certainly, but you might want to expedite the process by plunking down the extra change for a round-trip flight between Anchorage and Valdez. Once in camp, the accommodations in floored, heated tents—really canvas-sided cabins—make for "camping" in the loosest, cushiest sense of the word.

THE INTERIOR

Denali Horsepacking. Wolf Point Ranch, C/o American Wilderness Experience, P.O. Box 1486, Boulder, CO 80306. ☎ **303/444-2622** or 800/444-0099. Fax 303/444-3999. Approximate cost: $1,355. Dates: June–July. Trip length: 6 days. Begins and ends in: Denali Park. Relative difficulty: Moderate.

Historically, horses have not had an easy time of it in Alaska. They were originally brought to Alaska during the gold-rush era as pack animals, to lug the supplies over steep passes from Skagway north to the gold fields. It was fatally hard work, as it turned out. During the 1897–98 Gold Rush, more than 3,000 horses died along the White Pass Trail (from Skagway to Lake Bennett, in Yukon Territory) in an area that came to be known as Dead Horse Gulch. Historian Ethel Anderson Becker wrote of their suffering: "The glare of the snow blinded their eyes. Blizzards froze their lungs. Overloaded pack animals missed their footing as they dodged boulders or jumped sump holes, and lay legs up, screaming in agony and despair." Maybe it is this history of suffering—not to mention the long harsh winters—that has discouraged horsepacking outfitters from setting up shop in Alaska.

Nonetheless horses in summertime provide sturdy, reliable transport deep into the backcountry, in Alaska as in other mountainous regions. They can be particularly good vehicles in negotiating trail-less valleys, where bushwhacking on foot in alder and willow thickets and across swift-running streams can be debilitatingly difficult. Horses are better suited for the job. They're also better suited than humans as pack animals, just as they were back in the gold-rush era. The result is relatively high-end camping and wilderness dining.

This trip leads 60 miles into the Yanert Valley east of Denali, bringing into focus the sawtoothed upthrust of the Alaska Range and the ghostly, horizon-dominating spectacle of Mount McKinley. Tundra, wildflower-covered meadows, deep valleys, high-mountain passes—it's all here, well removed from the summer crowds of the eastern regions of the park. There are some who theorize that the sounds and strong smells of horses chase away wildlife, but don't count on it. Expect to spot Dall sheep feeding on steep mountainsides, very probably moose, and quite possibly bears. Previous riding experience is not essential for adventurous sorts, but it's advisable.

Skwentna Dog Mushing. Lucky Husky Racing Kennel, HC 89 Box 256, Willow, AK 99688. ☎ **907/495-6470.** Fax 907/495-6471. Approximate cost: $1,995. Dates: Jan–Mar. Trip length: 5 days. Group size: 2–4. Begins and ends in: Anchorage. Relative difficulty: Strenuous.

Skwentna, population 20 or so, lies out in the middle of nowhere, in the great plain formed by the Yentna and Kahiltna rivers that run from the glaciers of Mount McKinley. On a clear day, the Mount McKinley massif is a looming presence in the distance, its overwhelming size making it seem much closer than it is.

Like other checkpoints along the route of the Iditarod dog-sled race, Skwentna is a relatively somnolent place in summer. Fishermen and boatspeople stop briefly to gas up and resupply, then are on their way to lodges upriver. But in winter the action picks up: Snowmobilers, dog-sledders, cross-country skiers, and snowshoers, their overland passage enabled in winter by a well-traveled highway of snow, make their way to and through Skwentna. It is here that Ruth Hirsiger—Swiss by upbringing, Alaskan by cultural adaptation—leads dog-mushing trips, five days and 100 miles westward through the forest and over frozen bogs and riverbeds from Willow.

Hirsiger, a top-flight musher in short-distance races, is shooting for bigger things in 1997—a chance to compete in the Iditarod. That's no small undertaking; dog food is expensive, and you've got to pay the bills somehow. To help make ends meet, Hirsiger guides mushing trips, not always an easy undertaking, either. Accommodations at night are usually in log cabins or roadhouses, but there is the occasional night when it may be necessary to bivouac on a frozen swamp with the temperature 20° below or colder.

Cold is a part of mushing life, and mushers have a way of appearing much bigger than they are—looming presences in bulky, fur-trimmed outerwear hiding several layers of warm clothing. Well-insulated clothing is vitally essential. However, the cold of the Alaskan Interior is more often than not a clear cold, with the sun warming the midday air and with distant mountains crisply etched against a blue sky. Within this deep-winter environment, you learn to drive your own six-dog team, which can charge along as fast as 10 miles an hour when the trail is packed and smooth. If you ever wanted to get a taste of what Iditarod racing is all about, this is your chance.

Richardson Highway Bicycling. Alaskan Bicycle Adventures, 2734 Iliamna Ave., Anchorage, AK 99517. ☎ **907/243-2329** or 800/770-7242. Fax 907/243-4985. Approximate cost: $2,195. Dates: June–Sept. Trip length: 8 days. Begins and ends in: Anchorage. Relative difficulty: Moderate.

The Richardson Highway is Alaska's original highway, a one-time wagon trail stretching 360 miles from Fairbanks to Valdez, and it remains quite possibly its most scenic. If you like mountain views, this is your kind of highway, skirting or traversing the major mountain ranges of the state. Ride through the Alaska Range, crowned by Mount McKinley; past Wrangell–St. Elias National Park and its glaciated, 16,000-foot peaks; then through the Chugach Mountains at Thompson Pass, known for legendary snowfalls that have exceeded 5 feet in 24 hours. Unfortunately, too many

Alaskan visitors figure that the only way to see it all is by tour bus or RV, often blasting through in a single day, watching this special world rush by like a rapid-fire succession of dioramas in a natural-history museum.

There is an alternative, of course. As a cyclist, you must endure the noxious presence of RVs or tour buses (which pass by in a thick stream during the July peak season) hogging highway sections where shoulders are minimal. That unpleasantness aside, this is bicycle touring according to the blueprint: smooth road, few big hills to ride over (with some notable exceptions, like Thompson Pass and the climb up into the Alaska Range), spectacular scenery. You can pull over whenever the mood strikes, take a nap, smell and pick the wildflowers. Daily mileages of between 50 and 75 miles might sound like a grunt, but there's a comforting catch: You can wimp out whenever your body or spirit surrenders. A support van—known as the sag wagon or broom wagon—follows along just for that purpose. You might, however, find yourself riding longer than you thought possible; the surprise, in such mountainous country, is that the greatest daily elevation gain in a day's ride is 1,800 vertical feet.

This is road-bound travel and as such is obviously not wilderness adventuring in a truly rugged, remote context. Either you appreciate the occasional conveniences of roadside civilization, or you have chosen the wrong trip. Most nights are spent in comfortable motels or lodges. There is one night of camping, but as stated emphatically in bold type in the brochure, "you do none of the work!" Bikes are provided unless you want to bring your own; all you need bring is your own clothing, legs, lungs, and eyes.

Talkeetna Mountains Backpacking. Alaska Wilderness Journeys, P.O. Box 220204, Anchorage, AK 99522. ☎ **907/349-2964** or 800/349-0064. Fax 907/349-2964. Approximate cost: $725. Dates: tk. Trip length: 3 days. Group size: 4–8. Begins and ends in: Anchorage. Relative difficulty: Moderate to strenuous.

Walking a high ridgeline is, as Steve Weller of Alaska Wilderness Journeys says, "as good as it gets in Alaska." Above the treeline, you feel on a clear day as if you could see forever. That's particularly true when you can look over your shoulder with every step to see the hulking presence of the Mount McKinley massif commanding the western skies. The Talkeetnas are a humble range by big-mountain Alaska standards, being neither exceptionally high nor exceptionally rugged. They're a land between, with the more commanding Alaska Range (including McKinley) to the north and the Chugach Mountains to the south.

The ridges of the Talkeetnas are, simply, hikeable, unlike the more forbidding ridges of neighboring ranges. Sure, it might be a rough scramble at times to traverse steep, trail-less terrain, but it's do-able—nothing even close to technical mountaineering skills that might be required to hike ridges in the Alaska Range.

This is a short trip, just three days and two nights, and some of that time is consumed in driving between Anchorage and the small town of Talkeetna as well as in flying in and out of the mountains. As wild as this country is, the trip itself isn't entirely wild; one evening's dinner is at a remote lodge (see the Caribou Lodge, under "Wilderness Lodges," later in this chapter). This means that you can get by with a fairly light pack, making the scrambling easier and reserving more energy (for hardcore hiking junkies) for short after-dinner hikes. If three days sounds all too brief, you can combine this trip with others offered by Alaska Wilderness Journeys—a three-day raft down the Tazlina River, for example. Ridgelines and rivers—that truly is as good as it gets in Alaska.

SOUTHWEST

Shuyak Island Kayaking. Adventure Alaska, 2904 W. 31st Ave., Anchorage, AK 99517. ☎ **907/248-0400** or 800/365-7057. Fax 907/248-0409. Approximate cost: $1,875. Dates: June–July. Trip length: 9 days. Group size: 2–6. Begins and ends in: Anchorage. Relative difficulty: Moderate.

Erase preconceived images of what Alaska is supposed to look like—big mountains, big rivers, big glaciers, that sort of thing. Shuyak Island is different. "Seeing it from the air, you wouldn't be very impressed," says Claire Holland, the district ranger who oversees Shuyak Island State Park. It sits like an insignificantly small patch of dark green against the deep-blue ocean waters off the northern coast of Kodiak Island. But once on the ground, the perception changes dramatically.

Virgin Sitka spruce forests surround a maze of bays and inlets, rimmed by a stark, often storm-battered coastline. The island is, as Holland says, a "naturalist's dream," a world teeming with sea otters, sea lions, deer, and various species of birds, both resident and migratory—puffins, oystercatchers, cormorants, guillemots, ducks of all sorts, kittiwakes, and rhino auklets, among others. It's also a kayaker's dream. When the winds, tides, and storms pound the coastline, fine paddling can still be had on protected inner bays and coves. When the rough weather relents, the coast reveals another world entirely, a choice spot for sea-lion rookeries, possible whale sightings, and, on a clear day, certain sightings of the prominent volcanoes of the mainland coast, 30 miles distant across Shelikof Strait. Bill Herman, an Adventure Alaska trip leader, recalls one time watching orcas (killer whales) feeding on sea lions, "tossing them into the air like salmon."

Assume that you'll get wet. Shuyak's rich agglomeration of plant, animal, and bird life has a direct relationship to the island's considerable rainfall, conservatively measured at 50 inches or more in an average year. Technical kayaking skills in these relatively calm waters are not required to paddle the two-person kayaks, and camping know-how is not a prerequisite, either. However, this trip is not for total lightweights; you must be ready each morning to take on a full day of paddling and to help set up camp when evening comes. That's not hard work, but you must still be a game outdoorsperson, prepared at times to go *mano a mano* with the mercurial weather. In this microcosm of natural bounty, it's worth it.

YUKON RIVER DELTA

Yukon River Fish Camp. Yukon Starr, P.O. Box 126, Tanana, AK 99777. ☎ **907/366-7251.** Dates: June–Aug. Trip length: 3 days or more. Group size: 1–4. Begins and ends in: Fairbanks. Relative difficulty: Easy.

Cathy Fliris—seamstress by trade, dog musher by winter, fisherwoman by summer— is a runner by recreational habit. She's also a runner with an unusual tendency; she hits the road with a .44-caliber pistol strapped to her chest. That's just a part of life when life means subsistence survival in the Alaskan Bush, where a runner always runs the chance of a sudden encounter with an ill-tempered bear.

Understanding the Alaskan wilds is at least in part understanding the people who have forged a way of life deep in the Bush. In that context, this trip is not an adventure trip in the usual sense of the word. It is, instead, a quick and deep immersion in Bush life. During the summer months, Bill and Cathy Fliris operate a traditional Yukon River fish camp, scooping up silver and chum salmon from the river with a ferris-wheel-like fish wheel. Some fish they sell commercially, but most are rack-dried and stored, to be fed later to their team of sled dogs.

To reach the Flirises' camp, you must travel upriver from Tanana aboard the shallow-draft speedboat of Paul Starr, a full-blooded Athabascan. A former barge pilot, Starr has an insider's feel for the history and moods of the river. As you work your way against the flow, you'll pass other fish camps and a Native "spirit" camp, where local Natives come for soul-rejuvenating gatherings. Once at the Flirises' camp, don't expect luxury; this is makeshift, Bush-simple living, unretouched by any of the familiar trappings of tourism. You share with the Flirises their daily way of life—the fishing, the drying of fish, the splendid solitude of summer on the Yukon River banks—that so fascinated one German visitor that he stayed a full month. A month's stay isn't necessary; for a firsthand experience of what subsistence living is like, three or four days should do. Within that time, you may even run into a bear.

THE ARCTIC

John River Canoeing. Sourdough Outfitters, P.O. Box 90, Bettles, AK 99726. ☎ **907/692-5252.** Fax 907/692-5612. Approximate cost: $1,350. Dates: June–Aug. Trip length: 6 days. Group size: 4–8. Begins and ends in: Fairbanks. Relative difficulty: Moderate to strenuous.

Bettles is a dusty, sad-sack place on the banks of the Koyukuk River, just north of the Arctic Circle. Most people come to Bettles in order to leave Bettles; it's a major take-off point for adventure travelers headed into the Brooks Range. But, inevitably, more time is spent in Bettles than ought to be spent there as small planes come and go, carrying backpackers, canoeists, fishermen, and others in and out of the wilderness. Not a moment too soon, your call to fly comes; canoes are strapped to the pontoon struts of a float plane, a week's worth of gear and food is loaded on board, and you're winging it 100 miles north, to where the Hunt Fork meets the main flow of the John River.

The contrast between this sharply etched mountain basin and drab Bettles is striking, and it's just a start. For the next six days you follow the serpentine course of the John as it carves a path southward through the Brooks Range. This is wild country; in 100-plus river miles, you pass one dirt airstrip, the only sign of human intervention, and you've got to look hard to see it. In six days on the river you're highly unlikely to see another human being. You're very likely to see grizzly bears, moose, and caribou—certain to see their fresh tracks on any beach where you choose to set up camp for the night.

The John is a river that takes its time. A few rapids may approach Class II status early in the summer, but later in the summer extra paddling may be required to assure forward progress through languid stretches of water. The thrill here is not in any white-water challenge but rather in the profoundly wild wilderness and the chaotic geologic beauty of the surrounding mountains. Examine stones along the shore; most are works of natural art or sculpture and each, in its shape and striations, has a tale of geological history to tell.

There's nothing fancy about this trip. The food (mostly backpacker-style entrees like macaroni and cheese) is simple, the tent accommodations are simple, the means of transport simple. Time sneaks by, passing quietly and more quickly than you might imagine. Nearing the end of the trip, the river exits the mountains and passes by bluffs embedded with mastodon remains, where peregrine falcons soar and chatter. Within a few miles the John comes to an end at its confluence with the Koyukuk River, a few miles downriver from Bettles—sad, dusty Bettles.

3 Planning an Independent Wilderness Adventure

There's a funny thing about Alaska. The more remote the country and the more rugged the adventure, the more likely you are to encounter European travelers—English, French, German, Italians. You encounter and hear often about Europeans roaming around in faraway places: two Frenchmen bicycling the Yukon River in winter; two Italians heading off for three weeks on a river in the Brooks Range; an English couple cycling along the Dalton Highway from Fairbanks to Prudhoe Bay.

This doesn't necessarily mean that Europeans on the whole have greater wilderness savvy than Americans, but it probably does imply a greater willingness to rough it on personal terms, to take on the wilderness unguided. Put another way, though skill and experience are both essential to carrying off an independent wilderness trip in Alaska, proper preparation and adaptive ingenuity are probably just as important. If you aren't ready, willing, and resourceful in adapting to unpredictable wilderness conditions, you may, literally or figuratively, be up the creek without a paddle.

Probably the best way of going about an independent adventure is to enlist the services of any of a number of Alaska-based outfitters. These are outfitters in the traditional sense of the word—they provide support and gear for people heading off into remote regions. They can suggest itineraries, provide equipment, arrange flights to and from wilderness drop-off points, and assist in formulating a gear and food list. Among the companies that provide such outfitting services are **St. Elias Alpine Guides** and **Sourdough Outfitters** and **Alaska Air Taxi, K-2 Aviation,** and **Rust's Flying Service** (see "Recommended Air Services," below).

The services of an outfitter do not necessarily come cheaply. If you're looking for an inexpensive way to experience the Alaskan wilds on your own, backpacking in Southcentral Alaska or paddling in Southeast are probably the best ways to go. For equipment rentals, particularly backpacking and camping gear, good places to go are: **Gary King Sporting Goods,** 202 E. Northern Lights Blvd. (☎ **907/279-7454**), or **REI,** 1200 W. Northern Lights Blvd. (☎ **907/272-4565**), both in Anchorage; **Beaver Sports,** 2400 College Rd., Fairbanks (☎ **907/479-2494**); and **Adventure Sports,** 2092 Jordan Ave., Juneau (☎ **907/789-5696**). For sea-kayak rentals in Southeast, **Outdoor Alaska,** P.O. Box 7814, Ketchikan, AK 99901 (☎ **907/ 225-6044**). Kayak rentals must usually be reserved a month or more in advance.

Maps are available in many local sports stores, but if you know where you want to go and want to study maps before heading for Alaska, contact the **U.S. Geological Survey** (see "Preparing for the Alaskan Wilderness," earlier in this chapter). District or superintendent's offices for national parks, national forests, state parks, state forests, or wildlife refuges may also be able to provide maps and information.

A great way to go for independent travelers is to overnight in **public-use cabins,** most highly concentrated in Tongass National Forest in Southeast and in the Chugach Mountains in Southcentral Alaska. Some are road-accessible, but most are along hiking trails or remote waterways. These cabins are typically small and spare, with bunk platforms for sleeping and usually a stove and utensils for cooking. Most, however, are well maintained and many, especially in Southeast, require reservations well in advance. Cabin-permit fees generally range between $15 and $25 per night.

You can get information on public-use cabins from the **Alaska Public Lands Information Center** or by contacting **Alaska State Parks,** the **Bureau of Land**

Management, Chugach National Forest, or **Tongass National Forest;** a good number are also described in the regional chapters filling out the rest of this book, under the "Getting Outside" sections within a given town section.

4 Wilderness Lodges

The wilderness lodge, like other aspects of adventure travel, is an evolving concept. Not long ago, most lodges in remote locations were dedicated either to fishing or to hunting, or to both. But this is the age of eco-travel, introducing lodge operators to a whole new breed of guest. Families, elderly people, honeymooning newlyweds—the world where virile hunters and fishermen once prowled alone is now being infiltrated by a much different sort of sportsperson.

To be sure, many hunting and fishing lodges are still in healthy operation, and at almost all lodges, fishing remains a focal activity. At the wilderness lodge of the 1990s, however, hiking, canoeing, rafting, horseback riding, and wildlife viewing fill up the day. Many lodge proprietors are still fine-tuning their activities programs in accordance with the requests from clients; often you'll find that an activity not normally offered (a long hike, an overnight camping trip) can be arranged if you ask for it. It may simply be that the lodge operators, still getting the hang of adventure travel, never expected there to be an interest in a particular activity until somebody inquired about it.

In addition, the rude, bunk-style accommodations and hardtack-basic meals often associated with hunting or fishing lodges are giving way to accommodations that are often quite elegant and to meals of legitimately gourmet caliber. Many lodges take great pride in the lavishness with which they can surprise guests anticipating wilderness austerity. The wilderness may be wild, but it doesn't have to be uncomfortable.

There are, obviously, a good many wilderness lodges in Alaska. (As a matter of definition, "wilderness lodge" in this case refers here to a lodge inaccessible by road—accessible basically only by small plane.) Most are in Interior, Southcentral, and Southeast Alaska. (There may be more in Southwest Alaska than anywhere else, almost all of them catering to the spectacular fishing possibilities available off the Alaska Peninsula and Aleutians—see Chapter 11, "The Bush," for detailed information. We were only able to get to some of the less remote places this year; there will be more in the next edition of this book.) The following is a short sampling of recommended lodges, not only to give you a feeling for the broad range in price, accommodations, and activities, but also to provide some idea of where they fit within the full context of wilderness/adventure travel in Alaska. For other recommended lodges, see the "Where to Stay" sections in regional chapters in this book.

Caribou Lodge. P.O. Box 706, Talkeetna, AK 99676. ☎ **907/733-2163.** 3 cabins accommodate six. Five-day package $700 (a sample). Open year round.

Location is everything. A lodge doesn't have to be palatial or offer a dazzling smörgåsbord of activities in order to be appealing. So it is with Caribou Lodge, high on the tundral meadows of the Talkeetna Mountains, 30 miles east of Talkeetna. This is not a scruffy place, mind you; it just isn't anything more than it has to be. The entire compound consists of a small main lodge, three tiny cabins, and a shared shower and sauna. Hearty meals, a clean, comfortable bed, and a roof overhead—you don't need much more when you can rise in the morning to see a setting like this. Look to the west and Mount McKinley rises like a ghostly presence. To the east, at the doorstep of the lodge, lies a clear lake, mirroring the high ridges of the Talkeetnas in the distance.

Hiking across the trail-less tundra and watching for wildlife are the activities that consume the day. Wildflowers are most abundant earlier in the summer; August into early September is berry season. If you want, you can literally broaden your horizons by combining your lodge stay with guided backpacking trips of up to six days. And don't rule out a winter visit—if anything, the setting becomes more spectacular when winter sets in. This is excellent terrain for cross-country skiing, dog mushing, snowshoeing, or snowmobiling. What's more, the above-treeline location allows for excellent views of the northern lights during dark winter nights.

Chelatna Lake Fishing and Rafting. 3941 Float Plane Dr., Anchorage, AK 99502. ☎ **907/ 243-7767** or 800/999-0785. Cabins accommodating 16 guests in total. Open June–Sept.

The people who run Chelatna Lake Lodge seem determined to demonstrate to their guests that the wilderness need not be wild. Don't be misled by an old lodge that has been left more or less intact, a log structure filled with antiquated sofas, a craps table, and cases of beer. That's a sideshow relic for guests who can't relinquish the old-boy notion that a fishing lodge must be a rough-hewn, unkempt place, where men never shave and drink their whiskey straight-up. The rest of the Chelatna compound, including a handsome new main lodge, is spic-and-span New Age, with plush accommodations in recently built cabins and legitimately gourmet meals at night. The old boys might gag, but Chelatna Lake Lodge, located 100 miles northwest of Anchorage, is a place a yuppie could love.

Fishing remains the lodge's main raison d'être, as it was back when the old lodge was the only lodge. Each morning, guides and fishermen fly off in small planes to choice spots not far away. When the salmon are running, the fish are so ridiculously easy to catch that by lunchtime most fishermen are no longer, strictly speaking, fishermen; instead they're lolling around the beach cracking jokes and swilling beer. This is lazy man's fishing of the highest order: The guides disengage fresh catches from lures, gut and filet the fish, then prepare them on dry ice for shipping. As one recent guest commented, "You never have to touch your fish until you pull it out of your freezer back home."

But after your fill of lazy-man fishing, what's next? If you don't want to chill out at the lodge and behold the drop-dead view across the lake, rafting is a terrific alternative. The rafting program at Chelatna is still underdeveloped, primarily because most guests, men and women, come fixated on fishing. Short day trips on Lake Creek are the current offering, but Duke Bertke, the lodge proprietor, has contemplated overnight trips. If you are insistent and have enough allies among other guests to plead your case, you might talk him into arranging an excursion farther downstream. In its southward passage, the "creek"—more like a medium-sized river—gains more dramatic white-water force. It's a blast of wilderness reality that lodge guests, seeking respite from all that pampering, might appreciate.

Riversong Lodge. Riversong Adventures, 2463 Cottonwood St., Anchorage, AK 99508. ☎ **907/274-2710.** Fax 907/277-6256. Four-day/four-night package $1,415 (a sample). 10 guest cabins. Open year round.

Some 65 miles northwest of Anchorage, Riversong Lodge is a first-rate example of just how far the fishing-lodge concept has come from the roughing-it-in-the-wilderness days. To be sure, the reason people come here is to immerse themselves in the wilderness. But while the wilderness inspires them, it's usually the food at the lodge that ends up astonishing them—far superior to anything anyone would have a right to expect so far from civilization. Kirsten Dixon has been hailed by many restaurant critics as being the best chef anywhere in Alaska, let alone the best chef at a wilderness lodge. So good are the meals she cooks up that some guests fly in for the evening from Anchorage to do nothing but eat.

Of course there's more to Riversong than good food. Like so many lodges, fishing (primarily for salmon) tops the activity list, but there's more than that, too. Somewhat unusual for a wilderness lodge, Riversong offers extended guided trips into the outback of Southwest Alaska. Perhaps the most intriguing of these is a four-day trip (at $1,450 per person) into Lake Clark National Park, the great mystery among national parks in Alaska. Just across Cook Inlet from the popular Kenai Peninsula, the park is so rarely visited that even native Alaskans tend to scratch their heads in befuddlement when asked where it is.

So here's a sensible program: Take the trip into Lake Clark, where you can fish the remote Chilikidrotna River and hike in the surrounding mountains—a world you'll have almost entirely to yourself for four days. After that, return to the lodge, a log structure with outlying cabins sequestered in the woods, for a day or more. There are few things more satisfying than a good meal after several days in the wilderness—especially when it's a meal prepared by one of the most heralded chefs in Alaska.

Ultima Thule Lodge. Ultima Thule Outfitters, P.O. Box 109, Chitina, AK 99566 or 1007 H St, Anchorage, AK 99501. ☎ **907/258-0636.** Fax 907/258-4642. 4 multiple-room guest cabins. Seven-day package $2,800 (a sample). Open year round.

Rafting, hiking, fishing, camping, wildlife viewing, photography, horseback riding, mountaineering, backpacking, flightseeing, beachcombing, sea kayaking—that's an incomplete list of activities offered at Ultima Thule Lodge, located 100 miles west of Chitina. It's incomplete because if you come in winter, you can also go alpine skiing, ski touring, snowshoeing, ice skating, ice fishing, dog mushing, or "up-skiing." Up-skiing? Don't ask—simply suffice it to say that the Ultima Thule crew has combed the planet in search of all conceivable forms of outdoor fun and games. And who knows? Bareback whale-riding or white-water waterskiing may be next—the search no doubt continues. Just reading about what's possible at Ultima Thule is an exhausting exercise.

One reason that Ultima Thule can offer all that it offers is the location of the lodge, in the heart of Wrangell–St. Elias National Park. Even by big Alaskan standards, this is big country. The mountains are immense; Mount Logan, just west over the border in Canada, is said to be the world's largest mountain, in total bulk if not in height. The glaciers are long and deep, and the rivers run swift and murky with glacial silt—water that mountain people call glacial milk. Give a person a small plane and a big idea, and almost anything, as Ultima Thule seems set on proving, is possible.

If you dislike small-plane flying, Ultima Thule is not the place for you. Most activities, weather permitting, involve shuttling in and out of the surrounding mountains, landing on glaciers or gravel bars or on the beaches of the Gulf of Alaska. Unless you're planning an extended stay in the Wrangell–St. Elias backcountry—something, as you might expect, that Ultima Thule can set up for you if you want—you'll return by plane to the lodge each evening. This is a plush place as wilderness lodges go, the sleeping accommodations featuring down comforters and skylights for keeping watch on the northern lights. There's a sauna, too—probably the most welcome, muscle-relaxing feature of the lodge after 10 hours or more a day of romping around in the wilderness.

5 Further Reading

There is no shortage of books, from guides to personal narratives, on the Alaskan wilderness. An excellent source for books and maps is the **Alaska Natural History Association,** 605 W. Fourth Ave., Suite 85, Anchorage, AK 99501 (☎ **907/ 278-8440;** fax 907/274-8343). Books that may be helpful include *Alaska Parklands,* by Nancy Lange Simmerman (Seattle: The Mountaineers); its one- to two-page descriptions of state and national parklands in Alaska are adequate, but appendix material and nuggets of useful information on topography, climatology, edible flora, etc. make the book well worthwhile. *The Alaska River Guide,* by Karen Jettmar (Portland, Ore.: Alaska Northwest Books), is a guide for canoeing, kayaking, and rafting enthusiasts to the state's principal rivers and creeks. *The Alaska Wilderness Guide,* compiled by the editors of *The Milepost* (Bellevue, Wash.: Vernon Publications), includes brief descriptions of trails, rivers, lakes, and remote communities throughout the state. There's also an excellent directory of outfitters and wilderness lodges. *Fast and Cold: A Guide to Alaska Whitewater,* by Andrew Embick (Helena, Mont.: Falcon Press), is a large-format paperback as attractive to look at as it is informative. *Mountain Bike Alaska,* by Richard Larson (Anchorage: A T Publishing), is a good start on filling out the sparse information on mountain-biking possibilities in Alaska.

7

Southeast Alaska

Rich, happy people have lived in Southeast Alaska for thousands of years, fishing its salmon and hunting all through its primeval forests of trees up to a dozen feet thick. In canoes, they explored the hundreds of misty, mossy, enchanted islands where the animals, trees, and even the ice had living spirits. (Even for a modern non-Native, it's easy to forget you don't believe in such spirits in the grand quiet of the old-growth rain forests.) And, incredibly, after all those thousands of years of exploration among the teeming, extravagant life of Southeast Alaska, the region still is being discovered—literally.

A few years ago, an amateur spelunker looking at a map speculated that the limestone of Prince of Wales Island would be a likely place to find caves. On his vacation he went out to look, and discovered the deepest vertical cave in the United States in a place where no one had bothered to look before. In the annual explorations that have followed since, miles and miles of caverns have been mapped—caverns inhabited by strange, eyeless creatures and containing dinosaur bones, bear dens, and salmon spawning streams. The caves seemed to network all over the hundreds of square miles of the island, carved by rainwater that had been spiked with the acids of tree sap. Then someone realized that the geology of Southeast's other huge islands contained the same limestone. They started finding more caves.

You're probably not planning a spelunking vacation—my point is that the mysteries of Southeast Alaska run deep below the surface. Like the fractal geometry of the endlessly folded, rocky shoreline, discoveries seem to multiply the closer you look and the more you know. Passing by a stretch of shore on a ship, you could marvel at all the little beaches you pass—you'd surely stop watching after seeing hundreds of inviting spots pass in a day as your ship plowed on, day and night, to navigate the Inside Passage. But if you were to stop at random on any one of those particular, uninhabited beaches in a skiff or kayak, you'd find you could spend a day surveying just a few acres of rocks, the overhanging forest, and the tiny pools of water left behind by the tide. And if you gazed down into any one of those pools, you'd find a complex world all its own, with tiny predators and prey living out their own drama of life in the space of a few square feet.

So prepare to explore with unjaded eyes. Southeast Alaska is full, and what you find may be not only yours to remember, it may be yours alone.

Within Alaska, Southeast stands apart, and not only because most of it can't be reached by road. No other part of the state shares the mysterious, spirit-ridden quality of the coastal rain forest. No other area gets so much rain. (Precious few places anywhere on earth do, for that matter.) If Alaska sometimes feels like a different country from the rest of the United States, Southeast certainly feels like a different state from the rest of Alaska. Unlike most of the state, the economic base of Southeast is well diversified—fishing, timber, tourism, and government—and the region is generally more stable and prosperous than other areas. The weather, while wet, is mild—the climate is more akin to the Pacific Northwest than to the heart of Alaska. The Natives' heritage is richer—the Tlingit, Haida, and Tsimshian exploited the wealth nature gave them and amplified it by being successful traders with tribes to the south and over the mountains in today's British Columbia and Yukon Territory. In their early contact, the Tlingits even defeated the Russian invaders in the Battle of Sitka, and after white dominance was established, saved many of their cultural artifacts and stories.

Along with its other riches and complexity, Southeast Alaska also has many small towns and villages—too many to include in this brief chapter. They await your discovery.

1 Exploring Southeast Alaska

Another of the unique and inviting aspects of traveling in Southeast Alaska is that no roads connect the communities. People are forced to get out of their speeding cars and get on boats, where they can meet their fellow travelers and see what's passing by—slowly. The islands of the region form a protected waterway called the Inside Passage, along which almost all of the region's towns are arrayed. Thanks to the **Alaska Marine Highway** ferry system, it's easy and inexpensive to travel the entire passage, hopping from town to town and spending as much time in each place as you like. And if you're short on time, air service is frequent, with jets to the major towns and commuter planes to the villages.

Why are there no roads? A tectonic plate that underlies the Pacific Ocean brought the islands of the Southeast Alaska Panhandle from far afield and squished them up against the plate that carries the land mass of Canada. Along the line of the glancing collision, large glacial mountains thrust up and the islands themselves were stretched and torn into the fractured geography that makes the area so interesting. In short, it's just too difficult to build roads through those icy mountains and across the steep, jumbled terrain of the islands.

GETTING AROUND

BY FERRY   The state-run **Alaska Marine Highway System,** P.O. Box 25535, Juneau, AK 99802-5535 (☎ **800/642-0066;** fax 907/277-4829), founded in 1963, is a subsidized fleet of blue-hulled, ocean-going ferries whose mission is to connect the roadless coastal towns of Alaska for roughly the same kind of cost you'd pay if there were roads and you were driving. (Call for a free schedule.) There are also small state ferries in Southcentral and Southwest Alaska that don't connect to the ferry system in Southeast. The ferry system's strengths are its low cost, a convenient schedule, exceptional safety, and that it's about the most fun form of travel I can imagine—great for kids. Its weaknesses are crowding during the July peak season, sometimes many-hour delays, generally lackluster food, and a shortage of cabins, which means that most people camp on deck or in chairs during overnight passages.

The main line of the ferry system runs from Prince Rupert, British Columbia, north to Haines and Skagway, a voyage of about 38 hours if you never get off to visit any of the towns in between (which would be an act of sheer lunacy, in my view). The foot-passenger, or walk-on, fare is $118 for adults, and half that for children 11 and under.

The superb **B.C. Ferries** system, 1112 Fort St., Victoria, B.C., Canada V8V 4V2 (☎ **604/386-3431;** fax 604/381-5452), docks right next to the Alaska ferry in Prince Rupert, so you can easily connect to wonderful places such as Vancouver Island.

The Alaska ferry Columbia, the largest in the fleet at 418 feet, goes all the way south to Bellingham, Washington, taking about 40 hours in a nonstop run to Ketchikan, then continuing up to Haines. The walk-on fare is $164 to Ketchikan, $240 to Haines. The Bellingham trips, running only once a week, get booked early, so even foot passengers should make reservations during the summer. Three other large ferries also work the main line, giving service roughly five times a week to Prince Rupert, Ketchikan, Wrangell, Petersburg, Juneau, Haines, and Skagway. Sitka, which lies to the west of the Inside Passage, is bypassed by most ferries, receiving port calls from a main-line ferry once a week and from a smaller, connecting ferry, the *LeConte,* three times a week.

The two smaller ferries, the *LeConte* and *Aurora,* connect the larger towns to small towns and villages. These are commuter ferries, and if you have the time, taking one to the tiny towns they serve is a lot of fun. You can jump off and explore for an hour or so during port calls, or plan a longer visit to one of the quiet Bush communities, catching the next ferry or a scheduled Bush plane. The smaller boats mostly take local residents back and forth to their villages, so they're rarely crowded, and they are the definition of "off the beaten track." They don't have cabins. The risk of planning to visit towns during port calls, on the main line or the smaller ferries, is that if the ship falls behind its schedule you might not be able to get off as the crew does a quick turn-around to pick up time.

While touring the region, combining flying and the ferry can save time and reduce the chances you could spend the night sleeping in a chair on board. There are, however, some runs I wouldn't miss. Going to Sitka through Peril Straits, the ferry fits through extraordinarily narrow passages where no other vessel of its size ventures; the smooth, reflective water is lovely, and you may see deer along the shore. This is where the ferries can lose time—they can go through only when the current isn't running, so if they miss the tide they have to wait six hours. The Wrangell Narrows, between Petersburg and Wrangell, are also an incredible ride, day or night, as the ship accomplishes a slalom between shores that seem so close you could touch them, in water so shallow the schedules must be timed for high tide. Approaching Skagway through the towering mountains of the Lynn Canal fjord also is especially impressive.

Consider this as well: The ferries are crowded northbound in June and southbound in August. If you're flying one way, go against the flow and you'll have the ship more to yourself.

If you're bringing a vehicle or definitely need a cabin on the ferry system during the June-through-August high season, you *must* reserve well in advance. That doesn't mean that you can't get a car on board or pick up a cabin on standby, but you'd be counting on a lot of luck. Cabins on the Bellingham run book up more than six months in advance. Obviously, fares for taking vehicles vary according to the size of the car and how far you're going; a passage from Prince Rupert to Haines for a typical 15-foot car is $273, or $568 from Bellingham. You also have to buy a ticket for each person.

An overnight, two-berth cabin is roughly $30 on most sailings, or $92 from Prince Rupert to Haines, $227 from Bellingham to Haines, plus the cost of your ticket—

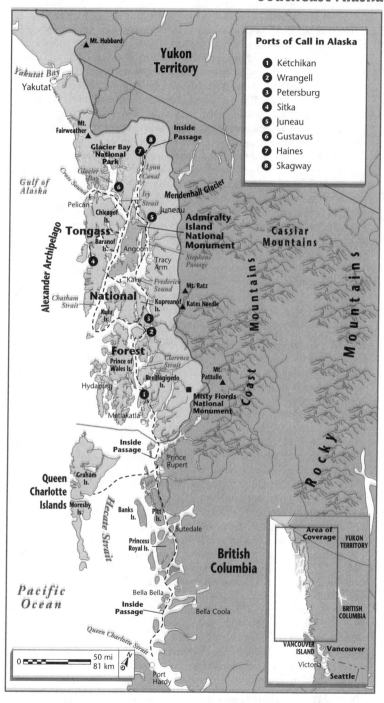

Southeast Alaska

Ports of Call in Alaska

1. Ketchikan
2. Wrangell
3. Petersburg
4. Sitka
5. Juneau
6. Gustavus
7. Haines
8. Skagway

Mt. Hubbard

Yukon Territory

Yakutat Bay
Yakutat

Mt. Fairweather

Inside Passage

Glacier Bay National Park

Glacier Bay

Cross Sound

Lynn Canal

Gulf of Alaska

Pelican

Icy Strait

Mendenhall Glacier

Chicagof Is.

Juneau

Tongass

Baranof Is.

Angoon

Admiralty Island National Monument

Cassiar Mountains

Tracy Arm

Stephens Passage

Chatham Strait

Kake

Frederick Sound

Mt. Ratz

National

Kulu Is.

Kupreanof Is.

Kates Needle

Forest

Prince of Wales Is.

Clarence Strait

Mt. Pattullo

Hydaburg

Revillagigedo Is.

Misty Fiords National Monument

Metlakatla

Coast Mountains

Rocky Mountains

Inside Passage

Prince Rupert

Queen Charlotte Islands

Graham Is.

Banks Is.

Pitt Is.

Moresby Is.

Hecate Strait

Butedale

Princess Royal Is.

British Columbia

Pacific Ocean

Bella Bella

Inside Passage

Bella Coola

Queen Charlotte Strait

0   50 mi
     81 km

Port Hardy

Area of Coverage

YUKON TERRITORY

BRITISH COLUMBIA

VANCOUVER ISLAND

Vancouver

Victoria

Seattle

the best deal on a room you're likely to find in Alaska. The cabins are small and come in two- and four-bunk configurations and, as staterooms, with sitting rooms attached. All have tiny private bathrooms with showers. Try to get an outside cabin so you can watch the world go by; inside cabins can be stuffy. The staterooms don't cost that much more, and provide your own private observation lounge. The best in the fleet are on the *Malaspina,* Cabins 105 to 107, near the bow, but they're all nice.

Do you need a cabin? If you do a lot of layovers to see Southeast's towns, you can time most of your passages during the day, but you're likely to have to sleep on board at least once. One of the adventures of ferry travel is finding a chair to sleep in or setting up a tent on deck with everyone else. The solarium, on the top deck, is the best sleeping spot on board and the recliner lounges second best; if the ship looks crowded, grab your spot fast, but don't worry—there'll always be somewhere to lay your head. Showers are available, although there may be lines. If you're tenting, the best place is behind the solarium, where it's not too windy. On the *Columbia,* that space is small, so grab it early. And bring duct tape to secure your tent to the deck in case you don't have a sheltered spot—using exposed deck space can be like camping in an endless gale. If all that sounds too rugged, or if you have small children and no tent, reserve a cabin.

If you can, bring your own food on the ferry. Ferry food isn't positively bad, but it's quite inconsistent from one ship to the next, and you can get awfully tired of it after several meals in a row. Also, during peak season the food lines are sometimes unreasonably long. If you make a stopover or have a long port call, pick up some bagels and deli sandwiches and have a picnic.

BY AIR   Air travel is the primary link between Southeast's towns and the rest of the world. The major towns all have jet service, provided by **Alaska Airlines** (☎ 800/468-2248). Juneau also receives less frequent flights from **Delta** (☎ 800/221-1212). Juneau is Southeast Alaska's travel hub, but Ketchikan and Sitka also have a number of daily flights. Wrangell, Petersburg, Gustavus, and Yakutat are served by a "milk run" flight that never seems to get very far off the ground as it hops between each little stop; on some of those flights, the cabin attendants barely have time to toss bags of peanuts before the plane lands again. Haines and Skagway, which have highway connections, don't receive visits from jets, but all the towns and all but the tiniest villages have scheduled prop service.

If you can possibly afford it, you'll want to take a flightseeing trip at some point during your trip; the poor man's way of doing this is to fly a small prop plane on a scheduled run between two of your destinations instead of taking the ferry. The plane probably won't go out of its way to show you the sights (it can't hurt to ask), but you'll see enough to gain an appreciation for the vast richness and extreme topography of the region. The largest providers are **L.A.B. Flying Service** (☎ 800/766-2222), in the northern Panhandle; **Wings of Alaska** (☎ 907/789-0790), all over Southeast; and **Ketchikan Air Service** (☎ 907/225-6608) and **Taquan Air** (☎ 800/225-8800), in the southern Panhandle.

Like the ferries, the planes can be quite late. Each of the airports in Southeast has its own challenges caused by the steep, mountainous terrain and the water. In bad weather, even jet flights are delayed or they "overhead"—they can't land at all at the intended destination and leave their passengers somewhere else. Your only protection against these contingencies are travel insurance, a schedule that allows plenty of slack in case you're significantly delayed, and low blood pressure.

BY ROAD   Three Southeast Alaska communities are accessible by road: Haines, Skagway, and the village of Hyder, which lies on the British Columbia border east of Ketchikan and is accessible from the gravel Cassiar Highway through Canada. Haines and Skagway are each a significant detour from the Alaska Highway, but if you want to visit both on your way up, you can save more than 350 miles of driving by taking your car on the ferry the 15 water miles between the two towns. This ferry route is not as heavily booked as the routes heading between either town and Juneau, but it's a good idea to reserve ahead anyway. It's possible to take a bus or rent a car from Haines or Skagway for travel to the rest of the state at the end of a ferry journey (Haines will save you about 60 miles over Skagway); details are listed in the sections on each of those towns. If you're driving the highway in winter, you should be prepared for weather as cold as 40° below zero. You'll need clothing and survival equipment in case of a breakdown hundreds of miles from help.

2 Outside in Southeast

Southeast Alaska has all the outdoors opportunities found in other areas of the state, except broad expanses of alpine or treeless Arctic terrain, and it has some that no one's thought of yet anywhere else, like commercial fishing demonstrations, the best of which is in Petersburg. Sea kayaking in the region is rivaled only by Prince William Sound or Kodiak, and you can do it from almost any town on the Panhandle (although I've never heard of sea kayaking in Skagway). The salmon, trout, and halibut fishing is great almost anywhere in the region you'd choose—bigger king salmon are caught on Southcentral Alaska's Kenai Peninsula, but in Southeast Alaska there are enough streams, lakes, and ocean-fishing spots that you never need to be crowded, unlike on the Kenai. For a few hundred dollars, you can charter a plane to a U.S. Forest Service cabin and not see another human for two weeks, feeding yourself on trout.

Even within Southeast Alaska, it doesn't matter that much where you go, but there are places that are best for different activities; for the details, see the listings of the individual towns.

FISHING   Anywhere you happen to be, you can find great fishing in Southeast Alaska. The lake cabins around Ketchikan provide some of the best opportunities for remote, all-alone fly fishing. Sea charters are great all over, but you can combine them with whale watching in Gustavus, Petersburg, and Juneau. Gustavus is known for huge halibut relatively near town. If you don't want to fish for salmon in a stream near town, you can charter a flight to a remote river where you catch one on every cast. For details on runs, seasons, regulations, and licenses, contact the **Alaska Department of Fish and Game,** Division of Sport Fish, 1255 W. Eighth St. (P.O. Box 25526), Juneau, AK 99802-5526 (☎ **907/465-4180**). In addition, every town of consequence has a Fish and Game office.

HIKING   The **Chilkoot Trail,** near Skagway, is a 33-mile-long museum, and a challenging three-day hike. Petersburg is a good starting point for more remote hiking, but there are trails from most towns.

SEA KAYAKING   Ketchikan, Sitka, Petersburg, Juneau, Haines, and Glacier Bay all have kayaking guides and great places to kayak. Glacier Bay is perhaps best for more experienced kayakers and outdoors people, Sitka is rich in sea otters and other wildlife, and Petersburg is a good place to see whales. Juneau's **Alaska Discovery,** 5449 Shaune Dr., Suite 4, Juneau, AK 99801 (☎ **907/780-6226** or 800/586-1911; fax 907/780-4220), is the most established ecotourism operator in the region.

SURFING   Well, okay, Alaska isn't known for its surfing. But if you were going to surf in Alaska, you'd go to Yakutat.

WHALE WATCHING   In summer, Petersburg and Gustavus are sure-fire, with Juneau a good second choice; in fall and winter, Sitka.

WINTER SPORTS   Do visit Southeast Alaska in the winter. It's not terribly cold, the crowds are gone, and skating and Nordic skiing are available in a lot of places, especially Juneau and Petersburg. Eaglecrest, in Juneau, is the region's only significant alpine skiing area.

3 Ketchikan: On the Waterfront

Had they known about it, the film noir directors of the 1950s would have chosen the Ketchikan (KETCH-e-kan) waterfront for Humphrey Bogart to sleuth. One can picture the black and white montage: A pelting rain drains from the brim of his hat, suspicious figures dart through saloon doors and into the lobbies of concrete-faced hotels, a forest of workboat masts fades into the midsummer twilight along a shore where the sea and land seem to merge in miles of floating docks. Along Creek Street, salmon on their way to spawn swim under houses chaotically perched on pilings beside a narrow boardwalk; inside, men are spawning too, in the arms of legal prostitutes. Meanwhile, the faces of totem poles gaze down on the scene disapprovingly, mute holders of their own ancient mysteries.

Today, the director hoping to re-create that scene would have his work cut out for him removing T-shirt shops and bright streetfront signs that seek to draw throngs of cruise passengers in to buy plastic gew-gaws. But Ketchikan's grittier past is barely out of touch, and not nearly out of memory. As a newspaper reporter covering a story here as recently as the late 1980s, I found a city where, if you were looking for a source, you'd go into a waterfront bar at 10 o'clock in the morning. They'd know where to find the guy you were looking for: which bar was his office at that hour of the day. Ketchikan was proudly tough. On returning in 1995, I found that the bars were catering to tourists and the shopfronts had filled with boutiques and tourist stores.

The ever-increasing flow of cruise ships created the change. Up to five ships at a time are in port during the summer, and always at least two. The streets simply pack with visitors at certain hours; then, Ketchikan feels more like a big museum or carnival. But later, in the evening when the cruise ships pack up and slide off to their next port, a sense of the old, misty, mysterious Ketchikan starts to return.

Whatever the feel of the place, visitors certainly have plenty to see here. Ketchikan is a center of Tlingit and Haida culture and there are two replica clan houses and totem pole parks, as well as the only museum dedicated to preserving the old, original poles from the days when the Tlingit and Haida peoples' cultural traditions were more intact. A walk through the streets is fun; there's an excellent walking-tour map provided by the local visitors bureau. Also, along with the plastic junk, there are some unique galleries here for shopping.

Ketchikan, as the state's fourth-largest city, is the transportation hub for the southern portion of Southeast Alaska, making it a great starting-off point for getting into some spectacular outdoor experiences, including Misty Fjords National Monument (see section 4, later in this chapter). Seaplanes based on docks along the waterfront are the taxis of the region, and a massive new interagency visitor center can get you started. Ketchikan also is one of the wettest spots on earth, with rain measured in the hundreds of inches, so any activity, outdoors or in the streets of the town, requires serious rain gear.

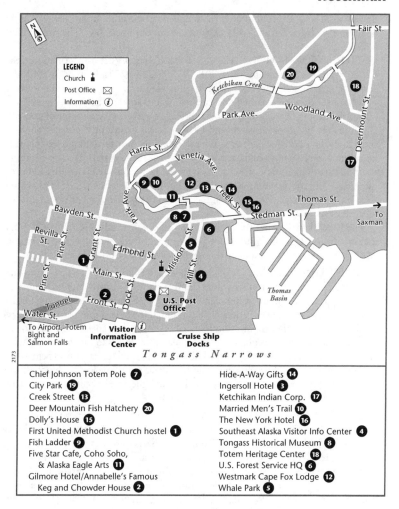

LEGEND
Church ✝
Post Office ✉
Information ⓘ

Chief Johnson Totem Pole ❼
City Park ❿
Creek Street ⓭
Deer Mountain Fish Hatchery ⓴
Dolly's House ⓯
First United Methodist Church hostel ❶
Fish Ladder ❾
Five Star Cafe, Coho Soho,
   & Alaska Eagle Arts ⓫
Gilmore Hotel/Annabelle's Famous
   Keg and Chowder House ❷

Hide-A-Way Gifts ⓮
Ingersoll Hotel ❸
Ketchikan Indian Corp. ⓱
Married Men's Trail ❿
The New York Hotel ⓰
Southeast Alaska Visitor Info Center ❹
Tongass Historical Museum ❽
Totem Heritage Center ⓲
U.S. Forest Service HQ ❻
Westmark Cape Fox Lodge ⓬
Whale Park ❺

ESSENTIALS

GETTING THERE   By Air   Alaska Airlines (☎ **907/225-2141** or 800/
426-0333) provides Ketchikan with nonstop jet service from Seattle and with a stop
only in Juneau from Anchorage. Several commuter lines run between Ketchikan and
the neighboring communities. **Ketchikan Air Service** (☎ **907/225-6608**), **Taquan
Air** (☎ **907/225-8800** or 800/225-8800), and **Promech Air** (☎ **907/225-3845** or
800/860-3845) are the largest. The airport is on a different island from the town and
can be reached only by a ferry that runs each way every half hour; believe the airline
when it tells you when to catch the ferry for your plane. The fare is $2.50 for foot
passengers, $5 for cars. You'll need a courtesy van, cab, or other vehicle to get to town
from the airport ferry. (See "Getting Around," below.)

By Ferry   The dock is out of town, although closer than the airport. Ferries run six hours north to Wrangell and six hours south to Prince Rupert, B.C. The fare for each is $38.

VISITOR INFORMATION   The ✪ **Southeast Alaska Visitor Information Center,** 50 Main St., Ketchikan, AK 99901 (☎ **907/228-6214**), finished in 1995 at a cost of $9.2 million, is not only a place to get guidance on your visit, it's also the best museum of the region's natural and cultural history and contemporary society. It's open daily in summer, Monday through Friday in winter. Plan a couple of hours to take it in. The enormous concrete-and-log structure is located on the waterfront near the cruise-ship dock. An information kiosk is located near the entrance, along with an auditorium showing a high-tech slide slow for $1. Downstairs is a trip-planning room, a luxurious library of outdoors material in various media, with a desk for questions. The trip-planning room, like the interagency Public Lands Information Centers in Anchorage, Fairbanks, and Tok, provides guidance for the outdoors for all areas of the state.

The **Ketchikan Visitors Bureau,** 131 Front St., Ketchikan, AK 99901 (☎ **907/ 225-6166**), operates an information center on the cruise-ship dock, at Front and Mission streets; it's open Monday through Friday during normal business hours.

ORIENTATION   Ketchikan is on huge **Revillagigedo Island.** The downtown area with most of the attractions is quite compact and walkable, but the whole of Ketchikan is long, strung out between the Tongass Narrows and the mountains. A waterfront road goes under various names through town, becoming North Tongass Highway as it stretches about 16 miles north of town. A tunnel divides the downtown and northwestern section of town. Saxman is 2¹/₂ miles to the south on the 14-mile South Tongass Highway. A large hill with a hotel and funicular rises behind the downtown section and Ketchikan Creek; on the far side is the lovely City Park and several other attractions. A good map, available at either visitor center, is a necessity, as the layout of the streets is quite confusing at first.

GETTING AROUND   You can spend a day downtown on foot, but if you have more time you'll need a rented car or you can join a tour. **Practical / All Star Car Rental** (☎ **907/225-8774** or 800/770-8778) delivers the car to you and picks it up when you're done. Fishermen and other locals use taxis, which are mostly minivans, and there are three competing companies, so the rates are not as outrageous as you'll find in some Alaska towns; try **Yellow Taxi** (☎ **907/225-5555**). A **city bus** runs from the airport parking lot and ferry downtown, operating from 5:30am to 9:30pm during the summer and 6:40am to 7pm in the off-season.

Retired schoolteacher Lois Munch, of ✪ **Classic Tours** (☎ **907/225-3091**), makes her tours fun: She wears a poodle skirt to drive visitors around in her '55 Chevy; a 90-minute tour is $35, and a 2¹/₂-hour tour, $50. Water-borne cruises of the town are available from **Alaska Cruises** (☎ **907/225-6044**). I'd recommend a closer look at the watery part of the city by sea kayak; **Southeast Exposure** (☎ **907/ 225-8829**) offers a three-hour tour, no experience necessary, for $50.

FAST FACTS   Ketchikan has a 5.5% **sales tax.** Several banks have **ATMs:** First Bank, at 331 Dock St.; National Bank of Alaska, at 306 Main St.; and Bank of America, at 2417 Tongass Ave. The **main post office** is at 3609 Tongass Ave. In **emergencies,** dial 911; the **police** can be reached at 907/225-6631 for nonemergencies. **Ketchikan General Hospital** is at 3100 Tongass Ave. (☎ **907/ 225-5171**). The *Ketchikan Daily News* publishes six days a week; *USA Today,* the *New York Times,* and Seattle and Anchorage papers are available at grocery and drug stores. Several **business centers** are available with copying and fax services, including The Local Paper, 516 Stedman St., and Mail Boxes Etc., 125 Main St.

SPECIAL EVENTS   Mayfest, spanning the entire month, has a variety of events to celebrate the coming of spring; you can get a schedule from the Ketchikan Visitors Bureau. The **King Salmon Derby,** almost 50 years old, takes place at the end of May and the beginning of June, run by the Greater Ketchikan Chamber of Commerce (☎ **907/225-3184**). The **Fourth of July** celebration will give you a true sense of the meaning of the holiday, with a long parade watched on Front Street by mobs of locals and cruise-ship passengers; after the parade there's a **Timber Carnival** at the baseball field near City Park on Park Avenue, an all-afternoon loggers' competition, admission free. The **Blueberry Arts Festival,** held the second Sunday of August, has booths, music, and food, and is put on by the Ketchikan Area Arts and Humanities Council, 338 Main St. (☎ **907/225-2211**). The council also organizes the **Winter Arts Faire** the first Saturday after Thanksgiving.

EXPLORING KETCHIKAN

TLINGIT, HAIDA & TSIMSHIAN CULTURAL HERITAGE   The Ketchikan area has two totem pole parks and a totem pole museum, as well as a wealth of contemporary Native art displayed all over town. Notable pieces stand at the whale park at Mission and Bawden streets and at the Westmark Cape Fox Lodge. Most of what you see in Southeast Alaska is Tlingit—the Haida and Tsimshian generally live to the south and east in British Columbia. But Ketchikan is near the boundary between the three peoples, and here their similar cultures mix. The **Ketchikan Indian Corp.,** 429 Deermount St., Ketchikan, AK 99901 (☎ **907/225-5158** or 800/252-5158), runs a three-times-daily, two-hour cultural tour, with dancing, for $35 during the summer.

The city-owned **Totem Heritage Center,** 601 Deermount St. (☎ **907/ 225-5900**), near City Park, contains the largest collection of original 19th-century totem poles in existence. The poles are displayed indoors, unpainted, many with the grass and moss still attached where it was when they were rescued from the elements in villages where they had been mounted up to 160 years ago. Totem poles were never meant to be maintained or repainted, instead disintegrating after about 70 years and being constantly replaced, but these were preserved to help keep the culture alive. Guides are on hand to explain what you're looking at and there are occasional demonstrations of Native arts. Admission is $3 in summer and open daily from 8am to 5pm; it's free in winter and open Tuesday through Friday from 1 to 5pm.

The ✪ **Totem Bight State Historical Park** was a New Deal–era work project to save disappearing Tlingit cultural artifacts by replicating them in an authentic setting. The park, now run by the state of Alaska Division of Parks (☎ **907/762-2600**), is unique among the clan houses and outdoor totem pole collections in Southeast for having excellent interpretive signs and a printed guide that explains what you're looking at. It sits at a peaceful spot on the edge of Tongass Narrows, at the end of short walk through the woods, 10 miles out of town on North Tongass Highway. The experience is aesthetic as well as educational, except for the logging clear-cut, ironically on Native-owned land, on the mountain right above the park. If you don't have a car, a number of companies have guided tours, available through the Ketchikan Visitors Bureau. **City Tours** (☎ **907/225-9465**) offers a two-hour Totem Bight and rain-forest tour for $20, leaving at 10am daily; if there are two or more of you, you can rent a car for less and make a day of it exploring Tongass Highway.

The **Saxman Totem Pole Park** stands on a lawn above the Tlingit town of Saxman, 2½ miles south of Ketchikan on the South Tongass Highway. It has artifacts similar to those at Totem Bight park, but an added resource: Master carvers are still at work here. Nathan Jackson, recognized in 1995 as a National Cultural

Heritage Fellow by First Lady Hillary Clinton—the "living treasure" award—carves in the small building to the right of the park. The drawback of the site for independent travelers is that **Cape Fox Corp.** (☎ **907/225-5163,** ext. 304), the Native corporation that owns it, caters mainly to cruise-ship passengers, and no interpretive material is available other than its two-hour, $30 tour, which also includes art demonstrations, a slide show, and, during the week, dancing. The timing of the tour is different each day, depending on the ships. Call for times and information.

OTHER ATTRACTIONS IN TOWN   Get the well-presented *Ketchikan Walking Tour Map* free from the visitor center; its three routes cover everything of interest downtown. Here are the highlights:

✪ **Creek Street** was the red-light district of Ketchikan until not that long ago; now it's a tourist attraction thronged with visitors. Prostitution was legal in Alaska until 1952; that history is so fresh, I have it on good authority that women who worked on Creek Street are still living in Ketchikan. Dolly Arthur, who started in business for herself on the creek in 1919, died in 1975; her house was kept as it had always been and opened as a museum soon after. **Dolly's House** is well worth the $3 admission; it's open at least 9am to 4pm during the summer.

Simply walking the boardwalk over the creek, into the forest above, and over the "Married Men's Trail" is a lot of fun, especially for children. The **Cape Fox Hill–Creek Street Funicular,** a sort of diagonal elevator, runs 211 feet from the boardwalk up to the Westmark Cape Fox Lodge on top of the hill. Take it up and then enjoy the walk down through the woods; the fare of $1 is not always collected, especially in the evening. Teenagers swim in the creek off the Stedman Street bridge at high tide, but I've never seen anyone stay in for long—the water is cold.

You can also walk beyond the boardwalk up Park Avenue to the **Deer Mountain Hatchery,** a small king and chum salmon hatchery where you can see the fry swimming in large tubs. Beyond the hatchery is **City Park,** where Ketchikan Creek splits into a maze of ornamental pools and streams; my young son found it a magical place.

On the downtown side of the creek, the one-room **Tongass Historical Museum,** 629 Dock St., presents the history and Native heritage of Ketchikan, along with an annually revolving exhibit. It's good for its size. Summer hours are 8am to 5pm daily and admission is $2 (free Sunday afternoon); in winter it's open Wednesday through Sunday afternoons only. The same building houses the beautiful **Ketchikan Public Library,** with big windows that look out on the foaming rapids of Ketchikan Creek. The children's section downstairs has a play area with lots of toys; it's a great place for families to rejuvenate. It's open Monday through Wednesday from 10am to 8pm, Thursday through Saturday from 10am to 6pm, and on Sunday from 1 to 5pm.

SHOPPING   Ketchikan has become a shopping and art destination thanks to the explosion of visitors. If you want something authentically Alaskan, however, you have to be careful. A journalist friend of mine met a boy out back behind one of the gift stores removing MADE IN TAIWAN stickers from the merchandise with a razor blade. Generally, items for sale are probably not made in Alaska unless they have one of two marks: a made-in-Alaska polar bear sticker or a silver hand sticker that marks authentic Native art. Of course, most of the many stores in Ketchikan are honest, and certainly competitive, and there's nothing wrong with buying a plastic what-not if you know what you're buying.

✪ **Coho Soho,** 5 Creek St., is worth a visit even if you aren't a shopper. Owner Ray Troll is Alaska's leading fish-obsessed artist. His gallery shows work by Troll and other Ketchikan artists from the same school of surreal rain-forest humor. In Troll's art, subtle ironies and silly puns coexist in a solidly decorated interior world. His popular T-shirts are in themselves both works of art and a comment on the commercialism of the region—"Curios Kill the Cat" shows a cat falling under a rain of plastic totem poles, igloos, and polar bear paper weights. The gallery, open in summer daily from 9am to 5:30pm, is upstairs from the Five Star Cafe, one of the best restaurants in town, and down the hall from **Parnassus Books,** a little cubbyhole worth a visit. Also downstairs is **Alaska Eagle Arts,** a serious gallery featuring the bold yet traditional work of Native artist Marvin Oliver. Down the boardwalk at 18 Creek St., George Brown demonstrates Haida carving in his store, **Hide-A-Way Gifts,** which carries carvings and Native crafts.

On Stedman Street—the cross street meeting the end of Creek Street—**Shotridge Studio** is worth a stop. Down near the cruise-ship dock, check out **Scanlon Gallery,** at 318 Mission St., which carries serious art, including affordable items in various media. The **Ketchikan Arts and Humanities Council,** at 388 Main St., maintains a gallery of regional work.

KetchiCandies, at 315 Mission St., makes and sells chocolates and other candies catering to many local addicts.

GETTING OUTSIDE

There's lots to do outdoors from Ketchikan, but most of it will require a boat or plane; the opportunities right on the road system are limited. See section 4 on Misty Fjords National Monument (later in this chapter) and the side trip to Prince of Wales Island (below) for more. In any event, your first stop should be the trip-planning room at the Southeast Alaska Visitor Information Center, where a forest ranger can provide detailed information on trails, dozens of U.S. Forest Service cabins, and fishing.

Many people wrongly assume that they can't afford a chartered, fly-in experience. Remember, once you're there you pay only $25 a day for a Forest Service cabin and cook whatever food you brought yourself. Charters typically cost around $250 an hour for a plane that can carry three passengers.

SPECIAL PLACES The U.S. Forest Service maintains more than 50 **cabins** around Ketchikan; all are remote and rustic, but at $25 a night, you can't beat the price or the settings. This is a chance to be utterly alone in the wilderness, and many of the lake cabins come with a boat. The cabins with the best fishing are on McDonald and Reflection lakes and Fish Creek; because of their popularity, days during the fishing season are allocated six months in advance by drawing. For details and a listing of many other cabins you can reserve without a drawing, contact the Southeast Alaska Visitor Information Center. It provides a free, 72-page Forest Service guide describing all the cabins, how to reserve them, and the flight time to get to each. A good rule of thumb is that a float plane charter will cost roughly $250 an hour and you'll have to pay for two round-trips to get out there and back; you can do it for as little as $350. Five flight services make these trips, including **Ketchikan Air Service,** 1249 Tongass Ave., Ketchikan, AK 99901 (☎ **907/ 225-6608**); **Taquan Air Service,** 1007 Water St., Ketchikan, AK 99901 (☎ **907/ 225-8800** or 800/225-8800); and **Promech, Inc.,** 1515 Tongass Ave., Ketchikan, AK 99901 (☎ **907/225-3845**). If you don't have the gear you need, they should be able to provide that, as well.

The Forest Service also has three-sided shelters, which cost nothing and don't need to be reserved. Some of these are well-kept local secrets, like the undeveloped natural hot springs at the **Lake Shelokum** shelter.

Ward Lake Nature Trail. This trail circles 1.3 miles around a smooth lake among old-growth Sitka spruce large enough to put you in your place. Ward Creek has trout and salmon. To reach the trail, campground, and picnic area, travel about 8 miles out North Tongass Highway and turn right just before the pulp mill. For a slightly more challenging hike, **Perseverance Lake Trail** climbs up boardwalks with steps to another lake 2.3 miles away.

Deer Mountain Trail. This is a challenging overnight, starting only half a mile from Ketchikan; there are dramatic views 1 mile up the trail and at the summit, after a $2^1/_2$-mile, 3,000-foot climb, but the trail also continues to a Forest Service cabin, across another summit, through some summer snow and ice, and ends at another trailhead 10 miles away. Check for information with the Forest Service at the Southeast Alaska Visitor Information Center.

✪ **FISHING**   The **Alaska Department of Fish and Game** produces a 24-page fishing guide to Ketchikan, with details on where to find fish in both fresh and salt water, listing 17 spots accessible from the roads. You can pick up a copy at the Southeast Alaska Visitor Information Center, or from the department: contact the ADF&G Public Communications Section, P.O. Box 25526, Juneau, AK 99802-5526 (☎ **907/465-4112**). To get out on the water for salmon and halibut, there are plenty of charters available. The Ketchikan Visitors Bureau can provide you with a list. For more remote fishing, you can fly out to meet a charter boat on **Taquan Air,** 1007 Water St., Ketchikan, AK 99901 (☎ **907/225-8800** or 800/225 8800), for around $300 per person.

If you want to devote your time in Ketchikan to fishing, there are two fishing lodges north of Ketchikan, listed in "Where to Stay," below. (There's also a fishing B&B.) Other fishing lodges are located on Prince of Wales Island and in Misty Fjords National Monument.

SEA KAYAKING   The islands, coves, and channels around Ketchikan are like an infinite fractal design; it's good, protected water for exploring in a kayak. **Southeast Exposure,** 507 Stedman St. (P.O. Box 9143), Ketchikan, AK 99901 (☎ **907/ 225-8829;** fax 907/225-8849), rents kayaks and guides trips from one to eight days long. A six-hour day trip is $70 per person; an eight-day trip, $1,135 per person.

WHERE TO STAY

Ketchikan charges an 11.5% **bed tax.**

HOTELS

Expensive

Best Western Landing. 3434 Tongass Ave., Ketchikan, AK 99901. ☎ **907/225-5166.** Fax 907/225-6900. 45 rms, 15 suites, 15 two-bedroom apartments. TV TEL. High season, $98–$170 double, $130–160 suites. Low season, $76–$160 double, $112–130 suites. AE, CB, DC, DISC, MC, V.

A well-run establishment with a wide variety of different types of rooms: simple hotel rooms; suites with sitting rooms and microwave ovens, refrigerators, and balconies; and full two-bedroom apartments with a TV in each room. The new wing has the best rooms. The only drawback is location. The hotel is near the ferry dock, not the sights, and while the courtesy van will take you downtown, there are long waits because the van also serves the Gilmore.

The restaurant, open from 6am to 9pm off-season, until 10pm in summer, serves good meals in a café setting for reasonable prices. One can order sandwiches all evening, or more expensive seafood or beef entrees. Kids are exceptionally well treated.

Drinks are available from the bar upstairs, Jeremiah's, which has live music Wednesday through Saturday.

❖**Westmark Cape Fox Lodge.** 800 Venetia Way, Ketchikan, AK 99901. ☎ **907/225-8001** or 800/544-0970. Fax 907/225-8286. 70 rms, 2 suites. TV TEL. $142 double with water view, $132 double with mountain view. Weekend rate $99. AE, DC, DISC, MC, V.

This is the most beautiful hotel in Southeast Alaska. Owned by the Native Cape Fox Corporation and run by the Westmark chain, the hotel is interwoven with red cedar and masterpieces of Tlingit art. It sits atop the hill that dominates Ketchikan at the end of a funicular that leads to Creek Street, surrounded by huge trees. Even if you can't afford to stay, the elegance and view are worth a visit. If you can, pay extra for the water view—you could spend the whole evening just looking out the window.

The restaurant and lounge share the wonderful view and the food is consistently good, making it probably the best in the less than stellar field of Ketchikan's restaurants.

Moderate

Gilmore Hotel. 326 Front St., Ketchikan, AK 99901. ☎ **907/225-9423.** Fax 907/225-7442. 36 rms, 35 with bath; 2 suites. TV TEL. High season, $66–$98 double, $124 suite. Low season, $40–$78 double, $98 suite. Additional person in room $10 extra. AE, CB, DC, DISC, MC, V.

This historic concrete structure facing the water on Front Street has been kept up in an appropriate style, but old hotels have small rooms and some of these are downright claustrophobic. Take a look at the room before you check in. Services include a courtesy van and free coffee in the lobby.

Ingersoll Hotel. 303 Mission St., Ketchikan, AK 99901. ☎ **907/225-2124,** or 800/478-2124 in Alaska. 58 rms. TV TEL. High season, $92 double. Low season, $52 double. AE, DC, DISC, MC, V.

This 1929 hotel is a slice of the real old Ketchikan. The carpets and trim are brown and the rooms are on the small side (but bigger than the Gilmore's). Waterside rooms have great views. There's free coffee in the lobby, and a courtesy van is available.

❖**New York Hotel.** 207 Stedman St., Ketchikan, AK 99901. ☎ **907/225-0246.** 8 rms. TV TEL. $79 double. MC, V.

It took six years to restore this 1924 building and fill it with antiques, but the loving work was worth the trouble: The New York is a special place to stay—very clean, with a balance of authentic atmosphere and modern comforts. The location is the best in town, right on the boat harbor and next to Creek Street. It's quickly developing a following, so reserve ahead.

FISHING LODGES

The Cedars. 1471 Tongass Ave. (P.O. Box 8331), Ketchikan, AK 99901. ☎ **907/225-1900.** Fax 907/225-8604. 12 rms. TV TEL. $85 double; $115 studio with spa; $160 suite. Fishing packages available. AE, DC, DISC, MC, V.

The Cedars is hard against the sidewalk of a busy street, but the back of the building is over the water, with a dock where float planes tie up; although its location is noisy, it combines being near downtown with being a fishing lodge. The rooms are good for the price and there are Jacuzzis, hot tubs, and saunas all over the place. The suites have great views and spiral staircases.

Salmon Falls Resort. 16707 N. Tongass Hwy. (P.O. Box 5700), Ketchikan, AK 99901. ☎ **907/247-2752** or 800/225-2752. Fax 907/225-2710. 52 rms. TEL. $147 double. Additional person in room $10 extra. AE, MC, V. Closed Sept 15–May 15.

This huge fishing lodge has its own waterfall (where silvers spawn in August) as well as a dock on Clover Passage with boats for all the guests. It's reachable from the Tongass Highway 16¹/₂ miles north of town, so you save the cost of flying to a comparable lodge off the island. The rooms are comfortable and well decorated; the new building is best. But it's the restaurant and bar that are really amazing: a massive log octagon held up in the center by a section of the Alaska pipeline with great views from all tables and excellent food. Nonfishermen will enjoy a drive out the road for dinner, even if they aren't staying here.

BED-AND-BREAKFASTS

Alaskan Home Fishing Bed and Breakfast Lodge. 11380 Alderwood St. N., Ketchikan, AK 99901. ☎ **907/225-6919** or 800/876-0925, 800/478-6919 in Alaska. 5 rms, 2 with bath; 1 suite. TV TEL. High season, $75 double; $125 suite. Low season, $65 double; $105 suite. Additional person in room $20 extra. Two-day/three-night fishing package $905. MC, V.

Music teacher Bob Holsten's home becomes a fishing lodge in the summer, as he takes guests on his 38-foot boat for salmon and halibut. The house is quite grand, with a sauna and Jacuzzi spa. Good meals, often Chinese treatments of local seafood, are provided for those who buy the fishing package; B&B guests can eat in for $20. The location, out North Tongass Highway, is much more convenient for fishermen than for sightseers. Services include a courtesy van, rental cars, free coffee, and bike rentals.

✪ **Captain's Quarters Bed & Breakfast.** 325 Lund St., Ketchikan, AK 99901. ☎ **907/225-4912.** 3 rms. TV TEL. High season, $75 double. Low season, $65 double. Additional person in room $20 extra. AE, MC, V.

These huge, quiet, immaculate rooms, with a sweeping view of the city and ocean, private telephone lines, and a self-contained, self-service breakfast room, rival the best in Ketchikan, but cost half as much. Marv Wendeborn custom-built the B&B with his own hands, carrying the nautical theme through fine oak woodwork. The house perches in a charming mountainside neighborhood just north of the tunnel where half the streets are stairs, a reasonable walk from downtown. Children aren't allowed, and there's no smoking in the house.

A HOSTEL

First United Methodist Church. Grant and Main sts. (P.O. Box 8515), Ketchikan, AK 99901. ☎ **907/225-3319.** 25 beds. $7 per person. Closed Sept–May.

Open only June through August, this church-run hostel, affiliated with Hostelling International, is just up from the tunnel in the downtown area. Use of the church kitchen is available. The office is open from 7 to 9am and 6 to 11pm.

CAMPING

Two Forest Service campgrounds with a total of 29 sites are located at **Ward Lake** (see "Special Places" under "Getting Outside," above).

WHERE TO EAT

Ketchikan isn't a place for great dining, but there is a selection of decent places to eat. Hotel restaurants at the Westmark Cape Fox Lodge, Salmon Falls Resort, and Best Western Landing (see "Where to Stay," above) also are good.

Annabelle's Famous Keg and Chowder House. 326 Front St. ☎ **907/225-9423.** Lunch $7.50–$16; dinner $12–$35. AE, CB, DC, DISC, MC, V. Daily 11am–4pm and 5–11pm. Closed Sun in low season.

The prices are high, but the turn-of-the-century decor, attentive service, and extensive seafood and steak menu make Annabelle's the chief competitor with the Westmark Cape Fox Lodge for the title of the best restaurant in Ketchikan. Full liquor license.

✪ Five Star Cafe. 5 Creek St. ☎ **907/247-STAR.** Lunch/dinner $1.25–$8.25. No credit cards. Daily 7am–6pm.

Like a place you'd find in a college town, the Five Star has good, reasonably priced sandwiches and soups in an atmosphere conducive to journal writing among the young patrons. The black-bean burrito was delicious and healthy. Local art hung about the walls is for sale, and Ketchikan Creek flows under and outside the windows. The building, which also holds two of the city's best galleries, was a brothel and dance hall at one time; the wood-inlay star in the floor is restored. No liquor license.

New York Cafe. 207 Stedman St. ☎ **907/225-0246.** Lunch $5–$7.25; dinner $5–$19. MC, V. 7am–9pm.

The food here is good and inexpensive and the decor perfect: a wonderfully restored little room on the street and boat harbor with an old-fashioned lunch counter. However, the service is inconsistent and there's nowhere to get away from the cigarette smoke. No liquor license.

Sea Breeze Cafe. 1287 Tongass Ave. ☎ **907/247-3082.** Lunch $6–$14; dinner $7.50–$33. AE, DC, MC, V. Daily 6:30am–11pm.

From the busy street north of the tunnel the Sea Breeze doesn't look promising. But the fisherman's chowder, at $11.95, makes a filling and memorable meal all by itself, and the pancakes are renowned in Ketchikan. You can eat on a deck over the water or at a table between a Formica lunch counter and the ocean, but nonsmokers are relegated to a narrow area facing the street. Full liquor license.

KETCHIKAN IN THE EVENING

The **Ketchikan Area Arts and Humanities Council,** 338 Main St. (☎ 907/225-2211), and the First City Players, puts on a popular summer melodrama, *Fish Pirate's Daughter,* in the small Main Street Theater. Tickets are $8.

Ketchikan is a hard-drinking town, and always has been. Trap doors remain in the floors of some Creek Street buildings—bootleggers would pass booze up through these from boats underneath. The bars on Front Street are generally authentic waterfront places, dark gritty rooms where you can meet fishermen and locals. The **Fo'c's'le Bar** has a sign that says TOURISTS TREATED SAME AS HOME FOLKS. **Annabelle's** is a more genteel, refurbished version of the Front Street bar. For a more refined evening and a beautiful setting, the lounge at the **Westmark Cape Fox Lodge,** at the top of the funicular on Creek Street, has an incredible view. Bowling, live music, and ball games on TV, as well as meals and drinks, are available at the **Roller Bay Cafe,** at 2050 Sealevel Dr. **Jeremiah's,** at the Best Western Landing Hotel, 3434 Tongass Ave., also has live music.

A SIDE TRIP TO PRINCE OF WALES ISLAND

If you have plenty of time, the Alaska Bush is a short ferry ride away from Ketchikan, ready to be explored by car. Prince of Wales Island, 135 miles long and 45 miles wide, is the third-largest island in the United States (after Alaska's Kodiak Island and Hawaii's Big Island). The island is unique in Southeast Alaska for having more than 1,000 miles of gravel road, primarily built by the U.S. Forest Service to facilitate logging. There are several villages, primarily logging towns, with limited visitor facilities, and first-class fishing lodges.

Fishing, in both salt and fresh water, is the island's main attraction. The Forest Service lists 32 good fishing streams and maintains some 20 cabins with access to fishing. The Forest Service also manages **spelunking** on the island: POW is a honeycomb of limestone caves, discovered only a few years ago, which are still being explored. Among them is **El Capitan,** the deepest natural pit in the United States, with a vertical drop of 598 feet. You can walk 300 feet into the cave on your own, or take the two-hour Forest Service tour, which runs four times a day, Wednesday through Sunday, during the summer. You'll need warm clothing and lights, and a hard hat is a good idea. You'll also need detailed directions to find it; contact the **Thorne Bay Ranger District,** 1312 U.S.F.S. Dr., Thorne Bay, AK 99919 (☎ **907/828-3304**). There also are good **canoeing** and **birdwatching** opportunities on Prince of Wales and a significant **totem pole** collection in Klawock.

Before going to Prince of Wales, stop at the trip-planning room in the **Southeast Alaska Visitor Information Center** in Ketchikan (see "Visitor Information" under "Essentials," above); pick up the Forest Service recreation guides and the $3 road guide and a copy of the *Ketchikan Daily News*'s free **Prince of Wales Island Guide,** and get current information from the ranger. The **Prince of Wales Chamber of Commerce,** P.O. Box 497, Craig, AK 99921 (☎ **907/826-3870**), can provide information on accommodations and businesses in the various villages.

You can fly to Prince of Wales on a float or wheeled plane with any of the air taxi operators in Ketchikan; some of them sell packages. **Taquan Air** (☎ **907/225-8800** or 800/770-8800) has kayaking, whale watching, diving, and fishing packages, as well as simple scheduled flights. Or you can go by ferry and take advantage of the island's roads. First, you must rent a car in Ketchikan, as the ferry runs to Hollis and there's not much there. The **Alaska Marine Highway** fare for a car and a person from Ketchikan to Hollis is $41. Craig and Klawock each have places to stay and eat.

Waterfall Resort is one of the state's largest and most luxurious fishing lodges, on the west side of Prince of Wales. It has cottages and rooms in converted cannery buildings as well as high-powered, 21-foot fishing boats with guides. Four-day trips, including the ride over from Ketchikan, start at $2,530 per person. The resort is under the same management as the Ingersoll Hotel (see "Where to Stay," above). **McFarland's Floatel,** P.O. Box 19148, Thorne Bay, AK 99919 (☎ **907/828-3335**), 2 miles across the water from Thorne Bay, has four large, two-bedroom cabins with bathrooms and kitchens for $140 a night. A boat will take you over, but you're mostly on your own, cooking your own meals. You can charter a guided fishing trip from the proprietor or rent a skiff for $65 a day.

4 Misty Fjords National Monument: Granite & Water

Among the vast, uninhabited islands, bottomless bays and fjords, massive trees and inconceivably towering cliffs of the southern Alaska Panhandle are 2.3 million acres of inviolate wilderness President Jimmy Carter set aside by a wave of his pen in 1978, a national monument. It's still waiting to be discovered. Unlike Denali or Glacier Bay national parks, Misty Fjords National Monument lacks a single star attraction to which visitors can make a pilgrimage; there is no one exceptional mountain or glacier, no holy grail to seek. For that reason, and its remoteness, the monument remains relatively unvisited. But what the monument does offer is found few places, if anywhere else at all: seemingly endless untouched wilderness with trees and geology so extraordinary and huge they force you to admit that your own imagination is sadly puny by comparison.

The only way to get there is by boat or float plane—there's no cheap way to see the bulk of the monument, which is the size of Connecticut. The only places to stay are in two luxury wilderness lodges or 13 rustic U.S. Forest Service cabins. One can get to the edge of the monument on an 18-mile trail from the little town of Hyder, which can be reached either by road from British Columbia or by a long ferry ride from Ketchikan, but that's a rare and challenging route. The most popular way to see the monument is on a tour boat from Ketchikan. It's also a good place for sea kayaking—that's how the four backcountry Forest Service rangers get around.

There are several noteworthy things to see. **New Eddystone Rock,** standing in the middle of Behm Canal, is a 237-foot-tall exclamation point of weathered rock, the remaining lava plug from an eroded volcano. **Rudyerd Bay** is like a place where the earth shattered open: The cliffs in its Punchbowl Cove rise vertically 3,150 feet from the surface of water that's 900 feet deep. Waterfalls pound down out of the bay's granite. The glaciers of the northern part of the monument also are impressive, although they require a plane to visit.

But don't go to Misty Fjords to see animals. You have a good chance to spot seals, but if you want to see whales, sea lions, sea otters, and the like, there are better choices in Southeast—Glacier Bay National Park, Tracy Arm, or Sitka, for example. Here the attraction is the land itself and its outrageous geology. Also, the name is accurate: It's misty. Or it could be pouring rain. This is among the rainiest spots on earth.

ESSENTIALS

GETTING THERE   By Boat   Charters are available from Ketchikan, but it's 50 miles to Rudyerd Bay, an expensive ride. A better choice probably is to go on one of the excellent boat excursions offered by Dale Pihlman's ✪ **Alaska Cruises,** 220 Front St. (P.O. Box 7814), Ketchikan, AK 99901 (☎ **907/225-6044;** fax 907/ 247-3498). The 32-passenger boats have comfortable table seating and lots of room to get outside. Guides provide accurate, interesting, and personal commentary. The tour travels up the Behm Canal, past New Eddystone Rock, then drifts through Punchbowl Cove during a hearty lunch (cooked on board), before finally coming to a floating dock at the head of Rudyerd Bay after 6^1/$_2$ hours. There passengers who have paid a $45 premium are picked up by a float plane and see the same terrain from the air on a 20-minute ride back to Ketchikan, a fascinating experience itself. Others take another five hours—and have dinner—on the return trip on the boat. The fare is $140 for the 12-hour version, $110 for children 11 and under. If you're susceptible to seasickness, try to have an alternative date to go in case of bad weather; the water is generally smooth in the fjords, but more exposed on the way there.

By Kayak   Southeast Exposure, 507 Stedman St. (P.O. Box 9143), Ketchikan, AK 99901 (☎ **907/225-8829;** fax 907/225-8849), offers guided trips to the monument, starting at four days for $655 per person. They also have kayaks for rent for $20 to $45 a day; a 90-minute training class is mandatory, and an unguided trip deep into the fjords isn't advisable for first-timers. The Forest Service produces a good kayaker's map showing camping spots, rip tides, and dangerous waters, available for $3 from the Southeast Alaska Visitor Center in Ketchikan. Alaska Cruises (see "By Boat," above) drops kayakers off at Rudyerd Bay for $175, or $50 more for anywhere else along the route.

By Plane   You can cover a lot more ground a lot faster this way, and flying over the cliffs, trees, and glaciers is an experience all its own. Several air-taxi operators in

Ketchikan take trips; **Taquan Air,** 1007 Water St., Ketchikan, AK 99901 (☎ **907/ 225-8800** or 800/225-8800), for example, does an excellent job. A two-hour, $169 trip leaves at 9:30am daily and lands on a lake; 90-minute flights leave at 11am and 1pm daily and cost $125 per person.

On Foot   Hyder is 18 miles by trail from the monument, but it's at the end of the long Portland Canal, so most of the monument is not readily accessible from there by boat. There's an as yet unregulated opportunity to watch black and brown bears feeding, however, from a Forest Service platform on Fish Creek, and the area has good birding. A van is available for a 15-mile drive to the breathtaking Salmon Glacier. Hyder can be reached by the Cassiar Highway from British Columbia or by ferry once a week from Ketchikan, a 12-hour run that costs $40.

VISITOR INFORMATION   The **Southeast Alaska Visitor Information Center,** 50 Main St., Ketchikan, AK 99901 (☎ **907/228-6214**), can give you a packet about Misty Fjords in the trip-planning room downstairs. The **Ketchikan Visitors Bureau,** 131 Front St., Ketchikan, AK 99901, (☎ **907/225-6166**), can provide the names of charter operators. The monument is part of the Tongass National Forest. **Monument offices** are at 3031 Tongass Ave., Ketchikan, AK 99901 (☎ **907/225-2148**).

WHERE TO STAY

There aren't many choices: This is wilderness, and the only commercial lodgings are on private in-holdings that the U.S. Forest Service would just as soon not exist. There also are 13 Forest Service cabins and several three-sided shelters. Many are little used and extremely remote.

FISHING LODGES

Yes Bay Lodge / Mink Bay Lodge. P.O. Box 6440, Ketchikan, AK 99902. ☎ **907/ 225-7906** or 800/999-0784. Fax 907/225-8530. Yes Bay (open May 15–Sept 15), 24 guests. Mink Bay (open May 1–Sept 1), 12 guests. $2,125 per person for a four-day package including air travel, meals, and fishing.

These are the only private businesses in the monument. Owned by the Hack family, which also has Promech Air in Ketchikan, they're beautiful, luxurious fishing lodges in a uniquely remote setting. Yes Bay is near MacDonald Lake, which also has a Forest Service cabin—you can fish fresh or salt water.

U.S. FOREST SERVICE CABINS & SHELTERS

The cabins cost $25 per night, but that's only a small part of the cost of using them. You also have to pay for a float plane to get there. I've listed the names of some of the air-taxi operators in "Special Places" under "Getting Outside," in the Ketchikan section, earlier in this chapter. While $250 an hour for flight time may seem steep, remember that in town or at a wilderness lodge you'd be paying for a hotel room and meals. A group of three could do three days at a Forest Service cabin for under $500.

This is remote country, and most locals wouldn't go into this bear-infested wilderness for a multiday trip without a gun for protection, or at least an anti-bear spray. (See "Bears" under "Safety" in "Health, Safety, and Traveler's Insurance" section in Chapter 3.)

Below are a couple of highlights. For a complete listing, contact the Forest Service at the Southeast Alaska Visitor Center or the Misty Fjords National Monument offices, listed above. All the lake cabins have rowboats.

Winstanley Island Cabin is a good destination for kayakers, and there's a chance of seeing bears. **Big Goat Lake Cabin** sits on a point in an alpine lake near a 1,700 foot waterfall; it's accessible only by plane, and because it's so beautiful, a lot of plane traffic comes by, so it's not as quiet as it might be. **Ella Lake** is relatively near Ketchikan, so the cost of the trip isn't as high as some others, but it's very secluded. You can fly to it, or take a boat to the 2.3-mile trail to the lake, then row across the lake to the cabin. Right off Rudyerd Bay, beautiful **Nooya Lake** has a three-sided shelter.

5 Wrangell: An Old-Fashioned Small Town

Wrangell just wanted to be a burly logging town, simple and conservative. Petersburg, 50 miles away up the twisting Wrangell Narrows, with its fishing fleet and government workers, was more sophisticated, and its boardwalks and clapboard houses had more charm. Wrangell was solid, blue collar, the kind of place where people stayed forever, knew each other, where the restaurants all were smoky and unconcerned about cholesterol. Approaching by ship, the whole town laid itself out, simple and straightforward, on the steep side of the island that bore its name, as it had for more than 150 years. As long as there were trees to saw into lumber, the future was safe.

Then, late in 1994, the sawmill shut down. Lumber had been a mainstay of the local economy since the 1890s and the mill was the only major employer. Now it was gone, and with it went a third of the town's payroll. People had to sell out cheap and leave the place where they were born and raised—an insular little town from which the outside world seemed all the more intimidating. The pressures of environmental protection were blamed; whatever the cause, the town needed a new economic reason to exist and ecotourism seemed the obvious choice. But this just wasn't a granola-eating town. "Environmentalist" was a swear word.

For the visitor, it's an interesting formula. Wrangell can't change its stripes—it's still a muscular town with narrow horizons—but the people are endearingly eager to please. There's a day's worth of sightseeing within walking distance and the U.S. Forest Service maintains some outdoor facilities along the island's logging roads, although not the wealth of wonderful opportunities to be found in Petersburg. Wrangell's greatest attraction for visitors may be its role as a starting point to reach the Anan Bear Observatory and the wild Stikine River; of course, there's good fishing, too.

Our family spent a jolly couple of sunny days here. (Sunny weather is not the norm.) We enjoyed playing in the two totem pole parks, and the Petroglyph Beach is a wonderful place for a family to explore and take a picnic. Wrangell has a nonthreatening, small-scale feel that allows a family to wander comfortably.

The town began as a fur-trading post and the Russians built a fort in 1834. The site was valuable for its position near the mouth of the Stikine, which was a Tlingit trade route into the Canadian interior. The British leased the area from the Russians in 1840 and their flag flew until the U.S. purchase of Alaska in 1867. Over the balance of the 19th century, Wrangell experienced three minor gold rushes and the construction of a cannery and the sawmill. A cozy, old-fashioned feel remains in parts of town, but fires have destroyed most of the town's historic or interesting buildings. In 1952 the downtown area was wiped out and its boardwalk waterfront replaced by today's drab gravel fill. Those old buildings that remain, dating to the turn of the century, can be found with the help of a walking-tour map available at the visitor center or museum.

ESSENTIALS

GETTING THERE   By Air   Wrangell is served by the "milk run," the daily jet service on **Alaska Airlines** (☎ **800/426-0333**) that links the communities of Southeast Alaska to the rest of the world. Scheduled commuter planes can carry you the short hop to Petersburg or Ketchikan, as well.

By Ferry   Wrangell is on the main line of the **Alaska Marine Highway System,** with landings almost daily in the summer. The voyage through the narrow, winding ✪ **Wrangell Narrows** north to Petersburg is one of the most beautiful and fascinating in Southeast Alaska; it's quite a navigational feat to watch as the 300-foot ships squeeze through a passage so slender and shallow the vessel's own displacement changes the water level on shore as it passes. The route, not taken by cruise ships, is also a source of delays, as the water in the narrows is deep enough only at high tide. The walk-on fare is $24 to Ketchikan, $18 to Petersburg.

VISITOR INFORMATION   A small visitor information center operated by the **Wrangell Chamber of Commerce,** P.O. Box 49, Wrangell, AK 99929 (☎ **907/ 874-3901**), is located on Outer Drive, near the city dock where cruise ships tie up. In addition to brochures from local businesses, it also provides excellent tabular listings of charter-boat operators, outfitters, and other local businesses. It's open in summer, Monday through Friday from 8am to 5pm, as well as Saturday morning and Sunday afternoon. The U.S. Forest Service also has an information desk at the entry of the **Wrangell Ranger District** offices, on the hill above town at 525 Bennett St. (P.O. Box 51), Wrangell, AK 99929 (☎ **907/874-2323**), where you can draw on detailed local knowledge of the trails and logging roads, obtain detailed two-page guides to each cabin and path, and buy a $3 road guide map.

ORIENTATION   A map is available at the visitor center. The main part of town is laid out north to south along the waterfront at the northern point of the island. **Front Street** is the main business street, leading from the small-boat harbor and **Chief Shakes Island** at the south to the city dock and the ferry dock at the north. Most of the rest of the town is along **Church Street,** which runs parallel a block higher up the hill. **Evergreen Avenue** and **Bennett Street** form a loop to the north which goes to the airport. The only road to the rest of the island, the **Zimovia Highway,** heads out of town to the south, connecting to logging roads built and maintained by the Forest Service.

GETTING AROUND   For the town of Wrangell, going on foot or bicycle will do. **Seacycle,** operating out of a shipping container near the city dock (P.O. Box 952), Wrangell, AK 99929 (☎ **907/874-2815**), is run by the Kulm family; unless there's a cruise ship in town, you'll have to track them down (they've got other jobs). They charge $5 an hour for a classic bike and $7 an hour for a mountain bike, with daily rates of $20 and $30, respectively. They also do diving tours. Cars are available for rent from **Practical Rent A Car,** at the airport (☎ **907/874-3975;** fax 907/ 874 3911), or they'll deliver to you. If you're going to get out of town for a hike or overnight on the island, a car or a very long bike ride are necessary. For a taxi, try **Porky's Cab Company** (☎ **907/874-3603**).

Rent a skiff of your own if you're comfortable running a small boat—you'll be much freer to enjoy the outdoors for fishing, wildlife viewing, or hiking. **Harbor House Rentals,** 645 Shakes St. (P.O. Box 2027), Wrangell, AK 99929 (☎ and fax **907/874-3084**), has boats for $125 to $150 a day.

FAST FACTS   Wrangell has a 7% **sales tax.** The National Bank of Alaska, at 105 Front St., has an **ATM.** The **post office** is at 105 Federal Way. In **emergencies,** call 911. For non-emergency calls to the **police,** call 907/874-3304. **Wrangell General Hospital,** at 310 Bennett St. (☎ **907/874-3356**), is a full-service health facility, with a clinic. The local *Wrangell Sentinel* comes out every Thursday. **Wrangell Drug,** on Front Street, also carries the *Seattle Times* and *Ketchikan Daily News.* Limited **photocopying** services are available at the **library,** 124 Second St., and Angerman's Special Tee's, at 34 Front St., has **fax service.**

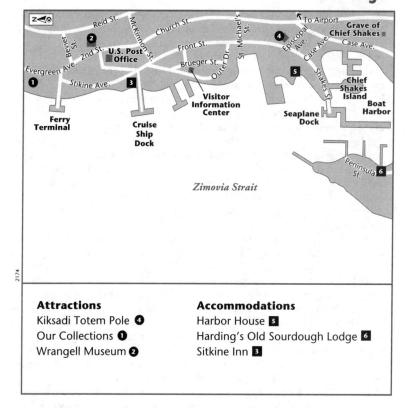

Attractions
Kiksadi Totem Pole ❹
Our Collections ❶
Wrangell Museum ❷

Accommodations
Harbor House ▣5
Harding's Old Sourdough Lodge ▣6
Sitkine Inn ▣3

EXPLORING WRANGELL & ENVIRONS

Wrangell's most interesting sights represent Tlingit cultural history and art. Although Sitka and Ketchikan have more and better-presented attractions along this line, Wrangell is much less visited—there's a more relaxed, intimate feeling.

✪ **Chief Shakes Island,** a tiny island in the middle of the small-boat harbor, is the site of a Tlingit clan house and collection of totem poles constructed, like those in Ketchikan, by the Civilian Conservation Corps during the 1930s. The setting and cultural resources on the island are fascinating; the tradeoff is that, as of 1995, the local tribal council was making no serious effort to show off or interpret the clan house to independent travelers. The house is open only when cruise ships are in town—then you can enter for $1 and hear a brief talk. If there's no cruise ship, you may find the manager of the island at the Alley Cat gift shop on Front Street (☎ 907/874-3747) and, for $10, have the clan house opened for your inspection. No matter—my son remembered much better watching a sea otter that lives near the island's footbridge feed its baby, and you can see the exterior of the clan house and the totems anytime.

Before whites arrived, Tlingits had already warred over this strategic trading location near the mouth of the Stikine River for centuries. The first Chief Shakes was a successful conqueror who enslaved his enemies, then handed down power through the female line, in the Tlingit way, for seven generations. The clan house was moved to the present site early in the 19th century. Charlie Jones was recognized as the last of the line, Chief Shakes VII, at a potlatch in 1940, but the position had lost most of its status almost 80 years before, when word of the Emancipation Proclamation arrived with the Alaska purchase and freed a third of the residents of the coast's Tlingit villages. Chief Shakes VI sent his slaves in canoes to dry halibut; they kept paddling home to Puget Sound, never looking back.

On Front Street near the center of town, the **Kiksadi Totem Park** was built by the Sealaska regional Native corporation in the mid-1980s on the former site of a clan house. The grass is a comfortable place to sit and the totem poles are worth a look.

The ✪ **Petroglyph Beach,** about a mile north of town, represents earlier evidence of indigenous people who may predate the Tlingit. Walk north on Evergreen Avenue and follow the signs down to the beach (don't go within an hour of high tide). The images, chipped into rocks on the beach, are of animals and geometric forms. Their purpose and the identity of their creators are lost to time. The great pleasure for a visitor is simply to search for them and wonder. It's a wonderful place for a family to spend an afternoon, in good weather. Don't take rubbings, however, as the experts fear that this practice is wearing away the images; try as well not to step on the markings.

Wrangell has two museums. The **Wrangell Museum** (☎ **907/874-3770**), operated by the Wrangell Historical Society, is located in temporary quarters in the basement of the gymnasium at 318 Church St. It's a typical small-town hodgepodge—an ancient totem pole is displayed along with an old lawn mower—but there are some significant artifacts. The staff is helpful and sells pamphlets on Wrangell history, including the excellent "Authentic History of Shakes Island and Clan" by E. L. Keithhahn, for $4. Admission to the museum is $2; in summer it's open on Monday and Tuesday from 10am to 6pm, Wednesday through Friday from noon to 5pm, on Saturday from 1 to 6pm, and when the ferry arrives on Sunday.

The other museum is a bit less conventional. Elva Bigelow, who admits to no more than 81 years, maintains her **Our Collections Museum** on Evergreen Avenue (☎ **907/874-3646**), on the way to the Petroglyph Beach. It's an all-inclusive gathering of her family's 60 years in Wrangell. There are old tools, outboard motors, a huge collection of dolls, bottles, a large diorama of the town assembled for the 1967 centennial celebration, old typewriters, wildflowers, and anything else you can imagine. Mrs. Bigelow loves visitors and her museum is open when cruise ships are in town, or you can reach her by phone and she'll gladly show it to you. Donations are appreciated.

There are two special events worth noting: A **salmon derby** is held the last two weeks in May, and the **Fourth of July** festivities last for days.

GETTING OUTSIDE

The **Garnet Ledge,** 7 miles across the water from Wrangell at the mouth of the Stikine River, still yields gems 130 years after its discovery. If you want to take garnets from the ledge you'll need to take along a rock hammer—and a child: Only children have the right to take the stones since the deposit's last owner deeded the mine to the Boy Scouts and the children of Wrangell in 1962. The ledge was exploited from 1907 to 1936 by the first all-woman corporation in the nation, a group of investors from Minneapolis. Information on the history and recreational mining of the ledge is available at the Wrangell Museum, and you can buy garnets from the ledge from children all over town.

Of course, you'll need a boat to get to the ledge; I recommend making a day of it on a ✪ **jet-boat tour** up the Stikine River. The ledge should be one stop, and also the Shakes Glacier and the Forest Service–owned Chief Shakes Hot Springs, where there's an indoor and an outdoor tub open for public bathing. The temperature is adjustable up to 125°F. The main feature of the trip, however, is a wild ride on the Stikine, the fastest-flowing navigable river in North America, through the Stikine-LeConte Wilderness. If your papers are in order, you can go all the way to Telegraph, B.C. Jet boats are the hot rods of the sea, capable of up to 50 m.p.h., and it's fun to zoom over the glacial water in one. Todd Harding's **Stickeen Wilderness Adventures,** P.O. Box 934, Wrangell, AK 99929 (☎ **907/874-2085** or 800/874-2085), is the leading operator. He is knowledgeable and safety-conscious and charges $135 per person, with a minimum of three passengers. Wrangell also has two dozen other licensed charter-boat operators. A list is available from the visitor center.

The ✪ **Anan Bear Observatory** is among the least regulated of Alaska's formal bear-viewing areas; however, it appears that the Forest Service may soon institute a permit system to control the numbers of people. There's a platform from which to watch black and occasional brown bears feeding on spawning pink salmon in Anan Creek in July and August. A single cabin books up immediately upon availability, 180 days in advance. Two rangers are on duty during the bear months, but you must take care of yourself by observing safe bear behavior. If you spend the night, I recommend taking a gun or other protection—I'm talking a lot of bears here! A guided day trip from Wrangell is available from **Harbor House Rentals,** 645 Shakes St. (P.O. Box 2027), Wrangell, AK 99929 (☎ and fax **907/874-3084**), for $100. A float plane also can take you the 29 miles southeast from Wrangell. **Sunrise Aviation,** P.O. Box 432, Wrangell, AK 99929 (☎ **907/874-2319;** fax 907/874-2546), is a Wrangell-based operator. The walk to the observatory is half a mile on a good trail. Contact the Forest Service Wrangell Ranger Station, listed above, for details.

Several Forest Service shelters, cabins, and trails can be reached from the Wrangell Island road system, some on lakes with rowboats for public use. The **Rainbow Falls Trail,** 5 miles south of town on the Zimovia Highway, is the most popular hike; it's 0.8 miles with a 500-foot elevation gain to a picnic area. You can continue another 2.7 miles and another 1,100 feet into alpine muskeg swamp on the **Institute Creek Trail** to the Shoemaker Overlook, where there are great views, a picnic area, and a shelter. Lake cabins on the road system are all fairly long drives on logging roads. **Thoms Lake** has the best fishing. The trail is owned by the Forest Service, but the cabin belongs to Alaska State Parks, 400 Willoughby Ave., Juneau, AK 99801 (☎ **907/465-4563**). If you're willing to charter a plane or boat, there are several Forest Service cabins with access to trophy-class fish, great wildlife viewing, or both, at **Virginia Lake, Harding River, Tyee Lake,** and **Eagle Lake.** Contact the Forest Service Wrangell Ranger Station, listed above.

WHERE TO STAY

Besides the accommodations listed here, the **Thunderbird Motel,** 223 Front St. (P.O. Box 110), Wrangell, AK 99929 (☎ **907/874-3322**), and **Rooney's Roost Bed and Breakfast,** 206 McKinnon (P.O. Box 552), Wrangell, AK 99929 (☎ **907/874-2026**), also provide good, inexpensive lodgings. Get a list of other bed-and-breakfasts from the visitor center. There's a $3-per-room **bed tax.**

✪ **Harbor House.** 645 Shakes St. (P.O. Box 2027), Wrangell, AK 99929. ☎ and fax **907/874-3084.** 3 rms, none with bath; 1 apartment. TV. $65 double; $93 apartment.

Each room in this house—set on pilings above the water near Chief Shakes Island—has some special feature: a nautical room has queen-size bunk beds and a porthole. Available are a furnished apartment and three rooms with a shared bathroom, two of which have TVs. The apartment has a sleeping porch facing the water from which you can often watch sea otters playing. Guests have a coin-operated washer and dryer, a coffeemaker, a microwave oven, and a refrigerator at their disposal. The family lives downstairs and runs a coffeehouse on the porch that faces the street.

Harding's Old Sourdough Lodge. 1104 Peninsula (P.O. Box 1062), Wrangell, AK 99929. ☎ **907/874-3613** or 800/874-3613. Fax 907/874-3455. 19 rms, 14 with bath. TEL. $55 double without bath, $65 double with bath. AE, DC, DISC, MC, V.

The energetic Bruce Harding runs his hotel almost single-handedly in the style of a fishing lodge. The attractive building with a wraparound porch is about a mile from the center of town in a slightly industrial area, but Harding will drive you where you want to go when he can get free. Probably the best meals in town are served here, family style—you eat what they cook—for $16 to $24 per person for dinner; nonguests can make a reservation. There's a large lounge, a sauna and whirlpool, and a wide variety of rooms, from a bunkhouse style to a massive suite. Laundry machines are at guests' disposal.

The Roadhouse Lodge. Mile 4, Zimovia Hwy. (P.O. Box 1199), Wrangell, AK 99929. ☎ **907/874-2335.** Fax 907/874-3104. 10 rms, 1 suite. TV TEL. High season, $65 double. Low season, $55 double. Additional person in room $6 extra. AE, MC, V.

About 4 miles south of town on the Zimovia Highway, the Roadhouse has a courtesy van and is close to the Rainbow Falls Trail and the Shoemaker recreational-boat harbor. Rooms are small but reasonably priced. Choose one on the water side, where there's a good view of the Zimovia Narrows, although with the exterior entryways you may keep the curtain closed for privacy. There's free coffee. The restaurant and bar also have a fine view and are decorated with nets and floats, old road signs, and miscellaneous stuff. With the salad bar and fish on the menu, it's as close as you'll get to fine dining in Wrangell, but I recommend sticking with the simpler fare.

Stikine Inn. 107 Front St. (P.O. Box 990), Wrangell, AK 99929. ☎ **907/874-3388.** Fax 907/874-3923. 31 rms, 3 suites. TV TEL. High season, $70 double, $80 suite. Low season, $60 double, $70 suite. Additional person in room $5.35 extra. AE, DC, DISC, MC, V.

The town's main hotel is close to the ferry dock and stands right on the water's edge. Rooms are spacious, comfortable, and clean, if some are outdated. We could hear the water lapping the shore outside the window as we fell asleep, but I've been told rooms over the bar are not a good choice—noisy. The Dockside Restaurant on the ground floor is the most popular in Wrangell; it provides adequate diner food with a good view but a very smoky atmosphere, even in the purported no-smoking section.

WHERE TO EAT

Wrangell lacks a good restaurant. Other than the three in the Stikine Inn, the Road-house Lodge, and Harding's Old Sourdough Lodge (see "Where to Stay," above), there are only two choices: the **Diamond C Cafe**, at 215 Front St., which is perhaps the least smoky in town, and the **Hungry Beaver Restaurant / Marine Bar** at 274 Shakes St., a dark place with the emphasis on bar.

6 Petersburg: Unvarnished Threshold to the Outdoors

There's a reason why Petersburg is short on tourist amenities—the residents like the town the way it is. They look with horror on the hoards of visitors, primarily off large cruise ships, in Juneau and Ketchikan, and they're glad big ships can't get into their harbor. They prefer Petersburg to continue making its daily bread from the sea, as it has from the start, free of boutiques, jewelry shops, and summer-only businesses.

Ironically, that very lack of attractions is the town's main attraction. Petersburg is real, and the outdoors opportunities to which it provides an entryway are sublime but still little used. Raven's Roost, a Forest Service cabin at the top of a mountain above the town—with views of glaciers, sea, islands, and the town below—isn't always booked up, as it would be in other places. The humpback whales haven't grown so habituated to watchers that they hold out a flipper for tips. When you walk down Nordic Drive, the principal street, you don't see many others like yourselves—you see Norwegian fishermen in pickup trucks and blond-haired kids on bikes.

The disadvantage, of course, is a lack of good restaurants, a narrow selection of places to stay, and not much to do in town except to look at the picturesque houses and boats. That's okay if you enjoy being on the water or in the woods, but Petersburg is not the place to come for shopping or sightseeing.

Petersburg is named for its founder, Peter Buschmann, who killed himself after living here for only a few years. But that shouldn't be a reflection on the town, which is in an ideal location and has had a prosperous history since that inauspicious beginning. Today its economy, based on fishing and government work—there's a large U.S. Forest Service office here—makes for a rich, sophisticated, and stable population.

In 1898 Buschmann founded a cannery on Mitkof Island facing the slender, peaceful Wrangell Narrows in what was to become Petersburg. As a proud old Son of Norway told me, Buschmann was a Norwegian and always hired Norwegians. Any Norwegian who came to him, he hired. They came from far and wide. In a short time the cannery failed. Perhaps an excessive payroll? My suggestion was met with an icy glance and a change of subject. In any event, the Norwegians stayed, brought their families, and built a charming town, which now has about 3,000 residents.

ESSENTIALS

GETTING THERE   By Ferry   Petersburg has the most welcoming ferry terminal in the system, with a grassy lawn and a pier that's a park to watch the boats and marine animals. To the north, you can go to Juneau direct, or by way of Sitka. In either case you'll pass through Frederick Sound, one of the best places in Alaska to see humpback whales. The narrow Peril Straits on the way into Sitka also are spectacular; so is Wrangell Narrows to the south, toward Wrangell. With all the lighted navigational markers, it's an impressive trip in daylight or darkness. The fare is $18 to Wrangell, $26 to Sitka, and $44 to Juneau.

By Air   Petersburg is on the **Alaska Airlines's** "milk run," the jet that stops in each of the little towns along the Panhandle (☎ 800/426-0333). Air services in small aircraft also are available at the airport above the town. **Wings of Alaska** (☎ 907/772-3536) is one operator.

VISITOR INFORMATION   The Petersburg Chamber of Commerce and the U.S. Forest Service jointly operate an excellent **visitor center** at the corner of First and Fram streets (P.O. Box 649), Petersburg, AK 99833 (☎ 907/772-3646). A ranger and a chamber representative answer questions, and in addition to the usual brochures, you can pick up a 36-page guide to the area's hiking trails and a birder's checklist by Peter J. Walsh. This also is the place to reserve a Forest Service cabin. **Viking Travel,** P.O. Box 787, Petersburg, AK 99833 (☎ 907/772-3818 or 800/327-2571; fax 907/772-3940), located on the waterfront near North Boat Harbor, is a good place to book tours, kayaks, and charters.

ORIENTATION   Petersburg is on Mitkof Island, divided from the much larger Kupreanof Island by the slender channel of the Wrangell Narrows. There are three small-boat harbors—the north, south, and middle—and so many docks, boardwalks, and wooden streets that the town seems to sit on the ocean. **Nordic Drive** is the main street, running from the ferry dock through town, then becoming **Sandy Beach Road** as it rounds Hungry Point to the north. At Sandy Beach, you can circle back, past the cannery worker's tent city and the airport, which stands above the town, to **Haugen Drive,** which meets Nordic again near **Hammer Slough,** right in town. To the south, Nordic becomes the **Mitkof Highway,** which runs south to the rest of the island.

GETTING AROUND   You need some mode of transportation to really enjoy Petersburg, because the best of the place is the outdoors. The **Tides Inn** and **Scandia House** (see "Where to Stay," below) rent cars, but only about a dozen cars are available in town and they get booked up well in advance. Two businesses offer **van tours** of the town and island. Judy Henderson, under the name **See Alaska Tours and Charters,** P.O. Box 1125, Petersburg, AK 99833 (☎ **907/772-4656**), offers a half-day trip in a six-passenger van that includes beachcombing and a nature walk for $35; **Alaska Scenic Waterways,** 114 Harbor Way (P.O. Box 943), Petersburg, AK 99833 (☎ **907/772-3777**), has a similar service.

Biking is a great way to see Petersburg. You can rent a bike for $3.50 an hour or $20 a day, or join a guided tour, from **Northern Bikes,** located in the lobby of the Scandia House Hotel (☎ **907/772-3978**). The hotel itself rents small boats; if you're comfortable handling a skiff, that's a good avenue to the outdoors. An 18-footer with a 40-horse outboard rents for $150 a day, gas included, $25 less for guests of the hotel.

FAST FACTS   Petersburg has a 6% **sales tax.** There's an **ATM** at the National Bank of Alaska, at the corner of Nordic Drive and Fram Street. The **post office** is at 12 N. Nordic Dr., at the corner of Haugen Drive. In **emergencies,** dial 911; the **police** can be reached at 907/772-3838 for other calls. The **Petersburg Medical Center,** at Second and Fram streets (☎ **907/772-4291**), is a full-service hospital. The *Petersburg Pilot* comes out every Thursday. Out-of-town newspapers are available at the **Rexall Pharmacy** on Nordic Drive. There's no business center as such, but **photocopying and fax** services are available at the **library,** at the corner of Nordic and Haugen drives.

SPECIAL EVENTS   Petersburg goes wild for the **Little Norway Festival,** which celebrates the May 17, 1814, declaration of independence of Norway from Sweden. There are lots of community events planned May 16–19, 1996. The **King Salmon Derby** offers a $30,000 purse May 24–27, 1996, and the summer-long **Canned Salmon Classic** is a chance to win $2,500 for guessing how many cans of salmon will be packed in Petersburg during the season; both are run by the Petersburg Chamber of Commerce (☎ **907/772-3646**). Some say the **Fourth of July** festival is even bigger than Little Norway, but all Southeast Alaska towns have big parties on the Fourth.

EXPLORING PETERSBURG

WHAT TO SEE & DO IN TOWN   A walk around Petersburg should include the boardwalk streets of Hammer Slough. Sing Lee Alley winds past the **Sons of Norway Hall,** where a large model Viking ship used in the Little Norway Festival is often parked. Birch Street follows the slough upstream past the old houses that hang over the water. Walk down to the **waterfront** past North Boat Harbor to see the frenetic activity of the huge commercial fishing fleet in the summer. At the north end of Nordic Drive, stop at **Eagle's Roost Park,** with a grassy area to sit and a stairway that leads down to the water. The eagles like to sit in the big trees here, but in fact you can see eagles almost anytime and anywhere along the water.

The **Clausen Memorial Museum,** at Second and Fram streets (☎ 907/ 772-3598), focuses on Petersburg and its history. It has a living, community feel; I especially enjoyed the stories written by children of their family's history in the town. The museum is open in summer Monday through Saturday from 10am to 4pm and on Sunday from 1 to 4pm, as well as sporadically in the winter; admission is $2 for adults, free for children 11 and under.

SHOPPING   I hope you're not going to Petersburg for the shopping—but there are a few nice shops if you're already there. Lyle and Carol Bennett's **Petersburg Gallery,** 12 Sing Lee Alley, shows Lyle's own paintings among other fine art and crafts. **Berthiel's** is Berthiel Evens's gallery at 233 Main St. **Sing Lee Books** is a cozy little bookstore in a big, white house by Hammer Slough. **Husfliden** is located in the loft of the Sons of Norway Hall, on pilings in Hammer Slough, selling craft supplies for traditional Scandinavian activities.

GETTING OUTSIDE

SPECIAL PLACES   There are so many great outdoors activities in Petersburg, I have listed only a few highlights. For other choices, many of which are as good as those I've written about here, or for the detailed trail and backcountry information you'll need, including cabin permits, call or visit the U.S. Forest Service at either of two locations in Petersburg—the visitor center, listed above, or the **Petersburg Ranger District** offices at Nordic and Haugen drives (P.O. Box 1328), Petersburg, AK 99833 (☎ 907/772-3871), above the Post Office.

Sandy Beach/Frederick Point Boardwalk. Our family enjoyed an afternoon at Sandy Beach, a long walk or short bike ride up Sandy Beach Road. There are picnic shelters and a place to sit in the sun. Around the point to the west are Native petroglyphs, although they're harder to find than those in Wrangell. A little farther up the road is the Frederick Point Boardwalk. We pretended to be trains with our three-year-old on the level, 4-foot-wide boardwalk, meeting some bicyclists and a wheelchair-bound group of elderly people along the way. The hike through a wetland forest leads after a mile to a mossy creek that empties across bedrock into the ocean, then continues in a primitive form a little farther to a few houses.

✪ **Raven Trail & Raven's Roost Cabin.** About 4 miles up a steep trail that begins behind the airport off Haugen Drive near the water tower, the Raven's Roost Forest Service Cabin sits atop a mountain with a sweeping view of the town and surrounding waters and islands. It's the sort of place that inspires artists and poets. Allow three hours for the climb along a boardwalk, then up a steep muddy slope, then along a ridge. Register with the Forest Service to stay at the cabin.

✪ **Petersburg Creek.** The lovely, grassy Petersburg Creek area can be an afternoon's family frolic among the meadows of wildflowers that meet the water, or the start to a challenging 21-mile, multiday hike into the Petersburg Creek–Duncan Salt Chuck Wilderness. You need a skiff or sea kayak, or to be dropped off by a charter, as the creek is on Kupreanof Island, across Wrangell Narrows from town; the state maintains a dock. The creek contains four species of salmon and two of trout. The trail is maintained by the Forest Service and has miles of boardwalks and two cabins, one at Petersburg Lake and one at East Salt Chuck, each with a boat for public use. (Contact the Forest Service for a permit, as noted above.) Petersburg Lake has trout and odds are good you'll see ducks, geese, loons, trumpeter swans, bald eagles, and black bears. The Kupreanof dock also provides access to the 3-mile, 3,000-foot trail that climbs Petersburg Mountain, a challenging hike that has spectacular views from the top.

On Mitkof Highway. Pick up the $3 Forest Service Mitkof Island Road Guide map at the visitor center; it shows what you'll find along the way, including king salmon fishing, swimming, ice-skating, views of swans, fish, and glaciers, and many other activities. Fourteen miles out you come to The Dip, a declivity in the road where high school seniors have long painted their names and classes on the road, then the quarter-mile boardwalk to **Blind River Rapids,** a great place to watch and fish for king salmon in June and July and silvers in September, and to watch eagles. At 18 miles you'll reach the **Blind Slough Recreation Area,** where locals go to swim in the amber water in the summer and skate in the winter. At 22 miles from Petersburg you reach the **Ohmer Creek campground,** with a 1-mile trail with interpretive signs on the life cycle of salmon, a floating bridge over a beaver pond, and access to king salmon in June and July and trout and some salmon in late summer.

LeConte Glacier. This impressive tidewater glacier is also a great place to see baby seals sitting on the ice. There are plenty of operators who can take you. The going rate is about $90 per person. Steve Barry, listed under "Whale Watching," below, does a good glacier trip too, as does Ron Compton, of **Alaska Scenic Waterways,** 114 Harbor Way (P.O. Box 943), Petersburg, AK 99833 (☎ **907/772-3777** or 800/279-1176). You can get a list of all the boats from the visitor center, or book through Viking Travel (see "Visitor Information" under "Essentials," above).

○ **WHALE WATCHING** Frederick Sound is one of the best places in the state to see humpbacks when they're feeding in the summer. Several charter operators offer trips in small, six-passenger boats, but Steve Barry secured his position as the dean of whale watchers in the summer of 1995, when a humpback jumped right into his boat. (No one was injured, but a few people fell in the water.) He has a hydrophone on board so you can hear the whales' songs while waiting for them to surface. When the song stops, you know they're about to break forth. You can book his trip directly at **Sights Southeast,** P.O. Box 934, Petersburg, AK 99833 (☎ **907/772-4503**), or through **Viking Travel** (see "Visitor Information" under "Essentials," above).

SEA KAYAKING These protected waters and the variety of things to see make Petersburg an especially good place for sea kayaking. **Tongass Kayak Adventures,** P.O. Box 787, Petersburg, AK 99833 (☎ **907/772-4600**), focuses on guided trips of three days to a week, which can get you out among the glaciers and whales, but also offers a five-hour paddle right around the harbor and Petersburg Creek, with no experience required. It costs $45 for adults and $30 for children 11 and under. Book direct with Tongass Kayak Adventures or through **Viking Travel** (see "Visitor Information" under "Essentials," above).

○ **A COMMERCIAL FISHING TOUR** Retired Petersburg high school principal Syd Wright runs a unique commercial fishing demonstration; people who've done it say it's the best, most authentic tour of any kind in Alaska. Wright is a crusty and well-loved local institution, always called upon for knowledge about the area's natural history. He takes six passengers on his crude, crowded work boat, trawls for shrimp and sole and pulls crab pots in Scow Bay, south of town, and then his wife, Vara, cooks it up with butter and garlic and a glass of wine; the passengers throw the shells out the window. Wright can identify all the weird creatures that come up in the trawl. The price is $98, but it's usually booked way in advance by cruise passengers on the

Alaska Sightseeing Tours ship *Sheltered Seas.* Wright can be reached direct at **Chan IV Charters,** P.O. Box 624, Petersburg, AK 99833 (☎ **907/772-4859**).

SPORT FISHING   There are a number of streams you can reach on the roads: see "Special Places" (above) or contact the visitor center. The boat harbor has a couple of dozen licensed charter fishing boats, mostly six-passenger vessels. As elsewhere, halibut and salmon are usually the target. You can get a list of operators at the visitor center, or book through **Viking Travel** (see "Visitor Information" under "Essentials," above). Dan O'Neil of **Secret Cove Charters,** P.O. Box 1455, Petersburg, AK 99833 (☎ **907/772-3081**), has a good reputation.

WHERE TO STAY

Petersburg is short on rooms, but if you can't find anything at the places listed below, try **Nordic House Bed and Breakfast,** 806 S. Nordic (P.O. Box 573), Petersburg, AK 99833 (☎ **907/772-3620;** fax 907/772-3673), or one of the other B&Bs listed with the visitors center. There's a 3% **bed tax.**

⊗ **Narrows Inn.** Nordic Dr. (across from the ferry terminal; P.O. Box 1048), Petersburg, AK 99833. ☎ **907/772-4288** or 800/665-8433. 22 rms. TV TEL. $65 double. Additional person in room $10 extra. AE, DC, DISC, MC, V. Closed in winter.

The small, twin-bedded rooms in this modest motel near the ferry dock look unpromising from the courtyard they face, behind the pizza parlor, but they're clean and well maintained, all have TVs and phones with free local calls, eight have kitchenettes (with refrigerators and microwaves), and the live-in hosts make a point of their hospitality. It's a decent, low-cost choice.

Scandia House. 110 Nordic Dr. (P.O. Box 689), Petersburg, AK 99833. ☎ **907/772-4281** or 800/722-5006. Fax 907/772-4301. 13 rms. TV TEL. $80 double without view, $95 double with view, $130 double with kitchenette. Additional person in room $10 extra. AE, CB, DC, DISC, MC, V.

The town's historic main hotel burned recently and was rebuilt in 1995 in the same style, although no one would mistake it now for a historic structure. The brand-new rooms are large and comfortable; eight of them have kitchenettes. There's free coffee, and a courtesy van is available. With its central location and community role, you'll probably find yourself here to rent a skiff, car, or bike even if you don't get a room. Book well in advance for the busy summer season.

Tides Inn Motel. 307 N. First St. (P.O. Box 1048), Petersburg, AK 99833. ☎ **907/772-4288.** Fax 907/772-4286. 48 rms. TV TEL. $85 double. Additional person in room $10 extra. AE, DC, DISC, MC, V.

This large, dark-brown hotel is comfortable and convenient. A block above Nordic Drive, it also rents cars, has free coffee in the lobby, and rents five rooms with kitchenettes at the same price as regular rooms—an excellent choice in a town short on restaurants. A new and old building face each other, so the rooms in between get little sunlight—ask for a room in the newer building, on the water side.

Water's Edge Bed and Breakfast. 702 Sandy Beach Rd. (P.O. Box 1201), Petersburg, AK 99833. ☎ **907/772-3736** or 800/TO-THE-SEA (800/868-4373). 2 rms. TV TEL. High season, $90 double. Low season, $80 double. Additional person in room $10 extra. Two-night minimum stay. No credit cards.

Guests gush about teacher Kathy Bracken's hospitality at her home on the beach a mile out of town. The rooms come with use of bicycles, a canoe, and laundry facilities, and Kathy offers free pickup at the airport or ferry terminal. Children under 12 aren't allowed, and there's no smoking in the house. Kathy offers packages with her husband, Barry, a semiretired marine biologist who leads tours on his 28-foot boat.

CAMPING

Tent City Campground. 1800 Haugen Dr. (at the intersection with Sandy Beach Rd.; P.O. Box 329), Petersburg, AK 99833. ☎ **907/772-9864.** Fax 907/772-3759. 50 wood-platform tentsites. $5 tentsite per night, $30 per week. Closed Oct–Apr.

The tent city was built to give the summer's cannery workers a place to stay. It's a mass of blue plastic tarps, with sites connected by a boardwalk. A lively little community of college students and transient workers.

WHERE TO EAT

You won't get a memorable meal in Petersburg, but there are adequate restaurants for your sustenance. **Pellerito's Pizza,** near the ferry dock, has the best pizza in town and a good view. Right next to it is **Joan Mei Restaurant,** with an attractive dining room serving Chinese and various other ethnic cuisines. A truly exceptional espresso and hot dog stand called **Oh My Cod** was operating on the waterfront in 1995, with clam chowder that was taking Petersburg by storm.

Helse. 17 Sing Lee Alley. ☎ **907/772-3444.** All meals $3–$7.75. No credit cards. Mon–Fri 7:30am–5pm, Sat 10am–3pm.

This health-food store/restaurant serves good, hearty sandwiches for lunch in a crowded, youthful setting. Each table hangs at one end from a rope and seating is on hard stools. Excellent coffee and the best place in town for lunch.

The Homestead. 218 Nordic Dr. (☎ **907/772-3900.** Lunch $4.25–$8.50; dinner $9.75–$23. AE, DC, MC, V. Mon–Sat 24 hours.

Your first clue that this is where the locals go is on the streetfront: There's no sign, just a window and lots of people eating inside. The Homestead—open around the clock—is for commercial fishermen coming off the boat in the middle of the night and looking for a glorious, juicy burger or deep-fried fresh halibut and a pile of greasy fries. The front room, with the lunch counter, is chokingly smokey; go past the kitchen to the back dining room, where the air is clearer. Kids are well treated.

7 Sitka: Rich Prize of Russian Conquest

The history that Sitka preserves is interesting not only because of the Russian buildings that record Alaska's early white settlement, but more deeply for the story of the cultural conflict of Alaska Natives—and by extension, all aboriginal peoples—with the invaders, and their resistance and ultimate accommodation to the new ways. Here, 18th-century Russian conquerors who had successfully enslaved the Aleuts to the west met their match in battle against the rich, powerful, and sophisticated Tlingit. A visit to Sitka teaches the story of that war, and also the cultural blending that occurred in the uneasy peace that followed under the influence of the Russian Orthodox church—an influence that continued after the Russians packed up and left upon the U.S. purchase of Alaska in 1867, and continues today.

Besides its historic significance, Sitka also is fun to visit. Somehow it has retained a friendly, authentic feel, despite the crush of thousands of visitors. Perhaps because cruise-ship travelers must ride boats to shore, or because Sitka is a slightly inconvenient, out-of-the-way stop on the Alaska Marine Highway's main-line ferry routes, the city's streets haven't been choked by solid rows of seasonal gift shops, as has occurred in Ketchikan, Skagway, and a large part of Juneau. It remains picturesque, facing Sitka Sound, which is dotted with islands and populated by feeding eagles. Historic photographs bear a surprising resemblance to today's city.

Beyond the town and its history, Sitka is a gateway to a large, remote portion of Southeast Alaska, in the western coastal islands. This area contains some of Tongass National Forest's least-used outdoors opportunities. Of course, the ocean halibut and salmon fishing are excellent and not overexploited.

The town's economy, traditionally based on commercial fishing, tourism, and timber, lost the third of those legs in recent years when the local timber mill shut down. After the mill closed, the U.S. Forest Service canceled a subsidized 50-year contract granted to a Japanese company after World War II to boost the Japanese and Alaska economies. Despite dire predictions, Sitka has recovered well from the economic blow and now seems a prosperous, active community, but the environment-versus-development debate remains rancorous, with the Forest Service standing at its center. In the fall of 1995, when Sitka voted on a resolution opposing clear-cut logging, the first vote count was a tie.

ESSENTIALS

GETTING THERE   By Ferry   Sitka sits on the west side of Baranof Island, a detour from the Inside Passage, and many ferries on the **Alaska Marine Highway System** bypass the stop. However, the ride through narrow Peril Straits is definitely worth the trip. Whether you're heading north to Juneau or south to Petersburg, you have to go through the straits. To see another side of the area, take one of the little "local" ferries that stop at all the villages on the way to Sitka. The fare to either Juneau or Petersburg is $26.

By Air   Alaska Airlines (☎ **907/966-2422** or 800/426-0333) flies jets daily to Seattle and Anchorage. If you need to save time, think about flying one way and taking the ferry back.

VISITOR INFORMATION   The Sitka Centennial Building, next to the Crescent Boat Harbor at 330 Harbor Dr., houses the **visitor center,** which, although only a desk, provides refreshingly straightforward printed information. The **Sitka Convention and Visitors Bureau** can be reached at P.O. Box 1226, Sitka, AK 99835 (☎ **907/747-5940;** fax 907/747-3739).

The ✪ **Sitka National Historical Park Visitor Center,** 106 Metlakatla St., Sitka, AK 99835 (☎ **907/747-6281**), run by the National Park Service, which maintains the major historic sites in Sitka, is an essential stop. The ✪ *Historic Sites of Sitka* **map** produced by the Park Service and Sitka Historical Society is an indispensable guide to the buildings and parks around town. You can easily see Sitka's history on foot with one of these maps.

ORIENTATION   Sitka, on the west side of Baranof Island, has a road leading a few miles north and south. The **ferry terminal** is located at its north end, on **Harbor Point Road;** the abandoned pulp mill at the south, on **Sawmill Creek Boulevard.** The town faces Sitka Sound. Across Sitka Channel is **Japonski Island** and the **airport** (don't worry, it only looks as if your plane is going to land in the water). **Lincoln Street** contains more of the tourist attractions. A free map provided by the Greater Sitka Chamber of Commerce at the visitor center will help you navigate the tangled downtown streets.

GETTING AROUND   Sitka is a walker's paradise. Competing shuttles charge $3 to get to town from the ferry dock or airport. **Sitka Cab** is available at 907/747-5001. **Rental cars** are available at the airport and the Potlatch Motel. Once you're downtown, you can walk, although the white buses and guides in red tunics of **Sitka Tours**

(☎ 907/747-8443) can show you around, as they do the cruise-ship passengers; a historical tour is $24, adding the Raptor Center it's $33, and children go for half price. Or go with **Sitka Walking Tours** (☎ 907/747-5354) to find some of the lesser-known places—Jane Eidler does a great job, charging $8 for a 90-minute walk. The **Sitka Tribe** (☎ 907/747-3207, or 800/746-3207) takes tours of the historical park twice daily for $10; a longer version, for $18, includes the Sheldon Jackson Museum and the Tlingit dances at the Centennial Hall.

FAST FACTS Sitka has a 4% **sales tax.** There's an **ATM** at the National Bank of Alaska, 300 Lincoln St., and another at the First National Bank of Anchorage, at 318 Lincoln. The **post office** is at 1207 Sawmill Creek Hwy., on the south side of town. Dial 911 for **emergencies;** call the **police** at 907/747-3245 for nonemergencies. The **Sitka Community Hospital** (☎ 907/747-3241) is at 209 Moller Dr. The *Sitka Daily Sentinel* is published weekdays. You can get a copy of *USA Today* or the *Anchorage Daily News* at the Westmark Shee Atika; the Sunday *Seattle Times* is sold at Lakeside grocery store, 705 Halibut Point Rd. The **Northstar Business Center** (☎ 907/747-3281) is at 332 Lincoln St.

SPECIAL EVENTS The **Sitka Salmon Derby** occurs at the end of May and beginning of June, when the kings are running; contact the Convention and Visitors Bureau. The ✪ **Sitka Summer Music Festival,** P.O. Box 3333, Sitka, AK 99835 (☎ 907/747-6774), a chamber-music series that began in 1972, is one of Alaska's most important cultural events, drawing musicians from all over the world during June. Performances and other events take place all month. Rehearsals are free. Alaska Day, commemorating the Alaska purchase, is a big deal in this former Russian and U.S. capital city; an **Alaska Day Festival** lasts several days in mid-October, closing everything in town; the Convention and Visitors Bureau has information.

EXPLORING SITKA
SITKA'S TLINGIT & RUSSIAN HERITAGE

✪ **Sitka National Historical Park.** 106 Metlakatla St. ☎ **907/747-6281.** Free admission. Visitor center open daily 8am–5pm.

In 1799 the Russian America Company established Redoubt St. Michael (now the **Old Sitka State Historic Site,** 7$^1/_2$ miles north of town) to control the lucrative fur trade; the Tlingit, who were sophisticated traders and had already acquired flintlocks, attacked and destroyed the redoubt in 1802, killing most of the Russians. Then the Natives immediately began fortifications on the site now within the national historic park, anticipating a Russian counterattack, which came in 1804. The attacking force was a Russian gunship and a swarm of Aleut kayaks, which towed the becalmed vessel into position to begin the bombardment. The Tlingits withstood the siege for six days, then vacated their fort at night, after taking heavy losses from the shelling and from a bomb-laden canoe. The Russians founded and heavily fortified the town of New Archangel, and in 1808 it became their administrative capital. But the Tlingit name is the one that stuck: Shee Atika, or Sitka.

The historic significance of the site was recognized early and President Benjamin Harrison set it aside in 1890. In 1905 a collection of totem poles from around Southeast were brought here (the originals are in storage and replicas are on display). The historic park emphasizes, as it should, the Native perspective. In the visitor center, a display explains the history, and Tlingit craftsmen labor in workshops making traditional carvings, jewelry, drums, and costumes. You can watch them work, but please don't act like you're in a zoo. An auditorium shows films and other programs.

Sitka

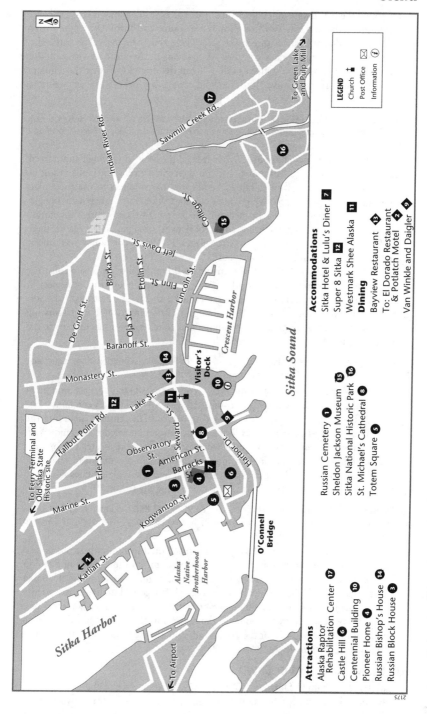

Attractions

Alaska Raptor
Rehabilitation Center **17**
Castle Hill **6**
Centennial Building **10**
Pioneer Home **4**
Russian Bishop's House **14**
Russian Block House **3**

Russian Cemetery **1**
Sheldon Jackson Museum **15**
Sitka National Historic Park **16**
St. Michael's Cathedral **8**
Totem Square **5**

Accommodations

Sitka Hotel & Lulu's Diner **7**
Super 8 Sitka **12**
Westmark Shee Alaska **11**

Dining

Bayview Restaurant **13**
To: El Dorado Restaurant
& Potlatch Motel **2**
Van Winkle and Daigler **9**

LEGEND
✝ Church
⊠ Post Office
ⓘ Information

I found the totem park and battle site most impressive. The totems stand tall and forbidding along a pathway through massive spruce and hemlock, where misty rain wanders down from an unseen sky somewhere above the trees. The battle site is along the trail—only a grassy area now—but among the trees and totems, with the sound of the lapping sea and raven's call, one can feel deep down what the Tlingits were fighting for; the spirits of the trees and ravens they believed in seem almost present.

✪ **The Russian Bishop's House.** Lincoln and Monastery sts. No phone; call Historical Park Visitor Center (see "Visitor Information," above). Free admission. Daily 9:30am–noon and 1–3pm.

Father Ivan Veniaminov, born in 1797, translated the Bible into Tlingit and trained deacons to carry Russian Orthodoxy back to their Native villagers. Unlike most of the later missionaries of other faiths, he allowed parishioners to use their own language, the key element to saving Native cultures. When the United States bought Alaska in 1867, few Russians remained, but the Russian Orthodox faith Veniaminov planted as a priest and later as Bishop Innocent remains strong in Native Alaska; there are 89 parishes, primarily in tiny Native villages. In 1977 Veniaminov was canonized as St. Innocent in the Orthodox faith.

In 1842 the Russian America Company retained Finnish shipbuilders to construct this extraordinary house for Bishop Innocent. It survived many years of neglect in part because its huge beams were fit together like a ship's. The National Park Service bought and began restoring the building in 1972, and today it's a fascinating visit. Downstairs is a self-guided museum; rangers take frequent tours upstairs to the bishop's quarters, which is furnished with period pieces.

✪ **St. Michael's Cathedral.** Lincoln and Cathedral sts. Free admission (donations requested). Mon–Sat 1:30–5:30pm, Sun for services, with longer hours in summer.

The first Orthodox cathedral in the New World stands grandly in the middle of Sitka's principal street, where it was completed in 1848 by Father Veniaminov (see above). The cathedral contains icons dating to the 17th century, including the miraculous *Sitka Madonna*. The choirmaster or another knowledgeable guide is on hand to answer questions or give talks when large groups congregate. The original building burned down in a fire that took much of Sitka's downtown in 1966, but the icons were saved and Orthodox Christians all over the United States raised the money to rebuild it exactly as it had been, completing the task in 1976.

✪ **Sheldon Jackson Museum.** 104 College Dr. ☎ **907/747-8981.** Admission $3 adults, free for students and children 18 and under. Mid-May to mid-Sept, daily 8am–5pm; mid-Sept to mid-May, Tues–Sat 10am–4pm.

Among the best collections of Alaska Native artifacts on display anywhere is kept here in a restored building, now run by the state museum, on the campus of Sheldon Jackson College. Jackson, a Presbyterian missionary and beloved figure in Alaska history, started the collection in 1888. This small octagonal building is like a jewel box, but the museum's overwhelming wealth is displayed in ingenious ways that prevent it from feeling cluttered. Some of the drawers in the white cabinetry open to reveal more displays. Some of the artifacts, despite their antiquity, are as fresh as if they had just been made.

OTHER ATTRACTIONS IN TOWN

The **New Archangel Dancers** (☎ 907/747-3225) are one of the most popular attractions in the state, since most cruise-ship passengers go to the crowd-pleasing shows in the Centennial Building. The all-woman troupe performs male and female roles in traditional Russian dances commemorating Sitka's Russian heritage (although they're not Russian—the Russians considered Alaska a worse assignment than Siberia and left on the first available boat upon the sale of Alaska to the United States in 1867). Shows are geared to ship arrivals—the times are posted at the Centennial Hall, or phone for information. Admission is $6. The **Sitka Tribe** (☎ 907/747-3207) sponsors performances of traditional Tlingit dances daily at the Centennial Hall; these are less well attended, but well worth seeing. The dancers explain the dances and interact with the audience; my son was entranced. For times, check at the hall or phone. Admission is $5. Also at the Centennial Hall is the **Isabel Miller Museum,** with exhibits on town history by the Sitka Historical Society.

Since 1980, injured eagles, hawks, owls, and other birds of prey have been brought to the **Alaska Raptor Rehabilitation Center,** 1101 Sawmill Creek Blvd. (take the dirt road up the hill to the left after the historical park), for surgery, convalescence, and release or transfer to a zoo. Visitors can see the patients in cages outside and receive a short lecture and guided tour inside with birds close up and displays about them. At $10 for adults and $5 for children, the admission price is high, but think of it as a donation to the center's good works; it's a private, nonprofit organization. Year round on Sunday afternoons only, the center is open to the public for free, without guides; otherwise it's open in summer, daily from 9am to 4pm.

I highly recommend the ✪ **"Historic Sites of Sitka" walking tour,** available at either of the visitor centers, but if you just want some of the highpoints, don't miss these. The brick **Pioneers' Home,** a state-run residence for retired people who helped settle Alaska, stands on a grassy park at Lincoln and Katlian, where the Russians had their barracks. Stop to talk to one of the old-timers rocking on the porch or visit their gift shop inside—many love to talk, and each has more of Alaska in his or her little finger than all the tour guides you'll meet all summer. Just north on Marine Street is a replica of a **Russian blockhouse;** across Lincoln Street to the south and up the stairs is **Castle Hill,** a site of historic significance for the ancient Tlingits, for the Russians, and for Alaskans. The American flag was first raised here in Alaska in 1867, and the Alsaka flag was first raised here when we became the 49th state in 1959. Walking east past the cathedral and Cascade Harbor, several quaint historic buildings are on the left—my favorite is **St. Peter's by-the-Sea Episcopal Church,** a lovely stone-and-timber chapel with a pipe organ, consecrated in 1899. At the east end of the harbor is a **public playground;** continue down the street to **Sheldon Jackson College** and the national historical park.

SHOPPING

There are some good shops and galleries in Sitka, mostly on Lincoln and Harbor streets. Three are across the street from St. Michael's Cathedral, on the uphill side: **Sitka's Artist Cove Gallery** at 241 Lincoln St., **Impressions,** and **Three Guys by the Church**—authentic Alaskan art. Just down the street is a T-shirt shop with a difference: original wearable art—**Fairweather Prints,** at 209 Lincoln St. Next door is a good bookstore, **Old Harbor Books,** which has a relaxing art and coffee shop in the back where I enjoyed an inexpensive breakfast. The **Sitka Rose Gallery** is in a lovely Victorian house at 419 Lincoln St. and has some serious fine art. The **Sheldon Jackson Museum Gift Shop,** 104 College Dr., features authentic Native arts and crafts from all over the state. A little off the beaten track, **Taranoff's Sitkawan Gifts** is at 208 Katlian St.

GETTING OUTSIDE

✪ **ON THE WATER**   The little islands and rocks that dot Sitka Sound are an invitation to the sea otter in all of us; you must get out on the water. Otters and whales are so numerous in the area that **Allen Marine Tours** (☎ 907/747-8100) guarantees a 50% refund if you don't see one on its Sea Otter and Wildlife Quest, which costs $80 (half price for children) for a 3¹/₂-hour cruise leaving on Sunday, Tuesday, and Friday from the boat harbor downtown during summer. You can also buy tickets on board or at various places around town, including **Greatland Travel** (☎ 907/747-7474). Whales are most often seen in the winter (see below), and there are so many bald eagles that you're pretty well guaranteed of seeing them from shore. But the lowly sea otter is the most common and, in my experience, most amusing and endearing of marine mammals, and you'll certainly see them from the boat. Otters seem so friendly and happy it's hard not to anthropomorphize and envy them.

✪ **St. Lazaria Island** is a bird rookery visited by tour boats where you can expect to see puffins, murres, and petrels. The public tubs at Goddard Hot Springs, 17 miles south of town, are another possible stop. Many boats are available for **wildlife tours** or **saltwater fishing;** the Sitka Convention and Visitors Bureau keeps a detailed list, including rates, of more than two dozen. Also, their "Sitka Through Four Seasons" brochure includes a checklist of what birds and animals you can expect to see when. Barbara Bingham's six-passenger boat is equipped with hydrophones to eavesdrop on the whales; her rates—$80 for a half day, $150 for a full day—seem to be typical; book direct through **Raven's Fire Inc.,** P.O. Box 6112, Sitka, AK 99835 (☎ 907/747-5777).

Or you could charter on a wooden sailboat that's a working **commercial fishing** vessel. Noel and Claire Johnson offer a $100 sightseeing cruise on their 56-foot gaff-rigged cutter, and also an overnight commercial long-lining trip for halibut, through **Southeast Alaska Ocean Adventures,** P.O. Box 6384, Sitka, AK 99835 (☎ 907/747-5011). **Waltzing Bear Charters,** 4600 Halibut Point Rd., Sitka, AK 99835 (☎ 907/747-3608), makes bare-boat and guided **sailing charters.**

Local boosters claim that Sitka has the best **sea kayaking** in the world, and I won't dispute it: These protected waters and little-used shorelines are inviting. The most established of providers is **Baidarka Boats** (☎ 907/747-8996). For the beginner, **Alaska Travel Adventures** (☎ 907/789-0052 in Juneau) takes several three-hour tours daily at $69 for adults and $45 for children.

ON & ABOVE THE SHORELINE   Humpback whales stop to feed in Sitka Sound on their way south in the winter migration. During the months of October, November, December, and March, I'm told you can watch from shore at the Sitka National Historical Park and see a dozen humpbacks. Even in summer, without the whales, there are good shoreline rambles in Sitka. Besides the historical park, there are two waterfront state parks out Halibut Point Road; **Halibut Point Park,** 4.4 miles out, is the larger of the two.

There are half a dozen U.S. Forest Service **hiking trails** accessible from the roads around Sitka. Get a copy of their trail guides from the Convention and Visitors Bureau, or the **Sitka Ranger District,** 201 Katlian St., Suite 109, Sitka, AK 99835 (☎ 907/747-6671). The 5¹/₂-mile **Indian River Trail** is a relaxing rain-forest walk starting close to downtown Sitka, off Sawmill Creek Road (take the unmarked road east of the Alaska State Troopers Academy). For a steeper, mountain-climbing trail to alpine terrain and great views, the **Gavan Hill Trail** is just past the house at 508 Baranof St., near downtown. It gains 2,500 feet over 3 miles.

U.S. FOREST SERVICE CABINS   The **Sitka Ranger District,** 201 Katlian St., Suite 109, Sitka, AK 99835 (☎ **907/747-6671**), maintains more than 20 cabins, available for $25 per night. They're either on mountain lakes, with rowboats provided, or on the ocean. All require either a boat or an aircraft to get to them, but once you're there you're truly in the wilderness by yourself. A Forest Service guide lists what you can find at each. **Bellair** (☎ **907/747-8636**) or **Mountain Aviation** (☎ **907/966-2288**) can fly you out.

WHERE TO STAY

The **bed tax** in Sitka is 8%. Besides those hotels listed here, I recommend the **Cascade Inn,** 2035 Halibut Point Rd., Sitka, AK 99835 (☎ **907/747-6904**), which is luxurious but inconveniently located. There's also an island lighthouse for rent, the **Rockwell Lighthouse** (☎ **907/747-3056**).

Ⓢ **Potlatch Motel.** 713 Katlian St., Sitka, AK 99835. ☎ **907/747-8611.** Fax 907/747-5810. 32 rms. TV TEL. $78 double. Room/car-rental packages available. AE, MC, V.

A clean, comfortable motel-style building located in the business district, a 10-minute walk to the sights. The rooms are reasonably priced and there's a coin-op laundry and a fish-cleaning and -freezing facility in the hotel, and free coffee in the lobby. We found the service kid-friendly. A courtesy van will take you to the ferry dock, airport, or even downtown.

Ⓢ **Sitka Hotel.** 118 Lincoln St., Sitka, AK 99835. ☎ **907/747-3288.** Fax 907/747-8499. 60 rms, 45 with bath. TV TEL. $49 double without bath, $59 double with bath. Additional person in room $7 extra. AE, MC, V.

Efforts to remodel and still advertise the lowest rates in town have left this old building with rooms of uneven quality—take a look before you check in. I can't recommend the rooms with shared bath, as the facilities were not well cleaned or maintained when I visited. However, with the central location and good views, many of the rooms with private bathrooms are a real bargain. There's free coffee in the lobby and the hotel rents bikes and has a coin-op laundry.

Super 8 Sitka. 404 Sawmill Creek Blvd., Sitka, AK 99835. ☎ **907/747-8804.** 34 rms, 1 suite. TV TEL. High season, $106 double. Low season, $90 double. Additional person in room $5 extra. AE, CB, DC, DISC, MC, V.

This is a first-class hotel right at the historic district, for $20 less than the Westmark. The Super 8 is small and quiet; many rooms have recliners, refrigerators, and VCRs. A coin-operated laundry and spa are in the building. The rooms also have air conditioning—perhaps you'll be in Sitka on one of the few days each year when it's needed. The lobby has coffee and a toast bar.

Westmark Shee Atika. 330 Seward St., Sitka, AK 99835-7523. ☎ **907/747-6241** or 800/544-0970. Fax 907/747-5486. 99 rms. TV TEL. $124 mountainside double, $128 harborside double. AE, DC, DISC, MC, V.

This large, upscale chain hotel stands in a central location in the heart of the historic district. Most rooms have good views, as do the restaurant and lounge. Better than half the rooms are reserved for nonsmokers. You can book tours and activities in the lobby. The service in the restaurant is friendly and efficient; the fine-dining menu emphasizes seafood.

BED-AND-BREAKFASTS

There are about a dozen B&Bs in Sitka, some more conveniently located if not as impressive as the two I've listed here. Two good downtown choices are the **Karras**

Bed and Breakfast (☎ 907/747-3978) and the **Biorka Bed and Breakfast** (☎ 907/747-3111). The Sitka Convention and Visitors Bureau produces a chart listing them all, with rates and facilities.

۞ Alaska Ocean View Bed and Breakfast. 1101 Edgecumbe Dr., Sitka, AK 99835. ☎ and fax **907/747-8310.** 3 rms. TV TEL. $79 double; $109 suite. AE, MC, V.

Bill and Carol Denkinger have a passion for making their bed-and-breakfast one you'll tell people about for years afterward. They've thought of everything—the covered outdoor spa where you can watch the eagles, toys and games for the kids, thick robes and slippers, an open snack counter and big full breakfast, even wildflower seeds to take home. The decor is feminine country style, and everything is just so. It's a bit of a hike to the sights, and a bike or car is a good idea. TVs are equipped with VCRs. The whole place is reserved for nonsmokers.

The Creek's Edge Bed and Breakfast. 109 Cascade Rd. (P.O. Box 2941), Sitka, AK 99835. ☎ **907/747-6484.** 3 rms, 1 with bath. TV TEL. $69 double without bath, $95 double with bath. Rates include full breakfast. AE, MC, V.

The house on a steep hill outside town has a deck with an amazing view of Sitka Sound. The rooms are decorated with antiques and have phones, but share a line. The more expensive room, with a private bath and its own deck, is something to write home about. No children, no smoking, and no alcohol are permitted.

HOSTELLING & CAMPING

A **hostel** is located at 303 Kimsham St. (P.O. Box 2645), Sitka, AK 99835 (☎ **907/ 747-8356**), quite a walk up from the downtown. The 20 beds are $7 per night, no linens available. It's open June through August; office hours are 8 to 10am and 6 to 10pm.

The Forest Service maintains two campgrounds, at the north and south ends of Halibut Point Road. Seven miles north of town, **Starrigavan Campground** has 28 sites. The fee is $8 nightly. The city maintains a 26-space **RV park** on Japonski Island, close to downtown. Full hookups are $16.

WHERE TO EAT

Bayview Restaurant. 407 Lincoln St. ☎ **907/747-5440.** All meals $5.50–$12. AE, DC, DISC, MC, V. Spring–fall, Mon–Sat 6:30am–8pm, Sun 6:30am–4pm; winter, Mon–Sat 7am–6pm, Sun 8am–3pm.

Although noisy and a bit cramped, the view of the boat harbor and reasonable prices make this second-story restaurant a popular place. The Russian-style halibut is a bit of a gimmick, but generally it's a good menu, well prepared and served. Beer and wine license.

Channel Club. 2906 Halibut Point Rd. ☎ **907/747-9916.** Dinner $12–$37. AE, DC, MC, V. Daily 5–10pm.

Located out the road north of town, the Channel Club's cuisine has won awards. The huge salad bar is a Sitka institution, sufficient for a meal all by itself. Full liquor license.

۞ El Dorado Restaurant. 714 Katlian St. ☎ **907/747-5070.** Lunch $5–$8; dinner $9–$14. DISC, MC, V. Daily 10:30am–11pm.

The menu has separate lists of American/Mexican and authentic Mexican dishes. The portions are large, the prices low, and the service jolly, efficient, and pro-kid. Our Mexican dinners were excellent—subtly flavored, despite the casual, small-town, family-restaurant atmosphere. Pizza also is available. Beer and wine license.

Lulu's Diner. 116 Lincoln St. ☎ **907/747-5620.** Lunch $5–$7; dinner $9–$14. AE, MC, V. Daily 6am–7pm.

This small, smoke-free, streetfront café is popular among locals for its hearty, reasonably priced burgers and sandwiches, but it also has a modest steak and seafood dinner menu for an early-evening meal. Beer and wine license.

♦ VanWinkle and Daigler. 228 Harper Dr. ☎ **907/747-3396.** Reservations recommended. Lunch $5–$9; dinner $16–$19. AE, MC, V. High season, Mon–Sat 11:30am–10pm, Sun 5–10pm; winter, hours vary.

A nice balance of the casual and fine, the dining room has shelves of old books but also tablecloths. The Pacific Northwest–style cuisine concentrates on Sitka-caught seafood. Portions are huge and service quick, but the cooking is still subtle and expert. The wine list and entrees are well priced. VanWinkle and Daigler are cousins—one mans the bar, the other the kitchen. Full liquor license.

8 Juneau: Forest Capital

Juneau (JUNE-oh) hustles and bustles like no other city in Alaska. The steep downtown streets echo with the mad shopping sprees of cruise-ship passengers in the summer tourist season and the whispered intrigues of the politicians during the winter legislative session. Miners, loggers, and ecotourism operators come to lobby for their share of Southeast's forest. Lunch hour arrives and well-to-do state and federal bureaucrats burst from the office buildings to try the latest trendy restaurant or brown bag on one of the waterfront wharves, sparkling water before them and gift store malls behind. The center of town becomes an ad hoc pedestrian mall as the crush of people forces cars to creep.

Even bears and eagles don't seem able to leave the place alone. Bears have always been a problem, wandering into town to dig through garbage and terrorize neighbors. And every couple of years an eagle makes off with a tourist's chihuahua, making a snack of Fifi and reigniting a civic debate between those who laugh at the news and those who are outraged at such insensitivity to the tragedy.

My Juneau is close at hand, but very different. At a magical age as a child, I lived here with my family in a house on the side of the mountains above downtown. My Juneau is up the 99 steps that lead from the cemetery to the bottom of Pine Street—the way I walked home from school—and then to the top of residential Evergreen Avenue, where the pavement gives way to a forest trail among fiddlehead ferns and massive rain-forest spruces. That trail leads to the flume—a wooden aqueduct bringing water down from the mountains—upon which we would walk into the land of bears and salmon, the rumbling water at our feet. It's still a short walk from the rackety downtown streets to a misty forest quiet, where one can listen for the voices of trees.

Juneau is Alaska's third-largest city, with a population of almost 30,000 (Anchorage and Fairbanks are larger), but it feels like a small town that's just been stuffed with people. Splattered on the sides of Mt. Juneau and Mt. Roberts along Gastineau Channel, where there really isn't room for much of a town, its setting is picturesque but impractical. Further development up the mountains is hemmed in by avalanche danger; beyond is the 1,500-square-mile Juneau Icefield, an impenetrable barrier. Gold-mine tailings dumped into the Gastineau created the flat land near the water where much of the downtown area now stands. The Native village that originally stood on the waterfront today is a little pocket of mobile homes several blocks from the shore. There's no road to the outside world, and the terrain forbids building one. Jets are the main way in and out, threading down through the mountains to the airport.

Gold was responsible for the location; it was found here in 1880 by Joe Juneau and Richard Harris, assisted by a Tlingit chief who told them where to look. Hard-rock mining continued into the 1940s. In 1900 Congress moved the territorial capital here from Sitka, which had fallen behind in the rush of development. Alaskans have been fighting over whether or not to keep it here for many decades since, but Juneau's economy is heavily dependent on government jobs, and it has successfully fought off a number of challenges to its capital status, most recently in 1994. The closest the issue came was in the 1970s, when the voters approved moving the capital, but then balked at the cost of building a whole new city to house it—a necessity since neither Anchorage nor Fairbanks (which have their own rivalry) would support the move if it meant the other city got to have the capital nearby.

There's plenty to see in Juneau, and it's a good town to visit because the relatively sophisticated population of government workers supports good restaurants and amenities not found elsewhere in Southeast. Also, Juneau is a starting point for out-doors travel in the area, and in all of Southeast Alaska. The crush of visitors can be overwhelming when many cruise ships are in port at once, and the streets around the docks have been entirely taken over by shops and other touristy businesses. Many of these are owned by people from Outside who come to the state for the summer to sell gifts made Outside to visitors from Outside. But only a few blocks away are quiet, mountainside neighborhoods of houses with mossy roofs, and only a few blocks farther the woods and the mountains.

ESSENTIALS

GETTING THERE   By Air   Juneau is served primarily by **Alaska Airlines,** with numerous daily nonstop flights from Seattle and Anchorage and to the smaller Southeast Alaska towns. **Delta** has flights, too. (See "Exploring Southeast Alaska," earlier in this chapter.) It's a travel hub, which is ironic since the mountainside air-port is tough to get into and can be a hair-raising place to land. The misty weather and the position of the airport have created a new verb: *to overhead*. It means that when you fly to Juneau, you could end up somewhere else instead; the airline will put you on the next flight back to Juneau, but won't pay for hotel rooms or give you a refund. Less drastic delays also are common. Don't schedule anything tightly around a flight to Juneau. Most of the commuter and air-taxi operators in Southeast also maintain a desk at the airport and have flights out of Juneau.

By Ferry   All main-line **Alaska Marine Highway** ferries (see "Exploring Southeast Alaska," earlier in this chapter) stop at the dock in Auke Bay, a 15-minute drive from town. There is an extreme shortage of parking at the ferry terminal.

VISITOR INFORMATION   The **Davis Log Cabin Visitor Center,** 134 Third Ave. (at Seward, downtown), Juneau, AK 99801 (☎ **907/586-2201;** fax 907/586-6304), is a replica of Juneau's first school, a log cabin with a little log belfry. Operated by the Juneau Convention and Visitors Bureau, the center shows a video and distributes the usual commercial visitor information, but it also distributes "55 Free Things to See and Do in Juneau," and a **Juneau Walking Tour Map.** The center is open daily from 9am to 5pm, year round.

A **visitor information desk** at the airport, near the door in the baggage-claim area, operates during the summer.

U.S. Forest Service headquarters for the 17-million-acre Tongass National Forest—encompassing the vast majority of Southeast Alaska—is in the federal building, the huge, square concrete building that dominates the skyline at Ninth Street and Glacier Avenue. The **Forest Service Visitor Information Center** is located in the

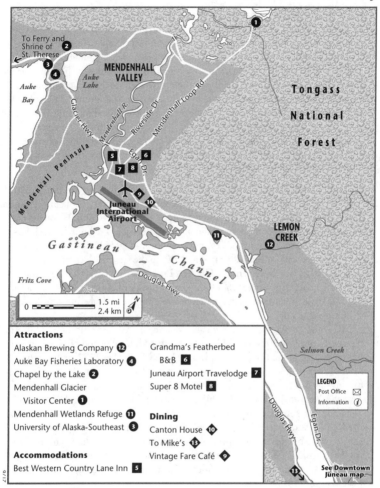

To Ferry and
Shrine of
St. Therese

MENDENHALL VALLEY

Auke
Lake

Auke
Bay

Glacier Hwy.

Mendenhall R.

Riverside Dr.

Mendenhall Loop Rd.

Tongass

National

Forest

Mendenhall Peninsula

Egan Dr.

Juneau International Airport

LEMON CREEK

Gastineau

Channel

Fritz Cove

Douglas Hwy.

0   1.5 mi
     2.4 km

Salmon Creek

Douglas Hwy.

Egan Dr.

LEGEND
Post Office ✉
Information ⓘ

See Downtown
Juneau map.

Attractions

Alaskan Brewing Company ⑫
Auke Bay Fisheries Laboratory ④
Chapel by the Lake ②
Mendenhall Glacier
    Visitor Center ①
Mendenhall Wetlands Refuge ⑪
University of Alaska-Southeast ③

Grandma's Featherbed
    B&B ⑥
Juneau Airport Travelodge ⑦
Super 8 Motel ⑧

Dining

Canton House ⑩
To Mike's ⑬
Vintage Fare Café ⑨

Accommodations

Best Western Country Lane Inn ⑤

Centennial Hall Convention Center, 101 Egan Dr., Juneau, AK 99801 (☎ **907/586-8751;** fax 907/586-7894). It maintains displays and shows films about the forest; it also answers questions and distributes information about the forest and takes reservations for cabins and permits for the Pack Creek Bear Observatory (see below under "Side Trips from Juneau").

Alaska Rainforest Tours, 369 S. Franklin St., Suite 200, Juneau, AK 99801 (☎ **907/463-3466;** fax 907/463-4453), is a unique booking and travel-planning agency catering to travelers who want to get into the outdoors and off the beaten track. Karla Hart, co-owner with her mother, fights politically for the protection of the Tongass rain forest. She says she got into the business to prove that the forest is worth something—standing. The company publishes an annual catalog of independent travel and outdoors experiences and runs the **Alaska Bed and Breakfast Association,** which books 60 B&Bs, primarily in Southeast.

ORIENTATION   Juneau has two main parts. The city outgrew its original site downtown, and housing spread to the suburban **Mendenhall Valley,** about a dozen miles out the **Egan Expressway** or the parallel, two-lane **Glacier Highway** to the north. The glacial valley also contains the **airport, University of Alaska Southeast,** and the village of **Auke Bay.** The road continues 40 miles, to a place called **"The End of the Road."** Across a bridge over the Gastineau Channel from downtown Juneau is the town of **Douglas,** mostly a bedroom community for Juneau. The older section of downtown, directly above the cruise-ship dock, is a numbered grid of streets overlying the uneven topography like a patterned quilt over a pile of pillows. The area below the hills to the west, near the massive federal building, is flatter and newer, much of it built on fill. As you look at Juneau from the water, **Mount Juneau** is on the left and **Mount Roberts** on the right; Mount Roberts is a few hundred feet taller, at 3,819 feet. **Franklin Street** extends south of town 5¹/₂ miles to the village of **Thane** and good hiking trails.

GETTING AROUND   A cab in from the airport will cost you nearly $20, but there are good alternatives. A Gray Line **airporter** meets every plane in the summer; tickets are on sale at the Hertz counter for $9.50. Or the **Capital Transit** city bus (☎ 907/789-6901) comes every hour at 11 minutes past the hour on weekdays during business hours and costs $1.25; however, your luggage has to fit under your seat or at your feet; call for bus information. A cab to the ferry dock costs even more than to the airport, but **Mendenhall Glacier Transport (MGT)** (☎ 907/786-5460) meets the boats with a blue school bus, and the price of $5 from town or the airport includes the driver's commentary. Call before 8pm the night before your ferry leaves to arrange a pickup.

MGT also does a two-hour town and Mendenhall Glacier tour for $12.50. **Alaska Native Tours** (☎ 907/463-3231) offers a three-hour city and glacier tour with an Alaska Native guide for $15. **Capital Cab** (☎ 907/586-2772 or 907/364-3349) offers normal taxi service and does tours for $45 an hour. Also, a 90-minute mining-history tour, with gold panning, operates in the summer through **Alaska Travel Adventures** (☎ 907/789-0052); the cost is $30 for adults and $20 for children.

Major **car-rental companies** are based at the airport. I cannot recommend the Rent-A-Wreck franchise; I rented a real wreck there and got rude service. You can get around downtown Juneau easily without a car, but if you're going to the Mendenhall Glacier or to any of the attractions out the road, renting a car for a day of your stay is a good idea. **Mountain Gears,** at 210 N. Franklin St. (☎ 907/586-4327), rents bikes.

FAST FACTS   The **sales tax** is 4%. There are numerous banks in Juneau with ATMs. The main **post office** downtown is in the federal building, 709 W. Ninth St., and in the Mendenhall Valley at 9491 Vintage Blvd., by the airport. In an **emergency,** dial 911; for nonemergency calls to the **police,** dial 907/586-2780. The **hospital** (☎ 907/586-2611) is 3 miles out the Glacier Highway. The *Juneau Empire* is published daily except Saturday; **out-of-town newspapers** are available at Big City Books, 100 N. Franklin St. Capital Copy, a **business center** with fax and copying services, is located at 123 S. Seward St. (☎ 907/586-9696).

SPECIAL EVENTS   The **22nd Annual Alaska Folk Festival** (☎ 907/789-0292) is a community-wide celebration drawing musicians, whether on the bill or not, from all over the state; it will be held April 8–14 in 1996. The **Juneau Jazz and Classics Festival** (☎ 907/364-2421), scheduled for May 15–25 in 1996, includes concerts at various venues. A gathering of some 1,000 Native dancers at the Centennial Hall, scheduled for June 6–8, 1996, is titled simply **Celebration** (☎ 907/463-4844). Later that month (June 28–30), **Gold Rush Days** (☎ 907/463-5706) includes logging and mining events and competitions anyone can join at Riverside Park.

The **50th Annual Golden North Salmon Derby** (☎ 907/789-2399) offers cash for the biggest fish, the money raised going for scholarships.

EXPLORING JUNEAU
DOWNTOWN
✪ **Alaska State Museum.** 395 Whittier St. ☎ **907/465-2901.** Admission $3 adults, free for students and children 18 and under. High season, Mon–Fri 9am–6pm, Sat–Sun 10am–6pm; winter, Tues–Sat 10am–4pm.

The museum contains a huge collection of Alaskan art and Alaska Native and historical artifacts, but it doesn't seem like a storehouse at all, because the objects' presentation is based on their meaning, not their value or quantity. Although the museum is small, each room is full of discoveries. A clan house in the Alaska Native Gallery teaches more than the outdoor houses you see in Wrangell or Ketchikan because it contains the authentic art that you'd really find there in its functional place. The ramp to the second floor wraps around the natural-history display, with an eagle screeching up in a tree, and at the top a state history gallery uses historical pieces to tell a story, not just impress. A visit to the museum will help put the rest of what you see in Alaska in context.

A Downtown Walking Tour
The **Juneau-Douglas City Museum,** at the corner of Fourth and Main streets, concentrates on the city's history, especially gold mining. There's a large relief map of the town, historic artifacts and displays, a video, and a hands-on display for children. Do pick up a historic walking-tour map and maps of the Evergreen Cemetery and the old Treadwell Mine. It's open in summer, Monday through Friday from 9am to 5pm and on Saturday and Sunday from 11am to 5pm; in winter, Thursday through Saturday from noon to 4:30pm. Admission is $1, free for children 18 and under. The **Alaska State Capitol** stands across Main Street in a nondescript brick building; it may be the least impressive state capitol in the most beautiful setting in the nation. Juneau has considered replacing it as an incentive to keep the rest of the state from voting to move it to another town. Free tours start every half hour, 9am to 4:30pm; the legislature is in session January to early May. Across Fourth is the **courthouse,** with a carved bear in front. This bear defines Alaskan taste in art: It replaced a steel modern-art sculpture called *Nimbus* that was removed by an act of the legislature, finally coming to rest at the state museum. The **state office building,** on the other corner, has a large atrium with great views and, on the eighth floor, a pipe organ that's played on Friday at noon. Off the eighth-floor lobby, the **state library** contains an excellent collection of historic photographs.

A block up and two blocks toward Mount Roberts on Fifth, you'll reach ✪ **St. Nicholas Orthodox Church,** at Fifth and Gold. This tiny, octagonal chapel was built in 1893 by local Tlingits. Under pressure from the government to convert to Christianity, they chose the only faith that allowed them to keep their language; Father Ivan Veniaminov (see "Exploring Sitka" in section 7 of this chapter) had translated the Bible into Tlingit 50 years earlier when the Russians were still in Sitka. Despite its size, the church is historically and architecturally significant, and still has an active Tlingit parish. Services are sung in English, Tlingit, and Slavonic on Saturday evening at 6pm and on Sunday morning at 10am. A well-trained guide is on hand the rest of the week during the day to answer questions; excellent written guides are available, too. Donations are accepted. **Holy Trinity Episcopal Church,** one block down at Fourth and Gold, has a cozy turn-of-the-century sanctuary with a steeply pitched tin roof and interesting stained glass; it's unlocked all day. A little-known piece of church history: As an undersized acolyte at age eight, I almost

Downtown Juneau

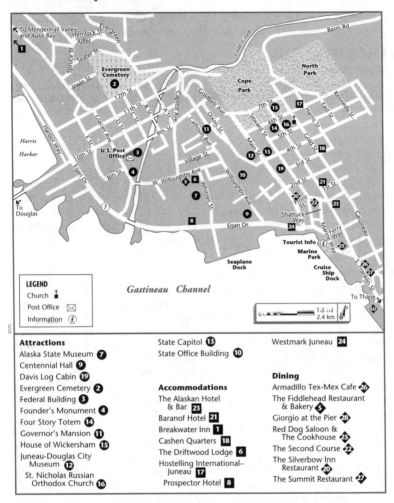

smashed the stained glass in the back of the church when I lost control of the heavy crucifix and had to run down the aisle to keep up with it.

A couple of blocks up, at 213 Seventh St., the **Wickersham House** (☎ 907/586-9001), a state-owned historical site, is sometimes open for tours; check at the visitor center for times or phone the house. Judge James Wickersham, elected the territory's nonvoting delegate to Congress in 1908, was a leading fighter for Alaska self-determination. Walk back down Main Street, turn left on Fifth, cross the footbridge, and turn right on Calhoun. On the left is the 1912 **Governor's Mansion;** although there are no tours, it's fun to see a sort of neoclassical southern plantation house on the side of a mountain in Alaska. If you're up for a longer walk, Calhoun, one of Juneau's prettiest streets, leads to Gold Creek, where you can turn right to peaceful **Cope Park,** which has tennis courts. Or continue across the creek until you reach the **Evergreen Cemetery** on your left; the wooded area on the opposite side is the old, Native part of the graveyard. Turning right instead of entering the cemetery, you come to the bottom of the steps that lead to the bottom of Pine Street, and the flume walk I described in the Juneau introduction.

The downtown shopping district is near the cruise-ship dock. At the top of the parking garage on the waterfront, the **Juneau City Library** has great views.

Shopping

Juneau, like Ketchikan and Skagway, has developed a shopping district catering primarily to the cruise ships; when the last of the 470 or more port calls are over late in the summer, many of the shops close their doors and their owners go home to the Lower 48. That doesn't mean that they don't sell good products, but to buy authentic Alaskan items you have to be careful—look for the MADE IN ALASKA polar bear sticker or the silver hand sticker, which authenticates Alaska Native art.

There are several serious galleries—here is a small selection: **Objects of Bright Pride,** at 165 S. Franklin St., is a beautiful little gallery with top-quality, authentic Native art; for most, it will be a place to look rather than buy, because real Native art is expensive. The **Gallery of the North,** 406 S. Franklin St., is large and carries many Alaska artists, specializing in sculpture. The **Decker Gallery,** 233 S. Franklin St., features Rie Muñoz, whose light-hearted watercolors of fishing and coastal town scenes are favorites of Alaskans; the **Rie Muñoz Gallery** has moved to 2101 N. Jordan Ave. **Mt. Juneau Arts,** 2 Marine Way, is a local artists' cooperative.

For regular gift shops, try the long-established **Ad Lib,** at 231 S. Franklin St., and **Galligaskins,** 207 and 219 S. Franklin St., a locally owned shop that began as a children's clothing store but now has gifts and T-shirts. I'm always more interested in bookstores than gift shops; **Big City Books,** 100 N. Franklin St., is a good shop and a locus of the Juneau literary scene.

In 1995 Sealaska Corp., the Native corporation representing Southeast Alaska, opened the **Cultural Arts Center** on the waterfront near the cruise-ship dock which includes an **Alaska Native Artists Market,** open in summer daily from 8:30am to 8:30pm. It was off to a slow start when I visited and not everything for sale there was either Native or art, so be aware of what you're buying.

BEYOND WALKING DISTANCE & THE VALLEY

The drive out the four-lane Egan Expressway to the Mendenhall Valley crosses tidal flats that are a place to see birds, especially bald eagles. The tidal marsh near the airport also is good birdwatching territory.

The **Gastineau Salmon Hatchery,** at 2697 Channel Dr. (☎ 907/463-4810), is open for visitors in summer, Monday through Friday from 10am to 6pm and on Saturday and Sunday from noon to 5pm; closed October 15 to May 15. Its saltwater aquariums contain indigenous marine life and there's a fish ladder with an underwater window through which salmon can be seen swimming upstream beginning in July. In May and June the tour includes the incubation process. There are displays and a shop to buy smoked fish. Admission is $2.75 for adults, $1 for children 11 and under. The **National Marine Fisheries Service Auke Bay Lab,** 11305 Glacier Hwy. (☎ 907/789-6000), also has a small saltwater aquarium; you can walk through free, Monday through Friday from 8am to 4:30pm weekdays.

All over the state you'll find Alaska's leading microbrews, Alaskan Amber and Alaskan Pale Ale; the **Alaskan Brewery and Bottling Company,** started by home-brewers Geoff and Marcy Larson in 1986, is now a booming business with a popular free tour and beer tasting. The list of the beers' awards fills pages. Tours are every half hour from 11am to 5pm, Tuesday through Saturday, May to September; Thursday through Saturday the rest of the year. The brewery is at 5429 Shaune Dr. (☎ 907/780-5866), in the Lemon Creek area halfway to the Valley.

At the head of Mendenhall Valley is the **Mendenhall Glacier,** the easiest glacier in Alaska to get to and one of the most visited. The Forest Service maintains a

The Tongass Battleground

A friend described this scene: a forest of tall, straight spruce and hemlock trees, widely spaced, the sunlight streaming down through the branches into a green, mossy glade. He stood on the soft forest floor beside the owner of the land, breathing deeply the fragrant air that seemed to cling to the trees all around him. He couldn't help smiling at such beauty and he noticed his host was smiling broadly, too. But when the landowner opened his mouth to speak, my friend realized he saw something entirely different. His joy was that these trees, worth several thousand dollars apiece, would soon be logged to provide him with an ample retirement.

That scene occurred in the Prince William Sound area, but the conflict it represents is the fundamental political and social conflict of the entire state, Southeast Alaska included. The vast majority of Southeast is in the Tongass National Forest, a land used to many different ends—including providing for a timber harvest. Of course, cutting down trees isn't compatible with looking at them, appreciating the wildlife that relies on them, or harvesting fish from the streams they protect from heat and erosion. And there are jobs and retirement incomes tied up in those uses, too.

The heavy rain and temperate climate of Southeast Alaska create perfect conditions for growing huge trees—western hemlock, red cedar, and Sitka spruce, Alaska's state tree, are the main commercial species. It's a rain forest. There are tree trunks up to a dozen feet across. And it has another unique feature—millions of acres that have never been cut, some of the last major tracts of old-growth forest in the United States. Once logged, those ecosystems are gone virtually forever, for the succession of forest development to maturity in this region takes longer than the span of a human life, and much longer than the duration of human patience.

It's likely no one will mention it to you during your visit, but you are one of the central figures in this controversy. Tourism and the visitor industry have grown fast in recent years. When a large pulp mill closed down for good in Sitka a couple of years ago, most people were surprised at how well the community came through the loss—the economy had already largely made a transition to tourism jobs. But the issue pits neighbors against each other. Some tourism operators ask, "Why cut down the trees for short-term jobs now when, if left standing, visitors will keep coming to look at them years from now?" Loggers answer, "That's my job you're talking about."

But even within the tourism industry there are sharp divisions, with ecotourism providers leading the way, and even suing in court to stop timber sales. Each town in Southeast defines itself, in large part, by its relationship to the issue: Ketchikan and Wrangell are pro-logging to the core, whereas liberal Juneau is populated by government workers who would rather kayak through forests than clear-cuts.

visitor center (☎ 907/586-8800) with rangers who can answer questions and show a video about the glacier and the Juneau Icefield; it's open from 8:30am to 5pm, daily in summer, Saturday and Sunday from October to May. The glacier is on the opposite side of a lake from the visitor center and parking lot; a wheelchair-accessible trail leads down to the lake, or there's a covered viewing area right by the lot. In late summer you can watch red and silver salmon spawning in **Steep Creek,** just short of the visitor center on the road.

There are several trails at the glacier, ranging from a half-mile nature trail loop to two fairly steep, $3^1/2$-mile hikes approaching each side of the glacier. At the visitor

Everyone agrees some trees can be cut without destroying the environment or ruining all the vistas—after all, Tongass comprises 17 million acres and is the largest national forest in the United States. But what the communities and the three branches of federal government are still tussling over is which trees to cut, and how many.

The U.S. Forest Service, under President Clinton, has put the brakes on timber harvest in the last few years. About half the timber jobs in Southeast have disappeared since 1990, despite strong prices for wood. But before that, the logging industry had been working in overdrive, driven by 50-year contracts the federal government signed with Japanese companies after World War II to stimulate economic growth in Japan and Alaska. Building roads and facilities to allow that logging required a government subsidy far beyond what the companies paid for the timber. Meanwhile, Native corporations that gained title to vast tracts of land in the 1971 Alaska Native Claims Settlement Act were fast liquidating their timber assets for business and tax reasons. No one thought the rate of cutting was sustainable—even today, cutting occurs faster than the trees can grow back.

One reason the Forest Service changed direction was a scientific study that showed that wildlife of the forest doesn't need just broken patches of trees left behind by loggers—animals like bears and wolves need whole, continuous ecosystems to keep their numbers healthy. But while the Forest Service reviews the question and works on a new logging plan to address the concern, the mills complain they aren't getting enough wood to stay in business—they've closed in Sitka, Wrangell, and Haines over the years, and only Ketchikan's mill remains active among large operations.

Then, with 1994's national elections and the Republican takeover of Congress, the political pot started stirring in the opposite direction again. Alaska's three-member congressional delegation—Sens. Ted Stevens and Frank Murkowski and Rep. Don Young—took the chairmanships of the resource committees in both the House and Senate, placing them in charge of these issues for the whole country. All three are adamantly pro-development. Even before Young gained his new power, a national environmental organization listed him as a member of its "dirty dozen" archenemies in Washington—and he wore the brand as a badge of honor, knowing it could only help him among conservative, pro-development Alaskan voters.

Since coming to power, Stevens, Murkowski, and Young have worked aggressively to force the Forest Service to speed up logging in Tongass and create more logging jobs, but as of this writing it was still too early to tell which side would win. People have fought over the wealth of Southeast since long before white explorers showed up on the scene. They probably always will.

center and a booth near the parking lot the Forest Service distributes a brochure, "Mendenhall Glacier: Carver of a Landscape," which includes a trail map. The ✪ **East Glacier Loop Trail** is a beautiful day hike leading to a waterfall near the glacier's face and parts of an abandoned rail tram and an abandoned dam on Nugget Creek; the trail has steep parts, but is okay for school-age children. The **West Glacier Trail** is more challenging, leaving from the skater's cabin and campground off Montana Creek Road and following the edge of the lake and glacier, providing access to the ice itself for experienced mountaineers with the right equipment.

Another way to see the glacier is a 3½-hour beginners' rafting trip in the lake and down the Mendenhall River, available from **Alaska Travel Adventures** (☎ 907/789-0052) for $83. In the winter, **skating** on the lake is wonderful, gliding among the icebergs, frozen into place. It's also a place for easy cross-country skiing.

The **University of Alaska–Southeast** sits on the edge of peaceful Auke Lake, looking across at the glacier (follow the signs off Mendenhall Loop Road). The **Chapel-by-the-Lake** is lovely and quiet, if you aren't there at the same time as a tour group, and the **Egan Library** contains a good collection of Native art; a printed guide explaining the works is available. The totem pole on campus, originally carved in Southeast Alaska for the 1964 New York World's Fair, is the best in Juneau.

OUT THE ROAD

On sunny summer weekends, Juneau families get in the car and drive out the road, or the Glacier Highway, as it's officially known. The views of island-stippled water from the paved two-lane highway are worth the trip, but there also are several good places to stop—besides those mentioned here, there are others for you to discover. The **Auke Recreation Area** is just past Auke Bay, and is a good place for picnics and beach walks. The **Shrine of St. Therese,** 10 miles beyond Auke Bay, stands on a tiny island reached by a foot trail. The stone chapel is inspiring for its natural setting and the mysterious way it has of sitting out there by itself. This is a good vantage from which to look around in the **Lynn Canal** for marine mammals. **Eagle Beach,** a few miles farther, is a welcoming picnic area in good weather, and it's fun to walk the beach and look for eagles and fossils in the rock outcroppings to the north. The road turns to gravel, then comes to **Point Bridget State Park,** at mile 38 (measured from Juneau)—the trail there is discussed under "Getting Outside," below. Two miles farther the road comes to an end, 40 miles from Juneau at pretty **Echo Cove.**

DOUGLAS ISLAND

The land across Gastineau Channel from Juneau is Douglas Island, and the town of Douglas is a couple of miles down to the left after you cross the bridge. A city bus goes hourly. **Sandy Beach,** next to the small-boat harbor, is nice and has good views of Juneau on a sunny day. About half a mile down the shore are the ruins of the **old Treadwell Mine,** which collapsed in 1917.

GETTING OUTSIDE

ON LAND

HIKING   A **trail guide** available from the Forest Service visitor center for $4 describes 29 different hiking routes in the Juneau area; that's good, because some popular hikes have been spoiled by the presence of too many visitors. The Juneau city **Department of Parks and Recreation** (☎ 907/586-5226) leads hikes in summer and cross-country skiing in winter on Wednesday and Sunday. If you're hiking on any of the mountains in winter or early spring, obtain some local knowledge first, as avalanches are frequent and deadly here.

I've mentioned two good hikes above, under Mendenhall Glacier. There also are hikes right from town, maintained by the state **Division of Parks** (☎ 907/465-4563).

The ✪ **Perseverance Trail** starts from the end of Basin Road, up Gold Creek from downtown Juneau. Walking from town adds about a mile. The trail is 3 miles of easy walking on the mountainside above the creek to the Perseverance Mine, at the Silverbow Basin, which operated intermittently from 1885 to 1921. A mile from the start of the trail, a challenging path to the top of 3,576-foot **Mount Juneau** branches off to the left; it's only for rugged hikers late in the season, and it's dangerous to diverge from the trail. An easier but still quite strenuous climb is **Mount Roberts**—just follow the stairway from the top of Sixth Street, a neighborhood called Star Hill. The summit is 4$^1/_2$ miles and 3,819 vertical feet away, but you don't have to go all the way to the top for incredible views and alpine terrain. The cross 2$^1/_2$ miles up the trail was first installed in 1908 by the Jesuit priest who led construction of the trail.

Outer Beach was always one of my favorite places to walk at low tide; the tide pooling is good around the point on the left, and looking across the water from Douglas Island to Auke Bay you can often see whales. You have to drive to get there; turn right on North Douglas Highway after crossing the bridge from Juneau. I've recently heard that excessive use by tour groups has taken some of the magic out of an afternoon at Outer Beach.

Out the road (see above) at mile 38 on the Glacier Highway, **Point Bridget State Park** is less used, but easy and beautiful, and from the beach toward the end of the trail you can see sea lions and maybe humpback whales. The flat 3$^1/_2$-mile trail leads through forest, meadow, marsh, and marine ecosystems. A mile short of the point it branches; to the left is a steeper walk to a small lake and beaver pond, ending at a cove. It's good for cross-country skiing, too. Pick up the free trail-guide brochure from the Forest Service visitor center in Centennial Hall.

The **Point Bishop/Dupont Trail** leads from Thane, at the other end of the road, 5$^1/_2$ miles south of Juneau. Although muddy, it's a flat trail leading through mossy old-growth forest. The old mining area of Dupont, on the water, is 1.6 miles along; Point Bishop, beyond the mouth of the Gastineau Channel, is 8 miles.

U.S. FOREST SERVICE CABINS   Four U.S. Forest Service cabins are accessible from Juneau's road system by trails ranging from 3.3 to 5.5 miles. The **Dan Moller** cabin is located on Douglas Island right across from town. They're all popular and three of the four have two-night maximum stays. Three more remote cabins require a boat or plane. Two are on **Turner Lake** in alpine terrain off Taku Inlet, each with a skiff and spectacular scenery. Cabin permits are $25 per night from the Forest Service visitor center in Centennial Hall.

ALPINE SKIING   The city-owned **Eaglecrest Ski Area** (☎ 907/586-5284) may not be Vail, but it was good enough to train Olympic silver medalist Hillary Lindh, Juneau's favorite daughter. If the winter is snowy, the slopes on Douglas Island, 12 miles from downtown on North Douglas Highway, are the locals' favorite place. An all-day lift ticket is $24 for adults; an adult equipment package rents for $20 a day. The views are incredible.

OUT ON THE WATER

KAYAKING & CANOEING   Juneau is a center for so-called ecotourism, which seems to mean experiencing the outdoors but leaving things as you found them. **Alaska Rainforest Tours** (☎ 907/463-3466; fax 907/463-4453), listed above, specializes in booking these kinds of trips. The most established operator is ✪ **Alaska Discovery,** 5449 Shaune Dr., Suite 4, Juneau, AK 99801 (☎ **907/780-6226** or 800/586-1911; fax 907/780-4220), with dozens of trips in Southeast and in the Arctic National Wildlife Refuge. One of the founders, Methodist minister Chuck Horner, helped save Admiralty Island from clear-cutting by taking people there; today Admiralty is a huge bear preserve and Horner's company, launched with those trips, is a huge ecotourism operator (more on Admiralty below). Most of Alaska Discovery's serious wilderness trips range from 5 to 12 days, and in price from $1,250 to $2,900 per person, but a five-hour wildlife-watching **sea kayak** paddle starting from the Aldersheim Lodge, 35 miles out the road from Juneau, is $95 per person, leaving daily at noon. Add $10 and a couple of hours for a van ride out from town to the put-in point. **Alaska Travel Adventures** (☎ 907/789-1749) does a 3¹/₂-hour kayak paddle around Auke Bay and the airport area, with the van from town included in the $65 price; the trip is geared to the cruise ships.

Several businesses rent kayaks, including **Kayak King,** 101 Dock St., Douglas (P.O. Box 21061), Juneau, AK 99801 (☎ 907/586-8220), and **Adventure Sports,** in the Nugget Mall (☎ 907/789-5696). A double rents for about $45 a day, a single for $35. Peter Wright, whose business is called **Kayak Express,** 4107 Blackberry St., Juneau, AK 99801 (☎ and fax 907/780-4591), specializes in drop-off charters.

FISHING & WHALE WATCHING   The closest I ever saw a humpback whale—within a few yards—was on the way back from king salmon **fishing** out of Juneau on a friend's boat. More than two dozen charter companies offer fishing from Juneau and Auke Bay; you can go to **watch whales** or fish, or both. Juneau is well protected behind layers of islands, so the water is generally very calm. The Juneau Convention and Visitors Bureau maintains a list of businesses with details on their services and prices. **Juneau Sportfishing and Sightseeing,** 76 Egan Dr., Suite 230 (P.O. Box 20438), Juneau, AK 99802 (☎ 907/586-1887; fax 907/586-9769), is one of the largest operators, with 17 six-passenger boats; they charge $189 per person for a full day of fishing or sightseeing. **Auke Bay Sportfishing,** 9159 Skywood Lane, Juneau, AK 99801 (☎ 907/789-2562; fax 907/789-2410), has 10 boats at around the same rates. If you have three or more people in your group, you may do better chartering a whole boat for $450 to $800 and being completely in control.

SAILING   Although Inside Passage wind can be fluky, the deck of a **sailboat** can be a great vantage point for seeing the area. **Alaska Yacht Rentals,** 4478 Columbia Blvd., Juneau, AK 99801, has four boats, 32 to 60 feet in length, for bare-boat or skippered charters, ranging from $350 to $1,200 a day. **58° 22—North SailingCharters,** P.O. Box 32391, Juneau, AK 99803 (☎ 907/789-7301), has a 30- and a 36-foot Catalina.

✪ A DAY TRIP TO TRACY ARM   The Tracy Arm fjord, in the Tracy Arm–Fords Terror Wilderness, south of Juneau, is a popular day cruise from Juneau as a relatively inexpensive substitute for a trip to Glacier Bay. The scenery is spectacular: Sawyer Glacier and South Sawyer Glacier, at the head of the fjord, calve ice into the water, and whales and other wildlife may show up along the way, all just as it is at Glacier Bay—John Muir even visited. But unlike Glacier Bay, you can do it in a day from Juneau and save yourself the cost of a flight to Gustavus. **Glacier Bay Tours** (☎ 907/463-5510 or 800/451-5952) offers a full-day cruise on a 74-passenger vessel for $124, with a half-day, fly-back option for an additional $74 more. Other large boats compete and you can shop for price, but a small charter boat may give you a better day; you'll be more in control and be able to get up-close and linger, watching the seals and falling ice in front of the glaciers. Ask **Alaska Rainforest Tours** (☎ 907/463-3466; fax 907/463-4453), listed above, to book you on the *Carpé Diem.* Or try the *See-More,* a 16-passenger boat built for these trips, which books through **Juneau Sportfishing and Sightseeing** (☎ 907/586-1887).

IN THE AIR

The glaciers around Juneau are rivers of ice flowing off a frozen ocean behind the mountains, the Juneau Icefield. You can fly over it in a fixed-wing plane, or land on it in a helicopter, a humbling experience that will teach you how small you really are. **Era Helicopters** (☎ 907/586-2030), a long-established company with an unmatched reputation, offers an hour-long tour with a 20-minute landing for $157. A lift is available and the aircraft are accessible for people with disabilities. **Temsco**

Helicopters (☎ 907/789-9501) offers a 50- to 55-minute tour, including 25 minutes on the icefield, for $142. Always wait for decent weather for a flightseeing trip.

The three-hour, $163 **Taku Glacier Lodge tour,** P.O. Box 33597, Juneau, AK 99803 (☎ 907/586-8258), or **Wings of Alaska** (☎ 907/789-0790) includes a 50-minute flightseeing experience, a chance to see a glacier and a 1923 wilderness lodge, and possibly see bears and other wildlife, and to eat at a salmon cook-out.

WHERE TO STAY

Juneau's **bed tax** is 11%. Hotel rooms are tight in the summer, so book ahead; the convention and visitors bureau can give you a complete list. For rooms near the airport in the moderate price range, I can recommend the **Best Western Country Lane Inn,** 9300 Glacier Hwy., Juneau, AK 99801 (☎ 907/789-5005, or 800/528-1234), or the **Juneau Airport Travelodge,** 9200 Glacier Hwy., Juneau, AK 99801 (☎ 907/ 789-9700), which has a small indoor swimming pool and Mexican restaurant.

EXPENSIVE

Baranof Hotel. 127 N. Franklin St., Juneau, AK 99801. ☎ **907/586-2660** or 800/544-0970. Fax 907/697-2211. 199 rms. TV TEL. High season, $142 double. Low season, $110 double. AE, DC, DISC, MC, V.

In winter the venerable old Baranof acts like a branch of the state Capitol building for conferring legislators and lobbyists; in the summer it's like a branch of the package-tour companies. The 1939 concrete building has the feel of a grand hotel, but some of the rooms, especially on the lower floors, are small and need upgrading; the upper-floor rooms are modern and have great views on the water side. Some of the suites are quite impressive. There are many room configurations, so make sure you get what you want. Kitchenettes are available. It belongs to the Westmark chain.

The ✪ **Gold Room** restaurant is among the best in town. The brass and black marble decor, with an art deco skylight, conveys a sense of grandeur and opulence only underlined by the small number of tables. The service is formally attentive and the food expensive but worth it. The hotel also has a café.

✪ **Grandma's Feather Bed.** 2348 Mendenhall Loop Rd., Juneau, AK 99801. ☎ **907/ 789-5566.** Fax 907/789-2818. TV TEL. 14 rms. $136 double. Rates include breakfast. AE, CB, DC, DISC, ER, MC, V.

Incongruously set on a busy highway near the airport, this is a ground-up re-creation of a luxurious New England country inn. Rooms have all imaginable amenities (12 have Jacuzzis); it's simply a building full of honeymoon suites, each an open invitation to lovemaking. There's a small restaurant in the lobby, where breakfast is served for guests and dinners are served to the public. There's a 24-hour courtesy car; no children, no smoking allowed.

Westmark Juneau. 51 W. Egan Dr. (P.O. Box 20929), Juneau, AK 99802. ☎ **907/586-6900** or 800/544-0970. Fax 907/463-3567. 105 rms. TV TEL. High season, $145–$155 double. Low season, $134 double. Additional person in room $15 extra; children 11 and under stay free in parents' room. AE, DC, DISC, MC, V.

A modern hotel with large, luxuriously appointed rooms. Both sides have views, of either the mountains or the Gastineau Channel, but the waterfront views are preferable and cost $10 more. All rooms have Spectravision movies. There's a good restaurant, the Woodcarver, in the lobby. The best of the downtown hotels.

MODERATE

Breakwater Inn. 1711 Glacier Ave., Juneau, AK 99802. ☎ **907/586-6303.** 41 rms. TV TEL. $99 single or double. Additional person in room $10 extra. AE, DISC, MC, V.

This two-story building near the small-boat harbor has standard American motel rooms, some with balconies, 21 with kitchenettes. The harborside rooms are afflicted with highway noise, but are lighter than those on the mountain side. The smoking-permitted room we looked at had burns in the carpet.

The hotel's restaurant overlooks the harbor with an upscale menu of seafood and beef and, for lunch, fairly pricey sandwiches and specials.

⊙ Prospector Hotel. 375 Whittier St., Juneau, AK 99801. ☎ **907/586-3737** or 800/331-2711, 800/478-5166 in Alaska. Fax 907/586-1204. 58 rms. TV TEL. High season, $90 double; $118 double with kitchenette. Low season, $75 double. AE, DC, MC, V.

A comfortable hotel right on the waterfront with rooms newly remodeled in 1995, the Prospector has the best rates for a good, chain-style room downtown. The lower level is a half basement and somewhat dark; the rooms facing the channel have great views, but also traffic noise. Rooms with kitchenettes are available.

The restaurant, T.K. Maguire's, also was recently remodeled. The extensive dinner menu ranges in price from $12 to $29, with lots of fresh fish and a special prime rib. Lunch is sandwiches in the $7 to $8 range, and fish specials.

INEXPENSIVE

Alaskan Hotel and Bar. 167 S. Franklin St., Juneau, AK 99801. ☎ **907/586-1000** or 800/586-1000. Fax 907/463-3775. 36 rms, 14 with bath; 4 suites. TEL. $60 double without bath; $80 double with bath. Additional person in room $10 extra. DISC, MC, V,

This 1912 hotel is on the National Register of Historic Places and has a great location, right downtown, but the rooms are small and a bit musty and noise is a problem—the bar downstairs has live music every night, and if you're not dancing you may not be sleeping either. Some rooms have TVs, and studio apartments with kitchenettes are available. Twenty-two of the rooms share four bathrooms. Laundry facilities are available.

⊙ The Driftwood Lodge. 435 Willoughby Ave., Juneau, AK 99801. ☎ **907/586-2280** or 800/544-2239. Fax 907/586-1034. 55 rms, 8 suites. TV TEL. High season, $78 double; $95 suite. Low season, $62 double; $87 suite. Additional person in room $7 extra. AE, DC, DISC, MC, V.

This three-story motel right downtown is popular with families and houses legislators and aides in the winter in its apartmentlike kitchenette suites. The rooms, although clean, are threadbare and the walls are of cinder block, but the managers are hospitable and the round-the-clock courtesy car saves guests a lot of money getting to the airport. Other pluses include a coin-op laundry and coffee in the rooms.

BED-AND-BREAKFASTS

There are many bed-and-breakfasts in Juneau; the visitor center has a list of 25, with rates. The **Alaska Bed and Breakfast Association,** 369 S. Franklin St., Suite 200, Juneau, AK 99801 (☎ 907/463-3466; fax 907/463-4453), books many of them and others. Here I've listed three that are exceptionally good:

Blueberry Lodge. 9436 N. Douglas Hwy., Juneau, AK 99801. ☎ and fax **907/463-5886.** 5 rms, none with bath. High season, $75–$85 double. Low season, $60–$65 double. Rates include full breakfast. Additional person in room $10 extra. No credit cards.

A beautiful log building in the woods near the Eaglecrest Ski Area, 6 miles from the bridge to Juneau, looks out on an eagle's nest and the Gastineau Channel's Mendenhall Wetlands Refuge—the family will lend you binoculars and rubber boots for both. The breakfast is deluxe, the rooms homey and very clean, and the atmosphere social, with two children and two dogs resident. You'll need to rent a car for the 10-minute drive to town. No plastic, but personal checks are accepted.

⑤ Cashen Quarters. 315 Gold St., Juneau, AK 99801. ☎ **907/586-9863.** 5 rms. TV TEL. High season, $75 double. Low season, $60 double; $100 two-bedroom unit. Additional person in room $10 extra. MC, V.

Conveniently located downtown, each room has its own entry and kitchen with a refrigerator stocked daily with breakfast foods. Laundry facilities are available. The 1914 house has been a hotel or boarding house since 1946.

☉ Pearson's Pond Luxury Inn. 4541 Sawa Cir., Juneau, AK 99801. ☎ **907/789-3772.** Fax 907/789-6722. 1 rm, 2 suites. TV TEL. High season, $99–$129 double; $119–$169 suite. Low season, $69–$99 double; $89–$119 suite. Additional person in room $20 extra. AE, CB, DC, MC, V.

Here's a mental game you can play: Imagine you're a slightly obsessed bed-and-breakfast host and you decide to give your guests every amenity you can possibly think of. Now go to Diane Pearson's house and count how many you missed. A private telephone line in each room? Kid's stuff—Pearson installed two lines per room so guests can make phone calls and connect to the Internet at the same time. Did you think of a private duck pond with a dock, a rowboat, and a fountain? How about stocking the pond with fish? How about VCRs, stereos, bicycles, massage, kitchenettes, a Jacuzzi, car rental, a business center, free coffee, and breakfast? To finish the game, you'll have to check in, but book far ahead, as the place is earning a deserved reputation. It's located in the Mendenhall Valley, far from downtown.

A HOSTEL

Hostelling International–Juneau. 614 Harris St., Juneau, AK 99801. ☎ **907/586-9559.** 46 beds. $10 per person.

The hostel is conveniently located in a white house among the downtown sights. The office is open from 7 to 9am and 5 to 11pm in the summer, 5 to 10:30pm in the winter. Kitchen and laundry facilities are available.

WHERE TO EAT

In addition to the restaurants listed here, the **Channel Bowl,** near the Fiddlehead, listed below, is what a friend described as "a good elbows-on-the-table-and-shovel-it-in type of place," where you can eat at the lunch counter or in the bowling alley and meet the locals. **The Bakery,** across from the cruise-ship dock, has good, healthy sandwiches on home-baked bread that you can take across the street to eat in the Marine Park. **Hot Bite,** a stand at the Auke Bay boat harbor, is a local secret, serving terrific sandwiches and charcoal-broiled burgers and huge, fancy milkshakes to locals getting on boats for the day. There are two good coffee shops: **Valentine's,** 111 Seward St., where you'll find the Capitol crowd, and **Heritage Coffee Co. and Café,** 147 S. Franklin St., with a younger group; both serve light meals.

EXPENSIVE

☉ The Fiddlehead Restaurant and Bakery. 429 W. Willoughby Ave. ☎ **907/586-3150.** Reservations recommended for the Fireweed Room. Main courses $12–$22; lunch $7–$15. 15% gratuity added for parties of six or more. AE, MC, V. Daily 6:30am–10pm.

In 1978 the Fiddlehead was the first restaurant of its quality in the region, offering skillfully prepared, garden-influenced seafood in a setting of casual fine dining, and it gained enough note to publish a successful cookbook in 1991; since then, however, it has also picked up some serious competition and is no longer Juneau's most "in" spot. The ferny thing is a bit dated. The upstairs Fireweed Room, open from 6 to 9pm, offers a more expensive and formal experience; downstairs is reasonably priced, and has a café atmosphere, but the food is still very good. Full liquor license.

✪ Giorgio at the Pier. 544 S. Franklin St. ☎ **907/586-3577.** Reservations not accepted. Main courses $16–$22. AE, MC, V. Lunch from 11:30am; dinner from 5:30pm.

Facing the water at the cruise-ship dock in a spectacular, specially designed dining room of light wood and tall windows, Giorgio's opened in 1995, starting a furious debate over which is the best restaurant in town—and receiving a lot of votes. (The Gold Room—see the Baranof Hotel in "Where to Stay," above—Fiddlehead, and Silverbow are the other candidates.) The cuisine is authentically northern Italian treatments of fresh Alaska seafood, a wonderful idea that's carried out to perfection. The service is highly professional. Full liquor license.

The Silverbow Inn Restaurant. 120 Second St. (between Main and Seward sts.). ☎ **907/586-4146.** Reservations recommended. Main courses $17–$30. AE, CB, DC, DISC, MC, V. 15% gratuity added for parties of six or more. Daily 5:30–9:30pm.

At this, the oldest bakery in Alaska, in an 1890 building decorated with antiques and stained glass, one is reminded of a private dining room. The award-winning menu is extensive, with seafood, beef, lamb, pork, chicken, and vegetarian main courses prepared in styles including French, West Indian, Créole, and Thai. As of 1995, however, the establishment was for sale. Beer and wine license.

The Summit Restaurant. 455 S. Franklin St. ☎ **907/586-2050.** Reservations recommended. Main courses $17–$20. AE, CB, DC, DISC, MC, V. Daily 5–11pm.

Yet another small, excellent seafood restaurant with a constantly changing menu, the Summit looks out on the water just above the cruise-ship dock. Try to reserve a table by the big window. The building is a converted brothel. Full liquor license.

MODERATE

The Cookhouse. 200 Admiral Way. ☎ **907/463-3658.** Lunch $6.50–$9; dinner $6.50–$21. AE, CB, DC, MC, V. Daily 11am–10pm.

This restaurant right in the tourist shopping district specializes in huge hamburgers and huge everything—no normal person can eat the portions. It works hard at a fun, informal, "Alaskan" atmosphere, but you'll mostly see other tourists. Full liquor license.

Gold Creek Salmon Bake. 1061 Salmon Creek Lane. ☎ **907/789-0052.** $22 adults, $15 children. MC, V. Tues–Sat 11:30am–1:30pm and 5–8pm, Sun–Mon 5–8pm.

A touristy salmon cook-out, but fun for families—marshmallow roasting, music, a nearby waterfall, and the Juneau Raptor Center, where injured birds are rehabilitated, are all part of the experience. It goes on rain or shine, but I'd wait for shine. A van brings patrons from downtown. Beer and wine license.

✪ The Second Course. 213 Front St. ☎ **907/463-5533.** Complete dinner $18–$24; buffet-style lunch $10. AE, MC, V. Mon–Fri noon–2pm and 5–9pm. Closed for dinner in winter, except for special arrangements.

Heidi Grimes does "New Asian Cuisine" that draws on Cantonese, Thai, Vietnamese, and other Far Eastern styles to create something completely new and different with fresh local seafood. Originally from Hong Kong, she ended up owning a restaurant because her cooking school didn't work out, but still changes the menu with constant experimentation. The storefront dining room, with white tablecloths and plastic garden furniture, is a bit odd, but perfectly comfortable. No liquor license.

INEXPENSIVE

⑤ Armadillo Tex-Mex Cafe. 431 S. Franklin St. ☎ **907/586-1880.** Lunch/dinner $6–$16. MC, V. Daily 11am–10pm.

Popular with locals and visitors alike for its convenient location, reasonable prices, unpretentious atmosphere, and good ranch-style Mexican food, this restaurant is known merely as "Tex-Mex." Chicken is the specialty and the homemade salsa, served free with chips, is famous. Beer and wine license.

JUNEAU IN THE EVENING

Juneau's **Perseverance Theatre** is Alaska's largest professional theater. During the winter season the troupe produces five serious offerings for Juneau audiences and multicultural shows such as *Yup'ik Antigone,* which toured internationally. During the summer it offers some 160 performances of a popular tourist melodrama, the ***Lady Lou Revue.*** The musical is a takeoff on a Robert Service story, with a handsome sled-dog driver, pretty saloon girls, and a dog team with dogs played by children. The revue is at Merchant's Wharf once or twice daily, May 15 to September 25; call 907/586-3686 for a recorded message on show times. Admission is $16. For information on the theater's other work, the office is at 914 Third St., Douglas, AK 99824 (☎ **907/364-2421**).

The new Sealaska Cultural Arts Center presents the ✪ **Naa Kahidi Theater** (☎ **907/463-4844**) in a mock clan house next to the cruise-ship dock. The professionally produced story-telling and dance performances are entertaining for a wide age range and present Tlingit, Haida, and Tsimshian artifacts as they were meant to be seen. The hour-long shows are presented as frequently as four times a day during the June-to-September season; tickets are $15 for adults, $9 for children at the box office.

You can also catch a movie in Juneau. The **20th Century** (☎ **907/586-4055**) is a classic old theater downtown.

A political scandal or two have put a damper on some of the infamous legislative partying that once occurred in Juneau, far away from home districts, but there still are good places to go out drinking and dancing. The **Red Dog Saloon,** at 278 S. Franklin St., is the town's most famous bar, with a sawdust-strewn floor and slightly contrived historic atmosphere. It's a fun place with lots of Alaskana on the walls and the live music doesn't entail a cover charge. The **Alaskan Bar,** a block away at 167 S. Franklin St., has cheaper beer and brass and wood decor, but there's a $2 cover on weekends for the blues, jazz, and folk music. For watching a game, try **Hootchies,** in the Mendenhall Valley. The major hotels have lounges, but the classiest bar in town is **The Galleon,** at 544 S. Franklin St., connected to Giorgio's restaurant. The owners spared no expense to make the bar a ship in a bottle—even the floor is like a wooden vessel's deck, with authentic caulking between the boards. They have jazz, country-and-western, and blues without a cover starting at 7pm, but the real show is the bar itself.

SIDE TRIPS FROM JUNEAU

ADMIRALTY ISLAND   The land mass facing the entrance to the Gastineau Channel is Admiralty Island, the vast majority of which is the protected Kootznoowoo Wilderness. Kootznoowoo, Tlingit for "fortress of bears," is said to have the highest concentration of bears on earth; despite the town of Angoon on the western side of the island, there are more bears than people on Admiralty. The **Pack Creek Bear Observatory** is the most famous and sure-fire place to see bears in Southeast. The area has been managed for bear viewing since the 1930s, when hunting was outlawed, and homesteader Stan Price, who lived there until 1989, habituated the bears to humans. There's a platform for watching the bears up-close as they feed on salmon spawning in the creek in July and August. They generally pay no attention to the people.

Only 25 miles from Juneau, **Pack Creek** is so popular that permits are allocated in a lottery for a maximum of 24 people to go during the day (from 9pm to 9am, no humans are allowed). The easiest way to go is to book with a tour operator who has permits; **Alaska Rainforest Tours** (☎ 907/463-3466; fax 907/463-4453) can help you. **Alaska Discovery** (☎ **907/780-6226** or 800/586-1911; fax 907/780-4220) has the most permits; their canoe trips are expensive, but they also have day trips (see "Out on the Water" under "Getting Outside," above). **Alaska Fly 'N' Fish Charters,** 9604 Kelly Ct., Juneau, AK 99801 (☎ **907/790-2120**), also has permits for its half-day, fly-in visits. Twelve permits per day go to the commercial operators and 12 for regular people; 8 of those 12 can be booked in advance with the Forest Service, and the other 4 are held out to be distributed two days before they're good, at 8am at the Forest Service visitor center at the Centennial Hall.

Or you can go somewhere else on Admiralty where you don't need a permit. After all, it is one of the largest virgin blocks of old-growth forest in the country, at over 900,000 acres. Two other sites near Pack Creek, on Seymour Canal, also have a lot of bears, but no permit system: Swan Cove and Windfall Harbor. There are 15 Forest Service cabins on Admiralty, 6 of them on the **Cross Admiralty Canoe Route,** which bisects the island from Mole Harbor, on the Seymour Canal, to the village of Angoon, where you can board the ferry. The lakes the route crosses also branch out to other remote cabins. For information and a $3 route map, contact the Forest Service visitor center at Centennial Hall, or **Admiralty Island National Monument,** 8461 Old Dairy Rd., Juneau, AK 99801 (☎ **907/586-8790**).

PELICAN   This tiny fishing village on the outside of Chichagof Island is extremely remote and entirely unspoiled. It may be more primitive than some people would really like, but for anyone who wants to see the Bush and experience its lifestyle for a few days—in a lush setting abounding in wildlife—it's an inviting stop. The ferry goes only every two weeks, so the only practical way to get there is on a float plane. Float-plane fares from Juneau are around $85 one way on **Wings of Alaska** (☎ 907/789-0790). Sitka also is a gateway.

The town, with around 250 people, is built on the water and the streets are boardwalks. There are a couple of bed-and-breakfasts, but Gail Corbin's **Lisianski Inlet Lodge,** P.O. Box 776, Pelican, AK 99832 (☎ **907/735-2266**), is the place to stay, with an old log cabin and a couple of rooms, and three meals provided. Corbin and her family guide kayaking journeys from the lodge, fishing trips in skiffs or a 21-foot cabin cruiser, or longer trips on board a 53-foot ketch that's also a commercial fishing boat—to nearby Glacier Bay National Park, for example. Forest Service–maintained hot springs are close by, too. Corbin charges $220 double for a room, $260 for the cabin, and is open May to September 15. Reserve in advance.

The **White Sulfur Hot Springs** are near Pelican—a 110° bath in a natural stone pool. A Forest Service cabin there rents for $25 a night; contact the Sitka Ranger District, 201 Katlian St., Suite 109, Sitka, AK 99835 (☎ **907/747-6671**).

9 Glacier Bay National Park: Ice, Whales & Wilderness

Glacier Bay is a work in progress; the boat ride to its head is a chance to see creation fresh. The bay John Muir discovered in a canoe in 1879 didn't exist a century earlier. Eighteenth-century explorers had found instead a wall of ice a mile thick where the entrance to the branching, 65-mile-long fjord now opens to the sea. Receding faster than any other glacier on earth, the ice melted into the ocean and opened a spectacular and still-unfinished land. The land itself is rising $1^1/2$ inches a year as it rebounds from the missing weight of melted glaciers. As your vessel retraces Muir's path, and then probes northward in deep water where ice stood in his day, the story of this new world unravels in reverse. The trees on the shore get smaller, then disappear, then all vegetation disappears, and finally, at the head of the bay, the ice stands at the water's edge surrounded by barren rock, rounded and scored by the passage of the ice and not yet marked by the waterfalls cascading down out of the clouds above.

In fact, the clouds sometimes seem as permanent a feature as the ice. And it's often windy and cold at the head of the bay, near the glaciers. Precipitation and cold add up to glaciers, but if you're not prepared for bad weather you could be disappointed. It rains a lot in Glacier Bay, and fog clings to the water and the ice. The mist and rain contribute their own beauty—at times the smooth, silver water, barren rock, white clouds, and ice create an ethereal study in white.

Glacier Bay, first set aside by President Calvin Coolidge in 1925, is managed by the National Park Service, which has the difficult job of protecting the wilderness while showing it to the public. This is a challenge, since this rugged land the size of Connecticut can be seen only by boat or plane, and the presence of too many boats threatens the park. The whales appear to be sensitive to the noise of vessels; since the 1970s, when in one year only a single whale returned, the park service has used a permit system to severely limit the number of ships that can enter the bay. But that decision has created a frothing controversy. With Alaska tourism booming, the state's powerful congressional delegation has pushed for more cruise-ship permits for the bay. As of 1995 it looked as if the park service would give in and allow a 72% increase. Already, any tour boat sees several other ships on a day's journey up the bay, but how much it bothers the whales really can't be proved.

If you go, you'll either be on one of those vessels or in an aircraft. There really is no cheap way to visit Glacier Bay, but many visitors feel compelled to go because it has become, like Denali National Park, a kind of Alaska requirement—something you're just supposed to do. It *is* a grand and fascinating place, but you can see Alaska without seeing Glacier Bay. In deciding whether you want to go, think about how many glaciers you really need to see while you're in Alaska. The glaciers at the heads of Glacier Bay's fjords certainly are impressive, but so are other glaciers in Alaska that are easier and less expensive to visit; if you're in Juneau, consider a trip to Tracy Arm. The uniqueness of the glaciers of Glacier Bay lies in their size and geological activity, in their number, and in the opportunity to see them fairly close up in a remote setting. On a Glacier Bay boat ride you'll also see wildlife—sea lions and eagles almost certainly, and possibly humpback whales—but as this is a national park, vessels cannot approach within a quarter mile of the whales. Outside the park, it's 100 yards. And there are other places with rich marine wildlife.

ESSENTIALS

GETTING THERE   You can't get to Glacier Bay by car or ferry. The only way to see the park is by flightseeing, by going there on a cruise ship, or by flying to the little town of Gustavus and picking up a boat or kayak there.

The ✪ *Spirit of Adventure,* operated by park concessionaire Glacier Bay Tours, is the main way for independent travelers to see the park. The fast, quiet tour boat carries up to 250 passengers in upper and lower lounges in a comfortable, table-oriented seating configuration. Bring heavy rain gear, as the windows can fog up and you'll want to spend as much time as possible outside. There's a snack bar and a simple lunch is provided. Bring binoculars or rent them on board for $2; they're a necessity. The boat leaves Bartlett Cove at 7am for a nine-hour cruise, for $153.50. Glacier Bay Tours offers a same-day trip from Juneau, on board **L.A.B. Flying Service** (☎ 800/766-2222), but it makes for a long day—you have to board the plane at 5:30am in Juneau—and the schedule leaves no time in Glacier Bay for anything but the boat trip. A better choice is to spend the night before the boat trip in Gustavus or at the lodge. **Alaska Airlines** (☎ **800/426-0333**) flies a jet once a day to Gustavus and commuter lines have many flights. The lodge offers frequent shuttle service for the 10-mile trip to the airport; if you stay in Gustavus, most of the inns will drive you there as well.

If your budget allows, there may be no better way to see Glacier Bay than on a small cruise ship on an excursion of a couple of days or more. **Glacier Bay Tours** (☎ **800/451-5952**) operates two such vessels. The *Executive Explorer* is a high-speed catamaran for more extensive overnight sightseeing trips, carrying 49 passengers. Fares range from $499 to $799. The ✪ *Wilderness Explorer* gets you out into the park in a pampered outdoors experience. Leaving Juneau on trips of varying lengths, it heads into the bay to allow passengers to hike, kayak, or boat in inflatables, never touching port again until it returns to Juneau. It's the balance between a crowded tour boat and a tent. The vessel carries 36 passengers, and the fare ranges from $469 to $1,109.

The other way to get to the park is by flightseeing. **Glacier Bay Airways,** P.O. Box 1, Gustavus, AK 99826 (☎ **907/697-2249**), offers flights from the Bartlett Cove visitor center. Other companies offer tours from various towns, Haines being the closest, served by **L.A.B. Flying Service** (☎ **907/766-2222**). You'll see the incredible rivers of ice that flow down into the bay, and may even see wildlife. What you give up is a lingering, up-close look and the awesome sense of having all that ice and rock above you.

VISITOR INFORMATION   The park service's address is **Glacier Bay National Park and Preserve,** Gustavus, AK 99826 (☎ **907/687-2230**). But the concessionaire, **Glacier Bay Tours,** operates most of the activities in the park. During the summer you can reach them at P.O. Box 199, Gustavus, AK 99826 (☎ **907/697-2226;** fax 907/697-2408); or year round at 530 Pike St., Suite 1400, Seattle, WA 98101 (☎ **206/623-7110** or 800/451-5952; fax 206/623-7809).

The park service interprets the park mainly by placing well-prepared rangers on board all cruise and tour vessels entering the bay. The park also maintains a modest visitor center with displays on the park on the second floor of the concessionaire's lodge at Bartlett Cove. The park's offices, a free campground, a backcountry office, a few short hiking trails, a dock, and other park facilities also surround the lodge in a wooded setting.

ACTIVITIES AT THE PARK

AT BARTLETT COVE   There are two short **hiking trails,** right at the Bartlett Cove compound, for an afternoon walk. A free trail guide is available at the visitor center. A ranger leads a daily nature walk, and there are displays upstairs in the lodge. In the evening the park service does a slide show.

OUT IN THE PARK   A popular way to see Glacier Bay is ✪ **sea kayaking,** and there are several remote yet protected places to paddle. I can only imagine what it's like to see humpback whales from a kayak. Most kayakers go up the protected eastern fjords via the *Spirit of Adventure,* or stay in the Beardslee Islands, near the Bartlett Cove lodge. The *Spirit of Adventure* beaches at several prearranged spots to put kayakers and hikers ashore. Make sure you calibrate the length of your trip to your outdoors experience—this is remote territory, and you can't just leave once you're out there. Also, everyone going into the backcountry is required to check in with the backcountry office by the lodge for orientation. **Glacier Bay Sea Kayaks,** P.O. Box

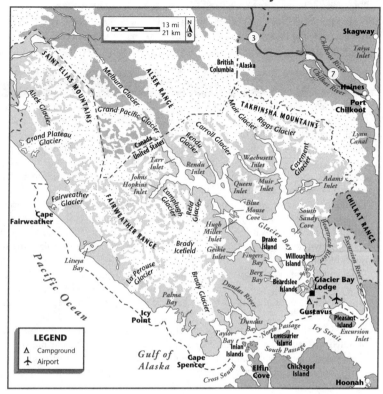

26, Gustavus, AK 99826 (☎ **907/697-2257;** fax 907/697-3002), is the park service concessionaire June 1 to August 31; it offers instruction and rentals for $50 a day, and drop-offs up the bay are $177.50 round-trip. Make sure to write or call ahead for information on what you'll need.

For guided kayak trips, **Alaska Discovery,** 5449 Shaune Dr., Suite 4, Juneau, AK 99801 (☎ **907/780-6226;** fax 907/780-4220), offers trips ranging from six hours to seven days. A six-hour guided paddle around Bartlett Cove and the Beardslees is $95; a seven-day tour, $1,800.

Hiking out in the park is possible for experienced, well-prepared outdoors people. There are no trails beyond Bartlett Cove. Contact the park service for current drop-off points and where to go from there.

WHERE TO STAY & EAT

Glacier Bay Lodge. Bartlett Cove (P.O. Box 199), Gustavus, AK 99826. ☎ **907/697-2226.** Fax 907/697-2408. 56 rms. TEL. $156 double. Additional person in room $9 extra. MC, V. Closed Sept 18–May 11.

Operated by park concessionaire Glacier Bay Tours, this is the only place to stay in the park, although Gustavus, 10 miles down the road, has some of the most attractive accommodations in Alaska, some for the same price or less. The lodge rooms are comfortable but, for the price, nothing special; they're in buildings accessed from the main lodge by boardwalks. Laundry and babysitting are available. The restaurant and bar have great views of Bartlett Cove. There are inexpensive main courses on the dinner menu, but mainly it's a fine-dining establishment with dishes in the $20 range. Breakfast is available as early as 5:45am and dinner as late as 10pm. The bar is open an hour later. For those on a budget, there are bunk rooms with six beds each for men and women. The lodge also provides showers for the free park service campground.

10 Gustavus: Country Inns & Quiet

The unincorporated town of Gustavus (gus-TAVE-us) remains an undiscovered treasure for visitors—or at least it succeeds in making itself feel that way. It's wonderfully remote, accessible for visitors only by air, but has a selection of comfortable and even luxurious inns and lodges, and several days' worth of outdoor activities—including excellent salmon and halibut fishing, nearly sure-fire whale watching, close access to Glacier Bay National Park with the sea kayaking and activities there, and places for casual hiking and bicycle outings. Cruise ships and ferries don't come here, leaving the roads free of their throngs of shoppers and the development they bring. Miraculously, the 300 townspeople have been smart enough to value what they've got and build on it. Even the new gas station is a work of art. Walking, biking, or driving down the gravel roads, everyone in a passing vehicle—every single person— waves to you.

The buildings, mostly clapboard houses and log cabins, are scattered widely across an oceanfront alluvial plain. Several of the founding homesteads were farms, and the broad clearings of sandy soil wave with hay and wildflowers. The setting is unique in Alaska.

The bad news: Visitors need to be willing to have their fun in the rain, well bundled up. Also, the remoteness and lack of tourist development means that Gustavus is expensive. Round-trip plane fare from Juneau is $140. Rooms aren't cheap and neither are meals. There's only one freestanding restaurant, and it can be inconsistently open, but you can buy a meal at the lodges and inns, for a price. And the most memorable activities in the outdoors all involve charters or rentals.

ESSENTIALS

GETTING THERE   The only way to get to Gustavus is by plane. **Alaska Airlines** (☎ 800/426-0333) has a daily jet, and several commuter lines fly more frequently, including **L.A.B. Flying Service** (☎ 800/426-0543) and **Glacier Bay Airways** (☎ 907/697-2249).

VISITOR INFORMATION   There are no public buildings in Gustavus because there is no government: Only the informal community association and the state government hold sway. **Puffin Bed and Breakfast,** P.O. Box 3, Gustavus, AK 99826 (☎ 907/697-2260 in summer, 907/789-9787 in winter, or 800/478-2258 in Alaska in summer; e-mail 73654.550@compuserve.com), has a booking agency. Generally, you'll rely on your host at the inn or B&B for information. Be certain you reserve a place before showing up at the Gustavus Airport.

ORIENTATION   There are just a few gravel roads. The main one starts at the airport and runs about 10 miles to **Bartlett Cove,** the Glacier Bay National Park base of operations. **Dock Road** branches off to the left, at the gas station, and leads to the ocean dock. Most businesses will give you a good free map, which shows everything in town, for exploring by bicycle.

GETTING AROUND   Many inns and B&Bs have courtesy vans and free bicycles. **TLC Taxi** (☎ 907/697-2239) also will carry you and your kayak.

FAST FACTS   There are no fast facts to provide: Gustavus isn't formally a town; it has no bank and other businesses are limited to a gas station, a small store, a restaurant, and a building-supply store, all on Dock Road. Bring cash and anything you may need.

EXPLORING GUSTAVUS

Everything to do in Gustavus involves the outdoors. ✪ **Whale watching** trips aboard the historic *Captain Conner,* operated by Glacier Bay Tours, leave the town dock for Point Adolphus twice a day. Icy Strait, where the vessel cruises, is one of the best places in the state to see humpbacks in summer. They come here because a swirl of currents makes it a rich feeding ground. The fare is $89, and you get your money back if you don't see whales. Other, smaller operators will provide a more intimate experience on smaller, less impressive boats. They'll also combine the trip with superb halibut and salmon fishing. Among the choices are: **Gustavus Marine Charters** (☎ **907/697-2233**), **Gusto Charters** (☎ **907/697-2561**), **Jon's Charters** (☎ **907/697-2374**), and several others; a boat typically charters for $200 for a full day. Or you can go on a sailboat with **Woodwind Adventures** (☎ **907/697-2282**). Or book with **Alaska Seair Adventures,** P.O. Box 299, Gustavus, AK 99826 (☎ **907/697-2215**), a family offering their Grumman Widgeon flying boat, a 41-foot yacht, and a comfortable house for guided packages starting at about $2,000 for three days.

For information on **sea kayaking,** see "Activities at the Park" in section 9 on Glacier Bay National Park, earlier in this chapter. Based in Gustavus, **Spirit Walker Expeditions,** P.O. Box 122, Gustavus, AK 99826 (☎ **907/697-2268**), leads guided one- to seven-day trips to the whale-watching grounds and beyond. The one-day trip is $100; seven days, $1,849.

✪ **Hiking and bicycling** in Gustavus are delightful. There are few cars because they have to be hauled here on a barge, but many inns provide bikes. The dirt roads are fun to explore, and the sandy beaches, accessed from the town dock, are a great place for a walk and a picnic. It's 14 miles from Good River Road along the shore around Point Gustavus to the Bartlett Cove national park center, 7 miles from the town dock along the beach to the airport. **Dave Walker** (☎ **907/697-2369**) leads hikes, 90 minutes for $12 and three hours for $20, and tells stories about the area.

WHERE TO STAY & EAT

There are a surprising number of good places to stay in Gustavus; I don't have room to list them all, but I've offered some good choices in different price ranges. I can also recommend the motel-style **Growley Bear Bed and Breakfast,** Dock Road (P.O. Box 246), Gustavus, AK 99826 (☎ **907/697-2730**), and the **Whalesong Lodge,** near the airport (P.O. Box 389), Gustavus, AK 99826 (☎ **907/697-2792;** fax 907/697-2743).

There isn't the same choice for food. There's a small store and there's a restaurant on Dock Road; however, the restaurant was inconsistently open when I visited in 1995. The full-service restaurant at the Glacier Bay Lodge (see "Where to Stay and Eat" in section 9, earlier in this chapter) is open all summer, and the inns that serve meals to their guests will sometimes make room for you if you call ahead.

EXPENSIVE

Annie Mae Lodge. 2 Grandpa's Farm Rd. (P.O. Box 80), Gustavus, AK 99826. ☎ **907/ 697-2346.** Fax 907/697-2211. 12 rms, 7 with bath. $80 double without bath or meals; $215 double with bath and all meals, $90 per additional person in room. AE, DC, MC, V.

The newly expanded lodge, with porches that wrap around, is secluded down a dirt side road overlooking a field of wildflowers through which runs a little creek. The main building is log and the cozy decor is country-style. The set menu emphasizes seafood. Courtesy car, free bicycles. No liquor license.

✪ **Glacier Bay Country Inn.** Tong Rd. (P.O. Box 5), Gustavus, AK 99826 (in winter, P.O. Box 2557, St. George, UT 84771). ☎ **907/697-2288** in summer, 801/673-8480 in winter. Fax 907/697-2289 in summer, 801/673-8481 in winter. 9 rms, 8 with bath. $238 double. Rates include all meals. Additional adult in room $69 extra; additional child in room $54 extra. Closed Oct–Apr.

Set on a 40-acre agricultural homestead well back in the woods, this inn is nationally renowned for its food and service. The quaint and quirky lodge building has lots of places to sit and watch the passing wildlife. Al and Annie Unrein also operate a travel service and, under the name Grand Pacific Charters, three boats for taking fishing, whale-watching, and Glacier Bay National Park trips—packages are available. Non-inn guests are welcome for dinner if there's room, but must call ahead. Courtesy car, laundry, free bicycles, car rental. No smoking, no liquor license.

✪ **Gustavus Inn at Glacier Bay.** Gustavus Rd. (P.O. Box 60), Gustavus, AK 99826 (in winter, 7920 Outlook, Prairie Village, KS 66208). ☎ **907/697-2254** in summer, or 800/649-5220 in winter. Fax 907/697-2255 in summer, 800/649-5220 in winter. 9 rms, 2 suites. $260 double. Additional person in room $130 extra. AE, MC, V. Closed Sept 16 May 15.

This is the original and still the best of the Gustavus inns—although that's a fine point, as several of them are extraordinarily good. Occupying an old homestead farmhouse at the center of the community, the inn offers lovely rooms in a pastoral setting with overflowing hospitality and superb, plentiful food. The Lesh family, running the inn since 1965, has published a cookbook, and people come just to eat. The inn is unique in having a bar with beer and wine for guests. Fishing, touring, and kayaking packages are available, as is a courtesy car, free bikes, and laundry service.

MODERATE

A Puffin's Bed and Breakfast. Rink Creek Rd. (P.O. Box 3), Gustavus, AK 99826. ☎ **907/697-2260** in summer, 907/789-9787 in winter. Fax 907/697-2258. E-mail 73654.550@compuserve.com. 6 cabins. $70 cabin for two, $75 with attached bath. Additional adult in room $20 extra; additional child (up to 11 years old) in room $8 extra. MC, V.

The cabins, with wood stoves and linoleum floors, all have their own bathrooms, but you might have to walk down a trail to find yours. The central room where breakfast is served is huge, with a cathedral ceiling. The proprietors also run a full-service travel agency and offer a multitude of packages for visiting Gustavus and Glacier Bay. Courtesy car, free bikes, coin-op laundry.

Good River Bed and Breakfast. Good River Rd. (P.O. Box 37), Gustavus, AK 99826. ☎ and fax **907/697-2241**. 4 rms, none with bath; 1 cabin, without bath. $70 double; $50 cabin. Additional person in room $20 extra. No credit cards. Closed Sept 15–May 15.

In contrast to the luxurious inns in Gustavus, this rustic B&B offers cozy little rooms in a house next to a creek and granola for breakfast. The nearby hexagonal cabin has a wood stove and a skylight, electricity and a hotplate, but no plumbing. Free bikes, fishing gear.

11 Haines: Eagles & the Unexpected

For years we always just passed through Haines on the way from the ferry up the highway. I didn't know what I was missing until I stopped and took a couple of days to really investigate. Now Haines is one of my favorite Alaska towns.

Haines is casual, happy, and slightly odd. It waits for one to find it, but once found, has wonderful charms. The mythical town of Cicely from television's "Northern Exposure" is closer to Haines than anyplace else I can think of. As I walked down a sidewalk, I saw a sign in a storefront that said to look in the big tree across the street. I looked, and there was an eagle peering back at me. At the Native cultural center, seeking an office or a ticket window or someone in charge, I wandered into a totem pole–carving studio where a carver was completing a major commission. He gladly stopped to talk. It turned out there wasn't anyone in charge.

The Chilkat Dancers have performed here for almost 40 years, and their efforts are among the most respected and authentic in carrying on the Tlingit cultural heritage. But their membership is undefined and their performances, while impressive, are also funny and slightly strange. Whites dance beside Natives and rehearsals are never held; the new generation learns by being thrown into the performances, sometimes before the age of five. Issues that are a big deal in some other towns just aren't in Haines.

Haines's chief feature, Fort William Seward, gives the town a pastoral atmosphere. The fort is a collection of grand, white clapboard buildings arranged around a 9-acre parade ground, in the middle of which stands a Tlingit clan house—out of place, yes, but wonderfully symbolic of Haines. The town is a friendly, accessible center of Tlingit culture as well as a retired outpost of seemingly pointless military activity.

And Haines has bald eagles—always plenty of bald eagles, and in the fall, a ridiculous number of bald eagles. More, in fact, than anywhere else on earth. They draw people into the outdoors here. There are well-established guides for any activity you might want to pursue, all cooperating and located together. And the weather is not as rainy as elsewhere in Southeast.

ESSENTIALS

GETTING THERE & DEPARTING   By Water   The **Alaska Marine Highway System** (see "Exploring Southeast Alaska," earlier in this chapter) is how most people get to Haines, and the cruise on the Lynn Canal from Juneau or Skagway is among the most beautiful in the Inside Passage. (The fare is $20 to Juneau and $14 to Skagway.) But there's a drawback—since this is the northern highway connection where nearly all vehicles get off or on, there are often delays. If you're just going to Skagway, a good alternative with more sailings is the **Haines-Skagway Water Taxi and Scenic Cruise** (☎ **907/766-3395**). May 20 to September 15 the 80-passenger vessel offers two round-trips daily. The ride takes an hour each way, and leaves from the Port Chilkoot cruise-ship dock, below the fort. The fare is $18 one way, $29 round-trip.

By Car   The **Haines Highway** leads 155 miles to Haines Junction, Yukon Territory, an intersection with the Alaska Highway. The road runs along the Chilkat River and the bald eagle preserve, then climbs into spectacular alpine terrain. One-way car rentals to Anchorage, Fairbanks, and Skagway are available from **Avis,** at the Hotel Hälsingland (see "Where to Stay," below), with a $300 drop-off charge.

By Bus   Gray Line's **Alaskon Express** bus (☎ **800/544-2206**) also stops at the hotel, with routes during the tourist season three days a week each to Skagway, Whitehorse, Anchorage, Fairbanks, and Beaver Creek. The fare to Anchorage is $200.

By Air   Three commuter airlines come to Haines. **L.A.B. Flying Service** (☎ **907/ 766-2222** or 800/426-0543) has frequent flights, charging $65 one way for the 30-minute trip from Juneau.

VISITOR INFORMATION   Haines's city-run **Visitor Information Center** is small but well staffed and stocked. It's open Monday through Friday from 8am to 5pm and on Saturday and Sunday from 10am to 1pm and 2 to 7pm. The center is run by the city's **Haines Visitors Bureau,** P.O. Box 530, Haines, AK 99827 (☎ **907/766-2234** or 800/458-3579), which also sends out a vacation-planning packet, and seemed to be able to answer any question.

ORIENTATION   Haines sits on the narrow Chilkat Peninsula near the north end of the Southeast Alaska Panhandle. Highways run north on either side of the peninsula; the one on the east side goes to the ferry dock, 7 miles out, and ends after 11 miles at **Chilkoot Lake.** The other is the **Haines Highway,** which leads to the rest of the world. The town has two parts: the sparsely built downtown grid and, down **Front Street** or **Second Avenue** a short walk to the west, the **Fort William Seward area.**

GETTING AROUND   Competing vans will bring you in from the ferry for $4 and give you a tour for a few dollars more. **Fort Seward Tours,** located at the Hotel Hälsingland (see "Where to Stay," below), is the biggest operator. Otherwise, your feet or a bicycle will get you around. Bikes are available from **Sockeye Cycle,** just uphill from the Port Chilkoot Dock on Portage Street in the Fort William Seward area (☎ and fax **907/766-2869**), for $6 an hour or $30 a day. **Haines Taxi** can be reached at 907/766-3079. **Avis** car rental has an outlet at the Hotel Hälsingland and **Affordable Cars** is at the Captain's Choice Motel (see "Where to Stay," below).

FAST FACTS   The local **sales tax** is 6%. There are two **ATMs,** at the First National Bank of Anchorage, Main Street and Second Avenue, and at Howsers Supermarket, a few doors down Main. The **post office** is located at 55 Haines Hwy. In **emergencies,** dial 911. The **police** can be reached in nonemergency situations at 907/766-2121. The **Lynn Canal Medical Center** is at Second Avenue and Willard Street (☎ **907/766-2521**). The *Chilkat Valley News* is published weekly.

SPECIAL EVENTS   In late June there's a race down the Haines Highway, the **Kluane to Chilkat International Bike Relay,** with hundreds of entrants; it's quite a downhill. The Fourth of July **Independence Day** celebration is big here as elsewhere in Southeast; in Haines, it includes the **Haines Rodeo** at the fairgrounds. The biggest event of the summer is the ✪ **Southeast Alaska State Fair** and **Bald Eagle Music Festival** (☎ **907/766-2476**), to be held August 7–11 in 1996; it's a regional small-town get-together, with livestock, cooking, a logging show, parade, music, and other entertainment.

EXPLORING HAINES

ACTIVITIES IN TOWN   The main feature of Haines is ✪ **Fort William Seward,** a collection of large, white, wood-frame buildings around a sloping parade ground overlooking the magnificent Lynn Canal fjord. (Get the informative walking-tour map of the National Historic Site from the Haines Visitors Bureau.) Historians aren't sure why the U.S. Army built the fort, starting in 1903—the popular explanation, that it was to guard the mountain passes leading to the gold fields, doesn't make much sense since the gold rush was over by then. In any event, the fort successfully deterred any attack on this little peninsula at the north end of the Inside Passage, and it was deactivated at the end of World War II (in which it played little part) without hostilities.

   In 1947 a group of five veterans from the Lower 48 bought the fort as surplus, with the idea of forming a planned community. That idea didn't really work out, but one of the new white families helped spark the Chilkat Tlingit cultural renaissance that

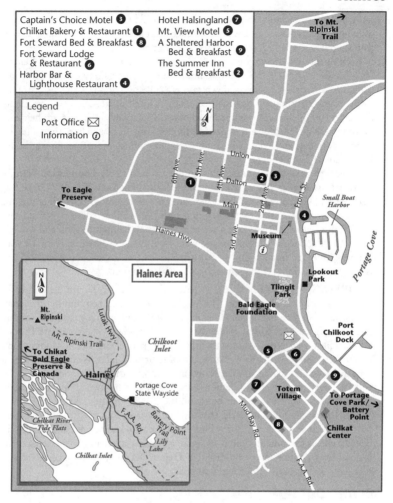

Captain's Choice Motel ❸
Chilkat Bakery & Restaurant ❶
Fort Seward Bed & Breakfast ❽
Fort Seward Lodge
& Restaurant ❻
Harbor Bar &
Lighthouse Restaurant ❹

Hotel Halsingland ❼
Mt. View Motel ❺
A Sheltered Harbor
Bed & Breakfast ❾
The Summer Inn
Bed & Breakfast ❷

Legend
Post Office ✉
Information ⓘ

started here in the 1950s. The Heinmillers, who still own a majority of the shares in the fort, were looking for something to do with all that property when someone had the idea of building a Tlingit tribal house on the parade grounds. The project, led by a pair of elders, took on a life of its own, and the ✪ **Chilkat Dancers** and **Alaska Indian Arts** cultural center followed. Lee Heinmiller, a member of the second generation, still manages the dance troupe his father started in 1957 as a Boy Scout project and participates in the performances with his pale, spreading paunch gleaming in abbreviated traditional Native dress. He has been adopted as a member of the tribe and given a name that accords high respect.

The dancers, who have been all over the world, perform at the **Chilkat Center for the Arts** (☎ and fax **907/766-2160**), an auditorium just off the southeast corner of the parade ground, and sometimes at the clan house. Times of the performances are geared to the arrival of cruise ships; check at the Visitor Information Center or the Alaska Indian Arts Cultural Center. Admission is $10 for adults, $5 for students, and free for children 4 and under. The cultural center is open from 9am to noon and

1 to 5pm and when cruise ships are in town, at the old fort hospital on the south side of the parade grounds, and has a small gallery, gift shop (see below), and a carvers' workshop where you may be able to see work in progress.

Back in the downtown area, the ✪ **Sheldon Museum and Cultural Center,** 11 Main St. (☎ **907/766-2368**), contains an upstairs gallery of well-presented Tlingit art and cultural artifacts; downstairs is a collection on the white history of the town. There's a uniquely personal feel to the Tlingit objects, some of which are displayed with pictures of the artisans who made them and the history of their relationship with the Sheldons. It's open in summer, daily from 1 to 5pm; in winter, on Sunday, Monday, and Wednesday from 1 to 4pm. Admission is $2.50 for adults, free for children 17 and under.

An entirely unique museum is the **American Bald Eagle Foundation Natural History Museum,** at Second Avenue and the Haines Highway (☎ **907/776-3094**), essentially a huge diorama of 100 eagles and other animal mounts which creates the hair-raising sense that you're standing in the middle of an incredible woodland convention of creatures. Dave Olerud sits in a wheelchair behind the desk and will talk your ear off about the museum if you want him to—he worked on it for 18 years and was paralyzed in a fall during construction. The museum opened in 1995 and is free, but donations are requested. It's open 10am to 6pm.

SHOPPING   Haines has several galleries with authentic Tlingit art and white interpretations of Native themes. It's more of a year-round community than some others, and the stores listed here are all locally owned and open regular hours in summer and winter. ✪ **Chilkat Valley Arts,** at 307 Willard St., represents 18 local artists, and has Native arts and crafts from other parts of the state, including some antiquities legally removed by Natives from their own land. Next door is **Inside Passage Arts,** also selling antique Native art, and with carving demonstrated in the gallery. Tresham Gregg also demonstrates carving in his two shops, on Portage Streetand next door to the clan house on the parade grounds, the **Sea Wolf** and **Whale Rider** galleries. **The Wild Iris,** inside the Alaska Indian Arts cultural center, sells only prints, jewelry, and clothing made by its owners, Fred and Madeleine Shields, except for some Eskimo ivory. Fred, a former mayor, also fixes eyeglasses and is good for an entertaining conversation. **Dejon Delights,** on Portage Street, sells excellent local smoked fish and salmon caviar.

GETTING OUTSIDE

There's a lot to do in Haines—good hiking, biking, kayaking, climbing, and rafting—with a special advantage over the rest of Southeast: It's not as rainy. Also, there's a small fraternity of outdoors guides that has grown up in Haines, on Portage Street and Beach Road next to the Port Chilkoot cruise-ship dock, a kind of one-stop shop.

✪ **EAGLE VIEWING**   Haines is probably the best place on earth to see bald eagles. The **Chilkat Bald Eagle Preserve** protects 48,000 acres of river bottom along the Chilkat River. From October to January, some 3,000 eagles gather in the cottonwood trees (also known as western poplar) on a small section of the river, a phenomenon known as the Fall Congregation. (A healthy 200 to 400 are resident the rest of the year.) The eagles come for easy winter food: A very late salmon run spawns here into December in a 5-mile stretch of open water, the Council Grounds. During the summer the gravels of the river flats store a massive reservoir of relatively warm water that percolates to the surface in the fall and winter, keeping it ice-free.

During the congregation, dozens of eagles stand in each of the gnarled, leafless cottonwoods on the riverbanks, occasionally diving for a fish. The best place to see them is from the bank just off miles 18 to 21 on the Haines Highway. Don't walk on the flats, as that disturbs the eagles. The preserve is managed by Alaska State Parks, 400 Willoughby, 3rd Floor, Juneau, AK 99801, but the Haines Visitors Bureau may be a better source of information for planning a visit.

Local guides offer trips to see the eagles by raft, bicycle, or bus—mostly in the summer, when the eagles are fewer but visitors more numerous. ✪ **Chilkat Guides,** on Portage Street (on the waterfront below the fort; P.O. Box 170), Haines, AK 99827 (☎ **907/766-2491**), does an excellent rafting trip twice a day during the summer down the Chilkat to watch the eagles. Safety is carefully attended to, but the rapids aren't threatening; there's a chance you'll be asked to get out and push. The company is run by young people who create a sense of fellowship with their clients. The four-hour trip, with a sandwich lunch, costs $70 for adults, $30 for children.

Sockeye Cycle (see "Biking," below) has guided bike tours to see eagles and Fort Seward on a 90-minute trip that costs $30, and **Alaska Nature Tours** (☎ **907/766-2876**) takes three-hour bus and walking tours to the preserve for $45 per person in summer.

HIKING   There are several good trails near Haines ranging from an easy beach walk to the south to a 10-mile, 4,000-foot climb of **Mount Ripinsky,** north of town (it starts at the top of Young Street). Get the "Haines Is for Hikers" trail guide from the Haines Visitors Bureau. The easiest for families is the **Battery Point Trail,** which goes 2.4 miles along the beach from the end of the shore road that leads southeast from the Port Chilkoot cruise-ship dock. **Mount Riley** is south of town, with three trail routes; get the trail guide or ask directions to one of the trailheads. The shortest route is 2.1 miles long, leading to great views at the 1,760-foot summit. **Seduction Point Trail** is 7 miles long, starting at Chilkat State Park at the end of Mud Bay Road south of town and leading to the end of the Chilkat Peninsula. It's a beach walk, so check the tides; they'll give you a tide table at the visitors bureau.

For a multiday trip including serious mountaineering instruction, contact **Alaska Mountaineering School,** P.O. Box 1081, Haines, AK 99827 (☎ **907/766-3366;** fax 907/766-2427). Its shortest trip, four days, is $490 per person.

BIKING   **Sockeye Cycle,** P.O. Box 829, Haines, AK 99827 (☎ and fax **907/ 766-2869**), leads a variety of guided trips—a couple of hours, half or full day, or even a nine-day trek. A three-hour ride along Chilkoot Lake costs $70. Or you can go on your own for $30 a day. The area is especially conducive to biking.

SEA KAYAKING   Next door to Chilkat Guides and Sockeye Cycle on Portage Street is **Deishu Expeditions,** P.O. Box 1406, Haines, AK 99827 (☎ **907/ 766-2427**), which offers instruction, short guided trips, longer expeditions, and rentals ($35 a day for a single, plus $20 for getting dropped off somewhere). Prices are reasonable: A two-hour guided paddle is $30; a full day, including lunch, $99.

FISHING   There are several charter operators in Haines, for halibut or salmon, or guided freshwater fishing for salmon, Dolly Varden, or cutthroat trout. The Haines Visitors Bureau maintains a list of operators, their specialties, and how to contact them. There's even a commercial-fishing opportunity: **Crew Fishing Alaska,** P.O. Box 1171, Haines, AK 99827 (☎ **907/766-2244**), will take you gillnetting for salmon. Of course, you may be able to find someone who'll pay *you* to do that.

FLIGHTSEEING   If you have money for one flightseeing trip in Alaska, this is a good place to choose. The Inside Passage is beautiful, and one mountain away is Glacier Bay National Park; the icefield and the glaciers spilling through to the sea are the sort of sight that you never forget. **L.A.B. Flying Service,** Main Street and Fourth

Avenue (P.O. Box 272), Haines, AK 99827 (☎ **907/766-2222** or 800/426-0543), offers a helicopter tour that actually lands on a glacier so you can walk around for 20 minutes. The two-hour trip is $145 per person.

WHERE TO STAY

Many towns have a lot of chainlike hotels and only one or two unique places with character. In Haines, the situation is reversed.

HOTELS

Captain's Choice Motel. Second Ave. and Dalton St. (P.O. Box 392), Haines, AK 99827. ☎ **907/766-3111** or 800/247-7153 outside Alaska, 800/478-2345 in Alaska and Canada. 39 rms. TV TEL. $98 double with one bed, $103 double with two twin beds; $128 upper-level double with one bed, $133 upper-level double with two twin beds. AE, DC, DISC, MC, V.

These red-roofed buildings house the one standard chainlike motel in town, with all the amenities that entails—objectively, probably the best hotel in town, but without the charm you'll find elsewhere. Many of the rooms have good views and more than half are reserved for nonsmokers. For $30 more you can get a big, upper-level room with a better view and furnishings. Courtesy van and car rentals are available.

Fort Seward Lodge. 39 Mud Bay Rd. (P.O. Box 307), Haines, AK 99827. ☎ **907/766-2009** or 800/478-7772. 10 rms, 7 with bath. $55 double without bath, $70 double with bath, $85 double with bath and kitchenette. All rates $10 less Oct–Apr. Additional person in room $5 extra. DISC, MC, V.

The rooms, although acceptable for the price, are on the small, dark side, except for the kitchenette units, which face the water—the pick of the litter. Some have TVs.

The restaurant and lounge were the old fort's PX, one of its more interesting buildings, and still have the wood gym floor. The lounge is a fun spot, popular with the crews of the cruise ships. The restaurant is open only for dinner. The all-you-can-eat crab is a good deal and well prepared.

Hotel Hälsingland. Fort William Seward parade grounds (P.O. Box 1589), Haines, AK 99827. ☎ **907/766-2000** or 800/542-6363, 800/478-2525 in Alaska and Canada. 50 rms, 45 with bath. TV TEL. $45 double without bath, $85 double with bath. AE, DC, DISC, MC, V. Closed mid-Nov to Mar.

There was no need to restore this historic building—it has been operating continuously as a hotel in the same family since 1947, a year after it stopped functioning as the commanding officer's quarters at Fort William Seward. But current owner Arnie Olsson has his work cut out with maintenance; while anyone can imagine commanding this strange outpost from the oddly shaped rooms, some of which have clawfoot tubs and nonworking fireplaces, some guests will notice the creaky, funky feel of the place rather than the charm. A courtesy van and car rental are available.

The **Commander's Room** restaurant has a wide selection of fresh seafood, views of the ocean and parade ground, and prompt, honest service. All-you-can-eat crab is on the menu. The vegetables, served on a steam table, were limp. It's open for three meals a day, and is probably the best place in town for dinner.

The small bar has five microbrews on tap; a pint is $4.50. It's a friendly, low-key place in the evening.

Ⓢ **Mountain View Motel.** Mud Bay Rd. and Second Avenue (P.O. Box 62), Haines, AK 99827. ☎ **907/766-2900** or 800/478-2902. 9 rms. TV. $71 double. AE, DC, DISC, MC, V.

It doesn't look like much from the outside, but the rooms are a real bargain for the price, especially the spacious, fresh ones in the newer wing. All rooms have refrigerators and coffeepots; the only major amenity they lack, oddly, is telephones.

BED-AND-BREAKFASTS

A Sheltered Harbor B&B. Portage St. and Beach Rd. (P.O. Box 806), Haines, AK 99827. ☎ **907/766-2741.** 4 rms. TV. High season, $80 double. Low season, $65 double. Rates include full breakfast. MC, V.

Upstairs from a gift shop across the street from the cruise-ship dock, these innlike rooms are a nice surprise, once you get inside. They're nicely decorated and come with a full breakfast.

Fort Seward Bed and Breakfast. 1 Fort Seward Dr. (P.O. Box 5), Haines, AK 99827. ☎ **907/766-2856** or 800/615-6676. 4 rms, 1 with bath. TV. High season, $82 double; $105 suite. Low season, $70 double. Additional person in room $15 extra. Rates include full breakfast. MC, V. Closed Oct 15–Apr 7.

The fort's surgeon's quarters overlook the parade grounds and the Lynn Canal with a big wraparound porch and an unspoiled historic feel; it might have become a B&B yesterday, but in fact Norm and Suzanne Smith have run it since 1979, becoming quite famous by word of mouth. It's not for smokers, or for those who don't like a homey B&B. Courtesy car available.

The Summer Inn Bed and Breakfast. 117 Second Ave. (P.O. Box 1198), Haines, AK 99827. ☎ **907/766-2970.** 5 rms, none with bath. High season, $70 double; $90 suite. Low season, $60 double; $80 suite. Rates include full breakfast. Additional person in room $15 extra. MC, V.

This lovely old clapboard house downtown has a big porch and living room, but the rooms are on the small side. Shannon Linebarger, the hospitable innkeeper, is a good baker. The house was built by a reputed former member of Soapy Smith's gang in 1912. No smoking or drinking here.

WHERE TO EAT

Two of Haines's best restaurants are in the Hotel Hälsingland and the Fort Seward Lodge (see "Where to Stay," above). Here are the other best places in town; there are lots of other places for a burger or a slice of pizza. **The Lighthouse Restaurant and Bar,** at Front and Main streets, is particularly popular with the locals.

✪ **Chilkat Restaurant and Bakery.** Fifth Ave. off Main St. ☎ **907/766-2920.** Lunch $4–$16; dinner $6.50–$23. AE, MC, V. Mon–Sat 7am–9pm, Sun 9am–9pm.

This pleasant, bright family restaurant allows no smoking, in contrast to most of the other smoky places in Haines. It started out as a bakery and has excellent baked goods, but now is a popular place for inexpensive lunches and dinners of steak or seafood. This would be my first choice with kids. No liquor license.

Port Chilkoot Potlatch. Fort William Seward parade grounds. ☎ **907/766-2003.** $20.75 per person. AE, DC, DISC, MC, V. Daily 5–8:30pm. Closed Oct–Apr.

Salmon bakes are touristy by nature, but this long-established event is a good salmon bake. The sockeye is grilled on alder and not overcooked or ruined with over-seasoning. Dining is at picnic tables, either in tents or in the clan house on the parade grounds. After you go through the line, waiters replenish your plate. One glass of beer or wine is included in the price.

A SIDE TRIP TO YAKUTAT

The village of Yakutat (YAK-a-tat) belongs to no region, lying midway between Juneau and Cordova and facing neither the Inside Passage nor Prince William Sound, but the wide Pacific. (It's closer to Gustavus or Haines than to anywhere else.) Yakutat is a fishing town and its few visitors are primarily serious sport fishermen who are after steelhead trout or salmon in the Situk River, a dozen miles south of town by car. Wilderness adventurers are coming more now: The town is close to the backsides of both Glacier Bay National Park and Wrangell–St. Elias National Park. Floaters on the Alsek and Tatshenshini rivers finish their trips in Yakutat; Chilkat Guides (see "Eagle Viewing" under "Getting Outdoors," above) offers such trips lasting 10 to 13 days through wild, uninhabited terrain, with a helicopter portage halfway through. (The renowned outfitter Mountain Travel • Sobek offers Tatshenshini River trips too—see Chapter 6, "Outside in Alaska.") A few professional surfers have conquered the North Pacific rollers that pound the black sand beaches near Yakutat; I haven't tried it myself, and I don't think you should, either.

Yakutat has no road or ferry service. The airport is served by the jets of **Alaska Airlines** (☎ 800/468-2248). The village of 700 residents has a bank and several restaurants, accommodations, and bars. For **visitor information,** you can contact the City and Borough of Yakutat, P.O. Box 160, Yakutat, AK 99689 (☎ 907/ 784-3323). **Totem Air** or **Fishing and Flying,** both at P.O. Box 51, Yakutat, AK 99689 (☎ 907/784-3563, or 800/352-3563), cater to visitors interested in seeing this extremely remote area, and will help with finding rooms.

12 Skagway: After the Gold Rush

It wouldn't be fair to say that Skagway is touristy—you might as well accuse Prudhoe Bay of being oily. This is a town with a curio shop that's been in business in the same location since 1897. In 1896 there was a single log cabin here, in 1898 it was a gold-rush boomtown, in 1899 the gold rush was ending, and in 1908—10 years after the town was founded—local businessmen started developing tourist attractions to revive their flagging economy. Picturesque gold-rush buildings were moved to Broadway, the main street, to create a more unified image when visitors arrived on the steamers. Gardens were planted. By 1920 tourism had become an important part of the economy. By 1933 historic preservation efforts had started. In 1996 you can see history in Skagway, and you can see the history of history.

With around 700 residents and more than 400,000 visitors annually, the "real" town has all but disappeared, and most of the people you'll meet are either fellow visitors or summer workers brought north to serve them. Most of the tourists are from cruise ships—it's not unusual for several to hit town in a single morning, unleashing waves of people up the wharf and into the one historic street. But there are plenty of highway and ferry travelers too, and outdoors enthusiasts here to do the Chilkoot Trail, just as the Stampeders did. There's a new gold rush going on, a new stampede 10 times larger than the original one they're coming to see—and probably richer for the town, too. With the approaching centennial of the '98 gold rush coming up, this new gold rush shows no signs of fading.

Is it worth all those visits? Skagway, spared from fire and recognized so long ago for its history, is probably the best-preserved gold-rush town in the United States. (Dawson City, the town all these Stampeders were heading for, is a strong competitor, but it's in Canada; see Chapter 10, "The Alaskan Interior.") What happened here in a two-year period almost 100 years ago was certainly extraordinary, even if the phenomenon the town celebrates is one of mass insanity based on greed, inhumanity, thuggery, prostitution, waste, and, for most, abject failure. In 1897 a group of prospectors showed up on the dock in Seattle with steamer trunks full of gold from the Yukon Territory's Klondike River, found the previous year. Even the mayor of Seattle joined the stampede. In the rush years of 1897 and 1898 Skagway, or its ghost-town sibling city of Dyea, were the logical places to get off the boat to head

Accommodations
Gold Rush Lodge **3**
Golden North Hotel **8**
Sgt. Preston's Lodge **4**
Skagway Home Hotel **7**
Skagway Inn Bed & Breakfast **5**
Westmark Inn **10**
Wind Valley Lodge **2**

Dining
Broadway Bistro **9**
Corner Cafe **6**
Red Onion Saloon **11**
Siding 21 Restaurant **1**

off on the trek to the gold fields near the new city of Dawson. Skagway instantly grew from a single homestead to a population of 15,000 to 25,000—no one knows exactly how many, in part because the people were flowing through so fast. But Dawson City ended up with 40,000.

While Canada was well policed by the Mounties, in Skagway there was no law—a hell on earth, as one Mounty described it. Soapy Smith, a con artist turned organized crime boss, ruled the city; the governor offered to put him officially in charge as a territorial marshall and rode with him in the 1898 Independence Day parade. Four days later Smith was shot dead in a gunfight with Frank Reid, who led a vigilante committee upset over one of Smith's thefts. Reid died of his wounds in the shoot-out, but Smith's gang was broken. Of course, the gold rush was about to end anyway. And for most of the years since then, Smith's gun and Reid's watch have been on display in Kirmse's Curios on Broadway, where you can see them today while you look for jewelry or a T-shirt.

In 1976 the National Park Service began buying many of Skagway's best old buildings for the Klondike Gold Rush National Historic District, and now it owns about 15. Broadway is a prosperous, freshly painted six-block strip of gold rush–era buildings, a few of which look like real businesses but turn out to be displays showing how it was back then. Other buildings restored by the park service are under lease to real businesses, and still others are still under restoration. Visitors also can ride a gold rush–era narrow-gauge railroad into the White Pass, hike the Chilkoot Trail, or join in some other, limited outdoors activities.

ESSENTIALS

GETTING THERE   By Ferry   The **Alaska Marine Highway System** (see "Exploring Southeast Alaska," earlier in this chapter) connects Skagway with Haines and Juneau; the fare is $14 to Haines, $26 to Juneau. If you aren't taking a vehicle to Haines, consider the more convenient **Haines-Skagway Water Taxi and Scenic Cruise.** From May 20 to September 15 the 80-passenger vessel offers two round-trips daily. The fare is $18 one way, $29 round-trip; in Skagway the ticket office is at Dejon Delights, Fifth Avenue and Broadway (☎ 907/983-2083), or you can buy them on board. Haines is 15 miles away by boat but more than 350 by road.

By Car   Since 1978 ✪ **Klondike Highway 2** has traced the route of the Stampeders through the White Pass, a parallel route to the Chilkoot Trail, into Canada. The road runs 99 miles, then meets the Alaska Highway a dozen miles southeast of Whitehorse. The border is at the top of the pass, 14 miles from Skagway. This is one of the most spectacular drives anywhere in Alaska; the views are basically equivalent to the White Pass and Yukon Route railway, but a lot cheaper. Make sure you do it in clear weather. Car rentals are available from **Avis** (☎ 907/983-2247 or 800/331-1212), with an office at the Westmark Inn Skagway (see "Where to Stay," below), or **Sourdough Van and Car Rentals** (☎ 907/983-2523), although Sourdough allows drop-off only in Skagway, Haines, or Whitehorse. Recreational vehicles are available from **ABC Motorhome Rentals** (☎ 800/421-7456).

By Bus   Two bus lines have daily summer service to Whitehorse, where you can make connections to Anchorage or Fairbanks three days a week. Gray Line's **Alaskon Express** (☎ 800/544-2206) stops at the Westmark Inn Skagway (see "Where to Stay," below); **Alaska Direct Busline** (☎ 800/780-6652) is cheaper.

By Air   Three commuter operators serve Skagway: **L.A.B. Flying Service** (☎ 907/983-2471), **Wings of Alaska** (☎ 907/983-2442), and **Skagway Air Service** (☎ 907/983-2218). The one-way fare from Juneau is around $75.

VISITOR INFORMATION   The ✪ **National Park Service Visitor Center,** in the restored railroad depot at Second Avenue and Broadway (P.O. Box 517), Skagway, AK 99840 (☎ 907/983-2921), is the focal point for activities in Skagway. Rangers answer questions, give lectures and show films, and four times a day lead an excellent guided walking tour. The building houses a small museum. The park service's programs are free. The visitor center is open June to August, daily from 8am to 8pm, closing two hours earlier in late May and September; it's closed in winter except when ferries are in town, but the park headquarters in the same building is open normal business hours and the staff is happy to answer questions or show the film. There's also a modest visitor center at the **Skagway Convention and Visitors Bureau,** P.O. Box 415, Skagway, AK 99840 (☎ 907/983-2854), with listings of local hotels and restaurants. It's open daily from 8am to 5pm, year round. It was to be moved in 1996 and at this writing no one knew exactly where it would wind up.

ORIENTATION   Skagway sits at the north end of the Lynn Canal fjord in a narrow mountain valley. The streets are a simple grid, with numbered streets starting at **First Avenue** at the water. The tourist attractions are on **Broadway. Klondike Highway 2** takes off up the valley to the White Pass, 14 miles away; an 8-mile gravel road branches off 2 miles up the highway to the **Dyea** historic area and the start of the **Chilkoot Trail.**

GETTING AROUND   Skagway's main sights can all be reached on foot. Don't miss the exceptionally good **Skagway Walking Tour Map,** provided free by the Skagway Convention and Visitors Bureau. If you want to go to Dyea or the gold-rush graveyard, a bike is a fun way to do it; you can rent a good mountain bike or join a guided trip (see "Getting Outside," below) at **Sockeye Cycle,** on Fifth Avenue off Broadway (☎ **907/983-2851**). No fewer than eight companies offer car, van, or bus tours of Skagway, but none goes to greater lengths for a unique experience than Steve Hites, whose **Skagway Street Car Company** (☎ **907/983-2908**), uses antique touring vehicles and whose costumed guides consider their work "theater." The two-hour streetcar tour is $34 for adults, a 90-minute van ride up the highway to the White Pass Summit is $27, and a five-hour tour into the Yukon Territory is $69; children are charged half fare. The company has been located at the Arctic Brotherhood Hall at Third Avenue and Broadway, but Hites planned to move into his own new building at 270 Second Ave. in 1996.

SPECIAL EVENTS   The Skagway Fine Arts Council puts on a **Folk Festival** in late April or early May (☎ **907/983-2276**). Skagway's **July 4th Parade and Celebration,** organized by the city, has been a big deal since Soapy Smith led the parade in 1898.

EXPLORING SKAGWAY

WHAT TO DO & SEE   The ✪ **White Pass and Yukon Route** railway, P.O Box 435, Dept. B, Skagway, AK 99840, (☎ **907/983-2217** or 800/343-7373), a narrow-gauge line that originally ran to Whitehorse, was completed after only two years in 1900. It's an engineering marvel and a fun way to see spectacular, historic scenery. Tickets are expensive, however, and I wouldn't recommend going in bad weather, when the pass is socked in and all you'll see out the window are white clouds. Also, they tell you not to get out of your seat (although many people do) and children may have a hard time sitting still that long. The ride begins at a depot on Second Avenue with the spine-tingling sound of a working steam engine's whistle. The steamer pulls the train a couple of miles, then diesels take the cars, some of them originals more than 100 years old, steeply up tracks that were chipped out of the side of the mountains. The summit excursion, which travels 20 miles with an elevation gain of 2,865 feet, then turns back, takes about three hours and costs $75. Children are charged half price. A 40-mile trip to Lake Bennett, where the Stampeders launched their boats for the trip to Dawson City, takes six hours and costs $124; that run links with a bus-train package to Whitehorse. But the Lake Bennett run has been canceled for 1996, and may or may not be running in 1997. (The whole line is up for sale.) The Lake Bennett train also carried hikers down from the Chilkoot Pass hike, and alternate arrangements were still in the planning stages late in 1995—check with the park service. The trains still drop off passengers for the hikes within the White Pass, listed below. These days the line operates only as a tourist attraction, and closes down for the winter in September.

Make sure to get a copy of the **Skagway Walking Tour Map** from either of the visitor centers. I also highly recommend the National Park Service guided walking tours, which leave their visitor center four times a day. In the National Park Service Visitor Center and next door, the park service maintains a small **museum** explaining the gold rush and displaying some artifacts and photographs. Of greatest interest is a collection of food and gear similar to the ton of supplies each prospector was required to carry over the pass in order to gain entry into Canada, a requirement that prevented famine among the Stampeders, but made the job of getting to Dawson City an epic struggle for each of them. The park service also has made a museum of the **Mascot Saloon,** at Broadway and Third Avenue, complete with statues bellying up to the bar. It's open daily from 8am to 5pm and, like all the park service's programs, it's free.

The city-owned ✪ **Trail of '98 Historical Museum and Archives,** temporarily housed in the Arctic Brotherhood Hall, on Broadway between Second and Third avenues, contains Skagway's best collection of gold-rush artifacts, most of which are well explained in labels. The museum started in 1961 and has been housed in a wonderful Victorian room upstairs from the city hall in the city's most impressive building, at Seventh Avenue and Spring Street, a granite structure originally built as a college during the gold rush and later used as a federal courthouse. The structure is worth a look, even though in 1996 it will be undergoing renovation. Outside the permanent museum building is a display of railroad cars, with informative historical markers. The museum is open in summer, daily from 9am to 5pm, and in winter by appointment; admission is $2 for adults, $1 for students and children. The **Corrington Museum of Alaska History** is located in Corrington's gift shop at Fifth Avenue and Broadway; admission is free, and the display is impressive and worth a stop. It's open, May 20 to September 15, from 9am to 7pm.

The **Moore Cabin,** near Fifth Avenue and Spring Street, is an important stop on the walking tour for the story behind it. Captain William Moore predicted that the gold rush would occur 10 years early and homesteaded the land Skagway would be built on, knowing that this would be a key staging area. He built this cabin in 1887. But when the rush occurred, the Stampeders simply ignored his property claims and built the city on his land without offering compensation. A block east, on Sixth Avenue, is **Mollie Walsh Park,** with a good children's play area, public restrooms, and phones. A sign tells the sad story of Skagway's first respectable woman, who chose to marry the wrong man among two suitors and was killed by him in a drunken rage. The other suitor—who'd previously killed another rival for her affections—commissioned the bust of Walsh that stands at the park.

The **Gold Rush Cemetery** is 1 1/2 miles from town, up State Street. Used until 1908, it's small and overgrown with spruce trees, but the charm and mystery of the place are largely lost because of the number of visitors and the shiny new paint and maintenance of the wooden markers. The graves of Soapy Smith and Frank Reid are the big attractions, but don't miss the short walk up to Reid Falls. A map is available at the visitor centers. The close dates on many of the markers are due to epidemics that swept through the Stampeders.

About 9 miles north of Skagway on a lovely drive or bike is the ghost town of **Dyea,** where Stampeders started the Chilkoot Trail. (See "Getting Around," above, for directions.) It's a lot more ghost than town—all that remains are a few boards, broken dock pilings, and miscellaneous iron trash. But on a sunny day the protected historical site is a perfect place for a picnic, among beach grasses, wild iris, and the occasional reminder that a city once stood here. The National Park Service leads a guided history and nature walk once a week; check at the visitor center. (See "Getting Outside," below, for other ideas on going to Dyea.)

The little-visited **Slide Cemetery,** in the woods near Dyea, is the last resting place of many of the 60 to 70 men who died in an avalanche on the Chilkoot Trail on Palm Sunday, April 3, 1898. No one knows how many are here, or exactly who died, or how authentic the wooden markers are. In 1960, when the state reopened the Chilkoot Trail, the cemetery had been completely overgrown and the markers were replaced. But it's a ghostly place, and the sense of anonymous, hopeless hardship and death it conveys is as authentic a gold-rush souvenir as anything in Skagway.

SHOPPING   With almost 100 years of experience, Skagway knows how to do gift shops—and now has more than 50. Of course, most are closed in winter, as the town has only about 700 year-round residents. ✪ **Kirmse's Jewelry and Curios,** at Fifth

Avenue and Broadway, has been in business since jeweler Herman Kirmse set up shop in a tent in 1897 and moved into its current building in 1899. Besides the jewelry and gifts, there are huge gold nuggets and Soapy Smith's gun on display. Across the street is **Curringtons,** a large gift store with an entire free museum attached. **Lynch and Kennedy,** at Fourth Avenue and Broadway, is in a building owned and restored by the National Park Service and leased to the current gift store; it carries art, jewelry, and high-quality gifts. The **David Present Gallery,** at Third Avenue and Broadway, shows work by 50 artists and craftspeople, including Seattle-based Present's own sculpture. **Inside Passage Arts,** on Broadway between Fourth and Fifth avenues, is a gallery of Alaska Native fine art from Southeast Alaska.

GETTING OUTSIDE

SPECIAL PLACES   The famous **Chilkoot Pass Trail,** used by some 20,000 to get from Dyea—9 miles from Skagway—to Lake Bennett, where they could launch boats bound for Dawson City, is now managed by the National Park Service and Canadian Park Service and is traversed by about 3,000 hikers a year. It's a challenging three- to five-day hike; people tend to underestimate it, which is odd, since the reason for going is to see and experience the difficulties faced by gold rushers. Contact the National Park Service before your climb and get a copy of the excellent trail guide published jointly by the two governments. With the number of people who hike it, and the gold-rush artifacts you'll find, the Chilkoot is not a wilderness trail, but more of an outdoor museum. Most of the 3,600-foot elevation gain comes in a 3-mile stretch that's the site of the famous photograph of a long line of men climbing the pass at a 45° angle. The whole trail is 33 miles long. Traditionally, hikers have been able to get back to Skagway from Lake Bennett on the **White Pass and Yukon Route** (see "Exploring Skagway," above), but that service has been canceled for 1996. Check with the Park Service for current arrangements, still up in the air at the end of 1995.

A **Skagway Trail Map** is available from the visitor center, listing 11 hikes around Skagway. An easy evening walk starts at the suspension footbridge at the north end of First Avenue, crossing the Skagway River to **Yakutania Point Park,** where pine trees grow from cracks in the rounded granite of the shoreline. Across the park is a shortcut taking a couple of miles off the trip to Dyea and to the **Skyline Trail and A.B. Mountain,** a strenuous climb to a 3,500-foot summit with great views. On the southern side of town, across the railroad tracks, a network of trails heads up from Spring Street between Third and Fourth avenue to a series of mountain lakes, the closest of which is **Lower Dewey Lake,** less than a mile up the trail.

There are two **U.S. Forest Service cabins** near Skagway, and official access to both is by the White Pass and Yukon Route railway. One is an old caboose parked next to the tracks 6 miles up the line at the trailhead for the 4-mile **Denver Glacier Trail.** The railroad charges $25 to take you there, and the cabin permit is $25 a night; some people walk it, being careful to get out of the way of the trains, but the railroad and Forest Service say that that's not safe. Another cabin is 1 1/2 miles off the track 14 miles up on the **Lawton Glacier Trail;** the train ticket is $50, and if you tried walking you'd find that there are places where you can't get off the track and could be run over by a train. The Forest Service maintains a summer office in Skagway, but it moves each year, so contact the park service visitor center, or the **Juneau Ranger District,** 8465 Old Dairy Rd., Juneau, AK 99801 (☎ **907/586-8800**).

BIKING   **Sockeye Cycle,** on Fifth Avenue off Broadway (☎ **907/983-2851**), leads bike tours, including one that takes clients to the top of the White Pass in a van and coasts down on bikes; the two-hour trip is $60. They also lead a tour of the quiet townsite of Dyea for $50, going over in a van. I rode to Dyea from Skagway on my own over the hilly, 9-mile coastal road; it was one of the most beautiful and pleasant rides I can ever remember.

HORSEBACK RIDING   Chilkoot Horseback Adventures leads half-day horseback tours of Dyea and West Creek Glacier, booked through Southeast Tours at Fifth Avenue and Broadway (☎ **907/983-2990** or 800/478-2990).

FLIGHTSEEING   Skagway, like Haines, is a good place to choose for a flightseeing trip. Glacier Bay National Park is just to the west; a small plane is a great way to see it, and less expensive, all things considered, than journeying to the bay and seeing it by boat. **L.A.B. Flying Service** (☎ **907/983-2471**), **Wings of Alaska** (☎ **907/ 983-2442**), and **Glacier Bay Airways** (☎ **907/697-2249**) have flights. **Temsco Helicopters** (☎ **907/983-2900**) takes 55-minute tours over the Chilkoot Trail and lands on a glacier for 25 minutes, although not a big Glacier Bay berg; those flights cost $142.

WHERE TO STAY

All the accommodations in Skagway are close walking distance to the historic district, except as noted. The **bed tax** is 8%.

EXPENSIVE

Westmark Inn Skagway. Third Ave. and Spring St. (P.O. Box 515), Skagway, AK 99840. ☎ **907/983-6000** or 800/544-0970. Fax 907/983-6100. 212 rms. TEL. $136 double. Additional person in room $15 extra. AE, DC, DISC, MC, V. Open summer only.

This property is the weak link in the generally reliable Westmark chain; you can get a better room and better service elsewhere for the same price or less. Nearly the entire hotel turns over every night as bus tours churn through. The rooms are small, lack TVs, and long-distance calling is only by credit card. I found the housekeeping and maintenance wanting, and the walls paper-thin. A courtesy car is available.

The large Chilkoot Room restaurant, reached through the lobby, offers fine dining in a light, Victorian atmosphere. The menu, mainly seafood, ranges from $15 for salmon cakes to $28 for king crab legs. Burgers and sandwiches, as well as cocktails and bottled microbrews, are sold in the hotel's Bonanza Bar.

MODERATE

Gold Rush Lodge. Sixth Ave. and Alaska St. (P.O. Box 514), Skagway, AK 99840. ☎ **907/ 983-2831,** 602/788-3469 in winter. Fax 907/983-2741. 12 rms. TV TEL. High season, $80 double. Low season, $45 double. Additional person in room $10 extra. DISC, MC, V. Closed Oct–Apr.

Harry and Vickie Bicker keep a clean, comfortable motel by the airstrip three blocks from the historic district and are noted for their hospitality. The rooms are on the small side, but nicely decorated. Courtesy car, free coffee, no smoking.

Golden North Hotel. Third Ave. and Broadway (P.O. Box 431), Skagway, AK 99840. ☎ **907/ 983-2294.** Fax 907/983-2755. 32 rms, 28 with bath. TEL. High season, $75 double. Low season, $50 double. Additional person in room $5 extra. AE, CB, DC, MC, V.

This big, white landmark on Broadway was built in 1898 and is Alaska's oldest operating hotel. It's a fun place to stay, with the old bathtubs and rooms with placards about gold-rush families, but it's not for everyone as the Victorian decor is threadbare and the rooms far from standard. A courtesy car is available. The dining room, open from 7am to 9pm, is small and smoky, with red tablecloths; the lunch menu is burger-and-sandwich fare and dinner is reasonably priced seafood and steak, with a halibut filet for $15. There's also a cocktail lounge with 1890s decor and a collection of sayings on the wall.

Sgt. Preston's Lodge. Sixth Ave. and State St. (P.O. Box 538), Skagway, AK 99840. ☎ 907/983-2521. Fax 907/983-3500. 30 rms, 19 with bath. TV TEL. $65 double without bath; $75–$85 double with bath. AE, DC, DISC, MC, V.

Set in several motel-style buildings on a grassy compound, many of the rooms are large and clean, but the eight new rooms reserved for nonsmokers are huge and light with high ceilings—the best rooms in Skagway, and quite a bargain for the price. Courtesy car, free coffee.

✪ Skagway Inn Bed and Breakfast. Seventh Ave. and Broadway (P.O. Box 500), Skagway, AK 99840. ☎ **907/983-2289.** Fax 907/983-2713. 12 rms, none with bath. High season, $72–$86 double. Low season, $65–$79 double. DISC, MC, V. Closed Oct–Apr.

Built in 1897, this perfect little Victorian inn has rooms named after the prostitutes who worked in them when it was a brothel—the owners researched old police records. There are six bathrooms for the 12 guest rooms, and they're kept immaculate. Some of the rooms are quite small; the Alice Room, above the street, is larger and has a porch, but costs more. The lobby is a welcoming parlor full of books where guests visit over tea. A courtesy van is available.

Wind Valley Lodge. 22nd Ave. and State St. (P.O. Box 354), Skagway, AK 99840. ☎ 907/983-2236. Fax 907/983-2957. 29 rms. TV TEL. High season, $75–$85 double. Low season, $55 double. Additional person in room $10 extra. AE, DISC, MC, V. Closed Oct 15–Mar 15.

These are excellent rooms for a reasonable price. The main building contains a pleasant lobby with a fireplace and gift shop and 12 smaller double rooms. The larger rooms in the new building are $10 more, and are among the best in town. The only drawback is the location—a mile from the sights on Broadway. Courtesy van, coin-op laundry, and free coffee are available.

HOSTEL & CAMPING

There's a free **National Park Service campground** at Dyea. For recreational vehicles, there are four parks in Skagway: two on Broadway, one on State Street, and one at the small-boat harbor.

Skagway Home Hostel. Third Ave. near Main St. (P.O. Box 231), Skagway, AK 99840. ☎ 907/983-2131. 2 rms, neither with bath; dorm beds. $12 per person. Possibly closed Oct–May (call ahead to determine if it's open).

Frank Wasmer and Nancy Schave have literally opened up their historic home to hostelers, sharing their meals, refrigerator, bathrooms, and hospitality side-by-side with guests. Guests have repaid them with consideration, and the place feels like the home of a huge family. Bunks are in separate male and female dorm rooms. The hostel is independent and you won't find it in the Hostelling International guide. Summer registration hours are 5:30–10:30pm. No pets, alcohol, or smoking.

WHERE TO EAT

I've already described the restaurants at the Golden North Hotel and Westmark Inn Skagway (see "Where to Stay," above). You may also enjoy lunch at **Mabel G. Smith's** (☎ **907/983-2609**), a year-round New Age bakery and card shop off Broadway serving one generally vegetarian lunch selection daily; people swear by it.

Broadway Bistro. In the Westmark Hotel, Third Ave. and Broadway. ☎ **907/983-6000.** Lunch $6–$8; dinner $9–$14. AE, DC, DISC, MC, V. Daily 6:30am–2pm and 5–8pm.

With its streetfront on Broadway, you wouldn't guess that this trendy Italian café is part of the Westmark Hotel. The pizza is good, but avoid the seafood or other more challenging cuisine. Beer and wine license.

Corner Cafe. Fourth Ave. and State St. ☎ **907/983-2155.** Lunch $4.50–$7; dinner $10–$15. No credit cards. Mar 15–Dec, daily 6am–9pm; Jan–Mar 14, daily 11am–7pm.

There are a lot of burger-and-fries diners in Skagway, but this one is open year round, popular with locals, and a little off the beaten track. It has a light dining room and a deck where you can eat in the sunshine. No liquor license.

✪ **Lorna's at the Skagway Inn.** Seventh Ave. and Broadway. ☎ **907/983-2289.** Dinner $17–$26. MC, V. May–Sept, daily 5–9pm.

Lorna makes it clear what she's about as soon as you walk into the Skagway Inn lobby: Her recent diplomas from Le Condon Bleu are posted by the entrance to the dining room. The intimate dining room is lovely, decorated with antiques, and seats only 25 people. The menu changes every night, but it always emphasizes Alaska seafood and country French cuisine. Beer and wine license.

❸ **Siding 21 Restaurant.** 21st Ave. and State St. ☎ **907/983-3328.** Lunch $5–$9.50; dinner $12–$15. DISC, MC, V. Daily 6am–10pm.

Built to look like an old-fashioned railway depot inside and out, this is a wonderful family restaurant. There's a complete children's menu and the regular menu is reasonably priced. The service is friendly and quick, and the no smoking section actually isn't smoky. It's located a mile out of town, next door to the Wind Valley Lodge. No liquor license.

SKAGWAY IN THE EVENING

There are two evening tourist shows in Skagway. Incredibly, the *Days of '98 Show* has been playing since 1927 in the Fraternal Order of Eagles Hall No. 25, at Sixth Avenue and Broadway (☎ **907/983-2545**). Jim Richards carries on the tradition each summer with professional actors from all over the United States. The evening shows begin at 7:30pm with mock gambling at a casino run by the actors. The performance, at 8:30pm, includes singing, can-can dancing, and the story of the shooting of Soapy Smith. The play money you win in the gambling hall can be used to bid for a garter from one of the can-can dancers in the show. Matinees are $12 and evening shows are $14; senior citizens pay $2 less and children are charged half price.

At the Arctic Brotherhood Hall, at Third Avenue and Broadway, the bearded **Buckwheat** performs Robert Service poetry and tells other stories nightly, mid-May to mid-September; admission is $6. The Skagway Street Car Company produces the show (☎ **907/983-2908**), and it may move in 1996.

The **Red Onion Saloon,** at Second Avenue and Broadway, is an authentic-feeling old bar with live music some nights. It was a brothel originally; look in the upstairs windows. The **Frontier Bar,** at Fifth Avenue and Broadway, is more of a gritty place for locals.

Southcentral Alaska   8

As teenagers, my cousin and I got a job from a family friend painting his lake cabin. He flew us out on his float plane and left us there, with paint, food, and a little beer. There was a creek that ran past the lake so full of salmon that we caught one on every cast until we got bored and started thinking of ways to make it more difficult. We cooked the salmon over a fire, then floated in a boat on the lake under the endless sunshine of a summer night, talking and diving naked into the clear, green water. We met some guys building another cabin one day, but otherwise we saw no other human beings. When the week was over, the cabin was painted—it didn't take long—and the float plane came back to get us. As we lifted off and cleared the trees, Anchorage opened in front of us, barely 10 minutes away. I doubt it could ever be as much fun as it was at that age, but fly-in fishing to a remote lake is one of the great summer experiences to be had in Alaska, and it's just a few minutes and a few hundred dollars from the busy streets of Anchorage. Southcentral Alaska is like that. You can climb an unnamed mountain and have dinner in a five-star restaurant on the same day.

Dominated by Anchorage, the state's largest city, with 40% of Alaska's population, Southcentral doesn't have an identity of its own. Anchorage is accused crushingly of being just like a city Outside, not really part of Alaska at all, although it sits in the lap of the wild Chugach Mountains. The Kenai Peninsula is famous for the crowding on its salmon streams, not the secret and grand places it contains. The Copper River country and Prince William Sound have their own definition, made up of the huge and spectacular land and the few little towns it hosts. As a region, Southcentral is more of an area on a map than an interconnected way of life.

For a visitor, that's an advantage, because Southcentral Alaska's diversity contains almost everything that people come to the state to see. The glaciers are most numerous and largest here. The mountains are the most massive, if not quite the tallest. The waters of Prince William Sound and the Kenai Peninsula have the same allure as Southeast Alaska, but are more accessible by road. The towns have art to see, if not much history. And in some of them, there's a new sophistication that's removed some of the crude edges that accompanies much Alaska travel. Many people who come to Alaska spend a lot of their time traveling great distances between regions to see the tallest mountain, the biggest river, and to say they've been to all parts of the state. If you have limited time—and who doesn't?—you can see a lot more staying in Southcentral.

The disadvantage, of course, is that there are more people in the way. The closer you get to Anchorage, the more the human development will remind you of the outskirts of any town in the United States, with fast-food franchises, occasional traffic jams, and even crime-ridden neighborhoods with the makings of youth gangs. But if that starts to bother you, do what Anchorage residents do—head up to the Chugach Mountains, down to the Kenai Peninsula, or out on Prince William Sound.

Anchorage lies at the center of the region, near the head of Cook Inlet. South of Anchorage, the **Kenai Peninsula** is one of the state's most populated areas. **Seward,** on the eastern side of the peninsula, is the gateway to **Kenai Fjords National Park,** a spectacular, rugged area on the Gulf of Alaska side of the peninsula. The **Kenai and Soldotna area,** facing Cook Inlet on the western central Kenai Peninsula, provide access to fishing in the Kenai River. **Homer,** near the southern end of the peninsula, sits on **Kachemak Bay,** which opens into Cook Inlet. The bay is a rich natural environment and Homer a quirky community popular with artists. **Prince William Sound** is southeast of Anchorage; with more than 2,700 miles of coastline, it holds a vast wealth of marine life and spectacular scenery, including many tidewater glaciers. **Whittier** is the Sound's closest access point to Anchorage; **Valdez** has its only direct highway access. **Cordova,** tucked away on the eastern Sound, is an undiscovered gem—its Childs Glacier, sliced by the Copper River, is one of Alaska's most impressive. North along the Copper River, the **Copper River country** is a vast region of some of the world's tallest and most massive mountains. West of that area, and north of Anchorage, the **Matanuska and Susitna valleys** are both a bedroom community to Anchorage and an access route to Denali National Park.

1 Exploring Southcentral Alaska

In Southcentral, uniquely in Alaska, you have your choice of modes of transportation. The Alaska Railroad runs from Seward north to Anchorage, with a branch from Portage to Whittier on Prince William Sound, and then farther north through the Matanuska-Susitna valleys to Denali National Park and Fairbanks, in the Interior. Highways connect all the region's towns except Cordova and Whittier, but you can take your car on the train to Whittier, and the ferry connects it with Valdez and Cordova. Jet airline service brings visitors into Alaska's hub airport, in Anchorage, and to Cordova. Commuter lines fan out from Anchorage to Kenai, Homer, Valdez, and other towns. Bus service also is available to many areas.

The easiest way to get around Southcentral is as residents do—**by car.** One good itinerary of 10 days to two weeks would be to fly to Anchorage and spend a few days taking in the sights—the museums, the coastal trail, perhaps a hike in the Chugach Mountains and a night out for a fine dinner and to the comic revue at the Fly-By-Night Club or one of the other choices for evening entertainment. Then rent a car to drive down the Seward Highway, taking plenty of time to get down to Homer, perhaps with a couple of days to stop for fishing or hiking on the way in the Chugach National Forest or in Cooper Landing or the Kenai/Soldotna area. In Homer, plan several days, getting out on Kachemak Bay to Halibut Cove, Seldovia, or the Alaska Center for Coastal Studies, or spending time hiking and boating in Kachemak Bay State Park. Visit the galleries and have at least one special night out eating. Then drive back to Portage and take the car on the train through the tunnel and travel on the ferry through Prince William Sound to Valdez, seeing the glaciers and wildlife. Spend a day in Valdez, then drive up the Richardson Highway, perhaps making a two-day side trip to historic Kennicott, in the spectacular Wrangell–St. Elias National Park, then returning on the Glenn Highway to Anchorage or continuing up to Fairbanks, if there's time.

Without a car, a possible 10-day itinerary would be to fly to Anchorage, spend a few days sightseeing as described above, then take the Alaska Railroad to Seward, visiting Kenai Fjords National Park by boat, and then having a second day in Seward in case of bad weather and to see the rest of what the town has to offer. Then head back to Anchorage and fly to Cordova, taking the tour to Childs Glacier, visiting the quaint and welcoming town, and perhaps getting outdoors on a bike, a hike, or a kayak. Then take the ferry to Valdez, spend part of a day there, and board a Stan Stephens Cruises tour boat to see Columbia Glacier and other glaciers in western Prince William Sound, either going all the way to Whittier and taking a train and bus to Anchorage or returning to Valdez and flying back to Anchorage. If there's time left, use Anchorage as a base for a fly-in fishing trip or take a flightseeing trip on a classically restored DC-3 over Denali National Park.

I offer these plans only as a starting point. Your own exploration of the region depends, of course, on your interests and how you like to travel. You'll find that Southcentral is the easiest part of the state to get around, and travel is more flexible than in other areas. But the height of summer, from mid-June to mid-August, is heavily booked, so you can't expect to just show up and get a choice room—often, any room is hard to get. Planning extra travel days because of the weather is not as critical as in Southeast Alaska, because Southcentral, while rainier than the Interior, is less likely to be socked in, and if you do get stuck, you can always drive. But leave plenty of time around any boating excursions, as rough weather can come at any time. Reputable tour and fishing operators simply won't go out in rough water and make you miserable; if you have a backup day, you can spend the rough-weather day on shore and try again the next day. Check on weather cancellation policies before you book any boat excursions.

2 Outside in Southcentral

Southcentral Alaska has all the outdoors opportunities found elsewhere in the state. The land ranges from crowded and well served by facilities, in parts of the Kenai Peninsula, to unexplored wilderness completely without facilities, out in Wrangell–St. Elias National Park. The best and most central place to get outdoors information is the Alaska Public Lands Information Center, at Fourth Avenue and F Street in Anchorage (see "Visitor Information" under "Essentials," in the Anchorage section, later in this chapter).

FISHING   The most famous place to fish, and the only place in the world to find such large king salmon, is the Kenai River, accessible on the Kenai Peninsula from Kenai, Soldotna, and other towns. But there's good salmon fishing virtually anywhere you choose to go in the region—including downtown Anchorage. The most famous halibut fishing, with flat fish topping out in the 300-pound class, is from Homer, but other towns have halibut charters, too. Anchorage is a good starting point for fly-in fishing.

FLIGHTSEEING   There are flight services in all the towns for flightseeing trips. Anchorage is a good starting point with lots of choices.

HIKING & BIKING   Southcentral has far more opportunities than I can describe in this format; you must get a copy of ✪ *55 Ways to the Wilderness,* by Helen Neinhueser and John Wolfe, Jr. Published by The Mountaineers, 1011 SW Klickitat

Anchorage

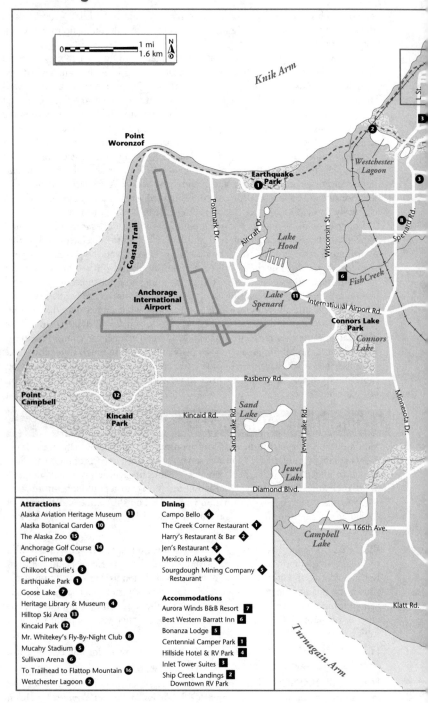

Knik Arm

Point Woronzof

Earthquake Park ①

Westchester Lagoon ②

L St. ③ ③

⑧

Spenard Rd.

Postmark Dr.

Aircraft Dr.

Lake Hood

Wisconsin St.

Fish Creek ⑥

Coastal Trail

Anchorage International Airport

Lake Spenard

⑪

International Airport Rd.

Connors Lake Park

Connors Lake

Minnesota Dr.

Rasberry Rd.

Point Campbell

⑫ Kincaid Park

Kincaid Rd.

Sand Lake Rd.

Sand Lake

Jewel Lake Rd.

Jewel Lake

Diamond Blvd.

W. 166th Ave.

Campbell Lake

Klatt Rd.

Turnagain Arm

Attractions

Alaska Aviation Heritage Museum ⑪
Alaska Botanical Garden ⑩
The Alaska Zoo ⑮
Anchorage Golf Course ⑭
Capri Cinema ⑨
Chilkoot Charlie's ③
Earthquake Park ①
Goose Lake ⑦
Heritage Library & Museum ④
Hilltop Ski Area ⑬
Kincaid Park ⑫
Mr. Whitekey's Fly-By-Night Club ⑧
Mucahy Stadium ⑤
Sullivan Arena ⑥
To Trailhead to Flattop Mountain ⑯
Westchester Lagoon ②

Dining

Campo Bello ④
The Greek Corner Restaurant ①
Harry's Restaurant & Bar ②
Jen's Restaurant ③
Mexico in Alaska ⑥
Sourgdough Mining Company ⑤
  Restaurant

Accommodations

Aurora Winds B&B Resort ⑦
Best Western Barratt Inn ⑥
Bonanza Lodge ⑤
Centennial Camper Park ①
Hillside Hotel & RV Park ④
Inlet Tower Suites ③
Ship Creek Landings ②
  Downtown RV Park

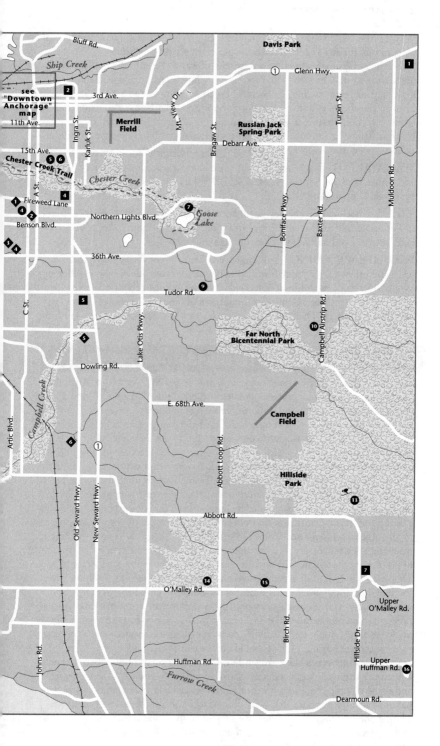

Bluff Rd.

Davis Park

Ship Creek

Glenn Hwy.

① 1

see "Downtown Anchorage" map

2

3rd Ave.

Ingra St.

Karluk St.

11th Ave.

Merrill Field

Mt. View Dr.

Bragaw St.

Russian Jack Spring Park

Turpin St.

Debarr Ave.

15th Ave.

5 6

Chester Creek Trail

Chester Creek

A St.

4

Goose Lake

7

Muldoon Rd.

1

4

Fireweed Lane

Boniface Pkwy.

Baxter Rd.

Northern Lights Blvd.

Benson Blvd.

3 4

36th Ave.

C St.

Tudor Rd.

9

5

5

Far North Bicentennial Park

Campbell Airstrip Rd.

10

Dowling Rd.

Artic Blvd.

Campbell Creek

E. 68th Ave.

Campbell Field

6

①

Abbott Loop Rd.

Hillside Park

13

Old Seward Hwy.

New Seward Hwy.

Abbott Rd.

7

14

15

O'Malley Rd.

Birch Rd.

Upper O'Malley Rd.

Hillside Dr.

Johns Rd.

Huffman Rd.

Upper Huffman Rd.

16

Furrow Creek

Dearmoun Rd.

Way, Seattle, WA 98134. It's the standard, comprehensive trail guide, and is well written, too. It costs $12.95 and is available in any Alaska bookstore.

The bike trails in Anchorage are a wonderful way to get into the outdoors without leaving town. Chugach State Park, near Anchorage, has many good alpine trails for hiking and biking. Chugach National Forest has short and long trails, some with historic significance, and cabins along the way on the Kenai Peninsula and in Cordova. The Matanuska Valley also has good alpine trails. Wrangell–St. Elias National Park is a vast area for wilderness trekking and biking on the abandoned right-of-way of the Copper River and Northwestern Railroad.

SEA KAYAKING   Kachemak Bay out of Homer, Resurrection Bay out of Seward, and Prince William Sound out of Whittier, Valdez, or Cordova all present good sea-kayaking opportunities.

SKIING   Anchorage is the best destination for downhill skiing, at Alyeska Resort in Girdwood and at two smaller ski areas; and for cross-country skiing, at several excellent areas and on trails that lace through the city.

WILDLIFE WATCHING   You can have a chance to see whales, otters, sea lions, seals, and other marine animals on cruise or charter boats out of Seward, Homer, Whittier, Valdez, and Cordova. Bears could show up anywhere, but the McNeil River sanctuary, out of Homer, is the place for guaranteed bears, for the lucky few who win permits in a lottery. Dall sheep are often seen on the Turnagain Arm south of Anchorage.

3 Anchorage: Alaska's Threshold

Steve McCutcheon came to Anchorage as a child in the city's first years. Anchorage started as a tent camp for workers mobilized to build the Alaska Railroad in 1915. A grid was laid out north and south of Ship Creek and lots were sold at auction; a few houses and businesses went up to serve the federal employees building and then running the railroad, as McCutcheon's father did. It was a remote, sleepy railroad town, enlivened by World War II and the construction of a couple of large military bases, but never more than strictly functional. As one visitor who came in the early 1940s wrote, the entire town looked like it was built on the wrong side of the tracks.

A couple of years ago, McCutcheon looked out the picture window from his living room on a placid lake surrounded by huge, half-million-dollar houses, each with a float plane pulled up on the green front lawn, and he recalled the year people started to take Anchorage seriously. It was the year, he said, when they started thinking it would be a permanent city, not just an encampment where you went for a few years to make money before moving on—the year they started building Anchorage to last. That year was 1957. Oil was discovered on the Kenai Peninsula's Swanson River, south of here. It was around that time that McCutcheon built his own house, far out in the country with no neighbors anywhere in the area, all alone on a lake. At that time you could homestead in the Anchorage bowl. Those who had the opportunity— my wife's family, for example—didn't do it only because it seemed improbable that flat, wet acreage way out of town would ever be worth anything.

Oil grew Anchorage like nitrogen fertilizer poured on a shooting weed. Those homesteads that went begging in the 1950s and early 1960s now have shopping malls and high-rise office buildings on them. Fortunes came fast, development was haphazard, and a lot was built that we'd all soon regret. I had the bizarre experience of coming home from college to the town I'd grown up in, and getting completely lost in a large area of the city that had been nothing but moose browse the last time I'd seen it. Visitors found a city full of life, but empty of charm.

In the last 10 years that has started to change. Anchorage is slowly outgrowing its gawky adolescence. It's still young, prosperous, vibrant—exhausting, at times, when the summer sun refuses to set. But now it also has some excellent restaurants, a good museum, and a nice little zoo, and things to do in the evening besides the tourist melodramas that you'll find in every town you visit. Some people complain that Anchorage isn't really Alaska—in Fairbanks, they call it "Los Anchorage" (In Anchorage, Fairbanks is known as "Squarebanks.") Yet the wilderness remains close by, right at the edge of town, and often intertwined with it. With around a quarter million people, Anchorage is the nation's 69th-largest city, yet it still has problems in the winter with moose—they're a general pest, especially for gardeners, as they seem to consider ornamental trees and bushes a tasty delicacy. Bears and eagles show up in town, though less frequently, and a system of greenbelts and bike trails, the city's best feature, brings the woods into almost every neighborhood. Good downhill skiing is available, as is some of the best Nordic skiing in the United States.

Anchorage stands between the Chugach Mountains, which are protected by Chugach State Park, and the silt-laden waters of upper Cook Inlet. The site of the city is broad and flat; it's mostly built on sediment. At the water's edge, mud flats of the same material, not yet made into land, stretch far offshore when the tide is at its low point, up to 38 vertical feet below high water. There's a downtown area of about 6 by 20 blocks, near Ship Creek where it all started, but the rest of the city spreads some 5 miles east and 15 miles south along broad commercial strips and freeway frontages. Like many cities in the western United States built in the era of the car, the layout is not particularly conducive to any other form of transportation. But the city's boundaries go even farther, far beyond the reach of cars, taking in the Chugach, Turnagain Arm all the way to Portage, and even reaching over to Prince William Sound. Most of that land is there only to be explored. I can't say for sure if all the mountain peaks in the municipality have been climbed, and far from all have been named.

Most visitors use Anchorage as a hub—that's its role for Alaskans, too—and they spend a day or two here before heading off somewhere more remote. Yet the city has enough personality and attractions to make more time interesting. The downtown area is pleasant, but if you just walk up and down its streets of tourist-oriented shops, you've missed most of the city. Get out on the coastal trail, go to one of the museums, take a day trip south to Portage, and explore the Chugach Mountains.

ESSENTIALS

GETTING THERE   You'll probably get to Anchorage at the start of your trip by air; it has by far the most flights linking Alaska to the rest of the world. You can also make the long drive up the Alaska Highway, or, if you're on a cruise ship, you'll likely come in on a tour bus from Seward.

By Air   The **Anchorage International Airport** is a major hub. Flights connect the city to Asia and the Russian Far East, but Seattle has the most frequent flights, with numerous domestic carriers flying nonstop all day. Within Alaska, most flights route through Anchorage, even for communities that are much closer to each other than either is to Anchorage. **Alaska Airlines** (☎ 800/426-0333) is the dominant carrier for Alaska destinations; it's the only jet operator to most Alaska cities. **Era Aviation** (☎ 800/866-8394) is a reliable carrier for Southcentral Alaska destinations, and can be booked through Alaska Airlines. Various commuter carriers link Anchorage to rural destinations not served by jet.

By Car   There's one road out of town to the north and one to the south, and the road to the south, the Seward Highway, is a dead end, leading only to the Kenai

Peninsula. The Glenn Highway is a four-lane freeway heading north to the inter-section with the Parks Highway, which leads to Denali National Park and Fairbanks. The Glenn continues as a two-lane road, meeting the Alaska Highway 330 miles from Anchorage at Tok. All major car-rental companies operate in Anchorage, at the airport or at other locations in town. In 1995 you could rent a midsize car for $55 a day, with unlimited mileage.

By Bus   Gray Line's **Alaskon Express** (☎ 907/277-5581, or 800/544-2206) links Anchorage to Seward, Valdez, and the Alaska Highway. The fare is about $200 to Haines. **Alaska Direct Busline** (☎ 907/277-6652, or 800/780-6652) goes from Anchorage to Fairbanks or the Alaska Highway. **Seward Bus Line** (☎ 907/224-3608) makes one trip daily from Seward to Anchorage and back.

By Rail   The **Alaska Railroad** (☎ 907/265-2494, or 800/544-0552) connects Anchorage to Seward, to the south, and to Fairbanks and Denali National Park, to the north. The run to Seward, which operates only in the summer, is incredibly spectacular; the fare is $50 one way, $80 round-trip. Heading north, you can ride the Alaska Railroad cars year round to Fairbanks (the summer fare is $135), or in the summer to Denali, in full-dome cars with Princess Tours or Holland America/Westours. For details, see Chapter 9 on Denali National Park.

By Boat   Anchorage does not have passenger vessel service except for a few cruise-ship calls a year.

VISITOR INFORMATION   The **Anchorage Convention and Visitor Bureau,** 1600 A St., Suite 200, Anchorage, AK 99501, operates five visitor information centers, distributing brochures and providing guidance for the whole state. The main location is the **Log Cabin Visitor Information Center,** downtown at Fourth Avenue and F Street (☎ 907/274-3531; fax 907/272-9564). It's open daily: June to August from 7:30am to 7pm, in May and September from 8am to 6pm, and October to April from 9am to 4pm; it's closed on New Year's Day, Thanksgiving, and Christmas. You'll also find a visitor center on the way into town by car, in Eagle River, at Easy Street and the Old Glenn Highway, and three at the airport, one in the baggage-claim area in the domestic terminal and two in the international terminal, in the lobby and in the transit area.

The ✪ **Alaska Public Lands Information Center,** 605 W. Fourth Ave., Suite 105, Anchorage, AK 99501 (☎ 907/271-2737), in the old concrete federal building across the intersection from the log cabin at Fourth and F, has guidance for anyone planning to spend time in the outdoors, as well as displays of interest even for those who aren't. The center occupies a grand room with high ceilings that used to be the post office. All the land agencies are represented, and there's information on the whole state. Similar centers are in Ketchikan, Tok, and Fairbanks.

The **Chugach State Park Eagle River Visitor Center,** at the end of Eagle River road, 12 miles up Eagle River Valley from the Glenn Highway exit (☎ 907/345-5014), is like a public wilderness lodge. In an old log building where a fire is often burning and cocoa or lemonade available, it contains hands-on naturalist displays about the area, and there are spotting scopes on the deck. Several excellent trails in Chugach State Park start here, from strenuous, multiday trips to easy nature walks. It's open in summer only, daily from 10am to 6pm. The **Chugach State Park Headquarters,** in the Potter Section House on the Seward Highway at the south end of town (☎ 907/345-5014), is open normal business hours all year.

The *Anchorage Daily News* maintains a free voice-mail **Daily Newsline** (☎ 907/277-1500) with hundreds of recorded topics, including fishing, hiking, skiing, and snowmobiling conditions, as well as basic visitor guidance, such as the Airport Information Line, at extension 5252.

ORIENTATION   Navigating Anchorage is easy if you just remember that the mountains are to the east. Maps are available at the visitor centers or in any grocery store. The major roads are on a north-south grid.

Many visitors never make it beyond the **downtown** area, the old-fashioned grid of streets at the northwest corner of town where the large hotels and the gift shops are located. Downtown's numbered avenues run east and west, with the numbers larger as you go south; letter-named streets run north and south, running through the alphabet as you go west. All street numbers start at First Avenue and A Street; many streets have east and west addresses. East of A Street, north-south streets have alphabetically arranged names—Barrow, Cordova, Denali, and so on.

Beyond downtown, most of the rest of Anchorage is oriented to commercial strips. Three major north-south thoroughfares run from downtown, through the **midtown** commercial area, to the shopping malls and residential districts of **South Anchorage.** These are, going west to east, **Minnesota Drive,** which becomes I and L streets downtown; **C Street** and **A Street,** which merge into C Street south of midtown; and the **New Seward Highway,** which is Ingra and Gambell streets downtown and heads out of town to the south. All three meet several major east-west roads: downtown, Fifth and Sixth avenues become the **Glenn Highway** to the east, the highway link to the north; in midtown, **Northern Lights Boulevard** and **Benson Boulevard** form a couplet running all the way across the city; south of midtown, **International Airport Road** goes to the airport—to get downtown from the airport, follow International Airport Road east, toward the mountains, then turn left on Minnesota Drive. **Dimond Boulevard** is the major east-west artery in South Anchorage. Minnesota Drive becomes **O'Malley Road** in South Anchorage, and then meets the New Seward Highway.

Some parts of Anchorage are outside the bowl defined by the Chugach Mountains. The communities of **Eagle River** and **Eklutna** are out the Glenn Highway, to the northeast; **Girdwood** and **Portage** are on the Seward Highway, to the south.

GETTING AROUND   If you just stay downtown, you can do Anchorage on foot. The **People Mover** city bus system (☎ **907/343-6543**) operates a free zone in the downtown core area; the transit center bus depot is at Sixth Avenue and G Street, and the fare for service all over town is $1. Buses generally come every half hour, but are much less frequent on weekends. Taxis are quite expensive in Anchorage because of the spread-out urban design. A ride downtown from the airport runs about $12; try **Alaska Cab** (☎ **907/563-5353**). There is no airport shuttle bus or People Mover service.

A bike is also a great way to explore, using the network of bike trails. The **Tony Knowles Coastal Trail** comes right downtown (see "Special Places" under "Getting Outside," below). **Anchorage Coastal Bike Rental,** at 414 K St. (☎ **907/ 279-1999**), is a couple of blocks from the trail, and charges $15 for three hours. **Downtown Bicycle Rental,** at Sixth Avenue and B Street and at Fifth Avenue and C Street, in the T-shirt shop (☎ **907/279-5293**), is also handy and charges $10 for four hours; it's open daily from 9am to 10pm. Both rent mountain bikes, tandem bikes, and kid trailers as well as street bikes.

To visit some of the best of Anchorage, or to get into the outdoors, you'll need to get beyond the downtown area. The easiest way is in a **rental car.** All the major rental agencies have offices in Anchorage, with a mid-size car renting for around $55 a day. The **Alaska Backpacker Shuttle** (☎ **907/344-8775** or 800/266-8625) offers rides to all the best trails around Anchorage, as well as to Denali National Park and the rail link to Prince William Sound at Portage; fares range from $7.50 to $20 in the Anchorage area, $35 to Denali, one way. **Alpina Tours** (☎ **907/783-2482**) offers combination guided day hikes and visits to some of the outlying sights in Girdwood, Portage, or even Seward, or half-day trips just to the Turnagain Arm sights without a hike; prices range from $30 to $75.

City tours are available from various operators; check with the visitor center. There isn't that much to see on a bus tour of Anchorage unless it's going specifically to one of the attractions I've listed below and you can get off. **Princess Tours** (☎ **907/ 276-7711**) offers a 5½-hour tour that includes several stops for $39. The most unique of these tour operations is the **Anchorage City Trolley Tour** (☎ **907/ 257-5603**), a bus that's been made to look like a San Francisco streetcar; it takes one-hour tours from the 4th Avenue Theater, on Fourth Avenue between F and G streets, for $10, every hour from 8am to 7pm during the summer. The same company offers Portage Glacier and Matanuska Valley tours.

FAST FACTS Anchorage has no sales tax. A **bank** is never far away and most grocery stores also have **ATMs.** In **emergencies,** call 911. There are many branches of the **post office** in town—in the downtown area it's downstairs in the brown building at Fourth Avenue and D Street. To reach the **Anchorage Police Department** for nonemergency problems, call 907/786-8500. For police business outside the city, call the **Alaska State Troopers** (☎ **907/269-5511**). There are four hospitals in Anchorage, two serving the general public: the **Alaska Regional Hospital,** at 2801 DeBarr Rd. (☎ **907/276-1131**), and **Providence Hospital,** at 3200 Providence Dr. (☎ **907/562-2211**). The *Anchorage Daily News* includes an extensive arts and leisure section each Friday, called "8." **Out-of-town papers** are available in street boxes, or at Carrs grocery stores; downtown, Sourdough News and Tobacco, at 735 W. Fourth Ave., carries 42 newspapers from across the United States, 12 from foreign countries, and all Alaska newspapers.

SPECIAL EVENTS The ✪ **Anchorage Fur Rendezvous,** in the second and third week of February, is a huge, city-wide winter carnival, the main event of which is the **World Champion Sled Dog Race,** a three-day sprint event of about 25 miles per heat. The **Iditarod Trail Sled Dog Race** starts from Anchorage the first Saturday in March, but the teams are loaded in trucks a few miles out of town and restarted in Wasilla for the 1,000-mile run to Nome (see the section on the Matanuska and Susitna valleys, later in this chapter). **The Taste** is a food fair in early June, on the Delany Park Strip near Ninth Avenue and I Street. The **Chugiak–Eagle River Bear Paw Festival** is a community celebration July 7–11 with a parade, rodeo, carnival, and other festivities. **Music in the Park** is a series of free concerts on Wednesday and Friday in July and August, held in front of the old city hall at Fourth Avenue and E Street. The **Great Alaska Shootout Men's Basketball Tournament** (Nov. 27–30, 1996) brings top-ranked college teams to the Sullivan Arena (see "Spectator Sports," below). The Saturday after Thanksgiving, a **Christmas Tree Lighting** takes place in town square, with Santa arriving behind a team of real reindeer.

EXPLORING ANCHORAGE

You'll likely find yourself in downtown Anchorage at some point, and there's plenty to do there. Many visitors make it no farther into the city. I've arranged this section starting with only the sights you can visit downtown, without a car; next is a description of the attractions that you'll need a vehicle to get to, but that still lie within the Anchorage bowl.

Downtown Anchorage

DOWNTOWN MUSEUMS

✪ **Anchorage Museum of History and Art.** 121 W. Seventh Ave. ☎ **907/343-4326.** Admission $4 adults, $3.50 seniors 65 and older, free for children 17 and under. High season, daily 9am–6pm; low season, Tues–Sat 10am–6pm, Sun 10am–5pm.

The state's largest museum doesn't have its largest collection, but unlike the Alaska State Museum in Juneau or the University of Alaska Museum in Fairbanks, the Anchorage museum has the room and staff to teach and to serve as a center of contemporary culture of a regional caliber. Here you can learn about the history and anthropology of the state in the excellent Alaska Gallery, for which a 90-page guide is available, or you can go to one of the art galleries to see what's happening in art in Alaska today. The Anchorage museum also gets the best touring shows. It's the only museum in Alaska that could require more than one visit. The cafe serves some of the best lunches to be had downtown. In the summer, Native dancers perform in the atrium daily at 12:15, 1:15, and 2:15pm.

The Imaginarium. 725 W. Fifth Ave. ☎ **907/276-3179.** Admission $5 adults, $4 seniors 65 and older and children 2–12. Mon–Sat 10am–6pm, Sun noon–5pm.

This is a science museum geared to children, where grownups can learn, too. The idea is that while they're running around having a great time, the kids may accidentally learn something; at least, the displays will excite a sense of wonder that is the start of science. It's the "in" place to go for good boys and girls in Anchorage, and visitors will enjoy it, too.

The Oscar Anderson House. 420 M St. ☎ **907/274-3600.** Admission $2 adults. Summer only, daily noon–4pm. Closed in winter.

This house museum, moved to this beautiful site in Elderberry Park over the water, shows how an early Swedish butcher lived. The house is perfectly quaint, surrounded by a lovely little garden. Canvases by Sydney Lawrence, Alaska's favorite landscape artist, hang on the walls—he was a friend of Anderson's. The tour guides will tell you about the ghost, too. If you come at Christmas, don't miss the Swedish Christmas tours, the first two weekends in December.

A STROLL AROUND DOWNTOWN ANCHORAGE

Anchorage Historic Properties, 645 W. Third Ave. (☎ 907/274-3600), a city-funded historical preservation group, offers a ✪ **Guided Walking Tour of Historic Downtown Anchorage** in summertime (June to August), Monday through Friday at 1pm. The volunteer guides are fun and knowledgeable. The one-hour tour covers 2 miles and costs $5 for adults, $4 for seniors over age 65, and $1 for children. Meet at the lobby of old city hall, 524 W. Fourth Ave., next door to the Log Cabin Visitor Information Center.

Here are some highlights of the downtown area; I've arranged them as a walking tour, but you can also scan the text for the sights that interest you.

Start at the **Log Cabin Visitor Information Center** at Fourth Avenue and F Street. Outside is a sign that shows the distance to various cities, a popular spot for pictures. Walking east, toward the mountains, the 1936 **old city hall,** at Fourth Avenue and E Street, is on the right; It's currently under renovation to house the convention and visitors bureau.

Crossing E Street, notice on the left side of Fourth Avenue that the McDonald's restaurant, yellow shopping mall, and brown post office mall are all modern—everything on the left side of Fourth Avenue from E Street east for several blocks collapsed in the 1964 earthquake. The street split in half, length-wise, with the left side ending up a dozen feet lower than the right. That land was later reinforced with a gravel buttress by the U.S. Army Corps of Engineers, but a block lower cannot be redeveloped because of the earthquake risk. This stretch of Fourth Avenue is where the **Iditarod Trail Sled Dog Race** and the **Anchorage Fur Rendezvous World Championship Sled Dog Race** start each year in March and February, respectively.

At Fourth Avenue and D Street, the **Wendler Building,** the old Club 49, is among the oldest buildings in Anchorage, but no longer the very oldest. (See the Oscar Gill House Bed and Breakfast, in "Where to Stay," below, for an explanation of that conundrum.) The bronze of the dog commemorates the sled-dog races that start here. Across D Street is a mural that depicts a relief map of Alaska, with the Iditarod Trail marked. It's on the side of ✪ **Cyrano's,** one of Anchorage's greatest, funkiest cultural institutions—it's a bookstore with character, a cafe and bakery, and a live theater showing some of the city's most challenging and original productions.

Turn right, walking a block south on D Street to Fifth Avenue. The **5th Avenue Mall,** a grand, four-story shopping center, is across the street; it includes Alaska's finest upscale shopping. On the opposite side of the building—turn left on Fifth Avenue and right on C Street to Sixth Avenue—is the **Wolfsong of Alaska** museum and gift shop. This nonprofit organization aims to educate and elevate the public about Alaska's most controversial mammal; inside you'll find displays, mounts, artwork, videos, and eager volunteers. Admission is free and it's open Monday through Friday from 10am to 7pm, on Saturday from 11am to 6pm, and on Sunday from noon to 5pm.

Turn right and walk west, past the mall, to Sixth Avenue and E Street, one corner of the beautifully planted **town square.** The Downtown Anchorage Association raised money for the improvements by collecting donations of $40 each for the granite bricks, with an inscription of the contributor's choosing. There are 13,344 (bet you can't find mine). The building on the north side that looks like a roll-top desk is the acclaimed **William A. Egan Civic and Convention Center;** inside you'll find a pleasant atrium, public restrooms, and whatever's going on in the ballrooms. On the east side of the square, the huge whale mural was painted freehand by Wyland in 1994; he painted similar whale murals in cities all along the west coast. On the west side of the square, the massive, highly decorated **❂ Alaska Center for the Performing Arts** dominates; it's Anchorage's most controversial building, completed in 1988 at a cost of over $70 million. The lobby is usually open, and whatever your opinion of the decor, a look inside will spark a discussion. Ask at the box office about tours. Thespians believe the building haunted by the ghost of painter Sydney Lawrence, who makes lights mysteriously vary and elevators go up and down with no one in them. An auditorium demolished to make room for the center was named for Lawrence. Check the box office also for current performances in the three theaters—this is Alaska's premier performance venue.

Continuing west on Sixth Avenue, **Humpy's,** the tavern on the left side of Sixth, has the largest selection of microbrews in town, if you're already thirsty, and is the trendiest yuppie hangout. The square green building next door is **city hall.**

Turn left through the pedestrian walkway between Humpy's and city hall. A mural depicting the history of Anchorage, facing the parking lot, was in progress at this writing. It is painted on the wall of the **Exxon Valdez Oil Spill Library,** a repository of most of what's known about the 1989 spill, which houses the offices of the trustees responsible for spending $1 billion won from Exxon by the government.

Walking west, between city hall and the spill library, to G Street, turn right and proceed to Sixth Avenue and G. (If you're up for a longer walk, you can turn left on G Street instead and explore the Delany Park strip and lovely South Addition residential neighborhood south of 9th Avenue.)

The **Alaska Experience Center** is on the northwest corner of Sixth Avenue and G Street, in the dome tent. A 40-minute Omnivision, wraparound movie about Alaska costs $7 for adults, $4 for children. It's certainly spectacular—too much so for some people, who get motion sickness. Sit toward the center at the back. An Alaska Earthquake display that really shakes is $5 for adults and $4 for children. They're open daily: from 9am to 9pm in summer, and from noon to 6pm in winter. Across Sixth Avenue is the transit center, for city buses.

Walk a block north, back to Fifth Avenue. The west side of G Street between Fourth and Fifth avenues contains some of the downtown's best **off-beat businesses: Side Street Espresso,** where you can get into a lively political discussion; **Darwin's Theory,** a good, old-fashioned neighborhood bar; the **Stonington Gallery,** probably the city's most sophisticated art gallery; and **The Great Alaska Train Company,** a retired couple's labor of love, which sells nothing but model trains and train memorabilia. There are others, too—it's a great little block. The Imaginarium, described above, is in the same building, on Fifth Avenue.

Going west on Fifth Avenue and crossing H Street, the **Holy Family Cathedral,** a concrete, art deco church, is the seat of the Roman Catholic archbishop. Keep going west, crossing L Street and walking down the hill to **Elderberry Park,** by the water. The yellow-and-brown house is the **Oscar Anderson House,** described above. There's good playground equipment here for a variety of ages, public restrooms, and comfortable places where you can sit and watch the kids and Cook Inlet at the same time and meet other parents. This is an easy access point to the ✪ **Coastal Trail** (see "Special Places" under "Getting Outside," below), where it tunnels under the Alaska Railroad tracks; even if you don't have time to go far on the trail, you may want to walk through the tunnel and see the ducks paddling around and, at low tide, the vast mud flats.

Now hike back up to L Street and turn left, going north two blocks to the **Resolution Park,** with the bronze **Captain Cook Monument.** Capt. James Cook stands on a large, wooden deck, but he's gazing out to sea—surely, when he discovered Cook Inlet in 1778 aboard HMS *Resolution,* he was looking toward land.

Follow Third Avenue east, passing the back of the **State Courthouse** on your right, and turn left on Christiansen Drive, then right again on Second Avenue. You'll descend into an area of old houses, some of which are still residences and some attorney's offices. Many are marked, and the historic significance of each is carefully catalogued—80-year-old houses may not be "historic" where you come from, but here we have to take what we can get. If you imagine houses like this over much of downtown, you'll know what Anchorage looked like before oil.

Continue east to E Street. At Second Avenue and E, a **monument** to Alaska's 1959 admission to the Union honors President Eisenhower; you can overlook the Alaska Railroad yards from here, and see part of the port of Anchorage and the neighborhood of Government Hill across the Ship Creek river bottom. This is where the tent city of Knik Anchorage, later shortened to Anchorage, was set up in 1914.

Walk up the hill on E Street to Third Avenue. The extensively landscaped parking lot on the left becomes the ✪ **Saturday Market** every weekend in the summer, a street fair drawing hundreds of vendors and thousands of shoppers. You can buy everything from local vegetables to handmade crafts to somebody's old record collection; lots of food booths and music are available, too.

Turn right, walk a block west on Third Avenue, then turn left on F Street. **F Street Station,** on the left, is a popular bar with an after-work crowd.

Proceed to Fourth Avenue and you're back at the Log Cabin Visitor Information Center, but don't stop. Turn right on Fourth Avenue. On the right side is the **old federal building,** a grand, white, Depression-era structure that now contains the Alaska Public Lands Information Center. Across the street is Anchorage's most attractive historic building, the restored ✪ **4th Avenue Theater.** It was built by Cap Lathrop, an early Alaskan business magnate, who created it as a monument to the territory and the permanence of its new society. Today it's a gift store and has a dinner-theater show; don't miss going in and looking at the bas-relief murals and the blinking big dipper on the ceiling, which during many a movie over the years was more entertaining than whatever was on the screen.

SIGHTS BEYOND DOWNTOWN

Alaska Aviation Heritage Museum. 4721 Aircraft Dr. ☎ **907/248-5325.** Admission $5.75 adults, $4.50 active military and seniors over age 62, $2.75 children. High season, daily 9am–6pm; low season, Tues–Sat 10am–4pm. Take International Airport Road toward the airport and follow the signs to the right as you near the terminal.

Old soldiers and aviators and anyone interested in mechanical things will enjoy this collection of classic planes in hangars and a small indoor exhibit near the Lake Hood float-plane base. A highlight is the shop where they rebuild wrecked classic aircraft—you can wander in and watch the work in progress. The display of Japanese and American military artifacts, from the war for the Aleutians, has impact. There are films too, and a pleasant picnic area with a dock on the lake.

Alaska Botanical Garden. Campbell Airstrip Rd. (off Tudor Rd.). ☎ **907/265-3165.** Free admission. Summer, daily 9am–9pm. From downtown, drive out New Seward Highway

(Gambell Street) to Tudor Road, exit to the east (left), turn right off Tudor onto Campbell Airstrip Road, and park at the Benny Benson School.

It's young and the volunteer staff still has a long way to go, but the garden already is a restful place to learn about native flora and see what else grows here while watching birds and squirrels from the peaceful benches. They've done a good job of integrating the garden into its forest setting. Kids love the paths and secluded spots.

○ **The Alaska Zoo.** 4731 O'Malley Rd. ☎ **907/346-3242.** Admission $6 adults, $5 seniors, $4 children 12–17, $3 children 3–12. Opens at 10am; closing time varies by season. Closed Tues in winter. Drive out the New Seward Highway to O'Malley Road, then turn left and go several miles; it's at least 15 minutes from downtown, without traffic.

If you're expecting a big-city zoo, you'll be disappointed, but the Alaska Zoo has a charm all its own. Anchorage residents have developed personal relationships with the animals, many of which are named, in their campy little Eden. Gravel paths wander through the woods past bears, seals and otters, musk oxen, mountain goats, moose, caribou, waterfowl—all the animals you were supposed to see in Alaska but may have missed. (Don't get the elephants or tigers in your pictures—they'll blow your cover.)

Heritage Library and Museum. C St. and Northern Lights Blvd. ☎ **907/265-2834.** Free admission. High season, noon–5pm; low season, noon–4pm.

Off the lobby of the white National Bank of Alaska building, this museum displays a large collection of oils and Native Alaskan art and artifacts in opulent surroundings. The bank's owners, the Rasmussen family, also helped found the city's museum, downtown on Seventh Avenue.

In Eagle River & Eklutna

Eagle River, 14 miles northeast from Anchorage on the Glenn Highway, is like a whole different town, with its own business district and local concerns. Most residents commute into town or to the nearby military bases. Other than the outdoor activities in the area, described below, there's not much to do in Eagle River. A new **Southcentral Alaska Museum of Natural History,** at 11723 Old Glenn Hwy. (☎ **907/694-8819**), is located in the drab Parkgate Building, across from McDonald's, with the visitor information center. It's a small but cheerful volunteer effort teaching about the minerals, fossils, and animals of the area—there are dioramas with mounted wild animals. Children and rock hounds should attend. Admission is $3 for adults; it's open in summer, daily from 10am to 5pm; in winter, Wednesday through Saturday from 11am to 5pm and on Sunday from noon to 5pm. About 25 miles out the Glenn Highway (take the Eklutna exit, then go left over the overpass), the Native village of **Eklutna** has a fascinating old cemetery in which each grave is enclosed by a highly decorated spirit house, the size of a large dollhouse. The spirit houses excite the imagination in a way no ordinary marker would. The **Eklutna Tribe** (☎ **907/688-6026** or 907/696-2828) leads a 30-minute tour of the cemetery, Russian Orthodox churches, and museum; it costs $3.50. Those not on a tour have to stay outside the cemetery fence. The park is open in summer only, daily from 8am to 6pm. Stop in at the **St. Nicholas Orthodox Church,** which is on the National Register of Historic Places. The 1920s **Chief Mike Alex Cabin** also is open for tours in the summer; Alex, who lived 1907 to 1977, was the tribe's last traditional chief.

SHOPPING

You can buy just about anything in Anchorage—at times it seems the entire downtown area has turned into one big gift shop. Some interesting shops are described above, in the walking tour. As elsewhere in Alaska, if you want something authentically Alaskan it's important to check—it should have the polar bear label, for

Alaska-made products, or the silver hand, which indicates Alaska Native work. Be prepared to pay more, especially for Native art and crafts.

The ✪ **Oomingmak Musk Ox Producers' Co-operative,** in the house with the musk ox on the side at Sixth Avenue and H Street, sells scarves and other knitted items of qiviut (KI-vee-ute), the light, warm, silky underhair of the musk ox, which is combed out, collected, and knitted in the Bush by village women. They're expensive—some caps cost over $100—but unique and culturally significant. The **Yankee Whaler,** in the lobby of the Hotel Captain Cook, at Fifth Avenue and I Street, is a small but well-regarded shop carrying Native arts. **Alaska Native Arts and Crafts,** better known as ANAC, in the post office mall at 333 W. Fourth Ave., is the traditional and original artists' outlet for Native work, in operation since 1938. **The Rusty Harpoon,** next door in the yellow Sunshine Mall, at 411 Fourth Ave., also has authentic Native items and reliable, long-time proprietors. **One People,** at 400 D St., carries folk art from all over the world, especially Native dolls, soapstone and ivory carvings, jewelry, and baskets. ✪ **Taheta Arts and Cultural Group,** at 605 A St., across from the museum, is both a shop and a workshop for Native artisans; some of the work you can see and buy there is quite rare. Farther afield, the **Alaska Fur Exchange,** at 4417 Old Seward Hwy., near Tudor Road, is an urban warehouse version of the old wilderness trading post, where rural residents bring in furs and crafts. They have a massive selection of Native crafts, and if you're in the market for pelts, go no further.

For furs in more finished condition, **David Green Master Furrier,** at 130 W. Fourth Ave., is an Anchorage institution. The **Alaska Fur Factory** is close by, at Fourth Avenue and D Street, as is the **Alaska Fur Gallery,** at 428 W. Fourth Ave., just down the block. There are others in the Anchorage Hilton Hotel and the 5th Avenue Mall.

✪ **Laura Wright Alaskan Parkys,** at 343 W. Fifth Ave.—there are several good stores there, in the Loussac-Sogn Building—makes and sells the bright, fabric coats really worn by Eskimos. Some have fur, but that isn't a requirement for beauty and authenticity.

There are lots of places to buy both mass-produced and inexpensive handmade crafts that aren't from the Bush. If you can be in town on a Saturday during the summer, be sure to visit the ✪ **Saturday Market** street fair, in the parking lot at Third Avenue and E Street, with food, music, and hundreds of miscellaneous crafts booths. You won't have any trouble finding shops on Fourth Avenue downtown. **Once in a Blue Moose** is one of our favorites, at Fourth Avenue and F Street; **Grizzly's Gifts** and **Trapper Jacks,** both under the same ownership, are the biggest, and have huge selections of gifts. **Remember Alaska,** with locations in the 5th Avenue Mall and Dimond Center, is well managed and attentive. The ✪ **Kobuk Coffee Company,** at Fifth Avenue and E Sreet, next to town square, occupies one of Anchorage's earliest business buildings; its a cozy little candy, coffee, and collectibles shop. In midtown, on International Airport Road between the Old and New Seward highways, **Alaska Wild Berry Products** is a fun store to visit: There's a chocolate waterfall and a big window where you can watch the candy factory at work. The chocolate-covered berry jellies are addictive and rich enough to make you dizzy if you eat more than a couple.

Downtown has several fine art galleries. The ✪ **Stonington Gallery,** at Fifth Avenue and G Street, is a real cultural resource that showcases originals and serious art by more than 100 Alaskan artists. On the same corner, **Aurora Fine Arts** also is a serious gallery, as is the **International Gallery of Contemporary Art,** at 625 W. Fifth Ave. The **Stephan Fine Arts Gallery,** with a main location at 600 W.

Sixth Ave. and smaller outlets in the Hotel Captain Cook and 5th Avenue Mall, is the largest in town, specializing in prints on wilderness and wildlife themes by such well-known artists as Bev Doolittle and Charles Gause. **Artique** is Anchorage's oldest gallery, at 314 G St., and has a large selection of ceramics and sculpture as well as prints and paintings.

GETTING OUTSIDE
SPECIAL PLACES
MUNICIPAL BIKE/FOOT/SKI TRAILS   My favorite thing about Anchorage is a ride or walk on a sunny summer afternoon on the ✪ **Tony Knowles Coastal Trail.** Leading more than 10 miles from the western end of Second Avenue along the shore to **Kincaid Park,** the coastal trail is a unique pathway to the natural environment from the heart of downtown Anchorage. You can join the wide, paved trail at various points; **Elderberry Park,** at the western end of Fifth Avenue, is the most popular. Two bike-rental agencies are in close proximity—see "Getting Around" under "Essentials," above. I've ridden my bike parallel with beluga whales swimming along the trail at high tide; toward the Kincaid Park end of the trail, I've often seen moose, or had them stop me. At **Westchester Lagoon,** 10 blocks south of Elderberry Park, the coastal trail meets the **Lanie Fleischer Chester Creek Trail,** which runs about 4 miles through the center of town to **Goose Lake,** where you can swim in a cool, wooded lake at the end of a hot ride—still, it's hard to believe, in the middle of the city. The trail follows a greenbelt the whole way, so you rarely see a building, and road and railroad crossings on all the trails have bridges or tunnels, so you're never in traffic. If you're just up for a short walk, the lagoon is a great place for a picnic, or to feed the ducks, and there are many other such spots along both trails.

✪ **Kincaid Park** itself is one of the best cross-country skiing areas in the country, and in the summer is a great place for mountain biking, running, or day hiking, and has an archery range. **Little Campbell Lake** is a picturesque swimming hole. The whole place is crawling with moose. You can reach the park either along the coastal trail or by driving south from downtown on Minnesota Drive (L Street) and then west on Raspberry Road, to the very end. The park is situated on 1,400 rolling acres of birch and white spruce on a point on Cook Inlet, south and west of the airport, with about 30 miles of groomed ski trails ranging from easy to killer. Seven miles are lighted and open until 11pm nightly. An **outdoor center** (☎ **907/248-4346**) is open Monday through Friday from 1 to 9pm and on Saturday and Sunday from 10am to 9pm; it's a warm-up house in winter and a popular venue for weddings in the summer, as the views across the inlet are spectacular.

THE CHUGACH MOUNTAINS   The mountains behind Anchorage are wonderfully accessible, and as beautiful as areas that people travel hundreds of miles from Anchorage to see. Almost the whole area is in either Chugach State Park or Chugach National Forest. There's plenty of alpine terrain to wander in, and it's possible to get off by yourself on multiday trips where you'll see few other people, or no one, and still be in cellular-phone range of Anchorage. You don't need a permit to camp, but you should get out of sight of trails. You can get ideas from the Alaska Public Lands Information Center, or from the park visitor centers (see "Visitor Information" under "Essentials," above). Get a copy of the tabloid newspaper visitor guide, *Ridgelines.* A backpacker shuttle is available in the summer (see "Getting Around" under "Essentials," above). The best trail guide to the entire region, a really essential purchase, is Helen Neinhueser and John Wolfe, Jr.'s ✪ *55 Ways to the Wilderness,* published by The Mountaineers, 1011 SW Klickitat Way, Seattle, WA 98134; it costs $12.95 and is available in any bookstore in the area.

✪ **Flattop Mountain,** right behind Anchorage, is a great family climb. It's an easy afternoon hike for fit adults, and younger children can go partway and still get to see memorable views above the treeline. From New Seward Highway, drive east on O'Malley Road, turn right on Hillside Drive and left on Upper Huffman Road, then right on the narrow, twisting, gravel Toilsome Hill Drive. The parking area at **Glen Alps,** above treeline, is a starting point for lots of winter and summer trips. If you don't feel like climbing, you can walk or bike the broad gravel trail that leads up the valley. Everything is above treeline; with the help of a copy of *55 Ways,* you can hike from here over the mountains to various alpine lakes, or over to Eagle River or to one of the trails leading down to Turnagain Arm.

You'll also find great hikes in the Chugach Mountains south of town, along the Seward Highway, at McHugh Creek, Indian, and several other spots; I've described them below in "A Road Trip to Turnagain Arm and Portage Glacier." North of Anchorage, on the Glenn Highway, there are trails at the head of Eagle River Road, around the park visitor center, and, from the Thunderbird Falls exit, 25 miles from Anchorage—there an easy mile-long hike leads to a crashing cataract of water. Continuing up the gravel **Eklutna Lake Road,** you come to a lovely state parks campground ($10 a night) and the beautiful, glacial lake for canoeing, hiking, and mountain biking. You can make a goal of the Eklutna Glacier at the other end. (This glacial melt is where Anchorage gets much of its water.) At Arctic Valley, off an exit halfway to Eagle River, the **Alpenglow Ski Area** (☎ **907/428-1208** or 907/ 249-9292) is a wonderful place in the summer for alpine day hikes away from any trail, or in the winter for above-the-treeline alpine skiing close to town. On top of the mountain to the left is an abandoned Cold War–era antimissile emplacement.

HILLSIDE PARK / FAR NORTH BICENTENNIAL PARK　The 4,000-acre, largely undeveloped park on the east side of town is a unique patch of urban wilderness. Wildlife, including bears and moose, live there among the trails for dog mushing, skiing, walking, and mountain biking. The Alaska Botanical Garden is in the park, as is the **Hilltop Ski Area,** 7105 Abbott Rd. (☎ **907/346-1446**), a beginner-oriented slope where you can rent equipment and get lessons in skiing or snowboarding. In the summer, they rent **mountain bikes,** $12 for half a day and $18 for a full day, and offer lessons. Hilltop is also the venue for summer **trail riding;** guided rides are offered for $25 an hour by **Alaska Wilderness Outfitters** (☎ **907/ 344-2434**) all summer, daily from 10am to 10pm. There are two ways to the park: Campbell Airstrip Road, off Tudor Road, is the way to the less developed part; or, on the south side, off Abbott Road (take Dimond east from the New Seward Highway), around Hilltop and Service High School. Besides Hilltop, there are challenging, lighted cross-country ski trails in the winter, good for walks and mountain biking in the summer.

POTTER MARSH　A large freshwater marsh at the south end of the Anchorage bowl, this is a great place for birdwatching. Boardwalks and interpretive signs help, but you can also pull out anywhere along the Seward Highway to set up a tripod for a camera or spotting scope. In the early winter, before the snow, it's the first and largest outdoor ice-skating pond.

EARTHQUAKE PARK　After the 1964 earthquake, a large waterfront parcel of land at the extreme western end of Northern Lights Boulevard was preserved to show how the earth goes mad above 9.0 on the Richter Scale. In the more than 30 years since, the humps and indentations in the land, which once looked like a frozen sea of mountainous waves, have been largely overgrown. But it's still a great place for children to romp around and explore, with lots of tiny, steep hills and pollywog ponds, and the sandy, muddy beach for digging. If you search intently, you may find some wreckage of houses in the area near the water, toward the east of the park, but most of that is gone.

ACTIVITIES

DOG MUSHING   In the last 15 years, sled-dog mushing has become a recreational sport as well as the utilitarian activity it once was in the Bush and the professional sport it has been for years. More and more sled-dog enthusiasts are offering a chance for visitors to drive their team, or at least ride in the basket. Of course, for real mushing, or anything remotely like it, you have to be here in the winter. **Birch Trails Sled Dog Tours,** 22719 Robinson St., Chugiak, AK 99567 (☎ **907/688-5713**), specializes in winter trips from their bed-and-breakfast 14 miles from Anchorage; if you have the time, they'll teach you to drive the team. **Mush A Dog Team** (☎ **907/688-1391**) offers a summer one-hour tour with gold panning for $25, and winter trips by appointment; they're located in Eagle River, on Hillcrest Drive, off the Glenn Highway South Birchwood exit. **Alaska Sightseeing Cruise West** (☎ **907/276-1305,** or 800/666-7375) has week-long packages to Anchorage for the Fur Rendezvous or Iditarod race.

FISHING   There are salmon, stocked and natural, in some of Anchorage's streams, and stocked trout in some lakes. Although it may not be the wilderness experience you've dreamed about, pulling in a 40-pound king under a highway bridge on Ship Creek may make up for it. From downtown, just walk down the hill to the railroad yard; fishing is best on a rising tide, and you'll need serious boots for the muddy banks. You can also catch stocked silver salmon in Campbell Creek and Bird Creek, in the late summer and fall. The **Alaska Department of Fish and Game** has a recorded information line on what's hot (☎ **907/349-4687**); for information on regulations or more detailed advice, call, write, or visit their office at 333 Raspberry Rd., Anchorage, AK 99518-1599 (☎ **907/267-2218**).

Serious fishermen will use Anchorage as a base, for a ✪ **fly-in fishing trip** on a remote lake or river all your own, or to go somewhere else in the state. Several companies offer fly-in trips; two of the largest and best established are **Ketchum Air Service** (☎ **907/243-5525,** or 800/433-9114) and **Rust's Flying Service** (☎ **907/243-1595** or 800/544-2299). They can take you out guided or on your own, just for the day or to stay for a while in a cabin. You can bring your own gear or they can provide it. You don't have to be an avid fisherman to enjoy one of these trips—there's nothing like the silence that falls as the float plane that dropped you off disappears over the horizon. Prices start around $200 per person for an unguided day trip.

If you want to be absolutely certain you're where the fish are when you're in Alaska, **Sport Fishing Alaska,** 1401 Shore Dr., Anchorage, AK 99515 (☎ **907/344-8674**), is an agency run by a former state fish biologist which, for a $95 fee, plans fishing vacations to Alaska.

FLIGHTSEEING   Small planes are the blood cells of Alaska's circulatory system, and Anchorage its heart. There are several busy airports in Anchorage, and Lake Hood is the world's busiest float-plane base. There are more than two dozen operators anxious to take you on a flightseeing tour—check the visitor center for names—but the most comfortable and memorable is probably the restored DC-3 operated by ✪ **Era Aviation** (☎ **907/248-4422,** or 800/866-8394). The plane re-creates the classic days of air travel—you can pretend to be Ingrid Bergman or Spencer Tracy while gazing out the oversize windows at a glacier. The daily summer flights from the South Airpark, off Raspberry Road, go to Mount McKinley for two hours for

$185 or to Prince William Sound for 90 minutes for $130; the route is tailored to the weather and viewing opportunities. Or for an even more unorthodox aircraft, try a champagne hot-air-balloon ride over the city at sunrise or sunset with **Hot Air Affair** (☎ **907/349-7333**).

GOLF   There are four courses in Anchorage and two in the Matanuska Valley, north of the city. The municipal **Anchorage Golf Course** (☎ **907/522-3363**), which has a good restaurant for dinner, O'Malley's on the Green, is on O'Malley Road near the zoo, uphill from the New Seward Highway.

RAFTING   There are several white-water rivers around Anchorage. **Nova Raft and Adventure Tours** (☎ **907/745-5753**) is a large, experienced operator offering multiday trips all over the state, and four different half-day floats in the Anchorage area, ranging from relatively easy-going Class II and III rapids on the Matanuska River to the Class IV and V white water of Six-Mile Creek, for which you may be required to prove your swimming ability before you can get in the boat. Self-paddling is an option on some trips. The half-day trips range in price from $50 to $125. **Eagle River Raft Trips** (☎ **907/333-3001**) offers access to the Eagle River, near Anchorage. Experts can float the river unguided; contact Alaska State Parks at the Eagle River Visitor Center or the Chugach State Park headquarters, listed above, for information and necessary warnings.

SKIING   Anchorage has three downhill ski areas: The **Alyeska Resort,** listed below, with Girdwood, is a destination; **Alpenglow** is a good local ski area above the treeline; and **Hillside** is a good place to learn to ski. The latter two are listed above in the Chugach Mountains Hillside Park sections. For Nordic skiing, Kincaid Park and Hillside Park, described above, are excellent. The bike trails are flat but convenient. Russian Jack Springs Park is right in town, at DeBarr and Boniface, and has a nice warm-up chalet.

SPECTATOR SPORTS

Anchorage has two ✪ **semi-pro baseball** teams, with college athletes playing short midsummer seasons: the **Anchorage Glacier Pilots** (☎ **907/274-3627**) and the **Anchorage Bucs** (☎ **907/272-2827**). If you've never been to a minor-league game, go—it's a blast. The quality may be uneven, but you may see diamonds in the rough: Tommy Seaver, Dave Winfield, Barry Bonds, and Wally Joyner all started out here. Check the *Anchorage Daily News* for game times; Mulcahy Stadium is at 16th Avenue and A Street, a long walk or a short drive from downtown; tickets are cheap. Dress warmly for evening games. A weekend day game is warmer, but then you won't get to see baseball played at night without lights.

The **University of Alaska–Anchorage** fields an NCAA Division I **hockey** team, the Seawolves, which plays at the Sullivan Arena (see "Anchorage in the Evening," below). The men's **basketball** team hosts a major Division I preseason tournament over Thanksgiving weekend, the **Great Alaska Shoot-Out,** and plays the regular season at the Sullivan Arena and at the University Sports Center, on campus on Providence Drive. Tickets are available from Carrs Tix (☎ **907/263-2787** or 800/478-7328).

WHERE TO STAY

Rooms can be hard to find in Anchorage in the summer—just how overheated the market is can be judged by the fact that winter rates are generally less than half the summer rates. I've provided full listings for my top recommendations in each price category below, but Anchorage also has almost all the chains and they all have the standard rooms you'd find anywhere in the country. At the top of the quality range downtown, there's the large **Anchorage Hilton** (☎ **907/272-7411** or 800/ 245-2527); at the **Sheraton Anchorage** (☎ **907/276-8700**), you'll save a little for being a few blocks off the downtown core. Also downtown, you're safe with the **Comfort Inn Heritage Suites** (☎ **907/277-6887**), with a swimming pool; the **Days Inn** (☎ **907/276-7226**), which has a courtesy van to the airport and many ameni- ties; the **Holiday Inn of Anchorage** (☎ **907/279-8671**), also with a pool; and the **Westmark Anchorage** (☎ **907/276-7676**) and **Westmark Inn** (☎ **907/ 272-7561**). Near the airport are the **Regal Alaskan** (☎ **907/243-2300** or 800/ 544-0553), **Super 8 Motel of Anchorage** (☎ **907/276-8884**), and the **West Coast International Inn** (☎ **907/243-3796**). The **Best Western Golden Lion,** at New Seward Highway and 36th Avenue (☎ **907/561-1522**), is located on the way into town from the south.

The **bed tax** in Anchorage is 8%.

VERY EXPENSIVE

Anchorage Hotel. 330 E St., Anchorage, AK 99501. ☎ **907/272-4553**, or 800/544-0988. Fax 907/277-4483. 21 rms, 5 suites. TV TEL. High season, $179–$189 double. Low season, $75–$95 double. $199–$209 suite. Additional person in room $10 extra. AE, CB, DC, DISC, MC, V.

The oldest hotel in Anchorage, recently renovated in an understated Old Anchorage decor, may not have the facilities to objectively justify the high rates, but something about the intimate, European style of the place keeps a loyal band of supporters com- ing back and swearing by it. The suites are really just larger rooms with more features. The hotel offers continental breakfast and complimentary newspapers; rooms with kitchenettes are available. The location is prime. The **Rumrunners** bar has live rhythm and blues without a cover charge.

✪ **Hotel Captain Cook.** Fifth Ave. and K St. (P.O. Box 102280), Anchorage, AK 99510-2280. ☎ **907/276-6000** or 800/843-1950, 800/478-3100 in Alaska. Fax 907/278-5366. 566 rms, 77 suites. TV TEL. High season, $200–$255 double; $275–$1,500 suite. Low season, $125–$155 double; $175–$1,500 suite. Additional person in room $10 extra. AE, DC, DISC, JCB, MC, V.

This is Alaska's great, grand hotel, where the rock stars stay. Former Gov. Wally Hickel built the hotel to demonstrate his commitment to the state's future after the 1964 earthquake. Today its three red towers, up to 20 stories tall, help define the skyline. Inside, the decor has a fully realized (maybe a little excessive) nautical theme, with art memorializing Cook's voyages and enough teak to build a square-rigger. The standard rooms are large and sumptuous, with great views from all sides; you don't pay more to be higher. A 1,700-square-foot suite was recently remodeled at a cost of $110,000. The lobby contains 16 shops, and there's a concierge, tour desks, barbershop and beauty salon, and business center. The full-service health club in the basement, with a decent-sized pool, racquetball court, and golf simulator, is popular with locals.

There are four restaurants, each with its own kitchen, and four lounges. **The Crows Nest,** at the top of the highest tower, is the city's finest restaurant, in the old-fashioned, formal style; the dining room is well divided to lend intimacy to the many booths and has stupendous views in all directions. The wine steward is dean of local oenophiles. Main courses range from $21 to $30, or there's a nightly fixed-price menu. **Fletcher's,** off the lobby, is an English pub serving good Italian-style pizza and sandwiches.

EXPENSIVE

Best Western Barratt Inn. 4616 Spenard Rd., Anchorage, AK 99517. ☎ **907/249-4909** or 800/221-7550. Fax 907/249-4917. 217 rms. TV TEL. High season, $109–$156 double.

Low season, $56–$98 double. Additional person in room $10 extra. AE, CB, DC, DISC, ER, JCB, MC, V.

This is a reliable airport hotel, a mile from the terminal—not convenient to downtown or the sights, but it has a van that will take you down to the downtown train depot. The rooms are standard for a good chain, with business-traveler features such as voice mail and a modem-compatible phone system. The prices in the restaurant are reasonable. Extras include Spectravision movies, concierge, exercise room, and free coffee in the lobby; laundry service and kitchenettes are available.

Inlet Tower Suites. 1200 L St., Anchorage, AK 99501. ☎ **907/276-0110** or 800/544-0786. Fax 907/258-4914. 158 rms, 22 suites. TV TEL. High season, $125–$145 double; $160–$175 suite. Low season, $64–$105 double; $84–$125 suite. Additional person in room $10 extra. AE, DC, DISC, ER, JCB, MC, V.

A 14-floor concrete building in a pleasant, older residential neighborhood eight blocks from the downtown core, this hotel is unique in that every room has a kitchenette—unusual in a high-rise with good views in every direction. Rooms above the ninth floor cost a little more. All the rooms are spacious and light, and the large, two-room suites would be comfortable for two couples. The hotel has a complex rate structure for various room types and five different times of year. Extras include refrigerators, microwave ovens and wet bars, courtesy van, coin-op laundry, beauty salon, exercise room, and sauna.

✪ **The Voyager Hotel.** 501 K St., Anchorage, AK 99501. ☎ **907/277-9501** or 800/247-9070. Fax 907/274-0333. 38 rms. TV TEL. High season, $149 double. Low season, $79–$99 double. Additional person in room $10 extra. AE, DC, DISC, JCB, MC, V.

Everything about the Voyager is just right: the small size; the central location; the large, light rooms, all with kitchens; the exceptional housekeeping; and the warm yet highly professional hospitality. There's nothing ostentatious or outwardly remarkable about the hotel, yet the most experienced travelers rave about it the loudest. No smoking.

MODERATE

🅢 **Bonanza Lodge.** 4455 Juneau St., Anchorage, AK 99503. ☎ **907/563-3590** or 800/478-3590. Fax 907/563-5560. 48 suites. TV TEL. Aug, $90 suite for two. Rest of high season, $80 suite for two. Low season, $55 suite for two. Additional person in room $10 extra. AE, CB, DC, DISC, MC, V.

Located in midtown, somewhat convenient to the airport but not the sights, this comfortable, family hotel is a converted three-story apartment building. All rooms are suites with full kitchens and large balconies. The site is in a largely industrial area, but it's completely screened by trees and nicely landscaped. Suites where smoking and pets are permitted are available; others are nonallergenic. The staff is friendly and competent, and the proprietors don't realize how reasonable their rates are in this market. There's a coin-op laundry and free coffee in the lobby.

✪ **Snowshoe Inn.** 826 K St., Anchorage, AK 99501. ☎ **907/258-SNOW** (258-7669). Fax 907/258-SHOE (258-7463). 14 rms, 6 with bath. TV TEL. High season, $80 double without bath, $90–$100 double with bath. Low season, $40 double without bath, $50–$60 double with bath. Rates include continental breakfast. Additional person in room $5 extra. CB, DC, DISC, MC, V.

Hardworking Norbert and Monique Lague's little hotel on a quiet downtown street is so clean it feels like you're the first one ever to stay there. The rooms are comfortable, light, and attractively decorated in bright fabrics. There are only two rooms for each shared bathroom and they couldn't be closer or more secure. There's no better bargain downtown. No smoking.

INEXPENSIVE

⑤ **Hillside Hotel and RV Park.** 2150 Gambell St., Anchorage, AK 99503. ☎ **907/ 258-6006** or 800/478-6008. Fax 907/279-8972. 27 rms. TV TEL. High season, $59–$84 double. Low season, $49–$69 double. Additional person in room $5 extra. AE, DISC, MC, V.

It looks grim from the outside, and the location, next to a busy highway in a low-rent commercial area, could be better, but once you're inside there's nothing to complain about, even without considering the low price. The rooms I saw were clean and well maintained and had features—like microwaves and refrigerators—you rarely see in this price range. The RV park is $20 with full hookups. There are coffee machines in the rooms and the lobby, and a coin-op laundry is available.

Inlet Inn Downtown. 539 H St., Anchorage, AK 99501. ☎ **907/277-5541.** Fax 907/ 277-3108. 87 rms. TV TEL. High season, $60–$80 double. Low season, $40–$50 double. Additional person in room $5 extra. AE, DC, DISC, MC, V.

The lobby and hallways of this old, concrete hotel are frankly seedy, but the rooms themselves, decorated in pink, were clean and well maintained when I visited. Although small, they're centrally located downtown and a good deal at the price. A couple can sleep in a room with one bed and pay only $60 in the high season. A courtesy van is available.

BED-AND-BREAKFASTS

There are probably hundreds of B&Bs in Anchorage, a reaction to a hot market for rooms that hasn't been satisfied by the regular hotels—it can be nearly impossible to find a hotel room at the height of the summer. Bed-and-breakfasts have become pretty sophisticated, most going far beyond the old idea of just renting out the spare room; some people are making it their livelihood. You can almost always get a better rate, and often a better room, at a B&B than at a hotel, and you'll learn more about Alaska by meeting your hosts.

I've listed only three B&Bs, to show the range of choices and to highlight some of the best. There are so many others that smart operators are catering to their own, narrow niches: **Moosewood Bed and Breakfast** (☎ **907/345-8788**), up in the mountains, has thought of every luxury that can be provided for vegetarians and people with disabilities; **Anna's Bed and Breakfast** (☎ **907/338-5331**) has bilingual hosts catering to German speakers; the host at the **Bering Bridge Bed and Breakfast** (☎ **907/272-0327**) speaks Russian and Hebrew; and **Arctic Feather B & B** (☎ **907/277-3862**) caters to gays and lesbians.

There also are several booking agencies that can put you together with the right bed-and-breakfast. **Alaska Private Lodgings,** P.O. Box 200047, Anchorage, AK 99520-0047 (☎ **907/258-1717;** fax 907/258-6613), is the most established of the agencies. It has a downtown office, below the 4th Avenue Theater, on Fourth Avenue between F and G streets. The **Bed and Breakfast Association of Alaska,** Anchorage Chapter, P.O. Box 242623, Anchorage, AK 99524-2623 (☎ **907/561-6652**), runs a **B&B Hotline** (☎ **907/272-5909**), which puts callers directly in touch with operators who have rooms open for the night; and they publish a B&B catalog of members.

✪ **Aurora Winds B&B Resort.** 7501 Upper O'Malley Rd., Anchorage, AK 99516. ☎ **907/ 346-2533.** Fax 907/346-3192. 5 rms. TV TEL. High season, $125–$195 double. Low season, $85–$135 double. Rates include full breakfast. Additional person in room $15 extra in high season, $10 extra in low season. AE, DC, DISC, MC, V.

The rooms in this massive house far up the hillside in South Anchorage are so grand and theatrically decorated you'll feel as if you're in a James Bond movie. The upstairs living room has a white stone fireplace (one of four) and a matching white grand piano. The downstairs theater has a saltwater tank containing a leopard shark. Each room has a sitting area and such other details as a second phone line so you can dial up the Internet and talk at the same time. But the McKinley Suite is downright incredible: It has an outfitted computer room and a palatial bathroom with a Jacuzzi and an "environmental habitat chamber." Extras for all guests include VCRs, an outdoor Jacuzzi hot tub, an exercise room, and a sauna.

✪ **The Oscar Gill House Bed and Breakfast.** 1344 W. 10th Ave. (P.O. Box 200047), Anchorage, AK 99520-0047. ☎ **907/258-1717.** Fax 907/258-6613. 3 rms, 1 with bath. TEL. High season, $75 double without bath, $95 double with bath. Low season, $65 double without bath, $75 double with bath. Rates include full breakfast. Additional person in room $10 extra. AE, MC, V (5% surcharge).

On the Delany Park strip, just a few blocks from downtown, this is truly the oldest house in Anchorage—because it was build in 1913, in Knik, before Anchorage was founded, and moved here on a barge a few years later. Oscar Gill was an early civic leader. The house was to be torn down in 1982, but was moved to storage by a historic preservation group; Mark and Susan Lutz saved it in 1994, moving it to its present location and, with their own labor, restoring it authentically as a cozy, friendly bed-and-breakfast. The house is full of appropriate antiques; it's a classic B&B experience. Free laundry machines available.

Sixth and B Bed and Breakfast. 145 W. Sixth Ave., Anchorage, AK 99501. ☎ **907/279-5293.** Fax 907/279-8338. 3 rms, 1 with bath. TV. High season, $78 double without bath, $98 double with bath. Low season, $38 double without bath, $58 double with bath. Rates include breakfast. Additional person in room $10 extra. AE, DISC, MC, V.

Right downtown, this is a fun, masculine place (yet clean and elegantly decorated) run by T-shirt and bike-rental entrepreneur Peter Roberts, his friendly black dog, Onyx, and perhaps a friend or two. For breakfast and snacks, there's free run of the food in the refrigerator. There are VCRs, free bikes and tennis racquets, and free laundry machines. Tommy Moe helped mount the "Far From Fenway Fan Club" flagpole; fortunately, neither the Red Sox curse nor his cries of "Oh, my back!" as he lifted it jinxed his subsequent Olympic gold medal in downhill skiing in 1994.

A HOSTEL

Hostelling International, Anchorage. 700 H St., Anchorage, AK 99501. ☎ **907/272-3635.** Fax 907/276-7772. 4 rms, 95 beds. $46 double; $15 bed for members, $18 for nonmembers. MC, V.

The main hostel is quite central, next to the transit center. Despite its size, it fills up in the summer and reservations are necessary. The backpackers' shuttle stops here, providing access to Denali National Park, the Whittier train shuttle, and the best of Southcentral's trails. A coin-op laundry, kitchen, and baggage storage are available. The office is open daily from 8am to noon and 5pm to midnight.

CAMPING

Anchorage is a big city—for a real camping experience, you need to head out of town. The 27-site State Parks' **Bird Creek Campground,** 25 miles south on the Seward Highway, is one of my favorites, next to Turnagain Arm. There are a couple of large Forest Service campgrounds near **Portage Glacier,** 50 miles south. Both agencies charge $8 a night. State Parks also has a 50-site campground in **Eagle River,** which costs $15; take the Hiland Road exit 12 miles from Anchorage on the Glenn Highway.

Within the Anchorage bowl there are several camper and RV parks. The munici-
pally owned **Centennial Camper Park** is near the Muldoon Road exit on the Glenn
Highway (☎ 907/333-9711 or 907/343-6397), just as you enter town from the
north. It has 80 dry sites; there's a dump station and free showers. Camping permits
are $13 a night. The **Ship Creek Landings Downtown RV Park,** in the railroad
industrial area down the bluff from downtown (☎ 907/277-0877), is the most
centrally located camping area. The **Hillside Motel and RV Park,** listed above, has
RV parking. Also, in recent years hundreds of RVs have parked in Walmart and
K-mart parking lots, especially off Dimond Boulevard in South Anchorage; as of this
writing, the stores didn't mind and RVers had created little summer communities on
the fields of asphalt.

WHERE TO EAT

Besides the sit-down restaurants listed below, there's lots of good take-out fast food
in Anchorage. (Of course, all the franchise places also are represented.) The best, most
original burgers are at **Arctic Roadrunner,** with locations on Arctic Boulevard at
Fireweed Lane and on Old Seward Highway at International Airport Road. **The
Lucky Wishbone,** at 1033 E. Fifth Ave., has the best fried chicken in town, and
great, old-fashioned milkshakes—they have a drive-through, but eat in for the
classic diner atmosphere, smoke free. The best deli, with legendary sandwiches, is
Atlasta Deli, in the shopping mall at Arctic Boulevard and Tudor Road; it's really
a gourmet experience, with over 100 meats and cheeses, and you can eat in. The best
(American-style) deep-fried burritos come from a van parked near the corner of
Benson Boulevard and Seward Highway, **Benny's Food Wagon** (it's been parked
there or nearby for at least 20 years). For sit-down, American-style Mexican fast food,
Taco King, at Northern Lights Boulevard and C Street, provides the best deal—a
tasty, filling meal is as little as $3.50. You won't find better **Asian take-out** than that
served by the van that parks in front of the Arco Building, at Seventh Avenue and
G Street, during the lunch hour. Anchorage is short on good Chinese food, but the
Fu-Do Chinese Restaurant, at 2600 E. Tudor Rd. (☎ 907/561-6611), is better
than most, and will deliver orders of $15 or more. The best pizza in town is made
at **Sorrento's,** 610 E. Fireweed Lane (☎ 907/278-3439), though their delivery is
awfully slow; **Omega Pizza** (☎ 907/272-6007) is also very good and faster.
Roscoe's Skyline Diner, 601 Hollywood Dr. (turn right after crossing the A and
C Street bridge over Ship Creek to Government Hill), has the best soul food and
barbecue in town.

In addition, there are coffee houses all over the city where people go for a cup of
java, a pastry, and to meet people and engage in conversation. They've become the
new agora of social interaction. The **Java Joint,** at Northern Lights and Spenard, is
the bohemian young people's hangout, with poetry readings and folk music. **Cafe del
Mundo,** at several locations downtown and at Northern Lights and Denali in
midtown, gathers an older crowd of business people, yuppies, stay-at-home parents,
and anyone else looking for a comfortable meeting place. **Side Street Espresso,** on
G between 4th and 5th, brings together artists, radicals, and other people who want
to trade ideas. And there are many others, each with its own personality—explore.

You'll find a good selection of formal restaurants in Anchorage, too. I've limited
myself to a few of the best, trying to provide choices of national cuisine and
location. I've left out a great many good restaurants, so please don't treat this list
as all-inclusive.

DOWNTOWN
Expensive
Club Paris. 417 W. Fifth Ave. ☎ **907/277-6332.** Reservations recommended. Main courses $14–$44; lunch $5.75–$15. AE, DISC, MC, V. Daily 11:30am–2:30pm and 5–11pm.

Walking from a bright spring afternoon, under a neon Eiffel Tower, into midnight darkness, past a smoke-enshrouded bar, and sitting down at a secretive booth for two, I felt as if I should lean across the table and plot a shady 1950s oil deal with my companion. And I would probably not have been the first. Club Paris will be too authentic for some, but it's the essence of old Anchorage boomtown years, when the streets were dusty and an oil man needed a class joint in which to do business. Beef, of course, is what to order, and it'll be done right. Full liquor license.

The Corsair. 944 W. Fifth Ave. ☎ **907/278-4502.** Reservations recommended. Main courses $22–$38. AE, DC, DISC, MC, V. Mon–Sat 5–pm.

This dark, nautical-theme restaurant with high-backed booths that wrap 270° around corner tables is the perfect place for a romantic rendezvous. The continental cuisine is consistently excellent and the award-winning wine list is the size of a phone book—there's a tasting on Tuesday night. Thursday night there's a special German menu. Meals unfold slowly—take someone you want to spend time with. Full liquor license.

✪ **The Marx Brothers Cafe.** 627 W. Third Ave. ☎ **907/278-2133.** Reservations recommended. Main courses $19.50–$28.50. AE, DC, MC, V. Daily 6–9:30pm.

A restaurant that began as a hobby among three friends nearly 20 years ago is still a labor of love, and has become a standard of excellence in the state. Dinner takes all night—you feel funny not ordering an appetizer—but you can spend the time watching chef Jack Amon pick herbs and vegetables for your meal from the garden behind the historic little building, one of the city's first houses. The cuisine is varied and creative, ranging from Asian to Italian, but everyone orders the Caesar salad made at the table by Van, one of the founders—he occasionally teaches Caesar salad workshops on the sidewalk outside. The decor and style are studied casual elegance. Beer and wine license.

✪ **Simon and Seafort's Saloon and Grill.** 120 L St. ☎ **907/274-3502.** Reservations essential. Lunch/dinner $14–$35. AE, MC, V. Daily 11:15am–2:30pm and 4:30–10:30pm.

Simon's, as it's known, is a jolly beef and seafood grill where hearty voices boom off the high ceilings and brass turn-of-the-century saloon decor. On sunny summer evenings the rooms fill with light off Cook Inlet, down below the bluff; the views are magnificent. After work on Friday, the well-stocked bar fills with young lawyers and other well-off downtown workers. To enjoy the ambience cheaply, order a sandwich and soup in the bar. In summer you'll wait all night for a table in the restaurant if you don't make reservations, preferably a few days in advance. Once there, I've never been disappointed by the salmon or prime rib, or anything else on the menu; the service is always efficient and highly professional. Full liquor license.

Moderate
Kumagoro. 533 W. Fourth Ave. ☎ **907/272-9905.** Main courses $11.80–$35; lunch $5.50–$13. AE, DC, DISC, JCB, MC, V. Daily 11am–10pm.

Anchorage has a lot of good, authentic Japanese restaurants, but this one, right on the main tourist street downtown, has the added advantage of convenience. The dining room is pleasantly low-key. The sushi is good enough to bring a friend of mine who is a Japanese food fanatic across town during his lunch hour. Beer and wine license.

☻ **Sacks Cafe.** 625 W. Fifth Ave. ☎ **907/274-4022.** Reservations not accepted. Main courses $12–$19.50; lunch $4.50–$9. AE, MC, V. Sun–Thurs 11am–10pm, Fri–Sat 11am–11pm.

We like to come here for a special meal because the food is creative and occasionally inspired, but the atmosphere is light and arty and the prices reasonable. There are only a few tables and the whole southern wall is glass—on a sunny afternoon the patrons themselves sometimes cook. At times the place takes itself a bit too seriously, but the (seasonal) mussels in white wine will make you forgive anything. A friend who set out to find the best sandwich in Anchorage found it here. Not a great place for kids, as you'll constantly worry about something getting broken, nor for large parties, as it won't take reservations and it tacks on an automatic gratuity. Beer and wine license.

Thai Cuisine. 440 H St. ☎ **907/277-8424.** Main courses $7–$23; lunch $6.50–$8. AE, MC, V. Mon–Sat 11am–10pm, Sun 4–10pm.

Anchorage has a lot of excellent Thai food. This may not be the best, but it's very good and has a convenient downtown location. The dining room has a light, clean feel and is popular for lunch. The spicy dishes are for those with a high pain threshold. Beer and wine license.

Inexpensive

Dianne's Restaurant. 550 W. Seventh Ave., Suite 110. ☎ **907/279-7243.** All items $4–$8. MC, V. Mon–Fri 7am–4pm.

Located in the base of a tall, glass office building, Dianne's has developed such a reputation for great baking, soups, sandwiches, and specials that at lunch hour it's clogged with people in suits and dresses. The line at the cafeteria moves fast, however, and the bright, casual atmosphere is fun and full of energy. My first choice for a healthy lunch downtown. No liquor license.

Downtown Deli and Cafe. 525 W. Fourth Ave. ☎ **907/276-7116.** All items $5–$12. AE, DC, MC, V. Daily 6am–9:30pm.

Tony Knowles made his Fourth Avenue sandwich restaurant the place to meet local politicians and people-in-the-know 20 years ago; when he was elected governor in 1994, President Clinton came for dinner. I didn't believe Clinton, however, when he said he enjoyed the reindeer stew—I found it fatty and floury. Stick with the generous sandwiches, good bouillabaisse, and traditional deli selections. Of late, the place has been so overrun with tourists that service has suffered, although I've never waited long enough to spoil my meal. Prices are reasonable, especially for dinner, when downtown is short on inexpensive sit-down places. Kids are treated well. Beer and wine license.

BEYOND DOWNTOWN

Expensive

☻ **Jens' Restaurant.** 701 W. 36th Ave. ☎ **907/561-5367.** Reservations recommended. Main courses $18–$22; lunch $7.50–$12.50. AE, CB, DC, DISC, MC, V. Mon 11:30am–2pm, Tues–Fri 11:30am–2pm and 6–10pm, Sat 6–10pm. Closed Jan.

This restaurant in a Spenard strip mall is an improbable playground for renowned chef Jens Hansen, who closes his doors each January to go on a gastronomic working vacation to exotic places. When we visited he was just back from Australia and a stew with emu and kangaroo meat was on the menu; earlier, he went through an insect thing. Other than the traditional Danish dishes served for lunch, the menu is French influenced and new every night. Hansen presides with a booming Scandinavian accent over the cognoscenti of Anchorage, which on a random night could include the newspaper editor, police chief, Catholic archbishop, and a group of Hell's Angels. Some nonmembers of the in-crowd feel slighted, and kids don't belong—highchairs are not available. Beer and wine license.

Moderate

✪ **Campo Bello.** 661 W. 36th, Suite 10. ☎ **907/563-2040.** Main courses $9–$16; lunch $7–$10. MC, V. Mon–Fri 11:30am–2:30pm and 5:30–9:30pm, Sat 5:30–9:30pm. From downtown, take C Street to 36th Avenue and turn right.

This midtown restaurant has sophisticated Italian cuisine in a low-key setting, with wonderfully hospitable service and low prices. It stands with the best of Alaska's restaurants, but charges half of what you would pay in a comparable establishment. The wild-mushroom cannelloni and calamari scaloppine were very good. Beer and wine license.

The Greek Corner Restaurant. 302 W. Fireweed Lane. ☎ **907/276-2820.** Main courses $11–$15; lunch $5–$9. MC, V. Mon–Thurs 11am–10pm, Fri–Sat 11am–11pm, Sun 4–10pm. From downtown, take C Street and turn right on Fireweed Lane.

An informal, family-operated Greek place on a busy commercial street in midtown. You're made to feel welcome, the service is quick, and the food is very reasonably priced. It's agreeably and comfortably low rent. Beer and wine license.

Harry's Restaurant and Bar. 101 W. Northern Lights Blvd. ☎ **907/561-5317.** Reservations recommended. Main courses $6.25–$17; lunch $6.25–$8. AE, DC, DISC, MC, V. Mon–Thurs 11am–10pm, Fri–Sat 11am–11pm, Sun 10am–9pm (brunch 10am–2pm). From downtown, take C Street to Northern Lights Boulevard and turn left; you can park in the bank parking lot on the immediate left.

Harry's strikes that nice balance by which you feel like you're in a nice sit-down restaurant for dinner, but you don't feel funny about ordering a burger, of which there's a large selection. The decor is dark wood, like a classic tavern, and the bar has 20 brews on tap, but that doesn't dominate; it's a good place to take children. The food is consistent but not particularly inspired. Full liquor license.

Mexico in Alaska. 7305 Old Seward Hwy. ☎ **907/349-1528.** Main courses $9–$16.75; lunch $7.95. AE, MC, V. Mon–Fri 11am–10pm, Sat noon–10pm, Sun 4–9pm. From downtown, take Gambell Street south (it becomes New Seward Highway); then continue on Old Seward Highway, which runs parallel on the right south of 36th Avenue.

Since 1972 serving strictly traditional, authentic cuisine of central-west Mexico—no American style, ever!—Maria-Elena Ball and her restaurant in South Anchorage have become a local institution, with regulars so devoted they loaned her large sums when her business got in trouble in the mid-1980s recession. Ball's hospitality is as famous as her food. The prices are reasonable. Beer and wine license.

Sourdough Mining Company. 1225 E. International Airport Rd. ☎ **907/563-2272.** Main courses $11–$31.75; lunch $7–$14. AE, DISC, MC, V. Mon–Sat 11am–11pm, Sun 10am–11pm.

Masses of people, many on package tours, flow through this huge, gold-mine-theme restaurant. The food is adequate, but the whole experience suffers from an assembly-line feeling. Full liquor license.

ANCHORAGE IN THE EVENING

THE PERFORMING ARTS Anchorage has become an ever-more-frequent destination for major popular and classical music performers; of course, the arts season begins in the fall and ends in the spring, but traveling performers often come through in the summer as well. Pick up a copy of the Friday edition of the *Anchorage Daily News* for current event listings in the "8" section; it's also for sale separately in boxes around town all week. (Kim Severson's restaurant reviews also are sophisticated and useful.)

The **Anchorage Symphony** has reached a second-tier level. There's also an opera company and the **Anchorage Concert Association,** which promotes a schedule of international-caliber music and other performing arts. The **Anchorage Festival of Music** presents a summer program of visiting classical musicians. And Anchorage has lots of community theater and limited professional theater, including the experimental, semiprofessional **Out North Theater.**

Most large events take place at one of two venues. The ✪ **Anchorage Center for the Performing Arts,** at 621 W. Sixth Ave., on town square, has three beautiful theaters ranging in size from 350 to 2,000 seats. A ticket office in the lobby is operated by **Carrs Tix** (☎ **907/263-2787,** or 800/478-7328), the main ticket agency in town, which is associated with Carrs grocery stores and has outlets at each store. Popular music and other large-venue performances take place at the 8,500-seat **Sullivan Arena,** at 16th Avenue and Gambell Street (New Seward Highway); call 907/279-2596 for a recorded listing of events.

JoAnne and Monty's Alaska Show (☎ **907/257-5600** or 907/278-8813) takes place nightly in the summer at the historic 4th Avenue Theater (see "A Stroll Around Downtown Anchorage" under "Exploring Anchorage," above). The warm musical performance introduces visitors to Alaska. It's a dinner show, with a buffet, and costs only $19.95. Dinner is served starting at 5pm. ✪ **Cyrano's Off Center Playhouse** is a small theater at Fourth Avenue and D Street that presents more challenging, intimate work, poetry readings, comedy, and lectures. The theater is connected to an excellent bookstore and cafe; it's a meeting place for the local art and literary community.

NIGHTCLUBS & BARS   For a fun, funny night out, nothing in town compares to ✪ **Mr. Whitekeys' Fly By Night Club,** on Spenard Road south of Northern Lights Boulevard (☎ **907/279-SPAM**). This drinking establishment seems to be an excuse for the goateed proprietor, a consummate vulgarian, to ridicule Anchorage in his crude, political, local-humor musical comedy shows, in which he co-stars with a fallen former Miss Anchorage. If you can laugh at dog poop, you'll love it. As Whitekeys accurately says in his press release, "Although the Whale Fat Follies has been featured in the worldwide media . . . it's still just a sleazy little show with cheap costumes, cheesy special effects, and a cast which is not qualified to work anywhere else in America." The summer show is at 8pm Tuesday through Saturday; tickets are $11, and reservations are necessary well in advance. After the show, the Fabulous Spamtones perform for dancing, with a guy on horns who can make his lips sound just like a horn even though he doesn't have one. Whitekeys, as you may suspect by now, is obsessed with Spam, but of late the Spam-heavy menu has been augmented by excellent food prepared by a serious chef.

The largest bar in town is **Chilkoot Charlie's,** at Spenard Road and Fireweed Lane (☎ **907/272-1010**), yet on the weekend the place is packed and there are lines for the 657-person standing-room capacity. There are three stages with live rock music, generally of the Top-40 variety. The place can be a little claustrophobic when crowded, with the low ceilings and dark, log-cabin/roadhouse atmosphere, but it's much safer than in past years. The cover is $3 on weekends, $1 or $2 during the week. Another big singles dance club is **Top of the Rock,** downtown at Third Avenue and E Street. The **Long Branch Saloon,** on Dimond Boulevard east of New Seward Highway, has country music every night and great burgers and other beef.

To watch a game, try the **Sports Edition,** in the Anchorage Hilton Hotel at Third Avenue and E Street. If you just want to talk, **Darwin's Theory,** on H Street between Fourth and Fifth avenues, is an unpretentious hangout; **Humpy's,** at Sixth Avenue and F Street, has 36 beers on tap and decent bar food; **F Street Station,** on F Street near Third Avenue, has a nice brass-and-wood decor and a relaxed atmosphere; **Simon and Seafort's,** on L Street near Fifth Avenue, has a great view of the water, good sandwiches, a massive menu of single-malt scotches, and lots of lawyers and other professional people after work.

MOVIES   There are several multiplexes in Anchorage playing all the current Hollywood output; check the *Anchorage Daily News* for listings. There's no movie theater downtown, but the **Fireweed Theater,** at New Seward Highway (Gambell Street) and Fireweed Lane, is a short cab ride away, as is the second-run **Denali,** on Spenard Road near Northern Lights Boulevard. The ✪ **Capri Cinema and Hollywood Canteen** (☎ **907/561-0064**) is the only art-movie house, in a strip mall at 3425 E. Tudor Rd. (go east from New Seward Highway on Tudor, and look on the left past Lake Otis Road). The funky little place is a treat, showing foreign and avante-guard films, and catering to alternative lifestyles.

✪ A ROAD TRIP TO TURNAGAIN ARM & PORTAGE GLACIER

One of the world's great drives starts in Anchorage and leads roughly 50 miles south on the Seward Highway to Portage Glacier. It's the trip, not the destination, that makes it worthwhile. The two-lane highway along Turnagain Arm, chipped from the foot of the rocky Chugach Mountains, provides a platform to see a magnificent, ever-changing, mostly untouched landscape full of wildlife. I've listed the sights in the style of a highway log, for there are interesting stops all the way along the road. It will take at least half a day, and there's plenty to do for an all-day excursion. Use your head-lights for safety and be patient if you get stuck behind a summertime line of cars; if you pass, you'll just come up behind another line ahead.

There are lots of bus tours that follow the route and visit Portage Glacier (see "Getting Around" under "Essentials," above). **Gray Line** (☎ **907/277-5581**) offers a seven-hour trip that includes a stop in Girdwood and the boat ride on Portage Lake for $55, twice daily in summer.

POTTER MARSH   Heading south from Anchorage proper, the Seward Highway descends a bluff to cross a broad marsh formed by water impounded behind the tracks of the Alaska Railroad. The marsh has a boardwalk from which you can watch a huge variety of birds. Salad-green grasses grow from sparkling, pond-green water.

POTTER SECTION HOUSE   Located at the south end of Potter Marsh, the section house was an early maintenance station for the Alaska Railroad. Today it contains offices of Chugach State Park, open during normal business hours, and a small gift shop. A few old train cars and an interpretive display outside will briefly interest the kids. Just south of here, on the left, the **Turnagain Arm Trail** starts, leading above the highway 9 miles south; there are lots of access points along the way.

MCHUGH CREEK   Four miles south of Potter is a state park picnic area and a challenging hike with a 3,000-foot elevation gain to a mountain lake. Without climbing all the way, there are spectacular views within an hour of the road.

BELUGA POINT   When the state highway department put up scenic overlook signs on this pull-out, 1¹/₂ miles south of McHugh Creek, they weren't messing around. The terrain is simply awesome, as the highway traces the edge of Turnagain Arm, below the towering cliffs of the Chugach Mountains. If the tide and salmon runs are right, you may see beluga whales. Belugas chase the fish toward fresh water. Sometimes they overextend and strand themselves by the dozens in the receding tide, farther along. Stranding doesn't appear to hurt the whales.

WINDY POINT   Be on the lookout in this section, 4 miles south of Beluga Point, on the mountain side of the road, where Dall sheep are frequently seen picking their way along the cliffs. It's a unique spot, for they get much closer to people here than is usual in the wild; apparently, they know they're safe. Windy Point is the prime spot, but you have a decent chance of seeing sheep virtually anywhere along this stretch of road. If cars are stopped, that's probably why; get well off the road and pay attention to traffic, which still will be passing at high speeds.

You may also see windsurfers in the gray, silty waters of the Arm. They're crazy. The water is a mixture of glacial run-off and near-freezing ocean water. Besides, the movement of water that creates the 38-foot tidal difference causes riverlike currents, with standing waves. At times, rushing walls of water up to 6 feet high, called bore tides, form in the arm with the incoming tide. You need perfect timing or good luck to see a bore tide. They normally occur 45 minutes to two hours after low water in Anchorage, depending on where you are on the road during the times of the month with extreme tides; you can get a free tide book at city hall in Anchorage, or check the *Anchorage Daily News.*

INDIAN VALLEY   You can stop off at the Indian Gold Mine, a touristy attraction right on the road, or head a short distance up the dirt road that joins the highway to Indian Valley Meats, a sausage-making outfit that processes wild game. **Turnagain House** is a good steak and seafood restaurant, open in the evening. Up the road by the restaurant is the **Indian Valley** trailhead, a gold rush–era trail that ultimately leads to the other side of the mountains, after two or three days; of course, you don't have to go the whole way, and the path, while often muddy, rises to alpine terrain less steeply than other trails along the Arm. Indian Creek has trout and, late in the year, silver salmon.

BIRD CREEK   The creek, with good salmon fishing, is less than 2 miles beyond Indian. The **Bird Ridge Trail** comes first, a steep alpine climb with southern exposures that make it dry early in the year. An excellent state campground is on the right, over the water; it costs $8 per night. The most famous attraction of the settlement is a funky little bar called the **Bird House;** collectors of campy roadside experiences should stop. For the next few miles the road is in danger of winter avalanches; highway maintenance crews use artillery to knock down the snow.

THE FLATS   Nine miles beyond Bird Creek, the highway descends from the mountainside to the flats. At high tide, water comes right up to the highway. At low tide, the whole Arm narrows to a winding channel through the mud. Since the 1964 Good Friday earthquake, the Arm has not been navigable; before the earthquake, there was never much reason to navigate it. The first to try was Capt. James Cook, in 1778, as he was searching for the Northwest Passage on his final, fatal voyage of discovery (he was killed by Hawaiians later that year). He named this branch of Cook Inlet Turnagain Arm because he had to keep turning around in its narrow confines before it petered out.

TURN-OFF TO GIRDWOOD   Seven miles after descending to the flat is the intersection with the road to Girdwood. The attractions of the town (listed below under "A Side Trip to Girdwood and Mount Alyeska") are worth a visit, but the shopping center here at the intersection is not chief among them. It houses the **Alpine Diner,** a gas station, convenience store, gift shop, and **Taco's Mexican**

Restaurant. To the consternation of the owner of the mini-mall, this is the traditional highway potty-stop in a long stretch of road without facilities. He finally persuaded the municipality to install a sewer. The Alpine Diner is a good spot for bakery snacks and coffee to go. The sandwiches are large, but you pay a premium for the convenient location. The menu also includes pizza, pasta, and breakfast. If you're spending the time to sit down for a meal, think about driving a few miles up the road to Girdwood, where there are several exceptional restaurants.

OLD PORTAGE   All along the flats at the head of Turnagain Arm are large marshes full of birds and what looks like standing driftwood. These are trees killed by salt water that flowed in when the 1964 quake lowered the land as much as 10 feet. On the right, 9 miles beyond the turn-off for Girdwood and across the highway from the railroad stop where you board the train for Whittier, a few ruins of the abandoned town of Portage are still visible, more than 30 years after the great earthquake.

There is good birdwatching from the turn-outs, but don't think of venturing out on Turnagain Arm's tidal mud flats. They suck people up and drown them in the incoming tide. A woman died a few years ago in the arms of rescuers, who were not strong enough to pull her out of the quicksandlike mud as the water covered her.

BIG GAME ALASKA   A couple of years ago an entrepreneur fenced off about 20 acres of this glacial valley to display deer, moose, bison, reindeer, and caribou in a more spacious setting than the Alaska Zoo, which has a greater variety of animals. Turn right about 1^1/$_2$ miles past Old Portage. Visitors pick up a cassette tape and map and drive the short course looking at the animals. It's a sure-fire opportunity to get a picture of one of these beasts, if you don't consider it cheating. Children, who often have trouble picking out wildlife in a natural setting, may enjoy seeing the animals close up and are not likely to care that the experience isn't authentic. A large log gift shop includes among its wares frozen bison burger and caribou steak. Admission is $5 for adults, $3 for children 4 to 12. In summer, it's open daily from 10am to 8pm; in winter, Wednesday through Sunday from 10am to 5pm.

PORTAGE GLACIER   The receding Portage Glacier is a rare chance to see geologic time running faster than human time. That is to say, the name attraction at this, the most popular of all Alaska attractions, has largely melted, receding out of sight of the visitor center. When the center was built in 1985, Portage Glacier was predicted to keep depositing icebergs into its 800-foot-deep lake until the year 2020. Instead, it withdrew from the lake last year.

Even so, the $8 million the National Forest Service spent on the **Begich-Boggs Visitor Center** wasn't wasted, and neither is a trip to see where the glacier used to be. The center is a sort of glacier museum. If you're in Alaska any length of time, you'll likely be seeing a lot of glaciers, and this is an excellent place to learn about what you're looking at. There's also a film, shown throughout the day, called *Voices of the Ice*. If you really like it, you can buy a copy on videotape.

The center is named after Hale Boggs, who was majority leader in the U.S. House, and Rep. Nick Begich, Democrat from Alaska. They disappeared together in a small plane in 1972 during Begich's first reelection bid. The plane was never found, but Begich, even though declared dead, was reelected anyway. Later, his opponent, Republican Don Young, won a special election. Almost 25 years later, Young still represents Alaska as its only congressman.

The lake is a good place for kids to throw rocks in the water—after two generations the boys of our family have never tired of it. Forest rangers promise that there should always be a small berg to aim at even though the glacier has receded beyond the lake—but you know how good their predictions are. Several short trails start from the area of the center, including one that leads less than a mile to Byron Glacier, in case you're interested in getting up close to some ice. Always dress warmly, as cold winds are the rule in this funnel-like valley.

A **cruise boat** operated by Gray Line of Alaska (☎ 907/783-2983), under license with the Forest Service, traverses the lake hourly to get right up to Portage Glacier, ice conditions permitting; it costs $21. If this is your only chance to see a glacier in Alaska, it's probably a good choice; if your itinerary includes Columbia, Exit, or Mendenhall Glacier, Glacier Bay National Park, or any of the other accessible glaciers, you won't be as impressed by Portage.

A restaurant and gift shop called the Portage Lodge offers basic cafeteria sandwiches and a variety of gift wares ranging from expensive jewelry and animal pelts to plastic souvenirs. There are no lodgings in Portage, but **two Forest Service campgrounds**, Black Bear and Williwaw, are on the road to the visitor center, with 51 sites between them; at the more developed Williwaw Campground there's also a place to watch red salmon spawning, in mid-August (no fishing).

A SIDE TRIP TO GIRDWOOD & MOUNT ALYESKA

The Girdwood area—actually still part of the Municipality of Anchorage—is a small town on the threshold of turning into a major resort. Originally a mining community, and more recently a weekend skiing area for Anchorage, it still has a sleepy, offbeat character. Retired hippies, ski bums, and a few old-timers live in the houses and cabins among the big spruce trees in the valley below the Mount Alyeska ski resort. They've all got their eye on the development bonanza expected to come with the discovery of skiing here as an international attraction—but so far the town is still an authentically funky community, worth an afternoon visit even in summer. In the winter, it's a destination.

The primary summer attractions are the hiking trails, the tram to the top of Mount Alyeska, and the Crow Creek Mine, described below. In winter, it's skiing. Mount Alyeska doesn't have the size or the fame of resorts in the Rockies, but it's certainly large and challenging enough—Olympian Tommy Moe trained here. Skiers used to more crowded slopes rave about the skiing here, with views of the Chugach Mountains and, between their parted, snowy rocky peaks, Turnagain Arm.

GETTING THERE

A rental car is the most practical route to Girdwood, 37 miles south of Anchorage off the Seward Highway, but there are van shuttles and tours that could bring you; see "Getting Around" under "Essentials" for Anchorage, above.

VISITOR INFORMATION

Check the Anchorage section. For Girdwood-specific arrangements, the **Alyeska Booking Company,** on Linblad Street (P.O. Box 330), Girdwood, AK 99587 (☎ 907/783-4FUN), takes care of accommodations, rafting trips, rentals, and so on. It also claims to be the headquarters of the Tommy Moe fan club.

EXPLORING GIRDWOOD

ALYESKA RESORT Owned by the Japanese Seibu company, Alyeska is trying to transform itself from a local ski area to an international resort. The work is going well, but it's not there yet—and that's good for skiers who enjoy a varied, challenging mountain with a long season, low lift-ticket prices, and no crowds.

The Skiing Mount Alyeska, at 3,939 feet, has 470 acres of skiing, beginning from a base elevation of only 250 feet and rising 2,500 feet. The normal season is early

November to April, and it's an exceptional year when there isn't plenty of snow all winter. The average snowfall is 556 inches, and in the winter of 1994–95 the mountain received an incredible 900 inches—75 feet! As it's near the water, the weather is temperate. Light is more of an issue, as the days are short in midwinter. There are 75 acres of lighted skiing on 19 trails, but the best Alaska skiing is when the days get longer and warmer in the spring. There are seven lifts, including the tram described below. An all-day lift ticket costs $29 for adults, $23 for students, and $17 for those under age 13 or over 60. Private and group instruction are available, and a basic rental package costs $18 a day. There are excellent Nordic trails as well. A **day lodge** is located at the front of the mountain, and there's a separate bar nearby. A new center for people with disabilities was opened in the fall of 1995 by **Challenge Alaska,** 720 W. 58th Ave., Anchorage, AK 99518 (☎ **907/783-2925** or 907/563-2635), a group dedicated to opening Alaska's outdoors to people with physical challenges. The center allows disabled skiers to use the mountain without assistance, skiing down to the lift to start and back to the center at day's end. The Alyeska Prince Hotel, described below, is around the side of the mountain, connected to skiing by the tram to the top.

The Tram At $12 per person for a six-minute summertime ride up the mountain, the tram leaving from the Alyeska Prince Hotel isn't cheap, but I think it's worth it for people who can't make the climb on foot. (In winter it's faster and comes with your lift ticket.) My three-year-old son called it "the spaceship bus," and that's exactly how it feels to float smoothly from the hotel up into the mountains. The view looks up and down the valley and below at the tree tops and, perhaps, the back of a grazing moose or bear. At the 2,300 foot level it stops at a station with an attractive but overpriced cafeteria and, in the evening, the **Seven Glaciers Restaurant,** so named for its view. But most important, this is an opportunity for everyone, no matter how young, old, or infirm, to experience the pure light, limitless surroundings, and crystalline quiet of an Alaskan mountaintop. Dress very warmly.

OTHER ATTRACTIONS The **Crow Creek Mine,** on Crow Creek Road (☎ **907/278-8060** for a recorded anouncement), opened in 1898 and operated until 1940. In 1969 the Toohey family took over the old buildings, now a National Historic Site, and they provide gold panning and walking tours of the 14 buildings. Crow Creek Road, off the Alyeska Highway, is quite rough and muddy in the spring. Gold panning costs $5 for adults, $4 for children 11 and under; just looking around is $3 for adults and free for children. It's open during the summer, daily from 9am to 6pm. Primitive camping is available.

TRAILS There are a couple of great trails starting in Girdwood. The **Winner Creek Trail** runs 5 miles through forest from behind the Alyeska Prince Hotel to a roaring gorge where Winner Creek and Glacier Creek meet; it's muddy and snowy in the spring. The winter ski trail takes a separate route, through a series of meadows, to the same destination. The **Crow Pass Trail** rises into the mountains and passes all the way over to Eagle River, after a 26-mile hike that takes several days. But you can make a long day hike of it to the pass and see the glaciers, wildflower meadows, and old mining equipment. The trailhead is up Crow Creek Road, off the Alyeska Highway.

You can also explore the area in a dog sled. **Chugach Express Dog Sled Tours** (☎ **907/783-2266**) has one- to three-hour tours ranging from $30 to $85. **Snowmobiling** is a hugely popular sport in Alaska, and is beginning to be extended to visitors; **Crow Creek Snowmachine Tours** (☎ **907/783-2660**) offers $125 half-day and $200 full-day tours into snowy mountains that aren't accessible any other way. They'll teach beginners.

WHERE TO STAY

If you don't want to pay the rates charged by the Alyeska Prince Hotel, there are other nice places to stay in Girdwood. Contact the **Alyeska Booking Company,** on Linblad Street (P.O. Box 330), Girdwood, AK 99587 (☎ **907/783-4FUN**), to find a bed-and-breakfast, with rates starting at $75 a night. **Alyeska Accommodations, Inc.,** on Olympic Circle (P.O. Box 1196), Girdwood, AK 99587 (☎ **907/783-2000**), offers condos and chalets ranging from efficiencies to four-bedroom houses, for $95 to $300 a night.

✪ **Alyeska Prince Hotel.** 1000 Arlberg Ave. (P.O. Box 249), Girdwood, AK 99587. ☎ **907/754-1111** or 800/880-3880. Fax 907/754-2290. 303 rms, 4 suites. TV TEL. Summer and Christmas, $230–$460 double; $800–$1,500 suite. Winter, $150–$300 double; $660–$1,000 suite. Additional adult in room $25 extra; children stay free in parents' room. Car-rental packages available. AE, DC, DISC, JCB, MC, V.

The hotel, completed in 1994, is unique in Alaska as a large, first-class hotel in a nearly pristine mountain valley. Two of the four restaurants—a cafeteria and the gourmet Seven Glaciers Restaurant—are 2,300 feet above the lobby on Mount Alyeska, at the end of a tram ride. The Japanese cuisine particularly has developed a reputation—it's a Japanese-owned property, and they really do it right. But check to see which of the restaurants will be open when you come, as there have been long seasonal closures since the hotel opened. The accommodations and service are as close to perfect as you're likely to find in Alaska—so perfect, in fact, as to seem inappropriately solemn at times. The standard rooms are not large, but have extraordinary views and lovely cherrywood furniture. The suites are magnificent. The swimming pool, with a cathedral ceiling and huge windows on the mountain, has no peer in Alaska. There are a few shops in the lobby. Additional amenities and services include in-room refrigerators and safes, hairdryers, a Jacuzzi and work-out room, tour desk, and concierge.

For summer visitors, you need a car. The hotel is convenient to nothing except its own spectacular surroundings. There is no courtesy van to the Anchorage airport, and the cab fare is a minimum of $50, each way, by special arrangement with Alaska Cab.

WHERE TO EAT

Other than the four restaurants in the Alyeska Prince, there are two good independent places to eat.

Chair 5. Linblad St., town square. ☎ **907/783-2500.** Main courses $6.25–$16; lunch $5.50–$8.50. AE, MC, V. Daily 11am–11pm.

This is where Girdwood locals meet their friends and take their families for dinner. In the bar, Bob Dylan accompanies a friendly game of pool and baseball on TV while men with ponytails sip microbrews. In the restaurant, families sit at tables amid stained glass and not-quite-antique collectibles. Managing chef Brad Hammond makes it work with good, simple meals, welcoming service, and a pro-kid attitude. The menu ranges from pizza to burgers to seafood, pasta, and beef. Full liquor license.

Double Musky. Crow Creek Rd. ☎ **907/783-2822.** Main courses $16–$32. AE, CB, DC, DISC, MC, V. Tues–Thurs 5–10pm, Fri–Sun 4–10pm. Closed Nov.

The Cajun cuisine has gained fame that attracts movie stars and journalists from all over the country, and Anchorage residents keep the restaurant going by making the 40-mile drive from Anchorage for dinner. It's located in the woods of Girdwood off Crow Creek Road. Full liquor license.

4 The Kenai Peninsula: A Microcosm of Alaska

Most of what you're looking for in Alaska you can find south of Anchorage, along a few hundred miles of blacktop. The Kenai (KEEN-eye) Peninsula, which divides Prince William Sound and Cook Inlet, is a microcosm of the state. It's got glaciers, whales, legendary sport fishing, spectacular hiking trails, interesting little fishing towns, bears, moose, high mountains—the major difference is that it's easy to get to, and that means it's not as exotic or remote as many of the other places where you find these things. People from Anchorage go to the peninsula for the weekend to fish, hike, dig clams, paddle kayaks, and so on. There's a special phrase for what happens when the red salmon are running in July on the Kenai and Russian rivers— "combat fishing." It's hard to imagine until you've actually seen fishermen standing elbow to elbow on a bank, each casting into his or her own yard-wide slice of river, and still catching plenty of fish. The peninsula also exerts a powerful magnetic force on RVs, those whales of the road that one finds at the head of strings of cars on the two-lane highways. The fishing rivers, creeks, and beaches on the west side of the peninsula, and the end of the Homer Spit, become sheet-metal cities of hundreds of Winnebagos and Itascas parked side by side during the summer. Often some local entrepreneur will be selling doughnuts or newspapers door to door.

Yet there are towns that still hold unspoiled charm and outdoors experiences where you can be on your own. You won't often be totally alone, but you might as well be, paddling among the whales in a kayak in Prince William Sound; tramping over the heather in Turnagain Pass, hiking, biking, or skiing one of the many maintained trails in Chugach National Forest; or boating to a base camp on the south side of Kachemak Bay. And the presence of people has some advantages—you have a better chance of finding good food and lodgings on the Kenai Peninsula than in less developed areas of the state.

Kenai is the largest town. It's only 10 miles from Soldotna, and together they form a unit with more than 25% of the peninsula's population of 44,000. They're also the least interesting of the peninsula's communities. Homer has wonderful art and character; Seward is smaller and quieter, but also charming and a gateway to Kenai Fjords National Park.

GETTING THERE / ORIENTATION   The Kenai Peninsula is served by a single major road, the **Seward Highway,** which forks 90 miles south of Anchorage. The great majority of visitors get to the peninsula in private cars on this road. At the fork, the **Sterling Highway** heads west to Cooper Landing, Kenai and Soldotna, and Homer, 235 miles from Anchorage. The balance of the Seward Highway goes to the east side of the peninsula to the town of Seward. All the major towns also are served by frequent **commuter air service.** Seward gets rail service from the **Alaska Railroad** during the summer and the **Alaska Marine Highway System** links Seward and Homer with outlying areas without roads. See the sections on the individual towns, below, for details.

VISITOR INFORMATION   Each town of significant size has a visitor information center, maps, guides, and other publications, and the peninsula as a whole also has the **Kenai Peninsula Tourism Marketing Council,** 10819 Kenai Spur Hwy., Suite 103-D, Kenai, AK 99611-7848 (☎ **907/283-3850,** or 800/535-3624), which is eager to send you information on businesses in the area. The Kenai Peninsula Borough is the county-level government for the whole area; it levies a 2% sales tax, and individual towns add varying amounts of tax of their own.

The Kenai Peninsula & Prince William Sound

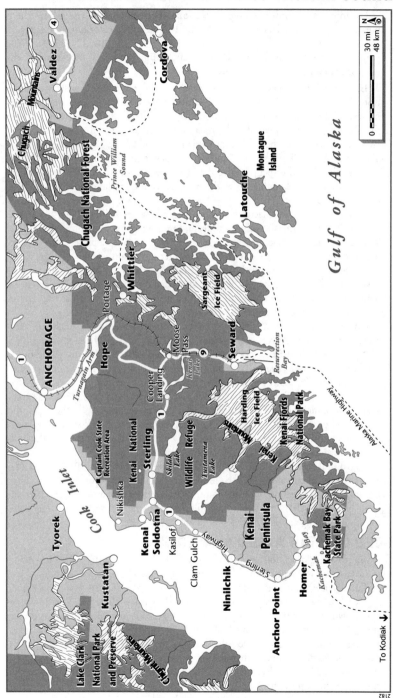

For information on the **Chugach National Forest,** which covers the northern portion of the peninsula, contact the **Alaska Public Lands Information Center,** at 605 W. Fourth Ave., Suite 105, Anchorage, AK 99501 (☎ **907/271-2599**), or the ranger district offices in Girdwood, on Monarch Mine Road, near the Seward Highway, or in Seward, at 334 Fourth Ave.

THE SEWARD HIGHWAY   The Kenai Peninsula's main lifeline is the road down from Anchorage, a 127-mile drive to Seward on a good two-lane highway, most of it through untouched public land without development or services. The drive is more than scenic, it's really a wonderful attraction in itself, designated a National Scenic Byway. I've written in the Anchorage section above about the 50-mile portion along Turnagain Arm to Portage. (The mileage numbers I give here count from Anchorage, the direction most people drive the first time, but the roadside mileposts start in Seward. To correlate this log to the mileposts, subtract the distance listed from Anchorage from 127.)

Beyond the Portage Glacier turn-off, the road traverses the salt marshes to the south side of the Arm, then climbs to fresh, towering alpine terrain over 1,000-foot **Turnagain Pass.** At the pass, 59 miles from Anchorage, there's a pit toilet and a parking area providing access to summer and winter mountain recreation. This is the Chugach National Forest, and there are a couple of campgrounds on this stretch. Seventy miles from Anchorage, the Hope spur road divides off to the west, described below; then the road climbs again through a series of curves up a narrow canyon before leveling out again above the treeline.

Now come a series of alpine lakes. Summit Lake, 81 miles from Anchorage, has a spectacular Forest Service campground, on the far side from the highway, and on the near side, **Summit Lake Lodge** (☎ **907/595-1520**), a wonderfully traditional rural roadhouse, open every day of the year from 7am to 11pm. It's the only permanent habitation for many miles in either direction.

The highway continues through similar terrain before descending into the trees again and branching at **Tern Lake,** 90 miles from Anchorage. To the right, the Sterling Highway leads to Kenai, Soldotna, and Homer. The Seward Highway continues to the left along a string of sparking mountain lakes, and through the little community of Moose Pass, 100 miles from Anchorage, with trails and Forest Service campgrounds. You also can stop at **Alaska Nellie's Inn** (☎ **907/288-3124**), a bed-and-breakfast and site of Nellie Lawing's cabin, a National Historic Site. Lawing was a pioneering big-game hunter whose hospitality was famous when she lived here, from 1915 to 1956. The highway continues from here through the forest, descending another 23 miles to Seward.

HOPE: GHOST OF A GOLD-RUSH TOWN

If you're headed down the Seward Highway to the Kenai Peninsula with a few hours to spare, a visit to Hope can make for a pleasant break. The town, on the south shore of Turnagain Arm, is at the end of a paved 17-mile spur 70 miles from Anchorage. A few white frame buildings remain from the days when Hope was a gold-mining boomtown after a strike in 1895. Many of the newer buildings in the town center are quaint, too. Four varieties of salmon run in Porcupine Creek, near the main street. The year-round population is less than 200; in the summer, the number goes up as Anchorage residents come to their cabins.

The gold rush–era ✪ **Resurrection Pass Trail** begins 4 miles above the town and runs over the top of the Kenai Peninsula to Cooper Landing. It's a beautiful, remote—yet well-used—hike or mountain-bike ride, rising through forest, crossing the alpine pass, and then descending again to a highway trailhead, where you'll need to have transportation waiting. The 40-mile trail has nine public-use cabins, available for $25 a night by mail or in person from the U.S. Forest Service at the Alaska Public Lands Information Center in Anchorage (see "Visitor Information," above) or in person at the ranger district offices in Girdwood or Seward. The cabins are well spaced to cover the trail in an easy five days and those that are on lakes have boats for fishing. They are reserved well ahead, but there are lots of good camping spots, too.

The **Hope and Sunrise Historical and Mining Museum** is a one-room log cabin displaying historic objects and photographs. It's open on Monday, Friday, and Saturday from noon to 4pm, and on Sunday from noon to 2pm. You can pan for gold at **BJW Mining and Gifts** for $5. Where the main street ends—the tidal meadow beyond was more of Hope before the 1964 earthquake—the **Seaview Cafe, Bar, Gift Shop and RV Park** acts as the town center. Don Ohr presides, and will gladly dispense town history and frontier wisdom. The cafe has modest meals. The bar has a wall with Polaroid photographs of everyone who lives here. In the small shop you'll find Native art, local crafts, and silver jewelry.

The U.S. Forest Service ✪ **Porcupine Campground** at the end of the road, just beyond the town, is one of the most beautiful in the Chugach National Forest. Twenty-four well-separated sites overlook Turnagain Arm, and it's the trailhead for a level 10-mile walk to **Gull Rock** and for a stiff climb that rises 3,600 feet to expansive views at **Hope Point.**

If for some reason you decide to seek lodgings for the night in Hope, the best choice is the **Bear Creek Lodge,** P.O. Box 90, Hope, AK 99605 (☎ 907/ 782-3141), with three pleasant cabins around a duck pond and two on a creek for $75 double; they have electric heat and wood stoves and share a bathhouse. There also are rooms with private bathrooms above the **Henry's One Stop** convenience store across the parking lot.

SEWARD: GATEWAY TO RESURRECTION BAY & KENAI FJORDS NATIONAL PARK

The main reason to go to Seward—now and historically—is Resurrection Bay and the access the port provides to the great mass of Alaska. Most visitors are on their way to the excellent ocean fishing, especially for silver salmon, or to Kenai Fjords National Park, which is described below. But the path left by generations of earlier travelers and settlers makes Seward a unique and attractive town in its own right. It's also a good starting point for hiking on publicly owned wild lands.

The old buildings—old by Alaska standards—are unique in Southcentral Alaska, and in some ways Seward is more like a town in Southeast with its mountainside grid of streets by the ocean. The grid is lined with old wood-frame houses and newer fishermen's residences. It's the sort of place where pedestrians casually wander across the road, hardly glancing for cars, for there likely won't be any, or, if there are, they'll be ready to stop.

Along the seashore, besides the large boat harbor that's the economic hub of the town, a beach of rounded gravel becomes a jolly city of tents and recreational vehicles at the height of summer. Late in the summer, campers can catch silver salmon out their front doors on this shoreline, possibly winning up to $10,000 in the famous derby. Your chances are better, of course, with one of the dozens of fishing charters available in the boat harbor. Even those who don't care much about fishing will likely enjoy tagging along on a charter: You'll have a decent chance of seeing sea otters, sea lions, and even whales.

Seward's history is among the oldest in Alaska. The Russian governor Alexander Baranov stopped here in 1793, named Resurrection Bay, and built a ship. It later sank—Baranov's men didn't have the appropriate materials to build a ship in this wilderness. The town was born in its modern form in 1903, when a company seeking to build a railroad north came ashore. There were already trails leading to the water; they were later surveyed as the Iditarod Trail, leading more than 1,000 miles to Nome. Today that route is discontinuous south of Anchorage, but you can follow it through Seward.

More relevant for current visitors and the local economy, the federal government took over the failed railroad-building effort in 1915, finishing the line to Fairbanks in 1923. Until the age of jet travel, most people coming to Alaska arrived by steamer in Seward and then traveled north by rail. The train ride to Anchorage, daily during the summer, is supremely beautiful.

ESSENTIALS

GETTING THERE   Seward can be reached by all modes of transportation.

By Car   See the Seward Highway log, above, for how to make the beautiful 127-mile drive down from Anchorage. All major car-rental agencies are represented in Anchorage; **Hertz** has an office in Seward, at Seward Waterfront Lodging, 500 Railway Ave. (☎ **907/224-6097,** or 800/654-3131).

By Bus   The **Seward Bus Line** (☎ **907/224-3608;** fax 907/224-7237) makes one trip daily, year round, starting in Seward and going to Anchorage and back; the fare is $30 one way. Gray Line's **Alaskon Express** (☎ **800/544-2206),** operating in summer only, instead leaves Anchorage in the morning and returns in the evening. Using one or the other, you can leave early or late.

By Rail   I think everyone should take the run between Anchorage and Seward on the ○ **Alaska Railroad,** 411 W. First Ave., Anchorage, AK 99501 (☎ **907/265-2494** or 800/544-0552), which runs daily in summer. It's even more spectacular than the highway route, passing close by glaciers and following a ledge halfway up the narrow, vertical Placer River gorge, where it ducks into tunnels and pops out at bends in the river. The terrain around the tracks is completely undeveloped and looks just as it did when the first person beheld it. The train has three cars: a dining car with good deli-style food, a car with commentary, and a quiet car. The railroad's young guides are well trained and provide an accurate and not overly verbose commentary. The fare for the summer-only run is $80 round-trip or $50 one way, a good value for a ride that I, at least, will never forget. The railroad also offers packages which include a boat tour of Kenai Fjords National Park, but I advise against trying to get down from Anchorage, do the park, and return in the same day; it's too much.

By Air   Small planes run between Anchorage and Seward. **F.S. Air** (☎ **907/248-9595**) is a Seward-based carrier.

By Ferry   The ferry *Tustumena,* of the **Alaska Marine Highway System** (☎ **907/224-5485** or 800/642-0066) connects Seward with Valdez and, to the west, Kodiak and all the way to the Aleutians (although Homer is a closer embarkation point for that trip). Sailings in either direction are quite infrequent—weekly or less. The terminal is at Fifth Avenue and Armstrong Street.

VISITOR INFORMATION   The **Kenai Fjords National Park Visitor Center,** at the boat harbor (P.O. Box 1727), Seward, AK 99664 (☎ **907/224-3175;** fax 907/224-2144), is worth a stop for park information and other outdoors opportunities (see the section on the national park, below, for more specifics on the visitor center). For information and permits in the Chugach National Forest, the **Seward Ranger District** is at Fourth Avenue and Jefferson Street (P.O. Box 390), Seward, AK 99663 (☎ **907/224-3374**). The **Seward Chamber of Commerce,** P.O. Box 749, Seward, AK 99664 (☎ **907/224-8051**), has three visitor centers: one on the Seward Highway as you enter town, another in a kiosk at the boat harbor, and a third in an old Alaska Railroad car at the corner of Third Avenue and Jefferson Street, downtown. Guides will provide objective information, but not advice on what's good or bad.

An automated voice-mail service called **Connections** (☎ **907/224-2424**) provides information about all kinds of local services, vacancies, and reservations and can put you through directly to the businesses described on the recordings.

ORIENTATION   The layout of Seward, strung along between mountains and bay, has a double focus. At the north end, the **Seward Highway** and **Alaska Railroad** enter near the small-boat harbor. In recent years this has developed like any seaside tourist town, with shops, restaurants, and tourist businesses clustered along the top of the boat basin. Many visitors feel no need to venture farther. Ten blocks to the south, however, is the heart of old Seward—the street grid of downtown, with historic buildings, more interesting hotels, restaurants, and the modest sights to be seen. North-south avenues are numbered; cross streets are named after presidents. To the south the dirt Lowell Point Road road runs a short distance before petering out at the trailhead to **Caines Head State Recreation Area.**

GETTING AROUND   You can easily cover downtown Seward on foot, although a little help is handy to get back and forth from the boat harbor. The **Chamber of Commerce Trolley** runs every half hour from 10am to 7pm daily in summer; it goes south along Third Avenue and north on Ballaine Street, stopping at the railroad depot, the cruise-ship dock, and the harbor visitor center. Bikes are a great choice in Seward. **The Charter Option,** at the small-boat harbor (P.O. Box 3125), Seward, AK 99664 (☎ **907/224-2026**), rents bikes as well as doing van tours and fishing charters. **Independent Taxi** (☎ **907/224-5000**) is one of the cab companies. If you're experienced with boats, rent a skiff for $15 an hour from **Miller's Landing**, on Lowell Point Road (P.O. Box 81), Seward, AK 99664 (☎ **907/224-5739**).

FAST FACTS   The **sales tax** in Seward is 5%. There are ATMs at the First National Bank of Anchorage, 303 Fourth Ave., and at the National Bank of Alaska, 908 Third Ave. In **emergencies,** dial 911. For nonemergency situations, call the **Seward Police Department** (☎ **907/224-3338**) or, outside the city limits, the **Alaska State Troopers** (☎ **907/224-3346**). **Seward General Hospital** is at 417 First Ave. (☎ **907/224-5205**). The *Seward Phoenix Log* is published each Thursday; you can usually find the Anchorage newspaper, too.

SPECIAL EVENTS   The big day of the year in Seward is the ✪ **Fourth of July,** when the whole town explodes with visitors, primarily from Anchorage. Besides the parade and many small-town festivities, the main attraction is the **Mount Marathon Race,** run every year since it started as a bar bet in 1915. The racers go from the middle of town straight up rocky Mount Marathon to its 3,022-foot peak, then tumble down again, arriving muddy and bloody at the finish line in town. Binoculars will allow you to see the whole thing from town, including the pratfalls of the runners on their way down. The **Jackpot Halibut Derby** runs during the month of July and the **Silver Salmon Derby** is the second and third week of August (10–18 in 1996). The chamber of commerce visitor centers can provide information about both.

Exploring Seward

WHAT TO SEE & DO IN TOWN   Explore downtown with the help of a **walk-ing-tour map** provided by the visitor center in the old rail car at Third Avenue and Jefferson Street. The **Iditarod Trailhead,** near the ferry dock on Railroad Avenue, is where pioneers entered Alaska. The **Resurrection Bay Historical Society Museum,** at Third and Jefferson, has historical memorabilia and curiosities, and a display on the Russian ships built here in the late 18th century; admission is $1, and it's open during the summer, daily from 11am to 5pm. The **University of Alaska–Fairbanks Seward Marine Education Center,** with displays, saltwater aquariums, videos, and demonstrations on marine science, is at Third and Railway avenues, open Tuesday through Sunday from 10am to 4pm; admission is free. The steep-roofed **St. Peter's Episcopal Church** is a delightful little chapel under the mountains at First Avenue and Adams Street. My family enjoyed using the **city library,** at Fifth Avenue and Adams Street, as a home base.

Dog-sled demonstrations and rides on a wheeled sled are available from **IditaRide Dog Sled Tours,** located on Old Exit Glacier Road, 3.7 miles out the Seward Highway (☎ **907/224-8607** or 800/478-3139).

SHOPPING   Stop at the ✪ **Resurrect Art Coffee House Gallery,** at 320 Third Ave. (☎ **907/224-7161**), in an old church that's also on the walking tour. The fine art is local and authentic and the coffeehouse is a meeting place and serves a good light breakfast or lunch. There's a children's area with toys in the choir loft. The ✪ **Bardarson Studio,** at the boat harbor (☎ **907/224-5448**), specializes in Dot Bardarson's watercolor prints, and also has a wonderful, welcoming attitude; there's a children's cave under the stairs and a husbands' recliner area with videos and reading matter upstairs. We all had a fine time. The biggest gift store in town is the **Alaska Shop,** downtown at 210 Fourth Ave.

Getting Outside

Here I've described things to do out of Seward other than the national park—which includes the fjords and Exit Glacier. See "Kenai Fjords National Park," below, for that information.

BOATING   Three Resurrection Bay sailing charters are available; the waters are beautiful, but it's a different experience than sailing in the Lower 48—if there's any wind, it's quite chilly. You can book a charter through the central agencies listed under "Fishing," below. **Adventure and Delights** (☎ **907/224-3960**) runs sea-kayaking trips from Seward, in both Resurrection Bay and Prince William Sound; they also have an office in Anchorage at 414 K St. (☎ **907/276-8282**).

FISHING   Seward is renowned for its saltwater silver salmon fishing, and there's a harbor full of large and small charter boats waiting to take you. There's also good halibut fishing. I prefer small boats, because you get to know the skipper better and have more of a feeling of being out there on your own. The going rate for a charter is $125 per person for salmon, or $140 for halibut, for which the boats have to go farther. There are several central charter agencies, which makes life simpler for visitors. **The Fish House,** P.O. Box 1209, Seward, AK 99664 (☎ **907/224-3674** or 800/257-7760; fax 907/224-7108), is the old, established booking agency, and has a big store for supplies at the boat harbor. Two other booking agencies are **The Charter Option** (☎ **907/224-2026**) and the **Charter Connection** (☎ **907/224-4446**).

You can fish from shore for silvers when they're running in the late summer, although your chances aren't as good as if you use a boat. The beach below the downtown area is a popular spot.

Seward

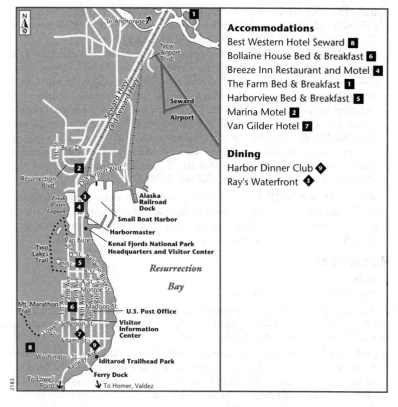

Accommodations
Best Western Hotel Seward **8**
Bollaine House Bed & Breakfast **6**
Breeze Inn Restaurant and Motel **4**
The Farm Bed & Breakfast **1**
Harborview Bed & Breakfast **5**
Marina Motel **2**
Van Gilder Hotel **7**

Dining
Harbor Dinner Club ◆**9**
Ray's Waterfront ◆**3**

HIKING There are several excellent hiking trails near Seward. You can get a complete list and directions at the Kenai Fjords National Park Visitor Center (see "Visitor Information," above). The **Iditarod National Historic Trail** starts as a paved path at Fourth and Railroad avenues. Through town it's a paved bike trail, then 15 miles of trail lead up through the woods starting about 2 miles out of town on Nash Road. **Seward Iditarod Trail Blazers,** P.O. Box 1923, Seward, AK 99664, can provide details. The Iditarod Trail doesn't become continuous—and used for the annual race—until Wasilla, north of Anchorage.

The **Mount Marathon Trail** is a vigorous hike to the top of a 3,000-foot mountain. The route of the famous Mount Marathon foot race is the more strenuous choice, basically going straight up from the end of Jefferson Street; the hikers' route starts at the corner of First Avenue and Monroe Street. Either trail rises steeply to the top of the rocky pinnacle and the incredible views there. Allow all day, unless you're a racer; in that case, expect to do it in under 45 minutes.

The **Caines Head State Recreation Area** has a 7-mile coastal trail south of town. It's best done as an overnight, or with someone picking you up in a boat at the other end, as it's only accessible at low tide. The trail has some gorgeous views, rocky shores, and a good destination at the end, the World War II gun emplacement at Fort McGilvray. There's a campground at Tonsina Point, 3 miles in, and a camping shelter at North Beach, at 4¹/₂ miles. It's a great hike. The trailhead is south of town on Lowell Point Road; pull off in the lot right after the sewage plant, then cross the road through the gate and follow the dirt road a bit until it becomes the actual

trail. The state **Division of Parks,** P.O. Box 107001, Anchorage, AK 99501
(☎ **907/762-2617**), produces a good trail guide you can pick up free at the
Kenai Fjords National Park Visitor Center at the boat harbor.

The ✪ **Lost Lakes Trail,** with its fields of alpine wildflowers and small lakes,
is the most beautiful hike in the area. There are two trailheads: One, in a subdivision 5¹/₂ miles out of Seward, is relatively difficult to find; the other, at the
10-site **Primrose Campground,** on Kenai Lake, 17 miles up the road, is easier to find
and starts out higher. Camping is $8. Most of the trail is in the Chugach National
Forest, and a Forest Service cabin is available on a 2-mile spur about 11 miles
along the 15-mile route starting at the Primrose trailhead. For a cabin permit and
detailed trail information, contact the Alaska Public Lands Information Center in
Anchorage or the **Seward Ranger District,** at Fourth Avenue and Jefferson Street
(P.O. Box 390), Seward, AK 99663 (☎ **907/224-3374**).

WILDLIFE WATCHING   The Moose Creek Fish Viewing Area, a platform to
watch spawning red salmon and occasionally black bear feeding on them, stands a
quarter mile off the Seward Highway 32¹/₂ miles from town. Get more information
from the Seward Ranger District.

WHERE TO STAY
Hotels
The tax on rooms in Seward is 9%.

✪ **Best Western Hotel Seward.** 217 Fifth Ave., Seward, AK 99664. ☎ **907/224-2378** or
800/478 1050. Fax 907/224-3112. 38 rms. TV TEL. High season, $178–$198 double. Low
season, $79 double. Additional person in room $10 extra. AE, MC, V.

Brad Snowden, who also owns the neighboring New Seward Hotel and the saloon
down the street, has created a hotel that's in a league of its own in Seward. The rooms
are large, fresh, and nicely decorated; many have big bay windows and all have VCRs,
refrigerators, and coffee makers. The view rooms on the front go for a premium; avoid
the south-facing rooms, which look out on the back of another hotel. A two-story
log cabin on a cliff over the boat harbor also is part of the hotel; with a large
hot-tub spa on the magnificent deck, it's one of the most beautiful and luxurious
accommodations in Alaska, renting for $299 a night.

The **New Seward Hotel** operates out of the same lobby as the Best Western. The
rooms are smaller and less expensive, with basement economy rooms with shared
baths as low as $60 a night. It has been called the "New Seward" since 1945, but was
remodeled in 1995 with pleasant country decor.

The Breeze Inn. At the small boat harbor (P.O. Box 2147), Seward, AK 99664-2147. ☎ **907/
224-5237.** Fax 907/224-7024. 66 rms. TV TEL. $105 double. Additional person in room $10
extra. AE, DC, DISC, MC, V.

Located right at the boat harbor, this large, three-story, motel-style building offers
good accommodations with the most convenient location in town for most visitors.
This is also, however, the busiest and thus not the quietest spot in town. The restaurant and lounge across the parking lot serve meals in a small-town, pool-hall
atmosphere.

The Marina Motel. 1603 Seward Hwy. (P.O. Box 1134), Seward, AK 99664. ☎ **907/
224-5518.** Fax 907/224-5553. 18 rms. TV TEL. High season, $110–$120 double. Low season,
$45–$55 double. Additional person in room $10 extra. DC, DISC, MC, V.

Comfortable, convenient rooms across the Seward Highway from the boat harbor are
a friendly, family-run business. Larger, lighter rooms with interior access, on the north

side, rent for more, but those on the south side are perfectly adequate. Rooms have coffee machines.

The VanGilder Hotel. 308 Adams St. (P.O. Box 2), Seward, AK 99664. ☎ **907/224-3525.** Fax 907/224-3689. 18 rms, some with bath; 2 suites. TV. $85 double; $135 suite. Additional person in room $10 extra. AE, DC, DISC, MC, V.

A charming if creaky old place founded in 1916 and listed on the National Register of Historic Places, the VanGilder is a retirement project for Don and Deane Decker. Authenticity means rooms tend to be small and unique, so choose carefully.

Bed-and-Breakfasts

Seward has many excellent B&Bs. Here I've listed some of the very best. Names and addresses of others are available at the Seward Chamber of Commerce Visitor Center.

Ballaine House Bed and Breakfast. 437 Third Ave. (P.O. Box 2051), Seward, AK 99664-2051. ☎ **907/224-2362.** 4 rms, none with bath. $75 double. Rates include full breakfast. No credit cards.

This 1905 house near the center of downtown makes the classic bed-and-breakfast, with its wooden floors, large living room, and tall, double-hung windows. It's on the National Historic Register and the town walking tour. Marilee Koszewski has decorated with antiques and handmade quilts, with a player piano in the dining room. Some of the rooms are small, and the three upstairs rooms share one bathroom. No smoking; no children under 7.

✪ **The Farm Bed and Breakfast.** Salmon Creek Rd. three miles from Seward (P.O. Box 305), Seward, AK 99664. ☎ **907/224-5691.** Fax 907/224-2300. 11 rms, 6 with bath. TV TEL. High season (including light breakfast), $40–$85 double without bath, $75–$85 double with bath. Low season (without breakfast), $40 double. Additional person in room $15 extra. MC, V.

A big, many-angled house, a set of three cottages, and a boat up on blocks contain 11 clean, daintily decorated rooms on 40 acres just north of town. You may see a moose wandering across the huge lawn. The rooms in the main house are larger (one is huge), but the cottage rooms have more privacy. There are accommodations for people with disabilities. The gregarious owner, Jack Hoogland, eagerly tells stories of his lifetime in Seward and the latest news from his trucking business. It's a great place for children.

✪ **Harborview Bed and Breakfast.** 900 Third Ave. (P.O. Box 1305), Seward, AK 99664. ☎ **907/224-3217.** Fax 907/224-3218. 8 rms, 2 apartments. TV TEL. High season, $85 double. Low season, $50 double. Year round, $75 apartment. Rates include continental breakfast. Additional person in room $15 extra. MC, V.

Really more of an inn than a B&B—there are no shared or common rooms—Jolene and Jerry King's eight immaculate, spacious guest rooms, decorated with Alaska Native fine art and with tables for dining, are an incredible value. The nondescript building is located midway between downtown and the boat harbor. Two other units, a few blocks away, are even more extraordinary. The Seaview rooms are a pair of large two-bedroom apartments right on the beach, with their own front lawn and barbecue.

Camping

A fun place to camp is the **beach** on Ballaine Avenue, which becomes a tent and RV city in the summer. With showers, it's operated by the city parks and recreation department (☎ **907/224-3331**), and charges $6 for tents, $8 for RVs. **Miller's Landing,** on Lowell Point Road south of town (P.O. Box 81), Seward, AK 99664

(☎ 907/224-5739), offers electric hookups for $17.50 a night and rustic, sleeping-bag cabins starting at $40 a night, with showers and many other services, including fishing charters and equipment rentals, including bikes, boats, and fishing poles.

WHERE TO EAT

Besides the two steak and seafood establishments listed below, **The Depot,** at the north end of the harbor, is a good fast-food place; it has burgers and fish sandwiches at reasonable prices and a pleasant dining room, part of which is a solarium.

۞ The Harbor Dinner Club. 220 Fifth Ave. ☎ **907/224-3012.** Main courses $3–$40; lunch $5–$8.50. AE, CB, DC, DISC, MC, V. Daily 11am–2:30pm and 5–11pm.

This Seward landmark has been in the Zantmire family since 1962 and the matriarch still lives upstairs. It's an old-fashioned family restaurant, with white tablecloths and a menu that ranges from fine seafood to a $3 hamburger. You need not spend a lot of money to eat in an attractive dining room. The sautéed seafood special, including shrimp, halibut, and tender scallops, was fresh and not overdone. The prime rib was large and well presented. Full liquor license.

Ray's Waterfront. At the small-boat harbor. ☎ **907/224-5606.** Main courses $14–$20; lunch $6–$10. AE, DC, DISC, MC, V. 15% gratuity added for parties of six or more. Apr 2–Sept, daily 11am–11pm. Closed Oct–Apr 1.

This popular, noisy steak and fish place looks out across the small-boat harbor. This is where the locals will send you, and for good reason: The salmon served on a cedar plank was done perfectly and smelled like a forest; the filet mignon had a subtle, smoky flavor. Service was professional, once we got seated; however, we waited 20 minutes past the time of our reservation to get a table and, despite empty tables, patrons were being sent to the bar for a wait. Full liquor license.

SEWARD IN THE EVENING

The **Liberty Theater,** at Fourth Avenue and Adams Street (☎ 907/224-5418), shows movies in the evenings and matinees. The **museum,** at Third Avenue and Jefferson Street, has slide shows on the history of Seward and the Iditarod Trail on Monday, Wednesday, and Friday at 7pm during the summer; admission is $2. The bar at the **Breeze Inn Motel,** at the boat harbor, is a place to trade fish stories after a day on the water; the saloon next door to the **New Seward Hotel,** at Fourth Avenue and Washington Street, is more of an upscale choice.

KENAI FJORDS NATIONAL PARK

The park is all about remote rocks, mountains, and ice that meet the ocean, and the animals that live there. For some it's a natural cathedral, and the experience of seeing the grand and rugged terrain takes on a spiritual dimension. Anyone will find the park and its surroundings impressive. And in few places are the chances better of seeing marine mammals or adding waterfowl to a birder's list.

But most of the park is remote and difficult to get to. A large vessel, such as a tour boat operating out of Seward, is the only practical way to see the marine portion of the park—the truly exceptional part. That's not cheap or quick if you really want the full experience, and there are better destinations for people subject to seasickness. The inland portion is accessible only at Exit Glacier, near Seward, unless you're an experienced mountaineer.

The park comprises 580,000 acres on the south coast and interior land mass of the Kenai Peninsula. The shore here is exposed to the Gulf of Alaska, whose wild, recurrent storms beat mercilessly against the mountainous shore, unbuffered by any land mass against the vast expanse of the Pacific to the south. The steep topography of the shoreline, created by the collision of the tectonic plates carrying the Pacific Ocean, on one hand, and Alaska, on the other, is uninhabited, although ancient Alaska Native archeological remains suggest there were settlements at times along the deep, fingerlike fjords that penetrate the mountains.

Behind the coastal mountains, and spilling over their shoulders, is an inconceivably vast plateau of ice, the Harding Icefield. Undiscovered until this century—and there's precious little to discover other than mile after mile of featureless ice—the icefield covers an area 37 by 20 miles, the entire southern Kenai Peninsula from Resurrection Bay to Kachemak Bay. It takes days for an experienced mountaineering party to cross. Each of the park's many glaciers is a small branch of this mother ice sheet.

Kenai Fjords National Park was created in 1980, when Congress passed the Alaska National Interest Lands Act, which set aside 106 million acres—about a third of the entire state—in protected parks and wilderness. Although development-minded Alaskans howled at the time, Kenai Fjords has proven to be far more valuable as an attraction for visitors than it could have been for any potential resource exploitation.

The park is not, however, entirely safe. In 1989 it was damaged by the *Exxon Valdez* oil spill. Oil took about 10 days to arrive from Bligh Reef, in Prince William Sound, 140 miles to the northeast, and when it did the destruction of wildlife was horrific. Many tens of thousands of birds and hundreds of sea otters perished. Although the oil quickly washed off the rocky, wave-pounded shore, some bird colonies never recovered entirely from the assault.

The damage of the spill is not perceptible to first-time visitors, however, and the tragedy has had a silver lining. Exxon Corporation's settlement with the state and federal governments, worth $1 billion, will allow, among many other projects, the construction of a $47.5-million sea life center in Seward that will allow visitors to see and learn about the marine biology of the area. Other allocations may be used to buy private holdings in the park which could otherwise be logged or developed.

ESSENTIALS

GETTING THERE   Seward is the threshold to the park. Exit Glacier is 13 miles from the town by road, the Kenai Fjords National Park Visitor Center is at the Seward small-boat harbor, and the tour boats that visit the park leave from Seward. Many visitors try to do the park in a day, coming from Anchorage by train or road, touring the park by boat, then returning that evening; I recommend against this. To really get to the park, you need to be on an all-day boat trip—most half-day trips barely leave Resurrection Bay and hardly see the park proper. More important, a lot of the visitors I saw riding the train back to Anchorage after a one-day marathon trip to Kenai Fjords were so tired they couldn't keep their eyes open for the extraordinary scenery passing by outside the train. A better plan is to spend a night in Seward and take in the full Kenai Fjords boat trip and Exit Glacier. See the section on Seward, above, for details on getting to and around the town.

VISITOR INFORMATION   The **Kenai Fjords National Park Visitor Center**, at the small-boat harbor (P.O. Box 1727), Seward, AK 99664 (☎ **907/224-3175;** fax 907/224-2144), is a place to ask questions of employees of the park or of the Alaska Natural History Association and to get the correct answer. (I've found that many tour companies inadequately train their guides, who tend not to be Alaska residents, and I've heard many inaccurate statements, even on the most reputable of the boat tours.) The visitor center also has a hall for daily lectures covering topics on the natural history of the park. There's a fine collection of books for sale about the flora, fauna, and geology of Alaska. You can also get information here on the many good hiking trails around Seward.

SEEING THE PARK

Kenai Fjords is essentially a marine park. On a boat tour, you'll see its mountains, glaciers, and wildlife. On any of the tours, you're likely to see sea otters and sea lions and you have a good chance of seeing humpback whales, orcas, mountain goats, and black bears. Birdwatchers will see bald eagles, puffins, cormorants, murres, and various sea ducks.

Depending on the time and money you have to spend, you can choose to take a half-day trip staying generally in Resurrection Bay or a full-day trip that travels to Aialik Bay or Harris Bay, in the heart of the park. The shorter trips generally cost about $60 per person, while the longer trips are up to $105. Find out exactly where the boat is going—some tour companies call their trips Kenai Fjords tours, but only scratch the end of the park and really are Resurrection Bay tours. Resurrection Bay contains plenty of impressive scenery—its cliffs are as if chiseled from the mountains—but the fjords' are even grander. Also, Holgate Glacier, in Aialik Bay, and Northwestern Glacier, in Harris Bay, at the heads of the parks' fjords, are great tidewater glaciers; Bear Glacier, at the edge of the park, and visited by the half-day tours, is less impressive.

How much wildlife you see also depends on the trip you take. The half-day cruises have less of a chance of seeing whales and will see puffins and other birds in lesser numbers. The longer trips, which make it into the heart of the park proper, will see birds and animals in greater numbers and variety. If you're lucky with the weather, you may make it to the exposed Chiswell Islands, which have among the greatest bird rookeries in Alaska, supporting more than 50,000 seabirds of 18 species. The daylong trips also have more time to linger and really see the behavior of the wildlife. Whatever your choice, binoculars will greatly enhance the trip.

An important factor in your decision is your susceptibility to seasickness. To reach the heart of the park, vessels must venture into the unprotected waters of the North Pacific. Large, rolling waves are inevitable on the passage from Resurrection Bay to the fjords themselves, although once in the fjords the water is calm. On a rough day, most boats will turn back for the comfort of the passengers and change the full-day trip into a Resurrection Bay cruise, refunding the difference in fare. Of course, they'd rather not do that, and the decision usually isn't made until the vessel is out there, probably after some of the passengers are already vomiting over the side. My advice is that if you get seasick easily, stick to the Resurrection Bay cruise, or take a boat tour in protected Prince William Sound; in any event, ask about the tour company's policy on turning back.

Most important of all, try to schedule loosely, so that if the weather is bad on the day you choose for your boat trip, you can wait and go the next day. Doing a trip like this in bad weather can take away a lot of the joy: You can't see as much, you're uncomfortable, and the animals and birds aren't as evident. If you pay upfront to hold a reservation on a boat—probably a good idea in the busiest months—find out the company's refund policy first.

Other questions to ask: How much deck space is there outside, so you can really see? What is the seating arrangement—airline style, or around tables? How many passengers will be on board and how many crew members to answer questions? Is lunch provided, and what does it consist of?

For those with the money, time, and outdoors skills, it's possible to charter a seaplane or a boat to one of four park service cabins; this is one of the most remote and spectacular trips I can imagine. Contact the park service visitor center for details and permits, which become available on January 1 for the entire year.

Here are some of the companies offering tours:

- **Kenai Fjords Tours / Kenai Coastal Tours** (☎ **907/224-8068** in Seward, 907/276-6249 in Anchorage, or 800/478-8068). These two names both belong to the same company. It's the biggest operation, with many years of experience and an excellent reputation. It offers a variety of trips, including the full-day trip to the park and half-day Resurrection Bay tours and dinner cruises. Its vessels are large and fast, well maintained, and well crewed. The office staff is efficient and knows its business; the refund policy is generous. The management has a philosophy of allowing passengers to really experience the wildlife by lingering and trying to create an individual feel instead of a herd atmosphere. The staff on board were friendly and solicitous, but the large boats have airline-style seating—comfortable, but less personal than table seating—and a vessel that holds 150 people can be only so personal. A good, simple cold lunch is provided.

- **Mariah Charters and Tours** (☎ **907/224-8623** in Seward, 907/243-1238 in Anchorage, or 800/270-1238). Mariah has two boats, each of which carries 24 passengers. It prides itself on a more personal feel than the big boats, but smaller vessels are more active in the waves, too. Passengers pack their own lunch. The company specializes in all-day tours that go all the way to Northwestern Glacier or Aialik Glacier and has a reputation for going on in weather when others turn back.

- **Major Marine Tours** (☎ **907/224-8030** in Seward, 907/274-7300 in Anchorage, or 800/764-7300). Making a specialty of its food, Major Marine features a dinner cruise of Resurrection Bay, but just barely enters the park proper, visiting Bear Glacier on a four-hour trip. The menu of crab, shrimp, rice pilaf, salad, and so on, with a full bar, gets good reviews. The *Star of the Northwest,* at 115 feet, is large and stable, with lots of outside deck space. But, again, if the weather's bad the dinner won't be such fun.

- **Fresh Aire Charters and Tours** (☎ **907/272-2755** in Anchorage). An Anchorage couple running a bed-and-breakfast drive guests to Seward for a winter or summer Resurrection Bay tour for only six passengers, for $175 per person. You almost have the boat to yourself.

- **Alaska Renown Charters** (☎ **907/224-3806**). The lowest-cost choice, this operator runs a single vessel, the 50-foot *Renown,* on a quick 2¹/₂-hour tour of Resurrection Bay—not the park. If you're short on time or money, it's a good way to get out on the water. The fare is $40 for adults, $20 for children.

EXIT GLACIER

When I visited Italy a few years ago, I got to the point that I thought I'd scream if I saw another painting of the Madonna. If your trip to Alaska is long, you may start to feel the same way about glaciers. But, although relatively small, Exit Glacier really is unique, and I enjoyed a visit even as a jaded life-long Alaskan. (And I've probably seen even more glaciers than Madonnas.) It's possible to walk quite close to Exit Glacier, see its brittle texture, and feel the cold, dense spires of ice looming over you. And the pattern of vegetation reclaiming the land that the glacier has uncovered is well explained by interpretive signs and a nature trail. At the same time, however, the area remains refreshingly primitive. The National Park Service's low-key presentation of the site makes it a casual, pleasant visit for a couple of hours; longer, if you do a hike. Kids enjoy the broad gravel trails, and as long as you don't let them go beyond the warning signs near the ice, there's not much trouble they can get into.

To get to the glacier, turn off the Seward Highway 3.7 miles north of town and follow the signs down the 9-mile gravel road. The road is open only in the summer and can be dusty. There are turn-outs in the broad bed of the wandering Resurrection River to the left of the road. Along this road you'll see the succession of vegetation in reverse, from mature Sitka spruce and cottonwood trees down to smaller alders and shrubs: It takes time for nature to reclaim the sterile ground left behind by a receding glacier. As you get closer, you'll see a sign bearing the year 1780; more signs count upward through the years, marking the retreat of the glacier through time.

If you don't have a car, **Exit Glacier Walking Tours** (☎ **907/362-3074**) takes three trips a day to the glacier from Seward for $7.95 per person, an excellent value. The tour lasts three hours and includes a guided nature walk. **Kenai Fjords Tours** (☎ **907/224-8068**) also takes daily trips to Exit Glacier, combined with a Seward town tour. It starts at 2pm, takes 2¹/₂ hours, and costs $19.

At the parking lot there's a simple ranger station and pit toilets. Ranger-led nature walks start here daily at 10am and 2pm during the summer. Often, a spotting scope is set up to see mountain goats up in the rocky cliffs. The short trail to the glacier starts here. In the summer, rangers wander around to answer questions. Along the way, there's a chance of seeing moose and possibly bears. At the glacier, the trail splits: The steep route goes up along the side of the glacier, and the easy route runs on the flat gravel at its face. Don't go beyond the warning signs; ice can fall off and crush you. An all-day hike, 8 miles round-trip, climbs along the right side of the glacier to the Harding Icefield—the glacier gets its name for being an exit from that massive sheet. It's a challenging walk with a 3,000-foot elevation gain, but is the only chance I'm aware of to visit an icefield on foot short of a technical mountain climb or a helicopter. Because of snow, the trail doesn't open until late June or early July. The icefield itself is cold and dangerous, and there's an emergency shelter maintained by the park service; don't head out on the ice unless you're an experienced climber with equipment. The park service guides a hike up the trail on Saturday starting at 8am.

The **Resurrection River Trail** begins from the road just short of the last bridge to the glacier. It's a pleasant walk, with lots of wildflowers in the fall. It's possible to follow the trail, linking with the Resurrection Trail, all the way across the Kenai Peninsula on a multiday trip. Unfortunately, the trail was heavily damaged by flooding late in 1995, so check with the Park Service for current conditions.

A free park service tent campground is located near the glacier, at Mile 8.5 on Resurrection River Road. There's also a park service cabin a mile from the glacier, open only during the winter when the road is closed. It's accessible by ski or dog sled. Contact the park headquarters for a $30-a-day permit.

COOPER LANDING

The little roadside community of Cooper Landing, in the wooded mountain valley along Kenai Lake and the Kenai River, begins about 8 miles west of Tern Lake, where the Sterling Highway splits from the Seward Highway, and continues sporadically along the highway for about 7 miles. (The Sterling runs generally west until Soldotna, where it heads south again.) The fresh, frothing upper Kenai River is the community's lifeline, bringing the salmon each summer that bring the visitors to fill hotels, restaurants, and the date books of guides. For nonfishermen, there's not much here—a couple of operators do rafting trips and some of the accommodations could provide a romantic mountain retreat. Cooper Landing is also the south end of the Resurrection Trail, described in the Hope section. Just west of the community, the Russian River meets the Kenai, the scene, during the July red salmon season, of a mad fishing and camping frenzy. A ferry takes anglers across the river from the highway, and the 180-site Russian River Campground is frequently full while the sockeye are running.

Cooper Landing has a post office, service stations, and small stores selling fishing gear and essentials, but it's not a center; for banking or anything else not directly related to catching a salmon, you'll have to drive to Sterling, 30 miles away to the west, or Soldotna, 44 miles away.

Each of the accommodations listed below can find you a fishing guide, or tell you where to put your line in the water. **Alaska Troutfitters** (☎ **907/595-1212** or 907/376-3474), at the Alpine Inn, offers guided fly fishing for $165 a day. They also rent drift boats and offer rafting tours—a 2¹/₂-hour trip is $35. The **Alpine Inn,** at Mile 48.2 of the Sterling Highway, in the heart of Cooper Landing, has 12 nice motel-style rooms with TVs and kitchenettes for $95 to $115 a night, double, in the high season. **Alaska Rivers Co.,** at Mile 50 (P.O. Box 827), Cooper Landing, AK 99572 (☎ **907/595-1226**), does a good job of their guided float fishing trips for low prices—$100 for a full day of fishing. They also offer rafting to just see the scenery and they rent cabins. For a rafting-oriented adventure with **Alaska Wildland Adventures,** see Chapter 6, "Outside in Alaska."

The most luxurious hotel on the Kenai Peninsula is up the dirt Bean Creek Road above Cooper Landing, the ✪ **Kenai Princess Lodge,** P.O. Box 676, Cooper Landing, AK 99572 (☎ **907/595-1425**). Built to service the company's cruise-ship and package-tour business, the hotel does have rooms open for independent travelers, for $175 to $185 double in the high season. When the ships stop running, but before the lodge closes in January and February, rooms rent for as little as $109. Each room is like a remote cabin, with balconies overlooking the wooded valley, wood stoves stocked with firewood, and many unique details; yet they are luxurious hotel rooms at a resort with exercise rooms, spas, and a fine restaurant. It would be worth a trip for nonfishermen to go just for a quiet stay. There's an attractive RV park, too.

Gwin's Lodge, at Mile 52, the west end of Cooper Landing (HC 54 Box 50), Cooper Landing, AK 99572 (☎ **907/595-1266**), is the town's old original log road-house; it's got loads of character, and stands just a mile east of the Resurrection trailhead and the Russian River Campground. The food ranges from long-famous burgers to the more recent steaks and seafood. The lodge also offers a shuttle van from Anchorage to bring anglers down to the river and rents a few cabins.

KENAI/SOLDOTNA & STERLING

These quintessential American towns, dominated by shopping malls and fast-food franchises facing broad highways, have only a single claim to fame, but it's a pretty good claim: The largest sport-caught king salmon in the world, almost 100 pounds, came from Kenai River. The Kenai's kings run so large there's a different trophy class for the river—everywhere else in the state, the Alaska Department of Fish and Game will certify a 50-pounder as a trophy, but on the Kenai it has to be at least 75 pounds. That's because kings in the 60-pound class—enough wild muscle to fight ferociously for hours—are just too common here. Fishermen prepared to pay for a charter will be in their element on the river.

Those not interested in fishing will find no more than an afternoon's sightseeing in these towns. There are outdoor activities other than fishing, however, primarily in the lake-dotted Kenai National Wildlife Refuge, which has its headquarters in Soldotna. The refuge has hiking and canoe trails. Kenai is a gateway to the remote wild lands on the west side of Cook Inlet, including the four million acres of Lake Clark National Park and Preserve.

Kenai came into being with the arrival of the Russians at the mouth of the Kenai River more than 200 years ago, but came into its own only with the discovery of oil on the peninsula in 1957. Today its economy relies on oil, commercial fishing, and, to a smaller extent, tourism. Soldotna, a smaller, newer, and even less attractive town, is the borough seat, and the primary destination for sport fishermen.

ESSENTIALS

GETTING THERE   By Car   From Anchorage, the drive on the Seward and Sterling highways to Soldotna is 147 miles. Allow at least three hours, without stops: In summer, traffic will slow you down; in winter, speeds are limited by ice and the fear of hitting moose, which can be fatal for the driver as well as the moose. Most of the major car-rental companies have offices in Kenai, at the airport.

By Bus   The only bus line coming to the area went out of business in 1995. Check with the visitor center to find out if anyone has picked up the service.

By Air   Commuter flights connect Kenai to Anchorage every hour. A reliable carrier is **Era Aviation** (☎ **907/283-9091,** or 800/866-8394), which can also be booked through Alaska Airlines.

VISITOR INFORMATION   The **Kenai Peninsula Visitor Information Center,** operated by the Soldotna Chamber of Commerce, P.O. Box 236, Soldotna, AK 99669 (☎ **907/262-9814**), is located on the south side of town; drive through the commercial strip and turn right after the Kenai River Bridge. It's open in summer, daily from 9am to 7pm; in winter, Monday through Friday from 9am to 5pm. The **Kenai Visitors and Cultural Center,** operated by the Kenai Visitor and Convention Bureau, on the left side of the Kenai Spur Highway past Main Street (P.O. Box 1991), Kenai, AK 99611 (☎ **907/283-1991**), has the usual visitor guidance, but also includes a free two-room museum built in honor of the 1991 bicentennial of the arrival of the Russians in the area. One room contains natural-history displays, and the other, Native, Russian, and Western cultural artifacts. They show free films, as well. In summer the center is open Monday through Friday from 8am to 7pm and on Saturday and Sunday from 10am to 7pm; in winter, Monday through Friday from 8:30am to 5pm and on Saturday and Sunday from noon to 5pm.

The **Kenai National Wildlife Refuge Visitors Center** is up Ski Hill Road in Soldotna (P.O. Box 2139, Soldotna, AK 99669 (☎ **907/262-7021**)—just south of the Kenai River Bridge, turn left, taking the dirt road uphill from the building-supply store. Besides providing outdoors information, the U.S. Fish and Wildlife Service maintains a good little museum of the area's natural history where a film is shown each hour. In summer, it's open daily from 8:30am to 6pm; in winter, Monday through Friday from 8:30am to 4:30pm and on Saturday and Sunday from 10am to 5pm.

ORIENTATION   Sterling is 14 miles east—toward Anchorage—from Soldotna on the **Sterling Highway.** It's just a wide place in the road—incredibly wide, as a matter of fact, and no one is quite able to explain why such a small town needs such a big road. Soldotna, too, is oriented along the Sterling Highway. The **Kenai Spur Highway** is the other commercial strip, connecting Soldotna with Kenai, 10 miles west. Continuing through town, it turns north 10 miles to Nikiski, and then to the Captain Cook State Recreation Area, 25 miles from Kenai. Kenai's central business area is oriented along the Kenai Spur Highway around the **Main Street Loop** and the airport; a couple of blocks south, on the water, is the **old town** area. **Bridge Access Road** leads south across the Kenai River and the Kenai River Flats bird-viewing area.

On the south side of the river, **Kalifornsky Beach Road,** also known as **K-Beach Road,** connects back to Soldotna or south along the shore.

GETTING AROUND   The area is so spread out, walking really isn't possible, and there's no public transportation. Everyone here owns a car, and you can rent one from most major agencies, located at the Kenai airport. If you plan only to fish, however, you may not need one, instead getting rides from your guide, host, or a taxi cab. There are several cab companies; try **Inlet Taxi Cab** (☎ **907/283-4711** in Kenai, **907/262-4770** in Soldotna). There are agencies offering organized tours. **Tours on the Kenai** (☎ **907/260-3369**) offers two three-hour tours, one concentrating on the fishing industry and the other on the Native and Russian cultural heritage of the area; the fare is $30 for adults. **Legacy Tours** (☎ **907/262-5724**) offers half-day history tours for $35.

FAST FACTS   The **sales tax** in Kenai and Soldotna is 5%; outside the city limits it's 2%. Kenai and Soldotna both have **banks.** In Kenai, the National Bank of Alaska is at the Kenai Spur Highway and Willow; in Soldotna, two banks are on the Sterling Highway commercial strip. In addition **ATMs** are all over the place—in Carrs and K-mart stores, for example. In **emergencies,** call 911. Who to call for nonemergency business with the police depends on where you are: in Kenai, the **Kenai Police Department** (☎ **907/283-7879**); in Soldotna, the **Soldotna Police Department** (☎ **907/262-4455**); or outside city limits, the **Alaska State Troopers** (☎ **907/262-4453**). The **Central Peninsula Hospital** is in Soldotna at 250 Hospital Pl. (☎ **907/262-4404**)—from the Sterling Highway, take Binkley Street to Vine Avenue. The *Peninsula Clarion* is published five days a week; out-of-town newspapers are available at Carrs grocery stores.

SPECIAL EVENTS   KENAI   The **Kenai River Festival** (☎ **907/262-5581**), in early June, has food, music, crafts, and games. The **Fourth of July** celebration is a big deal in Kenai. An **Annual Juried Art Show** occurs at the Kenai Fine Arts Center (☎ **907/280-7040**) in August.

Soldotna   In July, Soldotna celebrates **Progress Days,** with a parade and other festival events commemorating the completion of a gas pipeline in 1960—that's the area in a nutshell. The **Soldotna Silver Salmon Derby** takes place in late August, when the silvers come in; the prize for the biggest fish in 1995 was $5,000.

Ninilchik   The **Kenai Peninsula State Fair** (☎ **907/567-3670**), south on the Sterling Highway, is in mid-August.

EXPLORING KENAI & SOLDOTNA

In Kenai's old town, the **Holy Assumption Russian Orthodox Church** is the area's most significant building. The parish was founded in 1845 and the church was built in 1896. It's a quaint, onion-domed church; several related buildings are interesting for their interlocking log construction. Across the street are the remains of an early **Russian fort;** tours are available in the summer. The bluff over the beach is nearby. When the salmon are running, you can occasionally see white beluga whales chasing them upstream from here, sometimes in great numbers. Near here, you can get down to the beach for walks.

On Centennial Park Road, behind the visitor center in Soldotna, is the free **Homesteading Soldotna Historical Society Museum,** which celebrates the 50-year-old history of the town with a collection of old cabins set up as they were when pioneers lived in them; it's open in summer only, Tuesday through Sunday from 10am to 4pm.

A family looking for something to do while a parent is off fishing will do no better than the magnificent **public swimming pool** in Nikiski (☎ **907/766-8472**), 10 miles north of Kenai on the Kenai Spur Road. Built with taxes on the oil property in the area, the facility occupies a large dome and has a tall water slide, mushroom fountains of water, and a hot tub from which parents can watch their children play in the pool below. It's open Tuesday through Friday from 7am to 5pm and 6 to 8pm, and on Saturday and Sunday from 1 to 5pm and 6 to 9pm; the water slide is open Friday through Sunday only. Admission is $3, plus another $3 to use the slide.

GETTING OUTSIDE

✪ **FISHING**   Fishing the Kenai River is the whole point of coming to the area. Check at the visitor centers for information and regulation booklets. Or contact the **Alaska Department of Fish and Game,** at 34828 Kalifornsky Beach Rd. (☎ **907/262-2737**). Of course, you'll need a license, for sale in virtually any sporting-goods store.

King salmon, the monsters of the river, come in two runs. The early run, which sometimes has been limited to catch and release, comes from mid-May to June. These are the smaller fish, in the 20- to 40-pound range. The second run comes during the month of July, and has the massive fish that range up to 90 pounds. Most people fish kings from a boat, which makes them easier to catch and much easier to land. A charter averages $125 to $150 for a six-hour, half-day trip. There are dozens of guides, but no central charter agency. Contact the visitor center in Kenai or Soldotna to get in touch with a guide; many hotels and lodges also have their own guides. It's possible to rent a boat, but the river is swift and treacherous. The **Sports Den,** at 44176 Sterling Hwy. in Soldotna (☎ **907/262-7491**), is one of the larger charter operators, and also rents condos and equipment for all kinds of outdoor activities.

The area really goes crazy when the reds are in the river, mid-July to early August, and the kings are still in the river. You can fish red and silver salmon from the bank, although you have better chances from a boat. Silvers come in two runs. The first, late July to late August, is smaller; the largest group of fish arrive in September. Of course, the fish don't punch a time clock, so to know how they're running at any particular time you have to ask around. You can catch kings and silvers on lures, but reds go mostly for flies—a lot of people fish flies on spinning gear, with little lead weights to aid in casting. Salmon eggs work well as bait on kings and silvers, but check current regulations to determine if they're legal. Trophy-size rainbow trout and Dolly Varden char also come out of the river.

There are more than two dozen public access points over the 80 miles of the Kenai River. A **guide brochure with a map** is available from the state **Division of Parks** (☎ **907/262-5581**); you can pick up a copy at one of the visitor centers.

For fishermen interested in less competition and more of a wilderness experience, Kenai is a gateway for vast wild lands accessible by air on the west side of Cook Inlet. **Air Adventures** (☎ **907/776-5444**) and **High Adventure Air** (☎ **907/ 262-5237**) have packages with fly-in cabins.

SPECIAL PLACES   The **Kenai River Flats,** near the bridge in Kenai, are a tidal marsh populated by birds, and used by migratory birds each spring and fall. State Parks has developed a viewing area near the bridge. The **Kenai National Wildlife Refuge,** known locally as the moose range, is dotted by lakes on flat, wet lowlands. The **Swanson River Canoe Route** and **Swan Lake Canoe Route** are popular trips; the refuge visitor center has a free guide map. There also are several hiking trails in the refuge's uplands, and backcountry camping is permitted anywhere but close to a road or trailhead. Get guidance at the visitor center.

If you're not a fisherman, you may get quite sick of them after a little while any-where near the Kenai, especially if you're looking for a campsite. The **Captain Cook State Recreation Area** is the antidote, a lovely and little-used seaside area on Cook Inlet, 25 miles north of Kenai on the Kenai Spur Road. There are three campgrounds, one a site reached across a lake, and trails, beach walking, a canoe landing at the end of the Swanson River Canoe Route, and lake swimming.

A tour boat recently began taking trips to the remote western shore of Cook Inlet from Kenai. The destination, Tuxedni Bay, is good place to see birds, including puffins, otters, seals, and possibly whales. **Ship to Shore Tours (☎ 907/283-6052)** charges $135 for a full-day cruise on weekends, $42 for a much shorter weekday trip.

WHERE TO STAY

The **bed tax** in Kenai is 10%; in Soldotna you pay only the 5% sales tax; and out-side the city limits of either, only the 2% borough tax. Rates at all hotels are on seasonal schedules with three, four, or even more levels linked to the salmon runs.

There are several standard hotels in Kenai, the best of which looked to be the **Uptown Motel,** at 47 Spur View Dr. (☎ **907/283-3660,** or 800/777-3650); sum-mer rates are around $105 for a double. Across the street, the **Katmai Hotel,** at 10800 Kenai Spur Hwy. (☎ **907/283-6101**), offers perfectly adequate rooms, a little older and with exterior entries, for $89 double. The **Duck Inn,** midway to Soldotna at 35458 Kalifornsky Beach Rd., has tiny but clean rooms with TVs and phones above a bar and restaurant for just $70 double in summer.

Soldotna also has a variety of chain-style hotels. The **Best Western King Salmon,** at 35674 Kenai Spur Hwy. (☎ **907/262-5857**), is among the best, although far from the river.

Below I've listed some of the more interesting places in both towns.

Daniels Lake Lodge Bed and Breakfast. Near Cook Inlet State Recreation Area, north of Kenai (P.O. Box 1444), Kenai, AK 99611. ☎ **907/776-5578.** 5 rms, 2 with bath; 1 cabin. High season, $65–$95 double. Low season, $55–$65. No credit cards. Additional person in room $15 extra.

Located on the peaceful and sparsely built Daniels Lake, more than 20 miles north of Kenai, this lovely place has a boat and canoe you can use for trout fishing right out the back door, among the resident ducks. Beachcombing at the state recreation area also is nearby. There's an outdoor Jacuzzi, a sauna, and a laundry. No smoking.

Great Alaska Fish Camp. Moose River (HC1 Box 218), Sterling, AK 99672 (in winter, P.O. Box 2670, Poulsbo, WA 98370). ☎ **907/262-4515,** or 800/544-2261. Fax 907/262-8797 in summer, 206/638-1582 in winter. 19 cabins. Rates from $175–$249 (one day) to $2,995 (seven-day package). Rates include all meals, guide service, and travel from Anchorage. Closed off-season.

This is a top-flight lodge, offering kayaking, biking, and other "eco-tour" safaris as well as fishing (nonguests can rent equipment, too). Guests find a bottle of wine in luxurious cabins with private bathrooms. There are as many staff as guests and they take a video for you, providing an editing room if you want to cut the dull parts. It's located on a long stretch of riverfront where the Moose River meets the Kenai, in Sterling, east of Soldotna.

Kenai River Lodge. 393 Riverside Dr., Soldotna, AK 99669. ☎ **907/262-4292.** Fax 907/262-7332. 28 rms, 1 suite. TV TEL. High season, $108 double. Low season, $99 double. $250 suite. Rates include continental breakfast. Additional person in room $10 extra. Fishing packages available. MC, V.

Overlooking the river, next to the bridge in Soldotna, this motel has the advantages of good, standard rooms (with refrigerators) and a great location for fishermen. The grassy front yard descends right to the water, with a barbecue where you can cook up your catch. They operate fishing charters from the hotel. The suite is a large, luxurious apartment with a wall of windows facing the river.

⊖ **Log Cabin Bed and Breakfast.** 49840 Eider Rd. (P.O. Box 2886), Kenai, AK 99611. ☎ and fax **907/283-3653.** 8 rms. $80–$90 double. Rates include full breakfast. Additional person in room $10 extra. AE, MC, V.

Ted and Carol Titus built this huge log house specifically to be their new B&B, but with its large common room—with a cathedral ceiling and fireplace—it feels more like a luxurious wilderness lodge. Located off Kalifornsky Beach Road a little south of the bridge in Kenai, the house stands over an active beaver pond, with a deck and lots of windows to watch the beavers. The upstairs rooms, which cost $10 more, are well worth it—they're large and airy; the downstairs rooms are a half-basement. All the rooms are attractively decorated in a country style. In-room telephones are available, and there's a Jacuzzi.

Soldotna Bed and Breakfast Lodge. 399 Lovers Lane, Soldotna, AK 99669. ☎ **907/ 262-4779.** Fax 907/262-3201. 16 rms, none with bath, and three separate houses. TV TEL. $135–$145 double; $280–$870 complete house. Rates include full breakfast. Additional person in room $67 extra. Fishing packages available. Closed in winter. AE, MC, V (5% surcharge).

Right on the river, right in Soldotna, yet in a wooded setting, this inn run by the meticulous Charlotte Ischi has become *the* place to go for political dignitaries and oil industry executives. Each room is unique, with balconies over the river or the garden, and attractive wallpaper and furnishings. There are five clean bathrooms and four separate shower rooms among the 16 bedrooms. Smoking is not permitted in the inn. The grounds slope down to the river along a sheltered boardwalk, leading to a dock where you can fish or board one of the fishing charters run by Bill Ischi's Alaska Fishing Charters.

WHERE TO EAT

Franchise fast food dominates in Kenai and Soldotna; there also are plenty of burger-steak-seafood places. Here are some of the more unique highlights.

The Armenian Bakery / Grand Burrito. 44096 Sterling Hwy., Soldotna. ☎ **907/ 262-2228.** $6.30 buffet. No credit cards. Mon–Sat 11am–9pm.

I include this place partly because Armenian/Russian/Mexican fast food is a great example of the ethnic cuisine you find in the area—it's just about impossible to find Mexican without finding Italian, and vice versa, or other equally improbable combinations. The Armenian food—not that I'm an expert—is quite good, but most locals sit in the Mexican fast-food side, so I guess the Eastern European proprietors know what they're doing. No liquor license.

⊖ **Kitchen Express and Seafood Saloon.** 115 S. Willow, Kenai. ☎ **907/283-5397.** All items $6.20–$12.50. CB, DC, DISC, MC, V. Mon–Wed 7am–6pm, Thurs–Sat 7am–9pm, Sun 9am–3pm.

This light, casual restaurant near the airport has the ambience of an espresso shop, and, indeed, it has a coffee bar. But the menu, though limited, is more adventurous than most anywhere else in town, primarily revolving around shrimp, crab, and shellfish. There are lots of specials (in season) of salmon and halibut, too. And the prices are low. For meat-eaters, there are sandwiches. Beer and wine license.

Paradisos. Main St. and Kenai Spur Hwy., Kenai. ☎ **907/283-2222.** Main courses $10–$28; lunch $5.25–$16. MC, V. Daily 11am–11pm.

The cuisine is Greek, Italian, and Mexican—the usual hodge-podge. But the extensive menu is reliable, if pedestrian. The decor is quite elaborate and the service efficient. There's a large salad bar and lounge. It's a good family restaurant of the kind that's successful in a small town. Full liquor license.

Thai Town Restaurant. 44224 Sterling Hwy., Soldotna. ☎ **907/262-8426.** Main courses $7–$16; lunch $6. MC, V. Mon–Sat 11am–9pm, Sun 11am–4pm.

The authentic Thai food is prepared by members of the same family who have introduced Anchorage to their national cuisine and made many converts. The curries and soups are good, service is fast, and the dining room pleasant, if less than grand. No liquor license.

✪ Through the Seasons. Sterling Hwy. and Kenai Spur Hwy., Soldotna. ☎ **907/262-5006.** Lunch $5.25–$7; dinner $15–$24. MC, V. Tues–Sat 11am–3pm and 5:30–9pm, Fri–Sat until 9:30pm.

Although Homer now can do better, this has always been the Kenai/Soldotna area's best restaurant. It's at the intersection of two busy highways, but the attractive wood-sided building is nestled back in the trees. The menu specializes in local fish, prepared with light sauces in an atmosphere of casual elegance. Beer and wine license.

HOMER

Homer's leading mystic, Brother Asaiah Bates, maintains that a confluence of metaphysical forces causes a focus of powerful creative energy on this "cosmic hamlet by the sea." It's hard to argue. Homer is full of creative people—artists, eccentrics, and those who simply contribute to a quirky community in a beautiful place. Indeed, Brother Asaiah may be the quintessential Homerite, although perhaps an extreme example, with his gray ponytail, extraordinary openness and generosity, and flowery rhetoric about "the cosmic wheel of life." Homer is full of outspoken, unusual, and even odd individualists—people who make living in the town almost an act of belief. I can say this because I'm a former Homerite myself.

The geography of Homer—physical as well as metaphysical—has gathered certain people here the way currents gather driftwood on the town's pebble beaches. Homer is at the end of the road—the nation's paved highway system comes to an abrupt conclusion at the tip of the Homer Spit, almost 5 miles out in the middle of Kachemak Bay—and believers of one kind or another have washed up here for decades. There were the "barefooters," a communal group that eschewed shoes, even in the Alaska winter—Brother Asaiah came with them in the early 1950s. There are the Russian Old Believers, who organize their strictly traditional communities around their objection to Russian Orthodox church reforms made by Peter the Great. There are the former hippies who have become successful commercial fishermen after flocking here in the late 1960s to camp as "Spit rats" on the beach. And there are even the current migrants—artists and retired people, fundamentalist preachers and New Age healers, wealthy North Slope oil workers and land-poor settlers with no visible means of support—all people who live here simply because they choose to.

The choice is understandable. Homer lies on the north side of Kachemak Bay, a branch of lower Cook Inlet of extraordinary biological productivity—the halibut fishing, especially, is exceptional. The town has a breathtaking setting on the Spit and on a wildflower-covered bench high above the bay. The outdoors, especially on the water and across the bay, contains wonderful opportunities. And the arts community has developed into an attraction of its own, drawing more artists and creating the reputation of an "arts colony." There are several good galleries and the Pratt Museum, which has a national reputation.

Homer gets its name from a guy named Homer, which seems fitting since it's the sort of place where first names tend to be used. Homer Pennock came to the area around the turn of the century for the coal. Low-quality lignite is common on the north side of Kachemak Bay, which means "Smoky Bay," as the seams occasionally burned and created haze. The coal-fueled steamers landed at Seldovia, which was a metropolis at that time but today is a sleepy little village. A rail line led to the end of the Spit. Its last vestiges were destroyed in the 1964 earthquake and the coal is too wet and soft to be of any commercial value today, but locals still use it for heat in their wood- and coal-burning stoves. Storms break big hunks of it off underwater seams, washing the lignite ashore for the picking, especially on Bishop's Beach, at the end of Main Street.

Homer began to take its modern form after two events: In the 1950s the Sterling Highway connected it to the rest of the world, and in 1964 the Good Friday earthquake sank the Spit, narrowing a much larger piece of land with a small forest into the tendril that now barely stands above the water. If not for constant reinforcement by the federal government, the Spit long since would have become an island, and Homer would hardly exist. The Spit, and the boat harbor there, are the town's vital organs; the commercial fishing and visitor industry keep it alive.

ESSENTIALS

GETTING THERE   By Car   At about 235 miles, Homer is roughly 4¹/₂ hours from Anchorage by car, if you don't stop at any of the interesting or beautiful places along the way. It's a scenic drive. If you take a rental car, you may want to drive it both ways, as the drop-off fees from Anchorage to Homer are high. Take the Seward Highway, described above, 90 miles to the Sterling Highway, then hang a right and keep driving. There's also a long tradition of sharing rides to Anchorage; public radio station KBBI, 890am, broadcasts a ride line to connect those who need a ride with drivers.

By Bus   Service has always been available in the past, but the only operator was out of business at the end of 1995. Check with the visitor center, Gray Line, or Seward Bus Line (listed in the Anchorage or Seward sections) to find out if service has resumed.

By Air   Commuter airlines serve Homer's airport from Anchorage and Kenai. **Era Aviation** (☎ 800/866-8394) can also be booked through Alaska Airlines. Flights also go south from here to Kodiak. Several air-taxis use Homer as a hub for villages in Kachemak Bay, and this is a jumping-off place for the McNeil River Bear Observatory, fly-in fishing, and the outer coast of the Kenai Peninsula.

By Ferry   The **Alaska Marine Highway System** (☎ 907/235-8449, or 800/642-0066) connects Homer to Seldovia, Kodiak, and points west along the Alaska Peninsula and Aleutian Archipelago to Unalaska with the *Tustumena*. If you take the ferry anywhere, plan to fly back, as the sailings are infrequent and the stopovers sometimes brief.

VISITOR INFORMATION   The **Homer Chamber of Commerce,** P.O. Box 541, Homer, AK 99603 (☎ 907/235-7740 or 907/235-5300), maintains two **visitor information centers.** One is at 135 Sterling Hwy., on the right side past the intersection with Pioneer Avenue, open in summer, daily from 8am to 9pm. The other is in a little cabin on the Spit, and primarily sells tickets for the halibut derby the chamber puts on each summer, but also has a guide and brochures of businesses. You can get a copy of the *Homer News Tourist Guide* anywhere in town; it includes a map. The Alaska Division of Parks has a **ranger station,** P.O. Box 3248, Homer,

AK 99603 (☎ **907/235-7024**), located 4 miles from town as you approach Homer on the Sterling Highway. The **Maritime National Wildlife Refuge Visitor Center,** at 509 Sterling Hwy. (☎ **907/235-6961**), across from the intersection with Pioneer Avenue, is open in summer, daily from 9am to 6pm daily, shorter hours in winter. The refuge, consisting of most of the coastline of all of Alaska, is managed by the U.S. Fish and Wildlife Service. The visitor center has displays and films about marine natural history.

ORIENTATION   At the top of **Baycrest Hill,** coming into town on the **Sterling Highway,** you see the various parts of Homer—and the broad expanse of Cook Inlet, Augustine Volcano, and Kachemak Bay—arrayed before you in one of the most spectacular highway views anywhere. The chief feature of the town is **Homer Spit,** jutting out several miles into the bay. The ferry dock and all marine activity are at its tip. At the base of the Spit is the airport and a narrow commercial district that lies between man-made Beluga Lake and the Spit, on **Ocean Drive.** On the near side of Beluga Lake is the downtown area. The main street is **Pioneer Avenue,** which branches off from the Sterling Highway to the left as you pass the middle school entering town. On the ocean side of the highway is the Bishop's Beach area. On the other side of town from the Sterling Highway entrance, Pioneer Avenue turns into **East End Road,** which snakes far up the bay with great views of the water. On a bench above the town, more wonderful views, broad fields of wildflowers, and miles of great walks are to be had at the top of **East Hill Road,** off East End Road, and **West Hill Road,** off the Sterling Highway.

GETTING AROUND   You can't cover the town without a vehicle—at least a bicycle, and that would only be for strong riders. Most major car-rental agencies have offices at the airport. Bicycles are for rent at **Homer Saw and Cycle,** at 1532 Ocean Dr. (☎ **907/235-8406**). There are several taxi companies in town, including **CHUX Cab** (☎ **907/235-CHUX**). Run by the same folks as the Homer Referral Agency, listed below, **Homer Tours** (☎ **907/235-8996**) offers van and bus tours. **Day Breeze Shuttle and Tours** (☎ **907/399-1168**) offers a shuttle on the Spit and custom tours. For water transportation, there are many charters and water taxis available; they're described under "Getting Outside," below.

FAST FACTS   Homer has a **sales tax** of 5.5%; outside city limits you pay the 2% Kenai Peninsula Borough sales tax. There are banks, with **ATMs,** on Pioneer Avenue near Main Street and Sterling Highway near Heath Street. The **post office** is on the Sterling Highway at Heath Street. In **emergencies,** call 911; for nonemergency calls within city limits, call the **Homer Police Department** (☎ **907/235-3150**); outside the city, phone the **Alaska State Troopers** (☎ **907/235-8239**). Both have offices located across Pioneer Avenue from the intersection with Lake Street. The **South Peninsula Hospital** is at the top of Bartlett Street, off Pioneer Avenue (☎ **907/ 235-8101**). Homer has two weekly newspapers: the established *Homer News* and the more recent *Homer Tribune.* You can find the Kenai and Anchorage newspapers all over town.

SPECIAL EVENTS   Homer's **Winter Carnival,** in February, is its biggest community event of the year, a small-town celebration with a beer-making contest, beauty pageant, and hot rod races on frozen Beluga Lake, among other highlights. In early May, the **Kachemak Bay Shorebird Festival** includes guided birdwatching, art activities, and other events; it's organized by the Homer Chamber of Commerce and Maritime National Wildlife Refuge. **Concert on the Lawn,** put on usually the second Saturday or Sunday in August by KBBI radio (☎ **907/235-7721**), is a day-long outdoor music festival that brings together the whole town. The summer-long

Jackpot Halibut Derby, also put on by the chamber of commerce, has a top prize that usually exceeds $15,000 for the biggest fish of the summer. Winning fish are in the 300-pound class.

EXPLORING HOMER

Homer's history, though colorful, is too brief to have left any sites anyone could put up a fence around or sell a ticket to. The attractions of the town, even in town, come from its setting—the walks on the beaches and in the hilltop meadows—and from the art it has inspired. Pick up a copy of the walking tour of the downtown art galleries at the visitor center. Here I've described some of the highlights.

✪ **Pratt Museum.** Bartlett St. and Pioneer Ave. ☎ **907/235-8635.** Admission $3 adults, $2 seniors over age 65, free for children 17 and under. High season, daily 10am–6pm; low season, Tues–Sun noon–5pm. Closed Jan.

The Homer Society of Natural History's museum is as good as any you'll find in a town this size. The exhibit on the *Exxon Valdez* oil spill traveled to the Smithsonian in Washington, D.C., to acclaim. The Pratt is strongest in natural history and has a saltwater aquarium in which to see the life of Kachemak Bay close-up and even touch it, after you wash your hands, but the museum also has displays of local art, history, and culture. If you're wondering about all the fishing boats down in the harbor, at the Pratt you can find out about the different types of gear as well as the fish they catch. Also, the volunteers will enjoy imparting local secrets about where to go, what to do, and where to eat.

Commercial Galleries

✪ **BUNNELL STREET GALLERY** This cooperative, located in a perfect space in an old hardware store near Bishop's Beach at the lower end of Main Street, is one of the best in Alaska. Unlike most other Alaska galleries, which double as tourist gift shops, Bunnell was made by and for artists and the experience is noncommercial. You may be tempted to become a member of the nonprofit corporation that runs it, for membership comes with a one-of-a-kind plate made by one of the artists. As with all Homer art, the themes of the work tend to be fishy and the medium and style could be anything. The gallery is open afternoons and evenings, closed Monday during the summer and Tuesday as well in the winter. The gallery is closed completely in January and February. Don't miss the **Two Sisters Bakery** and coffee shop next door.

PTARMIGAN ARTS Located on Pioneer Avenue and sometimes staffed by the artist co-op members themselves, Ptarmigan Arts specializes in crafts, especially ceramics and fabrics, which are the most common media in Homer and which generally are more affordable than fine art. Occasionally you can see a demonstration by one of the resident artists. This was one of the first galleries that showed serious art in Homer.

UNDERWATER SEA ODYSSEAS and HOME OF THE WISDOM KEEPERS The name alone should be enough. On Pioneer Avenue, it features art that not only represents but uses sea plants and animals as a medium.

SEA LION GALLERY Wildlife artist Gary Lyon and his family own and staff this tiny gallery among the T-shirt shops on one of the boardwalks on Homer Spit. It's pleasant but a little odd to see very valuable works by Lyon and others displayed in this intimate setting. Lyon's work captures Alaska wildlife in spectacular detail, but also transforms his subjects with a distinctively dreamy vision. Open in summer only.

NORMAN LOWELL STUDIO & GALLERY Homesteader Lowell shows and paints his landscapes daily in the summer at his home above the Anchor River, about

Homer

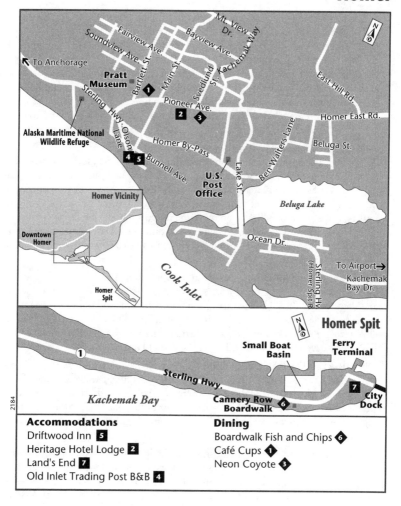

Accommodations
Driftwood Inn **5**
Heritage Hotel Lodge **2**
Land's End **7**
Old Inlet Trading Post B&B **4**

Dining
Boardwalk Fish and Chips ◆**6**
Café Cups ◆**1**
Neon Coyote ◆**3**

10 miles from Homer on the Sterling Highway—the turn-off is well marked. A visit provides a glimpse of old-time Alaska.

GETTING OUTSIDE

ON LAND ✪ **Tide Pooling**   Exploring Kachemak Bay's tide pools is the best way to really get to know the sea and meet the strange and wonderful animals that live in it, and it doesn't cost anything but the price of a pair of rubber boots. First, check a tide book, available for free or for a nominal price in virtually any local store, or ask a local to check one for you; you need a low tide of –2 or lower. This indicates that low water will be at least 2 feet below the normal low, some 25 feet below the high, exposing more of the lower intertidal zone that contains the most interesting creatures. At a –5 tide, you could find octopus and other oddities. Also, the lower the tide, the more time you'll have to look. Keep track of the time: The tide will come in faster than you imagine, and you could get stranded and quickly drown in the 40°F water.

The best place to go in town is reached from Bishop's Beach Park, near the lower end of Main Street. Walk west on the beach toward the opening of the bay to Cook Inlet. It's a good half-hour walk to the Coal Point area, where the sand and boulders end and bedrock makes out from the shore. This is where you'll find pools of water left behind by the receding tide, all full of life. Explore patiently and gently—look at the animals and touch them, but always put them back as they were and be careful not to crush anything underfoot. Identification keys are available for purchase at **The Book Store** on the Sterling Highway next to Eagle Foods. If you want to keep going, there's a sea otter rookery off shore about 3 miles down the beach.

Hiking   Kachemak Heritage Land Trust, at 395 E. Pioneer Ave. (☎ 907/235-5263), a nonprofit organization conserving land in Homer, leads naturalist day hikes all summer for $5 or $6 per person, or $10 per family; pick up a schedule at the office or the visitor center. If you want to hike on your own, there are trails on the bench above Homer. The **Homestead Trail** is an old road used by Homer's early settlers; it has several trailheads; one is at the reservoir on Skyline Drive—drive up West Hill Road from the Sterling Highway and turn right. The largely informal trail is lovely and peaceful, weaving through trees, across fields of wildflowers, and past old homestead cabins.

Driving or Mountain Biking   Several gravel roads around Homer make for exquisite drives or bike rides. East End Road goes through forest, the village of Fritz Creek, and then follows the bluff line through meadows toward the head of the bay. The road eventually turns into an all terrain vehicle trail, don't go beyond your vehicle's ability to get out. Skyline Drive has extraordinary views of high canyons and Kachemak Bay; drive up East Hill Road just east of Homer.

ON OR ACROSS KACHEMAK BAY   It's relatively inexpensive to get out on Kachemak Bay, and boating is the whole point of Homer. I've listed some of the options here; side trips to Seldovia and Halibut Cove are listed below. A daily boat, **Jakolof Ferry Service** (☎ 907/235-2376) runs to the south side of the bay, offering service to Halibut Cove and other remote points for kayaking, hiking, camping, biking, and cabins.

Fishing   Homer is known for ✪ **fishing for halibut,** those huge, flat bottomfish, and the harbor is full of charter boats that will take you out for the day for around $150 per person. People daily catch fish that are larger than they are, and halibut over 50 pounds are common. To get to where the fish are requires an early start and a long ride to fairly unprotected waters; people who get seasick easily shouldn't go, as the boat drifts on the waves during fishing. Using gear and lines that look strong enough to pick up the boat, you jig the herring bait up and down on the bottom. Halibut aren't acrobats like salmon and fighting one can be like pulling up a sunken Buick. **Central Charters** (☎ 907/235-7847 or 800/478-7847) is a booking agent for many operators, and also books tours, water taxis, the *Danny J* to Halibut Cove, rents sea kayaks, and even sells tickets for live theater. Two of the most experienced and largest operators are **Silver Fox Charters** (☎ 907/235-8792 or 800/478-8792) and **North Country Halibut Charters** (☎ 907/235-7620 or 800/770-7620).

The best **salmon fishing** is to be had in the Kenai River, 86 miles north on the Sterling Highway, or one of the other streams that drain the west side of the Kenai Peninsula to Cook Inlet, but there is some salmon fishing around Kachemak Bay. Salmon are fished with trolling gear year round, not only when they're running in the streams. **Dockside Tours** (☎ 907/235-8337 or 800/532-8338) books such charters. Also, a lagoon on the Spit is stocked with terminal run king and silver salmon by the Alaska Department of Fish and Game. These fish have nowhere to spawn, and some fishermen scorn such "fish-in-a-barrel" angling. At the end of the run, snagging is permitted, which is like mugging salmon. Check the **fishing regulations,** in booklets available at all sporting-goods stores or at the fish and game department, at 3298 Douglas (☎ **907/235-8191**).

⊗ Gull Island   Rainbow Tours' Gull Island trip is a tremendous value: For only $10 for an adult, the comfortable 67-foot *Rainbow Connection* takes passengers to the Gull Island bird rookery, lingering so close to the rocks it's possible to get a good view of the birds' nests with the naked eye. In season, you can see glaucus winged gulls, tufted puffins, black-legged kittiwakes, common murres, red-faced and pelagic cormorants, horned puffins, pigeon guillemots, and occasionally other species. The boat usually continues on to drop visitors off at the Alaska Center for Coastal Studies in Peterson Bay, listed below, so you get to see quite a bit of the bay for the price of Gull Island alone. **Rainbow Tours** has an office on the Spit, at the Cannery Row Boardwalk (☎ **907/235-7272**); it's a reliable, family-run company, and the wildlife commentary on the boat is accurate and well presented. A friendly crew mans a snack and beer and wine bar on board.

✪ Center for Alaska Coastal Studies   This nonprofit foundation is dedicated to educating the public about the sea. That means the group's emphasis isn't to make money, but to interpret Kachemak Bay for visitors. You'll go for a day-long exploration of the Peterson Bay area: If the tides are right, the volunteers will take you on a fascinating guided tide pool walk; if not, you can take a nature walk. You decide what you want to do. There's also a lodge with saltwater tanks containing creatures from the intertidal zone, and those who aren't up to the hikes can have a good day hanging around here. **Rainbow Tours** (☎ **907/235-7272**) books the trips and takes passengers at 9am daily on the *Rainbow Connection*, described above under Gull Island. At $55 per person, it's a bargain—you'd could pay that just for a boat to the other side of the bay. Pack your own lunch, as none is provided.

Kachemak Bay State Park   The park comprises much of the land across the water that makes all those views from Homer so spectacular. There's a network of state-maintained hiking trails and a remote **state park ranger station** in Halibut Cove Lagoon (☎ **907/235-7024**), open in summer. The park has about 25 miles of trails; a trail guide is available from the Division of State Parks, or the visitor centers. Once you're there, you are truly in the wilderness—you'll need to be ready to feed and shelter yourself and to deal with bears. Or you can go for a day trip, walk on a beach you have to yourself, and take a hike on one of the trails before being picked up at a prearranged time in the afternoon. Various water taxis can take you across and give you ideas on good places for beach walking, camping, and hiking. **Kachemak Bay Water Taxi and Tours** (☎ **907/399-3333**) charges $40 to $60 per person for that service.

Mcneil River State Game Sanctuary   McNeil River has the world's greatest known concentration of brown bears in June, July, and early August, when there's an easy meal to be had from the chum salmon trying to jump up a waterfall to return to spawn upriver. It's also the best place in the world to watch bears, as decades of protection and wise management have taught the bears—more than 100 at a time at the height of the run—to ignore humans standing within a few yards, even while the bears go on about their business of feeding, nursing, mating, and just being bears. If you've seen vivid photographs of bears catching flying salmon they may well have been taken here. It's such a valuable experience that permits to visit and tent in the campground are handed out by lottery by the **Alaska Department of Fish and Game,** 333 Raspberry Rd., Anchorage, AK 99518-1599 (☎ **907/267-2181**)

Hermits on the Homestead

Late in October the snow was holding back in the clouds like a strong emotion. The ground was frozen, the swamp grasses stiff, brittle, painted with frost. This was the one time of year when, with a stout four-wheel-drive truck, you could drive in to Ben's cabin. It stood on a small rise amid his hundreds of acres of swampy ground, the only spot where trees could get out of the dampness and grow. The heavy, lovingly peeled logs of the house lay horizontally amid big birch and white spruce trees. Ben had dragged these huge tree trunks from far afield, by himself, when he started his homestead nearly 40 years earlier so he could keep living trees nearer to his house.

I'm not using his real name. Ben was a private guy. He invited us generously, offered coffee from the percolator on top of the soapstone wood stove, but it was clear that he wasn't quite sure he remembered how to talk to people—where to look, for example—and he kept mumbling and looking at my feet or the sky. He showed us around the house—the huge rocks he'd dragged in to build a foundation, the cellar where he stored his food, the collection of moose racks. Food tended to walk by each fall—he never had to go far to get his moose, and one of the biggest he shot right on the doorstep. Everything about his home was exactly the way he wanted it, the product of immense effort to make it all with his own hands. I could see plainly how he'd spent his days all these years. But I could only imagine what his nights must have been like, all alone out here—the piles of *Reader's Digest* and *National Geographic* magazines, the insistent silence.

Late in the afternoon I finally asked Ben why he'd spent his whole adult life on this homestead, so far from other people. Why not move to town, where life is easier and there's someone to talk to? Well, he said, he did work construction in the summer for cash. But I knew that was an evasion. How, I asked, did he first end up out here, in the middle of nowhere, in a huge swamp? What made him want to be off by himself when he first came out here, so long ago? Pause—check the shoes, check the sky—well, he said, it seems there was a woman. She chose the other guy.

Years ago, *U.S. News and World Report* did an article about a homesteader on the Kenai Peninsula who was a Vietnam veteran—just one of the many mad hermits from the war who had hidden off in the Alaska woods by themselves, populating the wilderness with human time bombs. The subject of the story, a well-respected member of his little homesteading community, resented the characterization, and the magazine later paid him to settle his libel suit and printed a retraction. Everyone in the area knew the article was a bunch of baloney—Alaska homesteaders are as varied as people in the city. They aren't all crazed veterans any more than they're all victims of unrequited love, although those make the best stories. What they do have in common that's unique is a willingness to invest hard physical labor every day of their lives into the things the rest of us obtain effortlessly by turning a thermostat or a faucet handle.

Alaska's homesteaders came in waves. There were the prospectors from the gold rush who stayed. Then, after World War II, GIs with families looking for broad new opportunities came north and settled more land. The counterculture movement of the 1960s brought yet another group.

Federal homesteading laws written to open the Great Plains to agriculture in the 19th century made getting land difficult and required Alaska homesteaders to do a lot of anachronistic, absurd work—like clearing large tracts for farming that could never occur. To prove up the claim, the homesteaders had to survey the land, live on it, clear much of it, and then answer any challenges about their accomplishments at a hearing. If they passed the test, they received a patent to up to 120 acres.

The laws allowing homesteading on federal lands in Alaska were all repealed by 1986, but the state government still provides land to its citizens under laws that allow homesteading, lotteries, and sale of remote land. The parcels are very remote and smaller than the old federal homesteads, and the rules still don't make it easy—you have to live at least 25 months on the land in a five-year period, for example. Many families try, with a Hollywood dream of living in the wilderness, only to give up when they learn firsthand of the hardship, privations, and cold. I know from experience that I want never again to live in a home where the heating is wood or the water in jerry cans, and I've never done anything approaching building a homestead. Homesteading isn't like camping. Outdoors skills are essential, but won't help unless you also know how to repair engines below zero, build houses without power tools or proper materials, carry all your own water and firewood, and live poor, largely without an income or any of the things money can buy. You have to be willing to bathe rarely, be cold in winter and be eaten alive by mosquitoes in summer, and end up with land that isn't really worth anything.

Many successful homesteading experiences end with growing children. A couple may make it in the wilderness before having children, and young kids don't care if they can take a bath, so long as the parents don't mind being far from medical care and washing diapers by hand. But when children get to a certain age, they need to go to school and be around other children. The families often expect to go back to the homestead someday, but, somehow, they rarely do. I met a couple who worked and lived in town to educate their children; then, after they retired and the kids were through college, moved back out to their place along the railroad line north of Talkeetna. They didn't last through the winter—they'd forgotten how hard it was. Areas that were thriving little communities of neighbors in the 1950s or 1960s now are deserted, perhaps with one hermit left—like my friend Ben. Through it all, only about 160,000 acres of Alaska today—out of a total land mass of 365 million acres—shows any signs of human habitation. Less than 1% is in private ownership.

My wife's parents homesteaded in the 1950s and 1960s. They were in the post–World War II generation of families. Today the family still has some acreage, and a treasure trove of great stories—among them the tales of my late father-in-law's feats of strength and endurance, and my wife's memory of playing with dolls as a girl, and looking up to meet the eyes of a bear that had been watching her.

But my favorite is the story of Rose and her lover. They lived in the same area in northern California where Barbara's parents grew up. Everyone in town knew the story of the red-headed beauty who had an affair with an older man. Rose's parents refused to let her marry him and ruled that the couple couldn't see each other anymore. She entered a convent and he disappeared, never to be seen in the town again. Many years later, after moving to Alaska, Barbara's parents were boating in Kachemak Bay when they got caught by bad weather on the opposite side of the bay from Homer. On their own in an open boat and looking for shelter, they found a cabin on a remote beach of an otherwise uninhabited island. They were taken in and befriended by the hermit who'd homesteaded there for years. After warming up with a cup of coffee, they got to talking about where they'd come from and how they'd ended up in Alaska. When it came time for their host to tell his story, it was about a beautiful young woman he'd loved, named Rose.

more than 2,000 apply annually for fewer than 250 permits. There are outhouses and water comes from a rain barrel—it's remote camping. **Kachemak Air** (☎ 907/235-8924), listed below under "Flightseeing," can get you there, and knows where else to find bears if you can't get a permit. Mike and Diane McBride, of Kachemak Bay Wilderness Lodge (see "Where to Stay" section below), also operate a more comfortable lodging near the sanctuary.

Sea Kayaking   Kachemak Bay is popular for sea kayaking—the south side has many protected bays and inlets, and you're likely to see sea otters and may see orcas or other whales. The North Kayak Adventures (book through Central Charters, ☎ 907/235-7847) offers day trips, even for beginners, for $100. **Tutka Bay Boats** (☎ 907/235-7166) is operated by a couple who live on the south side of the bay. They offer guided sea kayaking, as well as water taxis, fishing charters, and accommodations. Another good idea would be to take the passenger boat *Danny J* to Halibut Cove, described below, and rent a kayak at **Quiet Place Lodge** (☎ 907/296-2212 or 907/235-7847), on the other side, where you'd be ready to set off paddling; the waters are protected and you can rent by the hour. Experienced kayakers can take a water taxi across and explore at will, camping on beaches over much of the bay; check with the Kachemak Bay State Park rangers for guidance.

Flightseeing   There are several good air-taxis in Homer, providing access to the really remote areas of the southern Kenai Peninsula and lower Cook Inlet that you can't easily reach by boat, but **Kachemak Air Service,** P.O. Box 1769, Homer, AK 99603 (☎ 907/235-8924), is really special. It offers scenic flights starring at $90 per person. Bill de Creeft, flying out of Homer since 1967, is experienced enough to qualify as a pioneer aviator, but he has nothing on his plane, a restored 1929 Travel Air S-6000-B, a luxurious biplane with mahogany trim and wicker seats, originally built in limited editions for executive travel by the airlines. De Creeft also operates a deHaviland Otter and a Beaver, the Alaskan bush pilot's traditional workhorses. They carry fishermen, hikers, kayakers, and those who just want to see the wilderness; and provide access to the McNeil River Bear Sanctuary and remote bear viewing in Katmai National Park.

WHERE TO STAY

Besides the hotels listed in detail below, you'll find good rooms at the following, in order of my preference: the **Baycrest View Inn,** at the top of Baycrest Hill before you come into town on the Sterling Highway (☎ 907/235-8485), with the best view you're ever likely to find at a motel; the **Best Western Bidarka,** at 575 Sterling Hwy. (☎ 907/235-8148), as you come into town, a large chain hotel with a restaurant and lounge; and the **Beluga Lake Lodge,** at 984 Ocean Dr. (☎ 907/235-5995).

The 5.5% **sales tax** applies to rooms.

Hotels

Driftwood Inn. 135 W. Bunnell Ave., Homer, AK 99603. ☎ **907/235-8019.** Fax 907/235-8039. 20 rms, some with bath; 1 suite. High season, $110 double. Low season, $60 double. Additional person in room $10 extra. AE, CB, DC, DISC, MC, V.

The inn, in a historic building a block from Bishop's Beach, resembles a lodge or bed-and-breakfast with its large fireplace of rounded beach rock in the lobby, the breakfast table, where cereal and coffee are available for a nominal price, and the owner's roving dog. The rooms are quaint, but some are tiny; some have ocean views, private bathrooms, cable TV, and telephones, while others have far fewer amenities. The walls are thin, so there's a no-noise policy during evening hours. The location, near the Bunnell Street gallery and the beach, is second only to Land's End, on the Spit. There's a coin-op laundry and free coffee in the lobby.

Ⓢ Heritage Hotel Lodge. 147 E. Pioneer Ave., Homer, AK 99603. ☎ **907/235-7787** or 800/380-7787. Fax 907/235-2804. 35 rms, 1 suite. TV TEL. High season, $60–$80 double. Low season, $50–$70 double. Additional person in room $10 extra. AE, CB, DC, DISC, JCB, MC, V.

Homer's first hotel was built in 1948 in a log building on Pioneer Avenue. Now it's considerably larger, but retains an old-fashioned feel. The hallways are narrow and the rooms are not large, but they are clean and those in the larger, new wing have all the facilities of a modern hotel. You're near the museum, downtown shops, and restaurants, but you'll have to drive to the Spit. Kitchenettes are available, and there's free coffee in the lobby.

✪ Land's End. 4786 Homer Spit Rd., Homer, AK 99603. ☎ **907/235-2500** or 907/235-0420. 49 rms, 12 suites. TV TEL. High season, $85–$150 double. Low season, $65–$105 double. Additional person in room $10 extra. AE, DC, DISC, MC, V.

Traditionally *the* place to stay in Homer, Land's End would be popular no matter what it was like inside because of its location at the tip of Homer Spit, the best spot in Homer and possibly the best spot in Alaska to site a hotel. It has been under constant renovation in recent years, and, although the wandering old buildings have lost much of their charm, the hotel now is quite comfortable. There are 11 different classes of rooms, ranging from cute shiplike compartments to two-story affairs; those in the lower price range look out on the parking lot, not the bay. It's near the boat harbor and you can fish right from the beach in front of the hotel. There's free coffee.

The **✪ Chart Room** restaurant, with excellent seafood, has comfortable light-wood furnishings and sits right on the beach, where you can watch otters, eagles, and fishing boats. The location is certainly the best in town, and the food, although uneven from year to year in the past, currently leaves nothing to be desired. This is the original quality restaurant in town—although it now has competition from its former chefs (see The Homestead and Café Cups under "Where to Eat," below). Main courses are in the $15 to $20 range.

Bed-and-Breakfasts

Homer has dozens of B&Bs, many of them really wonderful. A list is available from the Homer Chamber of Commerce Visitor Center, with names and addresses. Gert Seekins, at the **Homer Referral Agency** (☎ **907/235-8996;** fax 907/235-2625), books most of the B&Bs in town, and other activities; her old-time Alaska hospitality started the bed-and-breakfast movement in Homer. I can list only three, so I've attempted only to show the range of what's available.

✪ Magic Canyon Ranch Bed and Breakfast. 40015 Waterman Rd., Homer, AK 99603. ☎ **907/235-6077.** Fax 907/235-6077. 4 rms, 2 with bath. High season, $75–$90 double. Low season, $55–$70 double. Rates include full breakfast. Additional adult in room $25 extra; additional child in room $20 extra. No credit cards.

At the top of a canyon road off East End Road, the Magic Canyon has four rooms decorated in country fabrics, antiques, and quilts. Some have sweeping views over the bay and the pastures, and the llamas that graze on the 75-acre "ranch." The air is mountain clear and quiet between the high canyon walls. The Webb family share their comfortable living room with guests; they serve sherry in the evening and a full breakfast in the morning. There's a Jacuzzi spa on the porch. It's all so cozy and perfect it seems like it should be saved for honeymoons or other special occasions.

Old Inlet Trading Post Bed and Breakfast. 106-D W. Bunnell, Homer, AK 99603. ☎ **907/ 235-7558.** 3 rms, 1 with bath. High season, $55–$65 double. Low season, 25% discount. Rates include breakfast. Additional person in room $15 extra. No credit cards.

This bed-and-breakfast combines the artiness of the excellent Bunnell Street Gallery downstairs (see "Exploring Homer," above), and the historic feel of the old trading post/hardware store that the building used to house. The wood floors undulate with age and settling and the tall, double-hung windows, looking out at Bishop's Beach, are slightly cockeyed. Antiques and handmade quilts complete the charming ambience. They serve a full breakfast on weekends, and during the week you get a continental breakfast at the wonderful Two Sisters Bakery, downstairs.

Seaside Farm. 58335 East End Rd., Homer, AK 99603. ☎ **907/235-7850.** 4 rms, 9 cabins, 12 hostel beds. $55 cabin for two; $12 per person hostel bunk; $6 campsite. Additional person in room or cabin $12 extra. No credit cards.

Take a step back in time—all the way to the 1960s. Mossy Davidson's farm is populated by horses, sheep, geese, pigeons, and latter-day hippies, many of whom do chores in exchange for their room: 2¹/₂ hours of work equals a night in the hostel bunks and 90 minutes will earn a campsite in the pasture above the bay. Inhabitants congregate in an enclosure with a fire pit, a stove, running water (when the well isn't dry), and Jimi Hendrix posters. Rustic cabins and bed-and-breakfast rooms also are for rent; one lies all alone at an idyllic spot at the end of a path through the pastures and trees, quiet except for the waves lapping the beach. Davidson is a member of Homer's pioneering Kilcher family, which recently has spawned Jewel Kilcher, whom you may have seen performing on MTV. If you can catch Mossy floating through, she'll answer any question about Homer with a breezy smile and a Swiss accent.

Wilderness Lodges

Harmony Point Lodge. South of Seldovia (P.O. Box 110), Seldovia, AK 99663. ☎ **907/ 234-7858.** 3 cabins, none with bath. $225 per adult, $125 per child 4–12. Rates include all meals. Closed off-season.

The three rustic but attractively decorated cabins have a wonderful sense of isolation in the lodge's 7¹/₂ acres of thick woods above Seldovia Slough. The Dillon family makes a point of their hospitality—Ila cooks the meals and Tim takes guests fishing, kayaking, or to do whatever they want to do in this little-used paradise. The cabins lack electricity and share a shower at the sauna; each has its own pit outhouse.

✪ **Kachemak Bay Wilderness Lodge.** China Poot Bay (P.O. Box 956), Homer, AK 99603. ☎ **907/235-8910.** Fax 907/235-8911. 5 cabins. $400 per person. Rates include all meals. Minimum stay three days. Closed Oct 15–May 1.

I can think of no more idyllic a way to become acquainted with Alaska's marine wilderness than at this intimate, luxurious lodge, run for more than 20 years by hospitable and generous Mike and Diane McBride—I only wish it were affordable for more people, because it's the kind of place that could change your life. The McBrides' meals are legendary and their four cabins manage to seem rustic while having every comfort; it's easy to pretend you're the only guest. But their site, on China Poot Bay, is what's really special—it has excellent tide pooling, a black sand beach, and good hiking trails nearby. Experienced, environmentally conscious guide service is included, for kayaking, fishing, and wildlife watching.

WHERE TO EAT

Something about Homer has inspired culinary art as good as the visual art in the galleries, and today the town has the greatest concentration of good restaurants for a population of this size anywhere in Alaska—indeed, only Anchorage and Juneau have as many as good. Don't miss the **Chart Room** at Land's End, described above.

Anchor River Inn. Near the river on the Sterling Hwy., Anchor Point. ☎ **907/235-8531.** Main courses $7.50–$19; lunch $5.50–$9. AE, CB, DISC, MC, V. High season, 5am–midnight; low season, daily 7am–10pm.

Ten miles short of Homer on the Sterling Highway, the community of Anchor Point gathers around the road and the lovely Anchor River. This is one of its traditional, long-established businesses, a good old-fashioned family restaurant with filling meals of beef or seafood. People make the trip from Homer for the prime rib special. Full liquor license.

Boardwalk Fish and Chips. On the Spit. ☎ **907/235-7749.** All items $4.50–$8.45. No credit cards. High season, 11:30am–10pm; spring and fall, 11:30am–8pm. Closed in winter.

Eric Ringer had the idea years ago of using fresh local halibut with a light tempura batter to make inexpensive fish and chips at a small stand on the Spit. Now the restaurant has a large pleasant dining room on pilings right on the beach and it's busy all summer with tourists and locals. The milkshakes and burgers are good, too. Beer and wine license.

✪ **Café Cups.** 162 W. Pioneer Ave. ☎ **907/235-8330.** Lunch $6–$10; dinner $12–$20. MC, V. High season, daily 7am–3pm and 5–10pm; low season, Mon–Thurs 8am–3pm, Fri–Sat 8am–3pm and 5–9pm.

The facade of the yellow house on Pioneer Avenue, with its elaborate bas-relief sculpture, is truthful advertising for the arty restaurant and creative food to be found inside. The menu specializes in seafood and pasta; it's consistently good and reasonably priced, earning a reputation all over the state. The bohemian atmosphere may be a bit thick for some. The chef was formerly at Land's End, adding to the debate about whether "Cups," the Homestead, or the restaurant at Land's End is the best in town. Beer and wine license.

✪ **The Homestead.** Mile 8.2, East End Rd. ☎ **907/235-8723.** Dinner $17–$24. AE, MC, V. Daily 5–10pm.

Warmer than Café Cups and somewhat less adventurous, the Homestead is its equal in the quality of the seafood-centered cuisine. Again, like Café Cups, it's the work of Land's End refugees, inviting the enjoyable debate about which is best. Which side you come down on depends a little on who you are: The arty, literary, and New Age crowd in town definitely prefers "Cups," while more of the regular people I know like the Homestead. It's also farther from the tourists' beaten path, a pleasant drive out East End Road to the hip little town of Fritz Creek. Full liquor license.

⑤ **Neon Coyote.** 435 E. Pioneer Ave. ☎ **907/235-6226.** All meals $5–$9. No credit cards. Daily 11am–8:30pm. Closed Sun in winter.

The southwestern and new Mexican cuisine, served in a bright little dining room, is excellent and as inexpensive as fast food. In a sense, it *is* fast food—that's one reason locals favor it—because patrons order at a counter and get served quickly. But the black-bean burrito, only $5.50, tastes too good for that ignoble appellation. Beer and wine license.

HOMER IN THE EVENING

The ✪ **Pier One Theatre** (☎ 907/235-7333) is a strong community theater group housed in a small, corrugated-metal building on the Spit, just short of the small-boat harbor on the left. Instead of the ubiquitous gold-rush melodrama and Robert Service readings, Pier One presents original plays by Alaska playwrights and other serious theater—real art, not just schlock. They also produce dance, classical music, and youth theater events during the summer—check the *Homer News* for current listings. Performances usually play weekends only, with ticket prices around $9; they're available at **Central Charters** (☎ 907/235-7847) and various other places.

The small **Family Theater** movie house at Pioneer Avenue and Main Street presents first-run movies in a delightfully intimate atmosphere; listings and show times are on the marquee or in the *Homer News.*

There are lots of bars in Homer. The **Salty Dawg** is a small log cabin on the Spit with a lighthouse on top; it's a landmark and a good place to swap fish stories. The **Otter Room** at the Best Western Bidarka Hotel is a good place to watch a game. **The Waterfront,** on Bunnell Street below the Sterling Highway off Main Street, has live rock 'n' roll music with no cover charge beginning at 10pm; closing isn't until 5am and a beer only costs $2. Yes, fishermen party hard when they come in from the sea.

ONWARD FROM HOMER
✪ HALIBUT COVE

A visit to the tight, roadless little community of Halibut Cove, across Kachemak Bay from Homer, is like a dream for many visitors. An outing to Halibut Cove includes all the best things about a visit to the bay: a boat ride, the likelihood of seeing otters or seals, a top-notch restaurant, several galleries and open studios containing some of Alaska's best fishy, fine art, and even cozy, welcoming accommodations. The settlement sits on either side of a narrow, peaceful channel between a small island and the mainland; the water in between is the only road. Boardwalks connect the buildings and stairs reach down to the water from houses perched on pilings over the shore. The pace of life runs no faster than the tide.

It's also an essentially private community. Unless you have your own boat, an excursion boat is the only way to get there. The Jakolof Bay ferry goes, but the main route is by the boat owned by the community's restaurant. Once there, you have to leave according to plan, as there's no business district and everything is privately owned. You're really a guest the whole time you're in Halibut Cove—the community is open for visitors, however they arrive, only between 1 and 9pm, unless you're staying at one of the lodges.

The classic, wooden *Danny J* (☎ 907/296-2223, or booked through Central Charters at 907/235-7847) leaves Homer daily in the summer at noon, brings back day trippers and takes over dinner guests at 5pm, then brings back the diners later in the evening. The noon trip includes birdwatching at Gull Island. You also take the *Danny J* if you're spending the night in Halibut Cove. The noon trip is $35 for adults and the dinner trip is $17.50, but you're obliged to eat at the restaurant. Kids are $17.50 both times; seniors, $23 at noon and $14 for dinner.

On an afternoon trip, you can bring lunch or eat at the Saltry, described below, and then explore along the boardwalk that runs from the restaurant along Ismailof Island past the galleries, boat shops, and houses. There's also a barnyard where kids, who already will be in heaven, can look at rabbits, chickens, ponies, and other animals. Marian Beck, who owns the *Danny J* and the Saltry, shows her art and others' work at the **Experience Gallery.** Her mother, Diana Tillion, who, with her husband, Clem, pioneered the community, opens her **Cove Gallery** and studio to guests; she has worked in such fishy media as octopus ink. Alex Combs, a grand old

Picasso-like figure among Alaska artists, takes visitors at his studio; he mostly works in ceramics, producing huge sculptural pieces as well as affordable works.

The ○ **Saltry,** which operates in conjunction with the *Danny J,* would be among the area's best restaurants even if not for its idyllic setting, over the edge of the smooth, deep green of the cove's main watery avenue. The bread and sushi are specialties, but cooked seafood also is available.

The ○ **Quiet Place Lodge,** P.O. Box 6474, Halibut Cove, AK 99603 (☎ **907/ 296-2212** or 907/235-7847), is a family-owned bed-and-breakfast perched spectacularly on pilings that seem to climb up the side of the mainland across the water from the Saltry. The hosts lead fishing and exploring trips and rent kayaks and skiffs hourly or for up to three days. The cabins are comfortable but rustic, with their own wood stoves; the bathroom is shared. It costs $150 a night, with breakfast included, and is open May 1 to September 30.

SELDOVIA

Whether or not you enjoy little Seldovia depends on your expectations. It's a quiet little fishing village; if you enjoy quiet and fishing, this is the place to go.

The town of around 300 lies near the tip of the Kenai Peninsula, out at the end of Kachemak Bay. Today it's so sleepy as to sometimes seem completely asleep, but early in this century Seldovia was a metropolis, acting as a major hub for the Cook Inlet area with steamers coming and going with fish and cargo. The town's decline was steady until 1964, when the Good Friday earthquake destroyed most of what was left. Almost the whole city was built on boardwalks; the earthquake sank the Kenai Peninsula, and high tides began covering the walkways and the floors of the shops. The U.S. Army Corps of Engineers came to the rescue, but it's an agency known more for its efficiency than its imagination, and the boardwalks were replaced with more solid ground—fill of rock and gravel. The rebuilding since then has been without charm.

A short section of the old boardwalk remains. It runs along peaceful Seldovia Slough, where king salmon run in early summer and a sea otter is in regular residence—you can get a close look at him, if you're patient. The other roads and trails around town make for pleasant walks; you can see what a real Alaska fishing town is like without seeing many other tourists, wander in and out of the forest, beach walk, and maybe see wildlife—eagles certainly, and maybe bears.

Essentials

GETTING THERE   The trip across Kachemak Bay to Seldovia is one of the best parts of going there. The best way is by water on a tour boat. Two cruise boats go daily. **Rainbow Tours** (☎ **907/235-7272**) does a wonderful job and has a long reputation; you have a good chance of seeing otters, seals, sea lions, puffins, and eagles, and you may see whales. The fare is $36, and the boat stays a few hours in Seldovia—long enough for most people to see the town. Bring your own lunch, however, or you'll spend most of your excursion in one of Seldovia's two restaurants.

You can also fly on one of Homer's air-taxis and see the bay from above—something well worth doing. It's a cheap way to do a flightseeing trip, and an even better bargain if you book a package with Rainbow Tours to take the boat from Homer to Seldovia and fly back. **Homer Air** (☎ **907/235-8591**) is one good operator.

The **Alaska Marine Highway System** ferry *Tustumena* (see "Homer," above) also visits Seldovia from Homer, but stays too briefly.

FAST FACTS   Seldovia is a tiny town: There's no bank, and most businesses don't take credit cards. If you're going to stay overnight, bring lots of cash.

What to Do

The **Otterbahn Trail,** built by students at the Susan B. English School, leads through woods, wetlands, and beach cliffs to Outer Beach, where there's a picnic shelter. Allow a couple of hours. Maps are available in the town, but are not necessary. At the trailhead behind the school—just walk up the hill from town—is a sign proclaiming this THE-WE-WORKED-HARD-SO-YOU-BETTER-LIKE-IT TRAIL. Seldovia is great for mountain bikes—there are many miles of unused roads to explore—and the **Jakolof Bay Express** bus (☎ **907/234-7479**), which stops at The Buzz coffee shop, can bring you back from a ride. It's also a good area for **sea kayaking,** and **Kayak'atak** (☎ **907/234-7425**) offers rentals and guided trips. Seldovia also is considerably closer to the halibut grounds than Homer; drop by the **harbormaster** (☎ **907/234-7886**) for a referral.

There are several shops worth visiting, all on the main street, but it won't take long. The **Synergy Gallery** is an arts-and-crafts co-op in a log cabin and also serves as the Seldovia Chamber of Commerce visitor center. **Lost Horizon Books and Gifts** has a surprising selection of rare books; **Herring Bay Mercantile** is a large, new shop; **Alaska Tribal Cache,** owned by the Seldovia Native Association, has Native crafts, jelly made from local berries, and a showcase of items of historic interest. The Native association has clear-cut many acres of its land south of town, and Seldovia is known for the excellent berry picking to be found there. A tiny, picturesque Russian Orthodox church stands on the hill above the town, but admission is $4.50, payable to **South Shore Tours** (☎ **907/234-8000**).

Where to Stay

Dancing Eagles Bed and Breakfast. On the boardwalk (P.O. Box 264), Seldovia, AK 99663 (in winter, P.O. Box 240067, Anchorage, AK 99624). ☎ **907/234-7627** in summer, 907/278-0288 in winter. Fax 907/278-0288 in winter. 5 rms, none with bath; 1 cabin. June–Aug, $85 double; $125 cabin. May and Sept, $65 double; $125 cabin. No credit cards. Closed Oct–Apr.

The boardwalk leads to this large house, cabin, and outbuildings, themselves all nestled on rocks above the slough and connected by their own boardwalks. Judy Lethin likes to think of it as a place for healing; guests can use the wood-fired hot tub and sauna and engage the massage therapist on site. The rooms under the eaves upstairs are cute but very small; the cabin is huge, with a view of the boat harbor, and has cooking facilities.

Seldovia's Boardwalk Hotel. 243 Main St. (P.O. Box 72), Seldovia, AK 99663. ☎ **907/234-7810** or 800/238-7862. 13 rms. TEL. $88–$120 double. Additional person in room $20 extra. Closed Oct–Apr. No credit cards.

This Seldovia institution has light, comfortable rooms with private baths and phones. Despite the name, it isn't on the boardwalk, but does stand at the top of the small-boat harbor so rooms on the water side have a great view. They offer a $149 package from Homer, which includes a boat tour from Homer and a flightseeing trip back—quite a deal. There's a courtesy car and free coffee in the lobby.

Where to Eat

A drawback of spending much time in Seldovia is a lack of good restaurants. We got happy, gregarious service and decent food at the **Kachemak Kafe,** but they're not open for dinner. **The Buzz** is a great place for breakfast, with quiche and baked goods. Take picnics to the beach or the berry-picking fields. The best meals are at **Harmony Point Lodge** (☎ **907/234-7858**), described in "Wilderness Lodges" under "Where to Stay," in the Homer section, above. People not staying at the lodge can get a taste of its family-style dinner for $20 each, plus $6 for a ride to the lodge from town; reservations are required.

5 Prince William Sound: Kingdom of the Orca

Crossing Prince William Sound several years ago in a small boat, I thought I knew where I was—didn't care that much—among the tiny islands and rocks, comparing a chart to the broad, sparkling water's tussocks of bedrock and trees. Then I saw one mound, close at hand, that didn't belong. It shot forth a spray of water and a fin appeared. A humpback. We stopped the boat for pictures until the tail flipped up high, as it does when the whale is about to sound and disappear for a while. But what was that noise behind the boat? While we'd been watching the whale, a sea lion had swum up behind us. Its light-brown shape, just below the water, was the size of a large office desk, but it moved so fast, shooting toward us and then circling back in the opposite direction—as fast as the shadow of a sparrow. Finally we started up and went on our way, a warm afternoon sun on our backs as we continued east from Whittier, into the big, wide, gentle Sound. What'll we see next?

I have a friend who has kayaked the whole Sound. He knew a place—I don't know if it's still this way—where he would camp just above a pebbled beach and wait for the moon to come out. And in the night, orcas would come, swim up on the beach, scratch their tummies on the rocks, and wriggle back into the ocean. It was their secret spot—his and the killer whales'—and they'd meet there each summer. The beach was oiled in the *Exxon Valdez* oil spill, and my friend lost the heart to kayak much after all the death he saw there and all over the Sound while trying to save birds and animals that horrible summer of 1989. But now I'm sure the oil is gone from that beach. It's time to get back out there and meet the whales.

The waters of Prince William Sound are uniquely protected and diverse. On the western side, from Whittier, there are great tidewater glaciers at the heads of long, narrow fjords. In the center of the Sound, there's an infinity of islands, remote beaches, and hidden bays—and not many people. On the east, near Cordova, the Sound gets shallower and hosts millions of migrating birds. The islands and enclosing reach of the mainland keep the seas smooth in most of the Sound. That's one reason the oil spill was so devastating: These protected waters are a rich nursery, and that oil, once landed and stuck, would not soon wash away as it did out in the rougher Gulf of Alaska. Adding to the injury, an overly zealous cleanup operation killed much of the beach life that survived the pollution.

Today the oil spill is mostly history, although an expert or subsistence gatherer likely will be able to find buried oil remaining 10 years after the spill, as the experts always predicted. Natives and long-time residents have told me that they can tell the difference in the abundance of animals compared to what was there before—government studies support that perception—but most anyone else will only notice that a mind-boggling abundance still remains.

GETTING AROUND/ORIENTATION   Three major towns lie on Prince William Sound, each with a dramatically different character. Valdez is an oil town, the southern terminus of the trans-Alaska pipeline where tankers are loaded. You can drive there, on the **Richardson Highway,** and a day's boat ride will get you into the heart of the Sound. Valdez itself, however, is short on charm. Cordova is more attractive, a historic community on the eastern side of the Sound, with more untouched outdoor activities close at hand, but you can only get there by plane or boat. Whittier is a grim former military outpost, but quite a convenient gateway to the protected fjords and glaciers of the western Sound. It has frequent rail service through a mountain to the nearby **Seward Highway,** 40 miles south of Anchorage. One popular way to see the Sound is to take a boat from Whittier to Valdez—perhaps the state ferry, with your car on board—and then drive out of Valdez.

VALDEZ

On Good Friday, March 27, 1964, everything changed for the little gold rush–era town of Valdez (val-DEEZ). Under Miners Lake, west of town off a northern fjord of Prince William Sound, the largest earthquake ever recorded in North America occurred, setting off an underwater landslide that caused a huge wave to sweep over the waterfront, killing 32 people. The town sank and was practically destroyed. The U.S. Army Corps of Engineers rebuilt in a new, safer location, grading broad streets on a grid below the mountainside that slowly filled with nondescript modern buildings over the next two decades; a walking tour provides the locations of a few buildings that were moved to the new town site. Then, on March 24, 1989, on Good Friday 25 years after the earthquake, the tanker *Exxon Valdez,* on its way south from Valdez, hit the clearly marked Bligh Reef, causing the largest oil spill ever in North America. This time Valdez didn't suffer so much. The spill cleanup only added to the massive economic boom created by the trans-Alaska oil pipeline, completed in 1977, which ends here. Since the earthquake, Valdez had been transformed into something completely different—it had become a rich, middle-America company town.

The old town site is ghostly, although all that's there to see are an old foundation with a plaque listing the dead and the ruins of the dock. You can tour the oil terminal, too. But, other than an interesting history museum, and the access the harbor provides to the Sound, Valdez doesn't have much to hold a visitor. Because the town lies at the end of a funnel of steep mountains that catch moisture off the ocean, the weather tends to be overcast and rainy; but often it will be clear once you're out of Port Valdez on the Sound.

ESSENTIALS

GETTING THERE   By Car   The ✪ **Richardson Highway,** described in Chapter 10, "The Alaskan Interior," is unbelievably dramatic as it crosses Thompson Pass and descends into the narrow valley where Valdez lies. Try to do the trip in daylight, in clear weather, and stop at the roadside glacier. This is the only road to Valdez; the drive from Anchorage is roughly seven hours. **Avis,** at the airport (☎ **907/ 835-4774**), is the only major car-rental chain with a local office.

By Bus   Gray Line's **Alaskon Express** (☎ **800/544-2206**) runs to Anchorage daily in the summer, taking 10 hours for the trip; the fare is $61.

By Water   The **Alaska Marine Highway System** (☎ **907/835-4436** or 800/ 642-0066) calls on Valdez several times a week with the *Bartlett,* a small ferry connecting the three towns of Prince William Sound. The *Tustumena* comes from Seward less often. One time-tested way to see the Sound is to put your vehicle on the ferry in Whittier and take it off in Valdez, then drive north on the Richardson Highway; the fare is $72 for a car and $58 for a passenger. **Stan Stephens Cruises** (☎ **907/835-4731,** or 800/992-1297) operates a daily summer cruise with the *Glacier Queen* from Whittier to Valdez in the morning and back in the evening. The boat stops to look at the glaciers on the way. The one-way fare is $104.

By Air   Valdez is served by several commuter flights from Anchorage daily; **Era Aviation** (☎ **907/835-2636** or 800/866-8394) operates 40-passenger turbo-props on the route.

VISITOR INFORMATION   The Valdez Convention and Visitors Bureau maintains a **Visitor Information Center,** at 200 Chenega Ave., off Egan Drive (P.O. Box 1603), Valdez, AK 99686 (☎ **907/835-4636** in summer or 907/835-2984 in winter or 800/770-5954). It's open in summer, daily from 8am to 8pm, and normal business hours in the winter. They show a film about the earthquake for $2.50. A booking agency, **One Call Does It All** (☎ **907/835-4988** or 800/242-4988), reserves lodgings, fishing charters, and tours in the area. At the airport, an **Alaska Pipeline Visitor Center** has a few displays about the line and shows a film. This is where you catch the bus tours of the pipeline's marine terminal, described below.

ORIENTATION   The layout of Valdez is a grid. The **Richardson Highway** comes in from the east, becoming **Egan Drive,** the main drag. **Meals Avenue,** which runs to the boat harbor, and **Hazelet Avenue,** which runs to the city dock and ferry dock, are the major north-south streets. The airport is several miles out Richardson Highway; farther out on the Richardson, **Dayville Road** branches off to the south, leading to the other side of Port Valdez to the Alyeska Pipeline Marine Terminal, the tanker-loading facility and tank farm directly across the water from town.

GETTING AROUND   Once you're downtown, you can walk Valdez easily. To get to the airport, taxis are available from **Valdez Yellow Cab** (☎ **907/835-2500**). **Rental cars** are available at the airport. **Vortex Sports,** under the newspaper building on Galena Street (☎ **907/835-2925**), rents **bikes. Sentimental Journeys** (☎ **907/835-4988**) offers tours in a 1937 bus.

FAST FACTS   Valdez has no sales tax. There are two banks on Egan Drive, both with **ATMs.** In **emergencies,** call 911. For nonemergency business with the **Valdez Police Department,** call 907/835-4560. The **Valdez Community Hospital,** is located at 911 Meals Ave. (☎ **907/835-2249**). The *Valdez Vanguard* is published weekly, but the *Anchorage Daily News* is available in boxes the same day it's published.

SPECIAL EVENTS   In March or April, the **World Extreme Skiing Championships** (☎ **907/835-2108**) is held on the vertical faces of mountains north of Valdez; it's a daredevil competition, and someone seems to get killed or seriously injured every year. The **King of the Hill Snowboard Competition** (☎ **916/581-1259**) takes place after extreme skiing; it's the same kind of thing, but on snowboards. Three **fishing derbies,** for silver and pink salmon and halibut, happen each summer, in the appropriate season, with prizes totaling more than $60,000; check with the visitor center or buy a ticket at the boat-rental booth in the harbor. The **Prince William Sound Community College Theater Conference** (☎ **907/835-2678**) brings famous playwrights and directors to the community for seminars and events in August (16–19, 1996).

EXPLORING VALDEZ

The ✪ **Valdez Museum and Historical Archive,** at 217 Egan Ave. (☎ **907/835-2764**), contains an exceptional history display that follows the story of the area from early white exploration through the oil spill. It's a little light on Alaska Native culture, but there are other museums for that. Each gallery is well designed and some are fun, like the restored bar room. There's also a saltwater aquarium and an area with transportation relics, including an inspiringly shiny 1907 fire engine. Admission is $2. It's open in summer, daily from 8am to 7pm; in winter, Tuesday through Saturday from noon to 5pm.

A bus tour of the **pipeline marine terminal,** where tankers carrying up to a quarter of the nation's domestic oil supply are loaded, is operated by **Valdez Tours** (☎ **907/835-2686**). The two-hour ride begins four times a day from the pipeline visitor center

The *Exxon Valdez:* What Wasn't Learned

The landing pad on the stern of the troop ship *Juneau* was lined with admirals and executives as Vice President Dan Quayle's helicopter descended out of a lowering sky, off Smith Island in Prince William Sound. The weather was deteriorating, and Quayle wouldn't have much time to demonstrate concern about the *Exxon Valdez* oil spill before he would have to continue on his trip to the Far East. He was quickly carried ashore in a special landing craft and walked up onto the beach on a boardwalk handlers had ordered built over the oil-drenched rocks—they had prepared for days, obsessed by the fear of a TV image of the vice president falling down in the oil, and took every precaution.

This had been a seal haul-out area. A few days earlier, when it was still deserted, I'd landed on a boat chartered by my newspaper and stood in a brown oil-water emulsion that came halfway up my rubber boots. I'd tripped on something in the muck, reached down, and pulled out a dead loon. We realized that dead sea birds were all around our feet, hidden in the oil—cormorants, harlequin ducks, murres. Within a few weeks, an advance team of Exxon's newly mobilized cleanup workers arrived. The *Juneau* anchored to provide them lodgings until Exxon could build huge, floating work camps, with all the comforts of home, to be used for the balance of the summer.

Quayle looked around for five minutes, then said a few words to the sailors back on the ship and took off. That night he got good play on the evening network news. But there was no television in the narrow decks of the *Juneau*. Down in the workers' quarters, amid fetid racks of bunks, some of the men who'd been photographed with Quayle were talking in a tight, mutinous clump. They were from the Copper River country, homesteaders and rural firefighters who knew how to work hard. They were putting in 12-hour days spraying hot water on the rocks, surrounded by oily steam. By the end of the day they were cold, their faces filthy and their nostrils filled with black gunk. But what, they asked, were they really accomplishing? It all seemed pointless, a huge charade.

The National Oceanic and Atmospheric Administration, whose scientists are among the nation's most knowledgeable about oil-spill response, were soon asking the same question that summer of 1989. In the first weeks after the spill it was possible to wash thick pools of oil off the shore, but as time passed, rocky beaches were still deeply saturated with oil that was turning to gluey tar. Exxon had to create ever more severe methods of washing to get any off. They had little choice, spurred on by the state government and the U.S. Coast Guard and by the worst public relations nightmare anyone had ever imagined. Throwing unlimited money at the problem—ultimately more than $2 billion—the company invented new technologies, the height of which were barges with huge boilers that could spray a remote shore with near-boiling water at fire-hose velocities.

There was a massive rush on. The machines were built as fast as blank checks could provide and started blasting beaches all over the Sound. Indeed, oil kept

at the airport and costs $15 for adults, $7.50 for children. It's a tour of an industrial site. You don't get to enter any of the buildings. The highlights are a chance to see the big ships and an impressive scenic overlook, the only point where you can get off the bus.

coming off the shore. But the NOAA found, in the only controlled scientific study to come out of the whole cleanup operation, that the machines were killing every-thing in their path, and much of what was below the water line as well. The beaches stank of rotting death after a treatment. Worse, oil that had been contained to the beach was washed down into previously clean underwater habitats. The NOAA's follow-up work found that beaches that were blasted by boiling water didn't recover naturally. Like an empty lot denuded of vegetation, they were taken over by opportunistic species, the weeds of the sea. A few beaches that weren't cleaned to aid in studying cleanup impacts recovered faster, even if the oil that offended human eyes stayed on the surface longer.

The study didn't make much of a ripple in the public consciousness, or even catch much attention from cleanup decision makers. And I began to realize that this cleanup operation didn't have much to do with the environment after all. It was about people, and our need to convince ourselves that we can fix the environ-ment. It was a patch to one of our most deeply needed illusions—that we can un-derstand and control nature. It was protection from the question "If we can't put Humpty Dumpty together again, how do we justify our lifestyles?" But the truth was there to see—and it still is, in a sense. What I learned that summer, and what everyone should learn when they visit Alaska, is that nature is and always shall be beyond mastery. It can be destroyed, it can be kept at bay on the other side of a window, but it cannot be controlled, much less repaired.

As a newspaper reporter traveling the whole spill area from the earliest days, I knew from the start how hopeless the cleanup was. At first the spill was so large it took a day to travel in a boat from one side to the other. Then it was so large, only an airplane could cross it in that time. In the western part of the spill, on the Alaska Peninsula, I flew with a state bureaucrat whose job was to find oiled beaches so Exxon could send workers to clean them. The oil kept washing off one beach and hitting another. We flew all day in a jet helicopter beneath towering cliffs, banking in and out of unexplored bays and inlets, looking out the open helicopter door for oil down below. We landed now and then to get a closer look, but there was too much ground to cover, so we flew on and on, over endless miles of wilderness beaches, marking on a map what oil we could see.

Finally, we landed at one of the spots where they'd sent the workers the previous day. A crew of a dozen or so was there, picking up oily gravel and putting it in plas-tic bags to be flown out to Kodiak and then shipped to a hazardous-waste site in Oregon. Thinking back over the day of flying over miles of gravel beaches, I won-dered how many pebbles they thought they could pick up. But it was as if I was the only one who could perceive the tragic absurdity of the situation—everyone seemed to think their work was critical to restoring the Alaska Peninsula. Soon I shut up, feeling like I was in the midst of a scene of mass insanity.

And, in a sense, I suppose I was.

GETTING OUTSIDE

OUT ON THE SOUND   Stan Stephens, owner of the dominant tour-boat com-pany in town, is a crusty prophet—he predicted and was working to prevent an accident like the *Exxon Valdez* grounding right up to the very eve of the disaster, and he's still working for improved environmental safeguards for the oil companies. At the same time he runs a large, successful business selling an environmental experience to visitors. ✪ **Stan Stephens Cruises,** P.O. Box 1297, Valdez, AK 99686 (☎ **907/ 835-4731** or 800/992-1297), operates several boats, so you may not be on board with Stephens himself, but his skippers are knowledgeable Alaskans. You'll see the Sound and the animals that live in it—probably seals, otters, and sea lions, and maybe whales. Trips go to Cordova, Whittier, and Mearse Glacier, but the primary destination is the huge Columbia Glacier and Stephens's camp nearby, on Growler Island, where passengers get off and, on some trips, have a meal or even spend the night and go boating. Prices range from $63.50 for a 5¹/₂-hour cruise to $250 for a trip that includes both a night in Cordova and the Columbia Glacier. Stephens's biggest drawback has been that his star attraction, the Columbia, is melting too fast—it has receded up to a mile a year since 1981—and it hasn't been possible to get a vessel close or to see chunks calve off. Other tours now more often go to the fjord glaciers in the western Sound for those sights—which are closer to Whittier. But during the winter of '95–'96, the floating ice miraculously separated from the glacier face, offering the promise of much closer approaches for the first time in 15 years.

Jim and Nancy Lethcoe, who wrote the standard cruising guide to the Sound and have helped lead the fight to protect it, offer **sailing, sea kayaking,** and **hiking** trips in association with Stephens, sharing the same telephone number and address but keeping the name they've used for years on their sailing business, ✪ **Alaskan Wilderness Sailing Safaris.** They use the Growler Island camp as a base for their naturalist-guided outings, which are quite reasonably priced—$40 for a half day, $80 for a day, or $179.50 for an overnight ($100 for each additional day). You also can start off from Whittier, using Stephens's Whittier-to-Valdez boat, which stops at Growler Island.

Anadyr Adventures, at 203 N. Harbor Dr. (☎ **907/835-2814**), by the boat harbor, offers kayaking out of Valdez itself, but there's comparatively not that much to see right in the port; they also have longer trips and rentals for $45 a day for a single.

Fishing for salmon and halibut are popular in Valdez. You can fish from shore, in season, off Dayville Road on Allison Point on the far side of the port from Valdez. Salmon here are returning to the Solomon Gulch Hatchery and are primarily pinks in July and silvers in August. There are lots of fishing charters available in the boat harbor. **Popeye Charters** (☎ **907/835-2659**) is very reliable, and **Lil' Fox Charters** (☎ **907/835-4696**) and **Northern Magic Charters** (☎ **907/835-4433** or 800/ 443-3543) also are long-time operators. The **Valdez Charter Boat Association** produces a catalog of boats, available from the visitor center. The **One Call Does It All** booking agency (☎ **907/835-4988** or 800/242-4988) can help, too. If you're up to running your own boat, they're for rent on the docks from **Valdez Harbor Boat and Tackle Rentals** (☎ **907/835-5002**); a 16-foot boat costs $125 a day, plus fuel.

BIRDWATCHING & BEACHCOMBING   Between the airport and downtown Valdez, the Duck Flats, a tidal marsh met by a salmon spawning stream, lies along the Richardson Highway; it's a productive bird and marine habitat, busy with activity at spring and fall migrations, and a good place for birdwatching or picnicking at one of the two viewing areas all summer. The National Forest Service, which has a ranger station nearby, has set up a salmon-viewing station where you can watch fish do the deed in shallow, clear water.

A nice, short beach walk starts just east of the boat harbor, at the end of North Harbor Drive, and goes out to Dock Point.

RAFTING   Keystone Raft and Kayak Adventures (☎ **907/835-2606**) takes five trips a day down the amazing Keystone Canyon, a virtual corridor of rock with a floor of frothing water, past the crashing tumult of the 900-foot Bridal Veil Falls. It costs only $30 per person. The company also has numerous longer trips, ranging from a day to 10 days, on many of the region's rivers.

FLIGHTSEEING   There are plenty of fixed-wing operators at the airport, but I love the extra thrill of helicopters. **Era Helicopters** (☎ **907/835-2595** or 800/ 843-1947) has an office and helipad downtown, near the ferry dock at Hazelet and Fidalgo. A one-hour, $157 trip overflies Columbia Glacier and lands in front of Shoup Glacier.

WHERE TO STAY

Valdez charges a 6% tax on rooms.

Hotels

Keystone Hotel. 401 W. Egan Dr. (P.O. Box 2148), Valdez, AK 99686. ☎ **907/835-3851.** Fax 907/835-5322. 107 rms. TV TEL. $95 double. Rates include continental breakfast. Additional person in room $10 extra. AE, MC, V.

This building, made of modular units, was built by Exxon to serve as their offices for the oil spill cleanup operation, but wasn't completed until late summer of 1989, so the company occupied it for only about a month. In 1994, after standing vacant, a new owner remodeled it into a hotel, with smallish rooms that mostly have two twin beds or one double bed—they were clean and pleasant when I visited. The manager hadn't decided yet if they would be open in the winter. A coin-op laundry is available.

۞ Totem Inn. Richardson Hwy. as it enters town (P.O. Box 648), Valdez, AK 99686. ☎ **907/ 835-4443.** Fax 907/835-5751. 23 rms, 10 suites. TV TEL. High season, $85 double; $145 suite. Low season, $65 double; $95 suite. Additional person in room $5 extra. AE, DISC, MC, V.

This family-run motel has two different kinds of rooms, both good for the price. The basic motel rooms are about what you'd find anywhere, but have refrigerators. The suites are in a new building; they have two bedrooms and a kitchenette. An excellent choice for a large family or group, they're the largest in town. There's a coin-op laundry. The restaurant is a popular local hangout, with murals of Valdez. It's a very Alaskan meatloaf-and-mashed-potatoes kind of place, where the TV is always on and your cup of coffee is never empty. There's also a sports bar.

Valdez Village Inn. 111 Meals Ave. (P.O. Box 365), Valdez, AK 99686. ☎ **907/835-4445.** Fax 907/835-2437. 80 rms. TV TEL. High season, $129 double. Low season, $85 double. Additional person in room $10 extra. AE, MC, V.

Good standard rooms, a cut above the Keystone or Totem, but nothing especially memorable. There's a good coffee bar in the lobby. Avoid the 300-level, which is a half-basement, looking out on the bottom of parked cars. The weight room and Jacuzzi were out of order when I visited. Extras include free coffee, laundry, and a sauna. The **Casa Valdez** is the hotel restaurant, across the parking lot; its serves an extensive menu leaning on American-style Mexican food in an attractive dining room with booths.

Westmark Valdez. 100 Fidalgo Dr. (P.O. Box 468), Valdez, AK 99686. ☎ **907/835-4391,** or 800/544-0970. Fax 907/835-2308. 97 rms. TV TEL. High season, $149 double. Low season, $110 double. Additional person in room $15 extra. AE, DC, DISC, MC, V.

This is the only Valdez hotel on the water—it stands right above the entrance to the small-boat harbor, and the office for Stan Stephens Cruises and other tour operators are in an office just outside on a dock. The rooms don't all have views and the quality is inconsistent. Those that have been recently remodeled are top-notch; others are dark and out of date—if possible, take a look before you check in. Call ahead and ask for the "highway rate," which may save you a lot of money. The hotel maintains a tour desk, gift shop, and fuel dock.

The **Wheel House Restaurant** makes up for less-than-inspired food with a lovely dining room overlooking the harbor; main courses range from $12 to $17. The lounge is the best place in town for a quiet, friendly drink.

Bed-and-Breakfasts

Valdez has many bed-and-breakfasts, several quite good. A binder with descriptions is available for inspection at the visitor center, and there's a list in the visitor guide they hand out. Some are quite unique, like **Raven Charters,** P.O. Box 2581, Valdez, AK 99686 (☎ 907/835-5863), a large sailboat that's available for overnight lodging when it's not on overnight sailing charters; and **PWS Express,** P.O. Box 904, Valdez, AK 99686 (☎ 907/835-5807), which offers remote cabins in the Sound, with a low price that includes a two-hour boat ride to get there and a skiff for you to use once you arrive. Here are two good in-town B&Bs that show the range of what's available.

✪ **Cliff House Bed and Breakfast.** Off Hazelet Ave. near the city dock (P.O. Box 1995), Valdez, AK 99686, ☎ 907/835-5244. 3 rms $125–$135 double. Rates include continental breakfast. MC, V. Closed in winter.

Owen Meals, who gave his family's land for the new Valdez town site, built this architecturally brilliant house—it's modern, yet it fits perfectly into a priceless natural setting on its own 6-acre hill right at the waterfront in the center of Valdez. The family that now owns it lends binoculars to guests so they can watch the animals and ships in the water below—you could spend the day that way. Rooms are decorated with antiques and have private baths; two have TVs. The Cliff Room is something to write home about. Book well ahead. No smoking.

Wendy's B&B. 213 Porcupine St. (P.O. Box 629), Valdez, AK 99686. ☎ 907/835-4770. 5 rms, none with bath. High season, $70 double. Low season, $55 double. Rates include continental breakfast. MC, V ($5 discount for cash).

The house, actually run by Wendy's mother, Sheila MacDonald, is on one of Valdez's pleasant, suburban streets a few minutes' walk up from the waterfront. The rooms have cozy, Victorian-style decoration in a half-basement reached through a garage, but lack TVs and phones. There's a sauna and shared kitchenette.

Camping

Valdez is a popular RV destination, and there are lots of places to camp. **South Harbor Drive Campground,** on the harbor breakwater, is the young peoples' and cannery workers' tent village, and costs $5 a night. Camping at the **Allison Point** fishing area is $7 a night. The State Parks **Blueberry Lake Campground,** on the Richardson Highway before you get into town, has 15 tent sites and 63 RV spaces; it costs $8. Right on the boat harbor downtown, the **Bear Paw Camper Park** (☎ 907/835-2530) has full facilities and a tour desk; full hookups are $20, electricity only is $17, and dry camping, $14.

WHERE TO EAT

There isn't a top-flight restaurant in Valdez, but there are some good places to eat. You'll find good fast-food fish at the **Alaska Halibut House,** at Fairbanks and Meals

Avenue; it's open all day and a tasty and filling halibut basket is only $5.85. For an espresso or latte, healthy sandwiches and good seafood specials, **Cafe Valdez,** on the ground floor of an office building at 310 Egan Dr., is a local secret; it's open for a late breakfast and lunch only. Also see the Westmark Valdez and Village Inn, above, for descriptions of their restaurants.

Mike's Palace Ristorante. 201 N. Harbor Dr. ☎ **907/835-2365.** Main courses $6.25–$17; lunch $4–$7. MC, V. Daily 11am–11pm.

This is a good family pizza restaurant, a place where Valdez residents come for a casual evening out. The calzone is good, and everything is consistent. They've added Mexican dishes to the menu that I haven't tried. Formerly called the Pizza Palace, Mike's has a place in history: Capt. Joseph Hazelwood was waiting for a take-out pizza here when he slipped next door to the Club Bar for his last drink before getting on the fateful voyage of the *Exxon Valdez* that hit Bligh Reef. Beer and wine license.

Oscar's. 143 N. Harbor Dr. ☎ **907/835-4700.** Main courses $9.50–$15.25. MC, V. Daily 24 hours. Closed off-season.

Although unreliable in the past, this cafe was under new management in 1995 that had turned it into a light, friendly spot with quick service and food as good as you could expect from a 24-hour diner. The location is prime, on the boat harbor, to catch a meal before or after a day on the water. No liquor license.

The Pipeline Club. Egan Dr. ☎ **907/835-4332.** Main courses $4–$23.75. AE, DISC, MC, V. Open dinner only.

This is a traditional beef-and-seafood place with excellent steaks. The dark decor and low lighting create an eternal midnight to which my eyes never adjusted. The lounge is where Capt. Joe Hazelwood got loaded on vodka tonics before taking command of the *Exxon Valdez.* Full liquor license.

CORDOVA

The first time I ever went to Cordova, we arrived at the Mudhole Smith Airport in a small plane and happened upon an old guy with a pickup truck who offered to let us ride in back with some boards the 10 miles to town. The highway led out onto a broad, wetland plain—the largest contiguous wetland in the western hemisphere, as it happens. Our guide's voice, studded with profanity, boomed through the back window as he told us proudly about the diversity of the wildlife to be found out there. Then, absolutely bursting with enthusiasm, he leaned on the horn and bellowed, "Look at them f—king swans!" We looked; trumpeters paddling in the marsh looked back. He would have invited them along to the bar, too, if he'd known how.

Every time I've been to Cordova since, I've been taken under the wing of new friends. Although they usually don't express themselves the same way that first gentleman did, they are as enthusiastic to show off the amazing natural riches of their little kingdom. Tourists are still something of a novelty here, for Cordova not only is off the beaten track, it's not on the track at all—there's no road to the rest of the world. Boosters call their town "Alaska's Hidden Treasure." Forgotten treasure would be more like it, for Cordova isn't difficult to get to, and once there, the charm and attractions of the place are self-evident.

It's possible to feel a bit like an anthropologist discovering a tribe lost to time, for Cordova has the qualities small towns are supposed to have had but lost long ago in America, if they ever did have them. Walking down First Street, you pass an old-fashioned independent grocery store, the fishermen's union hall, Steen's gift shop, in the same family since 1909—not chains or franchises. People leave their keys in the car and their doors unlocked at night. When a friend of mine bought one of the quaint, moss-roofed, hillside houses a few years ago, he didn't receive a key—the simple reason was that the front door didn't have a lock.

Yet Cordova also possesses a surprising level of sophistication. The commercial fishermen who power the economy can afford to travel the world in the off-season, if they've had a good year. They like good food and an interesting place to live. They keep the bars lively at night when the salmon are running. Some are politically involved and well connected, battling the oil industry to protect Prince William Sound before the 1989 oil spill, then pushing after the disaster, which hurt Cordova worst of all, for the money won from Exxon to be spent on the Sound's environment.

They want Cordova to stay the way it is—with no road. Another faction in town, the merchants and tourism workers, want a road. The debate is hot, and a recent mayoral election between pro- and antiroad candidates was decided by a single vote. This has been going on for 50 or 60 years. The town's heyday was in 1911, when the Copper River and Northwestern Railroad opened, carrying copper ore down from the mine at Kennicott; it hit a low when the mine closed in 1938. Since then, boosters have been trying to get a road built on the old rail line, north along the Copper River to Chitina. They've only made it about 50 miles out of town so far, despite an effort a few years ago by former Gov. Wally Hickel to send maverick maintenance crews out to punch the road through by stealth. All he accomplished was to create a ruckus and get hauled into court by the environmental agencies.

The portion of the Copper River Highway that was completed and paved years ago provides access to the best birdwatching and, in my judgment, the most impressive glacier in Alaska, as well as trails and magnificent vistas and areas to see wildlife. The small-boat harbor is a doorway to Prince William Sound. And the town itself has to be experienced.

ESSENTIALS

GETTING THERE   By Air   The easiest way to get to Cordova is on **Alaska Airlines** (☎ **907/424-7151** or 800/426-0333), with daily jets to and from Anchorage and heading south to Southeast Alaska. If you're on a tight budget, standby fare is only about $75 round-trip, and the flights often have space left.

By Water   Cordova is served from Valdez or Whittier by the **Alaska Marine Highway System** (☎ **800/642-0066**) ferry *Bartlett;* the passenger fare from Valdez is $30, an inexpensive way to see a lot of Prince William Sound. **Stan Stephens Cruises** (☎ **907/835-4731** or 800/992-1297) offers an overnight trip from Valdez, including a bus tour to Childs Glacier operated by Copper River Northwest Tours, described below. Including lodging, the package is $250.

VISITOR INFORMATION   The well-informed **visitor information person** is also the director of the museum and library, and her office is in the same building, at 622 First St. (P.O. Box 391), Cordova, AK 99574 (☎ **907/424-6665**); hours are 1 to 5pm Tuesday through Saturday, year round. The **Cordova Chamber of Commerce,** P.O. Box 99, Cordova, AK 99574 (☎ **907/424-7260**), in the back of the fishermen's union hall on First Street, near Council, is open Monday through Friday from 8am to 4pm; they have visitor information and a recorded walking tour that you can listen to as it guides you around town. The **Cordova Ranger District** of the Chugach National Forest, upstairs in the old white courthouse at Second Street and Browning (P.O. Box 280), Cordova, AK 99574 (☎ **907/424-7661**), has displays and handouts about the area's natural history, as well as rangers who will sit down and help you figure out what you want to do and sell you cabin permits.

ORIENTATION   Cordova is nestled among mountains on the east side of Prince William Sound between Orca Inlet and Eyak Lake. The airport is about 10 miles out the **Copper River Highway,** on the massive Copper River Delta. The highway enters the forest along Eyak Lake and finally turns into **First Street**—which is also known as **Main Street, High Street,** or the Copper River Highway as it passes through the center of town. One block down, **Railroad Avenue** runs along the small-boat harbor. Continuing through town on First Street, you come to the **ferry dock** and the canneries. A good, free map is widely available.

GETTING AROUND   To get in from the airport, take the **van shuttle** run by The Reluctant Fisherman hotel (☎ 907/424-3272), listed under "Where to Stay," below, for $9 each way. **Taxis** are usually available as well from Wild Hare Cab (☎ 907/424-3939). Becky Chapek, who owns the local tour company, meets the ferry and will take you where you need to go for nothing. You can easily walk around downtown Cordova, but that's not where the most interesting sights are. To get out the Copper River Highway, you'll need a car, bus (described below), or, if you're vigorous, a bike. **Cars** are for rent from the Reluctant Fisherman Hotel or **Imperial Car Rentals** (☎ 907/424-5982), with pickup available at the airport; the going rate is $55 a day, without mileage charges. Bikes are for rent from **Cordova Coastal Tours** (☎ 907/424-3842), at the boat harbor below the fishermen's memorial; it charges $15 for 12 hours or $20 for 24 hours; the hardware store on First Street also rents bikes.

FAST FACTS   Cordova's **sales tax** is 6%. The National Bank of Alaska on First Street has an **ATM.** The **post office** is located at Railroad Avenue and Council. In **emergencies,** call 911; for nonemergencies, call the **police** (☎ 907/424-6100). The **Cordova Community Hospital** is on Chase Street (☎ 907/424-8000), off the Copper River Highway near the slough. The *Cordova Times* has been on hard times; if it's still published, it's weekly. You can find the *Anchorage Daily News* at the Killer Whale Book Store on First Street.

SPECIAL EVENTS   The **Cordova Iceworm Festival** is a winter carnival the first full weekend in February; the big iceworm or, to be precise, ice centipede, marches in a parade. The five-day ✪ **Copper River Delta Shorebird Festival** (☎ 907/424-7260) revolves around the coming of dizzying swarms of shorebirds—estimates range from 5 to 22 million—that use the delta and beaches near the town as a migratory stopover in early May. It's an opportunity to see immense waves of birds. The whole community gets involved to host birdwatchers and put on a full schedule of educational and outdoor activities. There's a **king salmon derby** in late June and a **silver salmon derby** in late August.

Exploring Cordova

Save some time to wander around town, possibly with the help of the historic-walking-tour booklet produced by the historic society or with the recorded walking tour from the chamber of commerce. Cordova is full of wonderful little discoveries to make on your own.

The free **Cordova Historical Museum,** at 622 First St., is a well-presented one-room display with some valuable artifacts reflecting Cordova's eventful past. The three-seat kayak and other artifacts of Prince William Sound Native peoples are of particular interest; Cordova is the home of the last few Eyak, a Native people whose language now has only one speaker left. The museum is open year round, Tuesday through Saturday from 1 to 5pm.

A chair lift to the top of **Eyak Mountain** can carry you to wonderful views 1,000 feet above the town, but you may have to track down one of the volunteers who run it; call 907/424-7766 and leave a message.

GETTING OUTSIDE

THE COPPER RIVER DELTA   The delta seems to go on forever, a vast patchwork of marsh, pond, a few trees, and the huge, implacable, gray river itself. A well-maintained gravel road leads across it, all in Chugach National Forest. There are public-use cabins available for $25 a night from the Cordova District Ranger station, and pull-offs for birdwatching platforms and interpretive signs. The road itself is the old bed of the Copper River and Northwestern Railroad. It leads 50 miles to the Million Dollar Bridge. Built by Michael Heney, a magician of a 19th-century railroad builder who also constructed the White Pass and Yukon Route in Skagway, the 200-mile Copper River line was an engineering miracle. The bridge over the Copper River went up in a race against time between two surging glaciers in 30-foot-deep, fast-flowing glacial water, in winter. The bridge stood 56 years, until the 1964 earthquake knocked down one end of one of the spans, augering it into the riverbed. But you can still drive across on a jury-rigged ramp and go a few miles farther on unmaintained road.

The best attraction, however, is just this side of the bridge: ✪ **Childs Glacier.** This is the most amazing glacier I've ever seen, and no one seems to know about it outside Cordova. It comes right down to the quarter-mile-wide river, where the flowing water cuts it off like a knife, eroding the base and bringing down huge chunks of ice. At the Forest Service viewing and picnic area across the river, salmon have been found high up in the trees and boulders in odd places. Why? When a big piece of ice falls off the glacier, it can create a wave large enough to flood the picnic area and uproot trees, not to mention hurling a few fish around. Several years ago such a wave injured some visitors it pulled into the river, and now the Forest Service warns that anyone who can't run fast should stay in the observation tower. You can hear the glacier clicking and cracking and, if you wait a while, see it put on a spectacular show.

Driving a **rented car** to the bridge and glacier and stopping for the birds and wildlife on the way is a good day's activity. Pick up the road guide from the Forest Service Cordova Ranger Station. Don't miss **Aleganik Slough,** where there's a 1,000-foot boardwalk for watching wildlife, or **Sheridan Glacier,** off the north side of the road. The ranger station also can provide you with a trail guide of hikes on the delta, and a wildlife-viewing guide. The animals you may see along the way include black and brown bears, moose, and mountain goats. The entire world population of dusky Canada geese nests on the delta, and you're sure to see eagles and trumpeter swans. Aside from Aleganik Slough, one of the best birdwatching areas is between the airport and town.

Copper River and Northwest Tours, P.O. Box 1564, Cordova, AK 99574 (☎ **907/424-5356**), takes trips on Monday, Wednesday, Thursday, and Saturday during the summer. On Wednesday it's timed to the arrival and departure of the ferry, so you can do the whole thing as a day trip from Valdez. Operated by the irrepressible Becky Chapek and her husband, Bill Myers, whose father cut ties on the Copper River line, the tours make numerous stops, spend an hour at the glacier for an excellent lunch prepared by Becky, and include a recorded narrative that's been checked for accuracy by the Forest Service and the historical society. The six-hour trip costs $35. They also drop off hikers along the road.

I think **biking** the highway would be a great adventure. There's a Forest Service cabin about halfway along, at Mile 22, and several other cabins on trails that branch from the road. Of course, you don't have to ride all the way to see lots of birds and wildlife. Unfortunately, the delta can be terribly windy, and that can make for hard riding. Be especially careful on the bridges in the wind. Bikes are for rent from Cordova Coastal Tours (see "Getting Around" under "Essentials," above).

Fishing, on the delta and in the lakes and streams around Cordova, includes all species of Pacific salmon, as well as Dolly Varden and cutthroat trout. The Cordova Ranger Station can offer guidance and regulation booklets and the **Alaska Department of Fish and Game** (☎ **907/424-3212**) has a Cordova office as well.

OUT ON THE SOUND   The waters of Prince William Sound around Cordova, although lacking the tidewater glaciers found in the western Sound, are calm, little used, and rich in marine life.

Since 1989 Dave Janka has operated the classic, wooden ✪ *Auklet,* P.O. Box 498, Cordova, AK 99574 (☎ **907/424-3428**), a 58-foot former Fish and Wildlife Service patrol boat, to carry researchers into the Sound from Cordova's Prince William Sound Science Center and other institutions. The boat also is his family's home. Recently he began bringing his experience and vessel to guided tours. He doesn't enjoy fishing and doesn't believe in hunting, so this is a wildlife and scenery experience. Within a few hours of Cordova, Janka knows where to find otters, sea lions, seals, and sometimes killer whales—and he'll know the whales you're looking at and the history of the pod. Half days are $80 per person, and full days, $150, including meals. Longer charters are available, but the accommodations on board are nautical, not luxurious. He also drops off kayakers. Book ahead, as otherwise Janka may be on a research mission when you get to town.

Several vessels are available for fishing charters, and each offers the strong possibility of seeing wildlife. **Cordova Fishing Charters** (☎ **907/424-5467**) and **Orca Bay Charters** (☎ **907/424-5777**) both charge $150 per person for a full-day trip.

Cordova is a good starting point for a sea-kayak trip, although Whittier, which is easier to get to and closer to Forest Service cabins, is more popular. **Cordova Coastal Tours,** P.O. Box 386, Cordova, AK 99547 (☎ **907/424-3842**), rents kayaks for unguided trips. It charges $25 for a single kayak for a day, $45 overnight; doubles are $40 and $65.

IN THE AIR   Cordova is all by itself, with untouched wilderness in all directions. An airplane or helicopter can get you out there for fishing, hunting, or just communing with nature. There are several Forest Service cabins in spectacular settings, accessible only by air. Flightseeing is available, but the most inexpensive way to do it, or to get deep into the Sound, is to take a mail plane to one of the villages or fish hatcheries. **Cordova Air** (☎ **907/424-3289**) is the largest operator. **Fishing and Flying** (☎ **907/424-3324**), located at the airport, is a friendly operation, and has remote cabins for rent; John Tucker, of **Wilderness Helicopters,** can be reached at the same number, for even-harder-to-reach spots.

HIKING AROUND CORDOVA   The Cordova Ranger Station can provide you with a trail-guide booklet with lots of ideas and maps. One of the best hikes is the **Power Creek Trail.** Take Power Creek Road along the north side of Eyak Lake to the end, 7 miles from town. The creek has spawning red salmon in July and attracts a lot of bears; watch, but don't get out of your car if you come upon one. The trail follows the creek through dramatic scenery 4.2 miles to a Forest Service cabin with a great view, available by permit for $25 at the ranger station. Strong hikers can continue to Crater Lake, which is connected by a trail back to Eyak Lake, 1 1/2 miles from town.

WHERE TO STAY

There are more establishments than those listed here, including several bed-and-breakfasts; get a list from either visitor center.

⑤ **The Northern Lights Inn.** 500 Third St. (P.O. Box 1564), Cordova, AK 99547. ☎ **907/424-5356.** 5 rms. TV TEL. $50–$65 double. Additional adult in room $5 extra; children stay free in parents' room. AE, MC, V.

These large, lovely rooms, with private bathrooms, antiques, and views, are an almost unreal value. They're upstairs in Becky Chapek and Bill Myers's historic, 1906 house a couple of blocks above the main street. Each room was lovingly renovated in 1995, and one has a kitchenette. There are VCRs, a coin-op laundry, and a freezer that's available for fish. The family also operates the well-run tour business in town.

Prince William Hotel. Second St. and Council (P.O. Box 908), Cordova, AK 99574. ☎ **907/424-3201.** Fax 907/424-2260. 16 rms. TV TEL. $75–$95 double. Additional adult in room $10 extra; children 11 and under stay free in parents' room. AE, MC, V.

Taken over by a fishing family and completely renovated in 1995, this former dive has been transformed into a clean, comfortable standard motel. The construction is cinderblock and the lower rooms look out onto an airshaft. The rooms have coffee machines; six rooms with kitchenettes are available.

✪ **The Reluctant Fisherman.** 401 Railroad Ave. (P.O. Box 150), Cordova, AK 99574. ☎ **907/424-3272.** Fax 907/424-7465. 50 rms. TV TEL. High season, $125 double. Low season, $95 double. Additional person in room $10 extra. AE, CB, DC, DISC, JCB, MC, V.

Mayor Margy Johnson presides at Cordova's main hotel with limitless energy. She and her husband, Dick Borer, have created one of the best waterfront lodgings in Alaska. The decor in the lobby, lounge, and restaurant capture the town's railroad and copper-mining history, with rich wood and pressed-copper ceilings. The hotel overlooks the small-boat harbor; the rooms are comfortable and modern. There's a gift shop and travel agency in the hotel; car rental and VCRs are available.

The ✪ **restaurant** serves the town's best dinners. Main courses range from $15 to $30. Order the Copper River king salmon in season, whether here or anywhere else in Alaska you find it on the menu; the river produces fish with a high oil content that create an exceptionally rich, beefy flavor.

WHERE TO EAT

Other than the restaurants listed here, try the **Reluctant Fisherman,** described above, and the **Baja Taco** (☎ 907/424-5599), a bus at the boat harbor with a covered dining area elevated on a small tower. The proprietor, who lives in Baja in the winter, specializes in salmon tacos. There also are a couple of other decent restaurants on First Street.

Ambrosia. First St. and Council. ☎ **907/424-7175.** Main courses $5.75–$18.75; lunch $5.75–$9.75. MC, V. High season, daily 11am–11pm; low season, daily noon–9pm.

This is a comfortable Greek and Italian family restaurant with an extensive menu, and pizza. The food is reliable and the portions large—as a friend said, if you order the carbonara, plan to share it, unless you just got off a week on a seiner. Beer and wine license.

Cookhouse Cafe. 1 Cannery Row. ☎ **907/424-5926.** All items $3–$7.75. MC, V. Daily 7am–3pm. Closed in winter.

A former cannery cookhouse on a dock with a working cannery—to find it go out toward the ferry dock—this clean, bright cafe with bench seating has a very agreeable feeling. The food is basic, but well prepared and inexpensive. No liquor license.

✪ **Killer Whale Cafe.** In the Killer Whale Book Store, First St. and Council. ☎ **907/ 424-7733.** All items $6.50–$8. No credit cards. Mon–Fri 7am–4pm, Sat 8am–4pm.

If not for the healthy sandwiches, salads, and soups, this cafe would still be a must for the atmosphere and the regulars—young fishermen, New Age practitioners, and other eco-people—found here drinking the excellent coffee. The bookstore belongs to oil-spill hero Kelly Weaverling, who became the only member of the Green Party to hold elective office in the United States when he was Cordova's mayor a few years ago. (He later lost to Margy Johnson, of the Reluctant Fisherman, by one vote.) The bookstore has a comfortable, arty feel and the restaurant seating is in a pair of lofts looking down on the books. No liquor license.

WHITTIER

I can think of only three reasons to go to Whittier: to get to Prince William Sound, to take the train through the mountain, or because you're collecting the oddest places in America. The great majority of the town, with a population of less than 300, lives in a single 14-story concrete building. (The balance lives in one other building.) The Begich Towers, as the dominant structure is called, was built during World War II, when Whittier's strategic location on the Alaska Railroad and at the head of a deep Prince William Sound fjord made it a key port in the defense of Alaska. Today, with its barren gravel ground and ramshackle warehouses and boat sheds, the town maintains a stark military-industrial character reminiscent of a Stalin-era Siberian outpost.

The claustrophobia of living with all your neighbors in a 1940s-era building with dark, narrow corridors is accentuated by the fact that Whittier can be reached from land only by a 30-minute **Alaska Railroad** (☎ **907/265-2313** or 800/544-0552) link through two mountains to the Seward Highway, near the abandoned town of Portage. For visitors, the train ride in funny old double-decked cars is well worth the trip (the fare is $16 round-trip, $70 round-trip for a car and driver to go through on the back of a flat car), but Whittier residents understandably have lobbied long and hard for a road. As one young town ambassador told me when I visited recently to look around, "You're thinking, 'Thank God I don't live here,' right?" The official boosters look more on the bright side: A brochure points out that having everyone live in one building saves on snow removal in a town that gets an average of 21 feet a winter.

The **Greater Whittier Chamber of Commerce,** P.O. Box 607, Whittier, AK 99693 (☎ **907/344-3340**), maintains a **visitor center** in an old railroad car near the boat harbor, where you can get a free cup of coffee to warm up from the rain, and maps, brochures, and guidance on finding a fishing charter or other way out on the water. On the ground floor of the Begich Towers is a one-room **museum** with artifacts of Whittier history; regular hours are 1 to 6pm, or find the proprietor of the video store (also on the ground floor) to let you in. Near the boat harbor, **Log Cabin Gifts** keeps a live reindeer in a decorated pen and has reindeer-theme gifts and bric-a-brac for sale inside.

For lunch, try **Hobo Bay Trading Company,** at the boat harbor, with good burgers and a children's menu. Seating is only on stools. If you need lodgings, you'll find adequate rooms with cinderblock walls above the store at the **Anchor Inn** (☎ **907/424-2354**). They have private baths, TVs, and phones. **June's Whittier**

Bed and Breakfast, P.O. Box 715, Whittier, AK 99693 (☎ **907/472-2396**), has rooms and suites at Apartment 513 of Begich Towers. She also offers fishing charters.

GETTING OUT ON THE SOUND Of course, you're probably in Whittier for access to Prince William Sound; for that, you're in a very good place. Whittier is the entrance to the western Sound. This part of the Sound contains some of its most pro-tected waters, up long, deep fjords, and among tiny islands and passages. You're likely to see marine mammals and eagles on a trip of any length. Glaciers lurk at the heads of many of the fjords, dumping ice in the water for the tour boats that cruise from Whittier. Whittier is a popular starting point for self-guided kayak trips. And the **state ferry** *Tustumena* (☎ **800/642-0066**) connects Whittier with Valdez and Cordova. It's fun to take your car on the train through the tunnel, then put it on the ferry in Whittier to Valdez.

Here are details on getting into the Sound:

Tour Boats The largest operator is **Phillips' Cruises and Tours,** with an office at 509 W. Fourth Ave. in Anchorage (☎ **907/276-8023** or 800/544-0529); its 26-glacier cruise on a three-deck tour boat is $119, with lunch included. **Major Marine Tours,** with its office at 509 W. Third Ave. in Anchorage (☎ **907/ 274-7300,** or 800/764-7300), operates a somewhat smaller vessel, specializing in a six-hour dinner cruise that passes 10 glaciers. **Stan Stephens Cruises** (☎ **907/ 835-4731** or 800/992-1297) runs a boat from Whittier to Valdez daily, stopping off for glacier viewing and for a visit to Stephens' Growler Island camp, in front of Columbia Glacier; the one-way fare is $104.

Fishing Charters Better than a dozen charter fishing boats operate out of Whittier. It's the closest saltwater fishing to Anchorage. You can get a list from the visitor center or book through **Anchor Services Unlimited** (☎ **907/472-2354**).

Sea Kayaking Whittier is a popular starting point for kayak trips to the beautiful and protected western Prince William Sound. Most of these kayakers are on their own, but **Prince William Sound Kayak Center,** P.O. Box 233008, Anchorage, AK 99523-3008 (☎ **907/276-7235**), offers guided three-hour trips, starting at $65 for a single person or $50 each for a couple. They also rent kayaks for unguided trips out of Whittier for $40 a day for a single, $60 double, but beginners shouldn't even think of doing it on their own. You can also rent a kayak and haul it down from Anchorage on the highway and train. They're available at **Alaska Mountaineering and Hiking**, at 2633 Spenard Rd. (☎ **907/272-1811**), and elsewhere.

To get beyond Whittier's long, steep fjord to the area that's enjoyable to paddle, you have to charter a boat to drop you off. There are six Forest Service cabins in the idyllic area popular with kayakers, off Port Wells. Unfortunately, they're so popular they often are reserved the maximum 190 days in advance at the Alaska Public Lands Information Center in Anchorage. On summer weekends there's also a shortage of good campsites in the area—the Forest Service can tell you where they are—because so many of the beaches were submerged by the 1964 earthquake.

Adventures and Delights (☎ **907/276-8282** or 800/288-3134) leads week-long and 10-day trips to the western Sound from Whittier and Seward; they cost roughly $1,450 to $1,750, including the charter out to the kayaking area. Or you can go to the same general area with either of the kayak operators listed in the Valdez section.

6 The Copper River Valley & Wrangell–St. Elias National Park

Looking at a relief map of Alaska, you'd think the portion drained by the Copper River so overweighted with mountains as to topple the whole state into the Pacific. The Alaska Range, in the center of the state, has the tallest mountain, but this Gulf of Alaska region, straddling the Alaska-Yukon border, has much more mass—the second- and fourth-tallest mountains in North America, Logan and St. Elias, and 9 of the tallest 16 in the United States. Four mountain ranges intersect, creating a mad jumble of terrain covering tens of millions of acres, a trackless chaos of unnamed, unconquered peaks. The Copper River and its raging tributaries slice through it all, swallowing the gray melt of the innumerable glaciers flowing from the largest icefield in North America. Everything here is largest, most rugged, most remote; words quickly fall short of the measure. But where words fail, commerce gives a little help: These mountains are so numerous and remote that one guide service makes a business of taking visitors to mountains and valleys that no one has ever explored before.

The dominant landowner in this forbidding region is Wrangell–St. Elias National Park. Over 13 million acres in area, it's the largest national park in the United States, about 25% larger in area than the entire country of Switzerland. The protected land continues across the border in Canada, in Kluane National Park, which is similarly massive. Driving 180 miles from Valdez to Slana on the Richardson and Glenn highways, you keep the Copper River and its tributaries, and the park boundary, on your right almost all the way. The other half of the Copper River country is to the left. There are a few tiny towns along the way, and tiny villages off in the Bush, but precious few people for all that land. The region isn't a destination for visitors looking for a standard hotel room at night or structured activities during the day, although most will enjoy the views on the drive through. But for travelers interested in outdoors exploration, this empty land is waiting.

WRANGELL–ST. ELIAS NATIONAL PARK

The park has two rough gravel roads that allow access to see the mountains from a car. On the south side, the old Kennecott Copper mine has big abandoned buildings to walk around (the name of the company is spelled differently from the place, Kennicott, where it was founded because of an early misspelling). But for those who don't want to put on a pair of hiking boots or get in a raft, the park holds few other attractions. After all, wilderness is the whole point.

APPROACHES TO THE PARK   Park headquarters is just north of Copper Center, on the old Richardson Highway (☎ **907/822-5235**). It's open Memorial Day to Labor Day, daily from 8am to 6pm; in winter, during normal business hours. You can write for information at P.O. Box 29, Glennallen, AK 99588. There also are three ranger stations, at the three access points to the park, all open only in the summer.

The **Nabesna Ranger Station** (☎ **907/822-5238**) is in Slana, on the Nabesna Road near the intersection with the Glenn Highway's Tok Cut-off, 65 miles from Tok and 60 miles from Glennallen. The Nabesna Road goes 46 miles into the park. Like the Denali Park Road, it's an avenue to see wilderness and wildlife, on mountain taiga, but here you can take your own car. The road can be rough and there are a couple of river crossings that may be impassible at high water; however, you should be able to make it at least to Mile 29. Pick up a copy of the road guide from the ranger station or the Alaska Public Lands Information Center in Tok (see Chapter 10). In this northern portion of the park, at the divide between the Tanana and Copper River drainages, the terrain isn't as fierce as elsewhere in the park. Hiking on the taiga is muddy, but not technical as in the steep mountains to the south. You can camp anywhere you want on park lands, but wilderness hiking in the park is only for proficient outdoors people who know what to bring, how to handle stream crossings and emergencies, and generally how to take care of themselves far from any other person.

The **Chitina Ranger Station** (☎ 907/823-2205) is at the most popular gateway to the park, the old mining town of Chitina (CHIT-na), 33 miles down the paved Edgarton Highway, which starts about 17 miles south of Copper Center on the Richardson Highway. The town of around 50 people has a post office and some services, as well as a bridge over the Copper River. When the reds are running, they're so numerous Alaska residents are allowed to fish for them by ladling them out of the water with long-handled dip nets.

The northern end of the unfinished and abandoned Copper River Highway runs south from here—the former road bed of the Copper River and Northwestern Railroad, with its tunnels still intact almost 60 years after the rails were removed. You can drive south along the river to fish, if you have four-wheel-drive and are an intrepid driver. It's a great mountain-biking route.

A more popular but very rough, narrow road continues 61 miles to the east to McCarthy—also on the remains of the Copper River line. Check with the ranger station for road conditions and a copy of the McCarthy Road Guide. Improvements were planned, but in 1995 you couldn't expect to do the trip in less than three hours, and flat tires were commonplace. That means the trip is best as a two-day affair, in order to have time to see the sights.

If you don't want to give your car that beating, **Wrangell Express Adventures** (☎ 907/823-2201) runs a van from the Chitina Saloon to McCarthy and Kennicott daily in summer at 9am, returning at 7pm. The fare is $30 one way, $55 round-trip. Whether you drive or take the van, you'll find that there's no bridge across the Kennicott River before McCarthy. The only way across is by riding a tram that's powered by your own hands, pulling yourself across or being pulled if someone on the bank knows proper tram etiquette. Another alternative is to fly from Glennallen, or any of the other larger towns in the region, avoiding the road and tram.

The **Yakutat Ranger Station** (☎ 907/784-3295) is the park's back door. This is the most rugged and undeveloped approach to the park, although some people have started using the area for sea kayaking. The peaks rising from the Pacific near here are the largest coastal mountains in the world, with a vertical rise greater than the Himalayas. For information on Yakutat, see Chapter 7, on Southeast Alaska.

WHAT TO SEE & WHERE TO STAY IN MCCARTHY & KENNICOTT   The point of enduring all that rough road from Chitina or absorbing the expense of flying from Glenallen is to reach the ghost-town communities of **McCarthy**—not quite a ghost town, with a few dozen residents left—and **Kennicott.** McCarthy was a rough little frontier town. The **McCarthy Lodge** (☎ 907/554-4402) has rooms with shared bathrooms, a restaurant, and a saloon; there's also a small museum and an art gallery in town. Kennicott, 5 miles away, uphill, by foot or shuttle from McCarthy, was a genteel company town for the rich copper mine that operated there from 1910 until its abrupt closure in 1938. When the ax fell, the residents just locked the doors and left, so there's more to see than you might expect. The 40 buildings, including a 14-story mill, were stabilized with a grant from the park service and have remained largely intact. They're privately owned, but people generally wander around to take a look at will.

The best place to stay in the area is the **Kennicott Glacier Lodge,** P.O. Box 103940, Anchorage, AK 99510 (☎ **800/582-5128**), which stands among the ghost-town buildings and was built in much the same style, with red walls, white trim, and a metal roof. Meals are served family style. It's a good starting point for hiking, near the confluence of the Root and Kennicott glaciers. A tour of the ghost town comes with the room. Including meals, rooms are $230 double, $65 per additional person; without meals, a double room is $159.

GETTING OUTSIDE IN THE PARK   Rafting   A popular activity in the park, river trips are offered by some 15 guide services, including **Alaska Wildland Adventures** (see Chapter 6, "Outside in Alaska"), and **Keystone Raft and Kayak Adventures** (see "Valdez" under "The Kenai Peninsula"; ☎ **907/835-2606**). Based in McCarthy during the summer, **Copper Oar,** P.O. Box MXY McCarthy, Glennallen, AK 99588 (☎ **907/544-4453**), has day trips in addition to expeditions. A Nizina Canyon Float takes all day; lunch and a bush plane ride back are included in the $195 price. A Kennicott River run takes only an hour or two and costs $45.

Hiking   Hiking trails and guides also are plentiful. **St. Elias Alpine Guides,** P.O. Box 111241, Anchorage, AK 99511 (☎ **907/277-6867**), is a company based in McCarthy during the summer that offers day hikes, mountain biking, rafting, backpacking trips, and alpine ascents, but specializes in guiding extended trips to unexplored territory. Bob Jacobs, president of the company, stopped guiding on Mount McKinley years ago because of the crowds. He claims never to have seen another party in more than 16 years of guiding expeditions in Wrangell–St. Elias, and has led more than 30 parties of customers up previously unclimbed peaks. Day hikes start at $50 per person, rafting at $195, and mountain biking at $80; it also rents bikes for $25 a day.

Hiking on your own in a wilderness largely without trails is a whole new kind of experience for experienced backpackers and outdoors people who are used to more crowded parts of the planet. You feel like an explorer rather than a follower. If you're not prepared to select your own route—a task only for those already experienced in trackless, backcountry traveling—use a trip synopsis provided by the National Park Service. Fourteen are available, cataloged on a Trip Synopsis List you can get from the headquarters. This is only for those who know how to take care of themselves in the woods, cross rivers, and deal with wilderness emergencies.

ALONG THE WESTERN PERIMETER OF THE PARK

The people of the Copper River region live on homesteads and tiny settlements, and in a couple of towns near the intersection of the Glenn and Richardson highways. Fourteen miles south of the intersection, **Copper Center** is a tiny Athabascan community on the old Richardson Highway. A historic roadhouse, the **Copper Center Lodge,** Drawer J, Copper Center, AK 99573 (☎ **907/822-3245**), is worthy of an overnight stop, if it's time for a rest on your drive. The big, old log building has been appropriately kept up, with wallpaper and antiques. It has the relaxed, imperceptibly slow pace of the deep countryside. Rooms with shared bathrooms rent for $80 a night; the restaurant has burgers, plus beef and fish main courses in the $15 range. The lodge goes back to the bizarre gold-rush origins of Copper Center and Valdez: About 4,000 Stampeders to the Klondike tried to take a virtually impossible all-American route from Valdez over the glaciers of the Wrangell–St. Elias region. Few made it and hundreds who died are buried in Copper Center. The original lodge was built on the leavings of those who wisely turned back. The existing building dates to 1932.

Glennallen is a regional hub; it stands at the intersection of the Richardson and Glenn highways and a few miles along the Glenn to the west. The volunteer-run **Copper River Visitor Center** is in a log cabin right at the intersection (☎ 907/822-5555); in summer it's open daily from 8am to 7pm. Glennallen has a bank with an ATM, a post office, a medical center, and government offices. It's a hub for the fishing and outdoor activities in the region, but there's nothing to do in the town itself.

The best accommodations in the area are at the **Caribou Hotel,** at Mile 187 of the Glenn Highway (P.O. Box 329), Glennallen, AK 99588 (☎ 907/822-3302). The rooms are the equal of an upscale chain. A double is $99 in the summer. They also have economy rooms in a surplused pipeline man camp for $44 double. The hotel's **Caribou Restaurant** is good for comfort food—meatloaf, roast beef, pork chops—and inexpensive. Across the highway, the **Hitchin' Post** restaurant has surprisingly good southwestern food in a pleasant little dining room. There's a drive-through and, incredibly, a good 89¢ taco. The **Tastee Freeze** is fine for a quick burger and cone. You won't find any alcohol, as its sale in Glennallen is illegal by local choice, but liquor stores are located a little outside of town on the Richardson Highway.

The land in the area west of the national park is largely controlled by the **Bureau of Land Management Glennallen District,** with an office in town on the north side of the Glenn Highway (P.O. Box 147), Glennallen, AK 99588 (☎ 907/822-3217). Information also is available from the public land information centers in Anchorage, Fairbanks, and Tok. Although not quite as large as the park—the BLM area is only as large as a mid-sized eastern U.S. state—these lands are more accessible to recreation and still very beautiful. There are several large alpine lakes, two National Wild Rivers, two dozen hiking trails, and six campgrounds, all accessible on the Richardson, Glenn, Denali, and Edgarton highways.

Guides are available for **rafting** and **fishing** in the rivers. **Alaska Whitewater** (☎ 907/822-5850 in summer, 907/337-7238 in winter, or 800/337-7238) offers floats ranging from a $65 half day on the Tonsina River to longer expeditions. **Gakona Fish Guides,** at Gakona Junction, 14 miles north of Glennallen (☎ 800/962-1933), offers half-day guided fishing trips on rafts or jet boats for $95. There's also a restaurant and lodge at the junction. The salmon are not as bright and firm this far inland as they are near the coast; they've begun turning red with their spawning changes.

7 The Matanuska & Susitna Valleys

For most visitors, the Mat-Su Valley, as the area is known, will be a place to pass through on the way somewhere else—along the Glenn Highway to Valdez or the Alaska Highway, or up the Parks Highway to Denali National Park from Anchorage. The Valley has not developed as a destination, and in some ways is less appealing now than it was 20 years ago. The Matanuska Valley developed from the Great Depression until the 1970s as a farming area. The New Deal relocated colonists from other areas of the country to settle the prime growing land. But as transportation links improved both within the state and to the Outside, farming in Alaska lost in competition to shipping goods in from Seattle. And farmland became more valuable as sites for subdivisions to house the booming population of Anchorage, only an hour's drive south on the Glenn Highway. With an adamantly antigovernment population that prevented any community planning, the rush of development that occurred turned the lovely meadows and rolling hills of birch into the worst kind of suburban sprawl of highway-fronting shopping malls and gravel lots.

A few farms still survive in the Valley, growing vegetables that command a premium in Anchorage grocery stores, and producing a little milk. And there are some areas worth a visit, if you have the time: **Hatcher Pass** is inspiring, winter or summer; several good salmon streams cross the Valley; and there are a few community museums and attractions to divert you on the drive through. In **Talkeetna,** at the northern end of the Valley, closer to the Denali region, you'll find a funky little town with a lot of history and spirit, too far from Anchorage to have been spoiled. It's a good place for a river jet-boat ride, salmon fishing, or a flightseeing trip to Mount McKinley. But other areas that should be appealing just aren't anymore. **Big Lake,** for example, simply has too much low-quality development and loud motor sports, with a weekend partying atmosphere that's not conducive to family recreation or anyone's idea of wilderness.

The entire area is enormous. The county-level government, the Matanuska-Susitna Borough, covers an area about as large as West Virginia. Most of the people live in the section near Anchorage, in and around the towns of Palmer and Wasilla, where the Matanuska and Susitna rivers drain into Cook Inlet. The Susitna is to the west and north, while the Matanuska flows down from the impressive Matanuska Glacier, parallel with the Glenn Highway, through the mountains to the northeast.

Palmer is a traditional small town, built by the Depression-era colonists. In recent decades it has been the victim of a long decline, as farms closed, highway travel was diverted up the Parks Highway, and shopping centers outside the business district drained away the downtown's economic life. The borough seat still resides in Palmer, and the town, swept by wind coming down the Matanuska Valley, retains a certain charm reminiscent of quiet farming towns of the American West.

About 10 miles west, **Wasilla** was created mostly by a building boom of the 1970s and 1980s, as people who work in Anchorage moved to the Valley for bigger lots, cheap housing prices, and a place where they could keep a horse, boat, or snowmobile out back. The town exists as a string of shopping centers along the Parks Highway, and you have to really look to find its center. The area is dotted with lakes surrounded by houses, where people waterski and fish in the summer and snowmobile and run sled dogs in the winter.

Hatcher Pass is in the Talkeetna Mountains on the north side of the Matanuska Valley, forming the top of a triangle with Palmer and Wasilla. The Talkeetnas aren't as tall as other ranges, but they have the striking, rugged beauty of cracked rock. A historic mining site nestles up in the pass, and it's a terrific place for summer hikes and winter recreation, including Nordic skiing and snowmobiling.

Talkeetna, at the northern end of the Susitna Valley, is a well-preserved gold-rush village, half of its 26 buildings on the National Register of Historic Places. An hour exploring along the two dirt streets is well spent. Talkeetna is served by the Alaska Railroad and is the main starting point for climbers heading up Mount McKinley—they fly from the landing strip to a glacier base camp. You can use it as a base for McKinley too, as there are good views of the mountain from here and flight services that can take you for a tour.

ESSENTIALS

GETTING THERE   By Car   Driving from Anchorage, from the south, you arrive in the Valley after 30 miles of freeway, when you cross the Matanuska River on the Glenn Highway bridge. Coming from Denali or Fairbanks, from the north, the Parks Highway follows the Susitna River drainage through various little towns before coming to the central Valley area. The Glenn Highway descends along the mountainous and much more dramatic Matanuska River from the northeast, coming from Glennallen.

By Bus or Train　Any of the bus lines and van services that connect Anchorage to Fairbanks, Denali National Park, or the Alaska Highway can drop you off in the Valley, as can the Alaska Railroad, on certain runs; but once you're there, you'll have no way to get around.

VISITOR INFORMATION　The **Mat-Su Visitors Center,** HC 01, Palmer, AK 99645 (☎ **907/746-5002** or 907/746-5000), is located on the right side of the Parks Highway just after the intersection with the Glenn Highway, as you enter the area from the south. It's open in summer, daily from 9am to 8pm; in winter, Monday through Friday from 10am to 5pm. The **Palmer Visitor Center,** at 732 S. Valley Way in the center of town (☎ **907/745-2880**), has a small museum on the 1935 colony project that developed the Valley. It's open June to August only, daily from 9am to 9pm. The **Denali/Talkeetna Visitor Center** is at the intersection of the Parks Highway and Talkeetna Spur Road (☎ **907/733-2223**), open in summer, daily from 8am to 7:30pm; in winter, Monday through Friday from 9am to 4pm.

ORIENTATION　The **Parks Highway** divides from the **Glenn Highway** about 7 miles south of Palmer on the Glenn and 7 miles east of Wasilla on the Parks. Turn left at the junction for Wasilla, Talkeetna, Denali National Park, and Fairbanks. Go straight for Palmer, Glennallen, and the rest of the world. If you're in either Palmer or Wasilla and want to get to the other, the **Palmer-Wasilla Highway** is the direct route. Hatcher Pass is on **Fishhook Road,** which meets the Glenn north of Palmer and the Parks in Wasilla. The Butte area, south of Palmer, is on the **Old Glenn Highway,** which runs from Palmer to an exit on the Glenn just south of the Knik River. The Knik area is on **Knik Road,** which meets the Parks in Wasilla. Talkeetna is at the end of 14-mile-long **Talkeetna Spur Road,** which intersects with the Parks Highway at Mile 98, 55 miles north of Wasilla.

GETTING AROUND　The only practical way to get around the broadly spread out Valley is by car. National car-rental chains are based in Anchorage.

FAST FACTS　The cities of Palmer and Wasilla each levy a 2% **sales tax.** You'll find **banks** on the Parks Highway in Wasilla and at 705 S. Bailey in Palmer; they have **ATMs,** as do most large shopping centers and grocery stores. In **emergencies,** call 911. For nonemergency business with the police, call the **Palmer Police Department** (☎ 907/745-4811), the **Wasilla Police Department** (☎ 907/ 373-9077), or, outside either town, the **Alaska State Troopers** (☎ 907/745-2131). The **Valley Hospital** is at 515 Dahlia Ave. in Palmer (☎ **907/746-8600**). In the Talkeetna area, the **Sunshine Community Health Center** is at Mile 97.8 of the Parks Highway, just south of Talkeetna Spur Road (☎ **907/733-2273**). The *Frontiersman* newspaper is published twice weekly, and the *Anchorage Daily News* is widely available.

SPECIAL EVENTS　The **Iditarod Restart,** on the first Saturday in March, enlivens Wasilla at the end of a long winter. The Iditarod Trail Sled Dog Race starts officially in Anchorage, but then the dogs are loaded in trucks and carried to Wasilla, where the trail becomes continuous to Nome. The restart is the real beginning of the race, and the area makes the most of it. The ✪ **Alaska State Fair,** August 23 to September 2, 1996, is the biggest event of the year for the Valley, and one of the biggest for

Anchorage; it's a typical fair, except for the huge vegetables. The good soil and long days in the Valley grow cabbages the size of a bean-bag chair. A mere beach-ball-size cabbage wouldn't even make it into competition.

EXPLORING THE ROADS OF MAT-SU

Here are the Valley's best sights, starting from Palmer and working west and north. The **Musk Ox Farm,** north of Palmer on the Glenn Highway (☎ **907/745-4151**), raises the beasts for their wool, and offers tours daily. A University of Alaska **research farm** is also open for tours, on the Trunk Road, off the Parks Highway just beyond the junction with the Glenn.

The **Independence Mine State Historical Park,** located in Hatcher Pass, 15 miles up Palmer Fishhook Road from the intersection with the Glenn Highway north of Palmer (☎ **907/745-3975**), is the site of a gold-mining operation that closed down in 1942. The mine buildings occupy a high mountain valley in the Talkeetna Mountains that's a great place for skiing or hiking, and quite beautiful. You do have to drive partway on a winding, gravel mountain road. The visitor center at the park is open from early June to Labor Day, daily from 11am to 7pm; admission is $3 for adults, $2 for seniors and kids. You can warm up or get a good lunch in a little restaurant just down from the mine.

The **Dorothy G. Page Museum,** at 323 Main St. in Wasilla (☎ **907/373-9071**), preserves the history of the area from before runaway development. The best attractions of the museum are the elderly volunteers themselves, real area pioneers who remember the history and love to talk about it. Several old buildings are open for tours daily from 10am to 6pm in the summer, and the museum is open daily from 8am to 5pm in the winter. Admission is $3 for adults, $2 for seniors, and free for children 17 and under. The **Iditarod Trail Committee Headquarters,** on Knik Road 2 miles south of Wasilla (☎ **907/376-5155**), has a museum, shows videos, and offers sled-dog demonstrations. Admission is free, and it's open in summer daily from 8am to 5pm. A pleasant side trip can be had continuing down the road to the tiny community of Knik, the precursor of Anchorage.

The **Museum of Alaska Transportation and Industry,** off the Parks Highway at Mile 46.7, west of Wasilla (☎ **907/376-1211**), is a place to stop for people interested in machines. Those who aren't can wait for those who are while having a pleasant picnic on the 10-acre grounds. There's a collection of old railroad cars, aircraft, and good junk, as well as a well-arranged indoor display area with an old fire truck, photographs, and various other items. It's open May to September, daily from 10am to 6pm; admission is $3 for adults, $1.50 for children.

GETTING OUTSIDE

There are some good float trips to be had in the Valley—see the **rafting** unit under "Getting Outside" in the Anchorage section, earlier in this chapter, for the names of operators. Hatcher Pass is a great place for **hiking,** where you can wander freely in the mountains above treeline or take one of three good trail hikes. We love cross-country skiing there in the winter, and it's a big spot for **snowmobiling,** too.

Fishing is popular in the Mat-Su area; however, low salmon returns have closed or limited several key rivers in the last few years. Call the **Alaska Department of Fish and Game** (☎ **907/745-5016,** or 907/745-0678 for recorded information) for current fishing information. **Mahay's Riverboat Service,** P.O. Box 705, Talkeetna, AK 99676 (☎ **907/733-2223**), is a top guide, with five-hour jet-boat charters for $115 per person, operating from a dock on the Susitna River in Talkeetna. Owner Steve Mahay is legendary, the only person ever to shoot Devil's Canyon in a jet boat.

Besides fishing, Mahay offers **river tours** ranging from 20 minutes to five hours, concentrating either on sightseeing and natural history or on thrills; prices start at $15 per person.

The Valley is a center of **sled-dog mushing,** both for racing and recreational dog driving. Raymie and Barb Reddington, of **Reddington Sled Dog Tours** (☎ 907/ 376-6730), take trips up the Iditarod Trail, ranging from half an hour to several days, and will teach you to mush, as well. **SNO-TREK Mushing Adventures** (☎ 800/ 495-6743), based in Willow, north of Wasilla on the Parks Highway, teaches guests to drive a team and takes them on multiday trips.

✪ **Flightseeing** from Talkeetna is an increasingly popular way to see **Mount McKinley.** This is also where climbers board planes to the mountain, and there's a park service ranger station to deal with those expeditions. **K2 Aviation,** with a main office at Mile 9 of Talkeetna Spur Road (P.O. Box 545-B), Talkeetna, AK 99676 (☎ **907/733-2291**), has for years been a renowned operator to Denali, with some of the most famous glacier pilots. It offers a flightseeing tour that circles the mountain and shows it off from every angle, and even landings on glaciers on the mountain itself, possible from November to mid-July. Depending on the length of the tour, prices range from $75 to $175 per person; add $40 to land on a glacier. **Geeting Aviation,** at the airport (P.O. Box 42), Talkeetna, AK 99676 (☎ **907/733-2366**), is another well-regarded mountain flying operation, with similar prices to K2's and float-trip drop-offs and remote cabin rentals also available.

WHERE TO STAY

Here are the best accommodations in the main part of the Valley. If you're headed for Talkeetna, try the **Swiss-Alaska Inn,** P.O. Box 563, Talkeetna, AK 99676 (☎ **907/733-2424**), or the **Whistle Stop Bed and Breakfast,** P.O. Box 128, Talkeetna, AK 99676 (☎ **907/733-1515**).

Hatcher Pass has two establishments, **The Motherlode Lodge,** listed below, which caters more to the snowmobile crowd, and the pleasingly rustic **Hatcher Pass Lodge** (☎ **907/745-5897**), which has cabins, a delightful little A-frame restaurant, and a sauna. It's right on the Nordic trails, and mostly gets cross-country skiers.

The Mat-Su borough charges a 5% **bed tax,** which is added to the 2% sales tax in Palmer and Wasilla for a total 7% bed tax within their city limits.

IN WASILLA

Best Western Lake Lucille Inn. 1300 W. Lucille Dr., Wasilla, AK 99654. ☎ **907/373-1776** or 800/528-1234. Fax 907/376-6199. 54 rms, 4 suites. TV TEL. High season, $89–$115 double;$165–$175 suite. Low season, $75–$85 double; $145–$155 suite. Additional person in room $10 extra. AE, DC, DISC, MC, V.

This attractive lakeside hotel right in Wasilla has the best standard hotel rooms in the Valley and, by some definitions, the only standard hotel rooms in the Valley. They're large and like new. The rates depend on whether or not you have a lake view. Also, the lower-priced rooms, without a view, have only one bed. Boats are for rent to get out on Lake Lucille. Extras include a Jacuzzi, sauna, workout room, self-service laundry, and free coffee in the lobby. The **restaurant** is one of the best in the area, with a nice view of the water. It's open for three meals a day, with the beef and seafood dinner menu ranging from $13 to $39.

IN PALMER

✪ **Colony Inn.** 325 E. Elmwood, Palmer, AK 99645. ☎ **907/745-3330.** Fax 907/746-3330. 12 rms, 1 suite. TV TEL. $75 double. Additional person in room $5 extra. AE, DC, DISC, MC, V.

Under the same ownership as the low-rent Valley Hotel—you check in there, at 606 S. Alaska St.—the Colony Inn is really special, full of antiques, with Jacuzzis and VCRs in all the large, clean rooms, and with managers proud of their hospitality. The building is on the historic register, as it originally was a dormitory for school-teachers in the Valley's early days. There's a coin-op laundry.

☉ Motherlode Lodge. Mile 14, Fishhook Rd. (P.O. Box 3021), Palmer, AK 99645. ☎ and fax **907/746-1464.** 10 rms. $65 double. Additional person in room $15 extra. AE, MC, V.

These clean, spacious, functional rooms, all with mountain views, are a great base camp for Hatcher Pass and Independence Mine, just 3 miles up the road. The 1946 building is completely self-contained, with a generator for power and water that comes from an artesian well. A range of mountain activities are available, including dog mushing, snow cats offering remote alpine skiing and tours, and the Nordic skiing that's so popular in Hatcher Pass. The **restaurant** has casual and fine dining areas, with a great view. The more expensive menu is surprisingly sophisticated, with main courses ranging from $14 to $19.

Sheep Mountain Lodge. Mile 113.5, Glenn Hwy. (HC 03 Box 8490), Palmer, AK 99645. ☎ and fax **907/745-5120.** 8 rms, most without bath; 2 cabins; hostel-style dorms. $90 double. Additional person in room $15 extra. MC, V.

Near the Matanuska Glacier halfway between Palmer and Glennallen, this pictur-esque log building has been in operation as a roadhouse since 1946. The current owners have kept it up to a higher standard than the usual roadhouse lodge and are trying to make theirs more than a room along the way. Some 15 miles of hiking trails are nearby, groomed as ski trails in the winter, and they have a good rest-aurant, a sauna, and a Jacuzzi. The separate cabins have private bathrooms. There's a hostel, too.

WHERE TO EAT

The best restaurants in the Valley are at the Best Western Lake Lucille and the Motherlode Lodge, described above, and at **Limani's Bar and Grill,** just west of Palmer on the Palmer-Wasilla Highway (☎ **907/746-6000**). Limani's offers good, inexpensive lunches and evening meals in a dark dining room. The dinner menu is extensive and reasonably priced, specializing in prime rib.

9

Denali National Park: Big Mountain, Big Crowds

Denali (den-AL-ee) National Park contains Mount McKinley, at 20,320 feet the tallest mountain in North America, but you don't need to go to the park to see the mountain, and you probably won't see it even if you do. And Denali encompasses a broad expanse of alpine tundra and taiga populated by bears, wolves, Dall sheep, caribou, moose, eagles, fox, beavers, and small mammals, but that's typical of much of Interior and Arctic Alaska. And in and around the park, opportunities exist for river rafting, flightseeing, hiking, and tourist activities—but again, you don't have to go to the park for that.

What makes Denali National Park a unique place to visit is the human management of the wilderness—in Denali, anyone, even for modest expense, can get into a relatively pristine natural environment and see wildlife in its natural state. A single National Park Service decision makes that possible: The only road through the park is closed to the public. This means that to get into the park, you must ride a crowded bus over a dusty gravel road hour after hour, but it also means that the animals are still there to watch and their behavior remains essentially normal. From the window of the bus, you're likely to see grizzly bears doing what they would be doing even if you weren't there.

More important and more valuable, you can get off the bus pretty much whenever you want to and walk away from the road across the tundra, out of sight of the road, and be alone in a primeval wilderness utterly undisturbed by human development. That makes many people nervous, because most of us have never really been away from other people, much less apart from anything people have made. But this is what visiting Alaska is about—learning, deep down, how big creation is and how small are you, one more mammal on the tundra under the broad sky. Sadly, experiencing such a moment usually costs thousands of dollars for anyone who isn't up to a rugged outdoor trek into the wilderness. At Denali, it costs $20, plus the cost of your accommodations. And when you're ready to go back to civilization, you just walk to the road and catch the next bus—they come every half hour.

It's little wonder that Denali is so popular when it offers such a valuable experience at such a low cost—or at least it wouldn't be

Denali National Park

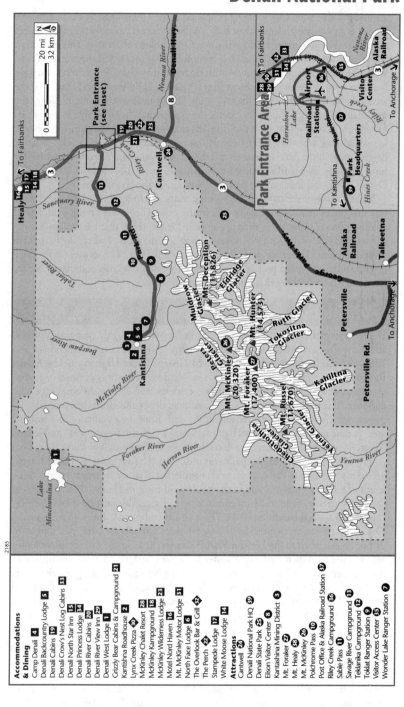

Park Entrance Area

To Fairbanks
To Anchorage
To Kantishna
To Talkeetna

20 mi
32 km

a wonder if that were why so many people go there. Unfortunately, the reason why Denali is mobbed with more than half a million visitors annually during its three-month season has more to do with mass psychology than with the chance to experience the wilderness. Denali has become a thing people feel they must do, and seeing Mount McKinley what they must do when they visit Denali. When they get home to Iowa or Ireland, they know they'll be asked "Did you go to Denali?"; if the answer is yes, they'll then hear the follow-up, "Did you see the mountain?" Since the mountain is usually shrouded in clouds, the chance that they'll be able to answer affirmatively to both questions is probably less than one in three; consequently, they're left wondering why they spent so much money to stay at the ticky-tacky roadside development at the park's entrance and then to ride on a bus over a bumpy road for most of a day. A friend overheard a tourist ask, as she boarded the train leaving Denali, "Why did they put the park way out here in the boondocks?"

Most visitors to the park are on package tours, churning through in an 18-hour stay that leaves no time to actually walk in the park. They arrive on the train, attend a dinner-theater show, sleep, then get up early for a tour bus that has time to go only partway into the park—in 1995 it was turning around short of where the bears were most often seen. Then they get back on the train and leave. The scenery on the drive is spectacular, and many package-tour visitors doubtless saw bears and the mountain, but I can't help thinking that they missed much more.

1 Orientation

Denali National Park and Preserve is a six-million-acre, roughly triangular polygon about the size of Massachusetts with an entrance 230 miles north of Anchorage and 120 miles south of Fairbanks on the paved **George Parks Highway** or the **Alaska Railroad.** Although Mount McKinley is visible from as far away as Anchorage, and excellent views are had from Talkeetna, you can't see it at all from the area of the park entrance. The **park entrance,** site of the railroad depot and all services accessible by private vehicle, stands on the far side of the park from the mountain, in a wooded area. A mile north on the Parks Highway, along a cliff-sided canyon of the **Nenana River,** hotels and restaurants have developed a kind of seasonal town on private land in the immediate area of the park entrance. Other services are at **Carlo Creek,** 14 miles south on the Parks, or at another gathering of roadside development 7 miles south of the park entrance, and in the year-round town of **Healy,** 10 miles north of the park entrance. From the park entrance, a road accessible only by shuttle bus (except under special conditions—see "Fees and Regulations" under "The Essential Details," later in this chapter) leads west 90 miles through the park, past a series of campgrounds, then to the **Eielson Visitor Center,** at Mile 66, with excellent alpine views of the mountain, and the **Wonder Lake area,** at Mile 85, with a campground and wooded views of McKinley, and finally to the **Kantishna mining district,** a collection of inholdings with wilderness lodges and a restaurant, at the end of the road another 10 miles farther—only owners of those businesses can use the road freely, a right won from the park service in court.

FAST FACTS There is no **bank** or automatic-teller machine in the Denali area—the closest is in Fairbanks, 120 miles away to the north. The **post office** is located near the park hotel. **Convenience stores,** with limited camping supplies, are located in the Chevronservice station near the park hotel and at the gas station near the large hotels a mile north of the park entrance. Outside the park, dial 911 in **emergencies;** within the park, phone 907/683-9100. The **Alaska State Troopers** (☎ **907/683-2232** or 907/768-2202) handle nonemergency calls from Cantwell, 28 miles south. A **health clinic** (☎ **907/683-2211**) is located in Healy, 10 miles north of the park entrance, open 24 hours a day for emergencies, or normal office hours for nonemergencies; you'll also reach them in emergencies by dialing 911.

2 Planning a Visit to the Park

CHOOSING AN ITINERARY

I have always enjoyed traveling without an itinerary, so you can believe me when I say that you *must* plan a trip to Denali National Park and reserve all accommodations, campsites, and trips into the park well in advance—for mid-July peak travel, make reservations by May. The park hotel is sometimes booked up by December for midsummer. Travelers who just show up at the visitor center without any reservations will have to spend at least a day—and probably two—outside the park before they can get a seat on a shuttle bus, a campground site, or a backcountry permit. It's quite a letdown to arrive at the park for a wilderness experience and have to spend the first few hours standing in line at the always-crowded visitor center trying to buy a bus ticket for two days later.

Of course, it can be difficult to know before you've been there exactly what you want to do, and Denali is especially confusing because the material distributed by the park service is not particularly clear, nor does it convey the paramount importance of reserving your place before you come. I've tried to help by preparing some sample plans for visitors with different budgets and degrees of "roughing it."

PAMPERED EXPLORERS   Arrive by train at the park, checking into accommodations either at the park, a mile north, or in Healy—shuttles and courtesy vans will get you around. Attend a ranger talk, the *Cabin Nite* dinner-theater show, or go on a short nature walk around the park hotel in the evening. Get to bed early, and the next morning take a shuttle bus before 7am into the park, riding to the Eielson Visitor Center to see the terrain and animals, and possibly to get a view of the mountain, arriving there in late morning. Now ride partway back toward the entrance before getting off the bus at a place of your choosing for a walk and to eat a bag lunch brought along with you (pack all trash out, of course), or take one of the park service guided walks. After enjoying the wilderness for a few hours, head back on the bus, finishing a long day back at the hotel. You can also take the Wildlife Tour or the Kantishna Roadhouse bus, which provide lunch, but you won't be able to get off and on the bus, and on the Wildlife Tour you'll have less chance of seeing animals because it doesn't venture as far into the park as the shuttle. Next day try a rafting ride, flightseeing trip, or other activity near the entrance to the park before reboarding the train.

FAMILY CAMPING & EXPLORING   Arrive at the park entrance by car with your camping gear and food for a couple of nights. Camp that evening at the Riley Creek campground near the visitor center and enjoy the evening ranger program or the lecture at the park hotel in the evening, or take one of the short hikes near the park entrance. Next day, catch a shuttle bus or camper bus into the park to one of the campgrounds there—either set up camp early at the eastern end of the park and then ride west for sightseeing, or ride the bus all the way to the Wonder Lake campground. Hike around the campground, or take the bus to one of the broad vistas of alpine tundra and explore. Next day, take the bus ride through the park to see the wildlife, hike the backcountry, then head back to the campground for another night, or out. Your final evening, spend the night at a hotel in Healy for a shower and a rest. Add a day outside the park, if you want, for rafting or horseback riding.

OUTDOORS ADVENTURE Arrive by train, bus, or car with your backpack, camping gear, and food for at least several days' hiking. Go immediately to the visitor center to orient yourself to the backcountry-permit process, buying the information you need for your trek (see "Hiking the Backcountry" under "Out in the Park," later in this chapter) and choose the unit area that looks most promising. If you're very lucky, you can get a permit for the next day; more likely, camp at the Marino Backpacker's Campground, 1.9 miles on the park road from the highway, and arrive at the visitor center the next day by the 7am opening to get your permit for the following day. Now you've got another day to wait; if you've reserved a shuttle-bus seat, you can get a preview of the park and see some wildlife, or outside the park, go on a rafting trip. The next morning you can start your backcountry hike, taking the camper bus to your unit, then traveling for up to two weeks in a huge area of wilderness reserved almost exclusively for your use.

WILDERNESS LODGES The lodge will fly you out—or, if it's in Kantishna, drive you through the park—and you'll immediately be away from the crowds in remote territory. The lodges all have activities and guides to get you out into the wilderness. If you're not staying in Kantishna, you may want to schedule a day to ride the shuttle bus into the park to see the mountain and wildlife anyway, with an evening in a hotel near the park or in Healy.

THE TALKEETNA OPTION Drive only as far as Talkeetna, about 110 miles north of Anchorage, and board a flightseeing plane from there to the park, perhaps landing on a glacier on Mount McKinley itself. You'll stand a better chance of seeing the mountain than anyone else, since you won't have to go on a certain, prearranged day when the weather may be poor. You'll also save yourself 130 miles of driving and the bus ride into the park, and the time and money required to go to the park. But you'll miss the wilderness and wildlife-viewing opportunities that can be had only on the ground in the park.

CLIMBING MOUNT MCKINLEY McKinley, because of its altitude and weather if not technical difficulty, is certainly among the world's most challenging climbs. Every year climbers die—most years, several. If you're looking here for advice, you're certainly not up to an unguided climb. A guided climb is a challenging and expensive six-week endeavor for experienced climbers in excellent condition. Climbs generally start with a flight from Talkeetna to a Kahiltna Glacier base camp. You must register with the park service's **Talkeetna Ranger Station,** P.O. Box 588, Talkeetna, AK 99676 (☎ **907/733-2231**). It can also provide names of qualified guides. There's a $150-per-climber fee to help cover the cost of all those who have to be rescued every year, but that will be one of your lesser costs.

WHEN TO GO: CROWDS OR SNOW

The park is populated by people beginning in mid-May, when there still is some snow; the humans migrate south again in mid- to late September, when winter is closing in. There is virtually no year-round settlement at Denali. In winter, nearly half a million summer visitors dwindle to only a few dozen residents—caretakers who watch over the hotels and other buildings and sled-dog-driving rangers who patrol the backcountry. (It's extraordinarily beautiful in winter, and that's the season when the mountain is most often visible.) While a winter visit may be impractical, you can improve your chances of getting away from others of your species by avoiding the peak month of July. All over Alaska, the tourism season really gets into high gear in mid-June and starts to wind down in mid-August, providing a month of relative quiet at the beginning of the season and another at the end.

In fall, the weather starts getting a bit nippy at night, but rain is less likely in Denali and the trees and tundra turn wonderful colors. (The peak visiting months of June and July are also, perversely, peak season for precipitation in the park.) By early September, visitors are so few that the park no longer takes telephone reservations. By mid-September, private cars can drive on the park road for three days—the park service holds a lottery to determine who will get that treat. The rest of the year, only credentialed professional photographers and researchers can drive their own cars on the road.

Another way to avoid the crowds is to book a stay in a wilderness lodge. Businesses in Kantishna, such as Camp Denali, have the right to drive over the road all summer. They make that ability a business asset by carrying their passengers over the park road in buses and vans. Kantishna Roadhouse offers a day trip (see "Where to Eat," later in the chapter). Outside the park, several other lodges fly in clients. The crowds are concentrated in the park; in comparison, similar terrain and animals just outside the boundaries are virtually unvisited.

Finally, remember that there are other beautiful places that are relatively unexploited by visitors; you're not obliged to go to Denali to see alpine terrain or to have a chance of seeing bears or caribou. The Denali Highway leads through the Alaska Range from Cantwell, 30 miles south of the park entrance, to Paxson, on the Richardson Highway, 135 miles to the east. It's a spectacular and little-used gravel road that in many ways is similar to the park road. Wrangell–St. Elias National Park, the nation's largest park, is barely used. The Richardson Highway and Steese Highway cross areas of broad, Arctic tundra with limitless vistas similar to those found in the park. In some ways, the Arctic is even more impressive than Denali, if you can afford a flight to the North or a drive up the Dalton Highway, through the Brooks Range.

3 The Essential Details

RESERVATIONS & VISITOR INFORMATION

In 1995 the park service put most of its dealings with the public in the hands of a concessionaire, ARA's **Denali Park Resorts,** P.O. Box 87, Denali Park, AK 99755, or 241 W. Ship Creek Ave., Anchorage, AK 99501 ☎ **907/272-7275** or 800/ 622-7275). (These are the main reservation numbers and addresses.) At the same time, they began charging for the bus that's the only way for most people to see the park. ARA now operates the buses and handles reservations for seats, for sites at the park service campgrounds (except the Marino Backpackers campground), and at the only hotel within the park, as well as reserving rooms in its two other hotels outside the park, rafting trips, and the dinner-theater show. **Destinations in Travel,** P.O. Box 76, Denali National Park, AK 99755 ☎ **907/683-1422** or 800/ 354-6020), also books packages and reservations for independent travel in the area.

The **park visitor center,** to the right less than a mile from the Parks Highway intersection, is the place to pick up bus tickets and campground permits from a desk manned by ARA employees. There's a perpetually long line for walk-in purchase, but a will-call desk speeds things up if you have reservations. Rangers man an information desk and can answer questions before you waste a lot of time in line; they also provide rudimentary information on local businesses other than ARA. The **National Park Service,** P.O. Box 9, Denali Park, AK 99755 (☎ **907/683-9640** for recorded information), provides a free map and a newsprint park guide *Denali Alpenglow* (get a copy in advance, if you can); you can talk to a real person by calling or visiting the interagency **Public Lands Information Center** (☎ **907/271-2737** in Anchorage or

---

Denali Lingo

Denali is the Athabascan name for the mountain; the park's name was changed from Mount McKinley National Park to Denali National Park, but attempts to change the name of the mountain itself were blocked in Congress by representatives from Ohio—President William McKinley was that state's favorite son. The **season** is mid-May to mid-September, but **off-season** rates often are available in September and sometimes in May. The park is still open in winter, but there are virtually no services or activities. The **Parks Highway** is the George Parks Highway, leading from Anchorage to Fairbanks, and providing access to the park entrance; it's distinct from the **Denali Park Road,** or park road, which is the 90-mile gravel road that leads into the park itself from the park entrance. The **park entrance** is the area around the visitor center where the Parks Highway and park road meet. The **backcountry** is the area beyond those environs, especially the bulk of the park beyond the checkpoint 14 miles west on the park road, where private vehicles may not travel. One needs a **backcountry permit** for remote overnight camping in the backcountry, but not for day hikes. Most park visitor operations are handled by a concessionaire, **Denali Park Resorts,** better known by the name of its owner, **ARA,** a large tourism company. The **front-country shuttle** is a free shuttle bus running a loop of a couple of miles between the visitor center and the park hotel, within the park entrance area. The green and garish pink **shuttle bus** is the main means of really getting into the park, running some 85 miles from the visitor center west to Wonder Lake. The yellow **camper shuttle** is the school-bus version of the shuttle bus, carrying campers and their gear into the park for a lower fare than the shuttle bus; four campgrounds are in the backcountry, and another four accessible by private car nearer the park entrance. The brown **Wildlife Tour bus** is a more heavily guided ride into the park than the shuttle, with lunch provided; used primarily by package tour groups, it costs more and doesn't go as far into the park as the shuttle. The **Natural History Tour bus** barely goes beyond the park entrance. The **park hotel** is the park service concession located in the park entrance area.

907/456-0527 in Fairbanks). The visitor center also has an auditorium showing a slide show and a gift shop with maps and publications. The park service still handles distribution of backcountry permits, for which there is no fee; these are available only at the park visitor center, and only one day in advance (see below).

If you have limited time, plan your visit around your bus and campground reservations, making them well in advance. Hotel reservations, while also extremely tight, are easier to get and less important to the purpose of your visit. In late August and early September, or early in the season, in June, you'll have a much easier time finding space (see "When to Go: Crowds or Snow" under "Planning a Visit to the Park," earlier in this chapter).

Here's the system for reservations. One-third of the available shuttle-bus seats and campsites (except at Marino, Sanctuary River, and Igloo Creek campgrounds) are available for reservation by phone, beginning sometime after the first of the year, until five days in advance of your visit. Reservations then close until two days before the date of the shuttle-bus ride or campground stay; then, beginning two days in advance, the remaining two-thirds of the spots are available in person only, at the visitor center, and are quickly booked up. When you get to the front of the line, if there's still a night available two days hence, you can book that night and book up to 14 continuous nights afterward at that campground or any other. (A backcountry permit qualifies to keep the 14 days continuous, but 14 days of camping or backcountry time is all you can have all year, total.) The doors of the visitor center open at 7am, and the line is already long when they do, forming by 6am in the peak season; the line stays long until the center closes, at 8pm. The chronic atmosphere of frustration and tension in the crowded, noisy visitor center is almost toxic.

Under this system, if you arrive without reservations, you usually must wait two days before getting a campsite or riding the bus. That means spending your time outside the park in private accommodations. I can't explain how this two-day waiting system benefits anyone other than the hotels and private campgrounds where the visitors must stay while they wait.

GETTING THERE

BY RAIL   The most popular way to get to Denali National Park is by train. The **Alaska Railroad,** P.O. Box 107500, Anchorage, AK 99510-7500 (☎ **907/ 265-2494** or 800/544-0552), which pioneered tourism to the park before the Parks Highway was built in 1972, has daily service in the summer from Anchorage and Fairbanks. Trains leave both cities at 8:30am, arriving at the park from Anchorage at 4pm and from Fairbanks at 12:15pm, crossing and going on to the opposite city for arrival at 8:30pm in each. The full train runs only from mid-May to mid-September, with slightly lower fares in May and September than during the summer. During the winter, the Alaska Railroad runs a single car from Anchorage to Fairbanks and back once a week; if you're here, ride it one way—it's a truly spectacular, truly Alaskan experience.

The advantages of taking the train to Denali are that it's a historic, unspoiled route through beautiful countryside, there's a good chance of seeing moose and caribou, it's fun and relaxing, and the food on any of the three sets of cars is good. The disadvantages are that the train is more expensive than renting a car if you have two or more people; it's slow, adding three hours to a trip from Anchorage to the park and five hours to a trip to Fairbanks; and once you arrive you have to rely on shuttles and courtesy vans to get around outside the park. Also, when the train is late, it's really late, and that can frustrate some people.

Once you've decided to take the train, you must decide which cars to choose. The Alaska Railroad locomotives also pull two sets of cars with full domes owned by **Princess Cruises** (☎ **800/835-8907**) and **Holland America Westours / Gray Line of Alaska** (☎ **907/277-5581 or 800/628-2449**). Each provides separate, distinct service and operates independently, as described below. You can't walk from one kind of car to another. Fares are $95 one way from Anchorage to Denali on the Alaska Railroad cars, $124 on the Princess cars, and $130 on the Holland America / Westours cars; packages are available.

The Princess and Holland America / Westours cars cater primarily to their cruise-ship and package customers, but do sell tickets to independent travelers. They offer a luxurious but controlled experience wherein each passenger has his or her own dome-car seat on a unique, beautifully appointed railroad car. You're expected to stay in your assigned seat, eat during a scheduled dining seating, and you may have to ride backward or sideways in cars designed with tables and living room–style furniture. Besides riding backward, you could spend almost eight hours sitting across a table from strangers whom you may or may not like. The Alaska Railroad cars are traditional railroad cars, with seats facing forward, and you can sit anywhere you want, you can move between cars and stand in the breezeway between cars, and you can eat when you want to. The food is not the luxurious fare the cruise lines strive for, but it's less expensive and still quite good, served in an old-fashioned, white-tableclothed dining car. A couple of dozen dome-car seats are available, with a 20-minute limit on staying in them—not the dome-to-yourself arrangement of the cruise-line cars. Well-trained guides provide intermittent commentary and answer questions in each car. Children will enjoy the Alaska Railroad cars more; adults can judge for themselves which approach is more appealing.

Between the two cruise-line car offerings, Princess's Midnight Sun Express Ultra Dome Rail Cars appeared clearly preferable to me. The decor was fresher and better maintained than in the Holland America / Westours cars, there was more head-room in the upstairs dome area, the fare was slightly lower, and on two of the three cars an outdoor platform was provided to get out of your seat and enjoy the fresh air. However, my personal preference would be for the Alaska Railroad cars; even if you can't sit in a dome the whole way, the windows still are large and clean, and I think half the fun of riding on a train is moving around and meeting a variety of people.

BY CAR You can rent a car and drive from Anchorage cheaper than taking the train, if there are two or more of you. Many of the views along the Parks Highway are equal to the views on the train, but large stretches, especially in the Matanuska and Susitna valleys, have been spoiled by the worst kind of roadside development—you don't see that on the train. The drive is about $4^1/_2$ hours from Anchorage, $2^1/_2$ from Fairbanks, on good two-lane highway. On the way north from Anchorage you pass through Denali State Park, about 135 miles along the highway. If the weather's clear, you get great views of Mount McKinley from the pull-outs here, which are about as close to the mountain as you can get on the park road within the national park, and much closer than you'll be at the park entrance. The state park also contains several campgrounds and hiking trails and a veterans memorial.

BY BUS The **Alaska Backpacker Shuttle** (☎ **907/344-8775** or 800/266-8625) carries passengers from Anchorage in a van that leaves from the hostel down-town. The fare is $35 one way. **Alaska Glacier Tours** (☎ **907/274-8539** or 800/327-7651) offers an endurance-testing one-day tour of the park from Anchorage. The van leaves Anchorage at 5:45am, arriving at the visitor center and putting you on a shuttle to the Eielson Visitor Center at 11am with a bag lunch, then driving back to Anchorage and arriving at half past midnight—a timetable that allows perhaps a total of an hour of standing on solid ground in almost 18 hours of hard driving. The fare is $159 round-trip for the tour, including the park fees, or you can use it just to get there for $75. **Fireweed Express** (☎ 907/452-0521) offers van service from Fairbanks for $25 one way, and will carry your bike for an extra $5.

BY AIR Flightseeing trips to Denali go from Talkeetna and from Anchorage—they're listed in the sections on those towns in Chapter 8. You can also charter to Denali from Anchorage or Fairbanks, although it's liable to be costly.

GETTING AROUND

If you drive to the park, you'll still need to take the **shuttle bus** to get into its heart, but you'll easily be able to access the broadly spread out commercial establishments along the Parks Highway. If you take the train, you'll find that virtually all accom-modations have arrangements to get you around. If your hotel doesn't have a courtesy van of its own, you can always take a scheduled shuttle. From Healy, the **Fireweed Express** runs to the park entrance hourly, charging $5 each way. **ARA** also operates a bus that carries guests from its Denali Park Resorts hotels, a mile north and 7 miles south of the park, to the park entrance; you can use the bus even if you're not staying at an ARA hotel—have the desk at your hotel call for a pickup.

Biking is one of the great undiscovered ways of seeing the park. Bicyclists can ride past the checkpoint where cars have to turn back, at Mile 14 on the park road. With well-planned campsites, you could make Denali the ultimate mountain-bike trip. **Denali Mountain Bike,** P.O. Box 448, Denali National Park, AK 99755 (☎ **907/683-BIKE**), rents bikes for $25 a day.

FEES & REGULATIONS

ENTRANCE FEES   The park service charges an entrance fee to come into Denali National Park, but there is no gate, no one collects the fee or asks for a ticket or receipt to show you've paid it, and many people probably never know about it at all. When you book a campground site or a bus ride, the fee is automatically added to your bill. Individual fees are $3, $5 for families, and they're good for seven days. Annual passes are available, but are unlikely to be worthwhile unless you're planning more than three visits, each separated by more than a week. U.S. residents 62 or older can obtain a lifetime family pass with a 50% discount on camping, called a Golden Age Passport, for $10. Disabled U.S. residents can get such a pass free, called a Golden Access Passport.

WHO CAN DRIVE THE PARK ROAD   Restaurants and lodges in Kantishna can use the park road to bring in customers, but everyone else is under strict controls. You can drive past Mile 14 on the park road only under certain circumstances:

- You have a three-day camping permit at Teklanika Campground (you must remain parked at the campground for the entire three days);
- You are a credentialed professional photographer or researcher with a special permit; or
- It is the last few days in September that the road is open and you have won a permit in a lottery that allows 1,600 cars free reign on the road.

After the three days of permit driving are over, the road is open to anyone as far as Mile 30 until the snow flies; then it's maintained only as far as the headquarters, 3 miles from the entrance.

CAMPING PERMITS & FEES   Each park service campground has different fees, regulations, and access limitations. All sites must be reserved, except the Marino Backpacker campground, which has a self-registration system. However, the Sanctuary and Igloo campgrounds can be reserved only in person—which means you'll most likely have to reserve your spot then wait two nights till a site is open. There's a one-time reservation fee of $4 per campground in addition to the campground permit fees. Campground fees and regulations are in "Denali Campground Facts," in the table below. Descriptions are in the "Out in the Park" section, below. Reservation procedures are given above. To get beyond the 14-mile checkpoint, you need to ride on the camper bus or go by bicycle. The $15 bus fare is a bargain, as it will allow you to explore the park for less than you'd pay if you weren't camping.

BUS FARES   Riding a bus over a bumpy gravel road is an integral part of the Denali experience. If that starts to bother you, just remember that most of what's attractive about the park wouldn't be there if free access by private vehicles were allowed—instead it would just be a busy, rural highway. For details on the trip, see "On (and Off) the Bus," later in this chapter. For fares and other details, see the "Denali Park Road Bus Facts" chart, on page 326.

Denali Campground Facts

Campground	Fee	No. of Sites	Access & Special Rules
Riley Creek	$12 per night	100 sites	Near park entrance. Private vehicle or free front-country bus.
Marino Backpacker	$6 per person	informal	Near park hotel. Free front-country bus. No parking or vehicle camping. Maximum 2 people per site. No reservations.
Savage River	$12 per night	33 sites	13 miles from park entrance. Private vehicle access or $15 camper bus.
Savage Group	$40 per night	3 sites	Group sites at Savage River. No discount for Golden Age or Golden Access passes.
Sanctuary River	$6 per night	7 sites	23 miles from park entrance. Tent camping only. Store food in lockers. Stove only, no fires. Reservations in person only. Access by $15 camper bus.
Teklanika River	$12 per night	53 sites	29 miles from park entrance. Minimum 3-night stay for vehicles. Access for private vehicles with camping permit or by $15 camper bus.
Igloo Creek	$6 per night	7 sites	34 miles from park entrance. Tent camping only. Store food in lockers. Stove only, no fires. Reservations in person only. Access by $15 camper bus.
Wonder Lake	$12 per night	28 sites	85 miles from park entrance. Tent camping only. Store food in lockers. Stove only, no fires. Access by $15 camper bus.

BACKCOUNTRY PERMITS   The permit system for staying overnight in the undeveloped backcountry is onerous enough to weed out those who aren't serious about a wilderness experience. For details on choosing your route and information for your trek, see "Hiking the Backcountry" under "Out in the Park," later in this chapter.

Permits are free, but can be obtained only 24 hours in advance and only in person at the backcountry desk in the visitor center. Since the unit areas book up quickly during the summer season, you may have to wait a while outside the park before you can start your hike. Camping at the Marino Backpacker campground during the wait is a good, inexpensive choice which does not require advance reservations.

The park is divided into 43 backcountry units, 29 of which are accessible from the park road. For your first night, you have to stay in one of these 29, as it isn't practical in one day to get into the park and hike across a roadside unit to camp in a unit that's off the road. Each unit generally has only a few permits available. You can reserve up to 14 days in the backcountry during the summer, planning a route from one unit to another and getting all the permits at the start. Because of this regulation, you may find the units you're most interested in already booked, even if you're first in line on the first morning they become available. Have second and third choices ready.

Before venturing into the backcountry, everyone is required to watch an orientation film called the *Backcountry Simulator*. The park service will provide bear-proof food containers in which you are required to carry all your food. Guns are not permitted in the park; a pepper spray for self-defense is a good idea and proper camping etiquette essential to avoid attracting bears.

4 On (& Off) the Bus

Your visit to Denali will likely revolve around your ride on the shuttle bus into the park to see the wildlife and get out for a walk in the wilderness. Some prior planning will make it a more comfortable ride.

You can buy shuttle tickets to the Toklat (TOE-klat) River 53 miles into the park, the Eielson (AISLE-son) Visitor Center at 66 miles, Wonder Lake at 85 miles, or Kantishna at about 95 miles. Of course, you have to go both ways unless you have a campground reservation, a backcountry permit, or accommodations in Kantishna—which means that you're in for a long drive. If you don't get off the bus along the way, the round-trip takes 6 1/2 hours to Toklat, 8 hours to Eielson, 11 hours to Wonder Lake, and 12 hours to Kantishna. In choosing your destination, you need to balance your stamina, your desire to save time for a day hike, and your desire to see bears and caribou, which in recent years have been sighted most often on the alpine tundra between Toklat and the Eielson Visitor Center. Going beyond Eielson to Wonder Lake provides more great views, including the classic image of Mount McKinley across the wooded lake. In general, however, I think Eielson is the best destination for most people, offering both the chance to see the mountain and some wildlife while leaving some time to get out and walk.

Reserve your ticket for as early as you can stand to get up in the morning. This strategy will give you more time for day hikes and enhance your chances of seeing wildlife; many animals are more active in the morning, especially on hot days. The first bus leaves the visitor center at 5am, the next at 6am, and then every half hour until the 2:30pm bus, which gets back at 10:30pm. By taking an early bus, you can get off along the way for a hike, then walk back to the road and get the next bus that comes along with a spare seat. If you were to take the 5am bus, you'd have 9 1/2 hours of slack time before you'd have to catch the last bus heading east. (To be on the safe side, double-check the time of the last bus with your bus driver when you get off.) The sun won't set until after 11pm May to July, so there'll be plenty of light.

Here's the hard part for families: Young children will go nuts on an eight-hour bus ride, and often can't pick out the wildlife—this isn't a zoo, and most animals blend into their surroundings. Older children also have a hard time keeping their patience on these trips, as do many adults. The only solution is to get off the bus and turn your trip into a romp in the heather. When you've had a chance to revive, catch the next bus. Besides, just because you buy a ticket to Eielson doesn't mean that you have to go that far.

Beginning early in June, a ranger-guided day hike in the backcountry leaves on a special bus from the visitor center each morning at 8am, a good alternative if you feel uncomfortable about backcountry hiking on your own. The **Discovery Hike** itself lasts about four hours and is fairly strenuous. You must sign up a day or two in advance at the visitor center.

Unfortunately, shuttle-bus tickets can be canceled only with two days' advance notice, and then at a cost of $6 each. The weather is unpredictable that far in advance.

Denali Park Road Bus Facts

Bus	Color	Purpose	Route	Frequency	Fare
Front-country shuttle/ ARA courtesy shuttle	Tan or blue and white	Park entrance transportation	Links Denali Park Resorts Hotels, Riley Creek campground, visitor center	Continuous loop	Free
Camper shuttle	Yellow	Access to campgrounds beyond the park entrance	From the visitor center to Wonder Lake Campground, 85 miles into the park	Several times a day	$15 adults, $7.50 children 13–16, free children 12 and under
Backcountry shuttle (or just "the shuttle")	Green with a pink stripe	General access to the park and wildlife viewing; limited commentary, depending on the driver; no food service	From the visitor center as far as Kantishna, 95 miles away through the park	Every 30 minutes to Eielson Visitor Center, every hour to Wonder Lake, less frequently to Kantishna	$20 to Eielson, $25 to Wonder Lake, $30 to Kantishna; children 13–16 half price, children 12 and under free
Wildlife Tour	Brown	Seven-hour guided bus tour with lunch provided; passengers may not get off en route	From the visitor center to the Toklat River, 53 miles into the park	Twice daily	$51, half price for children
Natural History Tour	Brown	Three-hour guided bus tour at the edge of the park	From the visitor center 17 miles into the park	Three times daily	$28, half price for children
Kantishna Roadhouse bus	Blue, with KANTISHNA ROADHOUSE on the side	All-day bus tour to a restaurant in Kantishna, operated separately from the park or concessionaire	From the park entrance 95 miles to Kantishna	Once a day	$99

If it's rainy, your chances of seeing wildlife are reduced and your chance of seeing Mount McKinley nil. Don't lose hope, however, as the park is large and the weather can be different at the other end of your long drive; besides, there's nothing you can do about it.

Before you leave for the visitor center to get on your bus, you need a packed lunch and plenty of water; you should be wearing sturdy walking shoes and layers of warm and cooler clothing with rain gear packed; you should have binoculars or a spotting scope at the ready; and you should have insect repellent handy. You may also want a copy of Kim Heacox's worthwhile booklet "The Denali Road Guide," available at the visitor center gift shop; it provides a milepost commentary you can follow as you drive. Most shuttle-bus drivers do a good job of providing commentary, too. If you'll be doing any extensive day hiking, you may also want to bring a detailed topographic map printed on waterproof plastic (available for $7 from the visitor center) and a compass; if you're just going to walk a short distance off the road you won't need such preparations.

Shuttle-bus etiquette is to yell out when you see wildlife. The driver will stop and everyone will rush to your side of the bus. After you've had a look, give someone else a chance to look out your window or to get a picture. Try to be quiet and don't stick anything out of the bus, as that can scare away the animals. Of course, you have to stay on the bus when animals are present. Most buses will see grizzly bears, caribou, Dall sheep, and moose, and occasionally wolves, but, as one driver said, the animals aren't union workers, and it's possible that you won't see any at all.

Here are some of the highlights along the road (check the visitor center or the park service information handouts to confirm times of the guided walks):

Mile 9 In clear weather, this is the closest spot to the park entrance with a view of Mount McKinley.

Mile 14 The end of the paved road at the Savage River Bridge. This is as far as private vehicles can go except under certain circumstances; a park service checkpoint stops anyone who doesn't have a proper permit.

Mile 16 Primrose Ridge is a popular place for a hike. This is as far as the Natural History Tour bus goes.

Mile 30 A large rest stop overlooking the Teklanika River has flush toilets, the last until the Eielson Visitor Center. Teklanika, like several others in the park and on similar glacier-carved terrain across the state, is a braided river—a relatively small stream wandering in a massive gravel streambed. It's thought that the riverbed was created by water from fast-melting glaciers at the end of the last ice age.

Mile 33 Craggy Igloo Mountain is a likely place to see Dall sheep. Without binoculars, they'll just look like white dots. Heathery, open terrain suitable for an outing begins here.

Mile 37.5 Tattler Creek, a good place for a steep day hike to see sheep and maybe bears.

Mile 38–43 A critical habitat area for bears; no backcountry use is allowed, and you have to stay on the bus. The area was designated years ago, when bears were using it heavily, but there hasn't been a particular abundance of bears there in recent years.

Mile 46 The top of Polychrome Pass, the most scenic point on the ride, with mountains of colored rock on each side of a broad alpine valley frequented by caribou. (There's also a rest stop with portable outhouses.)

Mile 53 The Toklat River, another braided river, is a flat plain of gravel with easy walking. The river bottom is habitat for bears, caribou, and wolves. A ranger leads a hike here of up to two hours, the Toklat Trek—check the visitor center for times. The Wildlife Tour bus turns around near here.

Mile 58 Highway Pass, the highest point on the road. In good weather, there's a nice view of Mount McKinley. The alpine tundra from here to the Eielson Visitor Center is inviting for walking.

Mile 64 Thorofare Pass, where the road becomes narrow and tortuous, is the area where most of the bear and caribou sightings were being made in 1995. Bus drivers know best where the animals are on any particular day; they exchange information among themselves.

Mile 66 The Eielson Visitor Center, the end of most bus trips, has flush toilets, a covered picnic area, and a small area of displays where rangers answer questions. Among the displays is one explaining why you probably can't see the mountain from this best of vantage points, just 33 miles from its summit. Mount McKinley creates its own weather, and is visible about a third of the time in the summer. Starting late in June, a ranger-guided tundra walk occurs daily at 1:30pm, lasting no more than an hour.

Mile 68.5 The road comes within a mile of Muldrow Glacier, one of the ice rivers that descends from Mount McKinley. The terrain on the way to Wonder Lake resolves from cliffs and bluffs to small hills of rolling, wet tundra, and finally descends into a spruce forest near Mile 82.

Mile 86 Wonder Lake campground, the closest road point to Mount McKinley, 27 miles away. The bus continues another half hour to Kantishna.

5 Out in the Park

ACTIVITIES The park service offers three guided hikes out in the park, beyond the 14-mile checkpoint. The daily **Discovery Hike** lasts four hours and goes somewhere different every day. You need to wear hiking boots and bring food, water, and rain gear. A special bus carrying the hikers leaves the visitor center at 8am, starting in mid-June. Reserve a place in advance. The **Toklat Trek** is an irregularly scheduled ranger-led walk in the Toklat River streambed; the **Tundra Walk,** at 1:30pm daily starting in late June, is a short guided stroll from the Eielson Visitor Center, at Mile 66 on the park road. Check in at the visitor center for late word on all the hikes before heading out on a long bus trip.

Fishing in the park is nothing special. There are grayling in some of the clear streams, but most of the water in the park is too thick with glacial silt to serve as fish habitat.

CAMPGROUNDS The park has eight campgrounds. Recreational vehicles can find a place, as can tent campers who want to be away from people out in the wilderness. The campgrounds range from 7 to 100 sites each. I've listed the fees and regulations for each campground in the table "Denali Campground Facts" under "The Essential Details," earlier in this chapter; here I aim to give you a feel for what each is like so you can choose which you'd prefer. I've listed private campgrounds under "Where to Stay," later in this chapter.

To get to campgrounds beyond Mile 14 on the park road, you have to take the $15 camper bus (unless you're staying three days or more at Teklanika). If it seems expensive, consider this: The ticket is like a free pass to travel all over the park, which would cost as much as $11 more if bought for the shuttle. If you need to get back to catch a train, reserve a return seat, as the camper bus normally picks up anyone who needs a ride and may be full.

First to the Top

On Sept. 27, 1906, renowned world explorer Dr. Frederick Cook announced to the world by telegraph that he had reached the summit of Mount McKinley after a lightning-fast climb, covering 85 miles and 19,000 vertical feet in 13 days with one other man, a blacksmith, at his side. On his return to New York, Cook was lionized as a conquering explorer and published a book of his summit diary and photographs. Even today, the Frederick Cook Society meets regularly to memorialize and celebrate the deed.

They spend even more effort trying to convince the rest of the world that it wasn't just a huge hoax.

In 1909 Cook again made history, announcing that he had beat Robert Peary to the North Pole. Both returned to civilization from their competing treks at about the same time. Again Cook was the toast of the world. Then his Eskimo companions mentioned that he'd never been out of sight of land, and his story began to fall apart. After being paid by Peary to come forward, Cook's McKinley companion also recanted. A year later, his famous summit photograph was re-created on a peak 19 miles away and 15,000 feet lower than the real summit.

In 1910 four prospectors from Fairbanks took a more Alaskan approach to the task. Without fanfare, they marched up the mountain carrying a large wooden pole they could plant on top to prove they'd made it. But on arriving at the top, they realized that they'd climbed the slightly shorter north peak; weather closed in, so they set up the pole there and descended. Then, when they got back to Fairbanks, no one could see the pole and they were accused of trying to pull off another hoax. In 1913 Episcopal missionary Hudson Stuck was the first to reach the summit for real—and saw the pole on the other peak.

Since then, more than five dozen climbers have died on Mount McKinley, and thousands of others have made it to the summit. Hundreds more try every year, flying to the Kahiltna Glacier from Talkeetna and then taking about a month to reach the top. Altitude and weather are the primary killers and deterrents to those who don't reach the summit—about half who try.

Still, no one has managed to re-create the feat Frederick Cook claimed to his death to have accomplished. But the 150 members of the Frederick Cook Society, based in New York, fight on to clear his name and establish Cook as the first to the Pole and the top of North America's tallest mountain. And they continue to gather evidence to discredit Peary, charging that Cook's difficulties were caused by a conspiracy of Peary supporters. As recently as 1994 the society funded an expedition to retrace part of Cook's route and validate his photographs and diaries.

Ninety years after Cook's telegram, the world isn't listening anymore.

(I am indebted to Dermot Cole's article on Cook in the April 1995 issue of *Alaska* magazine.)

Riley Creek   This is the traditional family campground in the woods right at the entrance to the park. With 100 sites, paved roads, flush toilets, and a sewage dump station, it's far from wilderness; but it is readily accessible, easy to get a permit, and young children won't care if it's not in the back country. For more ambitious campers, it's still a good stop for your first night in the park, when you need time to get your bearings before heading to a more remote area. The front-country shuttle bus stops in the parking lot, where there's a single pay phone. Riley Creek is a roaring tributary of the Nenana, running just below the campground; the best sites back onto the river. Riley is the only campground open all year, although the water is off in the winter.

Marino Backpacker Intended as a waiting area for backcountry travelers waiting for their permits, the Marino campground is essentially just a wooded area about a mile from the visitor center where backpackers can put up their tents. Sites are designated by stakes. There is no parking area and advance reservations aren't taken; you show up and self-register.

Savage River Just a mile short of the park road checkpoint beyond which vehicles cannot go, Savage River is both easily accessible and relatively remote, 13 miles from the park entrance. It's the best choice for car or RV campers who want to get away from the park entrance but don't have three days to spend camping at Teklanika. There are 33 sites. The bathrooms have flush toilets. Savage Group is the nearby group camping area. The taiga—sparsely wooded tundra—is good for exploring, and there's a chance of seeing wildlife.

Sanctuary River This small, primitive campground with seven tent sites is 9 miles beyond the road checkpoint. There are chemical toilets. The campground is in the woods near a ranger station.

Teklanika River At Mile 29 on the park road, this is the only campground for car or RV camping beyond the checkpoint. You can drive in if you agree not to move your vehicle for at least three days. With 53 sites, it's a large campground, but the sites are adequately separated by trees. It has chemical toilets.

Igloo Creek The last campground for 52 miles, Igloo Creek is a primitive tent camp with seven sites near a ranger station. It's the closest campground to the open terrain of alpine tundra.

Wonder Lake The 28 tent-camping sites at this campground near the end of the park road are in high demand, in the woods next to a placid mountain lake below spectacular views of Mount McKinley. Despite the remote location, it has flush toilets and a ranger station is only 2 miles away. Winter stays late at this end of the park, and the campground doesn't open until some time in June.

HIKING THE BACKCOUNTRY Trekking the backcountry on a multiday backpacking journey is challenging and rugged, but also the most authentic way to see the park and understand its meaning. Only people with strong outdoor skills who are in good physical condition should attempt a strenuous backcountry overnight, however, as there are no trails or other people to guide you. For this reason, I haven't included a list of needed gear and supplies.

You must be flexible about where you're going and be prepared for any kind of terrain, because you can't choose the backcountry unit you will explore until arriving at the backcountry desk at the visitor center and finding out what's available. This information, and a map of the units, are posted on a board behind the desk. Groups of four or more may have a hard time finding a place to hike, but there's almost always *somewhere* to go. A couple of rangers are there to help you through the process. (See "Fees and Regulations" under "The Essential Details," earlier in this chapter, for details on how to get a permit.)

Buy the $7 **Denali National Park and Preserve topographical map** published by Trails Illustrated, P.O. Box 3610, Evergreen, CO 80439-3425 (☎ **800/ 962-1643**), sold at the visitor center, which includes the boundaries of the 43 backcountry units. The map is printed on plastic and is indispensable for backcountry hikers. Also, you'll want to consult **Backcountry Companion,** by Jon Nierenberg, a book that describes each of the units. Published by the Alaska Natural History Association (605 W. Fourth Ave., Anchorage, AK 99501), it's for sale at the visitor center, or you can look at a well-thumbed copy kept at the backcountry desk.

The alpine units are most popular. That's where you get broad views and can cross heathery valleys walking in any direction. But to go far, you'll also have to be ready to climb over some rugged, rocky terrain. The wooded units are least popular, since bushwhacking through overgrown land is anything but fun. The best routes for making time are along the braided river valleys; you need to be ready for a lot of stream crossings. Tundra looks inviting to hike across, but it's soft and tiring walking and frequently has hidden hazards that can turn an ankle. Hiking in streambeds is the most efficient way to cross the Alaska Bush.

You can only reserve permits one day in advance, but you can reserve permits for continuation of your trip for up to 14 days at the same time. Units that aren't contiguous to the park road are more likely to be available, because you can't expect to make it that far on the first night of a hike. Because of the way the system is set up, the first night of a trip is the hard one to get; after that, each night gets progressively easier. You'll have to take the camper bus to get to your backcountry unit.

Before you decide to go to Denali, however, you may want to broaden your thinking—if you're up to a cross-country hike without a trail, there are tens of millions of acres in Alaska available for backpacking that don't require a permit. Check with the Public Lands Information Center in Anchorage or Fairbanks for ideas; or get off the road in virtually any area of public land and take off (taking proper wilderness precautions, of course, including telling someone where you're going).

6 Things to Do at the Park Entrance & Environs

RANGER PROGRAMS & ACTIVITIES   You may be anxious to get deep into the park as soon as you arrive, but the park service does offer lectures, guided hikes, and a sled-dog demonstration at the park entrance to keep you entertained and interpret the park while you wait for a bus or permit. I've highlighted a few choices that were offered in 1995. Pick up a copy of the park newspaper, *Denali Alpenglow,* at the visitor center for current offerings and times.

✪ Sled-Dog Demonstration   In the winter rangers patrol the park by sled dog, as they have for decades. In the summer, to keep the dogs active and amuse the tourists, they pull a sled on wheels around the kennel and a ranger gives a talk two to three times a day. It was the highlight of my three-year-old's trip to Denali. Although there's no substitute for seeing dogs run on snow, this is as close as you'll get in the summer. A free bus leaves the visitor center for each show, at the kennels near the headquarters at Mile 3.4 on the park road. Or you can join a guided 2-mile hike at the visitor center before the sled-dog show which heads up the Rock Creek Trail to arrive at the kennels for each demonstration.

Hotel & Visitor Center Programs   Rangers offer a talk and film at 1:30pm daily, and a lecture, possibly with slides, at 8pm, in the auditorium at the park hotel. There are ranger talks at the visitor center auditorium at 11am and 7pm.

Guided Hikes   Eight ranger-guided hikes and tours take off daily within the park, three in the backcountry (discussed in "Activities" under "Out in the Park," earlier in this chapter) and five around the park entrance. The longest of those in the entrance area is 3 miles, the **Mount Healy Overlook walk.**

CAMPGROUND PROGRAMS   The Riley Creek, Savage River, Teklanika, and Wonder Lake campgrounds have ranger programs almost nightly.

TRAILS   The park service is making a concerted effort to discourage the making of trails in the tundra or taiga of the park proper, but there are six easy, well-maintained trails around the park entrance area, the longest of which is the **Mount Healy Overlook,** a 5-mile round-trip. The others are strolls of 2 miles or less. A trail guide of sorts is printed in the *Denali Alpenglow* park guide handed out by the park service; "The Nature of Denali," available at the visitor center, is a natural-history guide to the trails.

FLIGHTSEEING   Getting a good, close look at Mount McKinley is best accomplished by air. Frequently, when you can't see McKinley from the ground, you can see it from above the clouds. It's an impressive mountain, standing huge and white far above most of the surrounding terrain. The best flights take at least 90 minutes and circle McKinley. **Denali Air** (☎ 907/683-2261) is the official concessionaire at the park, with an office at the airstrip in the park and six single- and two-engine planes. An hour-long flight going within a mile of the mountain costs $150. Other companies do tours as well, including **Fly Denali** (☎ 907/683-2889 or 800/563-2889), with flights for as little as $65, and **Denali Wings** (☎ 907/683-2245), operating out of Healy. **Era Helicopters** (☎ 907/835-2595 or 800/843-1947) has hourly flights for $170, including van pickup from the hotels. The drawback of a helicopter is you can't get near wildlife because the aircraft is so noisy.

✪ RAFTING & BOATING   Floating the swift, glacial water of the Nenana River Canyon as it passes the park entrance has become a major activity at the park, because it's convenient and fun. The entire trip is outside the park. Several companies compete for your business, most offering a choice of slow, Class II water, or a white-water trip with numerous Class III and IV rapids. Each trip takes 2 to 2½ hours and costs $40 to $47, or floating through both costs $53 to $60 and takes twice as long. Most of the companies fit you out with rain gear for the white-water trips, but you get soaked to the skin anyway; afterward, you'll need a shower, as the glacial silt sticks to your skin and hair.

The **Denali Outdoor Center** (☎ 907/683-1925) has an edge over the competition with a low price and by supplying dry suits to white-water passengers, so they remain warm and dry. Their office is on the right across from the McKinley Chalet Hotel as you head north on the Parks Highway through the business area nearest the park. For those who prefer to take a more active hand, the cooperative of five guides also offers inflatable kayak tours and schools and self-paddled raft runs. **Denali Park Resorts** (☎ 907/683-7234, or 800/276-7234), the park concessionaire, also does a fine job, and allows children as young as age 5 on the slow-water version of its raft trips with a half-off discount to kids 11 and under (age 12 is the minimum for the white-water trips for all the operators). The **Denali Park Paddling Center** (☎ 907/683-1925) specializes in inflatable and rigid kayak instruction and has half- and full-day trips as well as rentals to experienced kayakers who prove their abilities. **McKinley Raft Tours** (☎ 907/683-2392) offers the lowest priced four-hour trip, at $53. **Denali Wilderness Safaris** (☎ 907/768-2550), of Cantwell, offers jet-boat and air-boat tours, about 25 miles south of the park to a remote camp on Brushkasna Creek, for $85.

HORSEBACK RIDING   There is no riding in the park itself, but several opportunities in similar terrain outside its boundaries. **Beaver Lake Trail Rides** (☎ 907/683-1699), with a trail at Carlo Creek, 12 miles south of the park entrance, and **Sugar Loaf Wilderness Trail Rides** (☎ 907/683-2402), 11 miles north, both belong to Leonard Youngman, who keeps his three dozen horses in Wasilla in the winter. The Beaver Lake ride takes groups of five up a trail with an 1,800-foot elevation gain; trips range from 1 hour for $55 to 4¹/₂ hours for $100, all leaving several times a day. The Sugar Loaf ride is gentler, open country, with trips ranging from an hour to all day. The **Tumbling B Ranch,** at Carlo Creek, Mile 224 of the Parks Highway (☎ **907/683-2277**), has one-hour rides for $45, four hours for $90. **Wolf Point Ranch** (☎ **907/768-2620** or 800/367-8173 outside Alaska) offers four- and six-day pack trips for $910 or $1,350 per person, respectively.

BIKING   ✪ **Denali Mountain Bike** (☎ **907/683-BIKE**) leads multiday tours outside the park as well as renting bikes for $25 a day and offering the only bike-repair shop in 130 miles (Fairbanks is the next closest). But the real allure of mountain biking in Denali is that you don't have the same restrictions cars do—you can ride right past the checkpoint into the park. Park campgrounds have bike stands, and you can take a bike on the shuttle or camper bus. The longest stretch on the park road between campgrounds is 52 miles. On the downside, the buses kick up a lot of dust.

7 Where to Stay

Patterns of landownership and the furious pace of development around Denali have led to a hodge-podge of roadside hotels, cabins, lodges, campgrounds, and restaurants in pockets arrayed along more than 20 miles of the Parks Highway. There are rooms of good quality in each of the pockets, but the going rates vary widely. The most expensive rooms, and the first booked, are in the immediate area of the park entrance. Next are the hotels south of the park. Both these areas are entirely seasonal. The best deals are in Healy, 10 miles north of the park, where you can find a room for $50 less than a comparable room near the park entrance. Of course, if you don't have a car it's most convenient to stay in or near the park, but it's not essential, as various shuttles connect the areas. The other choice is to stay at a remote wilderness lodge. I've listed each of the four choices separately. Despite their high prices, rooms can be hard to find in the high season and it's wise to book well ahead.

The local **bed tax** is 7%.

NEAR THE PARK

I define this area, sometimes known as Denali Canyon, as the area extending about a mile north of the park entrance on the Parks Highway, plus the park hotel, which is within the park 1¹/₂ miles up the park road. Other than the hotels listed below, I can recommend two other accommodations in this area in the $120 to $130 price range: **Mount McKinley Motor Lodge,** P.O. Box 22011, Anchorage, AK 99522 (☎ **907/245-0200**), has attractive, modern rooms with TVs, set back in some trees; and **Sourdough Cabins,** P.O. Box 118, Denali, AK 99755 (☎ **907/683-2773**), has comfortable little cabins below the highway in the river bottom.

Denali Crow's Nest Cabins. Mile 238.5, Parks Hwy. (P.O. Box 70), Denali National Park, AK 99755. ☎ **907/683-2723.** Fax 907/683-2323. 39 cabins. $134 cabin for two. Additional person in cabin $10 extra. MC, V.

Perched in three tiers on the side of a mountain above the Nenana Canyon area, looking down on Horseshoe Lake and the other (big) hotels, the cabins are large and comfortable, especially those on the 100 and 200 level. You spend a lot of time climbing stairs, however, and despite the great views, the cabins are simple, not as luxurious as you might expect for the price. The excellent restaurant, **The Overlook,** is recommended separately under "Where to Eat," later in this chapter. Extras include courtesy van, two outdoor Jacuzzis, free coffee, and a tour desk.

Denali National Park Hotel. Mile 1.5, Denali National Park Rd. (P.O. Box 87), Denali Park, AK 99755. (For reservations, contact Denali Park Resorts, 241 W. Ship Creek Ave., Anchorage, AK 99501; ☎ **907/272-7275** in Anchorage, or 800/622-7275.) 100 rms. High season, $146 double. Low season, $93 double. Additional person in room $10 extra. DISC, MC, V. Closed mid-Sept to mid-May.

The only hotel within the park burned down in 1972; this "temporary" structure, cobbled together from old railroad cars and modular housing units, has served ever since, gaining an oddly historic feel of its own. The owner is the park concessionaire, which also owns the McKinley Chalet Resort and McKinley Village Lodge. The park hotel is a center of park activities, with hiking trails out the back door, and has more character than the other big hotels, but it needs remodeling and the rooms have no views. There's a courtesy shuttle, coffee in the rooms, and a tour desk.

The attractive **dining room** serves large portions. The lounge, in a pair of railroad cars, has a good, campy feel; smoking is permitted only in one of the two rail cars it occupies. For fast food, the snack bar is quite adequate. The gift shop has prices regulated by the park service.

Denali Princess Lodge. Mile 238.5, Parks Hwy. (P.O. Box 110), Denali National Park, AK 997555. ☎ **800/426-0050.** Fax 206/443-1979. 272 rms, 7 suites. TV TEL. High season, $165–$200 double. Low season, $99–$150 double. $250–$300 suite. Additional person in room $10 extra. AE, DC, MC, V. Closed late Sept to mid-May.

This is the best of the big hotels at Denali, with a resort-hotel feel—there's a lovely lobby, a couple of good restaurants, hot-tub spas on decks with a good view, and so on. But the rooms, while comfortable, are nothing special for the high price, even if they do have TVs and phones, which the major competition lacks. The hotel is used primarily for the cruise line's package tours, and is booked up most nights with their elderly passengers. If they're not full, you might fall into a good deal, but generally it's hard to get a room. There's a courtesy van, Jacuzzi, bicycle rental, beauty salon, and tour desk.

The huge **Summit Dining Room** has a great view. Main courses for dinner are in the $20 to $30 range.

Denali River View Inn. Mile 238.4, Parks Hwy. (P.O. Box 49), Denali National Park, AK 99755. ☎ **907/683-2663.** Fax 907/683-2423. 12 rms. TV. High season, $129 double. Low season, $79 double. DISC, MC, V. Additional person in room $5 extra.

Good standard hotel rooms with queen-size beds in a cedar-sided building set in the woods over the Nenana, separated a little from the rest of the gravel parking lots and big hotels. This is as well as you'll do for the price this close to the park. Extras include a courtesy van, free coffee in the lobby, and bicycle rental.

McKinley Resorts Chalets. Mile 238.5, Parks Hwy. (mailing address: 241 W. Ship Creek Ave., Anchorage, AK 99501). ☎ **907/276-7234** or 800/276-7234. Fax 907/258-3668. 343 rms. High season $177 double. Low season, $114 double. Additional person in room $10 extra. DISC, MC, V. Closed Sept 16–May 15.

The crowded lobby of this massive property, which sprawls across acres with buildings lettered A through Z and then some, has the ambience of a busy bus station, with constant announcements about shuttles going to some far-flung region of the hotel, the park, or an activity. Most of the rooms turn over nightly with Holland America / Westours packages; independent travelers occupy just a few of the overpriced rooms a night during high season. This is one of the three hotels owned by

ARA, the park concessionaire. There's an indoor pool, Jacuzzi, courtesy shuttle, coffee in the rooms, and a tour desk.

The **Chalet Center Cafe,** a large, light room with a cafeteria serving good sandwiches and healthy dishes, is the best place near the park for an inexpensive meal. There's also a **dining room** for full service and a lounge.

IN HEALY

Healy is 10 miles north of the park entrance, but a world away. It's a year-round community with an economy based on a large coal mine, only beginning to look south to the park for business. There are a number of hotels and bed-and-breakfasts; their rooms cost $20 to even $90 less than those near the park. They say the water tastes better, too.

Denali North Star Inn. Mile 248.5, Parks Hwy. (P.O. Box 240), Healy, AK 99743. ☎ **907/ 683-1560,** or 800/684-1560. Fax 907/683-4026. 296 rms, none with bath. TEL. $81 double. AE, MC, V.

This is an opportunity to learn how North Slope oil workers live—it's a British Petroleum camp, surplused and moved to Healy to house workers building a new power plant here. There was space left over, so they're renting rooms. Required by contract to keep a highly qualified chef, the camp will let you join in at the **cafeteria** for $17. The rooms are small, with narrow twin beds, and the shared baths each have a dozen showers, but this is the real Alaska, if you're up to it. Extras include a recreation room, free soft drinks and coffee, exercise room, free laundry facility, sauna, barbershop, and tanning salon.

✪ **Motel Nord Haven.** Mile 249.5, Parks Hwy. (P.O. Box 458), Healy, AK 99743. ☎ **907/ 683-4500,** or 800/683-4501 in Alaska. 16 rms. TV TEL. High season, $105 double; $120 for three or more in a room. Winter, $75 double. MC, V.

Brand new in 1994, this undiscovered gem has large, immaculate rooms off a hallway with a central sitting room—they're equal to the best in the Denali Park area, and a lot less expensive. It's open year round. Extras include free coffee and Anchorage newspapers.

Stampede Lodge. Mile 248.5, Parks Hwy. (P.O. Box 240), Healy, AK 99743. ☎ **907/ 683-2242.** Fax 907/683-2243. 29 rms. TEL. $80 double. Additional person in room $10 extra. AE, DISC, MC, V.

A former railroad barrack, renovated and under aggressive new ownership, the lodge has smallish rooms with phones on the wall. The 100-level rooms are in a half-basement. It's open year round serving the local trade, with a good **café and dining room.**

✪ **White Moose Lodge.** Mile 248, Parks Hwy. (P.O. Box 68), Healy, AK 99743. ☎ **907/ 683-1233** or 800/481-1232. 9 rms. $85 double. Rates include coffee, tea, and pastry breakfast. Additional person in room $10 extra for adults, $5 extra for children. AE, DC, DISC, MC, V. Closed Oct to mid-May.

This old, low-slung building among stunted black spruce contains an unlikely find—fresh, new rooms inside, and a hospitable host. These are excellent basic rooms for a reasonable price.

SOUTH OF THE PARK

There are several groups of accommodations south of the park. I've listed just a few. You may also want to try **McKinley Wilderness Lodge,** Mile 224, Parks Hwy. (P.O. Box 89), Denali National Park, AK 99755 (☎ **907/683-2277**), which has cabins with private or shared bath.

Denali Cabins. Mile 229, Parks Hwy. (P.O. Box 229), Denali National Park, AK 99755. ☎ **907/ 683-2643.** Fax 907/683-2595. (In winter, 200 W. 34th Ave., Suite 362, Anchorage, AK 99503; ☎ 907/258-0134.) 41 rms, 2 suites. High season, $119 double; $159 suite. Low season, $80 double. Additional person in room $10 extra. MC, V. Closed mid-Sept to mid-May.

These cabins—arranged around a grassy compound with a pair of hot tubs—are great for families; in the evening, the kids may well find someone their own age to play with on the boardwalks or lawns. Also, with a cabin you don't have to worry as much about waking the neighbors. There's a scheduled courtesy van.

Denali River Cabins. Mile 231, Parks Hwy. (mailing address: P.O. Box 81615, Fairbanks, AK 99708). ☎ **907/683-2500,** or 800/230-7275 or 800/456-5200. Fax 907/456-5212. High season, $140–$150 cabin for two. Low season, $95–$105 cabin for two. Additional person in room $10 extra. MC, V.

These brand-new cedar cabins along boardwalks above the Nenana River feel fresh and luxurious. But they have shower stalls, not tubs, and for the rate you may be expecting something more. The sauna does have a picture window on the river. The 17 cabins on the river, with decks over the water, are $10 more. A hotel with a restaurant and lounge is nearby. A sauna, Jacuzzi, free coffee, newspapers, and bike rental are available.

The Perch. Mile 224, Parks Hwy. (mailing address: HC2 Box 1525, Healy, AK 99743). ☎ and fax **907/683-2523.** 11 cabins, some with bath. $95–$100 cabin for two. AE, MC, V. Additional person in cabin $10 extra. Closed Sept 15–May 16.

These are small cabins in the woods with steep roofs and a shared bath house; a few have their own bathroom or a kitchenette. The main feature, however, is the **restaurant and bar** on the top of a hill that give it the name The Perch: It's a friendly, light place with excellent fish, beef, and bread for reasonable prices. It's open from 5 to 10pm, and prices range from $13.50 for perch (the house fish) to $40 for lobster.

PRIVATE CAMPGROUNDS

McKinley Kampground, Mile 248.5, Parks Highway, in Healy (☎ **907/683-2379,** or 800/478-AKOA in Alaska), is the only KOA campground in Alaska, and the best private campground in the Denali area. The campsites are surrounded by birch trees. There's a coin-op laundry, and other facilities. Basic tent sites are $15.75 to $18.25; $22.50 with electricity; $25 with water and electricity and $26 for full hookups. **Denali Grizzly Bear Cabins and Campground,** Mile 231, Parks Highway (☎ **907/ 683-2696**), has some wooded campsites and some in a gravel lot, for $16. Cabins are for rent too, starting at $21.50 for a small tent cabin. Cabins with their own bathrooms are $92.

WILDERNESS LODGES

For those who can afford it, there's no better way to be in the wilderness without giving up creature comforts than to book a few days at a wilderness lodge. I haven't starred any of the four selections as my personal favorite—they're all excellent. More important to your choice is how remote you want to be and how badly you need your own flush toilet.

Camp Denali / North Face Lodge. Kantishna Mining District (P.O. Box 67), Denali National Park, AK 99755. ☎ **907/683-2290** or 907/683-1568. 17 cabins (Camp Denali); 15 rms, none with bath (North Face Lodge). $240 per person cabin; $275 per person double. Rates include all meals. Additional person in room or cabin $100 extra. Minimum stay three nights in cabins, two nights in rooms. No credit cards. Closed early Sept to early June.

These pioneering eco-tourism establishments under the same ownership are deep in the park, located on an old mining inholding at Kantishna, close to Mount McKinley, and have the right to free use of the park road separate from the bus system. And they make good use of the unique opportunity, offering guests the chance to explore and understand the wilderness on guided natural-history hikes, biking, lake canoeing and, at Camp Denali, intensive sessions led by nationally reputed academics on the birds, botany, geology, and ecology of the park. All arrivals and departures are on fixed session dates, even aside from the intensives. Camp Denali cabins each have their own outhouse and share a central bath house. They're well known for their food. People come away from the experience feeling changed, or at least enlightened.

Denali Backcountry Lodge. Kantishna Mining District (P.O. Box 189), Denali National Park, AK 99755. ☎ **907/683-2594** or 800/841-0692. (In winter: P.O. Box 810, Girdwood, AK 99587; ☎ 907/783-1342.) 24 cabins. $260 per person cabin for two. Rates include all meals. MC, V.

This newly remodeled lodge on the Kantishna park inholding has a private bathroom in each cabin, and single-night stays are permitted (but if you have time, stay longer). The bus over the park road leaves the park entrance daily at 2pm, so if you're coming from Anchorage on the train you need to spend a night outside the park first. Guided hikes and naturalist programs are offered, and bikes, fishing gear, gold panning, and a mosquito-proof porch are available. The owner, Alaska Wildland Adventures, offers a variety of eco-tourism packages.

Denali West Lodge. Lake Minchumina, AK 99757. ☎ **907/674-3112.** 5 cabins with outhouses. $975 Fri–Mon stay, $1,300 Mon–Fri stay, both per person, double. Rates include daily guide service and all meals. DISC, MC, V.

This lodge offers real, Alaska Bush wilderness living, winter and summer. Located on a large lake 50 miles from Mount McKinley, west of the park, guests can count on seeing no one else on their daily hiking and boating outings—it's a very remote area. Two of the log cabins have sod roofs. In the winter, the Hayden family offers dog-mushing adventures; after instruction the guests drive their own teams, something few life-long Alaskans can say they've done. Getting to the lodge on a bush plane is not included in the price, but daily guiding in groups of two to four is.

Denali Wilderness Lodge. Wood River (mailing address: P.O. Box 50, Denali National Park, AK 99755). ☎ **907/683-1287,** or 800/541-9779 year round. Fax 907/479-4410. (In winter: P.O. Box 71784, Fairbanks, AK 99707; ☎ 907/479-4000.) 23 rms and cabins. $260 per person, double or cabin for two ($50 surcharge for a one-night stay).

The extraordinary log buildings were built by the late big-game guide Lynn Castle along the Wood River, and his amazing collection of mounted exotic animals from all over the world is in a sort of museum room. They don't kill the animals anymore: Now they're more valuable to look at alive, and the lodge has become an eco-establishment, flying guests in for as brief as a half day for flightseeing, horseback riding, hiking, and talks by naturalists and the like. But stay at least a couple of days to really experience the place. The 25-horse stable is the unique centerpiece. The cabins, while not luxurious, are quite comfortable and have flush toilets. The food is terrific. The location is distant from Mount McKinley, east of the park.

8 Where to Eat

Most of the good restaurants are listed above with the hotels where they're located, including **The Perch** and the **Chalet Center Cafe** at the McKinley Resorts Chalets, which I recommend.

Kantishna Roadhouse. Kantishna Mining District. ☎ **907/479-2436** or 800/942-7420. Reservations required. Full-day tour with lunch $99 per person. MC, V. One serving daily.

The family-style meals at the roadhouse are perhaps a pretext for the bus rides—since the roadhouse is located in the Kantishna inholding, it has the right to bypass the park service bus system and carry its own customers on its own buses. That allows those willing to pay $99 for the full-day tour with lunch in Kantishna to bypass the shuttle system and drive the length of the park road on a roadhouse bus. At the halfway point, in Kantishna, you can go gold panning or just stretch your legs.

Lynx Creek Pizza. Mile 238.6, Parks Hwy. ☎ **907/683-2547.** All items $6–$8.25. AE, DISC, MC, V. Daily 11am–11:30pm. Closed early Sept to late May.

This ARA-owned pizza restaurant is a center of activity for the less-well-heeled visitors to Denali, more for being the only place to get a slice and a cheap beer than for the quality of the food, which wouldn't be so popular if there were any competition. Beer and wine license.

✪ **The Overlook Bar and Grill.** Mile 238.5, Parks Hwy., up the hill above the Denali Canyon area. ☎ **907/683-2723.** Lunch main courses $9–$17; dinner $8.50–$28. MC, V. 11am–11pm. Closed mid-Sept to mid-May.

This is a fun, noisy place with lodge decor and a terrific view. The salmon and filet mignon were well seasoned and done to a turn, and the service was friendly, although the main course was slow to arrive. An extraordinary variety of microbrews is available. Full liquor license.

9 Denali in the Evening

The main evening event at Denali is ARA's **Cabin Nite Dinner Theater,** at the McKinley Resorts Chalets (☎ **907/683-2215** or 800/276-7234), a professionally produced musical revue about a gold rush–era woman who ran a roadhouse in Kantishna. You can buy the $35 tickets virtually anywhere in the area. The actors, singing throughout the evening, stay in character to serve big platters of food to diners sitting at long tables, doing a good job of building a rowdy, happy atmosphere for adults and kids. The only drawbacks to a jolly evening are the food—all you can eat, but no one at my table wanted to eat much of the overcooked fish and bland ribs—and the expensive ticket prices.

The **Northern Lights Gift Shop and Theater,** across the Parks Highway from the McKinley Resorts Chalets (☎ **907/683-4000**), shows the *Northern Lights Photosymphony,* an award-winning, music-accompanied slide show on a 40-foot-wide screen. Admission is $6.50. It's also a good gift shop, with a mixture of the usual T-shirts and higher-quality gifts.

For young people, you'll probably have more fun finding out where the young park employees are partying. They annually reconvene for work, adventures, and summer celebrations outside under the midnight sun.

The Alaskan Interior 10

A warm summer evening in a campground; a slight breeze rustling the leaves of ghostly paper birches, barely keeping the mosquitoes at bay; the sounds of children playing; a perpetual sunset rolling slowly along the northern horizon—this is Interior Alaska. You know it's time to gather up the kids, separate them according to who belongs to whom, and put them to bed; it's 11 o'clock, for heaven's sake. But it's too difficult to feel that matters, or to alter the pace of a sun-baked day that never ends, meandering on like the broad, silty rivers and empty two-lane highways. Down by the boat landing, some college kids are getting ready to start on a float in the morning. An old, white-bearded prospector wanders out of the bar and, offering his flask to the strangers, tries out a joke while swatting the bugs. "There's not a single mosquito in Alaska," he declares. Waits out for the loud, jocular objections. Then adds, "They're all married with big, big families." Easy laughter; then they talk about outboard motors, road work, why so many rabbits live along a certain stretch of highway. Eventually, you have to go to bed, leave the world to its pointless turning as the sun rotates back around to the east. You know it'll all be there tomorrow, just the same—the same slow-flowing rivers, the same long highways, the same vast space that can never be filled.

Interior Alaska is so large—it basically includes everything that's not on the coasts or in the high Arctic—you can spend a week of hard driving and not explore it all. Or you could spend all summer floating the rivers and still have years of floating left to do before you'd seen all the riverbanks. It's something like what one imagines the great mass of America's Midwest once was perhaps a century and a half ago, when the great flat lands had been explored but not completely civilized and Huckleberry Finn could float downriver into a wilderness of adventures. As it happens, I have a friend who grew up on a homestead in the Interior and ran away from home at age 15 in that exact same fashion, floating hundreds of miles on a handmade raft, past the little river villages, cargo barges, and fishermen. During an Interior summer, nature combines its immensity with a rare sense of gentleness, patiently awaiting the next thunderstorm.

Winter is another matter. Without the regulating influence of the ocean—the same reason summers are hot—winter temperatures can often drop to -30°F or -40°F, and during exceptional cold snaps, much lower. Now the earth is wobbling over in the other direction, away from the sun; the long, black nights sometimes make Fairbanks, the region's dominant city, feel more like an outpost on a barren planet, far off in outer space. That's when the northern lights come, spewing swirls of color across the entire dome of the sky and crackling with electricity. Neighbors get on the phone to wake each other and, rising from bed to put on their warmest parkas and insulated boots, stand in the street, gazing straight up. Visitors lucky enough to come at such times may be watching from a steaming hot-spring tub or a glass-roofed viewing room. During the short days, they, too, can bundle up and watch sled-dog racing or race across the wilderness themselves on snowmobiles.

Besides Fairbanks, the Alaska Interior is without any settlements large enough to be called cities. Instead, it's defined by roads, both paved and gravel, which are strands of civilization through sparsely settled, swampy land. Before the roads, development occurred only on the rivers, which still serve as thoroughfares for the Athabascan villages of the region. In the summer, villagers travel by boat; in the winter, the frozen rivers become highways for snowmobiles and sled-dog teams. White homesteaders and gold miners live back in the woods too, but except in alpine terrain, the land is generally impossible to hike when not frozen. Fairbanks itself is an entertaining, modern city worthy of visiting for several days, but it still maintains the Interior spirit.

1 Exploring the Interior

More than anywhere else in Alaska, having your own car in the Interior provides the freedom to find the out of the-way places that give the region its character. You can tour the region by bus—two lines connect Fairbanks with the Alaska Highway as far south as the ferry terminus at Haines or Skagway: Gray Line's **Alaskon Express** (☎ 800/544-2206) offers service along the Alaska Highway from Fairbanks to Haines and Skagway for around $200; **Alaska Direct Busline** (☎ 800/780-6652) also serves Dawson City. But that will show you only the larger, tourist-oriented destinations. If you have the time and money, you may enjoy picking out one of the remote gravel highways to drive, or just poking along between the larger towns, ready to stop and investigate the roadhouses and meet the people who live out in the middle of nowhere. You'll find them friendly and, often, downright odd—colorful, to use the polite term. I saw my all-time favorite roadside sign driving the Alaska Highway, years ago. Spray-painted on plywood, it said: SALE EEL SKINS ANVILS BAIT. I've always wished I'd stopped in to window-shop and meet the man or woman who came up with that business plan.

The down-side of driving your own car is that you have to cover a lot of ground, and much of the driving can be quite dull—certain stretches of the Alaska Highway and shorter sections on other highways last for hours of driving through brushy forest with no horizon visible. Furthermore, the paved sections have frost heaves— back-breaking dips and bumps caused by cycles of freeze and thaw—and the gravel roads are dusty and tiring and threaten your windshield or headlights with flying rocks. Also, bringing a private car from the Lower 48 adds a week to each end of your trip, and most people don't have that much time to spend.

A good alternative is to fly or take the train to Fairbanks, then rent a car for an exploration. But don't bother unless you have at least a couple of days to spend in addition to at least two days in Fairbanks. Renting a car one way is a great way to go, but there's a drop-off fee, typically around $300. One itinerary that makes a lot of sense is to rent a car in Fairbanks, explore eastward to Dawson City, drop the car in Skagway or Haines, and then board the ferry south before flying out from Juneau, Sitka, or Ketchikan; I'd allow a good 10 days for such a plan. Leaving off Dawson

City would cut that to a week. Travel information on getting to Fairbanks is listed in that section.

Vernon Publications' *The Milepost,* a highway guide to Alaska and northwestern Canada, has long been considered the indispensable handbook for Alaska drivers. It has mile-by-mile descriptions of all the major roads and is available for sale everywhere along the Alaska Highway. But in recent years, most of the book has been taken over by advertisements included in the text as listings. Consequently, the book is less useful than it once was, although still handy for directions, distances between towns, and the like.

INTERIOR'S MAJOR HIGHWAYS

At the **Alaska Public Lands Information Center** in Tok, the first major visitor center on the U.S. side of the border on the Alaska Highway, the first thing they usually hear is a question: "Do you have a road map?" The second thing is: "No, I mean a map that shows *all* the roads." The answer: "That's all the roads there are—welcome to Alaska." Paved, two-lane highways make a triangle, connecting Tok, Fairbanks, and Anchorage, with links to the Kenai Peninsula and Valdez. Otherwise, there are a few gravel highways reaching out a little way into the Bush, and that's it.

The roads Alaska does have are long and scenic. They have route numbers, but no one uses the numbers and few people even know them. Instead, they're known by names. Elsewhere in this chapter and in the chapters on Southcentral and Denali National Park, you'll find local details on all the roads. To help you decide your route, I've written descriptions for the major highways that link Alaska's cities here.

ALASKA HIGHWAY   Running nearly 1,400 miles from Dawson Creek, British Columbia, to Delta Junction, Alaska, a couple of hours east of Fairbanks on the Richardson Highway, this World War II road is paved, but that doesn't mean it's smooth. Like other northern highways, it's subject to bone-jarring frost heaves and potholes. There's some beautiful driving on the Canadian side, but the 200 miles from the border to Delta Junction is pretty boring.

PARKS HIGHWAY   The George Parks Highway, opened in 1972, is a straight line from Anchorage to Fairbanks, 350 miles north, providing access to Denali National Park. Although there are some vistas of the mountain, and beautiful terrain just south and north of the park, the Parks Highway is mostly just a transportation route, less beautiful than the Richardson or Glenn Highway and, on the southern portion, a conduit for a lot of ugly development.

GLENN HIGHWAY   This is the road you'd take if you were coming from the Alaska Highway or from Dawson City on your way to Southcentral Alaska, including Prince William Sound, Anchorage, and the Kenai Peninsula. It connects Tok to Anchorage, 330 miles southwest. (The section between Glennallen and Tok is sometimes called the "Tok Cut-Off.") The northern section, from Tok to Glennallen, borders Wrangell–St. Elias National Park, with broad tundra and taiga broken by high, craggy peaks. Glennallen to Anchorage is even more spectacular, as the road passes through high alpine terrain and close by the Matanuska Glacier and along a deep valley carved by the glacier's river. South of Palmer, the Glenn meets the Parks Highway and becomes a four-lane freeway 40 miles to Anchorage.

✪ **RICHARDSON HIGHWAY**   The state's first highway, leading 360 miles from tidewater in Valdez to Fairbanks, has lost much of its traffic to the Parks Highway, which saves over 90 miles between Anchorage and Fairbanks, and the Glenn Highway, which saves about 120 miles from Glennallen to Tok. That's unfortunate, because I think it's the most beautiful drive in the Interior. It begins with the heart-stopping drive through Thompson Pass, just out of Valdez, then passes the huge, distant peaks of southern Wrangell–St. Elias National Park. North of Glennallen, the road climbs into the Alaska Range for a series of broad vistas comparable to Denali National Park, but with the addition that the road snakes along the shores of a series of long, alpine lakes. Finally, it descends again to the forested area around Delta Junction and meets the Alaska Highway before arriving in Fairbanks.

THE YUKON RIVER   You can't drive it, but that doesn't mean the Yukon isn't a highway. It's by far the broadest, smoothest, and longest in the state. The Yukon is navigable over most of its 2,300 miles, including all 1,400 miles in Alaska. It starts in British Columbia, leads through Yukon Territory, then crosses the Interior to its mouth, across Norton Sound from Nome. Tugs, barges, skiffs, canoes, and rafts traverse the river in the summer, snowmobiles and dog sleds in the winter. You can reach the river on the Dalton Highway 140 miles north of Fairbanks, on the Steese Highway in Circle, on the Taylor Highway in Eagle, or on the Top of the World Highway in Dawson City, Yukon Territory. You can float between any of those towns—108 miles from Dawson City to Eagle, 158 miles from Eagle to Circle, and 300 miles from Circle to the Dalton Highway. Large-scale river tours run from Dawson City to Eagle, and smaller operations on the Dalton out of Fairbanks and in Circle.

2 Outside in the Alaskan Interior

The Interior is so vast, there are plenty of ways to get away from other people and see wildlife—primarily caribou, moose, bears, wolves, foxes, and a wide variety of birds.

RIVER FLOATING   Of course, there's white water in this huge region, but the essential Interior float trip is on a long, slow river such as the Yukon. A classic route could retrace the steps of the gold Stampeders who spread out across the state in a series of gold-rush finds after the 1898 Klondike gold rush. You can start above Dawson City and float down, or start in Dawson and float to Eagle, Circle, or even the Dalton Highway. Or you can connect any of those put-ins or take-outs, depending on how much time you have. I've provided canoe-rental information in the sections on Dawson City, Fairbanks, and the Dalton Highway. Also, check with the **Alaska Public Lands Information Center** in Fairbanks, Tok, or Anchorage for guidance on setting up your trip. You need to be experienced in the outdoors and in a boat; be prepared for emergencies and other contingencies, and leave word of where you're going with someone who will send out searchers if you don't come back.

HIKING   You can choose a trail, such as one of those on the Steese Highway or Chena Hot Springs Road, or you can simply head out into the wilderness in an area of dry, alpine terrain. Again, the **Alaska Public Lands Information Center** can provide essential guidance before you head out. The virtues of Interior hiking are the remoteness, the animals you'll see, and the low treeline, which provides millions of acres of upland tundra. On the down-side, much of the region is miserable swamp and the mosquitoes are voracious.

BIKING   Mountain biking has become an ever-more-popular way to the outdoors in Alaska, and a way to tour the countryside. The Denali Highway, a little-used gravel road from Cantwell to Paxson, runs through Alaska Range terrain highly similar to Denali National Park. The land belongs to the Bureau of Land Management, which has produced a road guide for bikers and has a number of campgrounds on the way. (Why, yes, you can get a copy at the **Alaska Public Lands Information Center.**)

3 Fairbanks: Alaska Heartland

If the story of Fairbanks's founding had happened anywhere else, no one would admit it, for the city's father was a swindler and its undignified birth contained an element of chance not usually admitted in polite society. It seems that in 1901 E. T. Barnette had it in mind to get rich by starting a gold-mining boom town like the others that had sprouted from Dawson City to Nome as the Stampeders of '98 sloshed back and forth across the territory from one gold find to the next. He booked passage on a riverboat going up the Tanana with his supplies to build the town, having made an understanding with the captain that, should the vessel get stuck, he would lighten the load by getting off with the materials on the nearest bank. Unfortunately, the captain got lost. Thinking he was heading up a slough on the Tanana, he got sidetracked into the relatively small Chena River. That was where the boat got stuck and where Barnette got left, and that was where he founded Fairbanks.

An Italian prospector named Felix Pedro found gold on the Tanana, and Barnette dispatched his cook off to Dawson City to spread the word. A stampede of hundreds of miners ensued when the cook's story showed up in a newspaper that winter, heading toward Fairbanks in weather as cold as 50° below zero. Barnette's town was a success, but the cook nearly got lynched when the Stampeders found out how far he'd exaggerated the truth. Then much more gold was found, and half the population of Dawson City came down the Yukon to Fairbanks. Barnette had made it big. He cemented the town's future with a little political favor to the powerful Judge James Wickersham—he named the settlement for Wickersham's ally in Congress, Sen. Charles Fairbanks, of Indiana, who later became vice president. Wickersham then moved the courthouse to Fairbanks, establishing it as the hub of the region. Barnette didn't get to enjoy his laurels, however, as he was run out of town for bank fraud.

Fairbanks is Alaska's second-largest city now, with a population of about 38,000, but it has never learned to put on airs. It sprawls, broad and flat, along big highways and the Chena, a friendly, easy-going town, but one where people still take gold and their independence seriously. There's another gold rush going on, north of the city, and plenty of prospectors are still searching the hills. And Fairbanks is the hotbed of the Alaskan Independence Party, whose platform advocates the state's secession from the Union and recognition as an independent nation—Gov. Wally Hickel was elected under its banner in 1990, although he didn't adopt all its positions. Fairbanks is an adamant, loopy, affable place; it doesn't seem to mind being a little bizarre or residing far from the center of things. And that makes it an intensely Alaskan city, for those are the qualities Alaskans most cherish in their myth of themselves.

Since you're a visitor, Fairbanks could strike you a couple of ways, depending on what you expect and what you like. Fairbanks could come across as a provincial outpost, a touristy cross between Kansas and Siberia, and you could wonder why you went out of your way. Or you could relax and take Fairbanks on its own terms, a fun, unpretentious town, full of activities and surprises, that never lost its sense of being on the frontier. There's plenty to do in Fairbanks, much of it at least a little corny. It's a terrific destination for families—my son would still be there if it were up to him. And there are good opportunities for hiking and mountain biking, and great opportunities for canoeing and slow river float trips.

Anchorage and Fairbanks maintain a great rivalry. In Anchorage we call it "Squarebanks," the edge of nowhere. In Fairbanks they say Anchorage is as close as you can get to Alaska without actually being there and call it "Los Anchorage." In the winter, Anchorage people note that it's -40°F in Fairbanks and wonder how anyone could stand it; in summer, under seemingly endless blue 85° skies, Fairbanksans wonder how anyone could live anywhere else.

ESSENTIALS

GETTING THERE   By Car   Fairbanks is a transportation hub. The Richardson Highway heads east 98 miles to Delta Junction, the end-point of the Alaska Highway, then south to Glennallen and Valdez. The Parks Highway heads due south from Fairbanks to Denali National Park, 120 miles away, and Anchorage, 360 miles south. The Steese Highway heads to the northeast, 162 miles over gravel roadbed to Circle, and the Dalton Highway heads 500 miles north to Prudhoe Bay. Exploring the region on your own requires a car. **Avis** (☎ **907/471-3101**) and **Hertz** (☎ **907/ 452-4444**) are located at the airport; **Affordable** is at 3101 S. Cushman St. (☎ **907/452-7341** or 800/471-3101).

By Bus   Gray Line's **Alaskon Express** (☎ **907/456-7741**) offers service three days a week from the Westmark Fairbanks down the Alaska Highway to Haines and Skagway (the fare is $200), with stops along the way, but not directly to Anchorage. **Alaska Direct Busline** (☎ **800/780-6652**) does go to Anchorage, and also has connections to Dawson City.

By Rail   The **Alaska Railroad** (☎ **907/456-4155**, or 800/544-0552) links Fairbanks to Denali National Park and Anchorage to the south, with connections to Seward in the summer. The fare is $50 to Denali and $135 to Anchorage. Luxurious full-dome cars also are available for a premium on those trains from **Princess Cruises and Tours** (☎ **800/835-8907**) and **Holland America / Westours** (☎ **907/ 456-7741**). Descriptions of the different cars are in Chapter 9.

By Air   **Fairbanks International Airport** has direct jet service on **Alaska Airlines** (☎ **907/474-9175** or 800/426-0333) from Anchorage, and has flights with various carriers to many of Alaska's Interior and Arctic communities.

VISITOR INFORMATION   The **Fairbanks Convention and Visitors Bureau** maintains a comprehensive visitor center in a large log building on the Chena River by Golden Heart Plaza, at 550 First Ave. (at Cushman Street), Fairbanks, AK 99701 (☎ **907/456-5774** or 800/327-5774), open in summer, daily from 8am to 8pm, and in winter, Monday through Friday from 8am to 5pm. Get maps, including a road map and the good downtown walking-tour map. It also maintains a registry of where hotel rooms are available in town and binders covering dozens of local bed-and-breakfasts, with information and photographs.

The ✪ **Alaska Public Lands Information Center,** at 250 Cushman St. (at Third Avenue), Suite 1A, Fairbanks, AK 99701 (☎ **907/456-0527**), open in summer, daily from 9am to 6pm, and in winter, Tuesday through Saturday from 10am to 6pm, is an indispensable stop for anyone planning to spend time in the outdoors, and an interesting one even if you're not. Besides providing detailed information on all of Alaska's public lands and answering questions and giving advice on outings, the center has a small museum about the state's regions and the gear needed to explore them. There are daily films and naturalist programs in a small auditorium.

Greater Fairbanks

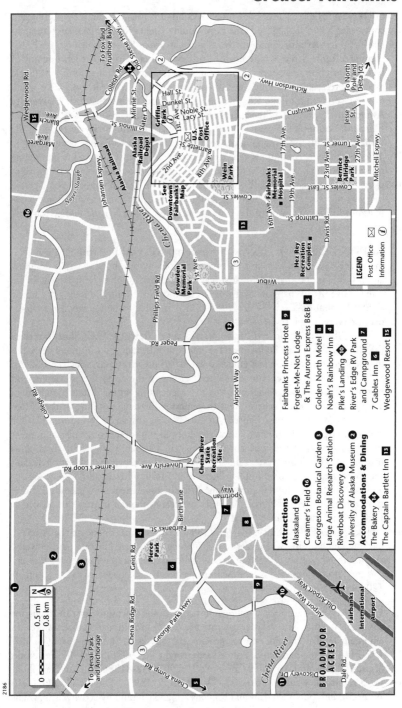

Attractions
Alaskaland **12**
Creamer's Field **16**
Georgeson Botanical Garden **3**
Large Animal Research Station **1**
Riverboat Discovery **11**
University of Alaska Museum **2**

Accommodations & Dining
The Bakery **14**
The Captain Bartlett Inn **13**
Fairbanks Princess Hotel **9**
Forget-Me-Not Lodge
& The Aurora Express B&B **5**
Golden North Motel **8**
Noah's Rainbow Inn **4**
Pike's Landing **10**
River's Edge RV Park
and Campground **7**
7 Gables Inn **6**
Wedgewood Resort **15**

LEGEND
⊠ Post Office
ⓘ Information

ORIENTATION   The old downtown section of Fairbanks is simple and compact, comprising a grid aligned along the slow, muddy **Chena River.** The main thoroughfares are **First Avenue,** along the river, and **Cushman Street,** which crosses it, becoming **Illinois Street** to the north. But development largely has left downtown behind, with businesses moving out to major suburban roads that form a rectangle of strip develop-ment around the city—the east-west strips of **Airport Drive,** south of the river, and **College Road,** to the north, and the north-south **University Avenue,** to the west, and **Steese Expressway,** to the east. The **University of Alaska–Fairbanks campus** lies west of Fairbanks proper, on **University Avenue,** in the **College** area, but the distinction between College and Fairbanks has lost meaning as development now continuously melds the two areas. Visitors may well be amazed by the system of high-speed freeways that belt Fairbanks and lead off in each direction, devoid of significant traffic. These are the product of skillful Fairbanks-based state highway bureaucrats and a powerful congressional delegation bringing home a bonanza of federal highway funds. You can judge for yourself if the money was well spent.

GETTING AROUND   It's possible to see much of Fairbanks without a car, staying in the downtown area and making excursions by bus, but the city is designed around the car and that's the easiest way to see the best sights. Rental agencies are listed above. Road maps are available free at the visitor center, showing the major sights. **Fairbanks Taxi** (☎ **907/456-3333**) is liable to be an expensive choice because everything is so far apart.

To see the widely scattered attractions without a car, try the **G.O. Shuttle Service** (☎ **907/474-3847,** or 800/478-3847), a unique bus, van, and car system geared to independent travelers. Besides guided tours of various attractions, which cost $24 to $65, the company offers on-call shuttle service to the airport, train depot, and major attractions for flat fares of $7 or $15, depending on the distance, and drives a regular route of the tourist areas throughout the day, stopping at the visitor center roughly every 90 minutes. An all-day pass costs $25 for adults, $20 for children. **Organized tours** also are available from four other companies; inquire at the visitor center. The lowest-cost option is the Fairbanks North Star Borough's three-route **MACS bus system** linking the University, downtown, North Pole, and shopping areas, and some hotels. The fare is $1.50, with an all-day pass for $3. Service is every 30 minutes, at best, and virtually nonexistent on weekends. Pick up timetables at the visitor center. All buses connect at the transit park downtown, at Fifth Avenue and Cushman Street.

The **Chena River Shuttle** (☎ **907/388-1032,** a cellular phone on the boat) is a relaxing and amusing way to get to sights along the water. The outboard-powered aluminum raft connects the visitor center with Alaskaland, the Riverboat *Discovery,* and the Pump House Restaurant, with stops in between. The fare is $2 per stop, or $20 for a 2¹/₂-hour round-trip.

FAST FACTS   Fairbanks has numerous banks, in the downtown area and along the commercial strips, with **ATMs;** you can also find ATMs in many grocery stores. In **emergencies,** dial 911. For nonemergencies, call the **Alaska State Troopers** (☎ **907/452-2114**) or the **Fairbanks Police Department** (☎ **907/459-6500**). **Fairbanks Memorial Hospital** is at 1650 Cowles St. (☎ **907/452-8181**). You can even phone for a **recorded weather forecast** (☎ **907/452-3553**). The *Fairbanks Daily News-Miner* is published daily and contains arts and community-activity listings. The *Anchorage Daily News* and *USA Today* are widely available in machines, and you can find other out-of-town papers at grocery and book stores all over town. For **business services,** a Kinkos Copy Center is at 418 Third Ave. (☎ **907/456-7348**).

SPECIAL EVENTS   A recording of current local happenings can be reached at 907/456-INFO.

WINTER   November 8–11, 1996, the **Athabascan Fiddling Festival** (☎ **907/ 456-7491**) draws together musicians and dancers from the Interior region for performances and workshops. In mid-February, the **Yukon Quest International Sled Dog Race** (☎ **907/452-7954**) starts or finishes in Fairbanks (Fairbanks has the start in even-numbered years; Whitehorse, Yukon Territory, in odd-numbered years). The challenge of the 1,000-mile race is equal to the Iditarod. In late February, in Nenana, the **Nenana Ice Classic** (☎ **907/832-5446**) starts with a weekend celebration; the classic is a sweepstakes on who can guess closest to the exact date and time the ice will go out on the Tanana River (see "A Stop in Nenana," below). In mid-March, the **North American Sled Dog Championships** (☎ **907/479-8166**), a sprint with two 20-mile heats and one 30-mile heat, begins and ends downtown. Toward the end of March, a spectacular ✿ **Ice Art Competition** (☎ **907/452-8250**) brings carvers from all over the world to sculpt immense chunks cut from Fairbanks lakes.

SUMMER   Festival Fairbanks (☎ **907/456-1984**) offers concerts in Golden Heart Plaza at 7pm every Wednesday evening, June to mid-August. **June 21,** the summer solstice, the local semi-pro baseball team, the Fairbanks Goldpanners (☎ **907/451-0095**) play a game under the midnight sun, beginning at 10:30pm. **Golden Days,** July 11–21, 1996, includes crafts fairs and a parade, and merchants dress in turn-of-the-century costume and put visitors "in jail" if they're not wearing a commemorative button. **Fairbanks Shakespeare** (☎ **907/457-POET**) presents a play each year for the last three weeks in July outdoors at the Birch Hill Recreation Area; admission is $10 for adults, $5 for children. The ✿ **Fairbanks Summer Arts Festival,** 2757 College Rd. (P.O. Box 80845), Fairbanks, AK 99708 (☎ **907/ 474-8869**), is July 26 to August 6, 1996; besides offerings for the public in music, dance, theater, opera, ice skating, and the visual arts, there are opportunities for instruction for all levels, without the requirement for audition tapes. The **Tanana Valley Fair** (☎ **907/452-3750**), August 3–10, 1996, shows off the area's agricultural production, arts and crafts, and entertainment, and includes a carnival and rodeo.

EXPLORING FAIRBANKS

DOWNTOWN   If you want to explore, pick up the walking-tour map available at the visitor center. Among the highlights is the **Golden Heart Park,** a waterfront plaza with a bronze of a Native family and plaques dedicated by various businesses and individuals—it gives a sense of Fairbanks's civic pride. The town's most interesting building is the Roman Catholic **Church of the Immaculate Conception,** across the river on Cushman Street. The white clapboard structure, built in 1904, has a pressed-tin ceiling inside, as well as stained-glass windows—an appealing if incongruous mix of gold rush and sacred decor. At Second Avenue and Lacey Street, a block from the Golden Heart Park, don't miss the **Fairbanks Ice Museum.** I don't know why no one ever thought of this before—a museum dedicated to winter, where summer visitors can find out what Alaska is like most of the year. There's a stunning high-tech slide show every hour from 10am to 9pm about the annual Ice Art Festival and a huge freezer containing ice carvings. Admission is $5. The museum was just getting started in 1995, and the idea has not yet come to fruition of a freezer you could enter and feel for yourself what a -40°F winter day feels like.

✪ **ALASKALAND, AIRPORT WAY & PEGER ROAD**　Built for the Alaska purchase centennial in 1967, Alaskaland is the boiled-down essence of Fairbanks. It's called a theme park, but don't expect Disneyland or anything like it. Instead, Alaskaland is a city park with a theme. It's relaxing and low-key, entrancing for young children and interesting for adults—you have to give in to the charm of the place. Admission to the park is free, and the tours and activities are generally inexpensive. It's open Memorial Day to Labor Day, daily from 11am to 9pm. Depending on the pace you like to keep and the age level of your group, you could spend a couple of hours to a whole day.

The **S.S.** *Nenana* is the park's centerpiece. Commissioned by the federally owned Alaska Railroad in 1933, it was the largest sternwheeler built west of the Mississippi, plying the Yukon and Tanana rivers until 1957. In 1967 the *Nenana* came to Alaskaland, but was unmaintained and had nearly collapsed from rot by 1982. It was about to be burned when a major community restoration effort began to save the ship. Today the *Nenana* is fully restored; 45-minute tours are offered for $3. The tour includes amazingly detailed historical dioramas of each riverside town the *Nenana* served.

Most of Fairbanks's history has been moved to Alaskaland. A village of log cabins contains shops and restaurants, each marked with its original location and place in Fairbanks's history. **Judge Wickersham's house** is kept as a museum, decorated appropriate to the period of the town's founding. President Warren Harding's ornate rail car, from which he stepped to drive the golden spike on the Alaska Railroad, sits near the park entrance. An exceptionally good **Pioneer Air Museum** is housed in a geodesic dome toward the back of the park. The aircraft are well displayed and there are displays and artifacts of the crashes of Will Rogers and Wiley Post and of Carl "Ben" Eielson, a key figure in Alaska aviation after whom a major air force base near Fairbanks is named. A large, round building at the center of the park is a **civic center,** where summer theater is often in session. On the third floor is a **fine-art gallery.** The **Pioneer Museum** contains early Fairbanks relics; a 45-minute narrated show of paintings tells the story of the gold rush six times daily; admission is $2 for adults, 50¢ for children 10 and over, and free for 9 and under.

If you have children, you certainly won't escape Alaskaland without a ride on the **little train** that circles the park twice, with a tour guide pointing out the sights; rides cost $2 for adults, $1 for children. Kids also will enjoy the large **playground,** with equipment for toddlers and older children, where lots of local families come to play, and the miniature golf course. The only carnival ride is a nice old **merry-go-round,** for $1.50 a ride. There's a boat landing where you can catch the Chena River Shuttle (see above under "Getting Around"), and a mining display with a waterfall.

Tour groups generally come to Alaskaland in the evening for the **Alaska Salmon Bake,** at the mining display (☎ **907/452-7274**), and the **Golden Heart Revue,** at the Palace Theater (☎ **907/456-5960**). The salmon bake has courtesy buses that bring people from the hotels and campgrounds from 5 to 9pm daily. The all-you-can-eat halibut, ribs, or brown-sugar salmon costs $18.95, or you can get a steak for the same price. Beer and wine are available. Lunch is served from noon to 2pm for $8.95. The revue, nightly at 8:15pm, covers the amusing story of the founding of Fairbanks with comedy and song in a nightclub setting; admission is $11.

There are a couple of other places to eat. **Souvlaki,** a Greek take-out place with a downtown location as well, is surprisingly good and inexpensive. **Gold Rush Ice Cream Parlor** has great ice-cream cones.

UNIVERSITY OF ALASKA–FAIRBANKS, UNIVERSITY AVENUE　The state university's main campus holds a lot of significance for Alaskans culturally,

Downtown Fairbanks

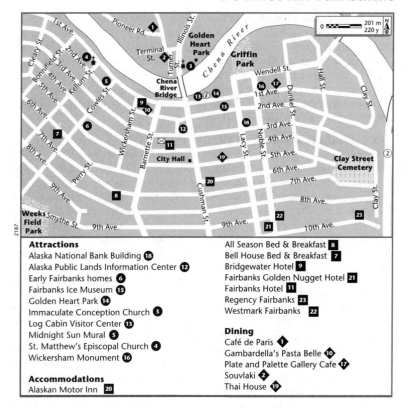

scientifically, and historically—it was the site of Alaska's constitutional convention. The Geophysical Institute here is the world's leader in the study of the aurora borealis, and when Alaska's volcanoes erupt and the earth quakes, these scientists' voices explain it in the media. There are several interesting attractions for visitors on campus, and the administration makes a real point of attracting and serving tourists. Free, two-hour **walking tours** meet at the museum Monday through Friday at 10am, June to August; call ahead (☎ **907/474-7581**) to confirm the time. If you don't want to take the time for a full tour, at least pick up a campus map at the museum so you can find your way around.

The ✪ **University of Alaska Museum** is the state's largest science museum, and also contains many cultural artifacts. In fact, its only weakness is that it tries to do so much in too small a space: A display on emission spectrums is side-by-side with a stuffed lynx, a woven root basket, and a broad-view aurora camera. The presentation is serious and scholarly. Don't miss the temporary exhibits, which have been superb in the past, and daily shows—they change annually, but in the past have included Native games and an aurora presentation. The museum is open daily: from 9am to 7pm June to August, closing at 5pm in May and September, and opening at noon on Saturday and Sunday in the winter. Just down the hill from the museum, at the computer center, is a Cray supercomputer that's one of the most powerful in the world; it's sometimes open for viewing.

The **Large Animal Research Station,** on Yankovich Road (☎ **907/474-7207**), is a farm where the university studies captive musk ox and caribou (it's more commonly known as the musk ox farm). Walking along the fence, you can see the animals behaving naturally in the large pastures, although they may be a long way off. Tours are given five times a week in the summer for $5; call for times. The **Georgeson Botanical Garden** and experimental farm, on West Tanana Drive, will be of interest to serious gardeners; plots are laid out to compare seeds and cultivation techniques, each with an explanatory monograph you can take. Children will enjoy looking at the pigs and cows in the barns. It's open Monday through Friday from 7am to 8pm; guided tours are at 2pm on Friday.

COMMERCIAL TOURIST ATTRACTIONS   There are some really exceptional commercial visitor activities in Fairbanks. The ✪ **Riverboat** *Discovery,* (☎ 907/ 479-6673) belongs to the pioneering Binkley family; they've been in the riverboat business since the Klondike gold rush, and family members still run the boat. The *Discovery* is a real sternwheeler, a 156-foot steel vessel carrying 700 passengers on as many as three trips a day—there's nothing intimate or spontaneous about the 3½-hour ride. What's amazing is that with so many people on board so often, the Binkleys still provide a fun, educational experience for a bargain price, $36.95 for adults and $25.95 for children. After loading at a landing with shops off Dale Road, near the airport, the boat cruises down the Chena and up the Tanana past demonstrations on shore—among others, a bush plane taking off and landing, fish cutting at a Native fish camp, and a musher's dog yard—in 1995 it was five-time Iditarod champion Susan Butcher's yard, and she'd often show off the dogs herself. Finally, the vessel pulls up at the bank for a tour of a mock Athabascan village. To avoid the crowds, take the evening sailing.

The Binkleys also own the **El Dorado Mine,** off the Elliot Highway, 9 miles north of town (☎ 907/479-7613), a working gold mine with a train that carries visitors through a tour, including a tunnel in the permafrost, and ends with gold panning— my son ended up with enough gold to fill a plastic locket and couldn't think about anything else for a week. The whole thing takes two hours, happens twice daily, and costs $24.95 for adults and $19.95 for children. The hosts of the tour are Dexter and Lynette Clark; they're real miners, perfect examples of the type—Lynette has even been involved in the Alaskan Independence Party.

Gold Dredge Number 8 (☎ 907/457-6058) is a tour of a gold camp on the National Register of Historic Places off the Steese Expressway north of town (turn left on Goldstream Road, and again on the Old Steese Highway). The 1928 dredge— similar to machines in Dawson City and Nome—is a remarkable invention that will fascinate anyone interested in mechanical things. Standing four stories tall on a barge, it would float in a pond it created, creeping across the terrain with its pond by digging at the front and dumping the spoils at the back. In between, the machine would digest the gravel and separate out the gold. The sterile areas of gravel you see in this area were created by these machines—nothing grows on the tailings for decades. After a 45-minute tour, you can pan for gold in the pay dirt yourself. Admission is $10; it's open May 31 to September 15, daily from 9am to 6pm. There's also a small museum, a restaurant, and a gift shop.

Alyeska Pipeline Service Co. maintains a visitor center—really just a booth where you can ask a question and buy a T-shirt—next to the **Alaska Pipeline,** 10 minutes north of town on the Steese Expressway. Here you can get right up close to the pipe, if you want to.

The town of **North Pole,** 13 miles east of Fairbanks on the Richardson Highway, is a bedroom community to Fairbanks—but if your group is like mine was, with young fans of Santa Claus in the car, you can't be within 13 miles of the North Pole without dropping in on him. You'll find Santa hanging out at a huge gift shop and RV park just off the highway as you enter North Pole. It's called, appropriately, **Santa Claus House** (☎ **907/488-2200**) and is open daily from 8am to 8pm. (The **Santa Land RV Park** is under different ownership; ☎ **907/488-9123.**) There are some reindeer in a pen, a tiny train for young children, and, of course, an opportunity to have your picture taken sitting in Santa's lap.

SHOPPING   Fairbanks has a few good shops downtown. ✪ **Arctic Travelers Gift Shop,** at 201 Cushman St., specializes in Native crafts, carrying both valuable art and affordable but authentically Alaskan gifts. The staff is friendly and knowledgeable and the store has a long and excellent reputation. The **Yukon Quest Trading Company,** at 522 Second Ave., supports the incredible 1,000-mile sled dog race from Whitehorse to Fairbanks; you'll find race memorabilia and a little museum. In the University District, at 3677 College Rd., **The Artworks** is a gallery for art and fine crafts from Alaska and Outside. Near the airport, at 4630 Old Airport Rd., the **Great Alaskan Bowl Company** makes and sells bowls of native birch. You can watch the work in progress. Gardeners may be interested in a stop at the **Tanana Valley Farmers Market,** at the fairgrounds on College Road; it operates on Wednesday from noon to 5pm and on Saturday from 9am to 4pm.

GETTING OUTSIDE

In this section, I've described the outdoors opportunities local to Fairbanks, but some other choices are barely farther afield: Make sure to look at the sections on Chena Hot Springs Road and the Steese Highway, later in this chapter.

SPECIAL PLACES   ✪ **Creamers's Field**   This migratory waterfowl refuge is an old dairy homestead right in Fairbanks, off College Road, saved from development in 1966 by a community fund drive. The pastures are a prime stopover point for Canada geese, pintails, and golden plovers in the spring and fall. Sandhill cranes, shovelers, and mallards show up all summer. The **Alaska Department of Fish and Game** (☎ **907/459-7200**) manages the refuge, including a small visitor center with bird displays, open Tuesday through Friday from 10am to 5pm and on Saturday from 10am to 3pm. I especially enjoyed the well-interpreted boreal forest nature walk; borrow a guide booklet from a stand at the trailhead when the visitor center is closed. Guided walks take place four times a week.

Chena Lakes Recreation Area   A pleasant destination for a family outing, managed by the local government, the Chena River Park and Chena Lake Park have flat walking and bike trails, a swimming beach, fishing, and a place to rent canoes, sailboats, and paddle boats. There are 80 camping sites, from pull-throughs for RVs to tents sites on a little island you can reach only by boat. In the winter it's a popular cross-country skiing area. Drive 17 miles east of Fairbanks on the Richardson Highway and turn left on Laurance Road as you leave North Pole.

CANOEING OR BIKING   There are lots of places for day trips. The Chena River is slow and meandering as it flows through Fairbanks, and you have your pick of restaurants on the bank. Or you could go up Chena Hot Springs Road (see that section, later in this chapter), or go to the Chatanika River, on the Steese Highway. The Alaska Public Lands Information Center can provide guidance and a list of companies that rent equipment. **7 Bridges Boats and Bikes** (☎ **907/479-0751**) rents canoes for $30 per day, and provides the essential service of dropping you off at the river and picking you up at your destination for $1 per mile out of town, with a $10 minimum. They're located near the Cushman Street Bridge and at the 7 Gables Inn (see "Where to Stay," below).

The same company rents bicycles: Street bikes are $10 a day; mountain bikes, $15. There are a lot of good mountain-bike rides to be had around Fairbanks, including the cross-country ski trails at the university or the trails at the Birch Hill Recreation Area, a few miles north of town on the Steese Expressway.

FISHING   Salmon fishing isn't as good as nearer the coast, where the fish are brighter, but kings and silvers are found in Fairbanks streams. You can also fish for pike, grayling, turbot, whitefish, and various kinds of trout. You can fish right in the Chena as it flows through town; the visitor center provides a brochure on where to fish and buy a license. The **Alaska Department of Fish and Game** is at 1300 College Rd., Fairbanks, AK 99702 (☎ **907/459-7207**). Guided trips by boat or plane will get you out into the country where you may see wildlife, too. Check at the visitor center for current operators; going prices seem to be $250 for a boat for half a day, $450 for a full day. To really get into the wilderness and have a trout or pike lake to yourself, try a fly-in trip. **Marina Air** (☎ **907/479-5684**) offers flights, including use of a cabin for the day, for as little as $250 for two people.

GOLF   They may not be what you're used to at home, but Fairbanks does have a couple of golf courses. The **Fairbanks Golf & Country Club** is at 1735 Farmers Loop Rd. (☎ **907/479-6555**).

WINTER RECREATION   Winters in Fairbanks can be awfully cold, but that just means you have to bundle up more (or at least that's what the locals claim). Cross-country skiing, snowmobiling, and sled-dog mushing are the main participatory sports. There are Nordic trails at the university, and 7 **Bridges Boats and Bikes** (☎ **907/479-0751**) also rents snowmobiles. There's also a minor ski area, **Moose Mountain** (☎ **907/479-8362**).

WHERE TO STAY

Fairbanks is a popular destination in the peak summer season and a good hotel room can be hard to find on short notice. Also, I inspected several establishments catering to the tourist trade which were well below acceptable standards (I can recommend all those listed here). If you can't find a decent room, take a look at the bed-and-breakfast section, below. Also, don't worry too much about being downtown, as that's not where most of the sights are anyway. Because of its Interior climate, Fairbanks can get quite hot during the day—it's the only place in Alaska where air-conditioning can be a significant asset.

The local **bed tax** is 8%.

VERY EXPENSIVE

✪ **Fairbanks Princess Hotel.** 4477 Pikes Landing Rd., Fairbanks, AK 99709. ☎ **907/455-4477** or 800/426-0500. Fax 907/455-4476. 198 rms, 2 suites. TV TEL. High season, $189–$220 double. Low season, $110–$150 double. $285–$500 suite. Additional person in room $10 extra. AE, DC, MC, V.

This is the best hotel in Fairbanks. The Princess cruise line finished it in 1993 to serve its packages. It's a well-thought-out, gray clapboard structure in a wooded area on the banks of the Chena, near the airport. The rooms, while not large, are elegant in shades of tan, and many look out on the river. The lobby is attractive, and the bar and Edgewater Restaurant have a large deck. The dinner menu is not extensive, with prices in the $20 to $25 range for entrees. Additional facilities include a courtesy car, health club, steam room, business center, and tour desk.

Westmark Fairbanks. 813 Noble St., Fairbanks, AK 99701. ☎ **907/456-7722** or 800/544-0970. Fax 907/451-7478. 225 rms, 13 suites. TV TEL. High season, $184 double. Low season, $120 double. Additional person in room $15 extra. AE, DC, DISC, MC, V.

Taking up a full block downtown, the Westmark Fairbanks—not to be confused with the seasonal and somewhat less expensive Westmark Inn on South Cushman Street—fulfills the role of the city's grand, central hotel, where banquets are held and couples have a night out on their anniversary. It's made up of a hodge-podge of different buildings and room configurations surrounding a central courtyard—you get a map when you check in. The rooms are typical of any upscale chain, the suites quite luxurious. A courtesy van, tour desk, and gift shop are other facilities.

The **Bear and Seal Restaurant** is among Fairbanks's best and is certainly its most formal, with a small dining room and service that draws out the meal all evening; but the prices are not out of sight, ranging from a $15 pasta selection to $31 for steak and crab. The **Birch Garden** restaurant is more of a hotel coffee shop, with dinners under $20.

EXPENSIVE

Bridgewater Hotel. 723 First Ave., Fairbanks, AK 99701. ☎ **907/452-6661.** Fax 907/452-6126. 89 rms, 5 suites. TV TEL. $130 double. Additional person in room $10 extra. AE, CB, DC, DISC, MC, V. Closed Sept 15–May 15.

This is a seasonal hotel in a concrete building on the downtown waterfront, trying for a classic hotel feel. The same company owns the Wedgewood Resort and Sophie Station hotels, geared primarily to package tours. Almost all the rooms go for the same rate, and there are big differences, so you may want to take a look before checking in. Some rooms are small, only those on one side have air-conditioning, and many have no tubs, but only shower stalls; ask for one of the large, front corner rooms. The price is reasonable for the location and the rooms. The restaurant is in the basement and opens only for breakfast and dinner. There's a courtesy van, coffee in the lobby, and a tour desk.

Captain Bartlett Inn. 1411 Airport Way, Fairbanks, AK 99701. ☎ **907/452-1888.** Fax 907/452-7674. 196 rms, 2 suites. TV TEL. High season, $140 double. Low season, $95 double. $175 suite. Additional person in room $10 extra. AE, CB, DC, DISC, JCB, MC, V.

Although it faces busy Airport Way, the Captain Bartlett succeeds in feeling like a rural Alaska roadhouse, from the log exterior and plantings to the historic photographs in the halls and the room decor—it makes you want to have fun. The rooms are comfortable, but the first floor is a half-basement without air conditioning, and most of the rooms have no tub, just a shower stall. You'll find a courtesy car, coffee in the rooms, Spectravision movies, and a business center available.

Slough Foot Sue's restaurant has hearty meals for low prices—at lunch, $5.95 will buy a big sandwich or all-you-can-eat 25-item salad bar. The seafood and beef main courses for dinner are in the $15 to $20 range. Patrons at the restaurant or bar can sit on a deck over the parking lot.

The **Dog Sled Saloon** deserves its fun reputation. You're expected to throw peanut shells on the floor, and you can barbecue your own burger or steak on the deck—$10 for a steak with a baked potato and corn on the cob. A 23-ounce draft costs only $2.50, and there's no cover for live music that starts at 5pm.

✪ **Wedgewood Resort.** 212 Wedgewood Dr., Fairbanks, AK 99701. ☎ **907/452-1442.** Fax 907/451-8184. 270 apartments. A/C TV TEL. High season, $150 apartment for two. Low season, $105 apartment for two. Additional person in apartment $10 extra. AE, DC, DISC, MC, V.

Off College Road near the Creamer's Field Refuge, most of a large apartment complex has been converted into guest suites, with large living rooms, separate dining areas and full kitchens, air conditioners, and balconies. The decor is dark and the rooms are in separate buildings without elevators, so the third floor can be a hike, but there couldn't be a better place for a family or businessperson to stay—the only difference from home is that someone else cleans up after you. Extras include full kitchens, courtesy van, newspapers, and coin-op laundries in each building. The restaurant and bar in the main lobby building are open May to September. The limited menu includes seafood, beef, and chicken main courses in the $15 to $20 range.

MODERATE

Fairbanks Golden Nugget Hotel. 900 Noble St., Fairbanks, AK 99701. ☎ **907/452-5141.** Fax 907/452-5458. 35 rms, 1 suite. A/C TV TEL. High season, $115–$150 double. Low season, $45–$95 double. No charge for additional people in room. AE, MC, V.

Right across the street from the Westmark downtown, this odd-looking building provides standard rooms that are clean and air-conditioned, and have a few extras, such as clocks, irons, and free coffee, for less than some of the big hotels.

INEXPENSIVE

☉ Golden North Motel. 4888 Old Airport Way, Fairbanks, AK 99701. ☎ **907/479-6201,** or 800/447-1910 in the U.S., 800/478-1910 in Canada. 41 rms, 21 suites. TV TEL. $75 double; $99 suite. AE, DISC, MC, V.

The Baer family, owners since 1971, keep the rooms in this two-story motel clean and up-to-date, making it a good bargain favored by Alaskans in town from the Bush to shop or just visiting Fairbanks by car. The rooms are small, but the reasonably priced suites are a good choice for families. They have fans, but no air conditioners. The location is near the airport. A courtesy van, coffee in the rooms, free pastry in the lobby, and kitchenettes are available.

Noah's Rainbow Inn. 700 Fairbanks St., Fairbanks, AK 99709. ☎ **907/474-3666** or 800/ 770-2177. Fax 907/474-3668. 100 rms, none with bath. TV. $40 double. AE, DC, DISC, MC, V.

This is a retired North Slope oilfield man camp—modular housing with tiny rooms—but when I visited, the huge shared bathrooms were clean. It's near the university and favored by young backpackers. For the price, you can't complain. A coin-op laundry and shared kitchen are available.

BED-AND-BREAKFASTS

Dozens of bed-and-breakfasts have sprouted like fireweed in Fairbanks, perhaps because the hotels are so tightly booked and good rooms for low prices are rare. B&Bs range from simple homes to luxurious accommodations, and in general are a much better value and provide a more memorable experience than a hotel. I've listed four of the very best here, but didn't have room for many more good ones, such as the **Stone Frost Downtown Inn** (☎ **907/457-5337**), **Such A Deal Bed and Breakfast** (☎ **907/474-8159**), and the **Cranberry Ridge Bed and Breakfast** (☎ **907/457-4424**). The **Bed and Breakfast Reservation Service,** P.O. Box 71131, Fairbanks, AK 99707 (☎ **907/479-8165** or 800/770-8165; fax 907/ 474-8448), represents more than 50 B&Bs. You can also get detailed information at the visitor center.

☉ All Seasons Bed and Breakfast. 763 Seventh Ave., Fairbanks, AK 99701. ☎ **907/ 451-6649** or 800/770-8165. Fax 907/474-8448. 5 rms. TV TEL. High season, $90 double. Low season, $65 double. Rates include full breakfast. Additional person in room $15 extra. AE, CB, DC, DISC, MC, V.

More of an inn than a bed-and-breakfast, this attractive house close to downtown was completely renovated in 1994 with its current function in mind. The design and decoration are inspired. The rooms are elegant and have VCRs and full bathrooms; there's a common room downstairs if you want to socialize, as well as a screened-in porch. It's quite a value. Complimentary newspapers are available.

⑤ Bell House Bed and Breakfast. 909 Sixth Ave., Fairbanks, AK 99701. ☎ **907/452-3278.** 3 rms, none with bath. $65 double. Rates include full breakfast. MC, V.

Kathryn LaSalle, a life-long Fairbanks resident, has lived in this steep-roofed clapboard house on a quiet lane of large birch trees for 30 years. There are a couple of cats and a piano, pump organ, TV, and fireplace in the parlor. It's like staying with your grandmother, just a few blocks from downtown. No smoking or alcohol—also as at Grandma's.

✪ Forget-Me-Not Lodge and the Aurora Express Bed and Breakfast. 1540 Chena Ridge Rd. (P.O. Box 80128), Fairbanks, AK 99708. ☎ **907/474-0949.** Fax 907/474-8173. 9 rms, 7 with bath. High season, $85–$135 double. Low season, $75–$110 double. Rates include full breakfast. Additional person in room $10 extra. MC, V.

Susan Wilson's late grandmother appeared to her in a dream and told her there would be a train on a bank below her house, on the family's 10 acres high in the hills south of Fairbanks. So Wilson went out and got a train—a collection that includes a pair of 1956 Pullman sleepers—and her husband, Mike, hauled the cars from the Alaska Railroad up onto the mountain and installed them below the house, right in the spot indicated. One sleeper is rented to groups of up to seven in its original form for $135 to $300 a night while another has been remodeled into four luxurious, Victorian rooms, each with a theme related to Fairbanks history, renting for $115 a night. Then there's the caboose, dedicated to Grandma—simply incredible. There are three rooms in the house too, including a large room with a Jacuzzi and a great view (it and the caboose are $135). Only the rooms in the house are open in the winter. It's worth making a trip to Fairbanks just to stay in this undiscovered, impossible gem.

7 Gables Inn. 4312 Birch Lane (P.O. Box 80488), Fairbanks, AK 99708. ☎ **907/479-0751.** Fax 907/479-2229. 7 rms, 2 suites. TV TEL. High season, $90–$105 double. Low season, $55–$70 double. Rates include full breakfast and coffee. Additional person in room $10 extra. AE, DC, MC, V.

This Tudor-style house in a subdivision near the university has been transformed into a luxurious if mazelike inn by its energetic owners and residents, Paul and Leicha Welton. They also run the canoe- and bike-rental business; if you're interested in going on a float trip, this is the place to stay, as they'll throw in the canoe. The less expensive rooms still have their own bathrooms, but you have to walk down the hall to get to it. All but one has a Jacuzzi tub, and every one has a VCR, with movies available for loan. There's also an apartment with a kitchen available.

A HOSTEL & CAMPING

There are a lot of RV parks in Fairbanks with full service and then some. Pick up a campground information list at the visitor center. **River's Edge RV Park and Campground,** at a wooded riverside bend of the Chena at 4140 Boat St., off Airport Way and Sportsmans Way (☎ **907/474-0286**), offers free shuttles and organizes tours. Full-hookup sites are about $23 a night. Or you can park right at **Alaskaland** (☎ **907/459-1087**) for $9. For tent campers looking for something a little closer to nature, there are superb **state campgrounds** on Chena Hot Springs Road (see below) and a borough-run campground at Chena Lakes Recreation Area (see "Special Places" under "Getting Outside," above).

Grandma Shirley's Hostel, 510 Dunbar St., Fairbanks, AK 99701 (☎ **907/ 451-9816**), offers a bed, with linens, towels, soap, and shampoo, for $15 a night. It's independent. There's no curfew, but the hostel is in a subdivision east of the Steese Expressway, distant from downtown.

WHERE TO EAT

I've described good restaurants above, in the listing on Alaskaland and at the Captain Bartlett and Westmark Fairbanks hotels. Here are some more. For a family pizza, try the popular **Pizza Bella** on Airport Way. The **Food Factory,** on South Cushman Street and at two other locations, is a fun burger place with a comprehensive selection of microbrews, many on tap. The **McDonald's** on Airport Way recently put in a Playland.

DOWNTOWN

✪ **Gambardella'a Pasta Belle.** 706 Second Ave. ☎ **907/456-3417.** Main courses $12–$15; lunch $4.25–$10.50. 15% gratuity added for parties of five or more, or for split checks. AE, MC, V. Mon–Sat 11am–10pm, Sun 5–10pm.

The quality of the southern Italian cuisine—the lasagne particularly—is a cut above everything else in Fairbanks, the prices are low, and the service efficient. You can eat in an attractive dining room on white tablecloths, but on a sunny day nothing could be more pleasant than to dine on the patio among the hanging flowers. Beer and wine license.

Ⓢ **Plate and Palette Gallery Cafe.** 310 First St. ☎ **907/451-9294.** Lunch $5.50–$7.50. No credit cards. Daily 11am–4pm.

There's no more delightful place for a health-food sandwich, salad, or vegetarian burger. The dining room is a serious art gallery, the various little chambers each containing a table or two and the diverse output of this college town's visual artists. Even the place mats are laminated children's art. Take your kids if you can trust them not to break anything, as children are exceptionally well treated and, in your own little room, you don't have to worry so much about noise. There's a New Age bookstore, too. No liquor license.

Ⓢ **Souvlaki.** 112 N. Turner St. ☎ **907/452-5393.** All items $3–$5.50. No credit cards. Mon–Fri 10am–9pm, Sat 10am–6pm. Closed at 6pm in winter.

In a somewhat run-down building across Cushman Street from the Church of the Immaculate Conception, Souvlaki has really delicious Greek food for reasonable prices. It's next to the *Fairbanks Daily News-Miner,* and is much favored by the journalists as a lunch hangout. You can get some of the same food at the restaurant's take-out place at Alaskaland. No liquor license.

Thai House. 528 Fifth Ave. ☎ **907/452-6123.** Lunch $6–$7.25; dinner $8–$12. No credit cards. Mon–Sat 11am–4pm and 5–10pm.

In a small storefront in the downtown area, this is a simple, family-run restaurant with authentic Thai cuisine that has made it a favorite in Fairbanks. No liquor license.

WITHIN DRIVING DISTANCE

Ⓢ **The Bakery.** 69 College Rd. ☎ **907/456-8600.** Lunch $6–$7.50; dinner $7–$14. No credit cards. Mon–Sat 6am–9pm, Sun 7am–4pm.

There are an infinite number of old-fashioned coffeehouses in Fairbanks—the kind of place where a truck driver or gold miner can find a big, hearty meal, a motherly waitress, and a bottomless cup of coffee. This is the best of the lot—quite a statement. The sourdough pancakes are mind-expanding, the service friendly, the prices low, and the baked goods approved by local constabulary—at least the parking lot is always full of police cars. Our children enjoyed it, and it's nice taking them to a low-key place where they can relax. No liquor license.

Pike's Landing. 4438 Airport Way. ☎ **907/479-7113.** Main courses $20–$55; lunch $6.50–$13.50. AE, DC, DISC, MC, V. Daily 11:30am–2:30pm and 5–11pm.

This huge steak and seafood house on the Chena River near the airport has a large deck over the river with many tables—a pleasant place to eat on a sunny day. The food is consistently good, if expensive; the restaurant has a full-time buyer who gathers the seafood and a full-time dessert chef. Full liquor license.

Two Rivers Lodge. 4968 Chena Hot Springs Rd. ☎ **907/488-6815.** Main courses $18–$27. AE, DISC, MC, V. Mon–Sat 5–10pm, Sun noon–10pm.

Chef Tony Marsico bought the restaurant in 1993 after cooking there for 13 years; he's published a cookbook and in 1995 was building a big riverside deck with a brick Tuscan oven. Generally, the menu is basic steak and seafood, but it's extensive enough to allow Marsico to stretch a little. The dining room is a log roadhouse lodge with one side opened up to provide a nice view of a pond. It's worth the 25-minute drive from Fairbanks for a special meal. Full liquor license.

FAIRBANKS IN THE EVENING

Fairbanks has a lot of tourist-oriented evening activities, as well as entertainment also attended by locals. Call the 24-hour event recording of what's playing currently, or check the *Fairbanks Daily News-Miner.* The best of the performing arts scene is at the ✪ **Fairbanks Summer Arts Festival** (☎ **907/474-8869**) and **Fairbanks Shakespeare** (☎ **907/457-POET**), both special summer festivals (see "Special Events" under "Essentials," above). There also are **movie theaters**—a large multiplex is located on Airport Way. The evening show at the **Palace Theater** is discussed with Alaskaland (see "Exploring Fairbanks," above).

The **Ester Gold Camp,** P.O. Box 109, Ester, AK 99725 (☎ **907/479-2500;** fax 907/474-1780), is an 11-building historic site, an old mining town that's been turned into an evening tourist attraction. The main event is a gold-rush theme show at the Malamute Saloon, with singing and Robert Service poetry, nightly at 9pm; admission is $11 and the drinks are reasonably priced. A pair of "photosymphony" slide shows takes place every summer evening as well—*Alaska: The Power of Beauty* at 7pm and *The Crown of Light: Northern Lights* at 8pm. There's also a restaurant that serves a buffet and has mess-hall seating for $14.95 for adults, $6.95 for big kids, and $3.95 for little kids. If you have crab, it's $19.95 for adults. The gift shop is open in the evening and there are simple, inexpensive rooms in the old gold-mine bunkhouse. A bus to Ester from Fairbanks takes you to the events for the price of $4.

Joel Mattson performs Service's oft-recited ballads and sings nightly at the penthouse bar in the **Polaris Hotel,** at First Avenue and Lacey Street (☎ **907/452-4456**). Admission is $5.

The **Howling Dog Saloon,** north of town in Fox (☎ **907/457-8780**), claims to be the "farthest north rock 'n' roll club in the world." That's questionable, but the bar does have quite a reputation for a good time. The hours are 5pm to 5am; the music is classic rock and blues; a selection of 20 microbrews is $4, while American beer is $2.75; and there's no cover charge. There are volleyball nets and the like outside. The saloon usually closes for a few months in midwinter. The **Dog Sled Saloon** at the Captain Bartlett Inn (see "Where to Stay," above) is an in-town club.

A STOP IN NENANA

Although there's little to justify a special trip, you might spend a pleasant hour or so wandering the deserted streets of Nenana, a little riverside town an hour's drive south of Fairbanks, as you travel the Parks Highway to Denali National Park or Anchorage. The town has a unique memory, keeping alive a sleepy, riverbank lifestyle Samuel Clemens might have found familiar. The Tanana River docks still serve barges pushed by river tugboats, carrying the winter's fuel and supplies to villages across the region. The Alaska Railroad still rumbles through, although it made its last stop at the depot in 1983, passing the spot where President Warren G. Harding drove the golden spike marking the line's completion on July 15, 1923. (The first president to visit Alaska, Harding died soon after the trip, supposedly from eating some bad Alaska shellfish—but we don't believe that, now *do* we?) Rotating fish traps made of spruce logs lazily scoop up salmon making their way up the Tanana, as they always have. Nothing much happens.

A log cabin **visitor center** stands at the intersection of the highway and A Street, the main business street. At the other end of A Street, by the river, the **old railroad depot** has been made, with little meddling, into a summer-only museum and gift shop. A block down Front Street, along the river, **St. Mark's Episcopal Church** is the town's most historic and loveliest building; its 1905 log-cabin construction remains unspoiled, even though it's still in use. The church predates most of the town, which was built as a railroad camp. It's left locked, but you can find out where to borrow a key at the visitor center. On the left of Front Street, you can see the **barge docks.**

Nenana's claim to fame these days is the **Nenana Ice Classic** (☎ 907/832-5446), a traditional statewide gambling event in which contestants try to predict the exact date and time of break-up on the Tanana. The pot builds to over $100,000 by spring, but it's generally shared among several winners who pick the same time. The town kicks off the classic each February with a celebration that includes dancing and dog-mushing races and the raising of the "four-legged tripod," a black-and-white log marker whose movement with the ice indicates that spring has arrived and that someone, somewhere, has won a lot of money.

There are accommodations in Nenana, but not much reason to stay. If you need a meal, the **Depot Cafe,** at Front and A streets, offers a basic burger-and-fries–oriented menu; the **Little Cabin,** near First and A, has soup and sandwiches. There are a couple of shops, a library, clinic and school, and RV park as well.

4 Chena Hot Springs Road

The 57-mile paved road east from Fairbanks is an avenue to an enjoyable day trip or a destination for up to a week's outdoors activities and hot-spring swimming. The road travels through the Chena River State Recreation Area, with spectacular hikes and float trips and well-maintained riverside campgrounds, and leads to the Chena Hot Springs, where there's a year-round resort perfect for soaking in hot mineral springs and for use as a base for summer or winter wilderness day trips. The resort is open to people who want to rent one of the comfortable rooms or to campers and day trippers, and it's equally popular in the winter as in the summer (the slow seasons are spring and fall). Japanese visitors especially make the pilgrimage in winter to see the northern lights, but Americans are discovering it as well. Of all the roads radiating from Fairbanks, this short highway will be most rewarding to most outdoors people, as well as providing the best remote lodgings accessible on the Interior road system.

The paved road leads through a forest of birch, spruce, and cottonwood, first passing an area of scattered roadside development and then following the Chena River through the state recreation area. It's a pleasant drive, around 1 1/4 hours from Fairbanks, but not particularly scenic. On a sunny summer weekend, the people of Fairbanks migrate to the riverside and the hiking trails; on a sunny winter weekend, they take to the hills on snowmobiles, cross-country skis, or dog sleds.

A pair of prospectors, the Swan brothers, discovered the hot springs in 1905, having heard that a U.S. Geological Survey crew had seen steam in a valley on the upper Chena. Thomas Swan suffered from rheumatism; incredibly, he and his brother poled up the Chena River from Fairbanks, found the hot springs, built a cabin and rock-floored pool, and spent the summer soaking. He was cured! More visitors followed, drawn by stories that whole groups of cripples were able to dance all night after soaking in the pools—by 1915 a resort was in operation, drawing worn-out miners and gold-rush Stampeders and many others as well. The resort has been in constant use ever since—you can rent one of the original cabins, if you want to rough it.

ESSENTIALS

GETTING THERE   The Chena Hot Springs Road meets the Steese Expressway about 10 miles north of downtown Fairbanks. You can rent a car in Fairbanks. The resort offers rides—$55 per person with a minimum of two.

VISITOR INFORMATION   For outdoors information, check the Fairbanks **Alaska Public Lands Information Center,** 250 Cushman St. (at Third Avenue), Suite 1A, Fairbanks, AK 99701 (☎ **907/456-0527**). A 16-page tabloid guide to the recreation area, the *Chena Trailmarker,* was published in May 1994 by the University of Alaska–Fairbanks Department of Journalism; I don't know if it will be updated for the 1996 season, but even the old edition will remain an essential resource, including detailed mile-by-mile trail and river guides. The state **Division of Parks,** 3700 Airport Way, Fairbanks, AK 99709 (☎ **907/451-2695**), manages the area and issues $25-per-night permits for the use of the public cabins. The **Chena Hot Springs Resort** owns and operates the springs; they are discussed below.

STOPS ALONG THE ROAD

There isn't much to see along the road, but two places are worth a stop. The **Two Rivers Lodge,** a fine dining establishment and bar, is listed in "Where to Eat" in the Fairbanks section. **Tacks,** at Mile 23.5, is an old-fashioned country store, greenhouse, post office, and lunch counter. The dining atmosphere is like a picnic, and people make a special trip from Fairbanks for the pies.

CHENA RIVER STATE RECREATION AREA

HIKING   The best trail hikes in the Fairbanks area are in the Chena Hot Springs State Recreation Area. The **Angel Rocks Trail** is an easy 3 1/2-mile loop to a group of granite outcroppings, with alpine views. The trailhead is well marked, at Mile 48.9 of the road. The 15-mile loop of the **Granite Tors Trail,** starting at Mile 39 of the road, is a bit more challenging, but you don't have to go all the way for an easy walk to alpine terrain. The towering tors, sentinels on the Plain of Monuments, are spires of granite that solidified in cracks in the surrounding earth which has since eroded away. For a longer backpacking trip, the **Chena Dome Trail** makes a 29-mile loop, beginning at Mile 50.5 and ending at Mile 49. A public-use cabin is along the way.

RIVER FLOATING   The Chena is an often-lazy Class II river as it flows through the recreation area and into Fairbanks; the faster-flowing water is found higher upstream, farther along the road. It's possible to float for days, all the way down to Fairbanks, but the road crosses the river four times and there are lots of access points, so you can tailor a trip to the amount of time you have. The third bridge, at Mile 44, may be the best put-in. The *Chena Trailmarker* provides detailed guidance. **7 Bridges Boats and Bikes,** 4312 Birch Lane (P.O. Box 80488), Fairbanks, AK 99708 (☎ **907/479-0751**), rents canoes for $30 per day, and will drop you off and pick you up for $1 per mile out of town, with a $10 minimum.

FISHING   Arctic grayling were overfished and a catch-and-release regulation is in effect in the Chena; there are bait restrictions too, so check with the **Alaska Department of Fish and Game** at 1300 College Rd., Fairbanks, AK 99702 (☎ **907/459-7207**). Several of the ponds are stocked with trout, which you can keep; signs along the road mark access points.

THE HOT SPRINGS

A family could have a relaxing outing here centered around swimming. The hot springs bubble up in fenced pools at 165°F, hot enough to heat the buildings, or to cook you. There's an indoor swimming pool with lots of windows kept at 80°—it's not large, and is sometimes crowded. A 95° spa and a 105° hot tub are also indoors; an outdoor spa is available, too. The facility is open Sunday through Thursday from 9am to midnight and on Friday and Saturday from 9am to 2am. Kids are kept out from 10pm to midnight Sunday through Thursday, and 1pm to 2am on Friday and Saturday. The locker room is clean and modern. Swim passes come with your room; for campers or day trippers, a day pass is $8 for adults, $6 for children and senior citizens. At 7pm, the prices drop $2.

WHERE TO STAY IN THE HOT SPRINGS AREA

✪ **The Chena Hot Springs Resort.** Mile 56.5, Chena Hot Springs Rd. (P.O. Box 73440), Fairbanks, AK 99707. ☎ **907/452-7867.** Fax 907/456-3122. 46 rms, 1 suite, 10 cabins. High season, $105 double. Low season (spring and fall), $70 double. Additional person in room $10 extra. Packages available. AE, CB, DC, DISC, JCB, MC, V.

The resort, scattered buildings around a nicely renovated log lodge, is well-managed to create as many ways to get into nature as possible. Everything from sleigh rides and horseback riding to swimming and ice skating happen every day in their appropriate season. Other activities include bicycling, gold panning, Nordic skiing, and snowmobiling. The resort has its own trails, in addition to the excellent trails in the state recreation area, and takes guided nature walks. But it's not the sort of place that pushes you out to get involved; the atmosphere is so relaxed that nobody would notice if you did nothing at all. Although there's no alpine skiing, the resort is the one place that has most fully developed Alaska's other winter assets. You could come here for a winter vacation, knowing that it would be snowy and you'd see the northern lights and have something to do every day. There's an aurora-viewing cabin on a mountain and a tracked vehicle that carries visitors on a cross-country aurora trek. There's also an indoor pool, hot tubs, and a launderette.

The resort belongs to the state of Alaska, and is for sale. A group of doctors bought and renovated it in good style, then gave back the deed to the state economic development bank that had loaned them the money.

The rooms range from the crude, original cabins built by the prospectors who discovered the area (which rent for $35, in summer only) to large, fairly luxurious rooms with private decks. The price range is broad, but all the accommodations I saw were a good bargain for the price. All lack televisions and phones—you'll be out of touch here. The larger cabins are simple but adequate for a family or large group looking for inexpensive lodgings; the chemical toilets are essentially a bucket with a toilet seat, emptied once a day. The lodge building contains the restaurant and bar; it's nicely done.

CAMPING AT THE HOT SPRINGS

The resort has an RV parking area with electric hookups and two campgrounds. A campground by a creek is especially lovely, with 31 sites; Site 8 is surrounded on three sides by the creek. There are chemical toilets. Dry camping is $8; with electricity, $10; and a free dump station is available.

CAMPING ALONG THE ROAD

Two beautiful campgrounds with water and pit toilets on the road by the Chena are managed by the state Division of Parks, and cost $6 per night. The **Rosehip Campground,** at Mile 27, has 38 sites, well separated by spruce and birch, with 6 suitable for RVs. Some sites are right on the river and some are reserved for more private tent camping, back in the woods. The **Granite Tors Campground** is near the trailhead at Mile 39; it has 23 sites, 7 suitable for RVs.

CABINS

There are four public-use cabins in the recreation area, available for a permit fee of $25 a night; contact the Alaska Public Lands Information Center or state Division of Parks. The **North Fork Cabin** is a quarter mile off the road at Mile 47.7. The others are all at least 7 miles into the countryside. The trails can be muddy and the country is remote, so be prepared.

5 The Steese Highway

The Steese Highway leads from Fairbanks 162 miles northeast to Circle, a village on the Yukon River about 50 miles south of the Arctic Circle (they were mistaken about the town's exact location when they named it—oh well). It's a historic gold-rush route, paralleling the Davidson Ditch, a huge aqueduct and pipe that carried water to the mining operations near Fairbanks. Small-time miners and prospectors still scratch the hills. They bring their gold into the bar in Central, where they can get a shower and the current metal price is posted on the wall. Circle Hot Springs is out here, too; you might find a few people paddling around the big outdoor pool. The Steese is one of the few ways to Bush Alaska on a road.

But the Steese is paved only for the first 40 miles, and you can only drive so fast on these rural gravel roads without bouncing into the ditch or getting your windshield broken by rocks kicked up by a speeding truck. Consequently, you'll spend most of your day in the car going out the highway—driving both ways in one day would be absurd. On the other hand, the overnight accommodations to be had on the highway are below many people's standards, and if you're not interested in a hike or float trip, there isn't that much to do. Circle Hot Springs is the main attraction—more on that below. If you go, above all take mosquito repellent.

ESSENTIALS

GETTING THERE The Steese begins as a four-lane expressway in Fairbanks. You can rent a car there.

VISITOR INFORMATION The **Alaska Public Lands Information Center,** 250 Cushman St. (at Third Avenue), Suite 1A, Fairbanks, AK 99701 (☎ 907/456-0527), can provide information on the outdoors, as can the federal **Bureau of**

Land Management (BLM), 1150 University Ave., Fairbanks, AK 99709 (☎ 907/ 474-2200). The **Fairbanks Convention and Visitors Bureau,** 550 First Ave. (at Cushman Street, by Golden Heart Plaza), Fairbanks, AK 99701 (☎ 907/ 456-5774, or 800/327-5774), is the best place to check for other information. For **road conditions,** call the state hot line (☎ 907/456-7623).

A HIGHWAY LOG

11 miles   The Steese and Elliot highways split, the Steese heading east into hilly, wooded land. The big piles of gravel and the machinery you may see in the trees are the many-years-old remains of the environmentally destructive form of mining practiced in this region, which requires the excavation and sorting of large amounts of gravel.

28 miles   Chatanika, an old gold-mining settlement, has a couple of roadhouses where you can stop for a burger, a beer, and, if necessary, a room or place to park your RV. The **Old F.E. Co. Gold Camp,** 5550 Old Steese Hwy., Fairbanks, AK 99712 (☎ 907/389-2414), is authentically unrestored, with corrugated metal walls and roof and simple rooms with a bathroom at the end of the hall for $55 to $65 as a double. They offer dog-sled, snowmobile, and cross-country skiing trips. The café is in a nice old dining room. The **Chatanika Lodge** has a large bar with a gun collection on the wall and money on the ceiling. You can order food and there are 10 basic rooms with TVs and a shared bath. There's little more in the way of any kind of services from here to Central

30 miles   The University of Alaska's **Poker Flats Rocket Range** is marked by a small rocket by the road. This is where the Geophysical Institute launches rockets to study the aurora and other high-altitude phenomena. Tours are occasionally planned; see the university description under "Exploring Fairbanks," in the Fairbanks section.

39 miles   The inviting state parks' **Upper Chatanika River Campground** sits on the river below a bridge on the highway, with 35 sites, pit toilets, and a hand pump for water. Camping is $6. There are grayling in the river and canoeing; get details from the Alaska Public Lands Information Center. The road is paved for another 5 miles, slowly rising along the Chatanika with some good views.

57 miles   The old **Davidson Ditch** water pipeline is along here—it's not much to look at, just a big rusted pipe. It carried water to mining operations nearer Fairbanks.

60 miles   The free, 21-site BLM campground at **Cripple Creek** is the last public campground on the highway. It's a popular place for recreational gold panning and a put-in for canoe trips.

86 miles   Twelvemile Summit—the drive becomes really spectacular from here to just short of Central, as it climbs over rounded, wind-blown, tundra-clothed mountaintops. There's a parking lot here for the lower end of the BLM's 28-mile **Pinnell Mountain Trail,** a challenging three-day hike over this amazing terrain. (The upper trailhead is at Eagle Summit.) There are two emergency shelters on the way to protect from the ferocious weather that can sweep the mountains. Get the free BLM trail guide from one of the agencies listed above. Over the next 20 miles the scars you see in the land are gold mines.

107 miles   Eagle Summit, at 3,624 feet, is the highest place on the highway, and the best place to be on June 21 each year—the summer solstice. Although still a degree of latitude below the Arctic Circle, the sun never sets here on the longest day because of the elevation and atmospheric refraction. People come out from Fairbanks and make a celebration of it. The midnight sun is visible for about three days before and after the solstice too, assuming the sky is clear.

CENTRAL

After descending from the mountains and entering a forest of spruce that continues to the Yukon, the road at Mile 128 suddenly reaches a stretch of pavement and is surrounded by the spectral white trunks of paper birches—like a breath of fresh air after hours bouncing over gravel. You're in the friendly little gold-mining town of Central. We were made to feel like we were the first tourists ever to make it this far—then we met the elderly couple who had driven a Model T from Texas. They were hitting it off with a group of young motorcyclists from Germany. From Central you can turn right for the 8-mile drive to Circle Hot Springs, or continue straight on the Steese for a featureless 34-mile drive to Circle.

The big annual event is the **miners picnic** in August. The town's main attraction is the **Circle District Museum,** which concentrates on the gold mining that has sustained the area since 1893. It's surprisingly good for a town of this size. Admission is $1 for adults, 50¢ for children; it's open Memorial Day to Labor Day, daily from noon to 5pm.

There are two restaurants, both with acceptable, rural diner food, but the **Central Motor Inn,** P.O. Box 24, Central, AK 99730 (☎ **907/520-5228;** fax 907/520-5230), is a bit more ambitious in its cuisine and the dining room is lighter and less dominated by the bar. They serve daily from noon to 11pm all year. The six rooms with TVs and private baths rent for $60 as a double (they accept Discover, MasterCard, and Visa). A shower is $3 and there's a coin-op laundry. The other establishment, **Witt's End,** at the corner of Circle Hot Springs Road and the Steese, has good, inexpensive food and a tiny grocery and liquor store, bar, and gas station. The Crabb family's **campground** is among the birch trees across the street (knock on the door of the house); camping is $5.

A SIDE TRIP TO CIRCLE HOT SPRINGS

Circle Hot Springs Resort. Mile 8, Circle Hot Springs Rd., (P.O. Box 254) Central, AK 99730. ☎ **907/520-5113.** Fax 907/520-5442. 24 rms, none with bath; cabins with and without water. $74–$100 double; $80–$110 cabin for two. Additional person in room $15 extra. MC, V. At Central, turn right off the Steese Highway and drive 8 miles.

The hot springs collect in a large outdoor pool. A one-day swimming pass, with a towel, is $7 for an adult, $5 for a child, free if you rent a room. The dressing rooms weren't well maintained when I visited, but it was fun to swim in hot water. In wintertime, Fairbanksans like to come out here for snowmobiling and swim outdoors in sub-zero weather, toasty warm in the water while their hair freezes.

It's funny how a place strikes people differently—I can't predict what you'll think. I have many friends who love the old-fashioned resort for its charm, history, and home-style meals. I found it ill-maintained and not completely hospitable. The shared bathrooms did not appear as clean as they should be and, while some rooms in the old wood building were attractively done in period style, others were simply not up to standards. The better cabins were large, although rustic, with their own facilities. RV parking on a gravel lot is $20 with power; the camping area isn't suitable for tents.

CIRCLE

Another 34 miles past Central along the winding gravel road is a collection of log buildings and fewer than 100 people—mostly Athabascans—at the town of Circle. The Yukon flows by, broad and flat like a big field of water; it looks as if you could walk right across it, but the gray water is moving swiftly westward. As broad as it is, you can only see the nearest channel from Circle. The boat launch has a sign with facts about the river. Boaters can put in here bound for the town of Fort Yukon or the Dalton Highway to the west; the Dalton Highway bridge is 300 miles downstream. Or you can use Circle as a take-out after coming down from Eagle, 550 miles away by road but only about 158 miles and five days to a week over the water.

You can camp on a little patch of grass by the boat launch. The **Yukon Trading Post** (☎ 907/773-1217), open year round, has a café, store, bar, liquor store, tire-repair shop, and post office, as well as operating boat tours. The **H.C. Company Store** has gas, groceries, and so on.

6 The Dalton Highway

Although it was built to service the trans-Alaska pipeline, one of humankind's largest construction projects, the glory of the 414-mile Dalton Highway is the wilderness it passes through. Running straight through Interior Alaska to the Arctic coast, the Dalton crosses all kinds of scenic terrain, including forested, rounded hills, the rugged peaks of the Brooks Range, and the treeless plains of the North Slope. This is still some of the most remote and untouched land on the globe. Wildlife shows up all along the way, from grizzly bears to sport fish to songbirds. The road passes through Alaska's history of mineral extraction, too—there's the gold-rush era town of Wiseman and the current oil industry complex at Prudhoe Bay. Also, the Dalton provides Fairbanks's closest access to the Yukon River.

But surely the reason most people drive all the way on the newly opened Dalton is because of where it goes, and not what's there. It goes to the very end of the earth, as far north as you can drive. It's quite a rough trip to nowhere, but a dramatic one if you have the time and endurance.

The Dalton is known to most Alaskans as the Haul Road—it was built to haul supplies to the Prudhoe Bay oilfield and the northern half of the 800-mile pipeline—but its real namesake is James Dalton, an oil engineer who helped explore the North Slope fields. Coldfoot, one of two truck stops on the highway, was originally established as Slate Creek in 1898 as a gold-mining camp. The town was abandoned around 1912 in favor of Wiseman, but revived in 1981, when the state decided to let a private operator offer roadside services. Now it's the northernmost truck stop in the United States. Just 15 miles up the road from Coldfoot, Wiseman now is home to about 25 people year round. A glimpse of the past can be found at the Wiseman Trading Company, which offers a museum and tours of Wiseman.

That's it for human settlement until you reach the modern industrial complex at Prudhoe Bay, where you come up against a chain link fence and must take a shuttle or tour to see the Arctic Ocean or the oilfield.

ESSENTIALS

GETTING THERE You can drive the highway yourself, staying in the few motels along the way or in a tent or motor home. The highway starts north of Fairbanks at Mile 73 of the Elliot Highway—take the Steese Highway 11 miles north from town to reach the Elliot. The gravel-and-dirt Dalton has a reputation for being notoriously bad, but now much of it is kept in good condition. Still, it's dusty, with soft shoulders, and flat tires are common. For **road conditions,** call the state hot line (☎ 907/456-7623).

This is a remote trip, and you must take some precautions. Services are as far apart as 240 miles. Drive with your headlights on at all times. Bring at least one spare tire, extra gasoline, car tools, and spare parts. A Citizen's Band radio is a good idea in case of an emergency. Insect repellent is an absolute necessity. Truck traffic is dominant and there are some steep grades, a few on corners, where truckers must go fast to keep their momentum. Slow down or even stop to allow trucks to pass you either way, and be careful on bridges, as some are not wide enough for two vehicles to pass safely. Also, get well off the road for views or pictures—don't just stop in the middle as some people do.

For people who want to let someone else do the driving, several companies offer a variety of packages, including flights to or from Deadhorse, or flying both ways. The packages include tours of some of the Prudhoe Bay facilities and a trip to the Arctic Ocean. Bus tours are offered by **Holland/America Westours** (☎ 907/456-7741 or 800/478-6388) and **Princess Tours** (☎ 907/479-9640 or 800/835-8907). Van tours are offered by **Northern Alaska Tour Company** (☎ 907/474-8600) and **Trans Arctic Circle Treks** (☎ 907/479-5451) See the "Prudhoe Bay" section in Chapter 11 for more details on tours.

VISITOR INFORMATION   Fairbanks's **Alaska Public Lands Information Center,** 250 Cushman St., Suite 1A, Fairbanks, AK, 99701 (☎ 907/456-0527), is the best source of information on the Dalton Highway. Rangers there have driven the road themselves. Much of the road runs through land managed by the federal **Bureau of Land Management,** 1150 University Ave., Fairbanks, AK 99709 (☎ 907/474-2200). Or try the **Fairbanks Convention and Visitors Bureau Visitor Center,** 550 First Ave., Fairbanks, AK 99701 (☎ 907/456-5774).

Along the highway there are two **visitor information centers** shared by land management agencies, one just north of the Yukon River bridge, which has no phone, and one in Coldfoot (☎ 907/678-5209 in summer).

ON THE ROAD

The bridge over the Yukon River at Mile 56 is the only crossing in Alaska, and many people drive the Dalton just to get to the Arctic Circle at Mile 115, where you'll find a colorful sign for pictures. A number of places along the highway have incredible views, including Finger Rock at Mile 98; Gobbler's Knob at Mile 132, which offers the first view of the Brooks Range; and Atigun Pass at Mile 245, where the road crosses the Brooks Range, winding through incredibly rugged country. The pass is the highest point on the Alaska road system and you may find summer snow.

The **Wiseman Trading Co.,** a museum and general store at Mile 188, offers a glimpse of the area's mining past. Check with the Coldfoot truck stop on the status of the store, which was still being worked on in 1995. **Arctic Adventures Touring Company,** run by Coldfoot Services, offers several tours of the area, including one that goes to Prudhoe Bay and another that lets customers pan for gold.

All along the highway are opportunities for animal and birdwatching. Animals that you might see include rabbits, foxes, wolves, moose, Dall sheep, bears, and caribou.

The 4-foot-wide **trans-Alaska pipeline,** which has fed the United States 25% of its domestically produced oil, parallels the road all the way to Prudhoe Bay. Finished in 1977, the pipeline climbs over mountain ranges and goes under and over rivers. The final stop on the road is a fence; on the other side is the **Prudhoe Bay complex,** where the pipeline originates, and access to the Arctic Ocean, a few miles away. The only way through the gate is with a tour operator. Longer tours of the area include a trip to the ocean and some oilfield operations, and provide general information and history on the oilfields and pipeline, but a shuttle to the water is available. Don't expect anything glamorous—it's an industrial site of Arctic oil rigs enclosed against the extreme winter cold. Tours are available from the Eskimo-owned **Tour Arctic**

(☎ **907/659-2368** or 907/659-2840) or from **Prudhoe Bay Hotel Tours** (☎ **907/ 659-2449**).

OUT OF THE CAR

Some of the world's most remote wilderness was opened up by the Dalton Highway. Experienced outdoors people can go it alone, but some package outdoor tours are available.

BOATING   Riverboat tours from the Dalton Highway bridge to a traditional Native fish camp on the Yukon River are offered by **Yukon River Tours** (☎ **907/ 452-7162**). The 90-minute trips run three times a day from June 1 to September 1. You can buy a ticket at the bridge. An overnight option is available. The camp also has a Native cultural center. Coldfoot Services offers rafting trips down the Middle Fork of the Koyukuk River between Wiseman and Coldfoot. To rent your own boat, see the Fairbanks section.

HIKING   The road has no established hiking trails, but most of the area is open to hikers who are willing to pick their own route. Open country can be found in the alpine Brooks Range, just north of the Chandalar Shelf at Mile 237, and on North Slope tundra. Forests make cross-country traveling more difficult south of the shelf. A popular destination is the Gates of the Arctic National Park and Refuge, to the west of the road, but consider going east. The country is more open and major rivers lie between the road and the park. Hikers who want to hike in the park without cross-ing the rivers can leave the road in the Wiseman area, where a short part of the road runs on the west riverbank. Topographical maps and advice on the Brooks Range area along the highway are available at the Alaska Public Lands Information Center in Fairbanks (see also "Gates of the Arctic National Park" section in Chapter 11). Remember, this is remote wilderness; be prepared and tell someone where you're going and when you'll be back.

FISHING   The Dalton is not a top fishing area, but there are fish in streams and lakes along the highway. Many of the streams have grayling, but you'll want to hike farther than a quarter mile from the road to increase your chances. A good bet is the Jim River area between Mile 135 and 144, where the river follows the road and fishing pressure is more spread out. Many of the lakes along the road have grayling, and the deeper ones have lake trout and Arctic char. Salmon fishing is closed along the road. For more detailed information, pick up the pamphlet "Sport Fishing Along the Dalton Highway" published by the **Alaska Department of Fish and Game,** available from the Alaska Public Lands Information Center or from Fish and Game, 1300 College Rd., Fairbanks, AK 99709 (☎ **907/459-7207**).

HIGHWAY SERVICE

You won't find anything luxurious, or even similar to standard chains, as you drive the Dalton; there are only three places along the 414 miles offering services.

Yukon Ventures Alaska, at Mile 56, just past the Yukon River Bridge (P.O. Box 60947, Fairbanks, AK 99706; ☎ **907/655-9001**), has a motel, restaurant, gift shop, fuel, tire repair, and some wrecker services. The motel, a former pipeline construc-tion camp, is clean and comfortable, and the food is basic trucker fare.

Coldfoot Services and Arctic Acres Inn, at Mile 175, just before the Brooks Range (P.O. Box 9041), Coldfoot, AK 99701 (☎ **907/678-5201**), offers a variety of services including lodging, a 24-hour restaurant, fuel, minor repairs, towing, a small campground, RV hookup, laundry, post office, gift shops, a small store, a bar, emergency medical services, tours, rafting, and gold panning. As at the Yukon, the inn is made of surplus construction worker housing—not fancy, but the rooms are clean and have private bathrooms.

After Coldfoot, the next service area is at **Deadhorse,** 240 miles north, with three hotels, fuel, restaurants, a post office, vehicle maintenance, a general store, and an airport. Deadhorse is the town that sits on the edge of the Prudhoe Bay oilfields, which are accessible only by tour. The main hotels are the **Prudhoe Bay Hotel** (☎ **907/659-2449**) and the **Arctic Caribou Inn** (☎ **907/659-2368**). I've included more on Prudhoe Bay in Chapter 11, on the Bush.

CAMPING

The Bureau of Land Management has several camping sites along the road, mostly just gravel pads left over from construction days. They are at:

- **Mile 60:** artesian well and outhouses.
- **Mile 98, Finger Mountain:** nice views, outhouse, and wheelchair-accessible trail.
- **Mile 115, Arctic Circle:** outhouses and picnic tables.
- **Mile 136, Prospect Creek:** no conveniences.
- **Mile 180, Marion Creek:** 25 campsites with well and outhouses.
- **Mile 275, Galbraith Lake:** outhouse.

7 The Alaska Highway

The 200 miles of the Alaska Highway from the border with Canada to the terminus, in Delta Junction, is pretty boring driving—hours of stunted black spruce and brush, either living or burned out. It's a relief when you hit the first major town, Tok (rhymes with Coke), 100 miles along. Don't get your hopes up. This is the only place where I've ever walked into a visitor center and asked what there is to do in town, only to have the host hold up her fingers in the shape of a goose egg and say, "Nothing." Another 100 miles (I hope you brought plenty of cassette tapes) and you've made it to Delta Junction. There's a little more to do here, but it's still not a destination. Another 100 miles and you're in Fairbanks.

Maybe I'm exaggerating, but after the spectacular Kluane Lake section to the south, the Alaska Highway in Alaska is mostly just ground that needs to be covered. Tok and Delta Junction provide accommodations on the way, but they're not why you're coming to Alaska.

CUSTOMS Canada is another country, with different laws. **Tourism Canada,** 235 Queen St., Ottawa, ON, Canada K1A 0H5 (☎ **613/957-0275**), can provide a brochure with details on Customs regulations. Here are a few highlights: **Firearms** other than hunting rifles or shotguns will cause you problems crossing into Canada; you may need **proof of citizenship,** and a driver's license doesn't always cut it, although it will in combination with some other identification; **children** with their parents may need a birth certificate, and children or teens under 18 unaccompanied by parents need a letter from a parent or guardian; products you buy made of **ivory, fur, or other wildlife** should be sent home ahead just to be on the safe side, as they could cause a problem going either way on the border; there are rules concerning **animals,** as well.

EAST OF TOK

The first 60 miles after entering the U.S., the road borders the Tetlin National Wildlife Refuge. A **visitor center** 7 miles past the border, at Mile 1,229, is open 7am to

7pm. The U.S. Fish and Wildlife Service also has two small campgrounds over the next 20 miles.

TOK

Originally called Tokyo Camp, a construction station on the highway, the name was shortened when it became politically incorrect during World War II. Since then, Tok's role in the world hasn't expanded much beyond being a stop on the road. With its location at the intersection of the Alaska Highway and the Glenn Highway to Glennallen—the short way to Anchorage and Prince William Sound—the town has built an economy of gas stations, gift stores, cafés, and hotels to serve highway travelers. The Tok Chamber of Commerce is trying hard to create more for visitors, and has a **Gold Rush Stampede** in early August, with a wild-game feed and raffle. But much of the town dries up when the summer tourists stop passing through.

ESSENTIALS

GETTING THERE   You're surely passing through Tok with your own set of wheels. If you get stuck for some reason, the Gray Line **Alaskon Express** (☎ 907/ 883-2291, or 800/544-2206) stops most days during the summer at the Westmark Inn; **Alaska Direct Busline** (☎ 800/780-6652) also serves Tok.

VISITOR INFORMATION   There are two large, luxurious visitor centers to serve highway travelers arriving at this entry to Alaska. The **Alaska Public Lands Infor mation Center,** in a large log building at the highway intersection that forms the town's locus (P.O. Box 359), Tok, AK 99780 (☎ 907/883-5667), open daily from 8am to 8pm in summer and from 8am to 4:30pm in winter, has interesting displays on the public lands and ecology of the area and a couple of rangers to answer questions. Next door, the **Tok Chamber of Commerce Log Visitors Center,** P.O. Box 389, Tok, AK 99780 (☎ 907/883-5887), has commercial information on Tok and anywhere else you may be bound on the highway, including videos and some displays.

ORIENTATION   The businesses all are along a couple of miles of the **Alaska Highway** and **Glenn Highway,** but there is a residential district for a couple of blocks north of the intersection.

FAST FACTS   There is no sales tax—there is no local government, for that matter. An **ATM** is to be found at the new Denali State Bank near the center of town. The **Alaska State Troopers** (☎ 907/883-5111) police the region; they maintain an office between the two visitor centers near the intersection of the Alaska Highway and Glenn Highway; in **emergencies,** phone 911. The **public health clinic** (☎ 907/ 883-4101) also is located at the visitor center. There is no **newspaper** in the area, but the *Anchorage Daily News* and *Fairbanks Daily News-Miner* are often available, and the Armed Services Network has a radio station, possibly the first you've heard in a while.

WHAT TO DO & SEE

Mukluk Land, under the big fiberglass mukluk 3 miles west of town (☎ 907/ 883-2571), is a homemade theme park that may amuse young children or even adults in a certain frame of mind; admission is $5 for adults, $2 for children and teens, and it's open June to August, daily from 1 to 9pm. Gold panning is an extra $5. The **Burnt Paw Gift Shop** has a free sled-dog demonstration on wheels June to August, Monday through Saturday at 7:30pm.

WHERE TO STAY
Standard Hotels & Motels

The motels are numerous and generally quite competitive in Tok. Shop around, if you want to take the time. There also are many bed-and-breakfasts—check at the visitor center.

☉ Snowshoe Motel & Fine Arts and Gifts. Across the highway from the information center (P.O. Box 559), Tok, AK 99789. ☎ **907/883-4511,** or 800/478-4511 in Alaska, Yukon, and part of B.C. 24 rms. TV TEL. High season, $62–$67 double. Low season, $52 double. Rates include continental breakfast. Additional person in room $5 extra. MC, V.

The 10 new nonsmoking rooms near the front are an extraordinary bargain. Each is divided into two sections by the bathroom, providing two separate bedrooms—great for families. The furnishings are fresh and modern. The gift store at the front is one of the best in town.

Westmark Tok. Intersection of Alaska Hwy. and Glenn Hwy. (P.O. Box 1300), Tok, AK 99789. ☎ **907/883-5174** or 800/544-0970. Fax 907/883-5178. 92 rms. TV TEL. $115 double. AE, DC, DISC, MC, V. Closed Sept 15–May 15.

The central hotel in town is closed in the winter, as its clientele is primarily the package-tour bus trade. It's made up of several buildings connected by boardwalks. The older rooms are narrow, without enough room at the foot of the bed for the TV, but nice enough. The new section has larger rooms with dark paneling. Ask for the "highway rate," which in 1995 was $79 to $89 for a double. There's a "factory outlet" gift store in the lobby. The restaurant is a few dollars higher in price than you'd pay elsewhere in town, but has a more attractive dining room, with light-wood decor; main courses are in the $15 to $20 range.

Young's Motel. Behind Fast Eddy's Restaurant on the Alaska Hwy. (P.O. Box 482), Tok, AK 99780. ☎ **907/883-4411.** Fax 907/883-5023. 43 rms. TV TEL. High season, $65 double. Low season, $60 double. Additional person in room $5 extra. AE, MC, V.

Although not as desirable as the Snowshoe or Westmark, the rooms in the new section—those with numbers higher than 11—are perfectly adequate standard overnight lodgings.

A Hostel & Camping

The **Tok Youth Hostel,** P.O. Box 532, Tok, AK 99780 (☎ **907/883-3745**), is made up of wall tents a mile off the Alaska Highway 8 miles west of town on Pringle Road. There are 10 beds and no showers. A bed is $7.50 for American Youth Hostel members, $10.50 for nonmembers. It's closed September 15 to May 15.

There are lots of excellent RV parks in Tok. One that provides great hospitality and lots of facilities, including a breakfast restaurant, and has wooded sites suitable for tent camping too, is the **Sourdough Campground,** just south of town on the Glenn Highway. They charge $18 for full hookups, $12 for dry camping, and take Discover, MasterCard, and Visa.

Don't fail to get the free state highway and campground map from the public lands center, which includes all the public campgrounds in Alaska. The 43-site **Tok River Campground** just east of town, managed by the state Division of Parks, lies along the river bottom below an Alaska Highway bridge. But if you're not ready to stop for the night, there are others along the highway which you can find on the map.

WHERE TO EAT

The restaurants in Tok are all of the "roadside diner" variety, with roughly similar prices and long hours. Those I've mentioned all take at least MasterCard and Visa,

Land of Fire

The flames stood up like mountain peaks beyond the trees to the south. Urgent eyes shot between the dirty, sweat-streaked faces of the firefighters working in the entangling brush along the Alaska Highway. It was suddenly obvious that their efforts to burn a fire line on the south side of the road were irrelevant—the fire's furious intelligence had already decided its course. This last line of defense to save the town of Tok would fail. The town had already been evacuated, but what of the homes and businesses?

It was July 1990, and I was in a group of journalists being led to the fire camp heliport to view the flames, and the last-ditch defense, from a Bureau of Land Management helicopter waiting there. On the way to the camp we stopped for pictures of the workers burning the fire line on the highway, and suddenly the main body of the fire was going faster than we could. Hot wind blew ash in our faces. Over the radios, panicked voices cracked the news of the lines breaching. The flames were moving down on us like a locomotive; they weren't distant mountains now, they were cliffs. Individual black spruce blasted into flame like crêpe-paper fireworks, *pop-pop-pop*. The crew ran east down the highway. Word came that the fire camp where we were heading to board the helicopter had burned over, incinerating firefighters' belongings. Between us and Tok, to the west, an arch of flames turned the highway into a tunnel, a billowing cathedral of flame. We were clear, and the fire was crossing the road behind us.

Now the fire crew chief counted his people. It was one of the Athabascan village crews—15 men and women who'd grown up together, worked together all their lives, each summer leaving the village together to fight fires, their people's chief cash crop. One firefighter was missing. The crew chief dropped his pack and tools and ran back toward the flames. The rest of us watched, in impotent silence, as he disappeared in the blinding smoke. Nothing on the radio. Gazing into the smoke. Then, finally, they emerged, first two orange, fire-resistant shirts glowing through the smudged air, then their dark, sooty forms silhouetted.

Back in Tok, a desperate house-to-house battle was going on. Canadian bombers dropped purple loads of fire-retarding chemicals and a fleet of fire trucks gathered from every town within hundreds of miles watered down roofs and swirling, red-hot ashes. Coordinating by radio, they were encircling each house, then falling back. They were overstretched and the fire had leaped all the lines.

Then, as capriciously as it had fanned the flames into great towers, the wind changed and the fire turned to the north. The town was spared. For weeks, black, apocalyptic smoke would blot the sun, as the fire galloped off over miles of unpopulated terrain. But the danger was over.

and all are located close together on the right as you come into town from the east on the Alaska Highway. The **Gateway Salmon Bake** has an attractive picnic set-up by the road and a dining room, and the food is good; it's a casual experience for families. Like all salmon bakes, it's touristy, but so what?—you're in Tok, after all. The **Northstar Restaurant** is favored by locals and has a barbecue in the parking lot specializing in ribs, but the dining room is small and smoky. **Fast Eddy's** is a popular spot, with a pleasant dining room and a menu with full meals and pizza as well as the standard burger fare. But the service and food are inconsistent.

The next spring, migrant farm workers came from all over the country to pick thousands of acres of morel mushrooms that sprouted among the blackened trunks. The natural cycle turned again, as it has for millennia. Black spruce, the gnarled, ignoble trees of Alaska's swampy Interior, grow no taller than a house top, even after 100 years. It seems almost a mercy for them to burn in their characteristic explosion of sappy flames. And it is—the cone of the black spruce opens only in the intense heat of a forest fire.

That's the way nature has provided for the forest to renew. It is reborn on hot summer days, when the thunderheads that float over the plains and valleys snap fires to life with strikes of lightning. The burns provide fresh, green browse for wildlife as the spruce slowly regrow. A healthy forest is a patchwork of mature trees and small burns of various ages supporting diverse species that rely on each kind of growth. A mosaic of small burns also blocks catastrophic fires that can tear across hundreds of thousands of acres of mature trees like an after-noon storm.

More than three million acres of Alaska burned during the summer of 1990—900 different fires in a single, smoky season, most of them never hindered by man. Yet fires touched less than 1% of the state's land mass, and other than the close call at Tok, inhabited areas were generally unthreatened.

Fire is a way of life in Alaska. All Interior Native villages have fire crews. Even if living a traditional subsistence lifestyle during much of the year, each village hopes for the call that will activate their crew for weeks of physically exhausting, hot, dangerous work at camps in remote, mosquito-infested wilderness. It's the largest engine of the tiny cash economies in many villages. Modern forestry demands that most fires be left unmolested—they couldn't all be fought, anyway—and the crews are dispatched only to areas where other resources are threatened. Their work is to dig, burn, or bulldoze lines that will divert the fire toward natural barriers, such as broad rivers, mountains, or patches of less-combustible hardwoods. It's an annual summer adventure for white firefighters, too. A friend of mine whose dreary winter job is as a hearing officer in tax disputes has the most exciting summer job I've ever heard of: He throws fire bombs from the open door of a helicopter to start remote fire breaks.

As you drive Interior Alaska's highways, you'll pass through long stretches where the land seems studded with thin black poles, the trunks of burned trees, for miles in every direction. East of Tok the green is creeping up from underneath, but the old black trunks will stand for years yet—the product of a single afternoon of fury, and of millennia of renewal.

FROM TOK TO DELTA JUNCTION

There's not much to look at, but you may be curious about the Bison Range as you pass the sign. In the late 1970s and early 1980s the state tried to start a massive barley-growing project in Delta Junction, selling would-be farmers tens of thousands of acres to clear so Alaska could become the barley basket of the Pacific. Among other prob-lems, introduced bison kept trampling the crops, so the state built another hay farm to lure the bison away from the barley farms. Meanwhile, the great majority of the barley farms quickly went bust. The landowners came out nicely, however, since they soon began receiving federal payments not to plant crops that far exceeded anything they ever made from barley. The bison are sitting pretty too, with their own 3,000-acre farm. Who says government doesn't work? In summer, there's slim chance of seeing a bison from the road.

DELTA JUNCTION

This intersection with the Richardson Highway, which runs from Valdez to Fairbanks, is the official end of the Alaska Highway. It's an earnest little roadside town, reeling from the 1995 announcement of the downsizing of Fort Greely, the army base just south of town that has sustained it. The trans-Alaska pipeline has a pump station near town, the only one open for tours—but this, too, is now slated for closure. West of town is a historic roadhouse. And there are several good campgrounds and opportunities for lake recreation. You can spend an enjoyable half day here as a break in your travels.

ESSENTIALS

A helpful **visitor center** run by the Delta Chamber of Commerce, P.O. Box 987, Delta Junction, AK 99737 (☎ **907/895-5068**), stands at the intersection of the Alaska and Richardson highways, in the middle of town. They have a small display upstairs and will give you a certificate attesting that you made it to the end of the Alaska Highway.

Delta has no taxes of any kind. The **National Bank of Alaska** has a branch right at the center of town, on the Richardson Highway, with an **ATM.** The **post office** is on the east side of the Richardson two blocks north of the visitor center. In **emergencies,** phone 911; for nonemergencies, call the **Alaska State Troopers** (☎ **907/895-4800**). The **Family Medical Center** is at Mile 267.2 on the Richardson Highway, 2 miles north of the visitors center (☎ **907/895-4879** or 907/895-5100). For **news,** you can pick up Armed Forces Radio, or find a copy of the *Fairbanks Daily News-Miner.*

WHAT TO DO & SEE

The **Buffalo Wallow square dance festival** occurs over Memorial Day weekend at the school. The biggest event of the year is the annual **Deltana Fair,** held for a weekend in late July or early August; it's a community celebration, with a parade, outhouse race, livestock, carnival, and games.

Trans-Alaska pipeline **Pump Station 9,** seven miles south of town on the Richardson Highway (☎ **907/869-3270**), has provided free, one-hour technical tours six times a day during the summer, the only one of the 12 pump stations open for tours. Late in 1995, however, pipeline owners announced the station may be closed in 1996 due to declining oil flow. The pump stations, powered by jet engines, keep the thick, viscous oil moving the 800 miles from Prudhoe Bay to Valdez. Call ahead to make sure the tours are still operating. Children and cameras are not allowed, and you must wear a hard-hat and goggles. **Rika's Roadhouse and Landing,** 10 miles northwest of town on the Richardson Highway (☎ **907/895-4201**), is part of a state historical park, with free guided tours of the log building every two hours from 11am to 5pm. A restaurant and gift shop are part of the site. The roadhouse was a stop on the pioneer trail that was the precursor of the Richardson Highway. Walk down the shoreline path to see an impressive suspension bridge crossing of the trans-Alaska pipeline over the Tanana River.

Alaska State Parks also maintains five campgrounds on the rivers and lakes in and around Delta Junction, with some limited fishing. The **Quartz Lake State**

Recreation Area, 11 miles northwest of town on the Richardson and down a 3-mile turn-off, has an 80-site campground on the shallow lake; the fee is $8 a night. The **Black Spruce Lodge** (☎ 907/895-4668) rents boats, canoes, and cabins on the lake.

WHERE TO STAY

There are several bed-and-breakfasts in Delta Junction in addition to these two motels—get information at the visitor center.

Standard Accommodations

Alaska 7 Motel. 3548 Richardson Hwy. (P.O. Box 1115), Delta Junction, AK 99737. ☎ **907/895-4848.** 16 rms. TV TEL. $60 double. Additional person in room $5 extra. AE, CB, DC, DISC, MC, V.

These rooms, with two queen-size beds, are large considering the bargain price. They're in need of remodeling, but acceptable if you're just looking for a bed for the night. There are refrigerators and free coffee in the rooms; kitchenettes are available.

Kelly's Country Inn. Intersection of Richardson and Alaska hwys. (P.O. Box 849), Delta Junction, AK 99737. ☎ **907/895-4667.** 21 rms. TV TEL. $70 double. MC, V. Additional person in room $5 extra.

The low-slung yellow buildings look odd from the outside, but the unique rooms are charming, with floral designs or arched wooden ceilings, and other unexpected touches. The proprietor is Chaddie Kelly, who has been here forever. Refrigerators and kitchenettes are available.

Camping

If you don't want to stay at one of the state campgrounds mentioned above— perhaps you need a shower or want to plug in an RV—try **Smith's Green Acres RV Park and Campground,** 1½ miles north on the Richardson from the visitor center (☎ 907/895-4369). Full hookups are $17; electric only, $15; dry camping, $12. There is an array of activities and facilities. They take Discover, MasterCard, and Visa.

WHERE TO EAT

There are two decent restaurants near the intersection that defines the town, each accepting MasterCard and Visa. The **White Raven** is a smoky but clean hangout for locals, with reasonable prices for roadside café food and an evening menu that includes a welcome break from the constant diet of beef generally found on the highway. **Pizza Bella** has a beer and wine license and reasonably priced pizza pies. Nine miles southeast of Delta Junction on the Alaska Highway, the **Cherokee Lodge and RV Park** offers burgers and sandwiches for lunch, steak and seafood for dinner, and has a full liquor license and liquor store, but does not accept credit cards.

8 Dawson City: Canada's Gold-Rush Town

Driving east from Tok toward Dawson City, by the third hour bouncing over gravel road, orange midnight twilight falls to the north and a huge moon rises to the east, lighting the silhouettes of rounded mountains, which stand all around in countless, receding layers, all quiet, all empty. The border to Canada is closed for the night; camping by the road, no vehicles pass in the alpine silence. Next morning, passing through Customs, you go on for an hour and a half more over the Top of the World Highway, no sign of humankind within the distant horizon other than the thread of gravel you're following. Turn another corner, and there it is—down below, a grid of city streets on the edge of the Yukon and Klondike rivers. Dawson City, once the second-largest city on the West Coast of North America, is still way out in the middle of nowhere 100 years later.

Suddenly the radio's working again, bringing in an urbane situation comedy originating in Toronto. At the gravel river landing, a free car-ferry pulls up. A moment later, on the other side, there are people all over broad, straight streets, looking at well-kept old buildings. Inside a museumlike visitor center, Parks Canada employees dressed in period costumes are providing tourists with directions and selling them tickets to shows. Looking back at the hill across the river, at the wilderness so close at hand yet so separate, it's suddenly possible to understand the incongruity and shock of the gold rush. Nearly 100 years ago the world suddenly went mad and rushed to this riverbank beyond the edge of civilization and created a sophisticated city. One day it was quiet riverbank; the next day, a city. It arrived as suddenly as it arrives in your windshield driving east on the highway.

Dawson City was the destination for some 40,000 Stampeders hoping to strike it rich on the Klondike River. Mining for gold and other minerals continues today, but the town's main focus is on the visitors who come to see a well-preserved gold-rush boom town. Parks Canada does a good job of keeping up the buildings that make up part of the Klondike National Historic Sites and providing activities that bring history alive; you can spend a full day and evening here, if you're interested in the period the town celebrates. Gambling in a historic setting happens every night. Dawson City has done a better job of avoiding the sense of commercialism that pervades Skagway, the other main gold-rush town in the region. From mid-September to mid-May, the town essentially shuts down, as the extreme weather of the region drives tourists and miners away.

For those who get their fill of gold-rush history quickly, the long drive may not be justified, although there are some mountain-biking and river-floating opportunities. Floating the Yukon down to Eagle is a popular trip, and other, more remote water is available to explore in the area, too.

ESSENTIALS

GETTING THERE   The main way visitors come to Dawson City is by making a long detour from the Alaska Highway. The paved Klondike Highway, also known as Yukon Highway 2, splits from the Alaska Highway a few miles west of Whitehorse, heading 327 miles north to Dawson City. Then the gravel Top of the World Highway heads west from Dawson City, crossing the border before connecting with the Taylor Highway, which rejoins the Alaska Highway 175 miles after Dawson City. The 502 miles for the detour compare to 375 miles if you stay on the pavement of the Alaska Highway, and bypass some of the Alaska Highway's most spectacular vistas, on Kluane Lake—although, if you're driving both ways, you could go on the Alaska Highway on the return. Below, you'll find a more complete description of what you'll find on the Top of the World and Taylor highways. Two facts are essential, however: The border is closed at night (open 8am to 8pm going east, 9am to 9pm going west) and from September 15 to May 15. Almost everything else in the area is closed during the winter, too.

If you don't want to drive, many package tours include Dawson City, and **Alaska Direct Busline** (☎ **800/780-6652**) has regular passenger service. **Air North** (☎ **403/668-6224**) in 1995 was flying Dawson City to Fairbanks on Tuesday, Fairbanks to Dawson City on Friday and Sunday.

VISITOR INFORMATION   The **Parks Canada Visitor Reception Centre,** at King and Front streets (☎ **403/993-5566**), is open daily from 8am to 8pm during

Dawson City

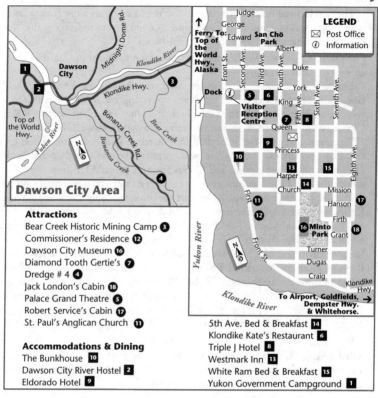

LEGEND
⊠ Post Office
ⓘ Information

Dawson City Area

Attractions

Bear Creek Historic Mining Camp ③
Commissioner's Residence ⑫
Dawson City Museum ⑯
Diamond Tooth Gertie's ⑦
Dredge # 4 ④
Jack London's Cabin ⑱
Palace Grand Theatre ⑤
Robert Service's Cabin ⑰
St. Paul's Anglican Church ⑪

Accommodations & Dining

The Bunkhouse ⑩
Dawson City River Hostel ②
Eldorado Hotel ⑨

5th Ave. Bed & Breakfast ⑭
Klondike Kate's Restaurant ⑥
Triple J Hotel ⑧
Westmark Inn ⑬
White Ram Bed & Breakfast ⑮
Yukon Government Campground ❶

the visitor season. It's a mix of information center, museum, and theater of historic films; it's an indispensable stop. The hosts are knowledgeable and provide free maps and guides, as well as selling tickets to all the Klondike National Historic Sites tours, events, and shows. If you plan to do all or most of the attractions, an events pass for $5.40 Canadian is a good deal. Generally, the prices for attractions are low, especially when you consider that Canadian dollars are worth about 30% less than U.S. dollars.

ORIENTATION   The town lies on a flat piece of land below a bluff on the bank on the Yukon River where it's joined by the Klondike River. **Front Street** runs along the river dike; behind it, a simple grid counts up to **Eighth Avenue** before the town runs out of room against the bluff. The whole thing is easily walkable. A few attractions are located out the **Klondike Highway,** which connects to Front Street on the south of the town. **Bonanza Creek Road** splits off to the right just after you leave town.

GETTING AROUND   Most people will have their own vehicle, but if you don't or if you don't want to drive, there are organized tours. **Gold City Tours,** on Front Street across from the riverboat *Keno* (☎ **403/993-5175**), offers a 3¹⁄₂-hour tour that includes Gold Dredge No. 4 and gold panning every afternoon in the summer for $31. They also have an airport limousine. **Mountain bikes** are a fun way to get to the outlying sights for strong riders—**Centennial Promotions,** at Front and York streets (☎ **403/993-6467**), has them for $7.50 an hour or $30 a day.

The free **George Black Ferry** crosses the Yukon 24 hours a day from a landing at the north end of Front Street, providing a connection to the Top of the World Highway, a provincial campground, and the hostel.

FAST FACTS   *Note:* All the prices in this section are listed in Canadian dollars, unless I've stated otherwise.

Dawson City is on Pacific time, one hour later than Alaska. You'll pay the 7% **Goods and Services Tax (GST)** for almost everything, but if you're not a Canadian you can apply to get up to $500 of it back at a Duty Free Shop or from Revenue Canada, Customs and Excise, Visitor Rebate Program, Ottawa, ON, Canada K1A 1J5; you must spend more than $100 and the rebate only counts for tax on goods and accommodations. There is one **bank** in town, the Canadian Imperial Bank of Commerce, at Second Avenue and Queen Street; it has an **ATM** (however, when I visited, the ATM had been out of order for several days, and if you need cash from your credit or charge card, you'll find that the bank takes only Visa—not American Express or MasterCard). The next closest bank is 330 miles southeast in Whitehorse or 175 miles southwest in Tok. Bring plenty of cash or traveler's checks. The **post office** is on Fifth Avenue near Princess Street, and a historic post office, with limited services, is at Third Avenue and King Street. In **emergencies,** call the **Royal Canadian Mounted Police,** on Front Street near Turner (☎ 403/ 993-5555), or the **ambulance** (☎ 403/993-4444). Dawson City once had eight **newspapers**, but today the *Klondike Sun* is published only monthly, on the second Thursday; other newspapers are available at Maximillian's, at Front and Queen streets. The CBC also provides **news,** at 560 AM, and a visitor radio station broadcasts on 96.1 FM.

SPECIAL EVENTS   The social event of the year in Dawson City is the **Commissioner's Grande Ball,** June 1, 1996. The **Yukon Gold Panning Championships** and **Canada Day Celebrations** are on July 1.

EXPLORING DAWSON CITY

GOLD-RUSH ATTRACTIONS   Parks Canada leads a **town walking tour** from the Visitor Reception Centre daily at 9am and 3:30pm for $2.25. The guides are well trained and can open historic buildings you won't get to look inside otherwise. Or you can use one of the maps they distribute to make up your own walking tour; there are interesting buildings almost anywhere you wander. Here are some of the highlights: On Front Street, just south of visitor centre, the steamer *Keno* sits on timbers, under restoration by Parks Canada; the free **Dawson As They Saw It** display of historic photographs is at Third Avenue and Princess Street; across the intersection, the **Bigg's Blacksmith Shop** is next to a gold rush–era building that is slowly sinking into the permafrost; at Front and Church streets, two blocks south, **St. Paul's Anglican Church** is a charming, creaky 1902 structure on the riverfront; next door, the **Commissioner's Residence,** an impressive mansion with a wraparound porch stands amid beautifully planted grounds; and in back of the house you'll find a log building which was part of the 1897 **Fort Herchmer,** and later a jail.

The ✪ **Dawson City Museum,** on Fifth Avenue between Church and Turner streets, is the best-presented gold-rush museum I've seen. The fascinating, tin-roofed, federalist-style building housed the Territorial Government starting in 1901, and upstairs one of the galleries still doubles as an impressive courtroom. The galleries downstairs display gold-rush artifacts in a way that makes them seem immediate and alive; guides dressed in costume lead tours further expanding on the teaching power of the objects and excellent placards. The clutter common to this kind of museum is confined to the "visible storage" gallery upstairs, where a rich collection is housed inside glass-fronted cabinets. A café serves soup, muffins, coffee, and tea, and there's a gift shop. Admission is $3.50; the museum is open Victoria Day to Labour Day, daily from 10am to 6pm. Next door is a free display of 19th-century locomotives from the short-lived Klondike Line Railway, which ran 32 miles up Bonanza Creek.

The **Jack London Cabin,** at Eighth Avenue and Grant Street along the foot of the bluff, is a replica with some logs from the original cabin where London probably spent his winter in the Klondike. (The rest of the logs are in a replica in Oakland, California, where London also lived.) A small museum with a guide who gives lectures is at the site. London found a gold mine of material for his classic adventure stories, but little gold, when he stampeded north.

Poet **Robert Service** spent more time at his cabin, at Eighth Avenue and Hansen Street, just down the road. Service wrote his ballads about the North while working as a bank clerk in Dawson City; he recited them for free drinks in the bars. Today you can hear them in tourist shows all over Alaska, but Tom Byrne is the granddaddy of Service readers; he's been reciting the poems from a rocking chair on the pleasant, grassy slope in front of the cabin since 1979, never canceling an outdoor show because of inclement weather. He has the right touch. Admission is $5 for adults, $2.50 for children; recitals are at 10am and 3pm.

Gold Dredge No. 4, 8 miles down Bonanza Creek Road south of town, is maintained by Parks Canada to show how these incredible earth-eating machines worked their way across the landscape, sifting gold out of the gravel; similar dredges are in Fairbanks and Nome. Hourly tours, from 9am to 5pm, cost $2.25. Another 7 miles up the road, the site of the original Klondike strike is marked. Parks Canada also manages the **Bear Creek Historic Mining Camp,** 7 miles up the Klondike Highway. The camp was headquarters for the company that owned the gold diggings; you can see the gold room, where the gold was melted into bricks. The tour takes place five times a day from 9am to 5pm and costs $2.25.

Other places of note in town, if you weary of the gold rush, are the outdoor **public swimming pool,** in the park just south of the museum ($3.50 for adults); the children's playground behind the museum; and the luxurious **Dawson City Community Library.**

ON THE RIVER   Dawson City is the largest town on the Yukon River after Whitehorse, and the most developed access point in or near Alaska. There are other good floating rivers in the region, too. The Yukon, the huge, spectacular water highway of the province and Alaska can take you far to the west at a relaxing pace: It flows 5 to 10 miles per hour. Two companies offer tour-boat rides, and three self-guided canoe or raft floats.

The *Yukon Lou,* with a log cabin office and dock on Front Street (☎ **403/ 993-5482**), takes 90-minute tours on a sternwheeler to Pleasure Island each afternoon, where passengers get off for a sled-dog exhibition, mining display, and other activities; it costs $15 for adults, $7.50 for children. The boat also takes an evening dinner cruise to the island for barbecued salmon; it's $35 for adults, $17.50 for children. Gray Line Yukon operates the *Yukon Queen* (☎ **403/993-5599**), which runs daily from late May to early September 108 miles down to Eagle. The modern 49-passenger boat leaves at 8:30am for a 4-hour, narrated ride to Eagle; once there, you can eat at the café and visit the museum. It returns the same day, going upstream in 5$^1/_2$ hours and serving a dinner of beef stew before arriving at 8pm back in Dawson City. Most passengers are on Holland America / Westours packages, but you can book a place if space is available. It's $77 U.S. one way, $129 round-trip; or you can fly back. The office is across Front Street from the Visitor Reception Centre.

One popular trip is to float three or four days in a canoe or raft to Eagle and come back on the *Yukon Queen;* there also are other more remote floats in the area, or you can keep floating down the Yukon to Circle, or even farther. The **Dawson Trading Post,** P.O. Box 889, Dawson City, YT, Canada Y0B 1G0 (☎ **403/993-5316**), rents canoes and camping gear, and operates a shuttle that can drop you off on the more remote Stewart or Klondike River for $25 an hour plus gas (they charge both ways). Or you can float down to Eagle. Canoes rent for $30 a day or $125 a week; the shop is open April 1 to mid-November, but answers mail all year. **Eagle Canoe Rentals,** P.O. Box 4, Eagle, AK 99738 (☎ **403/993-6823** in Dawson City or 907/547-2203 in Eagle), allows you to drop off the canoe at the end of your float. The Dawson City office is located at the Dawson City River Hostel on the west side of the river next to the free ferry landing. The price, including return of the canoe, is US$110 for up to four days to Eagle, US$160 up to five days to Circle; additional days are US$25. **Elmore Enterprises,** P.O. Box 145, Eagle, AK 99738 (☎ **907/547-2355**), offers 5- to 14-day raft trips over the same water.

WHERE TO STAY
STANDARD ACCOMMODATIONS

☺ **The Bunkhouse.** Front and Princess sts. (Bag 4040), Dawson City, YT, Canada Y0B 1G0. ☎ **403/993-6164.** Fax 403/993-6051. 31 rms, 5 with bath. $50 double without bath, $80–$95 double with bath. Additional person in room $5 extra. MC, V.

This is a unique place—it looks like a riverboat from the outside, and is fresh and new, but it's intended for a budget traveler. The rooms, all no-smoking with exterior entries, have varnished wooden floors and attractive fabrics; the beds are really bunks—no bed springs. Those that share bathrooms are quite small; the bathrooms are clean, but women may feel funny about the showers, which are in booths that enter into a shared room. The rooms with private bathrooms have telephones and TVs and are delightful.

El Dorado Hotel. Princess St. and Third Ave. (P.O. Box 338), Dawson City, YT, Canada Y0B 1G0. ☎ **403/993-5451.** Fax 403/993-5256. 53 rms, 4 suites. TV TEL. $117 double; $150 suite. Additional person in room $9 extra. AE, DC, DISC, ER, JCB, MC, V.

These are large, clean rooms in a year-round establishment. Those in the newer motel section are lighter and have exterior entries. The hotel is an old wood structure, without a sprinkler system and a little out of date. A courtesy car, coin-op laundry, and kitchenettes are available. The **Bonanza Dining Room** has burgers and sandwiches for lunch and mostly beef for dinner, although salads and pasta also are available, in a diner atmosphere. There's a bar on the other side of the lobby.

Triple J Hotel. Fifth Ave. and Queen St. (P.O. Box 359), Dawson City, YT, Canada Y0B 1G0. ☎ **403/993-5323.** Fax 403/993-5030. 45 rms. TV TEL. High season, $95–$110 double. Low season, $65–$75 double. Additional person in room $10 extra. AE, MC, V.

This rambling set of structures has three different kinds of rooms: large hotel rooms in the old, wooden main building (no sprinkler); smallish rooms in the low-slung motel building; and cabins. Some of the rooms are very good; others, nothing to brag about but still clean and serviceable (the cabin I looked at was a little musty). A courtesy car, coffee in the rooms, a coin-op laundry, and kitchenettes are available. The **restaurant** has a menu with a broad range of prices and varied cuisine; they make a specialty of the prime rib barbecue on Sunday.

✪ **Westmark Inn Dawson.** Fifth Ave. and Harper St. (P.O. Box 420), Dawson City, YT, Canada Y0B 1G0. ☎ **403/993-5542,** or 800/544-0970. Fax 403/993-5623. 120 rms, 9 suites. TV TEL. $152 double. AE, CB, DC, ER, MC, V. Closed Sept 15–May 15.

The newly renovated Westmark is the best hotel in town, especially the large rooms in the Robert Service Wing, which have elegant decorative touches. The older rooms are a bit out of date, but still superior to elsewhere in town. There's a coin-op laundry. A patio in the sunny courtyard is the site of a daily barbecue. **Belinda's Restaurant,** with light-wood decor and well-spaced tables, is open daily from 6am to 10pm; there's also a lounge. Ask for the "highway rate."

BED-AND-BREAKFASTS

There are several good bed-and-breakfasts in Dawson City. I particularly recommend the bright-pink **White Ram Manor,** at Seventh Avenue and Harper Street (P.O. Box 302), Dawson City, YT, Canada Y0B 1G0 (☎ **403/993-5772**), which has 10 generally small rooms with TVs, all but one with shared baths; but the great feature is the large deck with a hot tub, barbecue and picnic table, and the hospitable hostess, Gail Hendley. The **5th Avenue Bed and Breakfast,** on Fifth Avenue next door to the museum (P.O. Box 722), Dawson City, YT, Canada Y0B 1G0 (☎ **403/993-5941**), has five rooms—basic, but fresh and well done; two have their own bathrooms.

A HOSTEL & CAMPING

Dieter Reinmuth operates the **Dawson City River Hostel,** P.O. Box 32, Dawson City, YT, Canada Y0B 1G0 (☎ **403/993-6823**), across the Yukon from Dawson City on the free ferry. Bunks and camping are available. The provincial **Yukon River Campground,** just down the road, has 98 sites; the fee is $8. The **Goldrush Campground RV Park,** at Fifth Avenue and York Street (☎ **403/993-5247**), is a conveniently located lot right downtown.

WHERE TO EAT

I've described restaurants at the Westmark, El Dorado, and Triple J hotels, above, and the *Yukon Lou* Pleasure Island Restaurant dinner cruise. There are a few restaurants not associated with hotels, but nothing exceptional. **Klondike Kate's Restaurant,** in a historic building at Third Avenue and King Street (☎ **403/993-6527**), offers decent food for low prices, with a fully licensed bar. The patio is pleasant. **China Village,** at Third Avenue and Queen Street (☎ **403/993-5495**), is open almost all the time, offering "Chinese and Canadian cuisine" in a dark dining room with a pressed-tin ceiling.

DAWSON CITY IN THE EVENING

Some of Dawson City's most famous and fun activities are in the evening. **Diamond Tooth Gertie's,** at Fourth Avenue and Queen Street (☎ **403/993-5575**), operated by the Klondike Visitors Association, is a gambling hall and bar, with authentic can-can dancing floor shows at 8:30 and 10:30pm and 12:30am Tuesday through Sunday; it's open from 7pm to 2am, and admission is $4.75 for those 19 years and over only. There's no legal casino gambling west of here. The *Gaslight Follies* is more of a family evening; it's a two-hour vaudeville show at 8pm Wednesday through Monday in the **Palace Grand Theatre,** a historic building at Second Avenue and King Street that has been renovated by Parks Canada. Tickets—$13 to $16 for adults, $6 for children—are on sale at Mme. Tremblay's Store, at Third Avenue and King Street. Parks Canada also leads tours through the theater at 11am daily; it costs $2.25 at the Visitors Reception Centre.

WEST ON THE TOP OF THE WORLD & TAYLOR HIGHWAYS

There are few services, or signs of human habitation of any kind, on the 175 miles of gravel road ahead of you on the way to Tok, so fill your tank and pack some food before you leave Dawson City. Don't plan on making 60 miles an hour; in the Canadian section most of the road is fairly broad and smooth, but high speeds contribute to losing control and losing a headlight or windshield to a rock. On the U.S. side, the road is poorly maintained in places and you sometimes have to go quite slowly. Driving an old four-wheel-drive pickup, I covered the distance in under five hours; it'll take considerably longer with a car or RV you want to take care of.

Starting from Dawson City, take the free **George Black Ferry** across the Yukon River. It operates 24 hours a day, but the border crossing is open only from 9am to 9pm daily, from May 15 to September 15. The border opens and closes an hour earlier heading east because of the time zone change from Pacific to Alaska time (everything is an hour earlier in Alaska). Allow a good 90 minutes over the gravel road to cover the 66 miles to the border. See the Alaska Highway section for important information on **Customs.**

The Top of the World Highway is stunningly beautiful on a clear day. You drive over the tops of mountains, treeless alpine vistas spreading far to the horizon. Just after the border, there's a small roadhouse at a place called Boundary. Farther on the U.S. side, as you near the intersection with the Taylor Highway, the road descends into taiga—a landscape of small, stunted spruce near the altitude of the treeline.

The highway ends 79 miles from Dawson City at the intersection with the Taylor Highway. The Taylor runs from Eagle, a tiny mining town on the Yukon 65 miles north of this intersection, to Tetlin Junction, a spot on the Alaska Highway 97 miles south of here. The Taylor is rougher than the Top of the World Highway, but at points still beautiful, especially when it scales the sides of a gorge over a fork of the Fortymile River.

Eagle, at Mile 162, the north end of the Taylor Highway, is a historic little gold-rush town with fewer than 200 people, and the headquarters of the Yukon-Charley Rivers National Preserve, which starts a few miles downstream on the Yukon and extends almost to Circle, 158 miles and a week's float away. The National Park Service has a **visitor center,** P.O. Box 167, Eagle, AK 99738 (☎ **907/547-2233**), a good place to get information on the river and the only official place for information on the town; it's open Memorial Day to September, daily from 8am to 5pm. The headquarters is open during normal business hours year round.

After the road came in and Eagle's history started to disappear, residents founded a historical society. The isolation, and a lack of fires and floods, have kept the town's past safe, and everything that ever happened there seems to be preserved; as someone said, these days history is all they've got. The **Eagle City Historical Society,** P.O. Box 23, Eagle, AK 99738 (☎ **907/547-2325**), offers town tours Memorial Day to Labor Day, daily at 9am; the three-hour tour costs $3. Or for $10 for a group, they'll do the tour any time you like, winter or summer. The tour takes you through five buildings in the army's 1899 Fort Egbert, restored by the Bureau of Land Management (BLM).

Eagle is a good place to start or finish a Yukon River float trip, with a canoe- and a raft-rental company—see "On the River" under "Exploring Dawson City," in the Dawson City section, earlier in this chapter. From Dawson City to Eagle is 108 miles and takes three or four days; from Eagle to Circle is 158 miles and takes five days to a week. It's remote country, however, and not for novices. The BLM has a free

16-site campground in Eagle, and there are simple accommodations in a couple of lodges.

Heading south on the Taylor from the intersection with the Top of the World Highway, the free, BLM-maintained **Walker Fork Campground,** at Mile 82, has 20 sites and is a put-in point in the Fortymile National Scenic and Wild River system; from here you can float down to a bridge on the Taylor, or all the way to the Yukon and down to Eagle. Stop at the Alaska Public Lands Information Center in Tok for guidance, or contact the **BLM Tok Field Office,** P.O. Box 309, Tok, AK 99780 (☎ **907/883-5121**). Again, none of these trips is for beginners.

Sixteen miles farther, at Mile 66, the town of **Chicken** beckons with its two fiercely competitive businesses and little log post office. **The Goldpanner** is right on the road; the other business, a cafe, bar, liquor store, and gift shop all run by the same family, calls itself **"beautiful downtown Chicken,"** and is a little off the road. That's where to go, if you're of a mind, to get a good slice of pie and a burger, or visit the bar (checking your gun, as the sign directs) and find out why the gold miners around here never manage to save any of the money they dig out of the ground. There's no phone in town, and the toilets are outhouses, but you can wash your hands in the cafe.

The BLM's free **West Fork Campground,** with 25 sites, is 17 miles on, at Mile 49; it's another access to the Fortymile River system, upstream of Chicken and the Walker Fork campground. You may run across old and current mining equipment around here.

The intersection with the Alaska Highway is 12 miles east of Tok.

11 | The Bush

The Bush is most of Alaska. On a map of the state, the portion with roads and cities is really just a smallish corner. Yet most visitors—and, indeed, most Alaskans—never make it beyond that relatively populated corner. It's not uncommon for children to grow to adulthood in Anchorage, Fairbanks, or Southeast Alaska without ever traveling to the Arctic, the Aleutians, or the vast wetlands of western Alaska. The reason they don't is the same simple reason most tourists don't go to Bush Alaska—getting to the Bush is expensive, and there's not much there in the way of human activity once you arrive.

That's the point. Bush Alaska is one of the planet's last barely inhabited areas, where indigenous people still interact with the environment in their traditional way, and new places still remain to be explored by self-reliant outdoors people.

Although there are few people, the hospitality of those you meet in the Bush is special and warming. In Bush Alaska, it's not uncommon to be befriended and taken under wing by total strangers for no other reason than that you've taken the trouble to come to their community and are, therefore, an honored guest. Even in the larger towns, people look you in the eye and smile as you pass in the street, and if you have a questioning look on your face, they'll stop to help. Living in a small place where people know each other and have to work together against the elements makes for a tight, friendly community.

The cultural traditions of Alaska's Native people go beyond simple hospitality. Theirs is a culture based more on cooperative than competitive impulses, where honesty, respect, and consensus carry greater weight than in white society. Cooperation also requires slowing down, listening, not taking the lead—people from our fast-paced culture can leave a village after a visit wondering why no one spoke to them, not realizing that they never shut up long enough to give anyone a chance. (For more on the culture of Alaska's Native peoples, see Chapter 2.)

The Native people of the Bush also have terrible problems trying to live in two worlds. There's too much alcohol and too many drugs in the Bush, too much TV, but not enough of an economic base to provide for safe drinking water or plumbing in many villages. Even in some of the relatively prosperous village hubs described in this chapter, visitors will glimpse a kind of rural poverty they may not have seen before—where prices are extremely high and steady jobs interfere with traditional hunting and food gathering.

The world they survive in is extreme in every respect—the weather, the land, even the geography. There's a special feeling to walking along the Arctic Ocean, the virtual edge of the earth, on a beach that lies between flat, wet tundra and an ocean that's usually ice. The quantity and accessibility of wildlife are extreme too, as are the solitude and uniqueness of what you can do. Unfortunately, the prices also are extreme. With few exceptions, getting to a Bush hub from Anchorage costs as much as getting to Anchorage from Seattle. And once you're in the hub, you're not done. Getting into the outdoors can cost as much again. Most families and young people can't afford to make a Bush sojourn, instead satisfying their curiosity about the state's unpopulated areas on Alaska's rural highways. Most who can afford the trip usually make the most of their time and money with brief prearranged tours or trips directly to wilderness lodges. Only a few explorers head for the Bush unguided, although there are some good places to go that way—Nome, Kodiak, and Unalaska among them.

Covering the Bush also is a challenge for the writer of a book like this one. There are more than 200 Alaska villages, many lodges, camps, and guides, and a vast, undefined territory to describe. All that information would fill a larger book than this one, but would be of little use to the great majority of readers. I've taken the approach, instead, of providing sections on a few Bush hubs that are most accessible and popular with visitors, that have modern facilities, and can be used as gateways to much more of the state for those who want to step out beyond the fringe of civilization. For more complete information on even small Native villages, I recommend *The Alaska Wilderness Guide,* published by Vernon Publications of Bellevue, Washington. The core of that book is a directory of all of Alaska's villages, with the basic facts on what you'll find there.

If you find yourself in a town such as Nome, Kotzebue, Barrow, or Kodiak—a hub for outlying Native villages—there's a simple and relatively inexpensive way to get out and see how village people live. Mail and scheduled passenger planes—typically small, single-engine craft—make daily rounds of the villages from each hub. Without the difficulty, expense, and dubious interest of going for a longer trip to a village, you can fly out on one of these planes for a quick day trip, walk around and meet people, then fly back to the hub city on the same plane or the next one to come through. *One warning*—don't make such an excursion in lowering weather, as you could get weathered in at a remote village. A journalist friend of mine was weathered in for more than two weeks on one occasion. You'll find the air-taxi operators—true bush pilots—friendly, informal, and most willing to oblige you in working out your Bush adventure. To find out where to go, just walk into the office and tell them what you're interested in seeing and how much time and money you want to spend. It's also an inexpensive way to go flightseeing.

1 Exploring the Bush

Alaska's Bush is better defined by what it's like there than where it is. For the purposes of this book, following the most convenient and common conception, the Bush is everything beyond the roads—everything north or west of Fairbanks (erase the recently opened Dalton Highway from your mind for a moment). But there also are Bush villages in the Interior, in Southcentral, and in Southeast Alaska. There are even Bush villages you can drive to. After a while, you'll know a Bush community when you see one—it's a place where the wilderness is closer than civilization, where people still live off the land and age-old traditions survive, and where you have to make a particular effort to get in or out.

THE REGIONS

There are at least five commonly accepted regions in the Bush, which group easily into three:

THE ARCTIC The Arctic Circle is the official boundary of the Arctic. The line, at 66° 33' north latitude, is the southern limit of true midnight sun—south of it, at sea level, the sun rises and sets, at least a little, every day of the year. But in Alaska, people think of the Arctic as beginning at the Brooks Range, which is a bit north of the circle. The region includes Barrow, Prudhoe Bay, and, to the south, Gates of the Arctic National Park, which is in the Brooks Range. The Northwest Alaska region, which includes Kotzebue and, slightly south of the Arctic Circle, Nome, also is part of the Arctic in climate, culture, and topography. The biggest geographic feature in Alaska's Arctic is the broad North Slope, the plain of swampy tundra that stretches from the Arctic Ocean to the northern side of the Brooks Range. It's a swampy desert, with little rain or snowfall, frozen solid all but a couple of months a year.

WESTERN ALASKA This is the land of the massive, wet Yukon-Kuskokwim Delta and the fish-rich waters of Bristol Bay. The Y-K Delta, as it's known, was never really exploited by white explorers, and the Yup'ik people who live there have maintained some of the most culturally traditional villages—in a few, Yup'ik is still the dominant language. Bethel is the main hub city of the delta, which holds little attraction for visitors. Bristol Bay is known for massive salmon runs, and avid fishermen may be interested in its wilderness lodges, using Dillingham as a hub.

SOUTHWEST ALASKA Stretching from the Aleutians—really a region of their own—to the Alaska Peninsula, Kodiak Island, and the southern part of the mountainous west side of Cook Inlet, this is a maritime region, like Southeast, but far more remote. The hub of the wet, windy Aleutians is Unalaska and its port of Dutch Harbor. Katmai National Park and the adjoining wild lands are the main attraction of the Alaska Peninsula, although there also are fishing lodges on the salmon-rich rivers and on the lakes to the north, including areas in Lake Clark National Park and Iliamna Lake. (The McNeil River Bear Sanctuary is included in the Homer listing in Chapter 8, as that's its main access point.) The lakes and west side of Cook Inlet are accessed primarily by Kenai, Homer, and Anchorage flight services for fishermen and hunters. Kodiak is hardly a Bush community, but fits better in this chapter than anywhere else.

GETTING AROUND

With a few exceptions for strongly motivated travelers, who can take the ferry to Kodiak and Unalaska or drive to Prudhoe Bay, getting to each town in this chapter will require flying. Except for Bettles, which is the stepping-off point for Gates of the Arctic National Park, **Alaska Airlines** (☎ 800/426-0333) jets fly to all the towns described. Other, smaller operators serve each town, as well. MarkAir, which used to provide Alaska Airlines competition to many of the towns, went bankrupt and withdrew from Alaska in 1995. Throughout the chapter, I've listed the plane fare to various communities from Anchorage, based on flying coach and getting at least some kind of discount for advance purchase. Full Y-class fares are more. With the way airfares fluctuate these days, it would be unwise to use these numbers as anything more than rough guides for preliminary planning. To get the current best fare, use a travel agent.

Kodiak, which barely fits a chapter on the Bush, is the easiest to get to of the communities in the chapter, but it still requires either a 10-hour ferry ride from Homer or a $300 to $400 round-trip plane ticket from Anchorage. It's more similar to Southeast Alaska than to the other Bush towns listed. Unalaska, in the Aleutian Islands, is an interesting place to go way off the beaten path while staying in great comfort, but is short on the Native culture you may be looking for. A visit requires a $700 to $850 round-trip plane ticket. Kotzebue and Barrow are the most purely Native of the communities in the chapter. Nome has the advantages of Arctic surroundings and easy access to them on gravel roads, but is more of a gold-rush town than a Native village. Prudhoe Bay, at the end of the Dalton Highway, is an industrial complex without a significant identity of its own. Each of those Arctic communities costs around $400 to $600 to fly to. Bettles is a Bush village that has become the primary gateway to the deep wilderness of the spectacular Brooks Range. It is accessed by commuter plane from Fairbanks.

2 Outside in the Bush

The number of opportunities for outdoor solitude in the Bush are beyond comprehension, much less my ability to summarize them here. I've provided some ideas for the more popular destinations, and you can find more in Chapter 6.

BIRDWATCHING   In the Alaska Bush, serious birders can easily add birds to their lists they have scant chance of seeing anywhere else in the world. Nome, with its long gravel roads, may be the best destination for unguided trips. Unalaska is a good choice for sea birds you won't see elsewhere. Around Katmai National Park the birdwatching is good and you can even join in research. Kotzebue, the Pribilof Islands, and Saint Lawrence Island all receive visits from avid birders in the summer, too.

FISHING   Kodiak Island, the Alaska Peninsula, Bristol Bay, and the Lake Clark area have among the best salmon and trout fishing to be found anywhere. The only complaint I've ever heard is that it's too easy—there's not enough time waiting for a bite, and fishermen's arms get too tired fighting one big salmon after another. Poor things! Access is expensive, and that's why the fishing is so good—you need to fly in to a camp or wilderness lodge. The biggest halibut anywhere are caught off Unalaska.

HIKING   The green hills and mountains of the Aleutians are stunningly beautiful for walks across smooth heather, free of bears or many bugs. Kodiak has some good trails, and weekly guided hikes led by volunteers of the local Audubon society. Katmai National Park is a destination for dramatic backcountry hikes. The Brooks Range, part of which is in Gates of the Arctic National Park, is the ultimate destination for remote extended hiking trips away from trails among craggy, weathered peaks.

RAFTING & KAYAKING   The Noatak River and other rivers draining west from the Brooks Range are increasingly popular routes for remote float trips through massive areas of federal park and conservation lands. You can fly out of Kotzebue for an unguided trip or take a guide from Bettles or Fairbanks. Good kayak trips are guided from Nome, on the rivers, and from Kodiak, on protected ocean waters.

WILDLIFE VIEWING   I'm still boring my friends with the tale of the musk ox I saw from one of the roads out of Nome. I don't know of a better place to see wildlife without getting out of a car or off a bike. Katmai National Park has incredible bear viewing, as does Kodiak, where you also can see marine mammals in abundance. When I hiked for a week through the Brooks Range a number of years ago, I saw at least one bear every day.

3 Kodiak: Bears, Fish & History

The habitat that makes Kodiak Island a perfect place for bears also makes it perfect for people. Runs of salmon clog unpopulated bays and innumerable, unfished rivers; the rounded green mountains seem to beg for someone to cross them; the gravel beaches and protected rocky inlets are free of people, but full of promise. But, in this respect, bears are smarter than people. Brown bears own the island, growing to prodigious size and abundant numbers, but Kodiak is as yet undiscovered by human visitors. It's a part of the wonder of the place. I'll never forget flying over the luxuriant verdure of Kodiak's mountains and the narrow string of glassy Raspberry Strait on a rare sunny day, seeing no sign of human presence in the most beautiful landscape I had ever beheld. That's something the bears will never experience, despite their superior collective intelligence.

The streets of the town of Kodiak are a discovery, too. Narrow and twisting over hills with little discernible order, they were once the stomping grounds of Lord Alexander Baranov, the early Russian ruler of Alaska. And before Baranov, of the Koniag, the first people who lived off the incomparable riches of the island. Several early Russian buildings remain, and the Koniag are recovering their past too, with Native-managed archeology and a brand-new museum in Kodiak in which to keep the artifacts found.

Today commercial fishermen fill the town, providing, with the Coast Guard base, its economic base and energetic, prosperous, unpolished community. It's among the three most productive fishing ports in the United States. Kodiak is separate from the rest of Alaska, living its own salmon-centered life without often thinking of what's going on in Anchorage or anywhere else. It's off the beaten path because it doesn't really need anything the path provides; there's fishing and the money it provides, plenty to do in the outdoors, and a tight, interesting little town. For the visitor, Kodiak is what Southeast Alaska must have been long ago, before tourists ever thought of going there.

There are several Native villages on the island—a flight to one of them and back on a clear day is a wonderful, low-cost way to see remote areas of the island and to get a taste of how Alaska Natives live. Kodiak also has several wilderness lodges for fishing, wildlife watching, sea kayaking, and hunting, and even an archeological dig you can participate in.

ESSENTIALS

GETTING THERE   By Air   It's a one-hour flight from Anchorage to Kodiak on **Alaska Airlines** (☎ 800/426-0333), costing $300 to $400 round-trip. **Era Aviation** (☎ 907/487-4363 or 800/866-8394) has more frequent flights, but not on jets.

By Ferry   The ferry *Tustumena,* of the **Alaska Marine Highway System** (☎ 800/642-0066), serves Kodiak from Homer and Seward. It's a 10-hour run from Homer, the closest port with a road. The passenger fare is $48.

VISITOR INFORMATION   The **Kodiak Island Convention and Visitors Bureau** is at 100 Marine Way, Kodiak, AK 99615 (☎ 907/486-4782), near the ferry dock. It's open in summer, daily from 8:30am to 5pm; in winter, closed Saturday and Sunday. The **Kodiak National Wildlife Refuge Visitors Center,** 4 miles south of town, near the airport on Buskin River Road (☎ 907/487-2600), is headquarters for a refuge that covers most of the island, home of the famous Kodiak brown bear. There are remote public-use cabins all over the refuge, reachable by chartered plane. The center has displays and is a good place to stop for outdoors information.

It's open May to September, Monday through Friday from 8am to 4:30pm and on Saturday and Sun-day from noon to 4:30pm; in winter, Monday through Friday from noon to 4:30pm.

ORIENTATION   The Kodiak Archipelago contains Kodiak, Shuyak, and Afognak islands, and many other, smaller islands. The city of Kodiak is on a narrow point on the northeast side of Kodiak Island, surrounded by tiny islands. There are seven Native villages on other parts of the island. The airport and Coast Guard base are several miles southwest of town on **Rezanof Drive,** which runs through town and comes out on the other side. The center of Kodiak is a hopeless tangle of steep, narrow streets—you need the excellent map given away by the visitor center. The street along the top of the **St. Paul Harbor** is **Marine Way,** and also the location of the ferry dock and some of the sights. A tall bridge crosses to Near Island, where there's a pleasant park and the **St. Herman Harbor. Mill Bay Road** is a main commercial street leading through town. Several gravel roads, totaling 87 miles, fan out from Kodiak to scenic vistas, recreation areas, and salmon streams.

GETTING AROUND   You can walk the downtown area, where the main historic sites are, but to get in from the airport you'll need a ride. The **Airporter Shuttle** (☎ **907/486-7583**) costs $5. A **cab,** from Ace Mecca (☎ **907/486-3211**), runs around $14 from the airport. Several companies rent cars, including **Avis** (☎ **907/ 487-2264**), **Budget** (☎ **907/487-2220**), and **Rent-a-Heap** (☎ **907/486-5200**). Pickup is available at the airport or downtown. A car will help you explore the roads that lead from town, but that won't take too long. **Island Terrific Tours,** P.O. Box 3001, Kodiak, AK 99615 (☎ and fax **907/485-4777**), will pick you up at the airport by arrangement and show you around for $75.

FAST FACTS   The **sales tax** is 5% in the city of Kodiak, but there is no sales tax outside the city limits. There are several banks downtown; an **ATM** is at 202 Marine Way. The **post office** is near Lower Mill Bay Road and Hemlock Street. In **emergencies,** call 911. For nonemergency police business, call the **Kodiak Police Department** (☎ **907/486-8000**). The **Kodiak Island Hospital** is at 1920 E. Rezanof Dr. (☎ **907/486-3281**). The *Kodiak Daily Mirror* is published weekdays. The *Anchorage Daily News* is widely available, too. **Business services** are available at Mail Boxes Etc., at 202 Center St., Suite 315 (☎ **907/486-8780**).

SPECIAL EVENTS   **Russian Orthodox Christmas,** coming about two weeks after the Western celebration, includes the Starring Ceremony, in which a choir follows a star in the evening to sing at the homes of church members. The late-March **Pillar Mountain Golf Classic** (☎ **907/486-4782**) is played on a one-hole par-70 course which climbs 1,400 feet from tee to flag; dogs, guns, chain saws, and two-way radios are strictly prohibited. The **Kodiak Crab Festival** (☎ **907/486-5557**), on Memorial Day weekend, includes a carnival and survival suit races, and also the solemn blessing of the fleet and memorial service to lost fishermen. In early September, the **Kodiak State Fair and Rodeo** (☎ **907/486-2708**) has all kinds of small-town contests. The **Harbor Stars** (☎ **907/486-8085**), in mid-December, is a fleet parade of vessels decorated for Christmas.

EXPLORING KODIAK

A brief walking tour in the front of the local visitors guide will show you the sights and orient you to what's available in town. The **Fishermen's Memorial,** near the harbormaster's office at the head of the St. Paul Harbor, has a soberingly long list of Kodiak fishermen who have lost their lives at sea.

The ✪ **Baranov Museum,** at 101 Marine Way, is the oldest Russian building in North America, built in 1808 by Alexander Baranov. Inside is a museum of Russian and early Native artifacts collected by the Kodiak Historical Society. The gift store contains more than tourist junk: samovars, trading beads, grass baskets, and other interesting items. The museum is open in summer, Monday through Friday from 10am to 4pm and on Saturday and Sunday from noon to 4pm; in winter, Monday, Tuesday, Thursday, and Friday from 11am to 3pm, and on Saturday from noon to 3pm. Admission is $2, free for children 11 and under.

The ✪ **Alutiiq Museum,** at 215 Mission Rd., opened to acclaim in 1995. It's part of a general cultural reawakening of the Koniag Alutiiq people, whose culture was virtually wiped out by the coming of the Russians in the 18th century. The museum displays the findings of archeological digs around the Kodiak Archipelago, which are participatory efforts including Native people and visitors who want to get involved (see "Getting Outside," below). Museum hours are 10am to 4pm: daily in summer, closed Sunday and Monday in winter. Admission is $2 for adults.

Across the street, at Kashevarof and Mission, the **Holy Resurrection Russian Orthodox Church** was founded in 1794, although the present building dates only to 1945, when it was rebuilt after a fire. There are valuable icons and brass inside. Call the parish priest (☎ 907/486-3854) to arrange a tour. The **St. Herman's Theological Seminary,** a couple of blocks farther on Mission (☎ 907/486-3525), houses a museum of church artifacts and a bed-and-breakfast.

Native dance performances take place Monday through Saturday at 3:30pm at the **Kodiak Tribal Council Barabara,** at 713 Rezanof Dr. (☎ 907/486-4449).

GETTING OUTSIDE

ARCHEOLOGY   The **Afognak Native Corporation,** 214 W. Rezanof Dr., Kodiak, AK 99615 (☎ 800/770-6014), with the University of Alaska, offers visitors a chance to help in scientific excavations of Koniag sites on Afognak Island aimed at putting back together their cultural heritage. **Dig Afognak** visitors get to see the area and are instructed in the natural history as well as archeology, but they're also expected to work, digging and working in a remote lab. Accommodations are in heated tents. A six-day session is $1,650.

BROWN BEAR VIEWING   Two air services I'm aware of will give your money back if you don't see bears—a safe bet for them in Kodiak. The plan generally is to fly out and find a bear, then land on floats to look at it. **Kodiak Wilderness Adventures** (☎ 907/486-8101, or 800/556-8101), owned by Wilderness Air, offers a three-hour bear flight for $295 per person, or an eight-hour day with a guide for $480. They also offer fly-in fishing and float trips. **Uyak Air Service** (☎ 907/486-3407, or 800/303-3407) offers similar bear flights, and a guided bear-watching camp.

TWO RECREATION AREAS   North on Rezanof Drive a couple of miles, the **Fort Abercrombie State Historic Park** (☎ 907/486-6339) is worth a visit for the World War II history and the natural environment, even if you don't camp. There are bunkers and gun emplacements and a small visitor center. It defended against Japanese invasion, which made it only into the outer Aleutian Islands. The point the fort sits on also is a scenic place to enjoy big trees, tide pools, fishing, hiking, and lake swimming. There's a 14-site campground. Camping is $10 a night. Guided walking tours take place several times a week. The **Buskin River State Recreation Site,** 4 miles south of town on Rezanof Drive, has 17 sites, a hiking trail, and access to fishing.

FISHING   The roads leading from Kodiak offer access to terrific salmon and trout fishing. Some kind of salmon, somewhere, are available all summer. You can get a guide map from the visitor center or the **Alaska Department of Fish and Game,** at 211 Mission Rd., Kodiak, AK 99615 (☎ **907/486-1880**), where they'll also explain regulations and sell you a license. The guide also shows where to go for remote fishing, which on Kodiak is surely among the most prolific in the world. Various guide services are available as well—ask the visitor center for referrals. Air-taxi operators at the airport, or listed under "Brown Bear Viewing," above, can take you out, perhaps to stay at one of the public-use cabins. Or you can fish from a boat—**Eagle Adventures** (☎ **907/486-3445**) is but one of the charters available for salmon and halibut, starting at $125 a day.

HIKING   Pick up a copy of the *Kodiak Hiking Guide* at the visitor center for a variety of mountain climbs and day hikes from the road system. They'll also have field-trip program of the **Kodiak Audubon Society,** listing weekly guided hikes and birdwatching trips; or write to the society at P.O. Box 1756, Kodiak, AK 99615.

SEA KAYAKING   The Kodiak Archipelago, with its many folded, rocky shorelines and abundant marine life, is a perfect place for sea kayaking. **Wavetamer Kayaking,** P.O. Box 228, Kodiak, AK 99615 (☎ **907/486-2604**), offers short introductory paddles around the town for $40, and longer trips, including a day-long tour for $125, or multiday trips to Katmai National Park or elsewhere around the Archi-pelago. **Kodiak Kayak Tours** (☎ **907/486-2722**), easily mistaken for Wavetamers, which also calls itself Kayak Kodiak Tours, does a good job with its twice-daily four-hour paddles, suitable for beginners. Even on the short trips you'll see puffins, eagles, and sea lions.

If you're already an experienced kayaker, **Shuyak Island State Park,** 54 miles north of Kodiak, is the place to go. The 11,000-acre park is a honeycomb of islands and narrow passages in virgin Sitka spruce coastal forest. State Parks maintains four public-use cabins, which rent for $50 a night in the summer, and distributes a free kayaking guide with route descriptions. For information, contact the **Kodiak District Office,** S.R. Box 3800, Kodiak, AK 99615 (☎ **907/486-6339;** fax 907/ 486-3320).

WHERE TO STAY

The visitor center keeps a list of bed-and-breakfasts, of which there are many in Kodiak. I think a B&B is the best way to get to know a town like this. I've listed only one below, but among the other choices are **Wintels Bed and Breakfast,** P.O. Box 2812, Kodiak, AK 99615 (☎ **907/486-6935**), with four rooms, one with a private bath, and a Jacuzzi and sauna; and bear guide Dick Rohrer's **Ocean Side B&B,** P.O. Box 2219, Kodiak, AK 99615 (☎ **907/486-5835**).

The **bed tax** inside the Kodiak city limits is 11%.

Afognak Wilderness Lodge. P.O. Box 1, Seal Bay, AK 99697. ☎ **800/478-6442.** Fax 907/ 486-2217. 3 cabins. $400 per person. Rates include meals and guide service. MC, V. Closed Jan–Apr 15.

You'll have to fly out to Afognak Island, north of Kodiak. It's a dramatic landscape of spruce forest, with rich salmon streams, archeological heritage, and other attrac-tions for outdoors people. This lodge, operated by a couple who have been active in Seal Bay since 1964, is long-established and has great fishing, hunting, and wildlife-viewing opportunities. You can fish the streams on shore or go for halibut offshore. You're likely to see bears, otters, and lots of other wildlife. They guide hunts for huge brown bears, deer, elk, and ducks. Meals are large and served family style. The log cabins have indoor plumbing.

Buskin River Inn. 1395 Airport Way, Kodiak, AK 99615. ☎ **907/487-2700** or 800/544-2202. 51 rms. TV TEL. $115 double. Additional person in room $15 extra. AE, DISC, MC, V.

This standard airport hotel isn't convenient to the downtown sights—it's a $14 cab ride or you can rent a car—but there's a flip side: you don't pay the 11% bed tax because the hotel is outside the city limits. It's near the wildlife refuge visitor center, a hiking trail, and the nine-hole golf course at the Coast Guard base. Also, the Buskin makes a specialty of booking activities and offering package discounts for outdoors explorations of the island. The rooms all have refrigerators and hairdryers, and they'll pick you up at the airport. The **Eagle's Nest Restaurant** has an extensive beef and seafood menu, with reasonable prices.

Kodiak Bed and Breakfast. 308 Cope St., Kodiak, AK 99615. ☎ **907/486-5367.** 2 rms, neither with bath. $80 double. AE, MC, V.

This is a comfortable, homey place, with a nice porch to eat breakfast on sunny mornings, overlooking the harbor. Fish is often on the menu. The location is convenient, right downtown and next door to the more expensive Westmark. One of the hosts is a big, friendly dog.

Shelikof Lodge. 211 Thorsheim Ave., Kodiak, AK 99615. ☎ **907/486-4141** or 907/486-4116. 38 rms. TV TEL. $65 double. Additional person in room $5 extra. AE, CB, DC, DISC, MC, V.

This economy choice is right in town. The rooms are dark, but have queen-size beds, cable TV, and free local phone calls. There's a restaurant and lounge in the hotel, and free coffee in the lobby.

Westmark Kodiak. 236 W. Rezanof Dr., Kodiak, AK 99615. ☎ **907/486-5712** or 800/ 544-0970. Fax 907/486-3430. 81 rms. TV TEL. High season, $131 double. Low season, $111 double. Additional person in room $15 extra. AE, DC, DISC, MC, V.

This is the best hotel in downtown Kodiak, with good rooms perched on the hill overlooking the boat harbor, right in the center of things. Rooms in the wooden building generally have two double beds. Local calls are free and they operate a courtesy van. The **Chart Room** restaurant, specializing in seafood and with a great view of the source of the food on the menu, is a pleasant choice for a nice dinner out.

WHERE TO EAT

Besides the hotel restaurants listed above at the Westmark and Buskin River, try **El Chicano,** at 103 Center, which has good Mexican food in a dark dining room, and **Beryl's,** which started out as a candy shop and became Kodiak's favorite place for sandwiches, burgers, espresso, and ice cream.

4 Katmai National Park: Natural Ferocity

Most of the land of the Alaska Peninsula, pointing out to the Aleutian Archipelago, is in one federally protected status or another, centering on Katmai National Park, which was originally set aside in 1918. Katmai (CAT-my) lies just west of Kodiak Island, across the storm-infested Shelikof Strait. Bears and salmon are the main attractions today: Brooks Camp, with a campground and lodge within Katmai, is probably the most comfortable place for foolproof bear viewing in Alaska. Here, in July, you can sit on a deck sipping lemonade and watch 900-pound brown bears walk by, going about their business of devouring the spawning salmon that contribute to their awesome size. Staying the night will require you to win a camping permit in a lottery or stay in the pricey lodge, but you can go for a day trip, if you can afford round-trip airfare of over $500.

Katmai originally exploded into world consciousness in 1912, with the most destructive volcanic eruption to shake the earth in 3,400 years. When Katmai's Novarupta blew, it released 10 times more energy than Mount St. Helens's eruption of 1980 and displaced twice as much matter as 1883's Krakatoa. People could clearly hear it in Juneau, acid rain melted fabric in Vancouver, British Columbia, and the skies darkened over most of the northern hemisphere. All life was wiped out in a 40-square-mile area and buried as deep as 700 feet. But so remote was the area, then still unnamed, that not a single human being was killed. The Valley of Ten Thousand Smokes, the vast wasteland created by the blast, belched steam for decades after. Today it's dormant, but still a barren moonscape, making a fascinating day tour or hiking trip.

ESSENTIALS

GETTING THERE   The most common way to access Katmai is through the village of King Salmon, which lies just west of the park, and then by air-taxi to Brooks Camp. **Alaska Airlines** (☎ 800/426-0333) is one of several operators serving King Salmon from Anchorage daily. Various air-taxis operating float planes make the link to Brooks Camp. **Katmai Air** (☎ 800/544-0551, or 907/243-5448 in Anchorage), the operator owned by the Katmailand concessionaire; **Branch River Air** (☎ 907/ 246-3437); and **C-Air** (☎ 907/246-6318) also operate from King Salmon seasonally. Altogether, expect to pay more than $500 to get to Brooks Camp from Anchorage. It's also possible to visit the undeveloped areas of the park, especially on the incomparably grand and rugged east-side beaches, by air-taxi from King Salmon, Homer, or Kodiak.

VISITOR INFORMATION   The **park headquarters** is in King Salmon, P.O. Box 7, King Salmon, AK 99613 (☎ 907/246-3305). There's also a visitor center at the airport in King Salmon and at Brooks Camp. In Anchorage, you can get information, including the excellent 40-page *Bear Facts* guide, at the Alaska Public Lands Information Center, at Fourth Avenue and F Street.

GETTING AROUND   Once at Brooks Camp, there's a bus that carries visitors to the Valley of Ten Thousand Smokes, 23 miles by gravel road from the camp. **Katmailand, Inc.,** the park concessionaire, charges $50 per person, round-trip, for the all-day excursion, plus $7 more for lunch. One-way transfers for hikers are $30.

FAST FACTS   This is a remote area, but King Salmon does have **banking** services. In **emergencies,** call 911 outside the park, 907/246-3305 within the park. For nonemergency matters, call the **police** in King Salmon (☎ 907/246-4222) or the **Alaska State Troopers** (☎ 907/246-3346). The **Camai Clinic,** in Naknek (☎ 907/246-6155), is open during normal business hours, and the number goes to emergency dispatchers after hours.

EXPLORING KATMAI

The time to go to Katmai is when the bears are congregated near the Brooks River to catch salmon, the last week of June through the first week of August. This is when you're assured of seeing bears from the elevated platforms near the Brooks River falls, half a mile from Brooks Camp, even on a day trip. Other times in the summer, you could easily miss the bears altogether.

Brooks Camp, with the park service campground, visitor center, and lodge, is located where the Brooks River flows into Naknek Lake. Unfortunately, when it was built as a fishing lodge in the 1950s, the camp was placed on top of a valuable archeological site. The archeology is one of the attractions today, but the park service wants to move the camp to a more suitable location in the future. The most comfortable way to stay in the camp is at the **Brooks Lodge,** operated by Katmailand, Inc., with offices at 4700 Aircraft Dr., Anchorage, AK 99502 (☎ **907/243-5448** in Anchorage or 800/544-0551). The lodge has 16 units, with private bathrooms with shower stalls. Rooms are $260 double, $10 per additional person in the room. You have to pay by cash or check in Anchorage before you leave. Three buffet-style meals are served daily for guests and visitors who aren't staying in the lodge. Breakfast is $10; lunch, $12; and dinner, $22. For food, they take plastic at the lodge—American Express, MasterCard, and Visa. There's also a small store at Brooks Camp, the park service visitor center, and the free 18-site campground. The park service issues permits for the campground by lottery in the six-week bear-viewing season. The rangers also require special precautions to keep bears away from campers.

Bears aren't the only animals in Katmai. You're sure to see bald eagles, and birdwatchers can find many unusual species. The Alaska Peninsula is a prime summer habitat for tropical song birds, whose international decline is under serious study here by the U.S. Fish and Wildlife Service. **Earthwatch,** P.O. Box 403, Watertown, MA 02272 (☎ **617/926-8200;** e-mail info@earthwatch.org), has for several years provided funding and volunteers for the work, and provides serious bird enthusiasts the chance to spend two weeks studying birds and contributing to significant scientific work in a wilderness setting. Accommodations for the four-member teams are in a remote lakeside cabin. The trips cost about $1,500, starting from a base in King Salmon.

Backcountry hiking crosses a wilderness without trails and is only for experienced outdoors people. The most popular routes are on the desolate Valley of Ten Thousand Smokes, which provides awesome views but sometimes is swept by blinding sand storms. You'll go crazy without strong mosquito repellent, thick clothes, and a head net. Hikers need a permit from the park service for backcountry travel. There also are several lodges on inholdings along the park's huge lakes, and you can fly in for fishing or kayaking in rarely visited remote areas of the park. The park service has a list of dozens of fishing, hiking, and air guides.

A WILDERNESS LODGE

Koksetna Wilderness Lodge. General Delivery, Port Alsworth, AK 99653 (in winter: 1425 Fifth St., Colusa, CA 95932). ☎ **907/781-2227** in summer, 916/458-7446 in winter. 4 units in 2 cabins, none with bath. $200 double. Additional person in cabin $25 extra. Sun–Fri package $1,500 per person, including all meals and guide service. Closed Oct–May.

This family-operated lodge is on a sandy bay on the edge of Lake Clark, where the Chulitna River runs in, within Lake Clark National Park—north of Katmai, but this is the best place to slot this description that I could think of. The nearest neighbor is 10 miles away. Fishing in the area for salmon and trout is excellent, and guiding, fly-tying, gear, and other details are included. Meals are varied multicourse affairs served with wine and relying on local fish and on-premises greenhouses that provide fresh vegetables. The cabins have toilets, but the showers and bathtubs are in a shared bath house. There's a steam bath, as well.

5 Dutch Harbor/Unalaska: Aleutian Boom Town

After a lifetime of hearing how desolate the Aleutians (uh-LOO-shuns) were, I felt a bit as though I was leaving the edge of the earth the first time I traveled to Unalaska (oon-ah-LAS-ka). Shortly after I arrived, a storm started slinging huge raindrops horizontally through the air so hard that they stung as they splattered on my face. People went on about their business as if nothing special was happening—stormy weather constantly batters these rocks that pop up from the empty North Pacific. My expectations seemed justified.

But the next day the storm cleared like a curtain opening on a rich operatic scene— simultaneously opening the curtain of my dark expectations. Unalaska may lack trees, but it's not a barren rock—the island is covered with heather and wildflowers. Rounded mountains that invite wandering exploration rise from the ocean like the backs of huge beasts. For sightseeing, it has only a few hours of attractions, but for outdoor exploring, birdwatching, and halibut fishing, few places come close.

With the protected port of Dutch Harbor so far out in a ferocious ocean habitat rich in crab and bottomfish, Unalaska has grown in two decades from a tiny, forgotten Native village to the nation's largest fishing port. The pattern of growth followed the form of the early gold rushes. There was a wild, lawless time in the 1970s when crab fishermen got rich quick and partied like Old West cowboys. Then the overfished crab stocks crashed, only to be replaced, starting in the mid-1980s, by an even bigger boom, when waters within 200 miles of the U.S. shore were rid of foreign vessels and American bottomfishing took off. Big factory ships began unloading here and huge fish plants were built on flat ground chipped from the rock. Today that expansion has reached a more steady state, and more women and families are coming to town—another part of the gold-rush pattern. But domestication isn't done yet. It's hard to build on the Aleutians' volcanic bedrock, and housing and public services still lag far behind the boom. Most of the population lives in bunk houses and flies back to Seattle when the processing plants close for the season. Unalaska may be the best current example of the American cultural phenomenon of the settling of the frontier.

Ironically, Unalaska is Alaska's oldest town as well as its newest city. The value of a good port out in the middle of the ocean was recognized from the beginning by the Aleuts. In 1759 the Russians began trading here, and fought a war with the Aleuts from 1763 to 1766, the outcome of which was slavery for the Aleut hunters and the massacre of their people. The Russians built a permanent settlement here in 1792, their first in Alaska. Unalaska also was a key refueling stop for steamers carrying gold-rush Stampeders to Nome a century ago, which brought an epidemic that killed a third of the indigenous population. In 1940 Dutch Harbor—the seaport on Amaknak Island associated with the town and island of Unalaska—was taken over by the U.S. Navy to defend against Japanese attack. That attack came—in June 1942 Japanese planes bombed Unalaska, killing 43. The Aleut people were removed from the islands for the duration of the war and interned in inadequate housing in Southeast Alaska, where many died of disease. The military pulled out in 1947, but the remains of their defenses are interesting to explore. Today, thanks to a 1971 act of Congress settling Native claims, the Aleut-owned Ounalashka Corp. owns most of the island. Despite all the history, however, the old Russian Orthodox church and military ruins are all there is to see.

ESSENTIALS

GETTING THERE   By Air   Several operators fly to Dutch Harbor from Anchorage, including **Alaska Airlines** (☎ **800/426-0333**). You're likely to pay $700 to $850 round-trip. An air/hotel package makes sense and saves money—see the Grand Aleutian Hotel, described under "Where to Stay," below. (If it looks as if your plane is landing in the ocean, it's probably just sneaking up on a runway that wouldn't fit completely on the mountainous island.)

By Ferry   The **Alaska Marine Highway System** ferry *Tustumena* (☎ **800/642-0066**) comes seven times between April and September, leaving Homer Tuesday night and arriving in Unalaska, after stopping in Kodiak and the villages along the way, on Saturday morning. The passenger fare is $242, and an outside cabin, with facilities, is $328. I've never made the trip, but it must be an adventure. Of course, unless you want to spend only three hours early on a Saturday morning in Unalaska and then make the long return trip, you'll need to fly back.

VISITOR INFORMATION   The **Unalaska–Port of Dutch Harbor Convention and Visitors Bureau,** P.O. Box 545, Unalaska, AK 99685 (☎ **907/581-2612**), operates the Henry Swanson Visitor Center, on West Broadway between Second and Third, with information, maps, and gifts. Swanson, a late fox farmer, fisherman, and community leader, lived in the building.

ORIENTATION   The main historic part of the town is a tiny street grid on a narrow peninsula facing Iliuliuk Bay. The **Bridge to the Other Side** (that's the official name) leads to Amaknak Island, the site of the airport, big hotels, and the fishing industrial area of Dutch Harbor. Traveling down the road in the other direction leads a little way up into the mountains, a starting point for walks.

GETTING AROUND   Van taxis are the main way of getting around town for the hoards of fishermen. One company is **Blue Check Taxi** (☎ **907/581-2186**). You can rent a car, truck, or forklift from **North Port Rentals** (☎ **907/581-3880**) or a couple of other companies. The Grand Aleutian Hotel (see "Where to Stay," below) and the city department of Parks, Culture and Recreation (☎ **907/581-1297**) rent bicycles, which, in good weather, are a nice way to get around an island with only a few miles of roads.

   Aleut Tours (☎ **907/581-6001**) offers town tours in the summer, including all the major sights, with a Native guide driving the van. It lasts two to three hours, with pickup wherever you are, and costs $40.

FAST FACTS   The **sales tax** in Unalaska and Dutch Harbor is 3%. Key Bank has a branch near the Alaska Commercial Store, at the UniSea plant in Dutch Harbor, with an **ATM.** In an **emergency,** call 911; in nonemergencies, call the **Unalaska Department of Public Safety,** just above the bridge on the Unalaska side (☎ **907/581-1233**). Iliuliuk Family and Health Services (☎ **907/581-1202**) offers complete clinic services. The *Dutch Harbor Fisherman* is published weekly, and the *Anchorage Daily News* is available at the airport and a few places around town.

EXPLORING UNALASKA TOWNSITE

Unalaska's main sight is the **Holy Ascension Cathedral.** Completed in 1896 on the site of churches that had stood since 1808, the white, onion-domed church contains 697 icons, artifacts, and artworks—a significant collection that has been continuously in use by the Aleut congregation. The congregation was founded by Fr. Ivan Veniaminov, who translated the Gospel into Aleut and has been canonized as St. Innocent. The building was not well maintained and the buffeting of rugged weather and history left it in peril. Today the church is undergoing a $1.3-million restoration that will take a number of years. Early stabilization work in 1995 showed that it was on the verge of collapse from rot. The site and cemetery outside are very picturesque.

   There are several **World War II military ruins** around town, including some that are still in use—like a submarine dry dock that today fixes fishing boats. The activity at the port is interesting to see too, if only for the size of the vessels and harvest and the incredible investment in buildings and equipment.

GETTING OUTSIDE

The attractive thing about Unalaska is that, while it provides remote birdwatching for species you can't see elsewhere, hiking, and ocean fishing, you still can stay in complete comfort in a luxurious hotel. The island is out in the middle of nowhere, but it has an active, big-money economy, and that makes a difference in comfort and convenience for visitors.

You exploit this port far out in the ocean, like the Russian fur traders and factory trawlers, by using it for access to **fishing** and **birdwatching.** Of course, you can also do both at once, with sea lions and other marine mammals thrown in. Several rare bird species nest in the area, and Asian birds occasionally drop in as accidentals. The whiskered auklet and red-legged kittiwake are among the rare birds commonly found around Unalaska, but there also are huge rookeries with many species of birds, and you generally see lots of marine mammals, too. You can fly out for salmon fishing from black sand beaches, but Unalaska has become more famous for having the largest halibut caught in the state. In 1995 a local sport fisherman caught a 395-pound halibut from an 18-foot skiff within a half mile of town; to kill the behemoth he had to beach it and beat it over the head with a rock. A 70-pounder is considered small here.

The island's green heather and rounded mountains of wildflowers are inviting for **hiking.** You can walk pretty much in any direction, looking at the abandoned World War II defenses, or making a goal of a beach or one of the small peaks around the town, or, for the ambitious, even the top of an active volcano, Mount Makushin. There are no bears and not many bugs, but there is great berry picking and beach-combing. The weather can be a threat, however, and fox holes can trip you up; as always in remote outdoors areas, you must be well dressed, know how to take care of yourself, and leave word of where you're going and when you'll be back. Most of the island belongs to the **Ounalashka Corp.,** P.O. Box 149, Unalaska, AK 99645 (☎ 907/581-1276), the Native village corporation. Get a permit to hike, bike, or camp on their land from their office on Captains Bay, near the Grand Aleutian Hotel, open Monday through Friday from 8am to 5pm.

There are several charter and guide operators. The Grand Aleutian Hotel (see "Where to Stay," below) offers packages and halibut and salmon fishing, fly-in fishing and flightseeing, and guided kayaking and mountain biking. **Northwind Charters** (☎ 907/581-4688 or 800/347-4066) offers day-long birdwatching or fishing trips for $150 per person. **Fox Island Charters** (☎ 907/581-1624) and **Far West Outfitters** (☎ 907/581-1647) also do boat trips. For flightseeing and fly-in fishing, and hiking trips to the top of the active volcano of Mount Makushin, try **Volcano Bay Adventures** (☎ 907/581-3414). **Aleutian Airways** (☎ 907/581-1686) and **Peninsula Airways** (☎ 800/448-4226) also offer flight services in the area, including trips to outlying villages.

WHERE TO STAY

There are several other accommodations besides the two I've listed here, both of which belong to the huge UniSea fishing company. A list is available from the visitor center.

✪ **Grand Aleutian Hotel.** 498 Salmon Way (Pouch 503), Dutch Harbor, AK 99692. ☎ **907/581-3844** or 800/891-1194. 100 rms, 6 suites. TV TEL. $150 double. $195 suite. Additional person in room $15 extra. Packages available. AE, DC, DISC, MC, V.

It's almost unreal to arrive in this new, luxurious hotel in a hard-driving Alaska Bush community—the Grand Aleutian is among the best hotels in Alaska, to say nothing

The Aleutians: The Quiet After War

In 1995 the navy deactivated the secret naval base at Adak, in the outer Aleutian Islands, leaving only a few caretakers. Few civilians had ever seen the base, but the Anchorage newspaper carried a story about the dilemma faced by departing families with their pets. The dogs and cats had been handed down from family to family for years as the families rotated in and out; now, with the last families leaving, the animals would have to go, too. The little city that had been built was mothballed, along with the fast-food franchise that served the residents.

The Adak base had been hurriedly built more than 50 years before to fight back a Japanese invasion. With its closing, the book closed on a bizarre and bitter tale with few parallels in American history. The battle for the Aleutians was costly, pointless, and miserable, bringing ruin and disease to the Aleuts and death to thousands of Japanese and American soldiers. What began as a diversion became a ferocious fight for honor with little strategic meaning. When the fighting was done, it turned out that no one even wanted the land enough to stay. With the 50th anniversary of the war, Japanese and American soldiers met on the deserted islands they'd fought for and dedicated a monument. Then they left again—leaving behind the site of death and struggle to the fog, whipping wind, and migrating geese.

The Japanese attacked the islands of Kiska and Attu as the Pacific war was beginning to divert the main core of the American navy away from what became the Battle of Midway. But the Americans had intercepted and decoded Japanese transmissions, and weren't fooled. Meanwhile, the Japanese had sent 24 ships, including two aircraft carriers, on a fool's errand to bomb the new American naval base at Dutch Harbor / Unalaska and occupy islands in the western Aleutians. Those ships could have tipped the balance at Midway, among the most important battles of the war. Instead, the Japanese met stiff antiaircraft fire in two days of bombing at Dutch Harbor, and although 43 Americans were killed, the defensive function of the base was not greatly impaired.

The Japanese then took Kiska and Attu, meeting no resistance from 10 Americans staffing a weather station, or from a small Aleut village whose few inhabitants were all—even the children—sent to a prison camp in Japan to mine clay for the duration of the war. About half the prisoners survived to return to Alaska.

The Americans had their own plan to remove the Aleuts, but the idea of depopulating all the islands had been turned down. Now, with the Japanese attack, it was swiftly put into effect. All the Aleuts were rounded up and put on ships. As they pulled away from their ancestral islands, they could see the glow of huge fires destroying their villages. The U.S. military had torched the villages to deny the modest assets of the islands to the Japanese, should they advance further. With little thought given to their living conditions, the Aleuts were interned in abandoned summer camps and similarly inadequate facilities in Southeast Alaska. Shunned by the local communities and without the basic necessities of life, many died of the cold and disease. The U.S. Fish and Wildlife Service took Aleut hunters to hunt furs as virtual slaves, much as the Russians had done 200 years before.

The Japanese and American military fared not much better on their new real estate. Although the Aleutians quickly became irrelevant to the rest of the war, significant resources were committed to a largely futile air and sea battle in the fog and endless storms. Flying at all was difficult and extremely dangerous, and finding the enemy in the fog over vast distances close to impossible. The Americans couldn't spare a land invasion force at first, and had to rely on bombing Kiska and Attu to punish the Japanese and try to deter a further advance up the chain. To that end, they built the base at Adak, among others, so shorter-range fighter escorts could accompany the bombers. Construction in the spongy tundra was difficult in any case, made more so by the length of supply lines.

The Japanese high command never had any intention of advancing up the chain, but also saw no reason to abandon their new Kiska air base when it was causing the Americans to exert such effort—even if it had no strategic value to either side. The Japanese concentrated on fortifying Kiska, which became a honeycomb of underground bunkers and heavy antiaircraft guns and withstood constant bombing raids from the Americans.

Finally, on May 11, 1943, almost a year after the Japanese took the islands, Americans landed on Attu and a brutal 18-day battle for the rugged island began. The Japanese were massively outnumbered but heavily dug in. Finally, with only 800 soldiers left from an original force of 2,600, the Japanese mounted a banzai attack. Only 28 were taken prisoner—the rest were killed in battle or committed suicide. The Americans lost 549 killed, 1,148 wounded, and 2,132 injured by severe cold, disease, accident, mental breakdown, or other causes. In the end, it was the second most costly island battle in the Pacific, after Iwo Jima.

The battle for Kiska was less dramatic. The Japanese withdrew under cover of fog. After a massive bombardment of the empty island and the rallying of heavy reinforcements, the Americans landed to find that no one was there. Still, 105 American soldiers died in the landing in accidents and fire from their own forces.

After the Aleutian battle was over, American forces in Alaska declined drastically, but never went away altogether. Before the war, the absurd little Fort William Seward, in Haines, had been the totality of Alaska's defenses, with a couple of hundred men armed with Springfield rifles and no reliable means of transportation. Afterward there were large bases in several areas of the state. Military spending became the biggest economic boom the territory had ever seen, connecting it by a new road to the Lower 48 and bringing precious year-round jobs. A new wave of postwar settlers, many former GIs looking for a new, open field of opportunity, brought a population boom. The advent of the Cold War, and Alaska's prime strategic location in defense against the Soviet Union, brought ever-greater increases in military spending in Alaska. To this day the military is one of the largest sectors of the Alaska economy, and the state has been relatively unscathed in base closures except for remote outposts like Adak.

The end of the war was more bitter for the Aleuts. Everything they had in their villages had been destroyed. Many who had survived the terrible period of internment never returned to the islands where their villages had once stood, and some of the villages never revived. "When I came back to Atka after World War II, my buddy said, 'Why are you going back to the Aleutians? They say even the sea gulls are leaving there,'" Dan Prokopeuff is quoted as saying in *Alaska Geographic*'s book on Native people. "I told him I was going because it's peaceful and quiet."

Today Atka is the westernmost village remaining in the Aleutians. On Kiska there are only ruins of the Japanese fortifications; and on Adak, only a few caretakers.

of the Bush. For the same room in Anchorage, you'd pay considerably more. They have a courtesy van and bike rentals, the rooms are well designed and comfortable, the lobby grand, with a huge stone fireplace, and there's a piano bar. As you walk outside into a driving gale, it's like teleporting from a midtown Manhattan hotel back to an exposed rock out in the North Pacific. This may be why some call the hotel the "Grand Illusion," but I suspect they're alluding more to its economic viability, not its facilities. The ✪ **Chart Room** restaurant is first-rate, with sophisticated treatments of local seafood in the $20 to $30 range. The **Margaret Bay Cafe** is nice too, if pricey.

The Japanese-owned UniSea fish-processing company that built the hotel has developed a full scope of tour packages to keep it open, and booking one of those packages, including airfare, should save money over traveling independently. A basic two-night package starts at $711 per person, double occupancy—you could spend that just for your plane fare, if you're not careful. Birding packages range up to $1,227 per person, for four nights and two boat trips. They also have guided salmon and halibut fishing, hiking, mountain biking, and flightseeing.

UniSea Inn. At the small-boat harbor (Pouch 503) Dutch Harbor, AK 99692. ☎ **907/581-3844.** 44 rms. TV TEL. $115 double. Additional person in room $15 extra. AE, DC, DISC, MC, V.

Overlooking the harbor, in the midst of the surging UniSea processing operation, the UniSea Inn is a less expensive alternative to the Grand Aleutian. More fishermen stay there than tourists, but it's adequate if you just want a room. The sports bar in the same building could be noisy, so try to get a room that's not next to it. They have a courtesy van and bike rental.

WHERE TO EAT

The best restaurants in town are at the Grand Aleutian, but you can also find a meal at the **Ballyhoo Cafe,** at the airport, with standard American fare. At the Intersea Mall you have a choice of Italian or Greek at the **Dutch Harbor Cafe;** Japanese, including sushi, at the **Peking Restaurant;** or various Asian cuisines at **Linh's Cafe.** In Unalaska proper, you'll find Mexican food at **Paco's,** or Japanese, with sushi, and Mexican at **Stormy's.**

A SIDE TRIP TO THE PRIBILOFS

The Pribilof Islands of St. Paul and St. George sit out in the middle of the Bering Sea, due north of Unalaska, teeming with marine mammals and sea birds. Some 600,000 fur seals meet at the breeding rookeries in the summer, and two million birds of more than 200 species use the rocks. Birdwatchers go for one of the most exotic and productive wildlife-viewing opportunities in Alaska. **Reeve Aleutian Airways** (☎ **800/544-2248**) arranges packages to St. Paul ranging from $799 to $1,549. The accommodations are rustic.

6 Nome: Arctic Frontier Town

The accidents of history deposited the streets and buildings of this lusty little town on the shore of Norton Sound, just south of the Arctic Circle in Northwest Alaska, and gave it qualities that make Nome an exceptionally attractive place for a visitor to go. For once, the local boosters' motto—in this case, THERE'S NO PLACE LIKE NOME—is entirely accurate. For Nome, although itself nothing special to look at, combines a sense of history, a hospitable, somewhat silly attitude, and an exceptional location on the water in front of a tundra wilderness that's crossed by 250 miles of road. Those roads are the truly unique thing, for Nome is the only place in Arctic Alaska where a visitor can drive or bike deep into the open country, coming across musk ox, reindeer, rare birds, Native villages, undeveloped hot springs, and even an abandoned 1881 elevated train from New York City. Elsewhere, you're obliged to fly from rural hubs to get so far into the Bush, a more expensive and ambitious undertaking for casual explorers.

The accidents of history have been rather frequent in Nome—history has been downright sloppy. Start with the name. It's essentially a clerical error, caused by a British naval officer who, in 1850, was presumably in a creative dry spell when he wrote "? Name" on a diagram rather than name the cape he was sailing past. A mapmaker interpreted that as "Cape Nome." The original gold rush of 1898 was caused by prospectors in the usual way, but a much larger 1899 population explosion happened after one of the '98 Stampeders, left behind by an injury in a camp on the beach, panned the sand outside the tent—and found that it was full of gold dust. By 1900, a fourth of Alaska's white population was in Nome, sifting the sand. Small-time operators and tourists are still at it, and major gold mining rumbles on just outside town. A floating gold dredge of the kind that makes major historic sites in Fairbanks and Dawson City sits idle on the edge of town. In Nome, it stopped operation only a couple of years ago. Historic structures are few, however, as fires and storms have destroyed the town several times since the gold rush.

Nome has a particular, broad sense of humor. It shows up in the *Nome Nugget* newspaper and in silly traditions like the Labor Day bathtub race, pack ice golf tournament, and the Memorial Day polar bear swim. The population is half white and half Native, and the town is run largely by the white group. Some see Nome as a tolerant mixing place of different peoples, while the town strikes others as a bit colonial. Booze, outlawed in Kotzebue, the Native-dominated city to the north, creates a gold-rush–style saloon culture in Nome where alcohol abuse is a way of life. Front Street is one big party some nights.

But you can ignore that, instead taking advantage of the great bargains to be had on Inupiat art and crafts. And, most important, you can use one of the pleasant little inns or bed-and-breakfasts as a base to get into the countryside that beckons, down one of the gravel roads. Birdwatchers find the roads especially useful, and Nome is popular with birders.

ESSENTIALS

GETTING THERE   You can get to Nome only by air, and there's only one major carrier that flies there, **Alaska Airlines** (☎ **800/426-0333**), with a 90-minute jet flight either direct from Anchorage or with a brief hop from Kotzebue. The fare from Anchorage is likely to be in the range of $380 to $580, round-trip. Many visitors come on a package sold by **Alaska Airlines Vacations** (☎ **800/468-2248**), which visits Kotzebue then comes to Nome. But there's no need to be on a package in Nome.

VISITOR INFORMATION   The **Nome Convention and Visitors Bureau,** at Front and Hunter streets (P.O. Box 240), Nome, AK 99762 (☎ **907/443-5535**), is exceptionally well run, providing maps and detailed information for diverse interests, and screening videos for those interested. It's open mid-May to mid-September, daily from 9am to 9pm, to 6:30pm the rest of the year.

ORIENTATION   The town is an unpaved grid along the ocean. **Front Street** follows the sea wall, **First Avenue** is a block back, and so on. A harbor is at the north end of town and the gold-bearing beach is to the south. The airport is east of town. Three roads branch out from Nome. I've described them below, under "Getting Outside."

GETTING AROUND   Within the grid of town streets, you can walk most places. But you need a taxi, such as one from **Nome Cab** (☎ **907/443-3030**), to get in from the airport. All taxis operate according to a standard price schedule you can get from the visitor center; a ride to town from the airport is $5. To get out on the roads, you need a tour or to rent a car. Four car-rental agencies operate in town; the visitor center maintains a list, with rates. **Budget Rent-A-Car** (☎ **907/443-5598**) charges $65 a day for a compact car and $125 for a camper; **Stampede Rent-A-Car** (☎ **907/ 443-3838**) charges $55 for a Ford Escort or $75 for a van.

Two companies offer organized tours. ✪ **Nome Custom Adventures,** operating out of the Arctic Trading Post gift store at Front and Hunter streets (☎ **907/ 443-5134**), has the asset of a talented professional actor as the van driver and tour guide, Richard Beneville. He'll drive you anywhere in the area and share his quirky enthusiasm and extensive knowledge of the surroundings. Prices depend on how far you go. **Nome Tour and Marketing,** at the Nugget Inn, at Front and Bering streets (☎ **907/443-2651**), is a more traditional tour, with a dog-sled demonstration and gold panning, lasting 3$\frac{1}{2}$ hours. It goes twice a day, with times depending on flights into town, and costs $25 per person. The tour runs in summer only.

FAST FACTS   The **sales tax** is 4%. The **post office** and National Bank of Alaska have branches at Front Street and Federal Way. The bank has an **ATM.** In **emergencies,** dial 911; for nonemergency business with the **police,** call 907/443-5262. The **Norton Sound Regional Hospital** is at Fifth Avenue and Bering Street (☎ **907/443-3311**). The *Nome Nugget* is published weekly; the *Anchorage Daily News* is available at the airport.

SPECIAL EVENTS   The **Gold Rush Classic Snowmachine Race** (☎ **907/ 443-2155**), in mid-February, covers the Iditarod Trail—twice. Nome is the halfway point. The biggest event of the year is the ✪ **Iditarod Trail Sled Dog Race** (☎ **907/ 376-5155**), a marathon of more than 1,000 miles that ends in Nome in mid- to late March. The sled-dog racers and world media descend on the town for a few days of a mad party. Other dog-sled races continue into April. The **Bering Sea Ice Golf Classic** (☎ **907/443-5278**), in mid-March, showcases Nome's well-developed sense of humor—six holes are set up on the sea ice. The pressure ridges constitute a bad lie. Various similar silly events take place all year—you can get a list from the visitor center. For example, the **Polar Bear Swim** occurs in the Bering Sea on Memorial Day, ice permitting. The **Midnight Sun Festival** (☎ **907/443-5535**) celebrates the June 21 summer solstice, when Nome gets more than 22 hours of direct sunlight, with a parade, beauty pageant, and similar events.

EXPLORING NOME
WHAT TO SEE & DO IN TOWN

Most of Nome's original buildings were wiped out by fires or by storms off Norton Sound that tore across the beach and washed away major portions of the business district. A sea wall, completed in 1951, now protects the town. An interesting **Historical Walking Tour,** produced by the Alaska Historical Commission, is available from the visitor center; it takes less than an hour. Below the library, at Front Street and Lanes Way, the small **Carrie M. McLaine Memorial Museum** exhibits items found on the beach and some Native artifacts. Of greatest interest are copies of the *Nome Nugget* dating from the gold rush—the price, 50¢, is still the same today, indicating just how inflated the economy was in 1899. The museum is free and open in summer, Tuesday through Saturday from 11am to 4pm, only sporadically in winter.

In good weather—not the rule in Nome—a pleasant walk is to be had southeast of town, along the **beach.** Small-time miners are camped there, but the gold-bearing sand extends for miles more that you'll have to yourself on a walk. You can buy a gold pan in town and try your luck, but the sand has been sifted for nearly 100 years so don't expect to gather any significant amount of gold. On the other side of town, there's an impressive abandoned gold dredge of the kind that crept across the tundra, creating its own pond to float in as it went. It operated until quite recently. The **cemetery,** with white, wooden crosses on top of a little hill just out of town, also is worth a look.

SHOPPING

If you're in the market for walrus ivory carvings and other Inupiat art and crafts, you'll find low prices and an extraordinary selection in Nome. Jim West trades money for drinks for Native art from visiting villagers at his shop at the historic **Board of Trade Saloon** on Front Street, and consequently he has a legendary collection. The **Arctic Trading Post,** also on Front Street, is more of a traditional gift shop, and also has a good ivory collection. **Maruskiya's of Nome** wholesales walrus ivory. **Chukotka-Alaska, Inc.,** on West First Avenue, is an importer of art and other goods from the Russian Far East, and is really worth a look.

GETTING OUTSIDE

ON THE ROADS   The modest attractions downtown would hardly justify a trip to Nome, but the city's surroundings do. The roads provide unique access to a large stretch of the Seward Peninsula, and unlike other Arctic Bush areas, where you need to have someone take you where you want to go, all you have to do in Nome is rent a car or a camper and take off. You can bring a **mountain bike** from Anchorage too, for one of the best, most remote rides you'll ever have. No bikes are for rent in Nome, but **Bering C Bikes** (☎ 907/443-4994) repairs them and provides van support, with camping gear for bike tours—it's the same family that runs Inua Expeditions (see "On the Water," below). The **Alaska Department of Transporation** (☎ 907/443-3444) can provide current information on road conditions. You have a good chance to see moose, reindeer, owls, foxes, bears, and musk ox anywhere you drive, but check in with the visitor center or the **Alaska Department of Fish and Game,** at Front and Steadman streets, for where you're most likely to see animals. They can also give you guidance on fishing along the roads, and a Nome Roadside Fishing Guide.

Birdwatchers will find a paradise out on the roads. A bird list is available at the visitor center and they can tell you where to look—each of the three roads has a different habitat. The best times to visit for birding are right around Memorial Day, and from July to mid-August. Lana and Richard Harris were Nome's leading birders when I last visited, and the only local members of the American Birding Association. They maintain a birders' hot line on their home phone recorder (☎ 907/443-5528) and don't mind talking with visiting birdwatchers. There's a chance to see Siberian birds, and you can count on bluethroats, yellow wagtails, wheatears, Arctic warblers, and Aleutian and Arctic terns. Nome is the only place to see a bristle-thighed curlew without chartering a plane. You don't need a guide, although guided trips are available (see "Small and Specialty Tours" under "Package Tour or Do-It-Yourself?" in Chapter 3). As Lana put it, "If you haven't found a yellow wagtail, you haven't left the bar yet."

The only way to get a vehicle to Nome is to ship it in on a barge during the few ice-free months, and there aren't many people for all that land, so if you rent a car you'll have a huge expanse of spectacular territory to yourself, with wildlife-viewing opportunities as good as anywhere in the state. Or if you don't want to drive yourself, you can go with a driver who knows the area. Riding with Richard Beneville's Nome Custom Adventures (see "Getting Around" under "Essentials," above) just a few miles out of town, I had the unreal experience of seeing a musk ox wander out of the bushes and across the road in front of us—it's truly an animal that belongs only in an improbable science-fiction movie, yet there it was. Beneville knew where the wildlife was likely to be found, and knew the history and natural history of the area.

None of the three roads radiating from Nome has services of any kind—just small Native villages and a few dwellings, and some reindeer herders—so you must be prepared and bring what you need with you, including insect repellent. The visitor center provides a good road guide. Here are some highlights:

The **Nome–Council road** heads 72 miles to the east, about half of that on the shoreline. It turns inland at the ghost town of Solomon, an old mining town with an abandoned railroad train, known as the Last Train to Nowhere. The engines were originally used on the New York City elevated trains in 1881, then were shipped to Nome in 1903 to serve the miners along this line to Nome. This is a great scenic spot for birdwatching, and fishing is good in the Solomon River, all along the road. Council, near the end of the road, has a couple of dozen families in the summer; you have to get a boat ride across a river just short of the village.

The **Nome–Taylor road,** also known as the Kougarok road, runs north of town into the Kigluaik Mountains, 85 miles from Nome, petering out and becoming impassable. Lovely Salmon Lake, with a campground, is 38 miles out. A few miles farther, a road to the left leads to the Pilgrim Hot Springs, near the ruins of a Catholic church and orphanage. The two hot tubs are 100° to 125°F. Check with the visitor center before going, as the hot springs are privately owned and the open invitation may have changed since this writing.

The **Nome–Teller road** leads 73 miles to the village of Teller, which has about 200 residents, a gift shop, and a store. It's an opportunity to see an authentic Arctic Native village.

ON THE WATER   The **Inua Expedition Company of Nome**, reached in winter at P.O. Box 65, Brevig Mission, AK 99785 (☎ **907/443-4994** in summer, 907/ 642-4161 in winter), is the summer job of Keith and Annie Olanna Conger, who in the winter teach school in the tiny village of Brevig Mission. Keith, a biologist, leads the kayaking tours and teaches about the ecology of the land they paddle through. His $75 trips float down the Snake and Nome rivers for half a day; long, full-day trips float down the beautiful Pilgrim River to the Hot Springs, then drive back to town after a soak, for $150. They also do trips of up to eight days.

IN THE AIR   Nome is a hub for a bunch of Bush plane operators. It's a great place to get out and see some of the world's most remote areas from the air. Flightseeing charters are available, or you can just fly one of the mail-run routes out to the villages, spending a couple of hours touring for only $120. You can also fly 150 miles over to Russia, over the route where the first Americans arrived, up to 30,000 years ago. Jim Rowe, of **Bering Air,** P.O. Box 1650, Nome, AK 99762 (☎ **907/443-5464**), pioneered the service, and was a key figure, beginning in 1988, in the melting of the "Ice Curtain" that had separated Native families across the Bering Strait during the decades of the Cold War. Besides flightseeing and village flights, Rowe offers two- and three-day packages to Siberia, including a stay with a Russian family, evening plays and dances and swimming, and an intense cultural experience that builds long-term cross-border friendships. "Coming to Nome, for a lot of people is a culture shock—and that's a baby step compared to this trip," Rowe says. "You're basically going back to the 1940s."

Bering Air and the other air-taxis in town can also take you to **Saint Lawrence Island,** an even better birdwatching destination than Nome, with many Siberian birds, and one of the best-preserved communities of Eskimo culture to be found anywhere. People still live on whale meat hunted from walrus-skin boats. The village of Savoonga has a six-room lodge, with stoves and a refrigerator for food. This is very remote—don't expect many tourist services. For information on arranging a visit, contact Paul Rookok, president of the Saint Lawrence Economic Development Corp., P.O. Box 169, Savoonga, AK 99769 (☎ **907/984-6614**).

Nome's **Olson Air** (☎ **907/443-2229**) can fly you into the least-visited unit in the U.S. national park system, the 2.7-million-acre **Bering Land Bridge National Preserve,** which covers much of the Seward Peninsula north of the Nome road system. The **park headquarters,** on Front and Steadman streets (P.O. Box 220), Nome, AK 99762 (☎ **907/443-2522**), is a good stop for outdoors information— I don't think the rangers have much to do. The only attraction in the preserve is the Serpentine Hot Springs, which has spiritual significance to the Inupiat and is the site of traditional healing in the winter. In the summer, the bunk and bath houses are virtually never used, despite the dramatic surroundings of towering granite tors. It's so undiscovered, no permit or reservation is needed.

WHERE TO STAY

The **bed tax** in Nome totals 8%. There are two main hotels in town, neither of which is particularly good. I've described the adequate Nugget Inn below. I cannot recommend the Polaris Hotel at all. You'll do much better at any of the other establishments listed. Apartments are for rent by the day in various buildings, as well. Check with the visitor center.

Betty's Igloo Bed and Breakfast. First Ave. and K St. (P.O. Box 1784), Nome, AK 99762. ☎ **907/443-2419.** 3 rms, none with bath. $70 double. Rates include breakfast and tax. No credit cards.

The B&B is the lower half of a modern duplex, looking out on Norton Sound on the east end of town. The hostess puts out a self-service breakfast. It's a decent room with minimal interaction with the family upstairs.

June's Bed and Breakfast. 231 E. Fourth Ave. (P.O. Box 489), Nome, AK 99762. ☎ **907/ 443-5984.** 3 rms, none with bath. $65 double. Rates include breakfast and airport pickup. No credit cards.

June Wardle runs this traditional little B&B, proudly declaring, "I really am a gold digger's daughter." Her sourdough pancake starter came over the Chilkoot Trail in '98. The rooms are cozy, not commodious, but June's gregarious hospitality makes it special.

Nugget Inn. Front and Bering sts. (P.O. Box 430), Nome, AK 99762. ☎ **907/443-2323.** Fax 907/443-5966. 47 rms. TV TEL. $92 double. AE, MC, V.

This is the main tourist hotel in town, where those on packages stay. It tries for a gold-rush feel, but the rooms are small and dark and needed new carpeting when I visited. You can do better for less.

✪ Ponderosa Inn. Third Ave. and Spokane St. (P.O. Box 125), Nome, AK 99762. ☎ **907/ 443-5737.** Fax 907/443-3542. 10 rms, 1 suite. TV TEL. $75–$95 double; $120 suite. Additional person in room $15 extra. AE, CB, DC, MC, V.

Hidden in a pair of houses a few blocks back from the main drag, this inn has the best hotel rooms in town—those in the new section are light and spacious, and all have coffeemakers and refrigerators. The more expensive rooms have kitchens, and the suite is a large, two-bedroom apartment. Some rooms have only shower stalls, not tubs. There's a coin-op laundry, free coffee, and shared kitchen facilities. Book ahead, as experienced business travelers keep it full year round.

✪ **Trails End.** 49 E. First Ave. (P.O. Box 1834), Nome, AK 99762. ☎ and fax **907/443-5746,** or 800/443-4043 in Alaska. 3 rms (or 2 apartments). TV TEL. $75–$100 double. Additional person in room $25 extra. MC, V.

Dave McDowell will pick you up at the airport and drive you up Anvil Mountain for a great view, then leave you in the beautifully remodeled apartments, which are stocked with soft drinks and some food in the full kitchen. The upstairs one-bedroom apartment is $100; downstairs, you can rent one of the rooms of the two-bedroom unit for $75, or the whole thing for $130.

WHERE TO EAT

There's not a selection of great places to dine, but you can find an adequate family meal at various establishments along Front Street. The **Polar Cub Restaurant** and **Fast Freddies Restaurant** are basic, smoky, burger-and-fries diners overlooking the water. The **Twin Dragon** has good, reasonably priced Chinese food. The Korean family that owns it also owns **Nachos Restaurant,** an American-style Mexican place that I've been told is good. There are two Italian restaurants, **Pizza Napoli** and **Milano's Pizzeria,** serving about what you'd expect for a small-town family pizzeria.

Fort Davis Roadhouse, on the beach about a mile east of town (☎ 907/443-2660), is more of an experience. With views across the tundra and water, the large dining room with white tablecloths is quite pleasant. The menu is mainly beef and fried fish, but most people get the buffet—prime rib for $17 on Friday or seafood for $20 on Saturday. Service is attentive. Unfortunately, it's open only on Friday and Saturday evenings.

7 Kotzebue: Big Village

Although its 4,000 residents make Kotzebue (KOTZ-eh-biew) a good-sized town, with a bank, a hospital, and a couple of grocery stores, people call it a village instead. A village, in Alaskan parlance, is a remote Native settlement in the Bush, generally with fewer than a few hundred residents, where people live relatively close to the traditional lifestyle of their indigenous ancestors. Kotzebue is a support hub for the villages of the Northwest Arctic, with jet service and a booming cash economy, but it's populated and run by the Inupiat, fish-drying racks and old dog sleds are scattered along the streets, and Native culture is thriving. It does feel like a village.

For visitors, this characteristic makes Kotzebue unique, because you can see real Native Alaska—Eskimo culture—without leaving the comforts of Western society behind. Or if you don't mind giving up some of those comforts, you can get even closer to the Inupiat way of life. For adventurous outdoors people, Kotzebue offers access to huge areas of remote public land through which you can float on a raft or canoe.

It's important to realize from the outset, however, that outside of organized activities for tourists, there's nothing to do in Kotzebue. As I was told, "You have to shoot something or burn a lot of gas to have any fun around here." Kotzebue is not set up for independent travelers except those of the most intrepid ilk, and they will most likely use the town as a way to get into the remote public lands. Nome has more for the independent traveler interested in something in between an organized tour and a wilderness experience—there's more to do, a variety of lodgings, and the outdoors is less expensive to get to. But Nome is a white-run frontier town, not a village, and, unlike Kotzebue, it has bars and liquor stores, so it's noisier and there's a constant display of public drunkenness.

The sale of alcohol is illegal in Kotzebue, by local choice, and the dominant business in town is the NANA Corp., a regional Native corporation representing the roughly 7,000 Inupiat who live in a Northwest Arctic region the size of Indiana. NANA, which stands for Northwest Arctic Native Association, has successful operations in institutional catering and oil drilling, and is half owner of the Red Dog zinc mine that employs its members and supplies much of the world's supply of the mineral. It also owns the main hotel and tourist businesses in Kotzebue.

ESSENTIALS

GETTING THERE   The only way there is by air, and it's not cheap. Alaska Airlines (☎ 800/426-0333) has several daily jets from Anchorage and Fairbanks in the summer. You'll pay in the range of $380 to $580 from Anchorage. They also fly from Kotzebue to Nome. Once in Kotzebue, there are many air-taxis and commuter lines to the outlying villages (more on that below.) The cheapest and most convenient way to go to Kotzebue is to take a package offered by **Tour Arctic** and **Alaska Airlines Vacations** (☎ 800/468-2248), described under "Exploring Kotzebue," below.

VISITOR INFORMATION   The National Park Service staffs the **Kotzebue Public Lands Information Center** at Second Avenue and Lake Street (P.O. Box 1029), Kotzebue, AK 99752 (☎ 907/442-3890 or 907/442-3760; fax 907/442-8316). Since there is no town visitor center, the public lands center keeps information on local businesses, too. It's open May 21 to September 18, daily from 8am to 5pm, only sporadically the rest of the year; but the local headquarters of the park service, Fish and Wildlife Service, and Bureau of Land Management are open during normal business hours all year.

ORIENTATION   Kotzebue is 26 miles north of the Arctic Circle on the Chukchi Sea. The town, about a mile by 2 miles in size, sits on a low spit of land extending into the shallow Kotzebue Sound. The gravel streets are on a warped grid radiating from **Shore Avenue,** also known as **Front Street,** which runs along the water. Roads extend only a few miles out of town.

GETTING AROUND   You can walk pretty much everywhere you need to go. The main hotel is a 10-minute walk from the airport, but there are taxis available from **Polar Cab** (☎ 907/442-2233) and **Cab Company** (☎ 907/442-3555). If you're on the Tour Arctic package, buses will pick you up at the plane and deliver you and your luggage wherever you go.

FAST FACTS   The sale of **alcohol** is illegal in Kotzebue, but possession for personal use is permitted. At this writing, the community was considering going completely dry. Kotzebue has a National Bank of Alaska branch with an **ATM** at the corner of Lagoon Street and Second Avenue. The **post office** is at Shore Avenue and Tundra Way. In **emergencies,** dial 911. For nonemergencies, contact the **Kotzebue Police Department** (☎ 907/442-3351) or the **Alaska State Troopers** (☎ 907/442-3222). A large new **hospital** with a 24-hour emergency room is located at Fifth Avenue and Mission Street (☎ 907/442-3321).

SPECIAL EVENTS   The **Fourth of July** is something special in Kotzebue. Besides the Independence Day celebration, it's as early as you can count on all the snow being gone.

EXPLORING KOTZEBUE

There is only one activity in town, and it's part of an organized tour. **Tour Arctic** hosts around 10,000 visitors annually in its cultural and natural-history program, the centerpiece of which is the ✪ **NANA Museum of the Arctic.** For most people, the packages, sold through **Alaska Airlines Vacations** (☎ **800/468-2248**), are the best deal and the best way to get to the Arctic and learn about Native culture. The tour, owned and operated by Inupiats, teaches a lot about their culture and relationship with the land in five hours while keeping customers comfortable and insulated from the harshness of the Arctic. A show at the museum includes children dancing, a blanket toss, and a serious but high-tech slide show about the struggle to save Inupiat culture. The tour also includes a talk and demonstration in a tent about the clothing and survival techniques of the Eskimos. There's also a brief opportunity to walk on the tundra. Independent travelers in town for outdoor activities can attend the hour-long museum program only for $20; shows are timed to match the arrival of flights, at 3 and 6pm.

Day-trip packages are $332 from Anchorage—less than a full-fare ticket. The same tour with a night at NANA's Nullagvik Hotel is $447, based on double occupancy. A two-night trip that includes a tour of Nome is $495. Adding an excursion to the village of Kiana and a lengthy flightseeing trip over the Northwest Arctic region requires another night and an additional $255.

GETTING OUTSIDE

NEAR KOTZEBUE   Some rugged and curious travelers may want something a bit less pampered and scripted than the Tour Arctic program. **Arctic Circle Educational Adventures,** P.O. Box 814, Kotzebue, AK 99752 (in winter: 200 W. 34th Ave., Suite 903, Anchorage, AK 99503) (☎ **907/442-3509** in summer, 907/276-0976 in winter; fax 907/274-3738 in winter), offers a chance to stay at a fish camp similar to where Native people spend the summer gathering food for the winter—and participate in setnet fishing, fish cutting, food gathering, and other traditional subsistence activities, as well as hiking, town tours, and birdwatching. The camp is extremely rustic, only for people who don't mind using an outhouse or sleeping in a plywood shack, but presents an exceptional opportunity to briefly live as an Eskimo. Rates, including three meals a day, are $245 per person, but there's a discount for using your own tent. The season is mid-June to late August.

You can get an idea of what Native villages look like and see the **Kobuk Valley National Park,** including the Great Kobuk Sand Dunes, a desertlike area of shifting 100-foot dunes, from the air by buying a round-trip seat on one of the scheduled bush planes that serve the area. **Cape Smythe Air** (☎ **907/442-3020**) charges $152 for its loop that includes Shungnak and Kobuk and overflies the dunes (make sure to tell the pilot what you want to see). For $88 you can fly a shorter, northern loop to Noatak and Kivilina, over the **Cape Krusenstern National Monument.**

INTO THE BUSH   The Noatak River, originating in the Brooks Range in the Gates of the Arctic National Park and passing through the Noatak National Preserve, is becoming an ever-more-popular float trip. Although it crosses a stretch of the remote Arctic, it's calm, Class I water, the scenery is unique, and the camping spots are plentiful. You should, however, be experienced in the outdoors before heading out for a multiday trip in the Arctic and plan ahead, arranging details with the park service and your pilot before leaving Anchorage. Most visitors bring all their gear from Anchorage, as it has been virtually unavailable in Kotzebue, but recently Buck Maxxon, of **Arctic Air Guides Flying Service,** P.O. Box 94, Kotzebue, AK 99752 (☎ 907/442-3030), began renting rafts and canoes for $25 a day. An experienced bush pilot, he also will fly you out; how much you pay depends on where you put in your boats, but charter rates are typically $250 an hour, and you could need up to three hours of flying time, should you choose a long trip. You can take out the boats in Noatak and fly scheduled service, such as Cape Smythe Air (see "Near Kotzebue," above), back to Kotzebue for $55 per person. The public land information center also can provide you with a list of guides from Fairbanks or Anchorage who will take you down the river, for considerably more expense.

Lorry and Nellie Schuerch, of the village of Kiana, will take you up the Kobuk River in an enclosed, high-powered jet boat. You can visit the dunes, you'll likely see a lot of birds and wildlife, and you may be able to visit archeological sites. Their **Kobuk River Jets,** P.O. Box 89, Kiana, AK 99749 (☎ 907/475-2149), also offers fishing charters for sheefish and other species, and they'll put you up and feed you at their four-bedroom bed-and-breakfast, which has modern bathrooms.

WHERE TO STAY

Bayside Inn and Restaurant. 303 Shore Ave. (P.O. Box 870), Kotzebue, AK 99752. ☎ 907/442-3600. 12 rms. TV TEL. High season, $95 double. Low season, $80. AE, MC, V.

If you want to save $40 on your room over the Nullagvik, two doors down, these unadorned, white-walled rooms with shower stalls in the bathrooms likely will suffice. They have a coin-op laundry. The restaurant downstairs is popular with locals and a little cheaper than the other hotel restaurant, but also not as good.

Nullagvik Hotel. Shore Ave. and Tundra Way (P.O. Box 336), Kotzebue, AK 99752. ☎ 907/442-3331. Fax 907/442-3340. 78 rms. TV TEL. $135 double. Additional person in room $10 extra. AE, DC, MC, V.

The NANA-owned hotel is downright luxurious, considering it's in the Bush, where accommodations usually range from odd to uncomfortable. The rooms are large and up-to-date, have tables and chairs and two queen-size beds, and are cleverly designed so that all get at least some ocean view. It can be startling to see Eskimo women in parkys cleaning in the halls. There's a gift shop and a travel agency in the lobby.

The **restaurant** is clean and nicely decorated, and has a good view and excellent service—a combination found nowhere else in Kotzebue. Reindeer steak and Arctic salmon are on the menu for the tourists, although locals are more likely to order the less expensive sandwiches and beef.

WHERE TO EAT

Other than the two hotel restaurants described above, the only place I'd recommend is **Mario's Pizza and Deli,** 606 Bison St. (☎ 907/442-2666). I was told that the sushi was good in this Japanese-Chinese-Italian take-out place, but I couldn't believe that was possible, in Kotzebue, in this grubby little dining room, so I ordered barbecued pork instead. After a really excellent, spicy meal, I could only dream of how good the sushi might have been. The price range is $5.25 to $12, and they don't take credit or charge cards.

8　Barrow: Way North

The main reason visitors go to Barrow is its latitude. The Inupiat town is the northernmost settlement on the North American continent, above the 71st parallel. Here half-liquid land comes to an arbitrary point at the tip at the north of Alaska. The tundra around Barrow is dotted with lakes divided by tendrils of swampy tundra no more substantial than the edges of fine lace. On this haven for migratory waterfowl, the flat, wet land and the ocean seem to merge. Indeed, for all but a few months it's all a flat, frozen plain, ocean and land. For more than two months in the winter the sun never rises. In the summer it doesn't set, and the ice only recedes from the shore for a matter of weeks. Such extreme geography is a strong attractor—people want to stand in such a place, perhaps dip a toe in the Arctic Ocean.

And then what do you do next? If you're on a package trip, you can see an Eskimo blanket toss and other cultural presentations. Perhaps you'll have time to wander around and look at the drying skins on racks and other manifestations of traditional Inupiat life amid a modern, oil-enriched town. There are mounds where ancient Eskimo houses stood, the site of valuable archeological digs. Then you can get back on the plane and return to Fairbanks or Anchorage, for there isn't much else to do in Barrow.

The village of 3,000 is culturally unique. It's ancient, and still a center of whaling from open boats and a spring festival celebrating a successful hunt and distribution of the meat to the community. But Barrow also is the seat of the North Slope Borough, a county government encompassing a larger area than the state of Nebraska, in which lies North America's largest oilfield. The borough has everything money can buy for a local government, yet the people of the villages still must contend with crushing ice, snooping polar bears, and utter isolation.

Part of the effort to combine the town's two cultures was a vote in 1994 to completely outlaw alcohol—Barrow previously had allowed possession but not sale. Although social problems, such as domestic violence and crime, virtually disappeared in comparison to before the vote and the jail emptied, another close election in 1995 reopened Barrow to sale of booze. The anti-alcohol forces promised a quick vote to go dry again, but at this writing, alcohol was legal.

ESSENTIALS

GETTING THERE　　**Alaska Airlines** (☎ 800/426-0333) flies to Barrow daily from Anchorage and Fairbanks, and offers one-day and overnight tour packages. The packages are a good deal, competitive with round-trip tickets alone from Anchorage in the area of $550 to $650. Book them through **Alaska Airlines Vacations** (☎ 800/468-2248).

VISITOR INFORMATION　　A chamber of commerce **visitor center** near the airport operates in the summer only. The **Barrow Convention and Visitors Bureau,** P.O. Box 1060, Barrow, AK 99723 (☎ 907/852-TOUR), distributes a walking-tour map of Barrow. The **North Slope Borough Public Information Division,** P.O. Box 69, Barrow, AK 99723 (☎ 907/852-0215), produces a listing of tourism-related businesses in the area.

ORIENTATION　　Facing on the Chukchi Sea, Barrow has two sections, lying on each side of Isatkoak Lagoon. **Browerville,** primarily a residential area, is to the east, and **Barrow,** containing the offices and businesses, is to the west. The northern tip of Alaska, **Point Barrow,** is north of the town on a spit. Tour buses advertise visits to the "farthest north point navigable by bus," but the absolute end is farther out, beyond the road. All-terrain-vehicles are for rent in town, if you're going to be compulsive about it.

GETTING AROUND **Polar Taxi** (☎ 907/852-2227) provides cab service. There are a couple of car-rental agencies, but not much of anywhere to drive. **Extreme Tours** (☎ 907/852-2375) rents all-terrain-vehicles and provides ecological tours. The main tour business in town, however, is **Tundra Tours**, P.O. Box 189, Barrow, AK 99723 (☎ 907/852-3900, or 800/882-8478), which, with the Top of the World Hotel, is owned by the Arctic Slope Regional Corp., a Native corporation covering the region. Their tour is described below, and is the same one sold through **Alaska Airlines Vacations** (☎ 800/468-2248).

FAST FACTS Thanks to all that oil, there is no sales or bed tax in Barrow. There is a **bank** at Agvik and Kiogak streets. An **ATM** is located at the Stuaqpaq Alaska Commercial general store. In **emergencies,** call 911, or 907/852-6111. The **hospital** is on Agvik Street (☎ 907/852-4611).

SPECIAL EVENTS If the traditional bowhead whaling season has been a success, the **Nalukataq festival** in May celebrates the event. It's not every year that a whale is landed, and captains who do land the behemoths from their open boats are held in high honor for life.

EXPLORING BARROW

It makes most sense to visit Barrow on a package, because the Native cultural demonstrations are staged for the tours. Not many people go to Barrow independently, as it's costly and has few attractions or things to do. It's interesting to see an Arctic town dominated by the Inupiat—but, again, you can do that best on a tour.

Alaska Airlines Vacations (☎ 800/468-2248) coordinates with the Arctic Slope Regional Corp., whose Tundra Tours and Top of the World Hotel have the small market sewed up. You can have confidence that the Natives themselves are selling the tours and making the money, so it's not exploitative. Arriving visitors are met at the airport and carried to the edge of the Arctic Ocean for their moment at the tip of the continent, then see a traditional hunting camp. You see the exterior of some former government outposts, a research station and Cold War radar site. The culture program includes Inupiat dances performed to the beating of round, sealskin drums, and craft demonstrations, a blanket toss, and a chance to buy Native crafts while you watch workers making them.

The one-day tour is $383 from Fairbanks, $553 from Anchorage—less than you'd pay for a full-fare ticket alone. Including an overnight stay in the comfortable Top of the World Hotel, the package is $427 per person, double occupancy, from Fairbanks, $597 from Anchorage. Book the tour through Alaska Airlines Vacations, or with Tundra Tours.

WHERE TO STAY & EAT

The **Top of the World Hotel,** at 1200 Agvik St., Barrow, AK 99723 (☎ 907/852-3900), is the main accommodation in town, although there are a couple of others. If you book separately from the tour, a double room costs $145 a night, plus $10 for each additional person. There are several restaurants. The most famous by far, adjoining the hotel, is **Pepe's North of the Border,** at 1204 Agvik St. (☎ 907/852-8200); the incongruity of a good American-style Mexican restaurant in Barrow led to national media attention a number of years ago. You can get Italian food at **Arctic Pizza,** at 125 Apayauk St. (☎ 907/852-4222), and Japanese, American, and sushi at **Teriyaki House,** 1906 Takpuk St. (☎ 907/852-2276).

9 Prudhoe Bay: Arctic Industry

Touring an oilfield may not be your idea of what to do on vacation, but the Prudhoe (PREW-dough) Bay complex is no ordinary oilfield. It's a historic and strategic site of great importance and a great technological achievement. It's built the way you'd have to build an oilfield on the moon, with massively complex machinery able to operate in winters that are always dark, and very, very cold. But it might be simpler to build on the moon—here, the industry has to coexist with a fragile habitat for migrating caribou and waterfowl, on wet, fragile tundra that permanently shows any mark made by vehicles. It's quite an accomplishment.

You must sign up for a tour to get into the oil complex—everything is behind chain-link fences and security checkpoints. The town of **Deadhorse,** which serves the oil facility, barely deserves to be called a town, and certainly isn't anything you'd travel to see: It's simply a rectangular gravel pad with modular housing units that act as lodgings and other businesses. From the air it looks like part of the apron for the landing strip. If you want to go, fly up from Fairbanks or Anchorage for the day and take the tour from Deadhorse. There's no need to spend the night if you fly, as the tour takes six hours and there's nothing else to do and nowhere else to go. Or if you drive up on the Dalton Highway, you can engage a tour in Deadhorse, or just get a lift to the water, through the oil complex. See Chapter 10, on the Interior, for information on driving the Dalton. **Alaska Airlines** (☎ 800/426-0333) flies frequently to Prudhoe Bay. A round-trip ticket costs $550 to $700 from Anchorage, around $500 from Fairbanks.

Once at Prudhoe, by whatever means, the Native-owned **NANA Development Corp.,** P.O. Box 340112, Prudhoe Bay, AK 99734 (☎ 907/659-2368 in summer, 907/659-2840 in winter), provides visitor services, including a hotel, cafeteria, showers for RV passengers and campers, fuel and vehicle repairs, and tours and a shuttle service to the Arctic Ocean. Their 75-room hotel, the **Arctic Caribou Inn,** has accommodations starting at $85. It's near the airport in Deadhorse and serves as the starting point for the tours. The restaurant has a buffet for three meals a day. Access to the oil complex is provided by NANA's well-run **Tour Arctic.** A six-hour tour, which includes views of the pipeline, a pump station, oil rigs, a visitor center, a video, and a stop at the shore of the Arctic Ocean, costs $60. The one-hour round-trip just to the ocean allows time to walk on the beach, but doesn't tour the oilfield. It costs $20, and is mainly intended for those hearty travelers who drive to the northernmost point on the U.S. road system and want to make it all the way to the water before turning back.

Princess Tours (☎ 800/835-8907) and **Gray Line of Alaska** (☎ 800/478-6388) both operate trips from Fairbanks that fly one way and drive the other over the Dalton Highway in buses. Princess charges about $700 for the three-day/two-night trip from Fairbanks, and Gray Line, which is owned by Holland America Westours, charges $650 for a similar itinerary. It can also be arranged as an add-on to a longer tour, beginning in Anchorage or with a cruise. **Northern Alaska Tour Company,** based in Fairbanks (☎ 907/474-8600), offers the lowest-cost option, with van passage up the Dalton Highway, a Prudhoe tour, an optional visit to Barrow, and a flight back to Fairbanks. The Prudhoe trip is $445, and the Barrow option adds $215. All three Dalton tours spend a night in Coldfoot and a night in Deadhorse.

10 Gates of the Arctic National Park: High North Wilderness

The park protects 8.4 million acres of the Brooks Range, west of the Dalton Highway. West of the park, lands managed by the National Park Service continue, in the Noatak National Preserve, headquartered in Kotzebue, and beyond, to the ocean. To the northeast, the Arctic National Wildlife Refuge goes as far as the Canadian border on the Arctic Ocean.

The Brooks Range, which runs east and west, is the northern extension of the Rockies. It's an old, weathered gathering of unnamed, unclimbed, granite and limestone peaks. Above 2,100 feet on the south side of the range, the boreal forest gives way to alpine tundra, covering foothills and filling alpine valleys as the range rises to the froth of gray stone mountains that form the continental divide between the Interior and Arctic regions. If you're standing atop one of the peaks of this divide, mountaintops rise before you concentrically in every direction as far as the horizon. In the 7,000-foot range, these mountains are not particularly high, but they are so numerous, so remote, so cracked and angular, as to create a whole new conception of the size and infinite variety of the world. Big wild rivers wind everywhere through the mountain multitude and along the broad, heathery valleys full of berries and bears. But there are no people. Only 4,000 people a year pass through the park.

The only ways to see the park are on foot, in a raft, or by dog sled or snowmobile. Guides sell trips to see the massive caribou migrations that cross the range and operate rafting and sled-dog journeys, and some people trek it on their own. There are no roads, no dwellings, no campgrounds, no sign of people of any kind. For experienced outdoors people, who have already done wilderness trips away from any trail and know how to prepare for being far from help in case of emergency, there aren't many places more welcoming than the Brooks Range. For those who are fit and know they'd enjoy a wilderness trip, guides can lead you into the park for rafting or hiking or, for a truly rare and rugged adventure, on a dog sled. One lodge sits on a lake in the preserve, as a base for outdoors trips or a quiet place to see the range in comfort.

ESSENTIALS

GETTING THERE   There are a couple of ways into the park. The traditional gateway is through the ranger station at the village of **Bettles,** which has daily prop service to Fairbanks. Among the operators is **Frontier Flying Service** (☎ 907/474-0014). Or you can charter a plane straight from Fairbanks, where the park headquarters is located, into the park. Now that the **Dalton Highway** is open, there are several stops on the roadside where you can walk into the park, including the tiny gold-rush town of **Wiseman.** Get the detailed printed instructions for each of these access points from the park service.

VISITOR INFORMATION   The **Park Headquarters** is at 201 First Ave. (P.O. Box 74680), Fairbanks, AK 99707-4680 (☎ 907/456-0281). There also is a ranger station in Bettles. Knowledgeable guidance also can be obtained at the **Alaska Public Lands Information Center,** 250 Cushman St. (at Third Avenue), Suite 1A, Fairbanks, AK 99701 (☎ 907/456-0527), open in summer, daily from 9am to 6pm; in winter, Tuesday through Saturday from 10am to 6pm.

FAST FACTS   Bettles, with a population of less than 50, has a **clinic** (☎ 907/ 692-5035).

EXPLORING GATES OF THE ARCTIC NATIONAL PARK

Based in Bettles, **Sourdough Outfitters,** P.O. Box 90, Bettles, AK 99726 (☎ 907/ 692-5252; e-mail sour@nigu.sourdough.com), offers some 30 different trips, by backpack, canoe, raft, or dog sled. It also operates the Bettles Trading Post, the only store in town, and rents gear and gives advice for unguided trips. See Chapter 6 for more on their trips.

Several outfitters and guides leading trips to Gates of the Arctic are based in Fairbanks and use Bettles or other gateways to the Gates, including **Alaska Fish and Trails Unlimited** (☎ 907/479-7630), which offers hiking, rafting, canoeing, kayaking, and fishing in the Brooks Range; **ABEC's Alaska Adventures** (☎ 907/457-8907), with hiking and float trips; and **Alaska Iditarod Tours** (☎ 907/479-2275), which has sled-dog trips all over the Interior and in the Brooks Range.

Don't expect to use any of these services cheaply. Like all wilderness operations, few trips cost less than $1,000, and you're more likely to spend more than $2,000, all told.

Bettles Lodge, P.O. Box 27, Bettles Field, AK 99726 (☎ 907/692-5111), is the main accommodation in town. There are six rooms sharing two baths in the two-story log building, renting for $95 to $110 a night, and an apartment with a private bathroom for $145. Hostel bunks are $15. There's a coffeehouse and a bar at the lodge, too. They rent rafts and other gear, have three remote cabins, and arrange guided trips into the park.

Some 100 miles west of Bettles, in the Gates of the Arctic National Preserve, **Peace of Selby Lodge,** P.O. Box 86, Manley Hot Springs, AK 99756 (☎ 907/672-3206), offers the chance for people who aren't up to a rugged trek to stay in the Brooks Range in wilderness luxury at Selby and Narvak lakes. It's one of Alaska's most remote wilderness lodges, many dozens of miles from any settlement. It also offers trips from the lodge with a guide who has trekked Antarctica and is a member of the Explorers Club and a fellow of the Royal Geographical Society. Prices differ according to the level of comfort—the best room is $275 per person per day.

Index